FACILITIES PLANNING FOR PHYSICAL ACTIVITY AND SPORT

Guidelines for Development

Ninth Edition

Edited by
Thomas H. Sawyer
Bernie Goldfine
Michael G. Hypes
Richard L. LaRue
Todd Seidler

Developed by the
Council on Facilities and Equipment of the
American Association for Active Lifestyles and Fitness, An Association of the
American Alliance for Health, Physical Education, Recreation, and Dance
1999

KENDALL/HUNT PUBLISHING COMPANY
4050 Westmark Drive   Dubuque, Iowa 52002

All photos and illustrations found throughout the book belong to the co-authors, unless otherwise noted.

Dedication

This book is dedicated to all the hard-working professionals in the fields of dance, fitness, physical activity, physical education, recreation, and sport. As well as to those who have dedicated their careers to developing and building facilities for the professionals in the above fields.

Contents

Appendices

Glossary   455

Preface

Aside from Dr. Edward M. Hartwell's comprehensive report on gymnasium construction in 1885 and occasional articles in the The American Physical Education Review (the official publication of the American Association for Advancement of Physical Education [AAAPE]), no concerted effort was made by the profession to consider facilities (Rice, Hutchinson, & Lee,1958). In the early 1920s the Society of Directors of Physical Education in College (College Physical Education Association) appointed a committee, of which Dr. George L. Meylan was chairman, to consider physical education facilities. Its work was published in booklet form in 1923, entitled Physical Education Buildings for Education Institutions, Part I, Gymnasiums and Lockers (Hackensmith, 1966). The committee remained active, and following Dr. Meylan the chairmanship was held by Harry A. Scott until 1927, by A.R. Winters 1927-1928, and by Albert H. Prettyman 1928-1945 (Van Dalen, Mitchell, & Bennett, 1953).

In 1945 at the meeting of the Board of Directors of the American Alliance for Health, Physical Education, and Recreation in Washington, D.C., a favorable action was taken on a proposal by Caswell M. Miles, AAHPERD Vice-President for Recreation, that a grant be obtained to finance a national conference on facilities. Subsequently, a request for $10,000 to finance the 1st facilities conference was placed before Theodore P. Bank, president of The Athletic Institute, the project was approved and money appropriated to finance the 1st conference.

As a result of this conference the Guide for Planning Facilities for Athletics, Recreation, Physical and Health Education was published that same year. Thirty-eight years have elapsed since the first printing of the first Guide which resulted from the first workshop at Jacob's Mill West Virginia, in December, 1946. Since then there have been 20 printings of the Guide.

The second workshop was held May 5-12, 1956, at the Kellogg Center for Continuing Education at Michigan State University in East Lansing. The second workshop, like the first, was financed by The Athletic Institute. The 1956 edition of the Guide, which resulted from the second workshop, has been widely used in planning and constructing planning.

The 1963 edition was prepared by the third workshop, which was financed jointly by AAHPER and The Athletic Institute and was held January 15-24, 1965, at the Biddle Continuing Education Center, Indiana University in Bloomington. Two years later, April 29-May 8, 1967, another workshop was held at Indiana University. Among those invited were a number of outstanding college and technical personnel engaged in planning and conducting programs of athletics, recreation, outdoor education, and physical and health education. In addition, invitations were extended to a number of specialists responsible for planning and constructing facilities for these programs. These specialists included city planners, architects, landscape architects, engineers and schoolhouse construction consultants.

At the 1974 facilities committee meeting, five members were assigned the task of restructuring the Guide in such a way that it would serve as a more practical tool for school administrators, physical education heads, architects, planning consultants, and all others interested in planning new areas and facilities or checking the adequacy of those already in use.

During recent years, there have been many new developments in facility planning and construction. These have been due to a number of factors. The need for improving education, recreation, and fitness opportunities for the youth of the nation has been highlighted by many groups. The fine work of the President's Council on Physical Fitness is one illustration of the growing national interest in health, physical education, and recreation activities. Much of the research and attention devoted to facility planning and construction during the past three decades has been due to the increased leisure time in society and a growing realization that recreation and especially physical activity, is a fundamental human need essential to the well-being of all people.

The Athletic Institute and AAHPERD Council on Facilities, Equipment, and Supplies initiated the 1979 revision of the Guide following a careful review of the 1974 edition. A blue ribbon Steering Committee was appointed by the Council. Edward Coates of Ohio University, and Richard B. Flynn of the University of Nebraska at Omaha, were appointed as co-editors and contributing authors. Professionals well-known for their expertise in facility planning and construction, were invited to assist in a complete rewrite.

The 1984 edition of Planning Facilities for Athletics, Physical Education, and Recreation represents a continuing effort on the part of The Athletic Institute and AAHPERD to keep the text current and relevant. Richard B. Flynn of the University of Nebraska at Omaha, was selected to be editor, and contributing author. Chapter input was solicited from carefully chosen leaders in the field as well as from outstanding architects. Efforts were made to incorporate the most recent advances in facility planning and construction. Certain program areas, such as planning for the handicapped, were expended while outdated or irrelevant materials were deleted.

Richard Flynn was selected to serve as editor and contributing author for the 1992 edition. This edition carried the same title as the 1988 edition. Many of the same contributors volunteered to revise their sections. The text was revised but not expanded.

For the latest edition (1999) a new editorial team was put together by the Council of Facilities and Equipment to do a complete overhaul of the book. The editorial team consisted of Thomas H. Sawyer, Ed.D. (Indiana State University), Chair and Editor-in-Chief; Bernie Goldfine, Ph.D. (Kennesaw State University); Michael G. Hypes, D.A. (Indiana State University); Richard L. LaRue, D.P.E. (University of New England); and Todd Seidler, Ph.D. (University of New Mexico). There were 21 authors involved in writing the 29 chapters. A new edition will be available every third year.

The Council on Facilities and Equipment (CFE) was formerly the Council on Facilities, Equipment, and Supplies. The name was changed in 1993. The Council on Facilities and Equipment (CFE) focuses on concerns relating to facilities and equipment in relationship to physical activity. CFE works to develop policies, standards, guidelines, and innovations to insure the safest and most effective means for quality health, physical education, recreation, dance, sport, and fitness facilities for the young through the aging populations.

The purposes of the CFE are:

■ To initiate a national cooperative effort to improve the quality of the facilities and equipment for health, physical education, recreation, and dance.
■ To improve the quality of undergraduate and graduate instruction in facilities and equipment design and planning.
■ To present research findings and to review needed research projects for possible endorsement and development by the Council.
■ To prepare and disseminate information to aid members to keep abreast of current innovations, promising practices, comparative data and practical ideas.
■ To cooperate with related professions (Architecture, Engineering, Construction, Manufacturing), representing the Alliance in all matters within its purview and pro-posing and implementing joint projects with other Councils within AAALF.
■ To initiate and conduct state, district, and national conferences on facilities and equipment issues.
■ To plan and develop needed publications through the Alliance.
■ To provide consultant services for referral to potential users and developers of facilities.

The material in this text reflects the composite knowledge of many professionals who have contributed to past CFE projects, as well as of those individuals who were solicited to serve as authors, editors, and reviewers for this text. The American Alliance for Health, Physical Education, Recreation, and Dance (AAHPERD), American Association for Active Lifestyles and Fitness (AAALF), and Council on Facilities and Equipment (CFE) believe this book represents one of the most comprehensive resources available on the topic of planning facilities for fitness, physical activity, and sport.

Acknowledgments

Appreciation is expressed to the Editorial Committee members of the Council for Facilities and Equipment (CFE) for assuming initial responsibility for outlining the content and chapters for the text and selection of the chapter authors. While some served as authors/editors for specific chapters in the text, all served as reviewers for assigned chapter drafts. The Editorial Committee members were:

Dr. Thomas H. Sawyer, Chair and Editor-in-Chief, Indiana State University, Chair CFE, 1995-97

Dr. Bernie Goldfine, Kennesaw State University, Chair CFE, 1999-2001

Dr. Michael G. Hypes, Indiana State University, Chair-Elect CFE, 1999-2001

Dr. Richard LaRue, University of New England, Chair CFE, 1994-95

Dr. Todd Seidler, University of New Mexico, Chair CFE, 1991-92

Dr. Jan Seaman, AAALF Executive Director

Thanks also goes to Dr. Rob Ammon, Slippery Rock State University, who served as a chapter reviewer. His insightful comments and guidance were invaluable in the development of this book.

We are indebted to a number of authoritative sources for permission to reproduce material used in this text.

■ The National Collegiate Athletic Association for permission to reproduce drawings from selected 1997 NCAA rule books. It should be noted that these specifications, like others, are subject to annual review and change.

■ Athletic Business for permission to reprint selected drawings.
■ Selected architectural firms for supplying photographs, line drawings, artists renderings, and other materials.

Special recognition is due those professionals, who served as chapter authors or editors: Gordon Calkins, John Gartland, Bernie Goldfine, Thomas Horne, Larry Horine, Susan Hudson, D.J. Hunsacker, Christopher Ingersoll, James Karabetsos, Richard LaRue, David LaRue, Hervey LaVoie, John McNichols, Arthur Mittlestaedt, Thomas Rosandich, Jr., Todd Seidler, Donna Thompson, Ed Turner, Jack Vivian, Hal Walker, and Harvey White. These individuals worked diligently to present chapter material in an informative and useful manner.

Without the great assistance from a number of very special and important folks this book would not have been possible: Julia Ann Hypes who was responsible for the glossary and author information; Kendall/Hunt, for invaluable advice, counsel, patience, and encouragement during the final edit of the manuscript; Debra Conn, Copy Editor; and Indiana State University's Graphic Arts group, for their graphic design services.

Lastly, the editors wish to thank and acknowledge Jan Seaman, Executive Director of AAALF, for her continued encouragement and support during the preparation of this text.

Thomas H. Sawyer, Ed.D.
Editor-in-Chief

Meet the Authors

Editors

Thomas H. Sawyer
Editor-in-Chief
Contributing Author
(Chapters 1, 3, 4, 5, 6, 13, 15, 21, 22, 24, 25, 28)

Dr. Sawyer is a Professor of Physical Education, and Recreation and Sport Management, and Coordinator of the graduate sport management program in the Department of Recreation and Sport Management at Indiana State University. Dr. Sawyer has been a high school and university coach in the following sports: baseball, soccer, and track and field. He was an associate athletic director at a NAIA, Division II school, an intramural and recreational sports director at three different institutions of higher education, and a department head or chair of a department of HPE or PE in three different institutions.

He has 28 peer reviewed professional articles in national and international journals, 31 articles for-hire, and 74 other articles in state journals reviewed by editors. He has authored a variety of chapters in a number of textbooks. He has co-authored a management textbook and authored a trade book on sport nutrition.

Dr. Sawyer has given 53 peered reviewed professional presentations at state, regional, national, and international conventions, and 103 workshops at state, regional, and national meetings. His research areas focus on coaching education, facility and equipment development, sport law, and sport nutrition.

He has been actively involved in professional organizations serving as President, Indiana AHPERD; Chair, Council on Facilities and Equipment; President, American Association for Active Life Styles and Fitness; Treasurer, Society for the Study of the Legal Aspects of Sport and Physical Activity (SSLASPA); Executive Director, SSLASPA; Editor, Indiana AHPERD Journal; Chair, JOPERD Editorial Board; Editor, Journal of the Legal Aspects of Sport; and Editor, AAHPERD Law Review.

Dr. Sawyer is President of the Indiana Center for Sport Education, Inc. (ICSE). The ICSE provides the following services: coaching education seminars, liability seminars, legal consultation, and risk management audits.

Bernie Goldfine
Assistant Editor
Contributing Author
(Prologue, Chapter 23)

Dr. Goldfine is Associate Professor at Kennesaw State University. Currently, he is Chair-Elect of the Council on Facilities and Equipment. Dr. Goldfine has taught undergraduate courses in the area of facility design and management, served as a consultant on various athletic facility projects, and oversaw the design, planning, and management of a wide variety of athletic facilities while serving for 13 years as a high school athletic director. He has completed numerous presentations and articles for publication at the state, national and international levels as well as contributed to textbooks on facilities. Dr. Goldfine received a Bachelor of Arts from the University of California, Santa Barbara, a Master of Arts and Ph.D from the University of Southern California.

Michael G. Hypes
Associate Editor
Contributing Author
(Chapters 1, 3, 6)

Dr. Hypes is an Assistant Professor in the Department of Recreation and Sport Management and coordinator of the undergraduate sports-management program at Indiana State University. He is Chair-Elect for the Council for Facilities and Equipment, Vice-President for the Indiana Center for Sport Education, Inc., Assistant Editor of the Indiana

AHPERD Journal, Assistant Editor of the Journal of Legal Aspects of Sport, Director of Higher Education for Indiana AHPERD, was Assistant Editor of the Tennessee AHPERD Journal, and has held various leadership positions in professional organizations. He has completed numerous presentations and articles for publication at the state, national and international levels. Dr. Hypes received his Bachelor of Science and Master of Arts degrees in Physical Education from Appalachian State University and a Doctor of Arts from Middle Tennessee State University.

Richard LaRue
Assistant Editor
Contributing Author
(Chapters 8, 11, 16)

Dr. Larue is an Associate Professor of Management at the University of New England in Biddeford, Maine. He has several scholarly publications in journals and newsletters and completed 16 local, regional, and national presentations. Dr. LaRue is the AAHPERD Board of Governors Representative for AAALF, was the AAHPERD Board of Directors Representative for the Council on Facilities and Equipment, and on the Executive Committee of the CFE. He has been a consultant for several facilities, most recently the YMCA in Warren, PA. Dr. LaRue received a Bachelor of Arts in Teaching from the University of Northern Iowa, a Master of Science and a D.P.E. from Springfield College.

Todd Seidler
Assistant Editor
Contributing Author
(Prologue, Chapters 7, 29)

Dr. Seidler is coordinator of the graduate program in Sports Administration at the University of New Mexico. He spent six years as the coordinator of the graduate Sports Administration program at Wayne State University and two years as the coordinator of the undergraduate Sport Management Program at Guilford College. He is a past chairman of the Council on Facilities and Equipment within the American Alliance of Health, Physical Education, Recreation and Dance. Dr. Seidler is active as a consultant on facilities and risk management for sport

recreation. He presents, publishes and teaches classes in Facility Planning and Design, Facility Management, and Risk Management. Dr. Seidler received a Bachelor's degree in Physical Education from San Diego State University, a Master's and Ph. D. in Sports Administration from the University of New Mexico.

Authors

Gordon Calkins
(Chapter 20)

Dr. Calkins is a Professor of Physical Education at Virginia Military Institute. He has been a coach and boxing instructor for 23 years. Dr. Calkins coached 12 national champions and the VMI team placed third in the nation on two occasions. He is a registered coach with USA Boxing, the National Collegiate Boxing Association (NCBA) and is a Boxing Coaches Clinician for USA Boxing. Dr. Calkins has served as treasurer and registration chairman for the NCBA and is a member of the Sports Medicine committee of USA Boxing. He is also a retired Colonel with the United Stated Marine Core Reserves. Dr. Calkins received his Ed. D. from Virginia Polytechnic Institute and State University in 1977.

John Gartland
(Chapter 28)

Mr. Gartland is head coach of the Indiana State University women's cross country and track and field teams. He led the women's team to the Missouri Valley Conference outdoor track title in 1998 and was named the MVC Outdoor Coach of the Year. Gartland has received the Conference Coach of the Year award eight times and the NCAA District V Coach of the Year honors four times. Mr. Gartland received a Bachelor of Science from the University of Wisconsin—LaCrosse and a Master of Science from Indiana University.

Larry Horine

(Chapter 26)

Dr. Horine is Professor Emeritus at Appalachian State University in Boone, NC. He has been Supervising Director of Health, PE, Athletics, Recreation and Safety at the Panama Canal Zone Schools and College, Chairperson of the Department of HPER and Director of International Programs at Appalachian State University. Dr. Horine has been the consultant on several facility construction and renovation projects. He has also completed numerous presentations and articles for publication at the state, national and international levels. Dr. Horine received a Bachelor of Science in Physical Education, Master of Arts in Education Administration and Leadership, and an Ed.D. in Physical Education and Education Administration from the University of Colorado.

Thomas Horne

(Chapters 19, 20)

Dr. Horne is the Director of Facility Operations and Program Support within the Department of Physical Education at the U.S. Military Academy. He has been the Department of Physical Education representative for planning and development for the $85 million Arvin Physical Development Center, a $10 million pool and locker room renovation and numerous other construction/renovation projects at the U.S. Military Academy. Dr. Horne has completed presentations at the 1998 Athletic Business Conference, the Virginia Recreation and Park Society and has taught an athletic facilities course in Hong Kong, Singapore, and Kuala Lampur for the U.S. Sports Academy. Dr. Horne received a Bachelor's degree in Health, Physical Education and Recreation from Slippery Rock University, and Master's and Doctoral degrees in Physical Education from the Ohio State University.

Susan Hudson

(Chapter 17)

Dr. Hudson is a McElroy professor of youth leadership studies at the University of Northern Iowa. She has written numerous articles, books and monographs and has done over 40 paper presentations before conventions and professional groups. Dr. Hudson has held leadership positions as President of the American Leisure Academy, President of the American Association for Leisure and Recreation, and Vice-President for Recreation with the Southern District of AAHPERD. She is a project associate for the National Program for Playground Safety and a Facilities Unit Manager with the Girl Scouts of America—Cross Timbers Council. Dr. Hudson received a Bachelor of Arts in History from the University of California-Davis, a Master of Science in Recreation Administration from California State University—Los Angeles, and a Ph.D. in Leisure Services from the University of Utah.

D.J. Hunsaker

(Chapter 18)

Mr. Hunsaker is President/CEO of Counsilman/Hunsaker & Associates located in St. Louis, MO. Client contact, design programming, and strategic planning are just a few of his many responsibilities. Mr. Hunsaker was a design consultant for Georgia Tech (host of the 1996 Olympic swimming venue), Eisenhower Park (host of the 1998 goodwill Games), St. Peters Rec-Plex (site of the 1994 Olympic Festival) and Saanich Community Center (site of the aquatics venue for the 1994 Commonwealth games). He is past president of the Midwest Pool Management Corporation and the Swim Facility Operators Association of America. Currently, he is a board member of the National Swimming Pool Foundation and Chairman of Community Recreation Systems. Mr. Hunsaker is the recipient of four gold medal national awards for design excellence. He wrote the Official Swimming Pool Design Compendium for the National Swimming Pool Foundation. Mr. Hunsaker received a Bachelor of Science in City Planning from the University of Illinois.

Christopher Ingersoll

(Chapter 13)

Dr. Ingersoll is a Professor and Chair of the Department of Athletic Training at Indiana State University in Terre Haute, Indiana. He is Chair of the NATA Foundation Research Committee and Chair of the NATA Education Council Post-Certification Graduate Education Committee. He co-authored Athletic Training Management: Concepts and Applications. Dr. Ingersoll received a Bachelor of Science in Sport Medicine from Marietta College, a Master of Arts in Physical Education—Athletic Training from Indiana State University and a Ph.D. in Biomechanics from the University of Toledo.

James Karabestsos

(Chapter 2)

Dr. Karabestsos is an Associate Professor at Western Illinois University. He co-authored a chapter in Planning Facilities for Athletics, Physical Education and Recreation, and completed presentations at two AAHPERD Conventions. Dr. Karabestsos has been the Director of Campus Recreation at the University of Idaho, Assistant Athletic Director in charge of facilities at the University of North Dakota. He also participated in the planning of two major HPERD facility renovation projects at the University of North Dakota and the University of Idaho. Dr. Karabestsos received a Bachelor of Science and Master of Science from Northern Michigan University and an Ed.D. from the University of Northern Colorado.

Hervey Lavoie

(Chapter 14)

Mr. Lavoie is President of Ohlson Lavoie Corporation, Architecture and Planning located in Denver, CO. He plays an active role in the planning and designs of all projects the firm undertakes. He has conducted several seminars, published numerous articles and is a member of the American Institute of Architects and the International Health and Racquet Sports Association (IHRSA). Mr. Lavoie has been awarded the Athletic Business Facility of Merit in 1990 and 1995 "in recognition of an especially outstanding sports/recreation facility." He received a Bachelor of Architecture degree from the University of Detroit and Master of Architecture degree from the University of Colorado.

John McNichols

(Chapter 28)

Mr. McNichols is the head coach for the Indiana State University men's Track and Field and Cross Country programs. He led ISU to its first Indiana Intercollegiate cross country title in the fall of 1997, the cross country team won a Missouri Valley Conference Title in 1996, and in the spring of 1997 won the Missouri Valley Outdoor Track and Field title. Mr. McNichols was named MVC Coach of the Year for both seasons as well as the NCAA District V Coach of the Year for outdoor track. In addition to hid coaching duties, he has worked as a meet official at the 1984 Olympic Games in Los Angeles, the 1987 Pan American Games in Indianapolis, and the 1988 U. S. Olympic Trials in Indianapolis. He also served as a head marshal at the Atlanta Olympic Games. Mr. McNichols received Bachelor of Science and Master of Science degrees from Indiana University.

Arthur H. Mittelstaedt, Jr.

(Chapters 6, 25)

Dr. Mittelstaedt is the Executive Director of the Recreation Safety Institute Ltd. He has held positions in recreation and sports for governmental municipalities, for entrepreneurial enterprises, and for institutional groups. Currently, he serves as an Executive of two consulting firms. He has participated as an expert witness in liability suits, condemnation cases and zoning matters for local, state, and federal courts. Dr. Mittelstaedt has authored over 125 articles in recreation, sports and safety and has been a contributing author to several books. He has held several teaching positions in higher education. Dr. Mittelstaedt received a masters Degree in Public Administration and a Doctorate of Education from New York University.

Thomas Rosandich, Jr.

(Chapter 10)

Dr. Rosandich is the Vice President for Administration and Finance for the United States Sports Academy. His experience in facility design and review cover areas on a national and international level. Dr. Rosandich has completed several publications and presentations on sport facility design and equipment and was an equipment specialist for the American Institute of Sport Design. He most recently has submitted design reviews for The Mitchell Center at the University of South Alabama and the Molepole Sports Complex in Botswana. Dr. Rosandich received a Bachelor of Arts in Business Administration from Columbia Pacific University, and a Master of Sport Science from the United States Sports Academy, and is currently a Doctoral Candidate (ABD) at the United States Sports Academy.

Donna Thompson

(Chapter 17)

Dr. Thompson is a Professor at the University of Northern Iowa and Director of the National Program for Playground Safety. She has contributed to numerous books and monographs and written over 30 articles for publication. Dr. Thompson has held leadership positions as a Senior Fellow with the American Leisure Academy, President of the American Association for Leisure and Recreation and as a member of the Executive Committee for the National Playground Safety Institute. She has been 1st Vice-President of the Conestoga Council of Girl Scouts, on the National Advisory Board for Boundless Playgrounds and Secretary for the ASTM Public Use Playground Sub-Committee. Dr. Thompson received a Bachelor of Arts in Physical Education from Western Washington University, a Master of Arts in New Testament from Wheaton College, Illinois, and a Ph.D. in Physical Education from the Ohio State University.

Edward Turner

(Chapters 11, 12, 23)

Dr. Turner is a Professor in the Department of Health, Leisure, and Exercise Science at Appalachian State University in Boone, North Carolina. He has written over 80 journal and chapter publications, published 3 books and completed 48 state, regional, national, and international presentations. Dr. Turner has been a facility consultant on various sports projects and has taught sport facilities design and planning course for 30 years. Currently, he is a consultant for the $36 million Convocation Center at Appalachian State. He is a past-chair of the Facilities and Equipment Council. Dr. Turner has received numerous teaching awards, most recently he was the system wide recipient of the N.C. Board of Governors Award for Outstanding teaching, 1998. He is a member of AAHPERD, Phi Epsilon Kappa (life member) and the Creative Education Foundation. Dr. Turner received a Bachelor of Science from the Penn State University, a Master of Arts and Ph.D. from the University of Maryland.

Jack Vivian

(Chapter 27)

Dr. Vivian is President of JRV Management, Inc., a sport facility management company in Ann Arbor, MI. He has held several teaching positions in higher education as well as numerous administrative positions in sport. His areas of expertise include sport facilities planning, feasibility studies, design and management, and business turn-around consulting. In addition, he has written over 100 articles for publication and completed over 20 presentation at the state, national and international levels. Dr. Vivian received his Bachelor of Science in Physical Education from Adrian College, a Master's in Education, and a Ph. D. from Bowling Green State University.

Hal Walker

(Chapter 9)

Dr. Walker is an Associate Professor and Coordinator of the undergraduate and graduate sport management programs at Barry University in Miami Shores, Florida. He has served as a Director of Athletics, Division I Volleyball Coach, Department Chair, and Academic Dean while teaching at the college level. Dr. Walker has completed presentations at the national and international level on facility and event management, sport marketing, and risk management. He has been a consultant for sport related businesses, facility risk reviews, and sport facility planning and programming. Dr. Walker earned a Bachelor's degree from Brock University in Canada and a Master's and Ph.D. from The Ohio State University.

Harvey White

(Chapter 2)

Dr. White is a Professor and head of the Department of Physical Education, Recreation and Dance at New Mexico State University. He has written several papers for publication, completed presentations on facility planning, and received the National Honor Award from the Council for Equipment and Facilities in 1996. Dr. White received a Bachelor of Science in Physical Education from Pembroke State University, a master of Arts in Physical Education from Western Carolina University, and a Ph. D. in Sport Administration from the University of New Mexico.

PROLOGUE

Facility Planning and Design:
An Introduction

Todd L. Seidler, University of New Mexico ■ Bernie Goldfine, Kennesaw State University

Have you ever seen a facility with so many design problems that it left you shaking your head in disbelief? Each facility presents its own unique design challenges; if these challenges are not addressed and overcome, the result is a facility with design problems. Typically, the larger a building project, the greater the likelihood that mistakes will be made in the planning and design process. Often details are overlooked, and sometimes even major mistakes are made in the planning process and not discovered until after the facility is built and opened for use. For example, most of us have seen buildings with poor lighting, ventilation, or access control that could have been prevented with appropriate planning. In particular, one of the most common design flaws in recreational, physical education, and sports facilities is a lack of proper storage space. Surely, we have all visited buildings where hallways, classrooms, and even activity spaces were used for temporary or permanent storage of equipment.

A lack of planning has resulted in countless design flaws in sport and recreation facilities. Can you imagine a high school football team playing on an eighty-yard football field? What about a recreation center with access to the locker rooms available only by crossing the gym floor? Do you believe a facility designer would locate a locker room toilet one foot lower than the septic field it was supposed to drain into? How about a gymnasium with large picture windows directly behind the basketball standards? And how safe is an indoor track that has been constructed as part of a pool deck and has water puddles present in every running lane? Impossible? No.

These "Building Bloopers" are real and are not as uncommon as we would like to believe. Such mistakes can be embarrassing, expensive, amazing, and sometimes humorous (if it is not your facility). These and many other planning and design errors can usually be traced to insufficient planning. An example of

outrageous Building Blooper is Olympic Stadium in Montreal. Constructed as the track and field site for the 1976 Montreal Olympics, it has yet to be completed satisfactorily. Originally estimated to cost about $60 million, the price so far is upwards of $1 billion. And to top it off, a large percentage of the seats did not have direct sight lines to the finish line on the track.

Building bloopers are often caused by devoting insufficient time, effort and/or expertise to the planning process. The earlier in the process that mistakes are discovered and corrected, the less they are going to cost to rectify. It is cheap to change some words on a paper, somewhat more expensive to change lines on a blueprint, and outrageously expensive or impossible to make changes once the concrete has been poured. Furthermore, the impact of a poorly designed building is staggering when compared with other management problems. Problematic staff or other personnel can be relieved of their responsibilities. Funds can be raised for under-financed programs. However, the consequences of a poorly designed building will have to be endured for decades. Therefore, it is essential to devote all available resources early in the planning process.

All too often facilities are planned without in-depth consideration of the programs that they will support. Basically, a facility is a tool. The better it is planned, designed, and constructed, the better it will support the objectives of the programs it will house. Implementing a new program in an existing or poorly planned facility often requires designing the programs based on the limitations of the facility. Furthermore, poorly designed venues may limit or even prevent some activities from taking place. Conversely, a well-designed facility will support and enhance the programs. Planning and building a new facility is a great opportunity to ensure that it will optimally support the desired programs. Furthermore, if done properly, well-planned venues allow for flexibility when the popularity of activities and user demand fluctuate; additionally, they allow new activities to be added easily.

This book is intended to provide a basic understanding of the planning and design process as well as the unique features of many different areas and types of facilities. Although there is no such thing as a perfect building, with significant time, effort, and expertise devoted to the planning and design process, future Building Bloopers can be kept to a minimum. It is hoped that those of you involved with the planning of sports facilities will find this book to be a significant resource.

CHAPTER 1

History of the Council on Facilities and Equipment

Thomas H. Sawyer, Indiana State University ■ Michael G. Hypes, Indiana State University

---

Learning Objectives

After reading this chapter, the student will be able to

■ describe the historical development of the Council on Facilities and Equipment,

■ discuss the steps taken in developing standards for facilities and equipment, and

■ describe the difference between standards and guidelines.

Introduction

The Council on Facilities and Equipment (CFE) focuses on concerns relating to facilities and equipment in relationship to physical activity. CFE works to develop policies, standards, guidelines, and innovations to ensure the safest and most effective means for quality health, physical education, recreation, dance, sport, and fitness facilities and equipment for the young through the aging populations. This chapter describes the development of the CFE.

Initial Interest in Facilities

Aside from Dr. Edward M. Hartwell's comprehensive report on gymnasium construction in 1885 and occasional articles in the *The American Physical Education Review* (the official publication of the American Association for Advancement of Physical Education [AAAPE]), no concerted effort was made by the profession to consider facilities (Rice, Hutchinson, & Lee, 1958). In the early 1920s the Society of Directors of Physical Education in College (College Physical Education Association) appointed a committee, of which Dr. George L. Meylan was chairman, to consider physical education facilities. Its work was published in booklet form in 1923, entitled *Physical Education Buildings for Education Institutions, Part I, Gymnasiums and Lockers* (Hackensmith, 1966). The committee remained active, and following Dr. Meylan in the chairmanship was Harry A. Scott until 1927; A.R. Winters, 1927-1928; and Albert H. Prettyman, 1928-1945 (Van Dalen, Mitchell, & Bennett, 1953).

The halt in the construction of facilities during the depression was only temporary, and as soon as the federal government entered the picture, building programs were resumed on a grander scale than before. In its early stages many obvious and absurd mistakes were made in architectural planning (Van Dalen et al., 1953; Rice et al., 1958; and Hackensmith, 1966). This led to government provision of expert guidance in planning facilities. In addition, the National Recreation Association and the Recreation Division, Works Project Administration, issued many pamphlets as guides in planning recreation facilities. The College Physical Education Association also initiated the practice of collecting and filing architectural plans of college facilities that were made available to the profession on request (Hackensmith, 1966).

By the end of the 1930s, the degree of interest in the planning and construction of facilities was demonstrated by many publications on the subject, including Herbert Blair's *Physical Education for the Modern Junior and Senior High School* (1938), Emil Lamar's *The Athletic Plant* (1938), George Butler's *The New Play Areas — Their Design and Equipment* (1938), Fredrick W. Leuhring's *Swimming Pool Standards* (1939), and Ruth Eliott Houston's *Modern Trends in Physical Education Facilities for College Women* (1939).

Early Physical Education Facilities

Many gymnasiums were erected after the Civil War, starting with the Dartmouth building of 1867, which cost $24,000. Following that, Princeton replaced its earlier red shack with a $38,000 "gym," the finest of its day. Bowdoin's gymnasium had no heat, and the men dressed for class even in zero weather, changing to cotton shirts and tights and cloth slippers. In 1870 the University of Wisconsin built a $4,000 gymnasium (the first state university to build one). The Yale gymnasium of 1875 had eight long "bathtubes" lined with zinc, which the students used only on payment of a special fee. Then 1879 brought the wonder gymnasium of the age — Harvard's $110,000 Hemenway Gymnasium — followed in 1878 by the University of California's modest $12,000 Harmon Gymnasium. During the 1960's and 1970's many colleges that could not afford gymnasiums fitted up vacant rooms as drill halls (Rice et al., 1958).

In the women's colleges, physical education classwork got under way in this period by using the outdoors, corridors, assembly halls, and store rooms. One school used a privately owned gymnasium in the local community — Radcliffe at Sargent's Gymnasium. Vassar was the only college that started its physical education work with a special building constructed for the work. In 1860 it built a "Hall of Calisthenics" with footprints painted on the floor to indicate where the students should stand during their exercise periods. Mt. Holyoke had a gymnasium by 1865 that cost $1,900. Other gymnasiums that were constructed included one at Smith in 1875, Bryn Mawr, by 1885; Goucher, by 1888; and Mills College, by the end of the century. Goucher College constructed the first swimming pool for women in 1888, although it did not list swimming as an activity for students until 1904. Vasser built the second pool in 1889, and Smith installed a "swimming bath" in 1892 that could be used by two to five students at a time and was used for over 30 years; Bryn Mawr built its pool in 1894, and by the end of the century Radcliffe College had built one. There were no pools for women or men in any coeducational college or coeducational university of this era (Rice, 1929; Rice et al., 1958).

The coeducational colleges/universities lagged far behind the women's colleges in procuring facilities for women students. As a rule the women were permitted to use the men's facilities on occasion, and in many schools a large room in the women's dormitory was set aside for a women's gymnasium (Hackensmith, 1966).

American Alliance for Health, Physical Education, Recreation, and Dance

The American Alliance for Health, Physical Education, Recreation and Dance (AAHPERD) was founded on November 27, 1885, when William Gilbert Anderson, a physical training instructor in Brooklyn, New York, invited a group of people who were working in the gymnastic field to come together to discuss their profession. These 60 people talked informally of methods of teaching, the best system of measurements, normal-training classes, and the manufacture of apparatus. After a demonstration of new exercise methods, they embarked on the formation of a permanent organization that was named the Association for the Advancement of Physical Education (AAPE). Forty-nine people, all teaching physical education, enrolled as members of the organization with a pledge to meet the next year at the same place. The first convention ran full-circle with discussions, speeches, a demonstration, enrolling members, adoption of a plan of organization, and election of officers.

At the second meeting in 1886, a formal constitution was adopted and the name was changed to the American Association for the Advancement of Physical Education (AAAPE). The name was later changed to the American Physical Education Association (APEA). In 1937 the APEA and the Department of School Health and Physical Education of the National Education Association were formally amalgamated to form the American Association for Health and Physical Education (AAHPE). The following year, recreation was added to the title and the American Association For Health, Physical Education and Recreation (AAHPER) continued until 1974 when the American Alliance for Health, Physical Education, and Recreation was reorganized. Dance was added to the title in 1979.

The early years of the alliance focused on defining and exploring the field of physical education and encouraging its inclusion in the schools. By the close of the century, the organization had grown in number of members from 49 to 1,076 and was spreading throughout the nation. As the years went by, the alliance grew in structure, size, and scope as it worked toward the acceptance of the study of physical education.

In late 1896, the AAPE approved a plan to begin publishing a quarterly magazine, the *American Physical Education Review,* which became the *Journal of Health and Physical Education* in 1930 and now is the *Journal of Physical Education, Recreation, and Dance.* In 1930 the Association began publishing the *Research Quarterly.*

The years following World War II saw an emphasis on two key issues. One was the need for adequate and well-planned facilities, and the other was the pressing need for improved professional preparation of teachers. The alliance also continued its interest, which had developed during the War, in federal legislation relating to physical education and health services.

The decade of the 1950s was notable for a prodigious expansion of AAHPER activities, evident in three areas: conferences, consultant services, and publication. During this time AAHPER also provided significant support and service to the cause of fitness. In 1958, the Alliance developed the Youth Fitness Test, which was the first program of testing with national norms that applied to the fitness levels of America's school age children.

In 1965 a second national study was conducted, and the norms for the test were revised. It was during this year that the President's Council on Fitness joined with AAHPER, using the Youth Fitness Test, to initiate and promote the Presidential Physical Fitness Award.

In 1980 AAHPERD developed the Health Related Fitness Test, where the items on the test battery relate to a major health risk factor. From 1980 through spring 1988, the alliance sponsored its Youth Fitness Test and the Health Related Fitness Test. Physical Best was developed in 1988 and contains both the health related test and the teaching of fitness concepts.

The alliance went through growing pains in the late eighties and launched two major initiatives to explore its future. One, the Blue Ribbon Task Force, devoted three years of study to the structure and func-

tion of the alliance in an attempt to analyze its effectiveness for meeting member needs. Somewhat overlapping this effort was an experimental project focusing on autonomy. This project, called the AAHE Experiment, used a different method of accounting for cost of doing business and revenue sources. It allowed AAHE to experiment with more autonomous decision-making as well as taking responsibility for those decisions. This experiment along with the outcome of the Blue Ribbon Task Force resulted in Model III, a move toward autonomy for all national associations.

The American Alliance for Health, Physical Education, Recreation, and Dance (AAHPERD) is an educational organization designed to support, encourage, and provide assistance to member groups and their personnel nationwide as they initiate, develop, and conduct programs in health, leisure, and movement-related activities. AAHPERD seeks to:

■ Encourage, guide, and support professional growth and development in health, leisure, and movement-related programs based on individual needs, interests, and capabilities.

■ Communicate the importance of health, leisure, and movement-related activities as they contribute to human well-being.

■ Encourage and facilitate research that will enrich health, leisure, and movement-related activities, and disseminate the findings to professionals and the public.

■ Develop and evaluate standards and guidelines for personnel and programs in health, leisure, and movement-related activities.

■ Coordinate and administer a planned program of professional, public, and government relations that improves education in areas of health, leisure, and movement-related activities.

■ Conduct other activities for the public benefit.

AAHPERD is composed of six national associations, including:

1. American Association for Active Lifestyles and Fitness (AAALF)
2. American Association for Health Education (AAHE)
3. American Association for Leisure and Recreation (AALR)
4. National Association for Girls and Women in Sport (NAGWS)
5. National Association for Sport and Physical Education (NASPE)
6. National Dance Association (NDA)

Association for Research, Administration, and Professional Councils History — 1949-1995

The American Association for Active Lifestyles and Fitness (AAALF) evolved out of the General Division of the American Association for Health, Physical Education, and Recreation. In 1949 the General Division was created as the fourth division of AAHPER, joining the Health Education Division, Physical Education Division, and the Recreation Division. This reorganization plan consolidated the general sections to eliminate duplication of functions and service. At the time of its formation, the General Division included 12 sections, three of which originated in the AAHPER well before 1930.

These 12 sections were:

1. Aquatics
2. Administration and Supervision
3. Athletics — Boys and Men
4. Athletics — Girls and Women
5. Camping and Outdoor Education
6. Dance
7. Measurement and Evaluation
8. Professional Education
9. Professional and Public Relations
10. Research
11. Students
12. Therapeutics

The General Division's substructures fluctuated in number through the years, beginning with the addition of the Research Council in 1952. General Division councils and sections were differentiated by functions. The sections operated primarily to plan and conduct programs at the annual AAHPER conventions in their specialized interest area.

The General Division 1970 Operating Code stated that "the purpose of the General Division shall be to provide leadership and coordination to those groups developing programs and fostering education activities under its auspices" and to

■ Provide an organizational structure to serve groups whose professional interest and activities relate to two or more existing AAHPER divisions or whose professional interests do not readily lend themselves to inclusion in other divisions.
■ Promote flexibility to serving the many and varied professional interests and levels of the AAHPER membership by providing opportunity for growth of new and continuing professional interest groups.

■ Recognize inter-divisional professional interests and activities and to encourage communications and cooperation among the divisions of AAHPER.
■ Coordinate and lend intra-divisional support to professional interests and programs.

On April 16, 1973, the AAHPER Representative Assembly approved the Reorganization Committee's Model II to change AAHPER from an association to an alliance. This gave the eight AAHPER divisions and their structure self-determination of association status and placement. The premise was that the alliance would "provide unity with diversity," allowing the associations full control over their professional programs, while being a united structure of related disciplines. It is within these concepts and at that time that the Association for Research, Administration, and Professional Councils (ARAPC) had its origin. In October 1974, the Alliance Board of Governors defined the term "society" as an alliance structure, and further stated that all societies would be housed in ARAPCS, formerly the General Division of the American Association for Health, Physical Education, and Recreation. The name change took place during the early 1960's. ARAPCS was composed of those councils and a professional society that did not clearly fit into the other national associations — National Association for Sport and Physical Education, National Association for Girls and Women in Sports, American Association for Leisure and Recreation, and American Association for Health Education.

In spring 1994, ARAPCS changed its name to the American Association for Active Lifestyles and Fitness (AAALF). This name change was designed to more clearly define the focus and mission of the association. With its 12 councils and 1 society, AAALF has a broad range of interests and programs. All professional activities are carried on through the special interest areas of its councils. With this format, most of the income received by AAALF is allocated directly to the councils/society for their professional activities, which maximizes allocations for program content.

American Association for Active Lifestyles and Fitness

The American Association for Active Lifestyles and Fitness (AAALF), formerly ARAPCS, is one of six national associations within the American Alliance for Health, Physical Education, Recreation, and Dance (AAHPERD). The goal of AAALF and its 12 councils (Adapted Physical Education Council, Aquatics Council, College and University Administrators Council, Council on Aging and Adult Development, Council on Facilities and Equipment, Council on Outdoor Education, Ethnic Minority Council, International Relations Council, Measurement and Evaluation Council, Physical Fitness Council, Student Action Council) and one society (School and Community Safety Society of America) is to promote active lifestyles and fitness for all populations through support of research, development of leaders, and dissemination of current information. Membership provides the latest information in the field, professional development, career networking and contacts, annual national convention, regional workshops/conferences, publication opportunities, advocacy of mission, leadership opportunities, professional recognition, and headquarters support staff.

The Birth of the Guide for Planning Facilities for Athletics, Recreation, Physical and Health Education

At the meeting of the Board of Directors of the American Alliance for Health, Physical Education, and Recreation in Washington, D.C., in April 1945 favorable action was taken on a proposal by Caswell M. Miles, AAHPERD vice-president for recreation, that a grant be obtained to finance a national conference on facilities. Subsequently, a request for $10,000 to finance the first facilities conference was placed before Theodore P. Bank, president of The Athletic Institute. The project was approved and the money appropriated to finance the first conference.

As a result of this conference, the *Guide for Planning Facilities for Athletics, Recreation, Physical and Health Education* was published that same year. Thirty-eight years have elapsed since the printing of the first *Guide*, which resulted from the first workshop at Jacob's Mill, West Virginia, in December 1946. Since then there have been 20 printings of the *Guide*.

The second workshop was held May 5-12, 1956, at the Kellogg Center for Continuing Education at Michigan State University in East Lansing. The second workshop, like the first, was financed by The Athletic Institute. The 1956 edition of the *Guide*, which resulted from the second workshop, has been widely used in design and construction planning.

The 1963 edition was prepared by the third workshop, which was financed jointly by the AAHPER and The Athletic Institute and held January 15-24, 1965, at the Biddle Continuing Education Center, Indiana University, in Bloomington. Two years later, April 29-

May 8, 1967, another workshop was held at Indiana University. Among those invited were a number of outstanding college and technical personnel engaged in planning and conducting programs of athletics, recreation, outdoor education, and physical and health education. In addition, invitations were extended to a number of specialists responsible for planning and constructing facilities for these programs. These specialists included city planners, architects, landscape architects, engineers, and schoolhouse construction consultants.

At the 1974 facilities committee meeting, five members were assigned the task of restructuring the *Guide* in such a way that it would serve as a more practical tool for school administrators, physical education heads, architects, planning consultants, and all others interested in planning new areas and facilities or checking the adequacy of those already in use.

During recent years, there have been many new developments in facility planning and construction. These have been due to a number of factors. The need for improving education, recreation, and fitness opportunities for the youth of the nation has been highlighted by many groups. The extensive work of the President's Council on Physical Fitness is one illustration of the growing national interest in health, physical education, and recreation activities. Much of the research and attention devoted to facility planning and construction during the past three decades has been due to the increased leisure time in society and a growing realization that recreation, and especially physical activity, is a fundamental human need essential to the well-being of all people.

The Athletic Institute and AAHPERD Council on Facilities, Equipment, and Supplies initiated the 1979 revision of the *Guide* following a careful review of the 1974 edition. A blue-ribbon steering committee was appointed by the Council. Edward Coates of Ohio University and Richard B. Flynn of the University of Nebraska at Omaha were appointed as co-editors and contributing authors. Professionals well known for their expertise in facility planning and construction were invited to assist in a complete rewrite.

The 1984 edition of *Planning Facilities for Athletics, Physical Education, and Recreation* represents a continuing effort on the part of The Athletic Institute and AAHPERD to keep the text current and relevant. Richard B. Flynn of the University of Nebraska at Omaha was selected as editor and contributing author. Chapter input was solicited from carefully chosen leaders in the field as well as from outstanding architects. Efforts were made to incorporate the most recent advances in facility planning and construction. Certain program areas, such as planning for the handicapped, were expanded while outdated or irrelevant materials were deleted.

Richard Flynn was selected to serve as editor and contributing author for the 1992 edition. This edition carried the same title as the 1988 edition. Many of the same contributors volunteered to revise their sections. The text was revised but not expanded.

For the latest edition (1999) a new editorial team was put together by the Council on Facilities and Equipment to do a complete overhaul of the book. The editorial team consisted of Thomas H. Sawyer, Ed.D. (Indiana State University), Editor-in-Chief; Bernie Goldfine, Ph.D. (Kennesaw State University); Michael G. Hypes, D.A. (Indiana State University); Richard L. LaRue, D.P.E. (University of New England); and Todd Seidler, Ph.D. (University of New Mexico); There were 21 authors involved in writing the 29 chapters. A new edition will be available every third year.

Facility and Equipment Standards and Guidelines Publications

Dr. George L. Meylan was chairman of a committee to consider physical education facilities. The committee's work was published in booklet form in 1923, entitled *Physical Education Buildings for Education Institutions, Part I, Gymnasiums and Lockers* (Hackensmith, 1966). The list of early publications on facilities includes Herbert Blair's *Physical Education for the Modern Junior and Senior High School* (1938), Emil Lamar's *The Athletic Plant* (1938), George Butler's *The New Play Areas — Their Design and Equipment* (1938), Fredrick W. Leuhring's *Swimming Pool Standards* (1939), and Ruth Eliott Houston's *Modern Trends in Physical Education Facilities for College Women* (1939).

Council on Equipment and Supplies

In 1955 AAHPER established the Council on Equipment and Supplies, with Thomas E. McDonough (Emory University, Georgia) as chairman and Charles Heilman (Drake University, Iowa) as secretary. The purpose of the council was to assist physical educators, athletic coaches, and recreation leaders in the selection, purchase, and care of equipment and supplies. Since its organization the council has secured the cooperation of manufacturing companies and stimulated professional interest through exhibits of equip-

ment and supplies at conferences and conventions. In 1959 the AAHPER and the Athletic Institute cosponsored a third National Workshop on Equipment and Supplies for Athletics, Physical Education, and Recreation at Michigan State University, whose report was made available in 1960. In 1976 the name of the council was changed to reflect its work in the area of facilities — Council on Facilities, Equipment, and Supplies.

Council on Facilities and Equipment

The Council on Facilities and Equipment (CFE) was formerly the Council on Facilities, Equipment, and Supplies. The name was changed in 1993. The Council on Facilities and Equipment (CFE) focuses on concerns relating to facilities and equipment in relationship to physical activity. CFE works to develop policies, standards, guidelines, and innovations to insure the safest and most effective means for quality health, physical education, recreation, dance, sport, and fitness facilities for the young through the aging populations.

The purposes of the CFE are:

■ To initiate a national cooperative effort to improve the quality of the facilities and equipment for health, physical education, recreation, and dance.
■ To improve the quality of undergraduate and graduate instruction in facilities and equipment design and planning.
■ To present research findings and to review needed research projects for possible endorsement and development by the council.
■ To prepare and disseminate information to aid members to keep abreast of current innovations, promising practices, comparative data and practical ideas.
■ To cooperate with related professions (architecture, engineering, construction, manufacturing), representing the alliance in all matters within its purview and proposing and implementing joint projects with other councils within AAALF.
■ To initiate and conduct state, district, and national conferences on facilities and equipment issues.
■ To plan and develop needed publications through the alliance.
■ To provide consultant services for referral to potential users and developers of facilities.

Who Should Be a Member:

■ Those teaching courses or a unit within a course in facilities planning.

■ Any HPERD professional who has an interest in facility planning.

■ Any professional who plans, designs, and manages facilities, and manufacturers of equipment involving fitness, physical activity, and sport. CFE Membership Services:

■ Consultant service for potential users, planners, and designers of physical activity facilities and equipment.

■ Research on current trends in physical activity facilities and equipment.

■ Programs and site visits of facilities at the annual AAHPERD national conference.

■ Newsletter, *Focus on Facilities*, published semi-annually. It contains news about ongoing projects within the council and important happenings in facility and equipment development. Nonmembers may subscribe for a modest fee.

■ Awards given to members who contribute significantly to the CFE.

■ World Wide Web connection is http://www.aahperd.org/aaalf.html

Other CFE Activities:

■ Publication of state-of-the-art textbook used in educating undergraduates and graduates in the field of facilities and equipment; available from AAHPERD Publications.

■ Consultant lists published bi-annually. The lists include information on architects, builders, and consultants and is available for $2.50 (members) and $10 (non-members).

■ Facilities Bibliography Data Base a literature resource for facilities and equipment since 1990, available for $2.50 (member) and $10 (non-member).

The CFE is represented in the districts as follows:

▶ Six AAHPERD regional district representatives, along with the coordinator, serve our council at the district level. Some vital responsibilities of council representatives are:

■ To disseminate information within the district about council goals and programs.

■ To establish lines of communication with facility and equipment specialists in states within each district.

■ To promote facility and equipment workshops, clinics, and seminars to address expressed specific needs within each district.

■ To nominate facility and equipment professionals from their district who make outstanding contributions to the field of facility and equip-

ment development for the CFE Professional Service or Honor Awards.

■ Membership in the Council on Facilities and Equipment provides automatic membership with AAALF/AAHPERD. In addition to the benefits of the CFE membership, AAALF/AAHPERD benefits include twice yearly AAALF Newsletters, AAHPERD's UPDATE, a choice of four professional journals, discounts at the national convention and other professional events.

■ For membership information about the Council on Facilities and Equipment, please write or call: The Council on Facilities and Equipment/AAALF, 1900 Association Drive, Reston, VA 22091, (703)476-3430 or 1-800-213-7193 or e-mail: *aaalf@aahperd.org* or FAX (703)476-9527.

Leadership in Facilities and Equipment since 1920

The following professionals have been the leaders of the facility since 1920:

Leaders in Facilities, Equipment, and Supplies

1920-23	George L. Meylan
1924-27	Harry A. Scott
1927-28	A.R. Winters
1928-45	Albert H. Prettyman
1946-54	Caswell M. Miles

Chairpersons of the Council on Equipment and Supplies [CES]

1954-56	Thomas E. McDonough
1956-59	Charles Heilman
1959-60	D.K. Stanley
1960-61	Robert Weber
1961-62	James C. Loveless
1962-63	John A. Friedrich
1963-64	William Theunissen
1964-65	John Fox
1965-66	Maurice A. Clay
1966-67	Wayne Brumbach
1967-68	Richard B. Westkaemper
1968-69	Joseph M. Pease
1969-70	John Nettleton
1970-71	James Delamater

1971-72	Alexander Petersen
1972-73	O.N. Hunter
1973-74	Ghary M. Akers
1974-75	Richard B. Flynn

Chairpersons of the Council on Facilities, Equipment, and Supplies [CFES]

1975-76	James E. Sharman
1976-77	Edward Coates
1977-78	James Mason
1978-79	Marty McIntyre
1979-80	Margaret Waters
1980-81	Mike Collins
1981-82	Robert L. Case
1982-83	Edward T. Turner
1983-84	Ernest A. White
1984-85	Dan Gruetter
1985-86	Jack Lynn Shannon
1986-87	Larry Horine
1987-88	Armond Seidler
1988-89	Harvey White
1989-90	David Stotlar
1990-91	Maureen Henry
1991-92	Todd Seidler

Chairpersons of the Council on Facilities and Equipment [CFE]

1992-93	Brad Strand
1993-94	Marcia Walker
1994-95	Richard J. LaRue
1995-97	Thomas H. Sawyer
1997-99	Robert Femat
1999-2001	Bernie Goldfine

The CFES or CFE Award Winners

Honor Award

1979	Richard B. Flynn
1980	Edward Coates
1981	Edward Shea
1982	Martin McIntyre
1983	Margaret H. Aitken
1994	Armond Seidler
1995	Mason, James
1996	Harvey White
1997	Todd Seidler & Marcia Walker
1998	Edward Turner

Professional Recognition Award

1994	Edward Turner
1995	Larry Horine
1996	Alexander Gabrielsen
1997	Arthur Mittelstaedt
1998	Alison Osinski

Standards

A standard is something established for use as a rule or basis of comparison in measuring or judging capacity. A standard applies to some measure, principle, model, etc., with which things of the same class are compared in order to determine their quantity, value, or quality. A standard has a set of criteria used to test or measure the excellence, fitness, or correctness of something.

Standards for facilities and equipment are established by association, society, trade, or federal and state governments. The American Society for Testing and Materials (ASTM) is an example of a society that establishes standards. From the work of 132 technical standards-writing committees, ASTM (http://www.astm.org) publishes standard specifications, tests, practices, guides, and definitions for materials, products, systems, and services. ASTM also publishes books containing reports on state-of-the-art testing techniques and their possible applications. These standards and related information are used throughout the world (see Chapter 6 for greater details regarding the establishment of standards).

Guidelines

A guideline is a standard or principle by which to make a judgement or determine a policy or course of action. A guideline is developed after a standard has been established. The guideline is a series of procedures to ensure the maintenance of the standard.

Future of the Council on Facilities and Equipment

The CFE sees great potential for its newest version of the facility development book. The expanded book provides greater detail for the student, professionals in the field, consultants, and architects than previous editions. Further, the CFE will seek sponsorships to expand its semi-annual newsletter a quarterly newsletter of 8 to 16 pages. Finally, the CFE will continue to update its bi-annual list of consultants for sale to the membership and the private sector.

■ Summary

History is very important,as it tells others about the past experiences of people and organizations. The history of the CFE describes the beginning of an organization composed of professionals concerned about the construction of HPERD facilities. The development of these facilities has improved because of the efforts of the CFE and its leaders and members over the past 50 years.

Learning objective 1: The student will be able to describe the historical development of the Council for Facilities and Equipment.

The first gymnasium appeared in 1885 and construction on a grander scale continues today. The differences in the structures and contents are immense. As professionals began to gather more and more data, it became apparent that a national body should warehouse the literature, hold conferences to discuss the literature, and outline the material in a textbook to be revised periodically. The council continues to build upon its past experiences.

Learning Objective 2: The student will be able to discuss the steps taken in the developing standards for facilities and equipment

Standards are developed by national organizations The various national organizations bring together professionals in each area to develop appropriate standards for the development of stronger and safer facilities.

Learning Objective 3: The student will be able to describe the difference between standards and guidelines.

A guideline is a guide as to how something might be done, where as a standard is very specific and grounded in sound expert opinion and experience.

■ Self-Assessment Exercise

1. You have been asked by a colleague to give a presentation on the historical development of physical education, recreation, and sport facilities. Draft an outline of your presentation and a slide presentation using "presentations" software.
2. Describe for a group of young professionals what the Council on Facilities and Equipment is and how it is related to the American Alliance for Health, Physical Education, Recreation, and Dance.
3. Describe the evolution of today's American Association for Active Lifestyles and Fitness for an introductory class in sport management.

■ References

Hackensmith, C.W. (1966). *History of physical education.* New York: Harper & Row.

Rice, E.A., Hutchinson, J. L., & Lee, M. (1958). *A brief history of physical education.* (4th ed.). New York: The Ronald Press Company.

Rice, E. A. (1926). *A brief history of physical education.* New York: A.S. Barnes and Company.

Van Dalen, D. B., Mitchell, E. D., & Bennett, B. L. (1953). *A world history of physical education.* Englewood Cliffs, NJ: Prentice-Hall, Inc.

Notes

CHAPTER 2

Planning and Designing Facilities

Harvey White, New Mexico State University ■ James Karabetsos, Western Illinois University

Learning Objectives

After reading this chapter, the student will be able to

■ appreciate the evolution of facility planning,

■ understand the composition of a master plan and its importance in the growth of an organization,

■ write a program statement,

■ understand the role of selected professionals in the planning process (i.e., program specialist, facility consultant, architect, and engineers),

■ understand the significance of participatory planning,

■ understand the planning guidelines, and

■ select planning professionals.

Introduction

In the present economical climate, constructing health/wellness/fitness, physical activity, recreation, and sport facilities requires exorbitant sums of money. Capital expenditures exceeding $10 million, $15 million, and even $20 million are not unrealistic. These extreme costs and the fact that many of the building decisions must stand for the entire life of the structure (20-50+ years) intensifies the importance of good planning. As a result, careful analysis of users' needs over long periods of time has become a quintessential element in many of the present-day building projects.

In most instances, poorly constructed facilities can be directly attributed to ineffective planning. Errors in design, omission of ancillary features, and miscommunication of needs invariably lead to sub-par results, require expensive change orders, or result in costly overruns. Further, exacerbating the poorly planned facility dilemma are the delays and programmatic changes that are invariably called for to accommodate the altered construction plans brought about by these changes.

The planning of state-of-the-art health/wellness/fitness, physical activity, recreation, and sport facilities is not a simple process. Whenever one attempts to calculate future facility needs, interpret programmatic trends or forecast societal changes, miscalculations are possible and misinterpretations probable. However, the importance of these tasks should not be underestimated. The fact that many of these facilities end up hampering programs they had been designed to enhance typifies the problem of ineffective planning. The reality of these shortcomings highlights the exigency for initiating and utilizing a planning process which addresses problems on a long-range, systematic, and continuous basis.

A Historical Perspective

In the past, facility planning frequently occurred in a disconnected fashion. Oftentimes, facility administrators or planning/building committees designed their buildings independently of the other agencies within their organizations. This isolationism frequently led to vacuous areas of non-coverage or duplication of facilities and programs. These facility planners many times relied solely on hunches and "guesstimates" to design their edifices. Their intuitions and estimates frequently were off-target, and often the facilities they planned did not adequately serve the programs housed within them.

The more conscientious planners of past decades conducted rudimentary surveys to assist with their planning. However, the findings of these surveys too frequently were scant at best. On many occasions the results, on which planners predicated their facility designs, might not have even included input from user groups or program directors. Consequently, this type of "hard line" planning often resulted in disgruntled reviews and ambivalent acceptance.

Other types of planning approaches commonly found in past decades included political and "grass roots" planning. In the political planning process, the planner made the facility design decisions to influence certain segments of the population. These favors may have resulted in auxiliary benefits to specific programs or activities but often led to facilities that fell far short of expected standards in other areas. The latter strategy, grass roots planning, frequently evolved from negotiations with specific segments of the population and led to the selection of specific services or programs for which respective groups lobbied and were not necessarily based on an assessment of the overall needs of the prospective facility users.

Facility planners today operate in a different environment. The nature of physical education, recreation, and athletics is now characterized by a mix of declining resources, interrelated programs, and shared facilities. These types of complex circumstances necessitate that planning not be done in isolation. The complexity of meeting diverse needs of users and coordinating the efforts of all the agencies using a facility require that all individuals be included who can contribute in a meaningful way. This type of facility planning is called participatory planning. (See Guideline #3.)

Technology and Facility Planning

Technology is having a significant impact on facility planning as we enter the 21st century. Computers have become commonly used in processing quantifiable data (i.e., heating, ventilation and air conditioning control, security time-tables, lighting schemes, etc.) as well as providing input into the planning and design of facilities through computer-aided design (CAD) programs.

In the computer-aided design of facilities, software packages range from basic programs for simple walk-through maneuvers, which require only rudimentary graphics hardware, to high-end packages aimed at producing real-life images that can be controlled by operator head movements and tracking gloves. These virtual reality programs allow for animation of life-size figures, supported by sound cards that enhance the real-life effects of walk-throughs. The effects that provide a realistic setting are truly remarkable. High-end packages include sophisticated 3-D visualizations, which enable planners to look at different designs as they travel through a facility to see actual shapes and configurations that provide meaningful feedback. Wearing special headgear and/or stereoscopic glasses, users can simulate a situation or activity using backward/forward, up/down, pitch up/pitch down, and angle left/angle right and rotational movements. These movements are projected on a screen and approximate actual sport or recreational activities to varying degrees of reality.

Utilizing CAD technology in facility planning will continue to develop and assist with issues such as pedestrian traffic patterns, color selection, and spatial arrangements of furnishings/equipment, while conserving both time and expenses. Used today by aerospace firms and automakers, CAD programs will become less costly and increasingly more important in the planning and design of facilities. They will alter the methodology of facility planners while increasing their efficiency. The future use of advanced CAD programs will result in far better functioning and more aesthetically pleasing sport facilities in the end.

Planning Guidelines

The Council on Facilities and Equipment has adopted the following guidelines for planning facilities:

Guideline #1: Comply with the Americans with Disabilities Act (ADA)

Federal, state, and local legislation mandates the provision of certain services to all persons in our society, including those with various disabilities. In order for services to be provided to all individuals, architectural barriers within facilities must be eliminated. The Americans with Disabilities Act (ADA) of 1990 provides civil rights legislation for citizens with disabilities by prohibiting discrimination in places of public accommodation. The legislation requires the elimination of discriminatory practices toward all people with special needs.

The ADA legislation requires that facilities be designed to allow all patrons to have access to all activity sections of the facility. This mandate calls for the elimination of all obstacles that prevent parties from entering the facility or any architectural restraint that hampers moving inside the building. Accessibility also includes the capability to arrive at the site and requires a physical environment designed to enhance usability by individuals with special needs. If this standard can not be met, managers may be required to modify facility policies, practices, and procedures to reach that standard. The ADA applies to all physical education, recreation, and athletic facilities including gymnasiums, fitness facilities, health clubs, etc.

The planning for accessibility is a complex undertaking requiring much thought, cooperation among facility planners and users, and a removal of "attitudinal barriers" in order to meet the needs of all individuals. Federal health, education, and welfare regulations require that individuals with disabilities be consulted when designing public facilities. Supplementally, other good resource groups for facility designs include local chapters of national organizations whose primary purposes are to assist individuals who have special needs. A technical manual on the ADA can be found at the following website: http://www.usdoj.gov/crt/ada/taman3.html.

Guideline #2: Use a Master Plan (Comprehensive Plan)

It is recommended that today's planners use a well-contemplated, systematized strategy which takes into account the many variables (present and future) that may affect a facility to prevent debacles in facility construction because of slipshod planning. The document in which this information appears is called the Master Plan, or in municipal agencies, the Comprehensive Plan. This plan is a formal, comprehensive building scheme that identifies the organization's facility needs and establishes the priority in which construction of new or the renovation of existing facilities will occur.

The process of developing master plans involves the accumulation of vast amounts of information that may, directly or indirectly, affect the organization's mission. Usually the charge for developing facility master plans resides at the higher administrative levels of an organization and generally involves administrators, architects, program directors, community members, and engineers. The complexity of developing a master plan is influenced by the size of the institution or agency conducting the planning, human and financial resources available to support the planning process, and the master planning skills of individuals involved in the process. An example of the steps that may be followed in the process of developing a master plan for an educational facility is illustrated in Figure 2. 1.

The format of master plans may differ from one organization to another; however, they are basically composed of all the organization's anticipated long- and short-range acquisitions, renovations, and/or constructions. They include all possible community and regional developments, areas best suited for expansion possibilities, predicted demographic shifts, and programmatic need changes. The long-range projection of the Master (or Comprehensive) Plan is usually 5 or 10 years, and the short-range projection is generally one or two years. In some instances organizations also use long-term forecasts that project a 5-to-10 year outlook. The development and maintenance of a Master Plan is a continuous and ongoing process and is characterized by periods of highly intense planning. The components of the plan are directed toward specific planning goals that are identified in the organization's facility development program (see Figure 2.2).

The components of the Master Plan process presented above provide an abstract of transpositions that are to occur at some given point between the present and the future. The general rule when using projections in a Master (Comprehensive) Plan is to forego conservatism and propose the ultimate in design and imagination. A state-of-the-art facility is the goal. However, there is also a built-in cushion that allows some latitude for negotiations and cut-backs if future concessions are necessary. Although assurances do not exist, using this progressive approach increases the likelihood that buildings will be well designed and constructed to fulfill a 20- to 50-year life expectancy.

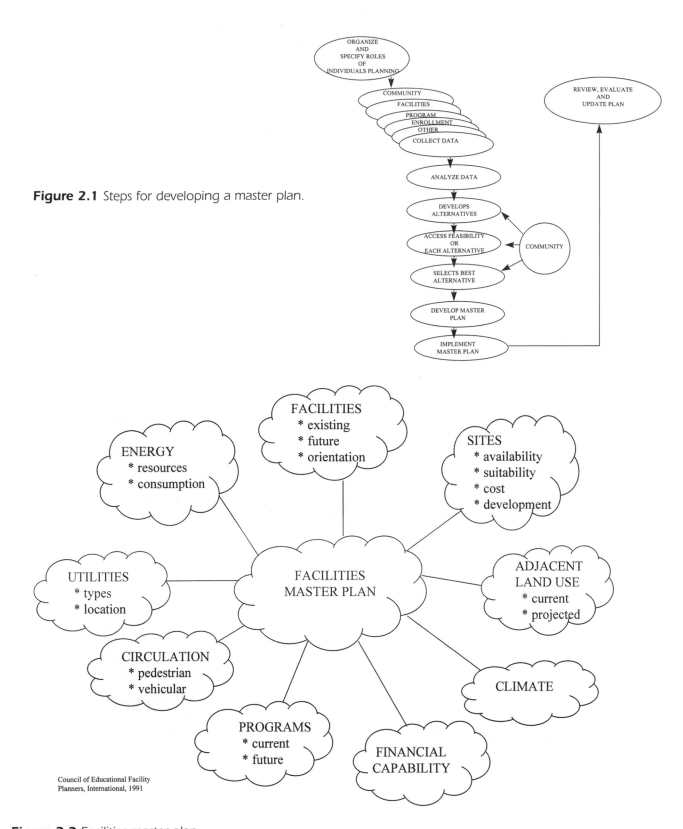

Figure 2.1 Steps for developing a master plan.

Council of Educational Facility
Planners, International, 1991

Figure 2.2 Facilities master plan.

The facility Master Plan should have as its primary concern the facility requirements and alternatives that are available to accomplish the specific goals and objectives of the institution's programs. With a view of what is available and what is needed to meet specified goals, facility planners can better understand the sequences that need to take place for alternatives to reach fruition. The Master Plan is paramount for planning, designing, constructing, utilizing, and evaluating quality facilities.

Guideline #3: Use a Participatory Planning Approach

The view that users, organizational units, and occupants have primary input into both new construction and/or renovation of existing recreational facilities is an essential precept in participatory facility planning. Furthermore, if the data obtained from these principal parties are clearly explained and adequately understood by the designers, the chances of a particular facility meeting the needs of the program constituents are substantially enhanced.

When designing facilities in this collegial environment, organizations commonly include all persons who are interested in or have a penchant for physical education, recreation, and athletic facility design. The specific thrust varies from one agency or organization to another. Community agencies take into account their large, divergent groups, and universities and colleges usually focus on the needs of the educational community. However, the importance of receiving input from representative user groups is the common thread that is interwoven into the fabric of this approach to facility planning.

A sample participatory, or team planning process, is illustrated in Figure 2.3.

Origination of the Idea (Basic Program Level). The idea typically emanates from individuals intricately involved in the outdated facility and the programs it houses.

Presenting the Idea to Higher Authority. Those conceiving the idea attempt to convince their departmental colleagues of the need for the project, whether

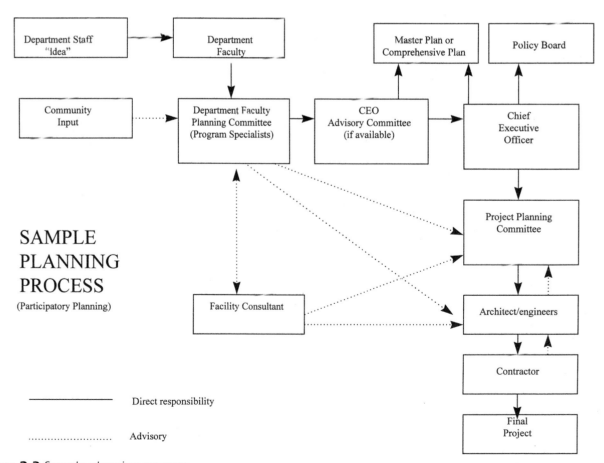

Figure 2.3 Sample planning process.

it is a new facility or simply remodeling an existing place.

If adequate support is generated, a departmental planning team is selected by the principal administrator of that unit (i.e., department chair, agency head, etc.). The mission of this planning team is to review the initial proposal, modify it, and embellish the substance of the report before presenting it to the next highest authority.

If the project is approved, selected department members who possess programmatic expertise will function as *program specialists* and advise both the Project Planning Committee and the Project Architect.

In Preparation for Highest Authority. Some colleges and universities, school systems, and recreation departments require a succession of complex steps to gain project approval, while others have relatively few and simple procedures. Regardless of organizational differences, a common feature should be the referencing of the organization's Master Plan to determine the reasonableness of the facility proposal. Referring back to the Master Plan will help assure consistency for the programs and facilities within the organization.

Gaining project approval from the policy board, the chief executive officer (CEO) appoints a project planning committee (see Guideline #5). This committee has a number of important responsibilities which assist the architect in planning the best facility possible.

A basic administrative principle should be understood clearly by all persons who participate in a participatory planning process. The chief executive officer, as the principal administrator of an organization, has the authority to intervene in the planning process at any juncture. Some CEOs exercise this right regularly while others prefer to maintain an "at arms' length" approach, relying on the committee to determine the results. The likelihood of this intervention taking place is predicated on several factors, the most significant being the management style espoused by the chief administrator.

Guideline #4: Research Your Funding Options

The single most important requisite when proposing a new or renovating an existing facility is to determine how the project will be funded. The project has a better chance of being approved by higher authorities if all available funding sources are researched and a precise funding strategy is developed in advance. This plan should include a listing of the different funding sources (i.e., governmental grants, private organizations, interested philanthropists, etc.)

which are available to support the project or identifying parties and/or organizations that have expressed a willingness to help provide the necessary funds.

Guidelines #5: Organize a Project Planning Committee

Once a facility project has been approved, a *project planning committee* is established to accumulate and organize all information for presentation to the architect. The makeup of this committee is usually members of the department (department specialists); an administrator; a principal member of the architectural firm to provide direction; users of the facility; selected construction specialists (engineers); and building specialists, as dictated by planning needs (see Figure 2.4). The facility consultant, whose responsibilities are defined in greater detail later in this chapter, should be an ex-officio member of this group.

Among the most important responsibilities of this committee are to gather information from user groups and use it to prepare a final coherent and systematic written program for the architect. This report is called the *program statement* (see Guideline #7) and is used by the architect to develop the facility design. To accomplish an acceptable end product, college and university physical education, recreation, and athletic groups should seek input from a wide variety of program areas such as adaptive physical education, aquatics, team/individual/dual sports, dance, outdoor recreation, exercise science, martial arts, and basic instruction classes. In municipal recreation planning, representation from indoor recreation, outdoor recreation, and therapeutic recreation is germane.

The project planning committee works with the architect and makes a majority of the crucial design decisions. This group has the responsibility of reacting to the architect's initial concepts and schematic drawings. It coordinates the design planning with the various users of the facility. In addition, it reacts to questions dealing with program statement interpretation, proposal changes, and possible deletions due to cost or program elimination. There should be no changes in plans without first having the input of this committee. When immediate answers are needed, the chairperson of this group may need to make some of these decisions alone.

Guideline #6: Understand when to Renovate, Retrofit, or Replace

The practice of buying-using-discarding has become unacceptable today. This not only applies to the day-to-day items that are recyclable, but to facilities as well. Due to the high cost of new construction, upper-

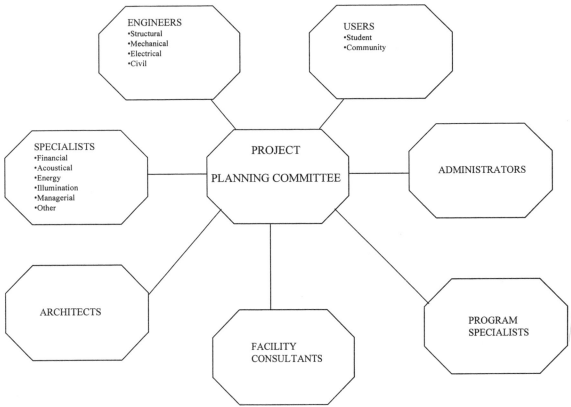

Figure 2.4 Organization of project planning commitee

level administrators, whether in the private sector, at a university, at a municipal agency, or in a public school system, have the responsibility of making the best decisions regarding the use of existing buildings. In meeting this obligation, it is necessary for administrators, with input from knowledgeable resource professionals, to consider the feasibility of either renovating or retrofitting an existing building, or of constructing a new facility.

By definition, the renovation of an existing facility is the rehabilitation of the physical features of that building, including the rearrangement of spaces within the structure. Retrofitting, on the other hand, is the addition of new systems, items, features, materials, and/or equipment to a facility that were not in place at the time the building was constructed. These changes may be minor, or they could be significant to the point of changing the primary function of the facility.

Administrators have a myriad of factors to consider to accurately ascertain whether renovation, retrofitting, or new construction is the most prudent alternative. One of the most important considerations is the impact that the construction process will have on ongoing programs. Consideration, for example, must be given to possible program modifications and adaptions that may be necessitated during the construction phase of the project.

A close scrutiny of the advantages and disadvantages of the existing structure and the possibility of a new building should be undertaken. Some of the factors that should be considered include, but are not limited to

■ Costs. The costs include construction to provide comparable space, compliance with safety codes and accessibility standards, and maintenance. The "50% rule" can be used as a guide: Do not retrofit/renovate if cost is greater than 50% of replacement.

■ Site selection. Site selection considerations include availability, sufficient space, location, parking, and available utilities.

■ Architectural and structural standards. There are many standards to be considered including aesthetics, meeting current and long-range program goals, energy efficiency, condition of footings and foundations, condition of heating and ventilation, air conditioning, and security system.

■ Educational considerations. The educational considerations focus upon meeting needs of current and future programs.

■ Community needs and restrictions. These include population needs, zoning requirements, the future plans for the area.

Before deciding on the wisdom of renovation, retrofitting, remodeling, or replacing, factors concerning the existing and proposed facilities should be evaluated in detail, both individually and collectively. It would also be beneficial for administrators to project a reasonable life expectancy of the facility, taking into account factors such as

■ increased or decreased populations served by the programs within the facility,
■ growth and development of areas surrounding the facility, and
■ the potential reorganization, community rezoning, or consolidation of schools in the district.

A decision on whether renovation or retrofitting is preferable to new construction should then be rendered, based on a composite of all the factors.

Guideline #7: Develop a Program Statement for the Architect

The program statement is a written document describing all the programs' current and proposed activities and events, plus their associated facility and/or space requirements. It describes the programs' goals and objectives and identifies any special facility needs the programs may have, (see Figure 2.5). In addition, the statement should also address the broader relationship of the physical education, recreation and athletic activities, and the proposed use of the facility.

Also referred to as the "building program" or "educational specifications," this program statement is the vehicle by which the needs of the organization's programs are communicated to the architect and the project planning committee. As a consequence, it is an extremely important document that provides linkage between the programs and the facility requirements.

The initial step in developing the program statement is to establish of goals and objectives to be achieved in each functional area of the programs. Goals are defined as desirable conditions sought, and objectives are defined as specific ends to be achieved in each of the programs.

The next step is to conceptualize the program(s) that are necessary to achieve the desired goals and objectives. Data to be included in the program statement are depicted in Figure 2.5. It is essential that the document be written in a clear, concise manner reflecting an optimal as well as minimal level of the programs to

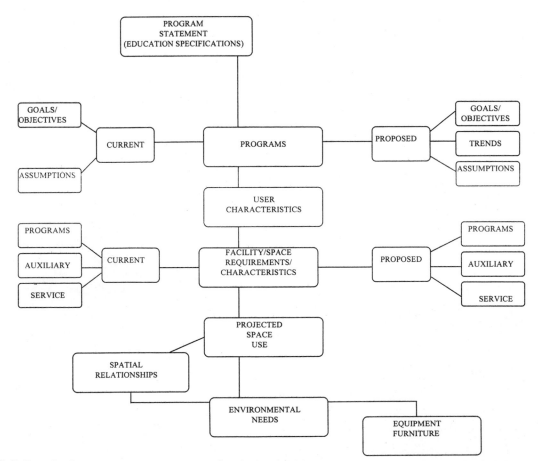

Figure 2.5 Developing a program statement for the architect.

be offered. The building program statement typically will be the result of a critical evaluation of the current programs determining whether the new programs should be emphasized, if old ones should be eliminated, or if old and new programs should be combined. All facility needs should be considered, both indoor and outdoor, and the location of buildings should be addressed in the report in terms of its importance on programming.

To ensure that the building program statement reflects the professional opinion of all members of the project planning committee (departmental personnel, administrators, facility consultant, specialists, and users), a rough draft should be circulated to all contributors for their review and comments prior to sending the statement to the architect. From this draft a final copy is developed and presented to the project architect.

Sample Building Program Statment Outline

Part I. Objectives of the Programs

    A. Instructional (professional and service)

    B. Recreational sports

    C. Adapted

    D. Athletics (interscholastic and intercollegiate)

    E. Club sports

    F. Community/school programs

    G. Others

Part II. Basic Assumptions to be Addressed

    A. Facilities will provide for a broad program of instruction, adapted activities, intramural sports, athletics, club sports, and others

    B. Demographics of the population who will use the facility

    C. Existing facilities will be programmed for use

    D. Basic design considerations: "What's most important?"

    E. Facility expansion possibilities will be provided for in the planning

    F. Outdoor facilities should be located adjacent to indoor facilities

    G. Consideration will be given to administrative and staff needs

    H. Existing problems

    I. Others

Part III. Comparable Facility Analysis

    A. Visit comparable facilities that have been recently constructed

    B. Compare cost, design features, etc.

    Part IV. Factors Affecting Planning

    A. Federal and state legislation

    B. Club sports movement

    C. The community education, or "Lighted School" program

    D. Surge of new non-competitive activities being added to the curriculum

    E. Expansion of intramural sports and athletic programs

    F. Sharing certain facilities by boys and men and girls and women (athletic training rooms and equipment rooms)

cont'd.

Sample Building Program Statment Outline—Cont'd.

    G. Coeducational programming

    H. Emphasis on individual exercise programs

    I. Physical fitness movement

    J. Systems approach in design and construction

    K. New products

    L. Others

Part V. Explanation of Current and Proposed Programming

    A. Instructional

    B. Intramural sports

    C. Athletics

    D. Club sports

    E. Adaptive programs

    F. Community/school

    G. Recreational programs

    H. Priority listing of programs

    I. Others

Part VI. Preliminary Data Relative to the Proposed New Facilities

    A. Existing indoor facilities, square footage broken down by area (e.g., equipment storage, training room, etc.)

    B. Priority listing of the proposed new indoor facilities and the function of each.

    C. Existing outdoor facilities broken down by area (e.g., football field, track, etc.)

    D. Priority listing of the proposed outdoor facilities and the function of each.

    E. Community facilities being used as resource or adjunct facility areas for current programs (e.g., golf courses, trap range, rifle range, bowling alleys)

    F. Others

Part VII. Space Needs and Allocation in the Proposed New Facilities

    A. Main gymnasium

    B. Spectator seating

    C. Lobby or concourse

    D. Administrative offices

    E. Faculty offices

    F. Conference rooms

    G. Laboratory/classrooms

    H. Other considerations (e.g., wall clocks, acoustical treatment of certain areas, mechanical, etc.)

Part VIII. Purposes and Uses of Auxiliary Space Areas

    A. Exercise/therapy

    B. Multipurpose gym

    C. Golf area

    D. Archery area

    E. Wrestling gym

Sample Building Program Statment Outline—Cont'd.

  F. Main dance studio

  G. Street shoe usage room

  H. Handball/racquetball courts

  I. Squash courts

  J. Others

Part IX. Service Facilities

  A. Locker rooms

  B. Shower rooms

  C. Toweling areas

  D. Toilets for locker area

  E. Equipment and supply storage areas

  F. Custodial storage areas

  G. Athletic training rooms

  H. Laundry

  I. Others

Part X. Projected Use of Present Facilities

Part XI. Spatial Relationships (relationship of areas to each other)

Part XII. Environmental Necessities

Part XIII. Equipment and Furniture List (all movable and fixed items identified in the document)

Guideline #9: Use Planning Professionals

Efficient facility planning requires the expertise and collaboration of many individuals. All participants are important to the process; however, their levels of involvement may vary depending on what phase of planning being undertaken at any particular time. The roles of three professionals are identified in the subsequent sections. However, it should be understood that their services are predicated upon on the client's needs and should be included in the contract agreement.

Program Specialists

The role of the program specialist in facility planning is very important. Program specialists normally are individuals who are actively engaged in the programs for which the facility is being designed. These program specialists should be individuals who are knowledgeable about the uses and problems of similar facilities. This involvement increases the likelihood that the contributions made by these individu-als in developing the Program Statement are both accurate and realistic. Examples of the type of input the program specialist offers include, but are not limited to the following:

■ Determines the number of activity and/or teaching stations needed to serve the instructional, intramural, recreation, athletic, club, and adaptive programs.

■ Helps in the selection of materials (e.g., hardwood floors and/or synthetic floors, lighting requirements, acoustical treatments, and maintenance issues).

■ Informs all appropriate persons and the general public about the program purposes and needs for the facilities; explains the facility plans.

■ Ascertains the various sizes of teams, classes, and groups that will use the facilities and knows the requirements of their activities and the implications they present in facility design.

■ Monitors changes relevant to facility planning (synthetic surfaces, all-weather tracks, coed athletic training rooms, coed and senior citizen classes, programs for the disabled, total commu-

nity use of recreational facilities, and rapid development of sports clubs are trends that may be considered in developing program statements).
■ Identifies, studies, and recommends desired traffic patterns for various individuals and groups, including spectators.
■ Provides the architect and planning committee with examples of facilities that meet desired needs. If the sites are too distant for visitation, slides or pictures may be taken as illustrations for the architect and planning committee.
■ Points out areas that represent quality as well as those that represent minimal quantitative standards.
■ Points out the special considerations necessary to allow persons with disabilities full use of facilities.

The program specialist may be assisted by facility consultants in identifying specific material needs, dimensions, space relationships, innovations, and other pertinent information.

Facility Consultant

A facility consultant is a professional in the field who is either employed by another organization or is self-employed in the facility-consulting business. This individual usually has had experience with facility planning and is familiar with recently constructed facilities in the country. The consultant is up-to-date with the latest innovations in facility construction materials, building concepts, and general programming. In many instances this professional should know the location of some recent renovation or construction projects and would be a good reference to the project planning committee when hiring an architect.

An outside consultant assists the project/building planning committee in developing alternatives and establishing priorities in its building project. As an objective expert, the consultant normally is looked upon as a person who can exert considerable influence.

A facility consultant may assist in selecting an architect and may serve as an advisor to both the architect and the project planning committee. The consultant's role becomes critical when the architect lacks a basic orientation to the specific programs for which the facility is being designed. When this occurs, the consultant's contribution to the success of the project becomes crucial. The Council on Facilities and Equipment [CFE] of the American Association for Active

Lifestyles and Fitness [AAALR] maintains a list of facility consultants who are identified by their areas of expertise.

Architect

One of the central members of the facility planning and design team is the architect. Since the architect's role is of paramount importance, a great deal of time should be spent on investigating the firm and/or individuals interested in the assignment. When selecting an architect, factors to consider are the firm's reputation, the project architect's experience, and an architect's interpersonal skills and ability to establish rapport with other members of the planning team. Ideally, the entire project planning committee should participate in the selection of the architect. Most states have laws that require architects to be licensed to practice architecture in the state where the facility is to be erected. The American Institute of Architects (AIA) can be helpful in providing information relative to those certified in a given geographic area.

Not to be discounted in importance when selecting an architect is the location of the firm. There is a decided advantage in selecting an architectural firm that is located near the proposed project. Besides the obvious political benefits of this selection, close proximity to the construction site allows for frequent visitations to the site, thus providing a greater safeguard against the possibility of construction errors. In recent years it has been common for local architects to enlist the assistance of larger national firms specializing in sports and recreation facilities. With project supervision as an integral function of the architect's responsibilities, the selection of an individual whose project management skills are well honed is preferred.

A common practice used to select architects is to implement a request-for-proposal (RFP) procedure. In this approach, firms are asked to submit proposals that explain how they would address the program statement. The proposals are submitted to the project planning committee, analyzed, and the selection of the architect is then made based on the assessment of all relevant considerations.

The architect's responsibilities are numerous and vital; they typically include, but are not limited to, the following:

■ Pre-design planning, where the architect:
  a. Solicits facility and equipment needs from all user groups.
  b. Develops a time schedule for each stage of the project.

c. Turns the program statement into an architectural or building program.

■ Schematic design, where the architect:
a. Translates the written program into a graphic representation of a building plan.
b. Designs and presents plans regarding space relations of various functions and accessibility to the facility for different functions. Shows how the facility will satisfy the needs as identified in the pre-design conference.
c. Studies the site, its topography, its relationship to the community and to traffic patterns, and the availability of utilities. Determines how the site might be developed.
d. Reviews applicable codes and laws to determine their effect on the design.

■ Design development, where the architect:
a. Develops the general design of the facility once approval from the highest authority is secured.
b. Prepares sketches of elevations and models to establish the visual character of the project.
c. Determines building materials and outlines their specifications along with the utilitarian value, aesthetic qualities, and mechanical and electrical systems.

■ Bidding, where the architect:
a. Assists the client in obtaining bids and awarding contracts.
b. Determines, with the client, how the project will be bid and the contractors who will be qualified to bid.
c. Answers questions for bidders and clarifies any aspects of the construction documents.
d. Provides copies of specifications, documents, and drawings for contractors, owners, and others who may need them.

■ Directing construction, when the architect:
a. Meets with the client and contractor to outline the project and discuss operating procedures.
b. Issues bulletins and change orders to accomplish changes requested by the client or required by field conditions.
c. Approves payments to contractors

■ Selecting Planning Professionals
The next task for the building committee after it has completed the building program and facility analysis chart, is to select a consultant, architect, and/or engineer. This may be the most critical aspect of the committee's task. Before the committee can begin this task, it must decide what type(s) of professional(s) it needs to complete the project.

Many architectural firms have either their own engineering department in-house or a working relationship with an engineering firm. It is best to allow the architectural firm to arrange for the most compatible engineering relationship.

It is advisable, however, to employ a consultant who is experienced in the area of facility planning to assist the committee and the chosen architect. Many times the consultant can be very helpful in this team effort because of expertise in designing specific spaces that may be unfamilar to the architect and committee. The consultant, if experienced, may be a very valuable asset when selecting an architectural and engineering firm.

Selecting the Consultant

What should the committee or selection body consider when selecting a consultant for a building project? The basic considerations in selecting the consultant, include determining:

■ educational background,
■ work experience,
■ planning experience,
■ proximity to project,
■ reputation,
■ ability to work with the building committee, architects, engineers, and contractors,
■ ability to understand and read blueprints and specification documents, and
■ ability to understand the organization's programs and the future of such programs and others.

The committee can develop a list of prospective consultants by contacting the American Alliance for Health, Physical Education, Recreation and Dance (AAHPERD, Reston, VA), Association for Fitness in Business (AFB, Indianapolis, IN), other similar facilities, or a local college or university that has a department of physical education, exercise science, kinesiology, recreation, or sport management. The selection process should be similar to that used to select an architect.

Inviting Possible Architectural Firms to the Project

It is important to invite all capable architectural firms to submit proposals for the project. The following steps should be taken when inviting the firms (see Figure 2.6) to submit proposals:

Figure 2.6
**Steps for Developing a List of Possible Firms
to Invite to your Project**

1. Send a standard letter of interest (See Figure 2.7) to all firms (recommend approximately 12)

2. Letter should state: (a) WHo you are? (b) WHY you are writing to them? (c) WHAT services you are interested in? (d) WHERE your project is to be located? (e) WHEN you will need this project constructed? (f) HOW you plan to proceed with this project?

3. Letter should give 5-7 statndard questions that each interested firm should address in their initial response. Questions such as:

    a. What were the five projects that you feel would be similar to our project in scope and dollar volume?

    b. Who are the key members of your design team who would be working on our project? Please include the resume for each person.

    c. What particular expertise does your firm and members of your design firm have that would benefit our project?

    d. How will your firm approach this project? What involvement would you see for members of our committee during each phase of the project?

    e. What exciting or innovative things have you done design-wise in your most representative past project which may or may not have a direct appplication to what we are hoping to do in our project?

    f. What fee percentage would you anticipate charging for your services?

    g. Should your firm be asked to interview and subsequently be selected for design services on our project, your firm would be asked to sign a standard AIA contract, does your firm have any concerns with signing this contract? If so, you should note those concerns in your response to the committee for its deliberations.

Send a letter of interest (see Figure 2.7) to all firms that have experience building projects similar to yours (recommend at least 12 firms).

The letter should include who you are, why you are writing to them, what services you are interested in, where your project is to be located, when you will need this project built, and how you plan to proceed with this project.

The letter should ask five to seven standard questions you wish each interested firm to address its their initial response, including:

■ What are the last five projects that would be similar to the project in scope and dollar volume completed by the firm?

■ Who are the key members of the design team who would be working on this project? Please include a resume for each person.

■ What particular expertise does the firm and its members have that would benefit this project?

■ How will the firm approach this project, and what involvement would the firm see for members of the committee during each phase of the project?

■ What exciting or innovative things has the firm done in terms of design that have a direct application to what we are hoping to do in this project?

■ What fee percentage would the firm anticipate charging for services rendered?

■ If the firm were asked to interview and subsequently be selected for design services on the project, it will be asked to sign a modified AIA contract. Will this be a problem for the firm? If yes, why?

Selecting an Architect or Architectural Firm

What should the committee consider when selecting an architect ? The basic considerations for select-

Figure 2.7
Sample Letter to Architectural Firms

July 28, 1998

Mr. Mark Twain
Principal
The TwainDesign Group
141 East Ohio Street
Hannibal, MO 36705-9087

Dear Mr. Twain

RE: Indian Joe Recreational Sports Center

Hannibal University is interested in seeking proposals from Architectural/Engineering firms to work with the University in planning for the following: Building a free-standing recreational sports complex (250,000 GSF) with fields on 20 adjacent acres.

The new facility to be known as, Indian Joe Recreational Sports Center, is estimated to have a total project cost budget not to exceed $25,000,000.00 (including A&E fees, moveable equipment, building costs, site costs, and demolition costs). The new facility will involve students, facility, staff, and alumni interested in recreational activities.

If you firm has had experience in facility design of the nature outlined herein, has designed facilities for higher education recreational sports. We encourage you to submit a proposal for our review (five copies).

Currently, out tentative schedule is as follows:

July 28, 1998	Issu this letter seeking interest for our project from architectural firms
September 15, 1998	Deadline for submittal or proposals by interested architectural firms
October 15, 1998	Completion of University's initial review fo submitted proposals and development of short list for interviews
October 25, 26, 1998	Architects to be interviewed by Hannibal University Architectural Selection Committee
November 3, 1998	Recommendations to be submitted to the VP for Business Affairs for Business Affairs and the President for review and selection
November 10, 1998	Award of design contract to successful A&E firm
December 1, 1998	Begin initial review of University's pre-program, Initial Site Selection Study, and begin meetings with building users

Further target dates would be mutually addressed after selection of an architectural firm is complete. The members of the Selection Committee would most likely include:

Dr. Huckleberry Finn, Physical Education Chair
Dr. Polly, Director of Recreational Sports
Dr. Tom Sawyer, Director of Athletics
Mr. Murray, Assistant Vice President for University Properties
Mr. Runion, Assistant Vice President for Facilities Management
Mr. Sutton, Facilities Management Campus Architect

Should your firm be interested in submitting a proposal for our review, the following topics must be clearly addressed: (1) Please submit a brief history of your firm with specific attention given to past expertise on projects of similar nature; (2) List all projects of like nature your team members have been involved with, plus list titl, address, owner, final design estimate, successful low bid, and length of construction period; (3) Please provide a tentative schedule for programming, schematic design, design development, and construction documents, plus an anticipated length of time for construction on a project of this nature; (4) Please provide a fee schedule for services as outlined, plus an anticipated length of time for contract; and (5) Appropriate references may be attached if you wish.

Also attached for your review is a copy of Hannibal University's facilities standards which are to be used during the planning for all projects on campus, and Hannibal University's standard contract with Architects/Engineers. You will be asked to sign such a contract if selected as our design architects.

If you have any questions, please feel free to contact me at (632) 456-8976. We look forward to your interest in what we consider to be an exciting project for Hannibal Unviersity.

Sincerely,

ing an architect, include determining whether the firm

■ is a member of the American Institute of Architects (AIA),
■ is licensed to practice in the state where facility is to be built,
■ has a good reputation,
■ can furnish references,
■ can provide examples of work on similar projects,
■ is in close proximity to the project to provide weekly visitations,
■ is able to work with the "building committee," consultants, and engineers,
■ is able to recommend reliable and respected contractors and sub-contractors, and
■ is able to provide strong competent supervision for the project.

The committee should develop a list of prospective architectural firms experienced in this area. A list can be solicited from the American Institute of Architects (AIA, Washington, D.C.) or the Association for Fitness in Business (AFB, Indianapolis, IN), or by contacting other similar facilities that have just been completed or are under construction (see Figure 2.6). After the list is completed, contact each firm and request a proposal outlining what the firm can do for the committee. Once the proposals have been gathered, reviewed, and ranked, select the top 5 to 10 firms for an interview. Interview the firms and select the one that can provide the best service and work cooperatively with the committee. After selection of the architectural firm, a contractual agreement will be completed and signed.

A legally binding contract should follow a standard form of agreement between the client and architect. The responsibilities of the architectural team include the building program review, evaluation of the site for the proposed building, schematic design, design development, construction documents, contractor bidding, and construction supervision.

Other Professional Involved in the Building Project

Other professionals will be working on the building, including civil, structural, mechanical, electrical, and acoustical engineers; interior designer; landscape architect; and general, electrical, and mechanical contractors. (See glossary for full descriptions.)

■ Summary

Poor facility planning often leads to needless expense and frequently produces inadequate results. Therefore, the importance of a properly planned building process cannot be overemphasized.

Learning Objective 1: The student will be able to have an appreciation of the evolution of facility planning.

Planners of the past relied on "guesstimates," rudimentary surveys, political planning, and "grass roots" approaches. However, modern-day planners use the participatory planning method because of the complex circumstances and diverse needs of users in multipurpose facilities.

Learning Objective 2: The student will be able to understand the composition of a master plan and its importance in the growth of the organization.

An organization's approach to facility planning can be enhanced with the use of the master plan (comprehensive plan) method. This invaluable planning guide helps avoid communication failure and provides all persons, from high-level administrators to program directors, with a "beacon" by which present and future building strategies can be guided.

Learning Objective 3: The student will be able to write a program statement.

The program statement reflects the opinion of all members of the project planning committee or building committee. It is the key document to assist the architect in the design development phase of the project. It includes objectives of the program (project), basic assumptions to be addressed, comparable facility analysis, factors affecting planning, explanation of current and proposed programming, preliminary data relative to the proposed new facility, space needs and allocation in the proposed new facility, purposes and uses of auxiliary space areas, service facilities, projected use of present facilities, spatial relationships, environmental necessities, and equipment/furniture list.

Learning objective 4: The student will be able to understand the role of selected professionals in the planning process.

The planning for new construction or renovation of an existing facility that serves multiple programs and fulfills the needs of diverse populations is a complex undertaking. It requires considerable interaction among current staff members, administrators, and planning professionals. This exchange includes the sharing of vital data (e.g., site, structural soundness, educational needs, and cost) that would be utilized in making important project decisions. The underlining principle of participatory planning ensures that individuals who have the programmatic interest and facility design expertise share in the process. This should help meet diverse program needs while instilling a sense of "ownership" in individuals that provides encourages support for the project.

The planning professionals that may be employed to assist in the facility planning process are usually associated with the programs to be hosted in the facility. The more complex the organizational structure and the diversity of needs to be met, the greater the need for individuals with specialized expertise. Program specialists are most likely existing staff members with a comprehensive understanding of the needs of all programs. The specialists usually take the leadership role in writing the program statement. When funds are available, facility consultants may also be employed. These professionals should have a general understanding of program trends and a working knowledge of facility design. Facility consultants are frequently called upon to assist the program specialist in writing the program statement. These individuals' primary function, however, is to serve as a liaison to the architect and the project planning committee.

The project architect is a central figure in the construction process. Because of the prominence of the architect's role, a great deal of thought should be given to the selection of this individual. The architect works with the project planning committee, consultant, and specialist to design the facility. For an agreed-upon fee, the architect is responsible for a number of specified items. Additional services can also be rendered; however, there is usually a commensurate increase in financial compensation for these additions. It should be noted that facility planning is a collaborative effort, and the input of all individuals involved in this process is valued.

Learning Objective 5: The student will be able to understand the significance of particpatory planning.

Participatory planning is pivotal to the success of a building project. It begins with the initial idea for a facility and continues through final acceptance, immediately before possession of the completed project (although evaluation of effectiveness of the design continues for years).

Learning Objective 6: The student will be able to understand planning guidelines.

Planning guidelines are the key steps to be taken in designing any building project. The steps include (1) complying with the Americans with Disabilities Act, (2) using the master plan, (3) using a participatory planning process, (4) understanding research funding options, (5) organizing a project (building) planning committee, (6) understanding when to renovate, retrofit, or replace, (7) developing a program statement for the architect, and (8) using planning professionals.

Learning objective 7: The student will be able to select planning professionals.

It is important to spend time to develop an appropriate selection process for planning professionals. The project (building) committee should understand what the specific considerations are for selecting each professional.

■ Self-Assessment Exercises

1. Explain the ADA.
2. What is a master plan? What purpose does it serve?
3. Explain the "participatory planning process."
4. Differentiate between renovation, retrofitting, and replacing.
5. What is the purpose of the program statement?
6. What are the factors an architect needs to consider when designing a new or renovating/retrofitting an existing facility?
7. What role does the architect, facility consultant, and program specialist assume in the planning process?

■ Case Study

As a student you have been exposed to a variety of professionals involved in planning, designing, and constructing the building. List and describe the criteria necessary in selecting a consultant, architect, architectural firm, engineer, and contractors.

■ References

AIA (1990). **Selecting the building team.** Washington, DC: AIA.

Bauer, R. L. (1986). **Facilities planning.** New York: Amacom, American Management Association.

Council of Educational Facility Planners (CEFP), International.(1991). **Guide for planning educational facilities.** Columbus, OH: Author.

Dahnke, H., Jones, D., Mason, T., & Romney, L. (1971). **Higher education planning and management manuals.** Boulder, CO: Western Interstate Commission for Higher Education and American Association of Collegiate Registrars and Admissions Officers.

Flynn, R. B. (Ed.). (1993). **Planning facilities for athletics, physical education, and recreation.** Reston, VA: Athletic Institute and American Alliance for Health, Physical Education, Recreation and Dance.

Hamer, J. M. (1988). **Facility management systems.** New York: van Nostrand Reinhold Company.

Joiner, D (May, 1991). The process: Programming, design and construction. **The Pressbox,** 16(5) 23-29.

■ Suggested Readings

Farmer, P. J., Mulrooney, A. L., & Ammon Jr., R. (1996). **Sport facility planning and management.** Morgantown, WV: Fitness Information Technology, Inc.

Horine, L (1998). **Administration of physical education and sport programs.** (4th ed.). Dubuque, IA: William C.Brown and Benchmark.

Parkhouse, B. L. (1997). **The management of sport: Its foundation and application.** (2nd ed.) St. Louis, MO: Mosby.

Sawyer, T. H., & Smith, O. R. (1999). **The management of clubs, recreation, and sport: Concepts and applications.** Champaign, IL: Sagamore Publishing, Inc.

Walker, M. L., & Stotlar, D. K. (1997). **Sport facility management.** Sudbury, MA: Jones and Bartlett.

CHAPTER 3

Site Selection

and Development Process

Thomas H. Sawyer, Indiana State University ■ Michael G. Hypes, Indiana State University

Learning Objective

After reading this chapter, the student will be able to

■ describe the process involved in site selection.

Introduction

The most successful building project has a well-designed site selection and development process. Projects without these elements are doomed to failure from the outset. There are 13 common steps that compose a strong site selection and development process, including research, regional analysis, site analysis, program, functional analysis, combined site and function, land use, refinement, site plan/overall design, construction documents, bidding, construction, and review. This chapter will provide practical information about each of the 13 phases.

Step 1: Research

The planning committee in its research should be concerned with (1) knowing and understanding the needs and desires of the people who are involved in and/or affected by the proposed project, and (2) knowing everything reasonably possible about the project function and/or activity and the space requirements.

Designers Design for People. At least four groups of people may need to be involved in the research and eventually satisfied, including clients (board of directors, etc.), users, affected neighbors and/or public, managers and operators, and possibly others. Each of the relevant groups must be identified and its needs, concerns, and desires understood. There will, almost certainly, be some conflicts between the various groups. Understanding these problems in advance may make it possible to resolve them during the design phase.

Maintenance and Operations. Maintenance and operational needs, small but significant, must be clearly understood. They can make a project successful or doom it to future failure. The following are some specific items to consider:

▶ Maintenance
  ■ Will maintenance be done by in-house labor or by contract?
  ■ Is special equipment used or needed (i.e., riding lawn mowers, etc.)?
  ■ Does maintenance staff have any requirements for any standard equipment requirements (i.e., motors, lights, shower heads, pumps, etc.) used or preferred by the maintenance staff?
  ■ How capable is staff to maintain sophisticated equipment.

■ What are maintenance space requirements, such as equipment — clearance around motors and pumps so maintenance can be performed, etc.

■ Are there any special fire protection requirements.

■ What special storage requirements are needed for inflammables and chemicals?

▶ Operations
■ Security — Is it needed? If so, what type (patrol, electronic, entrance only, dogs)? If patrolled, how — by foot, car, motorcycle, horse, bike, or boat?

■ Hours of operation — Is night lighting required?

■ Trash pickup — In-house? Contract? Kind of equipment used.

■ Deliveries — food, supplies, etc. When are separate entrances and exits needed?

■ Communications system— speakers, phone, radio?

■ Safety/first aid — Are special facilities needed? Where? Extent? Emergency vehicle access?

■ Peak use — How handled? Restrict use or provide overflow capacity?

▶ Special Programs
■ Will there be any? If so, what? Concerts at noon, employee training, visitor information and/or education, arts and craft shows, special exhibits?

■ Any special space requirements for programs? Lighting? Service areas? Other utilities?

▶ Facilities and Their Requirements
Most facilities have specific site requirements. Technical data must be gathered on all the proposed facilities. At a minimum, the following must be known:

■ Size — actual dimensions plus any buffer spaces or required accessory space.

■ Grade requirements — maximum and minimum.

■ Any special construction requirements — tennis courts, ice hockey rinks, etc.

■ Utility needs (i.e., type and amount).

Step 2: Regional Analysis

Sufficient data must be gathered about the off-site surroundings to ensure that the project will be compatible with surrounding environment, both man-made and natural. This part of the design process is referred to as the regional analysis. It should include:

■ Service area of the facility under construction (i.e., major facilities such as parks, large commercial areas facilities, and minor facilities usch as children's playgrounds, senior citizen centers, local library, etc.),

■ User demand (i.e., determining the kind of use desired [desires of clients, activity interests, demographic makeup of residents, and local leadership], and calculating the number of users),

■ Access routes (i.e., major and secondary routes),

■ Governmental functions and boundaries (i.e., contact the local planning agency and local government offices),

■ Existing and proposed land uses (i.e., gathering information about abutting land ownership, adjacent land uses, land use along probable access routes, off-site flooding and erosion problems, off-site pollution sources, views [especially of esthetic and historic interest], and significant local architectural or land use characteristics), and

■ Regional influences (i.e., check for anything unusual or unique that could either enhance or cause problems to the project).

Step 3: Site Analysis

The planning committee will need to consider various pieces of information prior to selecting the building site. The considerations for site selection (Fogg, 1986; Miller, 1997) include:

1. Access to the site (i.e., ingress and egress, surrounding traffic generators, accessibility via public transportation)
2. Circulation within the site (e.g., roads — paved and unpaved, bicycle trails, walks and hiking trails)
3. Parking
4. Water supply
5. Sewage disposal
6. Electrical service
7. Telephone service
8. Other utilities including oil/natural gas transmission lines, or cable TV
9. Structures to be constructed
10. Environmental concerns and conditions on and off property (e.g., noise, air, water, and visual pollution)
11. Easements and other legal issues (e.g., deed restrictions, rights of way, and less-than-fee-simple ownership)

12. Zoning requirements. Changing the zoning is usually time consuming and expensive and frequently not possible
13. Historical significance
14. Any existing uses (activities) on the site
15. Climatic conditions prevalent in the area by season (e.g., temperature; humidity; air movement — velocity, duration, and direction; amount of sunshine; precipitation — rain, sleet, snow; sun angles and subsequent shadows; special conditions — ice storms, hurricanes, tornadoes, heavy fog, heavy rain storm, floods, and persistent cloud cover)
16. Nuisance potentials (e.g., children nearby, noise, etc.)
17. Natural features (e.g., topography, slope analysis, soil conditions, geology, hydrology, flora, and fauna)
18. Economic impact of a site (e.g., labor costs, growth trends, population shifts, buying power index, available work force, property taxes, surrounding competition, utility costs, incentives, area of dominant influence [ADI], designated market area [DMA], and established enterprise zones)
19. Natural barriers and visibility
20. Supporting demographics (e.g., age, gender, occupation, martial status, number of children, expenditures, education, income, number of earners in the family, race, etc.) and psychographics (e.g., lifestyle data or lifestyle marketing)
21. Security concerns (e.g., proximity of police, fire, emergency medical personnel, hospitals)

The most important aspect of site selection is location, location, location. If the site is not in the most accessible location with a high profile for people to recognize, it will have a negative effect on the success of the venture.

Step 4: Program

Program, as used here, is the organization of the information needed for planning a project to provide an appropriate facility to meet the needs of the affected people (client, users, neighbors, and staff). Program needs should include a list of activities, facility needs for each activity listed, number of participants in each activity during peak periods, size of each facility ranging from minimum to ideal, and a description describing the relationship between activities and facilities (i.e., can certain activities co-exist with other activities at the same time in one facility?).

Step 5: Functional Analysis

Functional analysis is the process of analyzing and organizing the information provided in programming and relationships by translating that analysis into graphic symbols. It establishes the preferred or ideal physical relationships of all the component parts of a project. The process commonly consists of four parts — space diagrams, relationship charts and/or diagrams, bubble diagrams, and land use concepts. All the elements contained in the activity/program must be considered and their desired functional and physical relationships accommodated.

Steps 6 & 7: Combined Site, Function, and Land Use

Two issues are key relative to land use — people needs and site constraints. At this point the various constraints and opportunities presented by the site must become integrated with people needs. It is also the time when the reality of the site constraints may require changes in the program. This step combines site analysis (step 3) with functional analysis (step 5). If changes are made in the program, the changes must be incorporated throughout the functional analysis phase. This step in the site design process is where analysis of the site data is most completely utilized.

If the site selected is too small, the following options should be considered:

■ *Physical modification of the site.* This may be the least desirable option because it is almost always undesirable from an environmental standpoint, it frequently is not esthetically pleasing, and it is usually expensive.
■ *Expand the site if adjacent land is available.* This is frequently not possible and can be expensive.
■ *Change to another site.* This can be expensive and alternate sites may not be available.
■ *Cancel the project.* This is not usually desirable or possible.
■ *Creatively look at new ways of solving the problem.* Alternative 5 is the most difficult choice. It is always difficult to abandon the proven acceptable way of designing and operating facilities. When successful, however, it can often lead to outstanding innovative solutions.

Steps 8 and 9: Refinement and Site Plan/Overall Design

After the land use step has been completed, the planning committee needs to refine the focus of the building project before it moves to the site plan/overall design step. After the refinement is complete, then, and only then, should the planners consider site planning and overall design.

A site plan shows all the existing and proposed site features superimposed on a topographic base map at an appropriate scale. It functions as the coordinating plan that ensures that all the project parts fit together. This is the point in the site design process where imagination and creativity are really important. In addition, this plan is almost always the feature part of any presentation to the client and other interested parties.

Accompanying the site plan will be a number of drawings, including utilities (e.g., water sources, sewer lines, and electricity/communication), grading and drainage, circulation, scale drawings, relationships, and three-dimensional aspects.

Step 10: Construction documents (see chapter 4)

Step 11: Bidding (see chapter 4)

Step 12: Construction

The construction step of a project goes through several phases. The number of phases depends upon the scope of the project and the contracting agency. Two general guidelines govern the construction step — (1) the larger the project, the more steps required, and (2) governmental projects usually have more contractual controls. At least some, and perhaps all, of the following steps will be required during construction:

■ *Preconstruction conference.* A meeting between the contracting agency and the contractor(s) prior to the commencement of construction to review the contract items and make sure there is an understanding of how the job is to be undertaken.
■ *Construction.* Set up or mobilization as well as the actual construction of the facility.

■ *Change orders.* Defined as an official document requested by either the contractor or the contracting agency which changes the approved contract documents. These changes usually include an adjustment of the bid price and a benefit to the contractor. It is better to avoid all change orders. Where this is not possible, be prepared to pay a premium price and to accept delays in contract completion.
■ *Pre-final inspection and preparation of punch list.* The initial review of a completed construction project. This inspection should have all the affected parties' decision-makers present, including the owner or his or her representative, the architect, the contractor(s), and any subcontractors. At this time, it is also desirable to have the facility operation supervisor present. During this review a "punch list" is prepared of any work that needs completing by the contractor prior to call for a final inspection. All items that are not completed or not completed according to specifications should be included on the list. The punch list is then agreed upon and signed by all affected parties. The contractor must then correct and/or finish all the items on the list. When the punch list is completed, it is time to call for a final inspection.
■ *As-built drawings and catalogue cuts.* Defined as the drawings prepared by the contractor showing how the project was actually built. These drawings will be of great value to the operations and maintenance staffs. They must know exactly what facilities were actually built and their locations to be able to maintain the project effectively.

Catalogue cuts is printed information supplied by the manufacturers on materials and equipment used in the project construction. This material is necessary so that the operating staff will be able to learn about the material and equipment. In addition, it is needed for locating necessary replacement parts. It must also be included in working drawings and specifications of future renovations and/or expansion of the project.

Preparation of an operations manual. An operations manual contains written instructions on how to operate and maintain special equipment. The minimum data included should be how to start up, how to shut down, inspection(s) time intervals and what should be inspected, schedule of required maintenance, safety precautions, and whom to contact for specialized repair assistance.

Training on how to operate the project. This contract item is usually included only for larger projects that are unfamiliar to the people who will operate them.

Final inspection. The final inspection should concentrate on items not found acceptable during any previous inspections. The same review team that made the pre-final inspection should be assembled for the final inspection.

Acceptance of completed project. Assuming all the work has been completed as shown on the plans and described in the specifications, the project should be accepted and turned over to the owner or operator. Further, if the contractor has posted a performance bond guaranteeing the work, it should be released by the contracting agency.

If at all possible, avoid partial acceptances. Sometimes it is necessary to take over a part or parts of a project prior to completion of the entire project. If this becomes necessary, the contractor will have the opportunity to blame future problems and/or delays on having to work around the people using the project.

Maintenance period. When living plants are involved, many contractors have a maintenance period included after the acceptance of the project. This can last anywhere from 30 days or more (for lawns) to 90 days for flowers, and frequently one full growing season for ground cover, vines, shrubs, and trees.

Bond period. Most government projects and some larger projects require the contractor to post not only a performance bond, but a one-year (or some other specified period) warranty on the quality of the work. Usually the bond requires the contractor to replace or repair any defective or damaged items during the time covered by the bond. Typical items would be leaking roofs, infiltration of ground water into sewer lines, puddling of water in parking lots or tennis courts, etc.

Bond inspection and final acceptance. At the end of the bond period, another inspection is held by the original final inspection team. Prior to release of the bond, any problems that have been uncovered during this inspection must be rectified at no cost to the contracting agency. It is important to note that when the bond is released, the contractor no longer has any responsibility to the project.

Step 13: Review

The project has been completed and turned over to the client. Does the project do what it was designed to from the standpoint of the (a) client, (b) user, (c) affected neighbors and/or public, (d) manager and operator, and (e) design team? There are two basic kinds of information to be gathered — information on people and on physical conditions.

■ Summary

A very important process in the construction of a facility is the selection of the most appropriate site. Many variables must be considered when selecting a site, including variables include research, regional analysis, site analysis, program, functional analysis, combine site and function, land use, refinement, site plan/overall design, construction documents, bidding, construction, and review. If the site selection process is successful the building project will be well established.

■ Case Study

As a consultant for a new YMCA in Falmouth, Maine, you have been hired to complete a site selection report. The YMCA Board of Directors has four possible sites available to them. You have been requested to prioritize those sites. What steps will you take to complete the report?

■ References

Fogg, G. E. (1986). **A site design process.** Chicago: National Recreation and Park Association.

Miller, L. K. (1997). **Sport business management.** Gaithersburg, MD: Aspen Publishers, Inc.

■ Suggested Readings

Farmer, P. J., Mulrooney, A. L., & Ammon, Jr., R. (1996). **Sport facility planning and management.** Morgantown, WV: Fitness Information Technology, Inc.

Tharrett, S. J., & Peterson, J. A. (Eds.). (1997). **ACSM's Health/fitness facility standards and guidelines** (2nd ed). Champaign, IL: **Human Kinetics.**

Walker, M. L., & Stotlar, D. K. (1997). **Sport facility management.** Sudbury, MA: Jones and Barlett.

Notes

CHAPTER 4

Construction Documents and Bidding

Thomas H. Sawyer, Indiana State University

Learning Objectives

After reading this chapter, the student will be able to

- understand the various facility development phases,
- describe what construction documents consist of,
- outline the bidding process, and
- describe the construction phase.

Introduction

Construction documents control the actual constructed results. They consist of two separate parts: 1) working drawings and 2) specifications, the written companion to the working drawings. Upon completion of the working drawings and specifications, the project is bid, and if the bids are satisfactory the contract is awarded.

Schematic Design Phase

In the schematic design phase the architect prepares schematic design documents consisting of drawings and other documents illustrating the scale, and relationship of project components. These are based on the mutually agreed-upon program with the owner, the schedule, and the construction budget requirements and they are submitted to the owner for approval.

Design Development Phase

Based on schematic design documents and any adjustments authorized by the owner in the program, schedule, or construction budget the architect prepares further design development documents for approval by the owner. These consist of drawings and other documents to fix and describe the size and character of the project as to architectural, structural, mechanical, and electrical systems, materials, and other appropriate elements.

Construction Document Phase

Based on the approved design development documents and any further adjustments in the scope or quality of the project or in the construction budget authorized by the owner, the architect prepares construction documents for the approval of the owner. These consist of drawings and specifications setting forth in detail the requirements for the construction of the project.

Drawings

All working drawings must be clear, concise and understand-able to the people who are going to construct the building. Only as much detail as is necessary to build the project should be included. More detail might give the client more control but will definitely cost more money for design and will result in higher bids. All pieces must be clearly presented in such a manner that will allow accurate building.

All construction drawings must be accurate, clearly labeled, and dimensioned. If in doubt as to the need for a label or a dimension, include it! Normally, written numbers on the plan take precedence over field scaled distances.

A useful tool in outlining the numbers and kinds of con-struction drawings is a plan control list. Each drawing that is expected to be needed is listed by description. This enables the designer(s) to coordinate work and helps to ensure that all aspects of the project are included.

With the completed list of plans, an estimate of time required to complete the working drawing and the necessary scheduling of work assignments can be carried out. This plan control document will probably be revised during the preparation of drawings. In its final form it will become the drawing index listing for Sheet 2 of the working drawings package.

The more detailed and elaborate the working drawings, the higher the cost of preparing them and very frequently, the higher the cost of building the project. A rule of thumb: The smaller the job, the fewer the construction documents. Small contractors do not like excessive control and paperwork. They frequently will not bid on projects with elaborate specifications, and if they do, they bid high. Frequently, too much control will cause bids to be higher, but do not result in an increase in quality.

Sheet #	Title
1.	Title sheet
2.	Index, abbreviations, and symbols
3.	Location
4.	Site layout and survey control
5.	Grading and drainage
6.	Utilities (may be 2, 3 or 4 sheets with electricity and communications, water and sewer on separate sheets)
7.	Roads, parking, etc.
8.	Interior pedestrian circulation
9.	Planting plan
10.	Planting details
11.	Irrigation plan
12.	Irrigation details - pressure reducers, controllers, valves
13.	Site details - walks, drinking fountains, walls, drain inlets, etc.
14.	Lighting details - light fixtures, pull boxes, etc.
15.	Sign layout
16.	Sign details
17.	Architectural plans-
18.	Architectural detail
19.	Structural details
20.	Mechanical layout
21.	Mechanical details
22.	Plumbing
23.	Finish schedules

The construction drawings must be reviewed by the maintenance staff to 1) ensure compatibility of parts with existing facilities, 2) see if the project can be effective-ly maintained at reasonable cost, and 3) determine if alternative materials or design modifications would reduce the costs and/or simplify maintenance.

A detailed cost estimate is almost always necessary at this point in the design process. If costs estimated for the time of construction are too high, then the project may have to be reduced in scope and/or redesigned. Make sure that lifetime operations and maintenance costs are also considered in the estimate.

Specifications

The written portion of the construction documents comes in three parts:

1. Bidding and contract requirements (including the bid documents): Division "0"
2. General requirements: Division "I"
3. Construction Specifications: Divisions "2-16"

This part of the design process is often most disliked by de-signers because of the massive detail required. It is, however, of the utmost importance in ensuring that the design is actually built according to the way it was envisioned.

General Notes

■ Include everything in the specifications that you want to see in the final constructed product.
■ Make sure that Division "I" includes the contractor providing "as built" drawings, catalogue cuts, and, where appropriate, an operation manual and training of operating and maintenance staff.
■ Include only information necessary to the specific project -- especially if it is a small one. As with plans, small contractors don't like and frequently don't understand long, involved specifications; therefore, they will not bid or may increase their bids accordingly. The heavier, thicker, and more complicated the specifications, the higher the bid.
■ But the less detail you have in the specifications, the greater the opportunity for misunderstandings between the owner and contractor.
■ All phases of specifications are readily adaptable to computerization and/or word processing.

Much time can be saved if "canned" specifications are used, thus speeding up this tedious but crucial task. Computerization will probably lead to standardization of details and format.

The specifications book uses the standard Construction Specifications Institute format of 17 Divisions.

■ Division 0 Bidding and contract requirements
■ Division 1 General requirements
■ Division 2 Site work
■ Division 3 Concrete
■ Division 4 Masonary
■ Division 5 Metals
■ Division 6 Wood and plastics
■ Division 7 Thermal and moisture protection
■ Division 8 Doors and windows
■ Division 9 Finishes
■ Division 10 Specialties
■ Division 11 Equipment
■ Division 12 Furnishings
■ Division 13 Special construction
■ Division 14 Conveying systems
■ Division 15 Mechanical
■ Division 16 Electrical

All designers must keep current on the latest product information available in their field of expertise.

When the plans and specifications are completed the project is ready for bid.

Bidding Process

The bidding process includes (a) bidding and advertising, (b) opening and review of bids, and (c) award of contract. The bid documents include invitation to bid, instructions to bidders, the bid form, other sample bidding and contract forms, and the proposed documents (e.g., drawings and specifications).

Bidding and Advertising

Bidding is the process of receiving competitive prices for the con-struction of the project.

A bid form should be provided to ensure that all bids are prepared in the same manner for easy comparison. The bids can be received in many ways. The most common are:

1. Lump sum (one overall price),
2. Lump sum with alternatives (either add-ons or deletions), and
3. Unit prices.

A Typical Specification

Division 2
Site Work

02480	LANDSCAPING
02480.1	GENERAL
02480.1.1	Work included but not limited to the following.
02480.1.1.1	Furnishing plants, planting, and all necessary planting operations.
.2	Replacement of unsatisfactory plant material.
.3	Protection, maintenance, and warranty of work, etc.
02480.1.2	Related work specified elsewhere
02480.1.2.1	Section 02210 - Site grading
.2	Section 02441 - Underground sprinkler system
.3	Division 3 - Concrete
02480.2	REQUIREMENTS
02480.2.1	Coordination: Work to proceed as rapidly as pos-sible in coordination with other trades, but consistent with unavoidable seasonal limitations for landscape work.
02480.3	MATERIALS
02480.3.1	Planting soil mixture
02480.3-1.1	Components
	70% course sweet sand
	10% peat moss
	10% organic matter
	10% perlite
	Plus slow release fertilizer
02480.3.2	Fertilizer
02480-3.2.1	Slow release fertilizer (18-14-6) shall be added to the planting soil mixture, 450 grams (1 lb) per cubic meter of planting soil mixture.

All bids on large projects should be accompanied by some type of performance bond insuring that the contractor will perform the work as designed at the price bid. This ensures that bidders are sincere in their prices.

The time and place of the receipt of the sealed bids must be clearly shown on all bid packages. NO LATE BIDS CAN BE RECEIVED WITHOUT COMPROMISING THE ENTIRE BIDDING PROCESS.

Small projects (up to $25,000)

A bid of this size can normally be handled informally. The process of calling a selected list of local contractors will usually be suf-ficient and will probably get the best price.

Larger projects (over $25,000)

A formal bid process is usually necessary to ensure fairness, accuracy, and a competitive result. The process starts with advertising for bids. Advertising frequently is initiated prior to the completion of the plans, with an effective date for picking up the completed plans and specifications. The larger, more complex the project, the wider the range of advertising necessary. Governmental agencies usually have minimum advertising standards. They advertise in the legal advertisement section of the local paper and papers, in larger nearby cities, and in professional construction journal(s). In addition, designers or clients frequently have a list of contractors who have successfully built past projects and/or who have indicated an interest in bidding on future projects.

As a minimum, the advertisement should consist of

1. A description of the project and kind of work required,
2. The date and place plans can be picked up,
3. The cost of plans and specifications (usually only sufficient to cover printing costs),
4. The bid date and time, and
5. Client identification.

The approximate value of the project is sometimes included, although some designers and clients do not wish to give out this information. With complex projects it is desirable to schedule a pre-bid conference to explain the design and bidding process to prospective bidders. During the bidding period, questions are frequently raised by one or more prospective bidders. If the questions require design modifications or clarifications, the questions *must* be answered in writing in the form of an addendum to all holders of plans.

Opening and Reviewing of Bids

Bids are opened in front of witnesses, usually the contractors or their representative(s) and an attorney (normally required by a government agency). The designers or their representatives are usually at the bid opening. After the bids are opened and read, it is necessary to analyze them and decide to whom the contract is to be awarded. The technical analysis is usually done by the designers, who consider whether the bid is complete, the prices are reasonable, and the contractor is able to do the work. A recommendation is then made. The legal analysis by the attorney is done concurrently for such things as whether bonds are attached, all necessary signatures are included, and all required information is provided.

Award of Contract

Assuming favorable analysis by all involved and that the bids are acceptable to the client, the contract will be awarded. Most contracts are awarded to the lowest qualified bidder. Sometimes, however, the low bidder is not large enough or does not have the expertise to do the work required. Occasionally some bids are improperly prepared. In these situations, they may be rejected and the next lowest qualified bidder will be awarded the contract or the project is re-bid. This can lead to problems with the disqualified bids or bidders and is why an attorney should be present.

Figure 4.1 Construction phases of Western Illinois University Student Recreation Center.

Construction Phase

The architect shoud visit the site at least twice monthly at appropriate intervals to the stage of construction, and make the owner generally familiar with the progress and quality of the work in writing. The architect has other responsibilities, including

■ certifying the payments represented to the owner for payment;

■ accepting/rejecting work that does not conform to the contract documents;

■ reviewing and approving all submittals such as shop drawings, product data, and samples;

■ preparing all change orders and construction change directives, with supporting documentation and data deemed necessary;

■ conducting periodic observations to determine the date or dates for substantial completion, and receiving, reviewing, and forwarding all records and written warranties to the owner, along with issuing a final certificate for payment upon compliance with the requirements of the contract documents and;

■ interpreting and deciding matters concerning performance of the contractor.

Performance Bonds and Warranty

A *performance bond* is a bond of the contractor in which a surety (insurance company) guarantees to the owner that the work will be performed in accordance with the contract documents. If the work is not satisfactory or the contractor goes bankrupt, the project will be completed as specified in the contract documents by the insurance company.

A *warranty* is a guarantee the contractor provides with the building. Usually the contractor provides a 12-month warranty. The warranty is a legally enforceable assurance of quality or performance of a product or work or of duration of satisfactory performance. The documents should state at least a one-year warranty from the time the building is occupied by the owner. The facility manager should state the warranty date in writing, and at the same time place a note on the calendar 11 months from the occupancy date as a "final check" date of the facility, noting any problems in writing and literally placing the contractor on notice of the specific problems. This list is often called a "warranty punchlist."

■ Summary

It is important for planners to understand the document phases as well as the construction phases of a building project. Each phase has a specific purpose and is critical to the entire project. Planners need to be aware of the bidding process and the importance of awarding contracts to the most appropriate contractor.

Learning Objective 1: The student will be able to understand the various facility development phases.

The facility development phase starts with the owner's "wish book." The architects use the information in the wish book to put together the initial schematic design and cost estimates. After the schematic design is reviewed and cost decisions are made, the architects then begin the longer process of design development. This phase leads into the next phase of the project — final acceptance of the design and estimated cost.

Learning Objective 2: The student will be able to describe the construction documents.

The development of the construction documents is a longer phase including detailed drawings of all aspects of the project and preparation of the detailed specification document book. The detailed drawings and specification book is the final road map for the contractors to construct the project.

Learning Objective 3: The student will be able to outline the bidding process.

The bidding process follows the acceptance of the construction documents by the owner. The owner then advertises the opportunity to bid on the project to the contracting community. The contractors use the construction documents to prepare their bids. Bids submitted are reviewed for accuracy and the most appropriate bid is awarded a contract. The most appropriate bid is one that meets all specifications and is the lowest bid.

Learning Objective 4: The student will be able to describe the construction phase.

Before construction begins, the contractors show proof of a performance bond. Then the contractors and owner decide the procedures for payments, scheduling of construction meetings, changing plans, etc. After the procedures are agreed upon, construction can begin.

■ Case Study

As a student you are assigned the following tasks:

■ Describe the various facility development phases in a building project starting with the building committee.

■ Delineate each of the following: construction drawings and construction specifications. Why is this phase important?

■ Describe the bidding process and its components.

■ References

Indiana State University (1996). **Construction documents for ISU's Music Rehearsal Building.** Terre Haute, IN: Author.

Indiana State University (1995). **Construction documents for ISU's John T. Meyers Technology Building.** Terre Haute, IN: Author.

American Institute of Architects (1992). **Guidelines for construction documents and the bidding process.** Washington, DC: Author.

Notes

CHAPTER 5

Financing Facility Development

Thomas H. Sawyer, Indiana State University

Learning Objectives

After reading this chapter, the student will be able to

■ understand the various types of financing options available for construction of facilities, and

■ describe the financial team for a building project.

Introduction

Recreation and sport facilities are integral parts of communities. Schools, community organizations, teams, leagues, and special interest groups use the facilities for business, entertainment, recreation, and sports. Interscholastic, intercollegiate, and other educational entities, as well as professional teams, use facilities for a variety of entertainment, recreation, sport, and non-sport-related activities.

Sport arenas, stadiums, multipurpose facilities, and parks are financed in one of three common ways — public, private, or joint public/private. This chapter will focus on the financial methods used to build recreational and sport facilities. Several mechanisms are available in structuring public sector involvement in recreation and sport facility development, expansion, and renovation. The financial arrangements of a project are often the foundation for a successful facility. Budgets, cash flow, and financial statements depend on the facility's debt service arrangements. The objective of recreation and sport financial management in the public sector is to minimize public risk, which translates into maximization of municipal cash flow (Regan, 1997). The objective of private sport management is to maximize shareholder wealth, which translates into maximization of stock price (Regan, 1997).

Financing Options

Financing recreation and sport facilities requires cooperation between public and private entities. The common types of financing options are public, private, and joint public and private.

Public funding

A variety of *taxes* can be levied. The most common include hotel/motel tax, restaurant tax, auto rental tax, taxi tax, "sin" taxes (e.g., liquor, tobacco), sales tax, road tax, utility tax, property tax, business license tax, and team tax. The taxes most favorably viewed by local tax payers are the hotel, restaurant, and auto rental taxes, as they are more likely to be shouldered by tourists (Miller, 1997). Planners should understand from the outset that continual tax increases can generate citizen concern.

Another tax strategy used by governments to stimulate private sector investment and create employment in the community is to offer property tax abatements (Howard and Crompton, 1995). Abatement programs exist in approximately two-thirds of the states (Severn, 1992). Typically, they are awarded whenever they are requested (Wolkoff, 1985); therefore, they often are part of a city's incentive package in negotiations with professional franchises (Howard and Crompton, 1995). A tax abatement will exempt an organization's assets from property taxation for a given period of time. It may be for all or a portion of the tax. The length of time varies according to the state enabling legislation.

The issuing of bonds is the most common way for a city or county to generate the needed money for recreation and sport facilities (Miller, 1997). A *bond* is defined as "an interest-bearing certificate issued by a government or corporation, promising to pay interest and to repay a sum of money (the principal) at a specified date in the future" (Samuelson and Nordhaus, 1985, p. 828). According to Howard and Crompton (1995, p. 98) a bond is " a promise by the borrower (bond issuer) to pay back to the lender (bond holder) a specified amount of money, with interest, within a specified period of time." Bonds issued by a government or a subdivision of a state are referred to as *municipal bonds.* Municipal bonds are typically exempt from federal, state, and local taxes on earned interest. Bond buyers can include individuals, organizations, institutions, or groups desiring to lend money at a predetermined interest rate. However, according to Miller (1997), bonds are not a panacea for recreation and sport facility development for two primary reasons — debt ceiling or debt capacity, and tax-exemption concerns by the public.

There are basically two types of government bonds — full-faith and credit obligations, and non-guaranteed. A *general obligation bond* is a full-faith and credit obligation bond. The general obligation bond refers to bonds that are repaid with a portion of the general property taxes. There are two key disadvantages to issuing general obligation bonds — it requires voter approval, and it increases local debt.

Non-guaranteed bonds have been the most common type of bonds used in funding recreation and sport facilities (Howard and Crompton, 1995). These bonds are sold on the basis of repayment from other designated revenue sources. If revenue falls short of what is required to make debt payments, the government entity does not have to make up the difference. There are three main advantages for using this funding mechanism: voter approval generally is not required, debt is not considered statutory debt, and those who benefit the most from the facility pay for it.

Currently, there are three popular types of non-guaranteed funding mechanisms: revenue bonds, certificates of participation, and tax increment financing.

Revenue bonds can be backed exclusively by the revenue accruing from the project or from a designated revenue source, such as hotel/motel tax, restaurant tax, auto rental tax, or a combination of these taxes and others.

Certificates of participation involve a government entity buying the facility. The government entity then leases portions of the facility to the general public, and monies generated from the leases are used to pay off the facility's capital expenses. However, there is a moral rather than a legal obligation to appropriate funds if lease payments are inadequate or if the lessee goes out of business.

"Over half the states now have enabling legislation authorizing *tax increment financing* (TIF)" (Howard and Crompton, 1995, p. 102). TIF is available when an urban area has been identified for renewal or redevelopment. Real estate developed with the use of TIF is attractive to stakeholders, as tax increases are not necessary (Miller, 1997). The tax base of the defined area is frozen, and any increases in the tax base are used to repay the TIF bonds. The economics of any TIF are dependent on the development potential of a chosen site and its surrounding land (Regan, 1997).

Special authority bonds have been used to finance stadiums or arenas by special public authorities, which are entities with public powers (e.g., Niagara Power Authority, New York State Turnpike Authority, or the Tennessee Valley Authority) that are able to operate outside normal constraints placed on governments. Primarily, this has been used as a way to circumvent public resistance to new sports projects (i.e., Georgia Dome, Oriole Park at Camden Yards, or Stadium Authority of Pittsburgh [Three Rivers Stadium]) and construct them without receiving public consent through a referendum. Without having to pass a voter referendum, the authorities float the bonds that are sometimes guaranteed or accepted as a moral obligation by the state, (Howard and Crompton, 1995).

Additional sources beyond taxes and bonding available from the public sector include state and federal appropriations and public grants.

Private Funding

Private-sector investment is preferred by most stakeholders as a result of declining public monies and questionable economic impacts (Miller, 1997). Private-sector investments take on a variety of forms and degrees of contribution. The private-sector regularly contributes to financing of recreation and sport facilities, in ways such as the following:

■ *Donation of cash* — Cash is donated to the organization for a general or specific uses in return for a personal tax deduction.

■ *In-kind contributions* — An organization, business, or craftsman donates equipment or time to the project in return for a tax deduction.

■ *Naming rights* — Corporations vie for the right to place their name on the facility for a specific sum of money for a specific number of years (e.g., RCA Dome in Indianapolis, $2 million a year for 10 years; Conseco Arena in Indianapolis, $2.5 million a year for 10 years; Raymond James (Financial Inc.) Stadium in Tampa, $3.8 million a year for 10 years).

■ *Concessionaire exclusivity* — Companies purchase the exclusive rights for all concessions within a spectator facility for a specific number of dollars over a specific time period.

■ *Restaurant rights* — Corporations purchase exclusive rights for all the restaurants within a spectator facility.

■ *Sponsorship packages* — Large local and international firms are solicited to supply goods and services to a sporting organization at no cost or at substantial reduction in the wholesale prices in return for visibility for the corporation.

■ *Life insurance packages* — These programs solicit the proceeds from a life insurance policy purchased by a supporter to specifically benefit the organization upon the death of the supporter.

■ *Lease agreements* — These programs lease facilities to other organization during the off-season or lease additional spaces within the facility not used for the sporting activity, such as office space or retail space.

■ *Luxury suites* — These areas are designed for VIP use and leased by large corporations to wine and dine their clients as well as to provide them entertainment.

■ *Preferred/premium seating (i.e., club seating)* — This is VIP seating located within the luxury suites or in the club areas of the stadium, which are the most expensive seats in the facility.

■ *Parking fees* — These fees are generated from parking lots that surround the spectator facilities.

■ *Merchandise revenues* — This income is generated by the sale of shirts, shorts, hats, pants, t-shirts, sweat shirts, key rings, glassware, dishware, luggage, sports cards, balls, bats, etc.

■ *Food and beverage serving rights* — Companies purchase exclusive rights to soft drink, beer, and foods sold to spectators.

■ *Advertising rights* — Rights are sold to various entities that wish to advertise to the spectators within the sport facility.

■ *Vendor/contractor equity* — Vendor or contractor returns to the owner a specific percentage of the profit generated by the firms during the construction process.

■ *Bequests and trusts* — Agreements are made with specific individuals that upon their deaths a certain amount of their estates will be given to the organization.

■ *Real estate gifts, endowments, and securities* — Agreements are made with specific individuals to give to an organization real estate, stocks, or mutual funds to support an endowment for a specific project. Only the annual income returned by the endowment would be used, not the principal.

The newest private-sector funding strategy, as described by Daniel Kaplan (Sports Business Journal, 1998), is called *asset-backed securities* (ABS). In 1998, Ascent Entertainment, owner of Denver's professional hockey and basketball teams, issued $130 million in asset-backed securities to help pay for the $160 million Pepsi Center arena. Asset-backed securities are investments secured by expected revenue — in Ascent's case, contractually obligated fees from arena-naming rights, sponsorships, concession guarantees, and luxury-suite licenses. Unlike such traditional methods of financing as bank loans and bond issues, which generally require the commitment of all revenue generated by a facility, an ABS can be secured with just a portion of the revenue stream. Futhermore, an ABS issue does not require teams or owners to open their financial books to creditors.

The value of private-sector funding is best illustrated by the amount of revenue generated from private sources in the construction of The Ball Park in Arlington, Texas, which included $12.7 million from the ballpark's concessionaires, $6 million from first-year luxury suite revenues, $17.1 million from preferred-seat licenses, totaling $35.8 million (Brady & Howlett, 1996).

Private and Joint Public-Private Funding

Over the past decade public-private partnerships have been developed to construct large public sport facilities. Typically, the public sector lends its authority to implement project funding mechanisms, while the private partner contributes project-related or other revenue sources. The expanded revenues generated by the facilities and their tenants have resulted in increases in the level of private funding (Regan, 1997). Recent examples of partnerships, include the Alamodome (San Antonio), Coors Stadium (Denver), and Big Stadium (Saint Denis, France) (Regan, 1997).

Financial Team

All building projects need to assemble a proper financial team in order to design, organize, and finance a public, private, or public/private facility. A successful financial team should include the owner, facility manager, feasibility consultant, examination accountant, business plan consultant, financial advisor, facility consultant, architect, cost estimator, contractor, construction manager, senior underwriter, bond council, and owner's legal counsel (Regan, 1997). The financial team must work together to develop the goals and objectives of the community and/or owner. Successful facility financing is a partnership between the regional community, the owner, government, the financial institutions, and the investors.

■ Summary

A building project will just be a dream without a financial plan to bring it to reality. The planners need to consider not only the physical facilities but also how they will be financed.

Learning objective 1: The student will be able to understand the various types of financing options available for constructing a facility.

Three basic financing options are available for constructing public and private facilities: public sources, private sources, and a combination of public and private sources. The last option is the most acceptable by the taxpayer.

Learning objective 2: The student will be able to describe the financial team for a building project.

The most important part of financing construction of a facility is building a strong and representative financial planning team. The team should be diverse and include all areas in the financial community as well as elected officials. The more diverse, the stronger the acceptance of the final plan will be by the various constituencies.

■ Case Study

The city of Hannibal, Missouri, wants to construct a recreation and sports park near the Mississippi River (protected by a levy) in honor of Samuel Clemens, Tom Sawyer, and Huckleberry Finn. You have been employed as a facility consultant for the project. Describe (1) the components of a successful financial team you would develop, (2) public funding sources to be used, (3) private funding sources to be tapped, and (4) the partnership you would forge between the public and private sectors. Since Hannibal is a real town in Missouri, you should gather all the appropriate data from the primary source.

■ References

Brady, E., & Howlett, D. (1996, September 6). Economics, fan ask if benefits of building park outweigh costs. **USA Today**, pp. C13-C14.

Howard, D. R., & Crompton, J. L. (1995). **Financing sport.** Morgantown, WV: Fitness Information Technology, Inc.

Kaplan, D. (1998). ABS: A new way to pay. **Sport Business Journal,** 1(1), 3.

Miller, L. K. (1997). **Sport business management.** Gaithersburg, MD: Aspen Publishers, Inc.

Regan, T. (1997). Financing facilities. In M. L. Walker, & D. K. Stotlar, (Eds.), **Sport facility management.** Sudbury, MA: Jones and Bartlett Publishers.

Sameulson, P.A., & Nordhaus, W.D. (1985). Economics. New York: McGraw-Hill.

Severn, A.K. (1992). Building-tax abatements: An approximation to land value taxation. **American Journal of Economics and Sociology,** 51(2), 237-245.

Wolkoff, M.J. (1985). Chasing a dream: The use of tax abatements to spur urban economic development. **Urban Studies,** 22, 305-315.

■ Suggested Readings

Graham, P. J. (1994). **Sport business: Operational and theoretical aspects.** Dubuque, IA: Brown & Benchmark.

Rosentraub, M. S. (1997). **Major league losers: The real cost of sports and who's paying for it.** New York: Harper Row.

Sawyer, T. H., & Smith, O. R. (1999). **Club, recreation, and sport management: Theory and practice.** Champaign, IL: Sagamore Publishing, Inc.

Shropshire, K. L. (1995). **The sports franchise game: Cities in pursuit of franchises, events, stadiums, and arenas.** Philadelphia: University of Pennsylvania Press.

CHAPTER 6

Development of Standards

Arthur H. Mittelstaedt, Jr., Recreation Safety Institute
Thomas H. Sawyer, Indiana State University ■ Michael G. Hypes, Indiana State University

Learning Objectives

After reading this chapter, the student will be able to

■ understand the historical evolution of the standards process in the last 50 years,

■ gain insight into the impact on sports and related products and facilities by the emerging standards processes,

■ learn the procedures employed in the United States for developing standards,

■ identify the varied products and facilities for which standards have been formulated,

■ differentiate between a standard and other guidelines, criteria and requirements, and

■ understand the difference between mandatory/regulatory and voluntary standards.

Introduction

Standards are the basis by which fitness, physical activity, recreation, and sport products and facilities can be harmonized between companies, between sports associations and trade associations, and between countries. Standards that have been developed over the past 50 years have provided a uniform approach to producing devices and parts used in fitness, physical activity, recreation, and sport equipment, and in the construction elements of a facility. Standards have also provided sports specific organizations that represent classes and types of sports with a means of consistency among levels of a sport and variations of the game itself. This perhaps has been the weakest aspect of standardization as various sport organizations have similarities and differences that become the competitive edge for control of that market.

Mandatory and Voluntary Standards

Standards may be either mandatory or voluntary. The status of a standard depends on the sponsor's organizational standing (i.e., governmental or voluntary non-governmental). A mandatory standard is developed by a federal agency such as the Environmental Protection Agency (EPA) and Occupational Safety and Health Administration (OSHA). The voluntary standard is developed by a professional non-profit agency. A violation of a mandatory standard carries a penalty.

In addition to standards, other written documents control the unity and uniformity of equipment and facility development, including legal codes or regulations, technical specifications, guides, and literature and learned treatises.

Legal codes are developed by elected public officials such as the National Bureau of Standards, EPA, and OSHA. Further, each state or local government has its own building codes. *Technical specifications and guidelines* are developed by voluntary organizations such as the American Society of Testing and Materials (ASTM) or American National Standard Institute (ANSI), which create standards through committee or trade group processes. Many other professional, trade and organizational associations also promulgate standards, specifications, or guides that are used to measure a standard of care. *Literature and learned treatises* document common knowledge in a variety of ways, including professional journals, magazines, reference books, textbooks, and reports.

Standard of Practice

A *standard of practice* is a usual practice accepted by the national or local government regarding some aspect of equipment or facility design or usage. It is a usage or practice of the people, which, by common adoption and acquiescence and by long and unvarying habit, has become compulsory and has acquired the force of law with respect to the place or subject-matter to which it relates. A standard of practice results from a long series of actions, constantly repeated, which have, by such repetition and by uninterrupted acquiescence, acquired the force of a common consent or practice. Finally, it is considered a customary practice that prevails within a geographical area.

Standard of Care

In laws of negligence, the standard of care is that degree of care that reasonably prudent person should exercise in the same or similar circumstances. If a person's conduct falls below such standard, legal or customary, he or she may be liable in damages for injuries or damages resulting from his or her conduct.

Evolution of Standards

The development of standards began in earnest at the conclusion of World War II. The movement was enhanced by efforts by the National Bureau of Standards to establish partnerships with ASTM, ANSI, and other groups to standardize materials and methods used by private industry and government. During the 1950's and '60s, automation of the workplace increased the need for greater standardization of materials and methods. The computer age has again increased the need for yet greater collaboration between government and the private sector in the development of additional standards as well as the modification of previous ones.

The development of standards in the fitness, physical activity, recreation, and sport area began in the early 1970s. The F-8 Committee on Sports Equipment and Facilities was organized by ASTM. The initial standards promulgated by the F-8 Committee dealt with footwear and football helmets. Ten years after the F-8 Committee was developed, the Committee on Skiing and Amusements was established. Over the years a wide range of standards has been developed that influence fitness, physical activity, recreation, and sport. These standards have also made equipment and facilities safer for participants.

Though such standards have been through the gauntlet of objections and reservations, they are here to stay. Some fear standards may inhibit creativity, negatively affect the growth of the sport, and increase its cost. When participants are engaged in a sport they seem to want to use something to protect themselves. When they do, that something should meet reasonable and meaningful requirements demonstrating that it provides the protection. The cost of debilitating injuries is reduce by this common denominator.

Organizations Advancing Standards

American National Standards Institute (ANSI)

ANSI is another significant organization that develops standards. It is a nonprofit, privately funded membership organization that coordinates the development of U.S. voluntary national standards and is the U.S. member body to non-treaty international standards bodies, such as the International Organization for Standardization (ISO) and the International Electrotechnical Commission (IEC) through the Institute's U.S. National Committee (USNC). ANSI serves both the private and public sectors' need for voluntary standardization. The voluntary standards system contributes to the overall health of the economy and the competitiveness of U.S. industry in the changing global marketplace.

ANSI was founded in 1918, prompted by the need for an "umbrella" organization to coordinate the activities of the U.S. voluntary standards system and eliminate conflict and duplication in the development process. The institute serves a diverse membership of over 1200 companies; 250 professional, technical, trade, labor, and consumer organizations; and some

30 government agencies. The ANSI federation is guided by the national culture and the free enterprise system. For over 70 years, the U.S. voluntary standards system has been administered successfully by the private sector, through ANSI, with the cooperation of federal, state, and local governments. Standards exist in all industries, including telecommunications, safety and health, information processing, petroleum, banking, and household appliances.

ANSI's key functions as stated are to:

■ Coordinate the self-regulating, due-process consensus-based, U.S. voluntary standards system;
■ Administer the development of standards and approve them as American National Standards;
■ Provide the means for the U.S. to influence development of international and regional standards;
■ Disseminate timely and important information on national, international and regional standards activities to U.S. industry; and
■ Promote awareness of the growing strategic significance of standards technology and U.S. global competitiveness.

The benefits of ANSI are that it

■ Provides national and international recognition of standards for credibility and influence in domestic commerce and world trade,
■ Assists companies in reducing operating and purchasing costs and assures product quality and safety,
■ Provides national and international standards information essential for marketing worldwide, and
■ Promotes a self-regulated and strong privately administered voluntary national and international standards system.

ANSI's services to members and others in the world include the following:

■ "ANSI Reporter" provides leaders in the business and standards communities with timely information on important current national, regional, and international standardization activity; standards action that provides vital information for standards professionals on initiation of standards projects; notice of opportunity to review and comment on draft national, international, and regional standards and regulations; and notice of newly approved and published standards.
■ Access/consultation service with offices in Brussels and Washington provides an "on site" presence to access timely information on the latest developments and advice.

■ ANSI boards and councils, technical advisory groups, membership meetings involve thousands of professionals.
■ ANSI publishes over 9800 American national standards, and European standards, international standards, catalogs, handbooks, and other special publications.
■ ANSI aids national and international standards development process and programs, standards technology and program management, legal and antitrust issues.

A standards board is a standing organization within ANSI having planning and coordination responsibilities on a continuing basis for a defined scope of activity under the purview of, and advisory to, ANSI's Executive Standards Council (ExSC). Standards boards serve in a purely advisory capacity. They do not develop standards, nor do they have authority over the activities of accredited standards developers. Membership within ANSI is a prerequisite to service on a standards board. The standards board has responsibility for establishing overall planning and coordination for national and international standards activities in the safety and health area. Further, it reviews the standards activity of applicants for accreditation and the initiation of new standards activities by accredited standards developers. It reviews applications for accreditation of ISO U.S. Technical Advisory Group (TAG) Administrators and makes recommendations to the ExSC regarding approval of TAG Administrators, TAG membership lists and accreditation. The board also reviews lists of candidates for American National Standards and recommends the addition of directly and materially affected interests, and, it makes recommendations to the ExSC concerning suggested changes to ANSI procedures.

The scope of the standards board includes protection of the health and safety of employees and the public using buildings, machinery, and other equipment; hazardous materials; workplaces (including construction sites); vehicular traffic; public and recreation areas; homes and schools; and occupational and non-occupational hazards. Hazards include such things as explosion; fire; radiation (other than ionizing); mechanical, physical, chemical, and environmental hazards; disease; and inadequate or polluted air. Specifically included are personal protective equipment, including personal protection devices for attenuating noise, practices or devices to prevent or minimize fire, explosion or mechanical hazards, safe work practices, and provision for accident reporting and recording. Specifically excluded are building codes and acoustical (other than personal protective devices), electrical, process industry, and nuclear energy standards.

American Society of Testing and Materials (ASTM)

One of the first materials specifications was found in the Book of Genesis: "Make thee an ark of gopher wood; rooms shalt thou make in the ark, and shalt pitch it within and without with pitch." Prior to the 19th century's industrial revolution, craftsmen told their suppliers in similarly basic language what kinds of materials they desired. Craft experience was indeed key because artisans had no instruments to measure the tensile strength, chemical composition, and other characteristics of a given material.

The industrial revolution opened a new chapter in the history of material specifications. Locomotive builders, steel rail producers, and steam engine builders who used revolutionary new materials such as Bessemer steel could no longer rely on craft experiences of centuries past. Manufacturers encountered numerous quality problems in such end products as steel rails because suppliers furnished inferior materials. American rails were so poorly made, in fact, that many railroad companies preferred British imports, which were more expensive but reliable.

To avoid such problems, some manufacturers issued detailed descriptions of material to ensure that their supplies met certain quality standards. However, suppliers in many industries such as construction and metallurgy objected to standard material specifications and testing procedures because they feared that strict quality controls would make customers more inclined to reject items and default on contracts.

The Pennsylvania Railroad, the largest corporation of the 19th century, played a key role in the quest for standard specifications. Its efforts in this field were initiated by Charles Dudley, who received his Ph.D. from Yale University in 1874, and who later became the driving force behind ASTM. Dudley organized the railroad's new chemistry department, where he investigated the technical properties of oil, paint, steel, and other materials the Pennsylvania Railroad bought in large quantities. Based on his research, Dudley issued standard material specifications for the company's suppliers.

The Birth of Consensus

Dudley's efforts facilitated the formation of ASTM, which was committed to building a consensus on standards for industrial materials. From his experiences during the 1880s, which gave him a better picture of the antagonistic attitudes that marred relationships between the Pennsylvania Railroad and its suppliers, Dudley proposed an innovative system of technical committees. These committees provided representatives of the main parties with a forum to discuss every aspect of specifications and testing procedures for a given material. The goal was to reach a consensus that was acceptable to both producers and to the customer, (e.g. the railroad). Although many initial meetings ended in failure due to the inflexibility of the parties involved, Dudley's system held considerable promise and later formed the basis for ASTM's committee structure.

Dudley's call for consensus building, which he articulated in meetings of the American Chemical Society and the International Railway Congress, fell on fertile ground in the engineering community. His ideas contributed to the formation of the International Association for Testing Materials (IATM), which organized working committees to discuss testing methods for iron, steel, and other materials.

The International Association encouraged members to form national chapters. On June 16, 1898, 70 IATM members met in Philadelphia to form the American Section of the International Association for Testing Materials. The members grappled with two questions that were widely discussed throughout the engineering community at the turn of the century. First, how could standards for materials contribute to industrial progress? And second, how could producers and users of industrial materials reach a consensus on standards? ASTM's early history was in large part a quest to find answers to these pivotal questions.

The American Section's first technical committee on steel initiated a series of discussions of testing and material standards for the railroad industry, where most of its members were employed. During the first two years, the committee drafted specifications for steel used in buildings, boiler plates, and bridges. One of the first standard specifications in the history of the organization, "Structural Steel for Bridges," was approved by the committee and submitted to all members for a final ballot vote at the annual meeting in 1901.

The steel committee's early work attracted widespread attention in the engineering community and helped the American Section increase its membership from 70 to 168 during its first three years. At the fifth annual meeting of the American Section in 1902, they renamed the organization the American Society for Testing Materials and elected Dudley as its first president.

Expanding the Scope of ASTM

After the turn of the century, ASTM formed several new committees that expanded the organization's scope beyond the steel industry and responded to the growing need for standards in many areas. Committee C-1 on Cement, Lime, and Clay Products, for example, founded in 1902, played a key role in standardizing test methods in the cement and concrete sector.

The work of Committee C-1 was part of industry-wide efforts to develop uniform test methods. The committee defined basic testing procedures to measure tensile strength 7 and 28 days after the pour, researched the weather resistance of various cement formulas, and developed compression test standards that were widely adopted across the industry. During later years, committee members supported the formation of the Cement Reference Laboratory at the National Bureau of Standards, which standardized cement testing equipment used in research laboratories. World War I marked another watershed in the history of standard specifications. Many steel mills and cement plants that had traditionally supplied commercial materials now geared up for military production—foreign territory to most civilian manufacturers. Standard specifications greatly facilitated this conversion. ASTM specifications, for example, provided rolling mills with detailed technical information that was necessary to produce steel plates for tanks and ships. Cement producers used standard specifications to supply concrete for massive fortress construction projects on the Western Front.

ASTM Standards in New Industries

In the early 1920s, ASTM's main activities focused on the steel, railroad, and cement industries, and most of its members were based in the Northeastern part of the country. In the four decades after World War I, ASTM evolved into a truly national organization whose more than 100 technical committees formed an integral part of America's maturing economic base, contributing to the rise of new industries in such strategic areas as highway transportation, petrochemicals, electronics, and aerospace technology. ASTM's development from the 1920s to the 1960s helped facilitate the nation's rise to economic and military superpower status.

The period between the two world wars witnessed a phenomenal growth of mass-production industries, which formed the backbone of American economic strength for decades to come. Leading manufacturers availed themselves of ASTM standards, which gained wide acceptance well beyond the steel industry. General Electric, for example, a pioneer in the use of ASTM standards in the electrical industry, required suppliers to adhere to ASTM's new standard specifications for non-ferrous metals in the early 1920s.

The automobile, another innovation that came into its own during the 1920s, also benefited from the widespread adoption of ASTM standards. In this era, leading car manufacturers like General Motors, Packard, Hudson, and Studebaker copied Henry Ford's mass-production system, which depended on the uniformity of such materials as steel, rubber, paint, and oil—all areas where ASTM's technical committees launched a series of new activities.

The New Deal Era and World War II

The Great Depression of the 1930s marked a difficult period in U.S. history as well as in ASTM. To cope with its financial hardship, ASTM's leadership introduced austerity budgets and reduced the volume of technical papers presented in committees and at annual meetings. Despite cutbacks, technical papers remained one of ASTM's most important vehicles to disseminate the results of cutting-edge research conducted by committee members within the engineering community.

The trends of the 1930s—advances in test methods, close cooperation between government and industry, and mass production techniques—converged during World War II, when ASTM joined the industrial mobilization effort. Its first major contribution was the publication in 1942 of the society's most extensive *Book of Standards,* three volumes that made more than 1,000 standard specifications available to industry and government. Since more than half of these were purchase specifications, they could be written directly into tens of thousands of government contracts for war-essential materials. Existing ASTM standards also played an important role in the creation of an industrial base that was necessary to sustain the war effort.

ASTM in the Postwar Economy

The relationship between ASTM, the federal government, and private industry remained vital throughout the postwar era, most obviously in defense procurement. Building on positive experiences in voluntary consensus standards development during World War II, the Pentagon began to depend more on major technical societies to provide the bulk of standards used in defense procurement. Congress supported this practice with the passage of the Defense Standardization Act of 1952, which mandated the simplification of military specifications and standards, and strongly encouraged the Army, Navy, and Air Force to use established specifications developed by ASTM and other organizations. As a result, government defense specifications contained extensive references to ASTM standards.

In the civilian sector, one of the most important developments that transformed American culture and society during the postwar years was the explosive growth of suburbs, another area in which ASTM standards played a key role. Building contractors and architects, applying mass-production techniques to home construction on a massive scale to build suburban complexes in eastern metropolitan regions, southern California, and the southern states, developed a keen interest in material standards for construction materials. ASTM had been active in developing these standards for decades.

On the Threshold of a New Era

In 1961, 60 years after the American Section had turned itself into the American Society for Testing Materials, the organization renamed itself once again and became the American Society for Testing and Materials. The conjugation emphasized that ASTM was devoted to the development of standard material specifications, not only standard test methods. Internally, the society had evolved from a handful of technical committees devoted to steel and cement standards into a fairly complex organization comprising a management structure and more than 80 committees involved in a wide range of activities. After decades of sharing office space with other technical societies, ASTM finally moved into its own newly built headquarters at 1916 Race Street, Philadelphia, in 1964. The building accommodated the organization's staff, which supported technical committees, edited the annual Book of Standards and ASTM's member publications, organized meetings and symposia, and performed a variety of administrative functions.

A New Direction

William Cavanaugh, reflecting on the transformation of ASTM during his tenure as executive director, told members in 1985 that "those intimately familiar with the affairs of ASTM for the past 14 years or so would agree that the obvious and pervasive health of the organization today is the direct and traceable result of its ability to anticipate events through planning and to set in motion, in a timely fashion, policies to accommodate those events." Cavanaugh's philosophy enabled the organization to meet the extraordinary challenges of the 1970s and laid the groundwork for major new departures during subsequent decades.

Externally, ASTM reached far beyond its mainstay in industrial standards and entered rapidly growing markets for consumer products and environmental standards. Prior to Cavanaugh's appointment as managing director in 1970, ASTM had already launched several initiatives in these areas, highlighted by the formation of Committee F-8 on Sports Equipment and Facilities. Cavanaugh, determined to use ASTM's expertise in related fields, provided strategic guidance for these activities. In one of the most important programmatic statements of his career, he declared, "The genius of ASTM—meaning the consensus approach to standards—is applicable to a broad range of problems that are only very generally related to our traditional area of activity." This call for deploying the consensus principle in cutting-edge fields precipitated the formation of new technical committees, including F-15 on Consumer Products, E-34 on Occupational Health and Safety, F-13 on Safety and Traction for Footwear, and F-20 on Hazardous Substances and Oil Spill Response, to name only a few.

As in previous decades, ASTM's initiatives were closely related to seismic shifts in American society. This pattern continued with the social activism of the late 1960s, which precipitated the rise of a grass-roots consumer rights movement. Activists challenge manufacturers to tackle prevailing product quality and safety problems in cooperation with consumers, but also complained about their inability to match industry's power and influence in the standards development process. This formed the backdrop to the passage of the Consumer Products Safety Act in 1972, establishing a federal commission with the power to promulgate consumer product standards.

At about the time that ASTM was enjoying a new partnership with consumer advocacy groups, a new regulatory storm gathered on the horizon. The mid 1970s saw a rash of legislation aimed at federalizing the American standards development system—a formidable threat to the voluntary standards system that had prevailed since the early 20th century.

In response, ASTM launched a spirited defense of the voluntary system at several congressional hearings in Washington, D. C., declaring that the organization's consensus-building process, which had evolved through decades of committee work on industrial products, was a viable alternative to government-issued standards for consumer products. Responding to critics who charged that the voluntary system benefitted major corporations at the expense of other interests, Cavanaugh argued, "We cannot agree that the present standardization process poses grave economic hardships for small business. . . . There are many small business concerns involved in ASTM. In recognition of this fact, we have done everything possible to keep the cost of participation in the ASTM process at a minimum."

Organized consumer activism started to wane in the late 1970s, but its effects remain evident. ASTM established mechanisms such as the Consumer Sounding Board, by which consumers could provide input into the technical requirements of standards. The resurgence of the nation's consumer-good industry during the 1990s was partly a result of major improvements in product quality and safety that enhanced the competitiveness of U.S. manufacturers in global competition.

The environment was yet another area where ASTM established a major presence during the 1970s. As in consumer products, social activism and government intervention were important factors. Rachel Carson's *Silent Spring*, a penetrating analysis of pesticides such as DDT in the food chain published in 1962, helped trigger the modern environmental movement, whose participants were particularly concerned about air and water quality. Federal initiatives soon followed, including the passage of the Clean Air Act of 1970 that set standards for automobile emissions. Older ASTM committees, such as D-18 on Soil and Rock and D-19 on Water, which started to work on environmental standards during this era, developed strong relationships with the Environmental Protection Agency (EPA). EPA, which was formed in 1970, used ASTM standards for electrical generating plants, petroleum tests, and water as a basis for its own standards. Furthermore, industries with interests in environmental protection solicited the assistance of ASTM, leading to the formation of new technical committees such as F-20 on Hazardous Substances and Oil Spill Response and E-35 on Pesticides.

ASTM in the Global Economy

The rise of the "new economic world order" of the 1980s and 1990s that transformed modern standards development was an extraordinarily complex process. Economically, it was triggered by the rebirth of Japanese and Western European industry from the ashes of World War II, and by the formation of so-called "tiger economies" on the Pacific Rim during the 1970s. Technologically, globalization fed on new communication systems that allowed instant access to and exchange of information across continents. Politically, the lowering of tariff barriers in North America and Western Europe created vast new markets in which global producers competed head-on. The buzzwords of the new, interdependent world economy became cost efficiency, customer orientation, and the ability to respond quickly to changes in the global marketplace.

During the 1980s, ASTM introduced more restrictive time lines that helped technical committees stay focused on deliverables. To further accelerate the standards development process, ASTM formed the Institute for Standards Research (ISR) in 1988. ISR provides a mechanism to bring together the financial and technical resources of the private and public sectors to facilitate research that can be used to speed the development of standards. ASTM also initiated new standards-related programs to provide additional products and services to its members and customers, beginning in 1985 with the development of ASTM's Technical and Professional Training Courses. These courses provide continuing education in the performance and use of ASTM and other standards in areas such as petroleum, plastics, paint, steel, environmental subjects, and many other areas.

In 1993, ASTM expanded its services to include a new program on proficiency testing. ASTM's Proficiency Testing Program provides participating laboratories with a statistical quality assurance tool, enabling laboratories to compare their performance in conducting test methods within their laboratories and against other laboratories worldwide. Programs have been launched in metals (plain carbon and low-alloy steel, stainless steels, and gold in bullion), petroleum, plastics, and more.

The construction of ASTM's new headquarters building in West Conshohocken, Pennsylvania, a suburb of Philadelphia, was another milestone along the way toward a more efficient organization. In the late 1980s, it became clear that the old quarters on Philadelphia's Race Street could not accommodate state-of-the-art office technology that facilitated information management in a modern organization. The new building, which was completed in 1995, provided ultra-modern conference facilities for technical committees, ample work space for headquarters staff, and prepared ASTM to meet the challenges of the 21st century. "The new Headquarters building," a board member commented, was "a tangible indication of ASTM's movement toward the future and its responsiveness to the changing environment of standards development."

What is ASTM?

Organized in 1898, ASTM (The American Society for Testing and Materials) has grown into one of the largest voluntary standards development systems in the world. ASTM is a not-for-profit organization that provides a forum for producers, users, ultimate consumers, and those having a general interest (representatives of government and academia) to meet on common ground and write standards for materials, products, systems, and services. From the work of 132 standards-writing committees, ASTM publishes standard test methods, specifications, practices, guides, classifications, and terminology. ASTM's standards development activities encompass metals, paints, plastics, textiles, petroleum, construction, energy, the environment, consumer products, medical services and devices, computerized systems, electronics, and many other areas. ASTM Headquarters has no technical research or testing facilities; such work is done voluntarily by 35,000 technically qualified ASTM members located throughout the world. More than 10,000 ASTM standards are published each year in the 72 volumes of the *Annual Book of ASTM Standards.* These standards and related information are sold throughout the world.

Mission Statement

To be the foremost developer and provider of voluntary consensus standards, related technical information, and services having internationally recognized quality and applicability that

■ promote public health and safety, and the overall quality of life;
■ contribute to the reliability of materials, products, systems, and services; and
■ facilitate national, regional, and international commerce.

Strategic Objectives

■ To provide the optimum environment and support for technical committees to develop needed standards and related information;
■ To ensure ASTM products and services are provided in a timely manner and meet current needs;
■ To increase the awareness of the ASTM consensus process, the benefits of participation, and the value of ASTM standards and services in the global marketplace;
■ To strengthen both the national and international acceptance and use of ASTM products and services;
■ To make the ASTM process, resources, skills, and facilities available to the marketplace to accommodate its changing needs;
■ To ensure the fair representation and participation of key stakeholders in ASTM activities to secure technically sound standards; and
■ To maintain ASTM's fiscal stability in order to fulfill the Society's mission.

Website: http://www.astm.org

What Is a Standard?

As used in ASTM, a standard is a document that has been developed and established within the consensus principles of the society and that meets the approval requirements of ASTM procedures and regulations.

Some of the specific standards developed that relate to fitness, physical activity, recreation, and sport facilities and equipment are E-5 Fire Standards, F-6 Resilient Floor Coverings, F-8 Sports Equipment and Facilities, F-14 Fences, F-21 Filtration, F-24 Amusement Rides and Devices, F-26 Food Service Equipment. F-27 Snow Skiing, and F-30 Emergency Medical Services.

What Types of Standards Does ASTM Produce?

ASTM develops six principal types of full consensus standards. They are:

1. *Standard test method* — a definitive procedure for the identification, measurement, and evaluation of one or more qualities, characteristics, or properties of a material, product, system, or service that produces a test result.
2. *Standard specification* — a precise statement of a set of requirements to be satisfied by a material, product, system, or service that also indicates the procedures for determining whether each of the requirements is satisfied.
3. *Standard practice* — a definitive procedure for performing one or more specific operations or functions that does not produce a test result.
4. *Standard terminology* — a document comprising terms, definitions, description of terms, explanation of symbols, abbreviations, or acronyms.
5. *Standard guide* — a series of options or instructions that do not recommend a specific course of action.
6. *Standard classification* — a systematic arrangement or division of materials, products, systems, or services into groups based on similar characteristics such as origin, composition, properties, or use.

Why Are ASTM Standards Credible?

Many factors contribute to the quality and credibility of ASTM standards. Those factors include:

■ A voluntary, full-consensus approach that brings together people with diverse backgrounds, expertise, and knowledge;
■ A balanced representation of interests at the standards-writing table;
■ Intense round-robin testing to ensure precision;
■ Strict balloting and due-process procedures to guarantee accurate, up-to-date information; and

---

A Sample Standard

A961-96 Common Requirements for Steel Flanges, Forged Fittings, Valves, and Parts for Piping Applications

Scope

1.1 This specification covers a group of common requirements that shall apply to steel flanges, forged fittings, valves, and parts for piping applications under any of the following individual Product Specifications:

Title of Specification: A105/A105M Forgings, Carbon Steel, for Piping Components; A181/A181M Forgings, Carbon Steel for General-Purpose Piping; A182/A182M Forged or Rolled Alloy-Steel Pipe Flanges, Forged Fittings, and Valves and Parts for High Temperature Service; A350/A350M Forgings, Carbon and Low Alloy Steel, Requiring Notch Toughness Testing for Piping Components; A694/A694M Forgings, Carbon and Alloy Steel for Pipe Flanges, Fittings, Valves, and Parts for High-Pressure Transmission Service; A707/A707M Flanges, Forged, Carbon and Alloy Steel, for Pipe Flanges, Fittings; A727/A727M Forgings, Carbon Steel for Piping Components with Inherent Notch Toughness; A836/A836M Forgings, Titanium-Stabilized Carbon Steel, for Glass-Lined Piping and Pressure Vessel Service

1.2 In case of conflict between a requirement of the individual Product Specification and a requirement of this General Requirement Specification, the requirements of the individual Product Specification shall prevail over those of this specification.

1.3 By mutual agreement between the purchaser and the supplier, additional requirements may be specified (see 4.2.2). The acceptance of any such additional requirements shall be dependent on negotiations with the supplier and must be included in the order as agreed upon by the purchaser and supplier.

1.4 The values stated in either inch-pound units or SI units (metric) are to be regarded separately as a standard. Within the text and the tables, the SI units are shown in brackets. The values stated in each system are not exact equivalents; therefore each system must be used independently of the other. Combining values from the two systems may result in nonconformance with the specification. The inch-pound units shall apply unless the "M" designation (SI) of the Product Specification is specified in the order.

■ An atmosphere that promotes open discussion.

What is Meant by Full-Consensus Standards?

■ Full-consensus standards are developed through the cooperation of all parties who have an interest in participating in the development and/or use of the standards. Standards can be developed through varying degrees of consensus. Examples include:

■ Company standard — consensus among the employees of a given organization (principally within such departments as design, development, production, and purchasing).

■ Industry standard — consensus among the employees of a given industry (typically developed by a trade association).

■ Professional standard — consensus among the individual members of a given profession (typically developed by a professional society).

■ Government standard — consensus often among the employees of a government agency or department.

ASTM develops full-consensus standards with the belief that input from all concerned parties in the development of a standard will ensure technically competent standards having the highest credibility when critically examined and used as the basis for commercial, legal, or regulatory actions.

What Is Meant by Committee Balance?

Committee balance is when the number of voting producers on a committee exceeds the combined number of voting non-producers (users, ultimate consumers, and those having a general interest; that is, representatives of government and academia).

Is the Use of ASTM Standards Mandatory?

ASTM standards are developed voluntarily and used voluntarily. They become legally binding only when a government body makes them so, or when they are cited in a contract.

Who Uses ASTM Standards?

ASTM standards are used by thousands of individuals, companies, and agencies. Purchasers and sellers incorporate standards into contracts; scientists and engineers use them in their laboratories; architects and designers use them in their plans; government agencies reference them in codes, regulations, and laws; and many others refer to them for guidance.

Who Writes ASTM Standards?

ASTM standards are written by volunteer members who serve on technical committees. Through a formal balloting process, all members may have input into the standards before they are published by ASTM.

Anyone who is qualified or knowledgeable in the area of a committee's scope is eligible to become a committee member. ASTM currently has 35,000 members representing virtually every segment of industry, government, and academia.

What Are ASTM Technical Committees?

They are the specific arenas in which ASTM standards are developed. There are 132 ASTM main technical committees and each is divided into subcommittees. The subcommittee is the primary unit in ASTM's standards development system, as it represents the highest degree of expertise in a given area. Subcommittees are further subdivided into task groups. Task group members do not have to be ASTM members. Many task groups seek non-ASTM members to provide special expertise in a given area.

How Are ASTM Standards Developed?

Standards development work begins when a need is recognized. Task group members prepare a draft standard, which is reviewed by its parent subcommittee through a letter ballot. After the subcommittee approves the document, it is submitted to a main committee letter box. Once approved at the main committee level, the document is submitted for balloting to the society. All negative votes cast during the balloting process, which must include a written explanation of the voter's objections, must be fully considered before the document can be submitted to the next level in the process. Final approval of a standard depends on concurrence by the ASTM Committee on Standards that proper procedures were followed and due process achieved. Only then is the ASTM standard published.

How Long Does It Take to Develop a Standard?

It usually takes about two years to develop a standard, although some committees have produced their standards in a year or less. Progress depends entirely on the urgency of the need, the complexity of the job, and the amount of time committees devote to the work.

How Does Someone Initiate a New Standards Activity in ASTM?

A written request, which describes the proposed activity and lists individuals, companies, and organizations that might have an interest in it, should be submitted to ASTM headquarters. The ASTM staff then researchers the project to assess whether there is adequate interest, to discover if parallel activities exist in other organizations, and to determine where the activity would appropriately fit within the ASTM structure.

The process of organizing a new activity includes holding a planning and/or organizational meeting, depending on the activity's complexity. These meetings ensure that all affected interests have an opportunity to determine the need for the activity, participate in the development of a title, scope, and structure, and identity areas that need standardization.

Who Governs the Activities of ASTM Technical Committees?

The governing body is the ASTM Board of Directors, elected by vote of the entire membership. The board and its standing committees have established procedures to ensure that standards are developed on a full-consensus basis, that all dissenting parties receive due process, and that all ASTM standards follow style and format requirements. The "Regulations Governing ASTM Technical Committees" and the "Form and Style for ASTM Standards" are the documents that govern the ASTM standards development process. A full-time professional staff ensures that technical committees receive support in adhering to these procedures.

Does ASTM Publish Technical Information Other than Standards?

ASTM publishes special technical publications (STPs), which are collections of peer-reviewed technical papers reflecting the state-of-the-art in subjects spanning the scope of ASTM activities. Most STPs are based on symposia sponsored by ASTM technical committees. Other publications include compilations of ASTM standards, manuals, monographs, handbooks, retrospective publications, reference radiographs, standard adjuncts, data series. The Society also publishes a monthly magazine, *Standardization News,* and five journals: *Journal of Testing and Evaluation; Cement, Concrete, and Aggregates; Geotechnical Testing Journal; Journal of Composites Technology and Research;* and *Journal of Forensic Sciences.*

What Services Does ASTM Staff Provide?

The ASTM staff provides administrative support to the committee members, thus allowing them to concentrate on the technical aspects of standards development. An ASTM staff manager attends every committee meeting. It is the manager's responsibility to make certain that ASTM procedures are followed and to ensure that the committee members have maximum access to ASTM support services.

ASTM support services include meeting arrangements, promotion and public relations, symposia operations, technical and professional training, editorial assistance, publications marketing and distribution, member and committee services, customer services, accounting and financial services, and computer services. The ASTM Information Center contains all publications produced by ASTM and other sources of information.

Does ASTM Offer Continuing Technical Education?

ASTM provides continuing education and training in the use and application of ASTM standards through technical and professional training courses. ASTM members propose ideas for the courses, work with staff to establish course outlines, and serve as instructors. Attendees learn the practical application of standards and benefit from the instructors' technical expertise and knowledge of standards development.

Does ASTM Headquarters Assist Technical Committees with the Development of Research?

In 1987, ASTM formed the Institute for Standards Research (IRS). The purpose of the Institute is to provide a mechanism for conducting research to improve the quality and timeliness of ASTM standards. This mechanism includes fundraising, obtaining competitive bids for research proposals, and monitoring projects.

It does no research, but serves as the intermediary between the standards-writing community and the public or private agencies that could provide appropriate research and technical services, or supply funding for such research.

Are Members of ASTM Committees Liable for the Standards They Develop and That Are Published by ASTM?

No! A person claiming injury or damage as a result of an ASTM standard must base his claim on the publication of this information. Since ASTM is the publisher, any liability for the content of an ASTM publication is ASTM's, not its members', liability. The statutory law of Pennsylvania, where ASTM is chartered, expressly forbids the transfer of this liability to ASTM's members.

What Does it Cost to Be a Member of ASTM?

ASTM members pay a nominal administrative fee ($65/year for the individual membership; $350/year organizational memberships). ASTM does not charge any other fee for its service. The costs involved are the time and travel expenses of committee members, and the donated use of members' laboratory and research facilities. There are no project costs.

Occupational Safety and Health Administration (OSHA)

OSHA (a federal agency) has become extensively involved in standards development. The impetus to develop a new standard can come from a variety of sources: OSHA's own initiative, the U.S. Congress, information from the National Institute for Occupational Safety and Health (NIOSH), a referral from EPA's Toxic Substances Control Act (TSCA), public petitions, or requests from OSHA advisory committees.

The standard-setting process can begin in a number of ways — with publication in the Federal Register of a request for information (RFI), an advance notice of proposed rule-making (ANPRM), or a notice of proposed rule-making (NPRM). Through an RFI or an ANPRM, OSHA seeks information to determine the extent of a particular hazard, current and potential protective measures, and the costs and benefits of various solutions.

Recently, OSHA has begun to develop some new standards through a negotiated rule-making process. Under this process, the agency forms an advisory committee composed of representatives from the various interest groups that will be affected by the new standard. These labor and industry reps meet with OSHA to hammer out an agreement (consensus standard) that will serve as the basis for a proposed rule. This process is used to resolve long-standing differences that, until negotiated rule making, could not be resolved. OSHA is using this process to draft proposed rules for steel erection in construction and fire protection in shipyards.

Information from these sources, as well as injury and fatality data, is then used to develop a proposal. Formal proposals are published in the Federal Register with notice of a public comment period over the next 60 to 90 days. Occasionally, requests are made to extend the comment period or to hold a public hearing.

Finally, OSHA uses all this information to prepare and publish a final standard in the Federal Register — or, in some cases, to determine that no standard is needed. Standards usually take effect in 90 days or less, although some provisions (such as requirements for detailed programs) may be phased in over a longer period.

International Environment, Health and Safety (EH&S) and International Audit Protocol Consortium (IAPC)

New international environment, health, and safety (EH&S) requirements are also being developed. These requirements include Great Britain's BS7750, the European Union's (EU) environmental management audit scheme (EMAS), the International Standards Or-

ganizations's (ISO) 9000 quality assurance and quality management standards, and the ISO 14000, a global environmental management standard.

Companies are compelled to comply with these environmental management standards for reasons that reach beyond fear of legal reprisal — strong economic and political forces are at work. Consumers are increasingly demanding that companies' products and manufacturing processes be environmentally responsible. One of the goals of the ISO 14000 standards will be to provide a precise "green" measuring tool for a concerned public. Governments, particularly those in the EU, are also favoring the "green" company. Companies without an ISO 14000 certification could be shut out of some international markets.

American College of Sports Medicine (ACSM)

The ACSM has published a 2nd edition of the book entitled *Health/Fitness Facility Standards and Guidelines*, which suggests that the "book now sets a clear standard of comparison for use in legal proceedings."

However, IRSA, the Association for Quality Clubs (see below) has rejected the guidelines. The Association for Worksite Health Promotion (formerly the Association for Fitness in Business) is developing its own standards and certification process in a reaction to ASCM's failure to recognize the AFB's previous contributions to health and fitness certification standards.

There is a veritable alphabet soup of professional certifications from associations wishing to increase their memberships, improve their images, or turn a profit. The ASCM book defers to the state or local codes when it comes to more technical standards. These codes are based on BOCA or equivalent standards.

The ACSM is a medically based organization with a research focus. In the 14 years since the ACSM issued its initial exercise recommendations, the percentage of people complying has not changed substantially. The medical model works in a hospital or testing lab, but not necessarily in clubs or corporate health promotion or municipal fitness programs.

International Recognized Association of Quality Clubs (IRSA)

IRSA, the Association of Quality Clubs, is a not-for-profit trade association representing 2,500 health and sports clubs worldwide. It is the largest club association in the world. More than 1,800 IRSA member clubs offer some form of reciprocal access through the association's "Passport" program which provides members the opportunity to use another club when they travel.

A club must agree to abide by the IRSA Code of Conduct and comply with the association's, membership standards. A member of IRSA has the mission to enhance the quality of life through physical fitness and sports. It endeavors to provide quality facilities, programs, and instruction and strives to instill in all those served an understanding of the value of physical fitness and sports to their lives. To fulfill their mission, members pledge the following:

■ Open membership to persons of all races, creeds, and places of national origin,
■ Treat each member as though the success of the club depends on that individual alone,
■ Systematically upgrade the club's professional knowledge and keep abreast of new developments in the field,
■ Design facilities and programs with the members' safety in mind,
■ Continue to increase the value and benefits of services and programs,
■ Provide public-service programs to expand awareness of the benefits of regular exercise and sports,
■ Deliver what is promised, and
■ Conduct a business in a manner that commands the respect of the public for the industry and for the goals toward which the club strives.

ISRA has the following internationally recognized certifying agencies:

■ Aerobics and Fitness Association of America
■ Aerobic Pipeline International
■ American Aerobics Association/International Sports Medicine Association
■ American College of Sports Medicine
■ American Council on Exercise
■ Cooper Fitness Institute
■ IDEA: The Association for Fitness Professionals
■ National Academy of Sports Medicine
■ National Association for Fitness Certification
■ National Dance Exercise Instructors Training Association
■ National Federation of Professional Trainers
■ National Strength and Conditioning Association
■ Ontario Fitness Council
■ Sinai Corporate Health

United States Tennis Association (USTA)

The USTA represents the tennis industrial though many other groups exist, such as the U.S. Professional Tennis Association, the ATP Tour, Women's Tennis Association, Women's International Professional Tennis Council, International Tennis Federation, and others. Many of these associations are now working with ASTM in developing standards for tennis courts. These are also involving tennis court builders.

National Fire Protection Association (NFPA)

The NFPA publishes the Life Safety Codes and will be jointly developing and publishing the first edition of the International Fire Code by the year 2000. This agreement comes after negotiations between the ICC and NFPA. The ICC's three model code organizations, include the Building Officials and Code Administrators International, the International Conference of Building Officials, and the Southern Building Code Congress International. Representatives have been appointed by the ICC and NFPA to participate in the development of code. It will be processed through NFPA's International Conference of Building officials (ICBO).

ICBO is a leading code organization that established a uniform building code in 1927. That code contained a little over 200 pages of text, whereas the 1994 version involves three volumes and more than 2,600 pages. Modern codes are steadily moving to performance-type codes rather than the specification type because of the proliferation of types of materials, methods, and machinery used today. Such codes also reflect public policy, which has changed in the past 70 or more years; contemporary society has looked to codes not only to ensure safety of life and limb, but increasingly to safeguard public welfare or well-being and security. Goals for many public issues such as air and water quality, energy conservation, recycling, and disabilities have led to a number of codes that affect recreation, physical activity, and sport facilities.

Codes and standards are sometimes viewed as interchangeable terms. Indeed, a code meets the above definitions of a standard. Codes, or parts thereof, are frequently characterized as being either prescriptive or performance-based. Prescriptive code requirements are definitive and easily measurable, such as the minimum width of an exit corridor, maximum slope for a specific type of roof covering, minimum air gap for back flow prevention, minimum size of grounding conductor, etc. Performance code requirements, on the other hand, use terms that describe the desired result, such as watertight enclosure, smoke removal, safe-for-the-intended-use, etc. Some of these terms have companion standards as part of the code, such as those for smoke dampers, stairway identification signs, and waterproof paper, and others do not. Adopted standards in this context can be thought of as specification codes.

A review of the 1927 UBC reveals that 28 standards were incorporated by reference. These documents were promulgated by various organizations including ASTM, the American Concrete Institute, the National Board of Fire Underwriters, the National Fire Protection Association, and others.

Standards are incorporated into the UBC under a code change procedure involving a proposal, a review by a code change committee in a public hearing, and a vote at a final hearing by the assembled membership at the annual meeting. Anyone can propose a code change and argue for or against any code change. However, only Class A or governmental members are entitled to vote.

The Building Officials and Code Administrators International (BOCA) and the Southern Building Code Congress International (SBCCI), the respective publishers of the National Building Code (NBC) and the Standard Building Code (SBC), have similar histories of employing adopted standards in their codes. Together with ICBO, the International Code Council (ICC) has been formed as a consortium of these organizations. The ICC has targeted the year 2000 for the first edition of the International Building Code (IBC), with no further publications of the UBC, NBC, and SBC after 1997.

The standard and the manner it is to be utilized is to be specifically referenced in the IBC text as well as the following:

■ The need for the standard is to be established,
■ The standard is to be written in mandatory language,
■ It should be appropriate,
■ Uncommon terms should be specifically defined,
■ It should not require proprietary materials,
■ A proprietary agency for quality control or testing should not be required,
■ Details for preparing the test sample and the sample selection are to be provided,
■ The reporting format should be specified,
■ The measure of satisfactory performance should be defined,
■ Language in the standard should not state that the provisions override any conflicting requirements within the IBC,

■ The standard is to be promulgated through a consensus process such as ASTM or ANSI, and
■ The standard should be readily available.

European Committee For Standardization (CEN)

CEN is the European standards organization that coordinates all European country standards organizations. It has secretariats in various subject areas that in turn relate to ISO Technical Committees. CEN has been the initiator of EC 1992. This is the array of regulatory and standards initiatives that leads to the common European internal market. EC 1992 also requires testing and certifications requirements. It sets forth alternative approaches to testing, certification, and proving conformity with the regulatory directives that are set out. It identifies organizations that will perform conformity assessment functions and U.S. testing and certifying organizations. This has implications on many sports products and ultimately facilities used for international events.

International Standards Organization (ISO) or International Organization for Standardization (IOS)

The ISO is the worldwide body, and ANSI is the member body of this group representing the U.S. Approaching the 21st century, ISO sees a world in which global trade between nations continues to grow at a rate three to four times faster than national economies; a world in which the design, manufacture, marketing, and customer service operations of a growing majority of individual enterprises are distributed across many countries; and a world in which electronic communications have dramatically increased technical collaboration between experts in academia, governments, and industries from all countries.

The increasingly rapid development of technology in many sectors will continue to present major opportunities as well as underlying dangers for the general welfare of society. It will therefore be incumbent on all social and economic partners to collaborate closely in guiding the applications of appropriate technologies toward sustainable economic development and global prosperity.

In this rapidly evolving scenario, globally applicable standards will play a key role. Such standards, whether developed by ISO or others, will become primary technical instruments supporting international commerce. In this context ISO intends to be recognized globally as an influential and innovative leader in the developments of globally applicable international standards that meet or exceed the expectations of the community of nations. It will strive at all times to perfect the application of consensus and transparency principles in standardization, and in this way promote the values of rationality, utility, safety, and environmental protection for the benefit of all peoples.

Standardization is essentially an economic undertaking made possible by the achievement of widespread agreements on the coherent and mutually beneficial use of science, technology, and business know-how. The prime object of ISO and its governance is laid down in the ISO statutes (i.e., to promote the development of standardization and related activities in the world with a view to facilitating international exchange of goods and services and to developing cooperation in the sphere of intellectual, scientific, and economic activity). In the light of present and anticipated developments, the objectives of ISO may also be enumerated as follows:

■ ISO will produce international standards and actively promote their voluntary adoption and use in order to make worldwide industry and trade as efficient as possible;

■ ISO standards should be amenable for use in conformity assessment and promote quality and reliability at competitive prices at all levels of industry and trade for the ultimate benefit of consumers,

■ ISO standards will promote human and societal benefits whenever applicable in relation to health, safety, and environment, and in relation to general market and growing trade needs;

■ ISO standards will, when applicable, be suitable for reference in the regulatory and procurement activities of federal, state mid local authorities;

■ ISO will have an organization capable of quickly adapting to the changes and needs of the world community, which it serves;

■ In order to respond to the needs of the user community and demand for fast and cost-efficient production and implementation of standards, the organizational entities of ISO will combine the knowledge of standards making, and the knowledge of business operations, paralleling ISO member trends;

■ ISO will be organized in a democratic manner and attempt to accommodate the views and wishes of all its members with governance values respecting the need for balanced representation and consensus-based decision-making; and

■ In each of its undertakings, ISO must perform as well as, or better than, any other international standardizing organization in the world.

National Spa and Pool Institute (NSPI)

The National Spa and Pool Institute has for 30 years been the source of standards for the design, construction, and operation of public as well as residential pools and spas. The organization has a membership of designer-engineers along with manufacturers, builders, contractors, equipment, and chemical manufacturers and suppliers and retailers in every aspect of the pool and spa industry. Many representatives of Health Departments also belong.

In 1996, efforts began to rewrite the ANSI/SPI - 1-1991 standard for public pools as well as other pool and spa standards. This rewrite has undergone a conflict because of the various concerns for safety. At present the technical committee of NSPI has assumed the rewrite function and the broad base of interests originally invited to serve are now reviewers.

World Waterpark Association (WWA)

The federal government has had standards for waterparks since they became popular over a decade ago. In 1991 the WWA published with *Splash Magazine* a developers reference. Concurrently it established a risk management and safety committee. Representatives of this committee were invited by the National Spa and Pool Institute to sit on the public pool standards rewrite committee. After a year of deliberations, it was decided that water slides and flumes should have a stand-alone standard apart from any public pool standard. As a result, a committee WWA was established in 1997 to write a draft of a standard under the cooperative auspices of NSPI, which is an accredited member of ANSI. This standard is now being circulated.

Professional Involvement in Standards

Professionals in the fitness, physical activity, recreation, sport, and related fields are not as involved in standards as they could and should be. Standards organizations involve only a small percentage of the professionals directly involved in the teaching, researching, planning, administering, operating, and maintaining fitness, physical activity, recreation, and sport facilities and activities, regardless of jurisdiction or the type of entity. Many standards applicable to fitness, physical activity, recreation, and sport are developed by manufacturers, medical specialists, businessmen, lawyers, and others.

Professionals have not been aware of these standards organizations nor familiar with how to become involved. Organizations such as the American Alliance for Health, Physical Education, Recreation, and Dance and the National Recreation and Park Association have not specifically designated professionals to serve as their representatives to these organizations. It is imperative that in the future more professionals be appointed or volunteer to lend their expertise to the standards process.

Governmental Involvement in Standards

Governmental agencies have a long history of involvement in standards. Apparently, many of their efforts now tend to be catalytic in evolving standards. This is a significant change over the past 50 years. In most cases they have encouraged producers to regulate their own industries. Where such efforts have failed the government, both state and federal agencies have moved to provide regulations and supportive standards to protect the health, safety, and well-being of the public.

The government usually provides standards in the form of legislation that goes beyond the base line or minimum level of requirement. As a result, industries and professions are becoming more conscious in recognizing that if they themselves do not develop standards, somebody else will.

■ Summary

Standards provide a uniform base by which the requirements for equipment and facilities can be established. Standards are either mandatory or voluntary in implementation. The requirements are set forth as standards, or they can be produced in other forms such as legal codes, technical specifications, guides, or literature. Standards are also established through legal theories and even case law. They become standards through consistent practice and care.

Standards are created by many different types of organizations, all of which create the standard differently. These organizations are national and international in responsibility and influence trade and governmental relations around the globe. Particularly in sports, recreation, and related fields standards are more often set by nonprofessionals than by those involved day to day. Government still plays an important role in setting standards, particularly when industry does not pick up on the need to protect the public's health, safety and well-being.

Learning Objective 1: The student will understand the historical evolution of the standards process in the last 50 years.

The first set of standards were developed after World War II. The development of standards has been enhanced by automation, computerization, and partnerships between the private sector and government. The standards development process is extremely democratic in nature.

Learning Objective 2: The student will gain an insight into the impact of emerging standards processes on sports and related products and facilities.

Since the early 1970's participants in fitness, physical activity, recreation, and sport have learned to enjoy safer equipment and facilities. This increased safety comes from the development of standards that have, improved the football helmet, catcher masks, batters helmets, bicycle helmets, playground equipment, and landing areas and much more.

Learning Objective 3: The student will learn the procedures employed in the United States for developing standards.

The development of standards is a participatory process. The final standard is developed through give and take in order to reach a consensus. This process sometimes is long but the end result is often very effective.

Learning Objective 4: The student will be able to identify the varied products and facilities for which standards have been formulated.

Standards formulated for the areas of fitness, physical activity, recreation, and sport focus on equipment (e.g., helmets, masks, bats, clubs, strength-training equipment, cardiovascular equipment, playground equipment, and more), facilities (e.g., flooring, lighting, landing surfaces, filtration, and more), and instruction and supervision.

Learning Objective 5: The student will be able to differentiate between a standard and other guidelines, criteria and requirements that are promulgated.

A standard has been established by a governmental entity (mandatory or regulatory standards) or a professional nonprofit organization (voluntary standards). A guideline is a suggestion but does not have the same legal bearing as a standard.

Learning Objective 6: The student will understand the difference between mandatory/regulatory and voluntary standards.

A mandatory standard must be implemented, while a voluntary standard does not have to be implemented. Failure to implement a mandatory standard is punishable by statute. Failure to implement a voluntary standard may open the door to a negligence action by the plaintiff.

■ Self-Assessment Exercise

- What is ASTM? What is ANSI? What is OSHA? What is ACSM?
- What is USTA? What is NFPA? What is ICBO? What is ISRA? What is CEN?
- What is ISO? What Is NSPI?
- What is a standard? What is standard of practice? What is standard of care?
- How Is a standard developed?
- What type of standards do ASTM, ANSI produce?
- Who writes ASTM, ANSI standards?
- Are members of ASTM committees liable for the standards they develop? Which are published by ASTM?

■ Case Study

You have been selected to work on the F-8 Committee of the ASTM. You are representing the Council for Facilities and Equipment (CFE) of the American Association for Active Lifestyles and Fitness. Your colleagues on the CFE want to see a new standard developed for gymnasium flooring for basketball and volleyball. How will you proceed?

■ References

Innovation by consensus: ASTM's first century. (1998) [on-line]. Available http://www.astm.org/ANNIVER/consensus.htm

http://www.ansi.org

http://www.osha.gov

http://www.ascm.org

http://www.usta.com

■ Suggested Readings

Flynn, R.B. (Ed.) (1993). **Planning facilities for athletics, physical education, and recreation.** Reston, VA: American Alliance for Health, Physical Education, Recreation and Dance.

Kreighbaum, E.F., & Smith, M.A. (Eds.). (1996). **Sports and fitness equipment design.** Champaign, IL: Human Kinetics.

Tharrett, S.J. & Peterson, J.A. (Eds.) (1997). **ACSM's health/fitness facility standards and guidelines** (2nd ed.). Champaign, IL: Human Kinetics.

Notes

CHAPTER 7

Planning Facilities for Safety and Risk Management

Todd L. Seidler, University of New Mexico

Learning Objectives

After reading this chapter, the student will be able to

■ understand negligence and become familiar with the basic legal duties expected of facility managers,

■ understand the role that good facility planning has in the design and construction of safe facilities,

■ identify at least five methods of controlling access to facilities,

■ describe the importance of and identify the minimal guidelines for safety or buffer zones,

■ discuss the problem of traffic patterns within facilities and identify alternatives, and

■ understand the need for selecting the proper materials for floors, walls and ceilings.

Introduction

Sports and recreation facilities that are poorly planned, designed, or constructed often increase participants' exposure to hazardous conditions and not only render the facility harder to maintain, operate, and staff, but can also significantly increase the organization's exposure to liability. A poorly designed facility can usually be traced to a lack of effort or expertise of the planning and design team. It is not uncommon for a sport, physical education, or recreation facility to be designed by an architect who has little or no experience in that type of building. For those without the proper background and understanding of the unique properties of sport and recreation facilities, many opportunities for mistakes exist that may lead to increased problems related to safety, operations, and staffing.

Design problems commonly seen in activity facilities include inadequate safety zones around courts and fields, poorly planned pedestrian traffic flow through activity areas, poor access and security, lack of proper storage space, and the use of improper building materials. Often safety problems related to design are difficult, expensive, or impossible to fix once the facility has been built. It is essential that these facilities be planned and designed by professionals with activity-related knowledge and experience.

In order to protect themselves from claims of negligence, managers of sport and recreation programs and facilities have a number of legal responsibilities they are expected to perform. In this case, negligence is the failure to act as a reasonably prudent and careful sport or facility manager would act in the same or similar circumstances. In general, facility managers are required to run their programs so as not to create an unreasonable risk of harm to participants, staff, and spectators. One of their specific legal duties is to ensure that the environment provided is free from foreseeable risks or hazards. Unsafe facilities are one of the leading claims made in negligence lawsuits related to sports and physical activity. When discussing facility liability, Page (1988, p. 138) called it "one of the largest subcategories within the broad spectrum of tort law." More specifically, managers of sports facilities are expected to provide a reasonably safe environment and at least to carry out the following five duties:

1. Keep the premises in safe repair.
2. Inspect the premises to discover obvious and hidden hazards.
3. Remove the hazards or warn of their presence.
4. Anticipate foreseeable uses and activities by invitees and take reasonable precautions to protect the invitee from foreseeable dangers.
5. Conduct operations on the premises with reasonable care for the safety of the invitee.

According to van der Smissen (1990, p. 235), "The design, layout, and construction of areas and facilities can provide either safe or hazardous conditions, enhancing or detracting from the activity in which one is engaged." A facility that has been properly planned, designed, and constructed will greatly enhance the ability of the facility manager to effectively carry out these legal duties. A look at common safety problems in sports facilities has determined that they can usually be traced to two primary causes — poor facility planning and design and poor management.

When discussing safe facilities, Maloy (1997, p. 103) states, "Most liability problems dealing with safe environment, however, stem from maintenance and operation of the premises, not their design and construction." Even though this may be true, it is important to understand that there are many things that can be done during the planning process that will enhance the sport manager's ability to safely and properly maintain and operate the premises. A well-designed facility makes the management process more effective and efficient. According to Jewell (1992, p.111) in his book, *Public Assembly Facilities*, "Public safety begins with good architectural design . . . ." Therefore, the majority of this chapter will focus on the planning and design of safe facilities.

Planning Safe Facilities

In order to plan and build a facility that is safe, efficient, and that optimally supports activities likely to occur in each area, a thorough understanding of those activities is required. During the planning process, each individual space within the facility must be studied in an attempt to identify every activity that will, or might take place in that space. After this has been done, the requirements of the space necessary for each of the activities must be determined. For example, if it is determined that a multi-purpose room will house classes in aerobic dance, martial arts, yoga, and gymnastics, and will also act occasionally as a small lecture set-up with portable chairs, the needs of each of these activities must be met, even though some may be in conflict with others. After the design requirements have been identified for each activity, a master list for each area should be developed. This master list is then used to plan that area in order to reduce the number of design errors as much as possible. The following are areas where errors in planning often create hazardous situations within facilities:

Security and Access Control

When designing a facility the following two kinds of access will be addressed — controlling access to the facility and within the facility.

Controlling access to sport, recreation and fitness facilities is an important function of facility managers. Legal liability, deterrence of vandalism and theft, member safety and satisfaction, and maintaining exclusivity and value for those who pay for the privilege of using the facility are a few of the reasons it is necessary to deny access to those who don't belong. A properly designed and equipped facility along with the use of computer controls and a well-trained staff can make access control relatively easy to deal with.

Many facilities, especially older spectator facilities, can be a nightmare to control. Fire regulations require many outside doors for quick evacuation. When limited access is desired, how can these doors be secured, monitored and controlled?

When designing a facility it is often advantageous to plan for one control point through which everyone entering or leaving the building must pass. This control point is usually staffed during open hours so the appropriate fee is paid, ID card checked, or permission given to those who are eligible to enter. If a higher degree of control is desired, a door, gate, or turnstile can also be used.

Recently, many computer software programs have become available to help with access control. If patrons and staff are issued ID cards, such as in a club, school, or corporate setting, systems with magnetic strip or bar code readers can be used to quickly check a person's status. Swiping the ID card through an electronic card reader can determine if the user is eligible to enter. In systems designed for high traffic

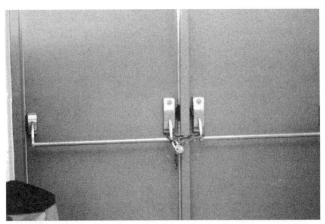

Figure 7.1 Example of an illegal control mechanism.

flow, the computer can be connected directly to a turnstile. If, after scanning the ID, the computer determines that the person be accepted for entry, it can send a signal to release the turnstile and allow entry. This, however, does not prevent an unauthorized person from using someone else's ID. For increased security, picture ID's are desirable to ensure that the person using the card is the legal owner. Other new systems of access control include software programs that, upon scanning an ID card, display a picture of the patron on a computer monitor. If a higher level of security is desired, some systems actually use biometric identification. These systems may scan a patron's fingerprint, palm print, or even retina and compare it to those in the computer's memory. These systems are not only used to admit members, but can also track attendance and adherence to fitness programs, determine patrons' attendance habits, and set staffing levels to provide services at the proper times of the day and to provide information for marketing efforts.

Another aspect of access control that is improving with advances in technology is the replacement of standard door locks and keys. Systems now exist that place an electronic card reader at each door. Instead of a key, each authorized person is issued a card that can be passed through any of the card readers. A central computer receives the information from the card and compares it with the information stored in memory. The computer determines if the person who was issued that card is authorized to open that particular door and either unlocks it or refuses access.

This type of system has many advantages. The computer can be programmed to allow access only to certain areas for each individual card holder. A part-time employee may have a card that works only on certain doors, while the facility manager's card can be programmed to open them all, like a master key. Also, the computer may be programmed so that certain cards only work during specified hours.

In the case of regular locks, if someone loses a key, it is often necessary to re-key many of the locks in the building. New keys must then be issued to everyone, often at great expense. With the card system, if someone loses an access card, that card can simply be turned off on the computer and a new card issued to the owner. The old card becomes useless.

Another feature of the card access system is that each time someone uses a card to open a door it can be recorded on the computer. For example, computer records may show not only that a certain door was opened on Thursday night at 10:17 but also whose card was used and if the person went in or out through the door. This information can be extremely valuable for facility security. The system can also be connected to the fire alarm and programmed to automatically unlock any or all of the doors when the alarm is triggered. Though it may be initially more expensive to install the card reader system than to install standard locks, it will usually pay for itself in increased efficiency, convenience, and long-term cost.

It is often desirable to *control access to certain areas within* a facility. Most buildings limit access to areas such as equipment rooms, office areas, mechanical rooms, or storage, but when a facility has more than one event or activity taking place at the same time, it may also be desirable to separate different parts of the building. For example, in a college activity center, it is not uncommon to have a varsity basketball game in the main arena while the rest of the facility is kept open for recreation. With good planning this can be accomplished by physically separating the spaces through the use of different entrances and exits, different floors, and locking doors, gates, and fences that can quickly restrict passage from one area to another. There are two basic concepts to be familiar with for controlling access within a facility: horizontal and vertical circulation control.

Horizontal circulation control is a common method of managing access to different parts of a facility when there is a need to separate areas on the same floor. In the above example, when the entire facility is open for recreation, an open access plan is utilized. However, when a basketball game is scheduled, certain doors, gates, and fences can be opened or closed in order to restrict access to the arena without having to close down the rest of the building.

Sometimes it may be most efficient to plan for access control through vertical circulation control. For example, it may be desirable in a certain arena to have limited access to the lower level. This level may include the playing floor, locker rooms, coaches' offices, training rooms, and storage areas. By limiting public access to the entire floor, it becomes much easier to secure each individual area. In some arenas, the luxury suites are located on one floor and access to that floor can be gained only by certain elevators, stairways, or gates. Patrons in general seating areas cannot gain access to the suite level, thereby enhancing security and also providing a feel of exclusivity for suite holders. If vertical circulation is needed for a large number of people, non-skid ramps with good handrails usually provide a safer method than stairs.

Safety Zones

Some activities require a certain amount of space surrounding the court, field, or equipment to enhance the safety of the participants. An inadequate amount of space for a safety or buffer zone can present foreseeable risks of injury. A number of lawsuits have been based on claims that an injury occurred as a result of an inadequate safety or buffer zone. Whether it is to separate two adjacent courts or to provide room between the court and a wall or another object, safety zones must be considered.

Basketball courts should have at least 10 feet (preferred), or 6 feet (minimum) of clear space around the court that is free from walls, obstructions, or other courts (NCAA, 1997). Anything less than six feet presents a foreseeable risk of collision. The area under the basket is especially important. If a full 10 feet of clear space between the end-line and the wall cannot be provided, padding should be placed on the wall to soften the impact where players are most likely to hit if they lose control while going out of bounds. It is recommended that wall pads be considered even when the safety zone is greater than 10 feet. One exception to the 10 foot guideline is for competitive volleyball. In this case it is recommended that a minimum of 12 to 15 feet of clear space on all sides be provided (NCAA, 1997).

Activity spaces and surrounding areas should also be designed to be free of obstructions such as doors, columns, and supports. If any such obstruction cannot be moved or eliminated from the activity area or safety zone, it must be padded. All other protrusions that may cause a safety hazard in the gymnasium should be avoided if possible. Common examples of such protrusions include drinking fountains and fire extinguishers, which, during the planning process, can easily be recessed into a wall. Standard doorknobs located in an activity area can also present a hazard, and alternative types of knobs that are recessed in the door are available. Such handles are commonly used on racquetball courts.

Another area where safety or buffer zones are important and often overlooked is in the weight room. Placing weight equipment too close together can pre-

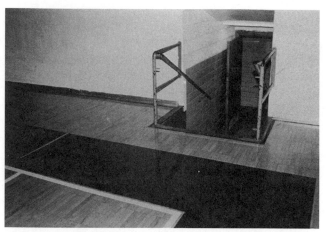

Figure 7.2 Failure to provide activity space free of obstruction.

sent a serious safety hazard. Most weight equipment should be spaced a minimum of three feet apart. This measurement should be made with the movement of the machine or exercise in mind.

Some exercises require a horizontal movement, and the safety or buffer zone should be measured from the extremes of this movement. An example occurs with many leg extension machines. As the movement is executed, the legs straighten and extend another two feet or so out from the machine. The safety zone should be measured from the point of full extension. Some exercises require more than a three-foot safety zone. Some free-weight exercises such as squats and power cleans require more room because of the amount of weight and relative lack of control typically encountered during such exercises. (See Chapter 21)

It should be recognized that an activity area such as a gymnasium may be used occasionally for activities other than those it was designed for. It is not uncommon for outdoor activities such as softball, ultimate frisbee, or track practice to be moved indoors during inclement weather. These activities must be considered when planning a safe gym. The main point is that not all activities will use the traditional court markings for their activity area. This means that the distance from out-of-bounds to the wall is not always a safety factor for those activities that ignore the floor markings. If these activities can be identified and planned for before construction, there is an opportunity to provide a safe environment for them also. Otherwise, it becomes a management concern and a potentially hazardous aspect of the facility that must be compensated for.

Allowing more than one activity to take place in one area can be dangerous. Playing more than one

Figure 7.3 Dangerous overlap of adjacent activity areas.

basketball game on two or more courts that overlap, such as using a side basket for one game and an end basket for another, produces a situation in which an injury is foreseeable. Overlapping fields are a common occurrence and can cause a significant safety hazard if activities are allowed to take place simultaneously. A common example is two softball fields that share a part of the outfields. If games are being played at the same time on each field, the outfielders are at risk of collision. Overlapping courts and fields should be avoided if at all possible. An alternative would be to turn the fields around.

Two activity areas adjacent to each other can be just as dangerous as those that overlap. It is not uncommon to see a baseball field located next to a track. Sometimes this can lead to joggers on the track having to dodge errant baseballs. All adjacent activity areas must be planned with the idea that activities may occur simultaneously, so that foreseeably dangerous situations can be avoided.

Pedestrian Traffic Flow

A common flaw in planning a facility that can cause safety problems is failure to properly plan for pedestrian traffic flow from one area to another. Requiring people to walk through an activity area in order to get to their desired destination can result in a needlessly high-risk situation. A very common example is when the main entrance to the locker room can only be reached by walking across the gym floor. The

Figure 7.4 Example of inappropriate planning for traffic control.

result is people entering and leaving the locker room while an activity is taking place in the same space.

Another example of poor traffic flow planning often occurs when pedestrians are forced to walk between two adjacent courts to get to another part of the facility. This also puts pedestrians in a situation where a collision with a participant is likely.

Planning pedestrian traffic flow within some activity areas is an important consideration. A weight room can be more hazardous if people do not have good, clear, open pathways to move around to different parts of the room. The design and layout of the weight room should take into account the

Figure 7.5 Example of lack of adequate staorge space.

movement of the users, especially during times of peak occupancy.

Storage

One of the most common complaints that facility managers report when asked about their facility is a lack of adequate storage space. The following is a typical example of how this often occurs. A new facility is planned with plenty of storage space in the early stages of planning. As the design is developed and the estimated cost of construction becomes clearer, it is determined that the project is over budget and something must be cut. Storage areas are usually the first spaces to go.

Without proper storage space, equipment will usually be stored in a corner of the gym, in one of the hallways or on the side of the pool deck. Besides the fact that improperly stored equipment is much more likely to be vandalized or stolen, it may also attract children (see *attractive nuisance* below) or others to use or play with it, usually unsupervised and not in the manner for which it was designed. Equipment such as mats and Port-a-pits, gymnastic apparatus, standards, nets, goals, chairs, hurdles, maintenance equipment, etc., are often seen stacked in the corner of gyms. No longer a common sight, trampolines were often pushed into a corner and left unattended. This improper storage and poor supervision led to many catastrophic injuries and deaths and has resulted in the elimination of trampolines from most programs to-

day. It is essential that adequate storage space be planned and constructed and that it be easily secured to prevent unauthorized use of the contents.

Proper Materials

Many factors must be considered during the selection of materials to be used in the construction of a sport or recreation facility. Among these are initial cost, functionality, durability and expected life span, ease, and cost of maintenance and aesthetics. Another often-overlooked factor is safety. Without proper consideration, building and finishing materials can play a large role in the inherent safety of the facility. The potential activities that may take place in every space must be studied thoroughly to ensure that the facility will optimally support each.

Flooring materials must be chosen with great care. Poor selection of the floor surface can contribute to significant safety hazards. One of the most dangerous examples commonly occurs in wet areas such as locker rooms, shower rooms, training rooms, and pool areas. The material selected for the floors in these areas should be a long-lasting, easily maintained, non-slip surface. All too often, these wet areas are constructed with a smooth finish, such as smooth or polished concrete, linoleum, or terrazzo. These are excellent surfaces in the proper situation and are usually selected for durability and ease of maintenance. But they all can become extremely slippery when wet. Many excellent non-slip surfaces can be used in areas

Figure 7.6 Inappropriate use of acoustical panels.

where they may get wet. One of the best surfaces for wet areas is rough finish ceramic or quarry tile. All wet areas should be designed to slope toward a floor drain to avoid standing water (see Chapter 9).

Wall surfaces also offer opportunities for hazards to be designed into a facility. A major hazard often introduced into a facility is the use of glass in or near activity areas. Glass in doors or windows or covering fire extinguishers is a common cause of injury. Even the use of strengthened glass, such as windows with wire mesh, should be questioned in activity areas. Even though it takes greater force to break this kind of glass, it still occurs and may cause severe injuries.

Another relatively common problem has occurred with the use of glass in what most people think of as a non-activity area. The trophy case in the lobby of most high school gyms is a good example. Planners often overlook the fact that lobby space is frequently used for activities, whether it's the wrestling team running in the halls during inclement weather, cheerleaders practicing, or just the everyday horseplay that occurs with teenagers. Safety glass of some sort should be used in this area. Mirrors used in weight rooms and dance studios must be selected and located with care. They should be high-strength, shatter-proof glass designed for activity areas. Weight-room mirrors should be mounted about 18 inches above the floor to avoid contact with a barbell that may roll against the wall.

It is also important to select proper ceiling materials. Acoustic ceiling panels can be excellent for classrooms and offices, but can become a maintenance headache and safety hazard when used in activity areas such as gyms. Acoustic panels are not meant to withstand abuse from balls and often break or shatter when hit.

The materials selected must be chosen with care in order to withstand the abuse likely to occur in each particular area. Lighting fixtures in activity areas must be appropriate to withstand the activities that will take place. In gyms where balls or other objects may hit the lights, each fixture must be designed to withstand potential punishment. The proper light typically has a plastic cover and a wire screen for protection. If the fixture is struck hard enough to shatter the bulb, the glass will be contained by the plastic cover and prevented from falling to the floor. Fixtures without this feature may shower broken glass on the participants below.

Supervision

Designing a facility so that it can be supervised efficiently is a great advantage, for two major reasons. First, a lack of proper supervision is one of the most common allegations made in lawsuits alleging negligence in sport and physical activity programs. The design and layout of the facility are often overlooked as a primary reason for poor supervision. Some facilities are easy to supervise and some are not.

Second, a poorly designed facility may require three staff members to properly supervise activities, whereas a well-designed building of similar size and offerings may require only one. Figuring the cost of paying even one extra supervisor, using the number of hours the facility is open each year over the life of the facility, can result in a dramatic increase in cost.

A well-designed facility can be adequately supervised by a minimum number of people. Design features that enhance efficiency of supervision include activity areas that are close together and easily monitored. Instead of spreading activity areas around the perimeter of the facility, one efficient method being used is to design a long central hallway or mall off of which are placed the activity areas. With proper windows or other means of observing, a supervisor can view many different areas in a short period of time.

Another innovation that is seeing increased usage is Closed Circuit Television (CCTV) systems. A well-designed system can allow a supervisor in one location to visually monitor many diverse locations, both within and outside of the facility. Often the supervisor is equipped with a two-way radio in order to stay in constant communication with attendants on duty inside and outside the building. If a problem is observed on the CCTV monitor, the supervisor can direct an attendant to respond immediately. A properly planned system may allow for a smaller staff than is usually required, while actually increasing supervisory coverage of the facility.

Figure 7.7 Emergency safety device.

Miscellaneous Considerations

All facilities must be planned in compliance with all applicable codes. This includes all Occupational Safety and Health Administration (OSHA), Americans with Disabilities Act (ADA), fire, safety and health codes that are appropriate for a given situation (see Chapter 8).

Humidity must be controlled throughout the facility. Excessive humidity not only reduces the comfort level but can cause corrosion and deterioration of building materials. Under the right conditions, high humidity can also condense onto activity floors, steps, walkways, etc., and create a dangerous condition (see Chapter 11). Lighting levels must be sufficient for the activity. Improper lighting can cause a hazardous situation. (see Chapter 11).

Signage can be an important part of a facility risk management program. Rules, procedures, and warning signs must be developed and posted in proper locations. (see Chapter 12).

■ Summary

This chapter focused primarily on planning and designing facilities for safety and risk management. It is important to understand that this is only a first step in running a safe program. Once the facility is open, it is essential that a complete risk management program be established and practiced on an ongoing basis.

One of the most common claims made in negligence lawsuits related to sports and recreation is that of unsafe facilities. Managers of sport, physical education, and recreation programs have a legal and moral obligation to make their programs as free from foreseeable risks as possible. As part of this, managers must be aware of how unsafe facilities can increase potential hazards for participants, staff, and spectators alike. In our increasingly litigious society, unnecessary injuries are likely to lead to lawsuits and increased exposure of the program's financial resources to loss. Safe facilities are essential, and a well-planned facility is safer as well as easier to supervise, manage, and maintain.

Many of the factors that go into making a facility safe are easy to implement if they are planned from the beginning. Once the concrete has been poured and the facility is open, it often becomes much harder or impossible to make changes. Planning and designing facilities with safety and risk management in mind can help prevent problems, headaches, injuries, and lawsuits in the future.

Learning Objective 1: The student will be able to understand negligence and become familiar with the basic legal duties expected of facility managers.

Negligence can be defined as carelessly performing a duty (commission) or carelessly failing to perform a duty (omission) that results in injury to a participant or damage to property. The key word is **carelessly**. It is the responsibility of a facility manager to maintain a safe environment for the participants whether they are employees, athletes, spectators, or clients/customers. Finally, five specific duties are to keep the premises in safe repair, inspect premises regularly, remove hazards or warn of their presence, anticipate foreseeable uses and activities of the facility, and conduct operations with reasonable care.

Learning Objective 2: The student will be able to understand the role good facility planning has in the design and construction of safe facilities.

Planning for a safe facility focuses on safety for the employee, physical activity participant, and spectator. The role of planners is to design the facility with safety as well as efficiency in mind. The facility planner should review other facilities, standards, and recent litigation to determine the safest design for a facility.

Learning Objective 3: The student will be able to identify five methods of controlling access to facilities.

The five ways to control access include the use of ID cards; replacement of standard door locks and keys with a card access system; horizontal circulation control; vertical circulation control; and limited access to mechanical, storage, office, and equipment areas.

Learning Objective 4: The student will be able to describe the importance of and identify the minimal guidelines for safety or buffer zones.

Safety or buffer zones are important to protect participants, employees, and spectators. The minimal guidelines for safety or buffer zones can be found in the various rule books published by the various organizing bodies.

Learning Objective 5: The student will be able to discuss the problem of traffic patterns within facilities and identify alternatives.

One of the most fundamental safety issues in any facility are the traffic patterns for the movement of participants, employees, and spectators. The planner needs to be aware of how the facility will be used at peak use times in order to design appropriate traffic patterns. Further, the planner needs to understand the various relationships spaces have to each other. Finally, the planner needs to consider exterior traffic patterns relative to pedestrian and vehicular traffic.

Learning Objective 6: The student will be able to understand the need for selecting the proper materials for floors, walls, and ceilings.

There are always safety issues regarding proper flooring materials for various spaces. The planner needs to be aware of current standards and litigation regarding the various flooring options. There are similar concerns about the appropriateness of materials used on walls and ceilings. The single most important question that needs to be asked is, "Is the selected material compatible with the proposed activities within the space?"

■ Self-Assessment Exercises

1. Why is it important for sport, physical education, and recreation professionals to be involved in the planning and design process of new facilities?
2. Define negligence.
3. What are the five legal duties that managers of sport facilities are expected to carry out?
4. What are the two primary causes of safety problems in sport facilities?
5. Why is it important to control access to sport and recreation facilities?
6. What are horizontal and vertical circulation and how can they affect a sport manager's efficiency?
7. What are safety zones and why is it important to understand their purpose?
8. Why is it important to provide adequate space for storing equipment and supplies?
9. How can a well-planned facility help in the supervision of a sport facility?
10. How can selecting the wrong materials increase potential hazards in a sport facility?

■ References

Appenzeller, H. (1993). **Equipment and facilities: Managing sports and risk management strategies.** Durham, NC: Carolina Academic Press.

Appenzeller, H. (1998). **Risk management in sport: Issues and strategies.** Durham, NC: Carolina Academic Press.

Berg, R. (1994). Unsafe. **Athletic Business, 18**(4), 43-46.

Hart, J. (1990). Locker room liability. **Strategies, 3**(3), 33-34.

Jewell, D. (1992). **Public assembly facilities.** (2nd ed.). Malabar, FL: Krieger Publishing Co.

Maloy, B.P. (1997). Safe environment. In D.J. Cotten, & T.J. Wilde, (Eds.), **Sport law for sport managers,** (pp. 103 - 112). Dubuque, IA: Kendall/Hunt Publishing Co.

Maloy, B.P. (1993). Legal obligations related to facilities. **Journal of Physical Education, Recreation, and Dance, 64**(2), 28-30, 68.

Page, J.A. (1988). The law of premises liability. Cincinnati: Anderson Publishing Co.

Seidler, T.L. (1997). Elements of a facility risk review (Chapter 3.5.) In H. Appenzeller (Ed.), **Management in sport: Issues and strategies.** Durham, NC: Carolina Academic Press.

Seidler, T.L. (1994). Omissions: Possible. **Athletic Business 18**(8), 59-60.

van der Smissen, B. (1990). **Liability and risk management for public and private enterprises.** Cincinnati: Anderson Publishing. Co.

■ Suggested Readings

Appenzeller, H. (1998). **Risk management in sport: Issues and strategies.** Durham NC: Carolina Academic Press.

Appenzeller, H., & Baron, J.D. **From the gym to the jury. Risk management newsletter.** Contact Herb Appenzeller, (336) 643-0701.

Berg, R. (1994). Unsafe. **Athletic Business 15**(4), 43-47.

Jewell, D. (1992). **Public assembly facilities.** (2nd ed.) Malabar, FL: Krieger Publishing Co.

Maloy, B.P .(1997). Safe environment. In D.J Cotten, & T.J. Wilde (Eds.), **Sport law for sport managers** (pp. 103 - 112). Dubuque, IA: Kendall/Hunt Publishing Co.

Maloy, B.P. (1993). Legal obligations related to facilities. **Journal of Physical Education, Recreation, and Dance, 64**(2), 28-30, 68.

Seidler, T.L. (1997). Elements of a facility risk review, (Chapter 3.5). In H. Appenzeller, (Ed.), **Management in sport: Issues and strategies.** Durham, NC: Carolina Academic Press.

Seidler, T.L. (1994). Omissions: Possible. **Athletic Business, 18**(8), 59-60.

Tharrett, S.J., & Peterson, J.A. (1997). **ACSM's health/fitness facility standards and guidelines.** (2nd ed.) Champaign, IL: Human Kinetics.

Notes

CHAPTER 8

Designing for Inclusion:
The Americans with Disabilities Act (ADA)
and Architectural Barriers Act (ABA)

Richard J. LaRue, University of New England

Learning Objectives

After reading this chapter, the student will be able to

■ understand the historical development of constitutional protection and civil rights of the disabled, including ADAAG of 1991, ADA of 1990, UFAS of 1984, ABA of 1968, and Section 504 of the Rehabilitation Act of 1973,

■ understand the concepts of designing for inclusion, architectural barriers, undue hardship, readily achievable, and reasonable accommodation,

■ understand the advantages and requirements of compliance, including incentives and enforcement. Further, the student will appreciate the implementation of the act, for all individuals,

■ understand the difference between standards and guidelines related to the ADA and other federal accessibility legislation, and

■ recognize the administrative responsibilities related to enforcement and the potential risk of failure to comply.

Introduction

The federal government and civil rights legislation related to persons with disabilities includes the following:

1. The Architectural Barriers Act (ABA) of 1968 was first developed as a minimum guideline for the United States Architectural and Transportation Barriers Compliance Board (Access Board), to be used as a baseline by other agencies responsible for issuing enforceable standards. The ABA, as amended, mandated that buildings or other facilities financed with certain federal funds must be accessible to persons with disabilities.

2. Section 504 of the Rehabilitation Act of 1973, as amended, set out the functions of the Access Board and further "specified that no otherwise qualified handicapped person shall, on the basis of handicap, be excluded from participation in, be denied the benefits of, or otherwise be subjected to discrimination under any program which receives or benefits from federal financial assistance" (Lumpkin, 1998, p. 229).

3. The Education Amendment Act of 1974 "mandated that all children must be placed in the least

restrictive environment (LRE), or the setting in which their optimal learning and development could occur" (Lumpkin, 1998, p.229).

4. All Handicapped Children Act of 1975 (Public Law 94-142) "mandated that athletics be provided to disabled school students" (Lumpkin, 1998, p. 300).

5. The Amateur Sports Act of 1978 "specified that the competitive needs of disabled athletes must be accommodated" (Lumpkin, 1998).

6. The Uniform Federal Accessibility Standard (UFAS) of 1984 is the standard currently used to enforce the ABA.

7. The Americans With Disabilities Act (ADA) of 1990 significantly expanded the role of the Access Board. Under the ADA, the Access Board has been responsible for developing accessibility guidelines for entities covered by the act and for providing technical assistance to individuals and organizations on the removal of architectural, transportation, and communication barriers.

8. The ADA Accessibility Guidelines (ADAAG) of 1991 are considered more stringent than the UFAS guidelines (both the ADAAG and the UFAS are under concurrent revision by the Access Board).

9. The Telecommunications Act of 1996 which requires the Access Board to develop and maintain accessibility guidelines for telecommunications and customer premises equipment (e.g., mandated closed-captioning options on the newest models of televisions).

The Americans With Disabilities Act

The Americans With Disabilities Act was signed into law on July 26, 1990, by then-President George Bush. The act provides for comprehensive civil rights protection to individuals with disabilities in the areas of employment, public accommodations, state and local government services, and telecommunications. Specifically, there are five titles that define the act. Of particular importance, when designing sport or recreational facilities, title III prohibits discrimination on the basis of disability by private entities in places of public accommodations and requires places of public accommodation and commercial facilities to be designed, constructed, and altered in compliance with the accessibility standards published in the law. The ADA extends prohibited discrimination beyond state and local governments that were previously prohibited from discriminating under Section 504 of the Rehabilitation Act of 1973. This coverage now includes all services provided by state and local governments, regardless of whether they receive federal money.

It is worth noting that the ADA uses the terms disabilities rather than the term handicaps, as used in the Rehabilitation Act of 1973 although for purposes of meaning, they are considered equivalent.

The Five Titles of the ADA

The following are the five titles for the American's with Disabilities Act (ADA):

1. *Title I.* Title I of the act prohibits discrimination against qualified individuals with disabilities in such areas as job application procedures, hiring, discharge, promotion, job training, and other conditions of employment. Employers must make "reasonable" accommodations for an individual's disabilities unless to do so would cause hardship for the employer. Employers must also post notices that explain the act (Miller, 1992). The Equal Employment Opportunity Commission (EEOC) is responsible for enforcement of title I of the ADA. The EEOC is further responsible for issuing interpretative guidance concurrently with Title I.

2. *Title II.* Title II prohibits exclusion of disabled persons from benefits, services, or activities offered by the government. It requires that public transportation be accessible (Miller, 1992).

3. *Title III.* Title III guarantees persons with disabilities access to privately operated places of business. The title may require changes of policies and practices to accommodate persons with disabilities by removing architectural barriers making all areas accessible (Miller, 1992).

4. *Title IV.* Title IV requires telephone companies to provide interstate and intrastate telecommunications relay service so that hearing-impaired and speech-impaired individuals can communicate with others (Miller, 1992).

5. *Title V.* Title V refers to the administration and handling of complaints under ADA. They include awarding reasonable attorney's fees in any proceeding under the ADA; prohibiting retaliation against or coercion of any person who makes a charge; allowing insurers to continue to rely on actuarial procedures in underwriting risks; authorizing state governments to be sued under the ADA; providing that state laws offering greater or equal protection cannot be preempted; and amending the Rehabilitation Act to conform its coverage of drug users to the provisions of ADA (Miller, 1992).

The Application of Title III of the ADA: Public Accommodation, Designing for Inclusion, Architectural Barriers, Undue Hardship, Readily Achievable, and Reasonable Accommodation

A place of *public accommodation* is defined as a facility, operated by a private entity, whose operations affect commerce and fall within at least one of the following 12 categories:

1. Places of lodging
2. Establishments serving food or drink
3. Places of exhibition or entertainment (stadium)
4. Places of pubic gathering (auditorium)
5. Sales or rental establishments
6. Service establishments
7. Stations used for specified public transportation
8. Places of public display or collection
9. Places of recreation (park)
10. Places of education
11. Social service center establishments
12. Places of exercise or recreation (gymnasium, health spa, bowling alley, golf course, or other place of exercise or recreation).

Public accommodation further refers to the private entity that owns, leases or leases to, or operates a place of public accommodation. Thus the ADA is directed not to the physical location, but to the individual or group that owns or otherwise operates the physical location (Cocco and Zimmerman, 1996).

A public accommodation must remove architectural barriers in existing facilities, where such removal is readily achievable. Examples of steps to remove barriers include

1. installing ramps,
2. making curb cuts in sidewalks and entrances,
3. repositioning telephones,
4. adding raised markings on elevator control buttons,
5. installing flashing alarm lights,
6. widening doors,
7. eliminating a turnstile or providing an alternative accessible path,
8. installing accessible door hardware,
9. installing grab bars in toilet stalls,
10. rearranging toilet partitions to increase maneuvering space,
11. repositioning the paper towel dispenser in a bathroom,
12. installing an accessible paper cup dispenser at existing inaccessible water fountain, and
13. removing high-pile, low-density carpeting.

Priorities for barrier removal. A public accommodation is urged to take measures to comply with barrier removal in accordance with the following order of priorities:

1. Provide access to a place of public accommodation from public sidewalks, parking, or public transportation. Include installing entrance ramp, widening entrances and providing accessible parking spaces.
2. Provide access to those places of public accommodation where goods and services are made available to the public.
3. Provide access to rest room facilities.
4. Take any other measures necessary to provide access to the goods, services, privileges, advantages, or accommodations of a place of public accommodation.

Where a public accommodation can demonstrate that barrier removal is not readily achievable, the public accommodation must not fail to make goods, services, facilities, privileges, advantages, or accommodations available through alternative methods, if those methods are readily achievable (ADA, 1990).

Designing for inclusion is a concept that supports full facility-full program access to all people. Two important aspects of this concept must be fully explored by both facility planners and program designers:

1. In real terms, the imminent first revision of the ADAAG regulations will likely mandate that "every inch of every facility [must] be accessible" (Cohen, 1997, p. 39). This is a major change from earlier requirements that allowed different standards for existing facilities versus new construction.
2. The ADA accessibility requirements apply not only to facilities but also to participation in certain sports programs. For instance, disabled individuals can only be excluded from intramural or team activities if their participation would result in the likelihood of danger to others (Munson and Comodeca, 1993).

A.

B.

C.

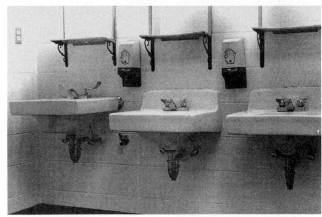

D.

Figure 8.1 A. Removing architectural barrier in shower. **B.** Removing architectural barrier for drinking fountain. **C.** Removing architectural barrier for toilets. **D.** Removing architectural barrier for sinks.

Undue hardship is defined as requiring significant difficulty or expense, considering the employer's size, financial resources, and the nature and structure of the operation (Miller, 1990).

Readily achievable means easily accomplishable and able to be carried out without much difficulty or expense. It constitutes a lower standard than *undue burden* (Cocco and Zimmerman, 1996). In determining whether an action is readily achievable the following factors are to be considered:

1. the nature and cost of the action needed under the act;
2. the overall financial resources of the facility or facilities involved in the action, the number of persons employed at such facility, the effect on expenses and resources, or the impact otherwise of such action upon the operation of the facility;

3. the overall financial resources of the covered entity; the overall size of the business or the covered entity with respect to the number of its employees; the number, type, and location of its facilities; and
4. the type of operation or operations of the covered entity, including the composition, structure, and functions of the work force of such entity; the geographic separateness, administrative or fiscal relationship of the facility or facilities in question to the covered entity (ADA, 1990).

To the extent that it is readily achievable, a public accommodation in assembly areas must provide a reasonable number of wheelchair seating spaces and seats with removable aisle-side arm rests. Further, this wheelchair seating must be dispersed throughout the assembly area seating, provide lines of sight and choice of admission at prices comparable to those for members of the general public, adjoin an accessible route that also serves as a means of egress in case of emergency, and permit individuals who use wheelchairs to sit with family members or other companions (who are not using wheelchairs). If removal of seats is not readily achievable, a public accommodation must provide, to the extent that it is readily achievable a portable chair or other means to permit a family member or other companion to sit with an individual who uses a wheelchair (ADA:36.308 Subpart C, 1990).

Reasonable accommodations under the ADA requires that employers and facilities make an accommodation if doing so will not impose an undue hardship on the operation of the business or facility (Miller, 1992). In general, this is also an alteration made by the employer or potential employer that puts individuals with disabilities on equal footing with individuals without disabilities (ADA:29CFR, 1990). Reasonable accommodations include, but are not limited to "making facilities readily accessible and usable to disabled persons; job restructuring, modifying work schedules and/or reassignment to a vacant position; acquiring or modifying equipment or devices; modifying or adjusting testing processes, training materials, and/or policies; providing qualified readers or interpreters" (Miller, 1992, p. 18).

Compliance

"Although the office of the ADA will determine what constitutes adequate compliance on a case-by-case basis, Title III is a reasonable and flexible law. In helping to bring about compliance, ADA office staffers would rather work with the business community than against it" (Miller, 1992, p. 18).

Methods for compliance (Miller, 1992, p.18) include the following:

■ Install ramps.
■ Make ramps in sidewalks and entrances.
■ Create designated, accessible parking spaces.
■ Rearrange tables, chairs, vending machines, display racks and other furniture.
■ Add raised markers to elevator control buttons.
■ Install flashing alarm lights.
■ Install accessible door hardware.

■ Install grab bars in toilet stalls.
■ Rearrange toilet partitions to increase maneuvering space.
■ Reposition paper towel dispensers in bathrooms.

With regard to reasonable accommodations and compliance, facilities that are used for both academic and leisure activities will likely be required to provide technology in class or laboratory spaces. Such technology would specifically enhance the academic accommodation of disabled students. *Eligible individuals* are defined as those who have a physical or mental impairment that substantially limits a major life activity. To qualify, individuals with a disability or learning-style challenge needing an accommodation may be required to self-disclose and offer proof of disability to receive some kinds of accommodations. Facilities that are used academically and for sport/recreation should consider permanent installation of computer (online) links, cable (for closed-captioning), multimedia carts (powerpoint, slides, etc.), as well as less technologically advanced services, i.e. signers, note takers, etc.

Short- and long-range planning are an integral part of an organization's stated intention to comply with federal accessibility regulations. If an organization claims "undue hardship" to avoid financial strife, it may be only a short-term "fix." It is important to note that the ADA is not passive legislation. As an organization strives to meet existing standards, it is possible that what was considered acceptable in 1998 may not meet future ADAAG specifications. Therefore, if an organization is already out of compliance because of an inability to fund a significant accommodation or barrier removal, etc., they may become hopelessly out of compliance when the latest ADAAG standards are set forth. It is imperative that organizations plan ahead, take advantage of federal tax incentives, and strive to meet or exceed the demands of future accessibility legislation.

Discrimination

Title III specifically prohibits discrimination on the basis of disability by private entities in places of public accommodation and requires places of public accommodation and commercial facilities to be designed, constructed, and altered in compliance with the accessibility standards published in the law.

Discrimination under title III includes:

■ failure to remove architectural barriers in existing facilities where such removal is readily achievable, and

■ where an entity can demonstrate that the removal of a barrier is not readily achievable, a failure to make goods, services, privileges, advantages or accommodations available through alternative methods if such methods are readily achievable.

■ Discrimination in new construction includes a failure to design and construct facilities for first occupancy after January 26, 1993, that are readily accessible to and usable by individuals with disabilities (ADA, 1990).

Exemption

Exemption to the act: Private clubs have limited coverage in the act. In determining whether a private entity qualifies as a private club, courts have considered such factors as the degree of member control of club operations, the selectivity of the membership selection process, whether substantial membership fees are charged, whether the entity is operated on a nonprofit basis, the extent to which the facilities are open to the public, the degree of public funding, and whether the club was created specifically to avoid compliance with the Civil Rights Act.

Accessibility Consultants

Private accessibility consultants or consulting firms are available to provide a wide range of services related to all aspects of federal legislation and compliance. Included below are just a few of both for-profit and not-for-profit individuals/organizations:

1. Access by Design—Accessibility Consulting Services
   (970)229-0672
   http://www.access-by-design.com

Access by Design is a business providing a full range of ADA accessibility compliance consulting services to public entities and the private sector.

2. Barrier Free Environments, Inc.
   P.O. Box 30634
   Highway 70, West-Watergarden
   Raleigh, NC 27622
   voice/TDD: (919)782-7823

Barrier Free Environments, Inc., provides consultation and technical stages of construction planning or product development.

3. The Center for Universal Design
   School of Design
   NC State University
   Raleigh, NC 27695-8613
   TDD: (919)515-3082
   http://www.design.ncsu.edu/cud

The Center for Universal Design environments for people of all ages and abilities is a national research, information, and technical assistance center that evaluates, develops, and promotes accessible and universal design in buildings and related products.

4. National Center on Accessibility (NCA)
   5020 State Road, 67 North
   Martinsville, IN 46151
   1-800-424-1877 or (317)349-9240
   FAX: (317)342-6658
   http://www.indiana.edu:80/~bradwood/nca-home.html

The National Center on Accessibility (NCA) a program of Indiana University Department of Recreation and Park Administration in cooperation with The National Park Service Office on Accessibility is "committed to the full participation in parks, recreation and tourism by people with disabilities." Among other areas of service, the center provides technical assistance to organizations that are designing and retrofitting their leisure areas and programs for accessibility.

5. Paradigm Design Group (PDG)
   801 Eighteenth Street, NW
   Washington, DC 20006
   (202)416-7645
   TDD: (800)795-4327
   FAX: (202)416-7647

Paradigm Design Group (Consultants for Accessible Architecture) offers consulting services tailored to architects, engineers, developers, property owners, building managers, private corporations, government agencies, and others who need specialized assistance.

■ Summary

The Americans With Disabilities Act is federal legislation that has been law since July 1992. The small business owner and the large city have all had ample time to minimally meet compliance through planning. More than this, employers and pubic accommodations should be following law because failure to comply is clearly discrimination. For the cost of a postage stamp an administrative complaint filed against an organization or community may cost thousands of dollars. And the act itself is more than beneficial to all people. If unsure of where to start, consult your state's attorney general's office on disability and ask for help. Countless organizations are committed to assisting willing public and private entities with implementation strategies. The burden is clearly ours to make this act more than just a few words on paper. The concept of accessibility is a concept that understands life's realities: we are all temporarily able-bodied.

Learning Objective 1: The student will be able to understand the historical development of constitutional protection and civil rights of the disabled, including ADAAG of 1991, ADA of 1990, UFAS of 1984, ABA of 1968, and Section 504 of the Rehabilitation Act of 1973.

Since 1968, the federal government has addressed the needs of persons with disabilities by enacting civil rights legislation that protect these individual's rights. Most significant, in recent years, was the Americans with Disabilities Act of 1990. This act and subsequent guidelines for accessibility (ADAAG) are powerful tools in support of designing for inclusion. A recent commitment by the Access Board to revise both the UFAS and the ADAAG guidelines concurrently has raised some concern with regard to the ability of some organizations to meet future accessibility standards. Only time and judicial precedence will likely establish the accessibility criteria of the future.

Learning Objective 2: The student will be able to understand the concepts of designing for inclusion, architectural barriers, undue hardship, readily achievable, and reasonable accommodation.

The ultimate goal of accessibility legislation is to establish equal opportunity for all people in the United States. The concept of designing for inclusion dates back at to the Architectural Barriers Act of 1968, when the federal government required all federally funded facilities and programs to meet minimal accessibility guidelines. The United States Architectural and Transportation Barriers Compliance Board (Access Board) has used the ABA and subsequent guidelines, i.e. the Uniform Federal Accessibility Standard (UFAS) of 1984 and ADAAG of 1991, to assist other federal agencies with establishing enforceable accessibility standards.

Learning Objective 3: The student will be able to understand the advantages and requirements of compliance, including incentives and enforcement. Further, the student will appreciate the implementation of the act for all individuals.

The various federal regulations about accessibility have consistently involved both incentives and enforcement characteristics. Most of the incentives have taken the form of tax credits. However, failure to comply with federal legislation can lead to costly penalties, both financially and in terms of public relations. Nonetheless, each organization must weigh its respective resources and limitations carefully to determine an appropriate plan of action. Potentially worse than failure to comply (a legal issue) is the act of discrimination (an ethical issue).

The implementation of accessibility legislation can serve to enhance the opportunities of disabled participants and further enhance the quality of all people. As humans, we are faced with the everyday possibility that our abilities can be reduced through accident or injury. In other words, we are all "temporally able-bodied." Designing spaces for inclusion will better prepare our facilities for a broader range of people and abilities.

Learning Objective 4: The student will be able to understand the difference between standards and guidelines related to the ADA and other federal accessibility legislation.

Most of the initial legislative acts, i.e. ABA and ADA, established guidelines that have served as a baseline for other federal agencies to establish enforceable standards.

Learning Objective 5: The student will be able to recognize the administrative responsibilities related to enforcement and the potential risk for failure to comply.

Compliance is an administrative responsibility, no less than fiscal management and personnel supervision. It is the responsibility of the manager or organizational leader to understand the law, legal enforcement, the judicial process, legal precedent, enforceable standards, and satisfactory compliance. Failure to comply is at least failure to perform responsibly. Failure to comply with the federal legislation regarding accessibility could result in loss of federal funding, significant financial penalties, and decay of the public trust.

■ Case Study

A. The Architectural Barrier

Debbie, a 13-year-old girl, had been in a wheelchair a little over three years when she first considered attending a resident sports camp for target sports. Injured in a bicycle accident, Debbie has a "low-level" spinal cord injury. However, she is physically active in school, and very bright. She wants to develop her competitive skills as both an archer and shooter. School and home have been easy environments to get around; how about at the camp?

Debbie's mother was the one that first suggested that Debbie attend the sports camp. The challenge was to determine if the sports camp she wanted to attend was accessible to someone in a wheelchair.

Consider that you are the director of this sports camp. What kinds of architectural barriers may exist, and how might you modify or make reasonable accommodations for Debbie? Are you prepared to make all the necessary accommodations so that Debbie can attend your camp? What are some of the significant costs that might affect full ADAAG compliance? If you are unable to afford some of the more important accommodations (undue hardship), how will you defend you decision to deny participation to Debbie?

B. The Communication Barrier

Jim has been hearing impaired from birth. Now, almost nine years old, Jim can sign, read lips, and verbalize quite well. However, he has no hearing at all and must completely rely upon visual or physical communication. Jim has registered for your swimming program and is looking forward to his first class in your facility.

When Jim arrives to your facility, will you be able to accommodate him? What kind of challenges will he face? What kinds of facility changes should you consider to ensure Jim the same quality of experience as other children enrolled in the program? Are there safety issues that must be addressed with regard to the pool environment? What legal obligation does your facility have to provide Jim with accommodating services for the hearing impaired? How do you intend to address Jim's challenges and your concerns?

C. The Employment Barrier

Darryl is a 45-year-old "low-level" quadriplegic who has applied to work at your facility's front desk. He has a bachelor's degree in psychology and a good record of prior employment. Darryl recently contacted you to get a copy of the job description for a front-desk employee. He has set up a meeting to discuss the position de-

scription requirements and reasonable accommodations that would allow him to perform the front-desk duties as prescribed. Though minor architectural barriers exist, the cost of reasonable accommodation would not be prohibitive. However, the fiscal budget has no reserves available in the capital budget that would fund any architectural changes to the facility. And without these modifications, Darryl cannot perform the duties of a front-desk employee.

1. What obligation does your facility have to remove the architectural barriers?
2. If funds do not currently exist in the budget, can you delay architectural changes until they are available?
3. What are Darryl's rights to employment, etc.?
4. What incentives exist that support the financial costs of barrier removal?
5. What incentives exist that support the legal need to act on barrier removal?
6. Develop a presentation for the facility's decision-makers detailing your recommended response to this case.

■ References

Section 504 of the Americans with Disabilities Act of 1990:42 U.S.C. 12204. Washington, DC: United States of America. Otherwise footnoted as ADA, 1990.

Americans with Disabilities Act Handbook (1992). Equal Employment Opportunity Commission and the United States Department of Justice.

The Americans with Disabilities Act: Your Personal Guide to the Law (1992). Washington, DC: Paralyzed Veterans of America.

Cocco, A. F. & Zimmerman, J. C. (1996). Guide to conducting a compliance review of the Americans with Disabilities Act. The CPA Journal, March.

Lumpkin, A. (1998). Physical education and sport: A contemporary introduction (4th ed.). Boston, MA: WCB/McGraw-Hill.

Miller, C. A. (1992). Equal access under the law: Removing barriers opens opportunities for the disabled. Recreation Resources, October.

■ Suggested Readings

The Americans with Disabilities Act Title III Technical Assistance Manual (1993). United States Department of Justice, Civil Rights Division, Public Access Section.

JFK health & fitness center, Edison, New Jersey (1994, January). Fitness Management, 32.

Cohen, A. (1997). Access baggage. Athletic Business, 21(11), 37-42.

Batchelder, J. (1997). Creating an ADA facility master plan. Facility Management Journal, March/April.

Bedini, L. A. (1995). Campers with disabilities: Encouraging positive interaction. **Camping Magazine,** March-April, 21-21.

Franke, A. H. (1994). The academic accommodation of disabled students. **Academe,** September-October, 96.

Green, F. P., & De Coux, V. (1996). Inclusion of students with disabilities in campus recreational sports programs. **NIRSA Journal,** Winter, 34-37.

Handley, A. (1991). The new club: The Americans with Disabilities Act: What your club needs to know. **Club Industry,** December, 49-56.

Herbert, D. L. (1992). **The Americans with Disabilities Act: A guide for health clubs and exercise facilities.** Canton, OH: Professional Report.

Kearney, D. (1995). Reasonable compliance. **Occupational Safety & Health,** 64(2), 62.

Leibrock, C. (1994). Dignified options to ADA compliance. **Facilities Design & Management,** 13(6), 56.

Lyberger, M. R., and Pastore, D. L. (1998). Health club facility operators' perceived level of compliance with the Americans with Disabilities Act. **Journal of Sport Management,** 12, 139-145.

Mamis, R. A. (1994). ADA checklist. **Inc.,** 16(9), 132.

McGovern, J. (1992). **The ADA self-evaluation: A handbook for compliance with the ADA by parks and recreational agencies.** National Recreation and Parks Association.

Morrissey, P. (1993). **The educator's guide to the ADA.** Alexandria, VA: American Vocational Association.

Munson, A. L., & Comodeca, J. A. (1993). The act of inclusion. **Athletic Management,** July, 14.

Rabin, J. (1993). Wheels in motion. **Athletic Management,** July, 4.

Schmid, S. (1996). Accessible play: Parks designed for disabled users are a hit in two cities. **Athletic Business,** August, 20.

Story, M. F., Mueller, J. L., & Mace, R. L. (1998). **The universal design file: Designing for people of all ages and abilities.** Raleigh, NC: The Center for Universal Design.

Tarr, S. (1992). Adapting equipment for special needs. **Strategies,** 24-27.

United States of America v. Ellerbe Becket, Inc., United States District Court District of Minnesota Fourth Division, Civil Action No. 4-96-995. [On-line], Available: http://www.usdojogov/crt/ada/ellerbe.htm (September 30, 1998).

Wong, G. M. & Goering, J. R. (1997). Sports law report: Sitting targets—two prominent ADA cases lead to changes to a new arena. **Athletic Business,** 21(9), 20.

Zibula, P., & Navarn, F. (1991). **The disabled employee: The four-way win. Athletic Bussiness,** 20. Access by Design-Accessibility Consulting Services, 970/229 0672. [On-line]. Available: http://www.access-by-design.com

Access Currents: Current news from the U.S. Access Board, United States Architectural and Transportation Barriers Compliance Board, 1331 F Street, NW, Suite 1000, Washington, DC 20004-1111 1-800-872-2253 TTD: 1-800-993-2822. [On-line]. Available: http://www.access-board.gov

ADAAG Accessibility Guidelines for Buildings and Facilities: [On-line]. Available: http://www.access-board.gov/bfdg/adaag.htm

Adaptive Environments Center, Inc. and Barrier Free Environments, Inc., Checklist for Existing Facilities version 2.1, (The Americans with Disabilities Act: Checklist for Readily Achievable Barrier Removal). [On-line]. Available: http://www.usdoj.gov/crt/ada/checkweb.htm

Barrier Free Environments, Inc., P.O. Box 30634, Highway 70 West-Watergarden, Raleigh, NC 2762. voice/TDD: (919)782-7823.

The Center for Universal Design: Environments for people of all ages and abilities. School of Design, NC State University, Box 8613, Raleigh, NC 27695-8613. voice/TDD: (919)515-3082. [On-line]. Available:http://www.design.ncsu.edu/cud

Equal Employment Opportunity Commission (EEOC). [On-line], Available: http://www.eeoc.gov/laws/ada.htm

Federal Communications Commission (FCC) offers technical assistance on ADA telephone relay service requirements. FCC also has jurisdiction over compliance with Section 255 of the Telecommunication Act [On-line]. Available: http://www.fcc.gov/dtf/dtfhome.html

Job Accommodation Network (JAN on the web) includes a points of interest page that is a thorough listing of resources related to employment, disability, government web sites, web tools and other web sites related to job accommodation. [On-line], Available: http://www.jan.wvu.edu

National Center on Accessibility, A program of Indiana University Department of Recreation and Park Administration in cooperation with The National Park Service Office on Accessibility. 5020 State Road 67 North, Martinsville, IN 46151 (317)3499240 1-800-424-1877 FAX: (317)342-6658. [On-line]. Available: http://www.indiana.edu:90/~bradwood/ncahome.html

Paradigm Design Group: Consultants for Accessible Architecture, 801 Eighteenth Street, NW, Washington, DC 20006 (202)416-7645 TDD: 1-800-795-4327

US Department of Justice, Americans with Disabilities Act, ADA Home Page [On-line]. Available: http://uskoj.gov/crt/ada/adahom1.htm

Notes

CHAPTER 9

Indoor Surfaces — Ceilings, Walls, and Floors

Hal Walker, Barry University

Learning Objectives

After reading this chapter, the student will be able to

■ demonstrate knowledge of the primary surface design areas of a facility,

■ demonstrate knowledge of the types of materials available for these surfaces and their characteristics,

■ identify various advantages and disadvantages of surface materials that should be taken into consideration for flooring, wall, and ceiling materials,

■ explain recommended maintenance and upkeep practices for various surface materials,

■ demonstrate an understanding of an appropriate selection process for facility flooring options, and

■ understand the role of a facility manager in the selection of appropriate surface materials for sport facilities.

Introduction

Indoor surface material choices are central to the overall success of any facility. The cost, type, installation, and maintenance of these materials are directly linked to facility usage, appearance, longevity, and overall facility "success." Three main areas of indoor surfacing are floors, walls, and ceilings. This chapter will provide information on the types of materials available for these surfaces, along with some advantages and disadvantages based on use in specific areas. The importance of selecting the correct surface material, based on need, budget, and aesthetics, will be the focus.

Facility surface choices are generally divided into three distinct areas: service/ancillary areas, the main floor, and office/administrative areas. The correct selection of indoor surfacing materials, along with the proper installation and maintenance over the facility life-span, can have a profound impact on a facility. These surface choices can determine optimal facility use features as well as the incidence of sport injuries. Surface options are extensive, with many companies offering countless choices in innumerable textures, materials, colors, and performance characteristics. Yet of the hundreds of products on the market, no one surface is ideal for all activities a facility plans to offer. There is plenty of room for error in making the correct surface decisions. As a result, optimal surface choices must be made with extensive deliberation and clear communication among facility planning members. Available budget, planned activity offerings, longevity, maintenance costs, and climate are but a few of the factors that must be considered in making the correct surface choices.

Selection of Indoor Surface Materials

Indoor surface materials must be carefully chose for the nature of the facility and the activities that are planned. As mentioned above, the primary surfaces are floors, walls, and ceilings. The following text will outline the types of materials available for these surfaces, their characteristics, and some advantages and disadvantages of each.

Generally speaking, the planned activity in a given area should dictate the type of flooring surface. Many, if not most surfaces, however, are used for more than one purpose. Three distinct areas must be considered in facilities currently being built. The first is service/ancillary areas such as locker rooms, shower rooms, bathrooms, etc. These areas require surfaces that take into account heavy moisture content. The second area is the main arena or activity focus of the facility. Typically these require either a hardwood floor or a resilient synthetic material. Offices, administrative areas, and classrooms account for the third facility location (Flynn, 1993). Special areas require different materials, layouts, and treatments. For example, basketball courts should be made out of a non-slip material, whereas a dance area should have a finished treatment that allows individuals to slide across the floor (Flynn, 1993).

Durability, flexibility, and cost are three considerations that have allowed synthetic floors to challenge traditional hardwood flooring. Synthetic surfaces may take the form of grass or non-grass surfaces. The two most popular synthetic surfacing materials are polyvinyl chlorides (PVCs) and polyurethane. Polyurethane is either poured in place or produced in prefabricated sheets that are adhered on the site, while PVCs are typically prefabricated. The general perception is that polyurethane possesses most of the desirable characteristics sought in a multipurpose facility surface (Flynn, 1993).

It is essential to understand that there are countless types of wooden floors, and the costs can vary dramatically. Costs also vary extensively among other surface alternatives, such as synthetics and carpets. Costs often depend on the materials used, the thickness of the surface selected, and the condition of the existing surface. Thicker synthetic surfaces, for example, although they may absorb more shock and offer greater resilience, are generally more expensive (Flynn, 1993).

In the past, the third area — administrative offices and classrooms — have been satisfactorily covered with some type of tile such as vinyl, vinyl asbestos, asphalt, rubber, or linoleum. Many believe consideration should now be given to using carpet in some of these spaces. Hard maple floors are the most expensive to install initially; however, over a long period of time these flooring options become more than competitive when compared with most synthetic surfaces. The cheapest flooring surface option is generally viewed as indoor-outdoor carpeting (Flynn, 1993).

Floors

Sport flooring surfaces, according to Viklund (1995), are categorized as *point-elastic* or *area-elastic*. Point-elastic surfaces maintain impact effects at the immediate point of contact on the floor, with the ball, object, or individual. Area-elastic surfaces allow for dispersion of impact, where a bouncing object or jumping individual is felt approximately 20 inches around the point of impact.

Viklund (1995) also states that resilience is another factor to consider when analyzing performance characteristics of various flooring options. Resilience is the shock absorption ability of a floor based on the amount of force applied to the surface area. For comparison, concrete is a base value, with no resiliency (0 %). Point-elastic surfaces (synthetics) have a low absorption level (10% to 50%), with most in the 25% to 35% range. Resilience is influenced by both the thickness and the hardness of the floor material and the sub-flooring under the surface (Viklund, 1995).

Area-elastic floors also need to be evaluated based on activities planned for the space. Area of deflection must be considered with regard to the primary use of the facility surface. Area deflection is the amount of impact that is felt in the vicinity of the points of contact. With area-elastic flooring, it must be decided that the area of deflection will not adversely impact the activities of other individuals concurrently on the surface. According to Viklund (1995), area of deflection is not a major concern for recreational use; however, it could be a major consideration for competitive or varsity play.

Another important consideration for most organizations in making flooring choices is a concept known as the "rolling load." Rolling load is the capacity of a

Type of Flooring	Life Expectancy	Initial Cost
Vinyl Tile	15 years	$15,000
Synthetic Surface	20 years	$40,000
Wood Flooring	50 years	$65,000

Initial Cost/ Life Expectancy	Maintenance Cost Annually	Total Cost Annually
$1,000/yr (vinyl)	$1,210	$2,210
$2,000/yr (synthetic)	$200	$2,200
$1,300/yr (wood)	$2,666	$3,966

floor to withstand damage from external forces such as bleacher movement, equipment transport, or similar activities (Viklund, 1995). Any surface utilized for multiple purposes must be able to withstand the movement of equipment or materials over the surface area during transition from one activity to another.

A variety of floor surfaces can be used successfully on a main gym floor. This surface choice is typically dictated by the planned activities for this area. Options are generally broken down into three surfaces: hardwood, vinyl, and synthetics. Each surface option has strengths and weaknesses. Many existing athletic facilities have chosen either a hardwood or a standard vinyl tile. According to Bishop (1997), wood flooring with proper maintenance can last 50 years, compared with 20 years for a synthetic surface and 15 years for a vinyl tile. The following chart illustrates initial cost, life expectancy and annual maintenance cost for vinyl tile, synthetic surface, and wood flooring for a 5,000 square foot gymnasium (Bishop, 1997).

Vinyl tile floors have a life expectancy of approximately 10 to 15 years, but begin to show their wear after the first few years. Vinyl floors are also very hard and have poor absorption qualities. This can also lead to athletic injuries if high humidity levels are prevalent, or if water spills are not managed properly. Unlike other sport surfaces, which require only washing and damp mopping, a vinyl tile floor must be stripped, sealed, and waxed at least three times annually. Synthetic floors also require regular cleaning, but may require line repainting or a touch-up every five years (Bishop, 1997). Hardwood floors are generally designed with an intricate sub-flooring to provide shock absorption and can be expected to last the life of the school. Wooden floors must always be kept clean to provide proper traction. They must also have

the lines repainted or touched up and be sanded down every three years. Synthetic floors do not allow for as much sliding as hardwood floors. As a result, if the activities on the floor involve sliding actions, a wood floor is the better choice. Wood floors can also be designed in a number of ways including sub-floor systems, channel systems, cushioned systems, and spring systems (Flynn, 1993).

Current research demonstrates that the type of sub-flooring used is a more important factor than the top layer of the floor. Three types of sub-floor constructions are recommended. The first is a suspension floor, which is made out of plywood, foam rubber, or some other type of synthetic material, and is available in a variety of patterns. The finished floor rests on top of the sub-floor material. The second type of sub-floor construction is a spring floor. This involves coiled metal springs, covered by a plywood sub-floor, with the finished floor resting on the plywood. The third type is referred to as a padded floor. Padded materials such as foam or other synthetics are laid over concrete or plywood and then covered with the finished floor (Stoll & Beller, 1989). Naturally, the more materials needed to install the floor, the higher the cost. Even though cost is a primary concern, safety should be also be considered throughout the decision-making process.

Synthetic floors are softer than wood floors and better acoustically. Wood floors, depending on their suspension systems, can also have "dead spots." Dead spots are areas on the floor that can cause objects impacting the floor surface to perform inconsistently. For example, a change in the characteristics of the floor would cause a basketball to have a variable bounce. Synthetic floors are evenly laid and are less likely to have "dead spots," although inconsistent ball performance can still occur. Quality installation will maximize optimal surface performance with any surface choice. Upkeep of all gym floors calls for constant maintenance. Rubberized synthetic floors, however, have a higher maintenance cost than wooden floors.

Many different floor coverings related to sport and recreational activities are offered in today's market. Some examples include ceramic tile, cushioned wood flooring, and rubber compound flooring. The selection criteria for certain flooring materials should include

■ Economic feasibility in its initial and life-cost cycles. Floor covering choices entail much more than the initial up-front cost. Many now realize that the initial cost for materials and installation is only a small component of the total investment needed. Life-cycle cost considerations not only include the initial expense and installation, but the number of years the flooring is expected to last, cost for removal or disposal of the floor, lost revenues during remodeling or replacement, and maintenance costs over the course of the surface life (Hard Questions, Critical Answers, 1998).
■ Ease of maintenance and replacement.
■ Potential performance capabilities for both intended and possible use.
■ Overall compatibility in appearance to surrounding materials in the facility (Barkley, 1997).

If floor plates are to be utilized, they should be taken into consideration early in the process and should be covered for both ease of maintenance and safety. If electrical outlets are installed in the floor (which is highly recommended), they should be covered and flush with the floor's surface.

When selecting a surface, it is a wise choice to consult other facilities that have similar needs and use patterns to explore all flooring options based on performance characteristics. It is also important to consult with individuals who work with and maintain these other facilities (e.g., maintenance personnel, students, public, etc.) since they will likely have a different perspective regarding the suitability of various facility surfaces.

Surface Selection Process

As stated earlier, choosing the appropriate floor surface is a major decision in the design or renovation process. Floor materials and construction can influence athletic performance, determine how well multiple uses are served, and impact the incidence of sports injuries. Floor surfaces come in innumerable materials, textures, colors, and performance charac-

teristics. Yet, of the hundreds of products on the market, no one surface is perfect for all uses and there is plenty of room to make the wrong choice (Viklund, 1995, p. 41).

A logical and systematic approach should be followed in conducting a search for the appropriate surface. These guidelines will assist in the decision-making process. According to Viklund (1995, p. 46), the steps in the following "flooring checklist" are recommended:

1. Select the room or space to be considered.
2. Prioritize the sports/activities that will occur within the space.
3. Decide whether the preferred floor should be area elastic or point elastic.
4. Review the performance criteria for the selected floor type.
5. Test flooring options by reviewing samples and comparing costs.
6. Compare life-cycle costs for flooring options.
7. Play on the different surfaces.
8. Check the manufacturers' referenced projects.
9. Make the final decision.
10. Flynn (1993, p. 77) recommends the following steps in the surface selection process:

Definition. Define the characteristics required to meet specified needs (e.g. bounce characteristics, sunlight effects, etc.). Many of these questions are addressed by manufacturers in their literature.

Solicitation. Cost should not be a limitation for one's initial research and review of possible flooring systems. Request as much information from as many manufacturers as deemed reasonable. The review of this information will allow for a broader knowledge of different systems and a basis for comparison. Obtain material estimates and project costs from various manufacturers. Manufacturers should also provide references, a list of installers, and the location of like facilities for comparative analysis.

Comparison. After reviewing manufacturer materials and comparing all possible systems, categorize all materials by type and desirable qualities, e.g., natural vs. synthetic, resiliency, initial cost, longevity, and any additional factors significant to your decision-making process. A table that compares the various positive and negative attributes of each surface option is often helpful in making the right surface choice for your facility.

Visitation. After the field of choices has been narrowed down based on established criteria, make a site visit to each of the facility surfaces being considered.

A closer inspection and discussion with personnel at each facility is also likely to be helpful in making the best choice for your facility. Explore performance as well as maintenance factors, as initial cost and utility are but two of numerous factors in making a wise surface choice.

Selection. At this point, select a system based on upon all research efforts. Take into consideration all performance criteria and always keep in mind that surface choices are a significant factor in the overall success of a facility.

Quality. A specific surface may be selected; however, rach option has numerous levels of quality. Once more, take into consideration the quality of the materials, workmanship, guarantees, facility use factors, and any other considerations when making this important decision.

Manufacturer. Choosing a manufacturer is also significant. How long has it been in business? What type of technical support does it provide? What are its methods of quality control, both in the manufacturing process and in the field? What is its reputation? How soon can it provide you with the requested materials? What guarantees does it provide? Ask many questions of each company being considered. Always remember that references are important, however, be careful to do your homework in the inquiry process. One should never rely too heavily on references provided by the company being considered, as it will obviously be more than willing to provide positive references. Unsolicited references should be sought for all finalists in the bidding process you choose to, or are mandated to follow. It is common for manufacturers to provide products to clients in exchange for positive reviews.

Installer. An installer should be recommended by the manufacturer to help ensure that the installer is familiar with of the manufacturer's product. Ask the installer questions similar to those you asked the manufacturer. Facility visits are very helpful in deciding upon an installation company.

Maintenance. Maintenance is a considerable portion of the operating budget and it is important to define exactly what is involved. What type of maintenance is required? How often will the surface need to be refinished, covered, lacquered, etc.? Facility planners should never underestimate the expense of properly maintaining facility surfaces and figure this expense into the overall surface cost and choice made.

Figure 9.1 Wood floor protective coverings.

Initial cost. What is the "total" initial cost of the system? Make sure there are no hidden costs that will arise later. If two systems are considered similar, yet one is more costly than the other — why? Is it the quality of the system, materials, or both? Sometimes product name or reputation is a reason for cost inflation.

Life-cycle cost. This comparative analysis considers the initial cost, operational costs, maintenance costs, and if necessary, replacement costs during the estimated life cycle. These figures will generate the anticipated total costs. Generally, a higher initial cost system will be comparable to less expensive systems when all factors are considered.

Bidding. When bidding is required, pay attention to written specifications to ensure the product and installation methods are accurately described. This will help avoid misunderstandings.

Installation. It is in the owner's interest to require the manufacturer to perform periodic on-site supervision of the installer. This will help ensure compliance with the manufacturer's specifications.

Walls and Ceilings

Facility walls serve a greater function than simply delineating specific areas. Walls act as barriers to sound, heat, light, and moisture. When selecting wall surfaces, consideration should be given to the acoustical properties of the material as well. Generally speaking, moisture-resistant walls with sound acoustical properties are ideal. The acoustical treatment on walls should be high enough so that it will not impede the utilization of wall space and will not be damaged by users, or objects striking the surface. There is also a trend towards the utilization of colors, pictures, and graphics on wall surfaces. These color schemes have positive psychological value and often make the environment more aesthetically pleasing (Flynn, 1993).

Roof design, local building codes, and the nature planned activities should determine ceiling construction. Ceilings should be insulated to prevent condensation and also be high enough to allow for all planned activities. One may also wish to paint the ceilings to improve the physical look of the facility and enhance light reflection. Bright white ceilings are strongly advised against in areas where light-colored objects are used (e.g., shuttlecocks and volleyballs). It is difficult to visually follow these objects against a bright white ceiling background. A light color is recommended for ceilings; however, most facilities find an *off-white* color to work well. A 24 foot minimum height (to the lowest suspended object) is required in any teaching station designed for a variety of activities (Flynn, 1993). Whenever possible, facility planners should attempt to exceed this minimum ceiling height, as lower heights can still contribute to game interference, equipment lodging (e.g. shuttlecocks), and greater ceiling fixture expenses as a result of occasional contact with equipment (e.g. volleyballs).

Acoustical ceiling materials are needed in instructional spaces and areas with many planned activities. Dropped ceiling panels require considerable maintenance since they are susceptible to damage by objects or individuals. Since most acoustical instruments are not necessarily made out of the hardest materials, they need to be placed out of range of flying objects. In some cases low-ceiling activity areas, dropped ceilings may be equipped with spring-loaded clips that will return the acoustical panel back into place after contact. It should be noted that false ceilings with catwalks above them have been effectively constructed to allow for easier maintenance, and repair of lighting and ventilation arrangements (Flynn, 1993).

Walls in the main gym or activity area should have a minimum height of eight feet and should always be padded for safety reasons. Electrical outlets should be provided every 50 feet and should also be protected by padding (Flynn, 1993). For access, small inserts can be cut out of the padding and affixed with fasteners for easy removal and replacement. All padding should be checked with regularity, as it can wear and harden with age and still cause significant injury upon contact. Keep in mind that some unobstructed flat wall space should be kept available as appropriate, for teaching and/or lecture space. In some cases all walls should be kept unobstructed; however, this

would be based on the specific activities planned for the space (such as indoor soccer).

As mentioned earlier, the ceiling should have a minimum height of 24 feet to the lowest obstacle, with an off-white color usually appropriate. Investigate clear-span ceiling design without minimum support pillars and substructure girders to achieve better safety, viewing, aesthetics, and more open and usable space. If one chooses to mount or store equipment in the ceiling area, structural reinforcement may become necessary at these sites (Flynn, 1993). It is very important to consider all factors when constructing or remodeling the primary features of a facility.

The following chart provides a guide for floor, wall and ceiling choices for a variety of rooms within your facility (Flynn, 1993, p. 19).

Windows

The use and aesthetic value of windows are often overlooked in the planning of indoor facilities, as well as when making surface choices. Windows can provide durable and attractive enclosures as well as divisions of space within a facility. Facility planners must keep in mind, however, that windows may face daily exposure to the elements, as well as frequent contact with objects used in activities planned for the space (Johnson and Patterson, 1997).

The selection process for windows according to Piper (1998) is based on a number of factors, some of which include 1) Lighting. The three most common ways for controlling the light passing through windows are tinted glazing, heat absorbing glazing, and low-emissivity coatings; 2) keeping the elements out, 3) heat loss, 4) aesthetics, 5) security, and 6) view. Windows are often overlooked when making wall surface choices; however, they should be incorporated into the overall building's aesthetic plan, as well as into the activities scheduled within.

Additional Floor, Wall and Ceiling Considerations

Floors

■ an adequate number of floor drains in the proper locations
■ proper floor sloping for adequate drainage
■ water-resistant, rounded base, where the flooring and wall meet in any locker or shower area
■ flush-mounted floor plates placed where they are needed

ROOMS	FLOORS							LOWER WALLS								UPPER WALLS						CEILINGS			
	Carpeting	Synthetics	Tile, asphalt, rubber, linoleum	Cement, abrasive & nonabrasive	Maple, hard	Terrazzo, abrasive	Tile, ceramic	Brick	Brick, glazed	Cinder Block	Concrete	Plaster	Tile, ceramic	Wood Panel	Moistureproof	Brick	Brick, glazed	Cinder Block	Plaster	Acoustic	Moisture-resistant	Concrete or Structure Tile	Plaster	Tile, acoustic	Moisture-resistant
Apparatus Storage Room						1	2			1		2	1	C											
Classrooms			2				1					2		1		2			2	1			C	C	1
Clubroom			2				1					2		1		2			2	1			C	C	1
Corrective Room		1					2			2	1					2		2	2	1	2				1
Custodial Supply Room	.				1				2																
Dance Studio					1																		C	C	1
Drying Room (equip.)					1			2	2	1	2	1	1					1		1					
Gymnasium		1					1			2	1					2		2	2	1	2	*	C	C	1
Health-Service Unit			1				1					2		1		2			2	1					1
Laundry Room				2					1	2	1	2	2		1	C	*				*			*	*
Locker Rooms		3		3			2		1		1	2	2	3	1	*		1	1	2				C	1
Natatorium		2					1		2	1	3	2		1		*	2	2	1		*	*	C	C	1
Offices	1		3			2						2		1		1			2	1					1
Recreation Room			2				1			2		2		1		1			2	1	2	*		C	1
Shower Rooms				3			2	1		1					2	1	*	2	1	2	2	*		1	*
Special-activity Room			2				1				2				1	1		1	1	1				C	1
Team Room	1			3			2	1	2	1	2	2	3	1	*	1		1	2					C	1
Toilet Room				3	-	2	1		1	2	2	2	1		*	1		1	1	1					1
Toweling-Drying Room				3		2	1		1			2	1		*	2	1	2	2		*			1	*

Note: The numbers in the Table indicate first, second, and third choices. "C" indicates the material as being contrary to good practice. An * indicates desirable quality.

Figure 9.2 Suggested indoor surface materials.

■ provision of non-skid, slip-resistant flooring in all wet areas (i.e., pool, shower, etc.)

■ lines painted as appropriate, prior to any sealers being applied (Patton et al., 1989).

Walls

■ an adequate number of drinking fountains, fully recessed into the walls

■ a minimum of one wall of any exercise room with full-length mirrors

■ all "corners" in the shower and locker room areas rounded

■ all wall coverings aesthetically pleasing, as well as matching the decor and color scheme of the facility

■ electrical outlets placed strategically within the wall, firmly attached, and accessible, if the wall is protected with padding

■ in wet or humid areas, materials that are easy to clean and impervious to moisture (Patton et al., 1989).

Ceilings

- ceiling support beams that are engineered and designed to withstand stress
- adequate ceiling heights for all planned facility activities
- ceilings, except in storage areas, that are acoustically treated with sound-absorbent materials
- easily accessible ceilings and access areas for purposes of routine repair and maintenance
- acoustical materials that are impervious to moisture when used in moisture-dense areas (Patton et al., 1989).

Service and Ancillary Areas

Locker Rooms

All surfaces in the locker area should combine a level of easy maintenance and a strong consideration of hygiene. All surfaces should be durable and able to withstand moisture and the accumulation of dirt. Aesthetics is also an important factor, since many use the look of the locker rooms to judge the facility as a whole. Locker room areas should contain hot and humid/wet areas, as well as dry dressing areas, typically within close proximity. Floors in wet areas should always be designed with safety, aesthetics, and maintenance in mind. For obvious reasons, non-slip tile is the best surface for these floors. Since soap and dirt often have a tendency to build up, a beige or brown-colored grout is recommended to keep the tile looking clean. All wet-area floors should be pitched away from the dry areas and directed toward a drain. Some alternative sources include epoxy sealants over waterproof sheet rock or concrete block. These surfaces have proven in the past to work satisfactorily in the dressing room, sink, and common areas. It should also be noted that all corners of these areas should be rounded so moisture cannot penetrate the seams (Patton et al., 1989).

Moisture is the enemy in any building, even those without large shower areas. Precautions during the design process as well as the life span of the facility are important to minimize negative effects of humidity, moisture, and microbe growth. Migration of moisture into contiguous areas must be controlled, and measures must also be taken during the construction process to ensure that all building materials are not moisture-damaged prior to installation. An effective and efficient heating, ventilation, and air control system (HVAC) must maintain a balance between humidity control and energy savings (Straus and Kirihara, 1996).

Prevention is the key in controlling microbiological gardens from growing in the building. Clearly, the most prevalent hazard is moisture, which can range from large pools of water from roof leaks or broken water pipes to invisible rain that is absorbed into building materials, or moisture that condenses on facility surfaces. Dust also serves as a nutrient source for microbial growth. Although chemicals are a common method to combat these problems, moisture is the real culprit and should be the primary focus of effective and routine maintenance procedures (Straus and Kirihara, 1996).

In drier areas of the locker room, the floor is a major concern for interior decorators and designers. Mildew and mold are constant problems, and materials in these areas should be able to withstand long periods of moist conditions and show little or no signs of delaminating. A 100% nylon carpet is recommended for flooring material in a health and fitness setting. The carpeting provides an aesthetically pleasing appearance and is easily maintained with daily vacuuming and periodic shampooing. It should also be noted that the nylon carpets will have a longer life and will be more easily maintained if they are mildew resistant and Scotch-guarded (Patton et al., 1989).

Wall coverings in locker room areas usually consist of epoxy-coated paint, vinyl, or wallpaper. The chosen material should be strong and not show dirt. Consideration should also be given to corners and wall-to-wall moldings to reduce the number of black marks and cuts that typically appear, with heavy use.

Ceilings are usually finished with moisture-proof, hand-finished paint. As mentioned earlier, acoustical materials should also be used in conjunction with paint to reduce the noise level in the locker rooms (Patton et al., 1989).

Steam Rooms

The type of building materials and the way they are applied are central to a low-maintenance steam room. It is recommended that you hire a contractor with previous experience in the construction of wet areas. The floor surface of a steam room should be covered with a liquid rubber material applied over a concrete slab. A layer of fiberglass fabric is laid over the rubber material, followed by an additional coat of liquid rubber. The floor should also slope toward the drain for proper water drainage. This system both protects against water leaks and expands with floor movement. Steam room walls and ceilings should be covered with a cement building board and fiberglass tape. This wall surface should also be placed on galvanized metal studs or wormanized lumber (a process by which the wood is treated for insects). It is important to slope ceilings as well, to enable moisture to runoff rather than dripoff. This system has proven to be durable and helps to prevent against rot and mildew. As with other wet areas, tile should be both attractive and durable. A textured non-slip tile should be used on the floors; glazed ceramic tile is often chosen for walls and ceilings (Patton et al., 1989).

Aerobic/Exercise Facilities

In direct correlation with the emergence of aerobic exercise has also grown a concerted effort to reduce impact-related injuries. Spring-loaded hardwood floors are one of the more popular surfaces, followed closely by heavily padded carpet surfaces that are sealed and plastic-laminate-bonded to inhibit moisture leaks into the pile textures. This type of flooring allows for regular steam cleaning and avoids hygiene problems from accumulated perspiration in a carpeted or padded area. Important considerations are compliance (shock absorption), foot stability, surface traction, and resiliency (energy return). Furthermore, synthetic and especially made floors may be used as alternatives (Patton et al., 1989).

Finding a balance between all facility surface areas is a considerable challenge for the facility planning team. For example, one of the best shock-absorbing floorings is any type of thick sponge pad. Regular foam may develop dips after prolonged use, but some new synthetics have been especially developed to hold their shape. One such surface is microcell foam, which is available at one-fourth the cost of wood, but it should be noted that some difficulties may arise because of its interlocking sections. These types of synthetic floors are usually soft enough that individual mats are not needed for floor exercises. However cleaning may present unique problems with these floor types. Bacteria growth may also be a problem, in particular if the surface is textured or not properly maintained (Walker & Stotlar, 1997).

Although the quality of polyurethane surfaces has improved in the last 10 years, these surfaces are not considered resilient enough by some because they are simply poured directly over concrete surfaces. Maintenance is also an issue as these surfaces are often plagued with cracking and peeling. The life cycle of these surfaces is also much shorter than wood.

Carpeting is relatively easy to install and newer sport varieties have special shock-absorption properties. These should be used with foam cushioning and never applied directly over concrete surfaces. Carpet is versatile, inexpensive, and works well, especially in multi-purpose areas. It should be noted, however, that carpets are highly susceptible to staining, can be easily discolored or stretched, and retain odors. The expected life span of most carpets is two to four years, depending on the usage.

Historically, wood floors have been the most popular choice. Wood is aesthetically pleasing and provides a high degree of flexibility within most multi-purpose activity areas. Wood floors, however, depending on the sub-flooring utilized, are often extremely hard, not resilient enough for high-energy exercise, and prone to warping in excessive humidity (Walker & Stotlar, 1997).

Strength Training Areas

Another area of increased popularity is the strength training room. The dark and dingy weight rooms of the past are being replaced with colorful new flooring options. The type of flooring needed depends on the type of equipment selected. If a weight area is primarily equipped with machines (Nautilus, Universal, etc.), an easily maintained, durable carpet is sufficient. If the room is dominated by free weights, a resilient rubber surface is recommended. This surface comes in the form of sheets or tiles and is simply glued on top of the existing concrete slab. The desired appearance of strength training rooms is an important consideration. The correct ambiance must be established to entice members to join and maintain their memberships. The color schemes of the walls, equipment upholstery, and flooring must all be coordinated to appeal to the user. Consultants or interior designers can be provide assistance in this area (Patton et al., 1989).

Racquetball Courts

The overall playing surface for a racquetball court requires 800 square feet. Traditionally, racquetball courts are covered with a wood floor surface. Maple floors are attractive, provide favorable ball bounce, and absorb shock to the feet, but they have one disadvantage. When moisture enters the wood, it will buckle the system and cause a swelling in the floor. This becomes an important factor if subterranean facilities are built in areas with porous soil. The only other viable system is a synthetic one. New polyurethane materials have been implemented with satisfactory results. These floors are poured and trawled over the concrete floor slab (Patton et al., 1989).

The most popular wall systems to choose from are reinforced fiberglass concrete, plaster, panels, poured-in-place cement slab, and shatterproof glass. Before deciding on a wall system, one should consider material cost, land considerations (moisture and stability), overall appearance, maintenance, and ball action. Plaster is often viewed as a mainstay, as it has been around for years; however, maintenance costs usually prove to be expensive. Poured-in-place concrete slabs have not been used very often. The cost is prohibitive, and obtaining a straight wall from a slab that is poured on the ground and then erected is difficult to accomplish. Reinforced fiberglass concrete has a promising future, but many applications have proven inconsistent. Plexiglass walls provide an aesthetic appeal but are too costly for some facilities. Finally, the floor system with perhaps the best reputation is a panel system designed from compressed wood. The quality of panel systems varies widely, so facility planning members must be careful in selecting a system with a satisfactory quality-to-price ratio (Patton et al., 1989).

Racquetball court ceilings are often constructed from the same materials used for the walls. A popular alternative involves a combination of the wall material for the front half of the ceiling and acoustical tile for the back half. The acoustical tile has been found to be successful in deadening the sound of the ball. Another alternative is to use sheet rock covered by paint or a glazed material (Patton et al., 1989).

Offices and Teaching Areas

Most offices and teaching stations employ a smooth-surfaced glazed block, or a similar smooth surface on walls ranging from 8 to 10 feet. Smoother walls are easier to maintain and clean, more durable, and safer. As mentioned earlier, walls are important aspects of many teaching stations and must be planned appropriately. Many walls are utilized as rebound areas, barriers for equipment storage, and sound barriers, as well as for fitness testing and measurement (Flynn, 1993). Many varieties of wall barriers are available and must be considered based on facility needs and area utilization.

■ Summary

Facility surfaces are an integral part of any athletic complex. The primary surfaces within a facility are floors, walls, and ceilings. Activities planned for each area of the facility should dictate surface selection, even though surfaces are often utilized for more than one purpose.

Learning Objective 1: The student will be able to demonstrate knowledge of the primary surface design areas of a facility.

Facilities have three distinct areas or divisions. The first is the service/ancillary areas such as locker rooms, bathrooms, exercise rooms, etc. These areas require surfaces that are able to withstand heavy moisture content. The second area is the main arena or activity of focus. The third holds offices and administrative areas.

Learning Objective 2: The student will be able to demonstrate knowledge of the types of materials available for these surfaces, along with their characteristics.

Flooring surfaces are categorized into three areas: wood, vinyl, and synthetics. The two most popular forms of synthetic flooring are polyvinyl chlorides (PVCs) and polyurethane. It is important to note that countless types of wood flooring are available, and the costs vary depending on the system that is utilized. Facility walls serve more functions than simply dividing specific areas. Walls serve as barriers to sound, heat, light, and moisture. When selecting wall surfaces, consideration should be given to the acoustical properties of the material. Moisture- resistant walls with acoustical properties are usually favored. There are also several issues to consider when selecting materials for ceiling construction, including the activities planned for the area, roof design, and local building codes. Ceilings materials should allow for acceptable acoustical standards, be high enough for planned activities, and be insulated to prevent condensation.

Learning Objective 3: The student will be able to identify various advantages and disadvantages of surface materials should allow for flooring, wall, and ceiling materials.

Facility surfaces are available in many colors, textures, and materials, and with varying degrees of performance characteristics. When trying to find the correct fit for your facility, please keep in mind the following four concepts in the decision making process:

1. Economic feasibility of the initial and life-cycle costs,
2. Maintenance and replacement ease,
3. Performance capabilities for intended use and possible future use, and
4. Overall compatibility in appearance to other surrounding materials in the facility.

Learning Objective 4: The student will be able to explain recommended maintenance and upkeep practices for various surface materials.

After selecting the best materials for walls, floors, and ceiling, it is imperative to learn how to best maintain the surfaces. Quality surfaces need quality maintenance. The better the maintenance, the longer the original surface will last before major renovation is required.

Learning Objective 5: The student will be able to demonstrate an understanding of an appropriate selection process for facility flooring options.

Many options are available for flooring. The selection should be based on program needs and functionality. If the facility is multi-purpose, a number of people will have a vested interests in the flooring selection. The key to the selection process is involvement of all the stakeholders.

Learning Objective 6: The student will be able to understand the role of a facility manager in the selection of appropriate surface materials for sport facilities.

The central stakeholder in any facility is the manager responsible for scheduling, maintaining, and managing it. He or she should have the greatest knowledge about flooring options.

■ Self-Assessment Exercise

1. What are the three important surface area considerations when planning facility construction or renovation?
2. Name three distinct areas, or divisions within facilities currently being built.
3. Name the two most popular synthetic flooring materials.
4. What are the three main types of surfaces currently employed for primary gym floors?
5. What are three types of recommended sub-floor construction?
6. Name four considerations in the selection of a flooring material.
7. Name the considerations in making an appropriate surface choice.
8. Describe the functions walls serve and name two highly sought after properties in wall materials.
9. Name three important considerations that should be used to determine a ceiling's construction.
10. According to Piper (1998), what are some factors that should be included in the selection process for windows?
11. Locker room materials should possess what important qualities?
12. What is the key to controlling microbiological gardens?
13. What are two of the more popular surfaces for aerobic exercise facilities, and what are important considerations when choosing flooring materials?
14. What are some popular forms of wall systems for racquetball courts?

■ References

Barkely, J.T. (1997). Surfacing. **Cornerstones: A Fitness, Recreational Facility and Parks and Recreation Web Magazine** [On-line]. Available: http://www.sanfordgroup.com/editoriall..library/fitness_facilitysurfacing.html.

Bishop, W. (1997). Athletic flooring. **Cornerstones: A Fitness, Recreational Facility and Parks and Recreation Web M.agazine** [On-line]. Available: http://www.sanfordgroup.com/editoriall...library/athletic_flooring.html.

Brickman, H. (1997). Helping hardwood perform. **Athletic Business**, 67-70, 72.

Flynn, R.B. (Ed.). (1993). **Facility planning for physical education, recreation, and athletics.** Reston, VA: American Alliance for Health, Physical Education, Recreation and Dance.

Hanford, D.J. (1998). What's going down. **Building Operation Management** [On-line]. Available: http://www.facilitiesnet.com/NS/NS3b8ch.html.

Hard questions, critical answers. (1998). **Building Operation Management** [On-line]. Available: http://www.facilitiesnet.com/NS/NS3b8cb.html.

Johnson, D.K., & Patterson, D.S. (1997). Window and curtain walls: Out with the old? **Building Operation Management** [On-line]. Available: http://www.facilitiesnet.com/NS/NS3b7lb.html.

Julicher Sports-Sports flooring, http://www.julichersports.com/wood.html.

Lundin, B.L.V. (1997). Floor plans. **Building Operation Management** [On-line]. Available: http://www.facilitiesnet.com/ NS/NS3b7ce.html.

Patton, W., Grantham, W.C., Gerson, R.F., & Gettman, L.R. (1989). **Developing and managing health/fitness facilities.** Champaign, IL: Human Kinetics.

Piper, J. (1998). Complete performances. **Building Operation Management** [On-line]. Available: http://www.facilitiesnet.com/NS/NS3b8ci.html.

Piper, J. (1997). Form meets function. **Building Operation Management** [On-line]. Available: http://www.facilitiesnet.com/NS/NS3b7cg.html.

Sports surfaces. (1994). **Athletic Business**, 63-67, 70-75, 80, 82.

Straus, D.C. & Kirihara, J. (1996). Indoor microbiological garden. **Building Operation Management** [On-line]. Available: http://www.facilitiesnet.com/NS/NS3b86h.html.

Stoll, S. & Beller, J. (1989). **The professional's guide to teaching aerobics,** (p. 94-98, 150). Englewood Cliffs, NJ: Prentice Hall.

Viklund, R. (1995). High-performance floors. **Athletic Business**, 41-47.

Walker, M.L. & Stotlar, D.K. (1997). **Sport facility management.** Sudbury, MA: Jones and Bartlett.

Walls/ceilings-Acoustical tile. (1994). [On-line]. Available: http://www.ces.ncsu.edu/homecare2/data/IS/C0108.html.

Notes

CHAPTER 10

Facility Maintenance

Thomas J. Rosandich, Jr., United States Sports Academy

Learning Objectives

After reading this chapter, the student will be able to

■ provide guidelines for planning maintenance facilities into the sports and recreational facility,

■ understand the types of maintenance facilities required in a multipurpose sports facility,

■ understand the physical requirements and characteristics for these facilities within the sports facility,

■ identify strategies for positioning maintenance facilities within the sports facility, and

■ describe maintenance concerns to be considered with the overall design of the facility.

Introduction

Most maintenance managers will agree that maintenance requirements are almost invariably not given adequate consideration when facilities are designed. Even when some consideration is given to maintenance during the design phase, changes in design during construction often nullify the original plans. The construction contractor is most usually concerned with getting the building completed in the manner that will generate the most profit, and as such, is not usually concerned with maintenance and repair requirements once the warranties expire (Heintzelman, 1976). Further, there is a natural tendency on the part of architects to focus on the visual aesthetics of the design, often at the expense of more utilitarian concerns such as cost efficiency in operations (Beisel, 1998).

Given that the largest cost of a sports facility is borne through the many years of operation following construction and commissioning, maintenance professionals (typically the designated facility maintenance manager) need to participate in the design process. These maintenance professionals should remain involved until the project is completed. So while there should be no question at this point that the maintenance manager can have a lot to offer in terms of the planning of the facility, further discussion are in order as to the practical considerations for operations and maintenance (O&M) in the project planning. This chapter looks at some of the design requirements for the sports facility from the perspective of the maintenance manager. The first part relates specifically to maintenance and support areas and the second to general "generic" maintenance concerns for the facility as a whole.

Design Considerations for Maintenance and Operations

Physical education, athletic, and recreational facilities should be maintained in a sanitary and hygienic condition. The very nature of many of the activities conducted within these facilities and the many uses of water within them magnifies the need for consistent, superior custodial care. Unless custodians are provided with adequate and convenient facilities and equipment, the prospects of achieving the desired level of sanitation are significantly diminished (Bronzan, 1974).

Among the facilities required by the maintenance and custodian staff for the care and operation of sports facilities include workshops; storage for tools, spare parts, and supplies; janitorial closets; laundry facilities; office and administrative space; and staff break rooms with locker facilities. The following discussion looks briefly at design considerations for these specific O&M areas within the multipurpose sports facility.

Central Custodial Complex

The size and configuration of the custodial complex in any sports facility is contingent upon a number of factors, the first of which is the size of the building and the nature of the programs being conducted. The needs of a small, privately held health club, for example will vary markedly in both size and scope from those of a multipurpose municipal facility or a university sports complex.

But even between facilities of comparable size, the nature of the organization that owns them will have a significant impact on the size and composition of the custodial complex and the way that it is managed. For example, the physical education, intercollegiate sports, and recreational facilities of a major university can be very similar and size to that of a national sports complex or a municipal stadium. However, in the university situation, there will typically be less space given over to O&M within the sports facility itself because it is likely that elsewhere on campus will be a centralized buildings and grounds operation will be responsible for the heavy maintenance activities of the entire university. Thus within the sports facility there may, at most, be a small work space with a storage area for tools and spare parts, which would be totally insufficient for a free-standing, independent operation of comparable size.

Free-standing sport facilities, such as a municipal civic center or a national sports complex, will typically have a self-contained operation for O&M activities. Instead of a small work area for on-site repairs, a

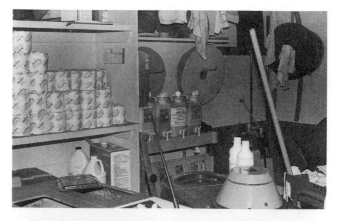

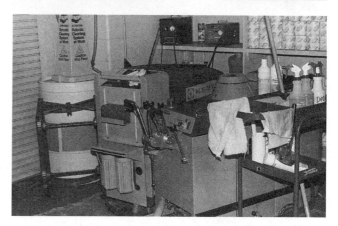

Figure 10.1 *Example of a central custodial complex.*

free-standing sports facility will need expansive work spaces with a much larger variety of tools and storage for spare parts. Nevertheless, O&M facilities of all types do have a number of elements in common.

One approach for the allocation of administrative and support space for O&M operatives is described by Bronzan (1974). In large facilities, a central custodian headquarters should be planned to include a toilet, shower, lavatory, and dressing area with individual lockers. This unit should also have a separate break and meal area equipped with a sink, hot-and-cold water supply, microwave oven, and a small refrigerator. Additionally a small, apartment-size breakfast table and chairs should be provided.

While there is no question that a properly furnished break area and locker room facilities for the O&M staff are appropriate, there is a definite need for a separate O&M office. The area for the administrative office in a typical collegiate facility should be about seven square meters. It is important to note, however, that this space allocation for the administrative office is a minimum, and that the size of the space allocated will grow as the complexity and size of the O&M operation grows. The administrative area should have enough office space to accommodate a desk, filing cabinets, and communications equipment. With today's communication technology capabilities, the administrative office must have a networked computer (either a networked personal computer or a terminal in the case of a mainframe operation) with a printer. Traditionally, the office of the O&M supervisor has been physically located in the workshop or storeroom area. However, because of advances in the application of communications equipment and powerful management tools such as networked micro-computers, the physical presence of the supervisor in the workshop area is no longer a necessity (de Booij, 1993).

A further case can be made that, because of the coordination required between the different administrators who manage the sports facility, the office of the maintenance supervisor should be located in the same area as other administrators. Regardless, however, of where the office of the maintenance manager is physically located, the office (and those of the other facility administrators) should be hard-wired for communications and micro-computer networking.

There is little point in having the maintenance manager's office hard-wired for data and communications if the work areas of the operatives are not. Thus each of the main components of the O&M complex, such as the workshop area, storage for spare parts and supplies, and the administrative office, should similarly be hard-wired for data and communications and should have a desk area that can accommodate a micro-computer and communications equipment.

With the exception of the manager's office as outlined above, ideally the rest of the maintenance offices and workshops will be grouped together in one of the service areas of the building. General characteristics of the O&M area include direct or easy access to the exterior of the building, preferably with a loading dock to facilitate the handling of deliveries, which will often arrive by truck. The landing area at the loading dock should be spacious enough to allow the easy movement of cargo pallets and bulky containers and to allow sorting and organization of materials being received before they are moved into storage.

The storerooms and workshop areas should be located close to each other. This will reduce work-hours wasted in retrieving parts and supplies before they are used. In addition to easy access to the exterior of the building, the custodial complex should be easily accessed via wide and level (i.e., without impediments) corridors. Wherever feasible, the doors between service and storage areas should "line-up" so custodial operatives do not have to turn corners with cumbersome loads.

Access to the central custodial complex and its various work and storage areas should be through double doors. If some material other than steel is used for these doors (for aesthestic reasons, for example), they should be equipped with kick plates and bumper guards. The service or freight elevator in the case of a multi-story building should also be situated in close proximity to facilitate logistic operations. Such elevators should have a ceiling, if possible, of 10 feet and should be as wide as possible. Quite simply, such elevators are going to have to handle the largest pieces of equipment being moved between floors of a multi-story sports facility and should be planned accordingly. Such appropriate logistical considerations will typically yield dividends in the cost-efficient use of personnel and are discussed further below.

However, while easy access to the custodial complex is desirable, the area must still be secured against unauthorized entry. Bear in mind that the typical sports facility will have large numbers of participants and spectators passing through the building and having them entering service areas, either intentionally or otherwise, is undesirable.

These are the general guidelines for O&M facilities within the building. Each individual area is discussed below.

Maintenance Workshops

Among the most obvious concerns of the maintenance manager during the design phase of the sports facility are the work and support areas that will be utilized by the maintenance crews. The size and location of their work areas will have a significant impact on how well O&M workers can do their job. The argument could be made that perhaps the most important of all of the facilities in the custodial complex is the workshop area.

The workshop itself should be situated against an outside wall of the building in the service area, which will allow an exhaust fan to vent outdoors the hazardous fumes and odors generated by activities conducted within. Preferably it should also be situated immediately adjacent to the loading dock entrance and service reception area and have access to the core of the building.

The floor should be of hardened concrete and have a non-corrosive drain. There should also be sufficient open floor space between such permanent fixtures as the storage bins and shelving, work bench, and slop sink to allow free movement around large pieces of equipment that may be brought to the workshop for servicing. The door into the workshop area itself should be a lockable sheet metal type without a floor sill or threshold. Because of the level of noise generated in the workshop area with power tools, the walls should be of sufficient thickness to inhibit the transmission of sound to surrounding spaces. The walls should also be finished with a stain-resistant and easy-to-clean surface.

As stated earlier, the actual size of the workshop area will depend on whether it is a self-contained operation and how much activity it will be required to handle. Regardless of the size, however, some common characteristics should be considered. The first is a spacious workbench equipped with vises, small mounted power tools such as grinders, and a non-skid surface. The workbench area should be well lit by fluorescent lighting in the 100 lumen range that are mounted directly overhead. There should be sufficient electrical outlets around the room, particularly in the workbench wall near the vises and bench-mounted power tools. Also depending on the type of operation, sufficient floor space may be needed to mount free-standing equipment such as pipe-threaders and certain types of woodworking tools.

The maintenance workshop area should be both air conditioned and well ventilated. Because maintenance personnel use highly toxic and volatile substances such as paint, solvents, and cleaners, the workshop areas and central storage areas have exhaust fans that operate automatically and are vented to the outside (Bronzan, 1974).

Another area that needs to be considered is the tool room (also known as a tool crib). While maintenance workers frequently have a set of commonly used tools assigned to them, such as those contained in a lockable tool box, many specialized or very expensive tools and equipment are not assigned to individual craftsmen on a permanent basis. Examples of the specialized tools required for building maintenance may include welding equipment, a variety of metering devices (such as volt meters), and certain power tools. Because these types of tools and equipment are typically high-value items, access needs to be controlled and sign-out procedures employed as with any other inventory item. It is therefore cost effective from a labor standpoint to have the tool room physically located near the workshop area and/or combined with other stockroom activities such as the spare parts store room.

Storage

Storage falls into a gray area between strictly O&M concerns and sports activity and program concerns. On the one hand storage space is needed for tools, spare parts, and consumables such as cleaning supplies and dispenser items (toilet paper, paper towels, and hand soap) to support O&M activities. On the other hand, sufficient storage space is needed to support program activities in the building, such as that required for sports equipment, uniforms, and ancillary activities.

Experienced administrators of the various activity programs and experienced supervisors of storage and distribution rooms agree that the most prevalent fault in the planning of these facilities is the failure to allocate sufficient space. As a result, programs suffer in one way or another, and students do not enjoy all of the benefits they should receive. Operations costs increase disproportionately (Bronzan, 1974). Thus it is useful to consider all the storage requirements for a sports facility for both O&M and sports and activity programs concurrently.

Storage for O&M Operations

A wide variety of spare parts and consumable supplies is required to keep any building functioning properly. Examples of spare parts required for a typical sports complex can range from light bulbs, ballasts, filters, and fan belts for air handling units to replacement modules for scoreboards. Consumables similarly include a wide variety of materials ranging from equipment lubricants, chemicals such as chlorine for the pool, cleaning supplies required for custodial work, and dispenser items required for the restrooms and locker rooms. Secure tool storage and space for storing bulky maintenance equipment such as scaffolding and/or hydraulic lifts are also needed.

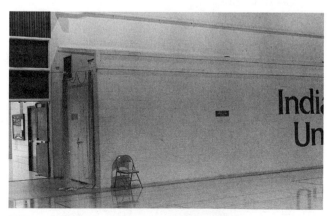

Figure 10.2 Storage area, Indiana State University.

There are a number of considerations in determining the size and location of storage and supply rooms to support O&M operation. Obviously, whether the O&M operation is self-contained is one of them. Another is whether the supply room is run on an open-stock or closed-inventory basis and how much inventory is dispersed to other storage locations around the facility such as in janitorial closets.

If the nature of the organization is such that the sports facilities are a self-contained operation, then the space required for the storage of O&M related equipment and supplies will obviously be greater. More space must be set aside for larger quantities of tools and supplies and for bulky equipment such as scaffolding. If the sport facilities are, for example, part of a centralized O&M operation on a university campus, it is likely that the high-value tools and equipment such as lifts and scaffolding will be kept elsewhere at a central location.

Whether the supplies are run on an open-stock or closed-inventory basis is another consideration. Low-value, high-usage standard stock items such as nails, nuts and blocks, paints, and lubricants are frequently designated open-stock items. Maintenance personnel can obtain them directly from bins without a requisition form, and there is no control over who takes them or what job they are used on. Such items can be stored right in the workshop area, for example, which will further enhance efficiency of the O&M operation. While such an arrangement reduces the need for separate storage space and an inventory clerk, it also invites increased pilferage by employees (Heintzelman, 1976).

Perhaps the best use of an open-stock situation is in operations where maintenance is centralized, such as on a large university campus. As explained earlier, it is likely that a central O&M complex will serve the whole campus with sufficient volume and value of materials to require a closed-inventory system within the central maintenance complex. Thus the sports facility, which is at best a peripheral operation, will likely have a smaller workshop area and tool crib with an open stock of standard-issue items.

A self-contained sports facility such as a municipal stadium or national sports complex, on the other hand, will likely have a closed-inventory system or a combined open-stock, closed-inventory system. Because high-value tools and spare parts required for O&M operation must be retained on the premises, there is a need for access control and accountability and thus for an established inventory system and issue clerk. However, in terms of operational efficiency, it still makes sense in this type of an operation to place some items such as standard issue nuts and bolts in workshop areas and to disperse restroom cleaning supplies and equipment to the janitorial closets. The point is, however, that the space given over to this storage will be markedly greater.

In terms of the physical characteristics of storage areas and supply rooms, these should be situated in close proximity to the areas that they service. For example, tool and spare parts issue should be close to the workshop area, with the space required determined by the criteria discussed above.

The storerooms require temperature and humidity control, as inventory items frequently have specific requirements for storage. The floors should be of hardened concrete with a non-slip surface that is easy to clean. The room should be brightly lit with luminaries located between rows of shelving to ease identification of inventory, which is frequently described on small punch cards or tags affixed to the shelving.

For limited-access storage, there should be a distribution window that can be easily secured when the inventory clerk steps away from the service area to retrieve an item. Near the distribution window should be space enough for a desk and filing cabinet, which should be hard-wired for communications and networked computer equipment (de Booji, 1993). The distribution window should have a counter upon which any transactions can be completed.

Doorway access to the stockroom should be planned to accommodate the largest pieces of equipment or machinery that will enter the area. Unless otherwise indicated, a doorway that is at least 60 inches wide and 84 inches high is recommended, with thresholds that are flush with the floor. The doors will also require good-quality, tamper-proof locks and should be of fire resistant, sheet metal (Bronzan, 1974).

Shelving is an obvious requirement for the storage of supplies and inventory. Bronzan (1974) goes on to describe the requirements as adjustable, steel shelving with a depth of between 18 to 24 inches and a width of 36 to 48 inches. The first shelf should be at least six inches off the floor and the top shelf no less than 12 inches from the ceiling. So far as possible, shelves should be adjustable and standard sizes used.

Sports Equipment Storage and Repair

In most sports facilities, storage and work areas for sports activity and team equipment is separate from that used for general facility O&M. Regardless, many of the physical descriptions of the space required and fixtures contained in the storage rooms used for spare parts and supplies in the O&M operations are also applicable to storage areas for the sports and activity program. It should be noted that virtually all professional teams and most collegiate programs have professional equipment managers whose responsibility includes inventory control and servicing of team clothing and equipment. Just as a maintenance professional should be included in the design process to review the facilities program from an O&M perspective, so too should the equipment manager be consulted with respect to sport equipment storage and repair areas.

Bronzan (1974) recommends that the space given over to the storage of sports equipment include a small area to facilitate the repair of program-related equipment. A well-equipped work area can result in considerable savings over an extended period of time, and sports operations tend to work at a higher level of efficiency with this capability.

Examples of equipment that should be housed in a workshop of this type include a small workbench similarly equipped to that in the main facility workshop area described above. Some of the equipment will vary because the nature of the work to be done is quite different. Examples of equipment that should be included in this work area are racquet stringing machines and sewing machines for uniforms. Additionally, the laundry facility will typically be located in or near the equipment manager's facility.

As custodial workers are frequently asked to set up and remove equipment used in various sports activities, of particular interest to the maintenance manager are the location and characteristics of equipment storage rooms situated about the building. Generally, an equipment storage facility should be located adjacent to each major activity area in the building. Each of these auxiliary storage units should be designed to accommodate equipment anticipated to be used in that particular area, such as hydraulic basketball and other game standards in the main gymnasium, racing lanes and recall lines in the swimming pool area, and gymnastics equipment and mats in their specific area. In all cases, design considerations include doors of sufficient size to accommodate bulky equipment (preferably "lined up" to reducing the number of corners to be negotiated when moving equipment), no door sills or thresholds, and appropriate shelving needs.

Janitorial Closets

The janitorial closet is the staging area for all custodial, or housekeeping work. If the custodian works out of a room that is disorganized and dirty, it is likely that the cleaning effort will suffer accordingly. Also, much of the damage to custodial equipment occurs in the janitorial closet. An example of this is how mop buckets are frequently wheeled into the closet and not emptied, or floor scrubbing equipment is not cleaned

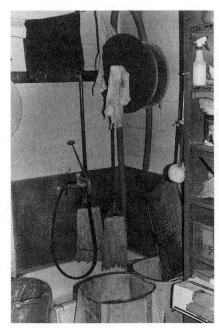

Figure 10.3 Example of a janitorial closet.

after use. Thus every effort should be made to design janitorial closets that will facilitate the custodial work (Walker, 1990). In determining the number of janitorial closets, a number of variables need to be considered. To Heintzelman (1976), these are

■ the number of floors within the facility,
■ the type of floor finishes to be maintained,
■ the proposed use of the areas, and
■ the number of restrooms in the facility.

There should be at least one 6-square-meter custodial room for each 930 square meters of floor space, and at least one such room on each floor of the facility. The room should be designed with a large enough open area where equipment can be assembled and checked and janitorial carts properly stocked prior to starting a job (Walker, 1990). Each janitorial closet should have a service sink with a pop-up drain and a temperature-mixing type of faucet; floor sinks are preferable to large wall sinks for this purpose. Shelves and hanging boards should be constructed in each janitorial closet to facilitate the storage of supplies and tools (Flynn, 1985). Hanging boards, however, should be designed so that wet mops do not rest flush against the wall. Lastly, the janitorial closet should have a good level of illumination (at least 50 lumens) so that equipment can be properly cleaned after the job and before being stowed, and the fine print on chemical containers can be read (Walker, 1990).

While the foregoing is a general guide to the dimensions required for janitorial closets, the general rule of thumb is that the closet should have sufficient space both relative and particular to the area that is being served. High-volume activity areas with greater traffic flow have greater requirements and will need a larger space to accommodate the supplies and equipment needed to properly service them (Bronzan, 1974). Additionally, areas serviced on a seven-day cleaning schedule will require 35 to 40% more supplies than those cleaned on a five-day schedule, which would suggest a larger space allocation (Heintzelman, 1976).

As an example of how the size of a janitorial closet should be determined in part by the area being serviced, consider the open floor space required to store floor maintenance equipment. A closet located in a corridor that features tile flooring would require an area large enough for power scrubbing equipment, whereas one in the vicinity of a carpeted office complex could get by with the smaller area required for a commercial-grade vacuum cleaner. Janitorial closets should also be located in or next to restroom and locker room complexes for a number of reasons. First, this location provides a water and sewage source for the mop sink and thus is cost effective from a design and construction standpoint. The second reason is that locker rooms and restrooms typically must be cleaned more often. Thus work hours are saved if the supplies and equipment are positioned near these areas. And finally, such a location facilitates storage of restroom cleaners, maintenance supplies, and dispenser stock.

As another example of the need to service high-volume traffic areas, a small room should be located near each entrance of the building to store maintenance supplies and tools (Flynn, 1985). Quite simply, everyone who enters or leaves the building will do so through one or more designated entries, which leads to excessive wear in these areas. The first 12 feet on the inside of an entry doorway is called "the walk-off area" and functions exactly as the name implies: it is within this radius that dust, dirt, oil from the parking lot, and water from rain and melting snow are deposited. Thus a well-conceived maintenance plan will call for the regular policing of this area to prevent soiling materials from spreading beyond the walk-off area. To facilitate this frequent cleaning, a small custodial storage area should be situated nearby.

The failure to provide janitorial closets in the proper location and of the proper size can be illustrated by the following example. A building was constructed in which the janitorial closets were only 1.5 square meters in size, most of which was taken up by the mop sink. As a result, most of the supplies and power cleaning equipment had to be stored in the basement of the building, and carting supplies and

equipment to the place where they were needed each night amounted to 30 hours of labor per five-night workweek. This amounted to an additional three-fourths of a worker-year labor expense (currently over $12,000 per annum), which would have been unnecessary if the facility were properly planned. Additionally, because of operating conditions that arose from this situation, pilferage of supplies and theft of equipment increased, leading to the additional requirements of building a lock-up room in the basement of the building and the administrative controls (and expense) to run it (Heintzelman, 1976).

Laundry Room

In most physical education, sport, and recreational facilities, it is now more cost effective to establish in-house laundry facilities than to contract out for cleaning uniforms and towel services. As the operation of the laundry most frequently devolves to the custodial staff, and the laundry facility itself is most likely to be situated within the maintenance support areas of the building, it is appropriate to consider planning guidelines for the laundry operation along with the rest of the O&M facilities.

So far as possible, the laundry facility should be physically located on the ground level of the building against an outside wall to facilitate venting of the dryer. Non-skid concrete floors are recommended, since the floors in the laundry should be hardened and impervious to water. Floors should be sloped to a drain trough that leads to non-corrosive drains. The slope should be 1/8 inch per linear foot. The planarity of the floor is important, since puddles can be dangerous. Floor materials should extend up the walls at least 12 inches, with corners rounded or covered. The thickness of the floor should comply with the equipment manufacturer's recommendations, but in any case, the floor should be able to withstand heavy, vibrating equipment.

As with other maintenance and service areas, the laundry facility should have double-hinged, double-doors without a threshold or a sill to facilitate the installation of laundry equipment during construction and the subsequent movement of laundry carts and supplies in and out of the premises. As a laundry is a noisy place, the walls and ceilings should have good sound absorption or non-transmission properties and yet be impervious to water. The wall finish should also be easy to clean and stain resistant.

While the floor space required for the laundry is contingent upon the size of the machines and the projected work load, sufficient space should be included in the plan for the storage of supplies and sorting/folding tables. Lizarraga (1991) provides guidelines by noting that the size of the laundry facility is determined by the size of the workload. The capacity of laundry equipment is determined by weight (pound). To calculate the number and the size of the machines that will be required, compare the anticipated daily quantities of articles to be cleaned multiplied by their respective weights with the poundage capacity of the machines under consideration, which will give the number of loads they can handle per day. Most process formulas will handle two loads per hour. Facilities with multiple goods classifications (i.e., nylon game uniforms and cotton-blend towels) should opt for two or more machines. Drying equipment needs to be matched up with the washers/extractors and typically has a larger capacity. For example, a 50-pound dryer is a good match with a 35-pound washer.

Once the number and types of machines have been determined, it is a relatively simple matter to size them, as the dimensions of the units can be easily obtained from prospective vendors. The machines should be mounted a minimum of two feet away from the walls and with a minimum of 18 inches between machines. Generally, however, sufficient space should be left around them for circulation and work and for equipment servicing as may be required. Combine this with the space required for processing the work and storage, to determine the net useable footage required for the laundry.

As with all equipment, access to utilities needs to be considered in the plan. While hot and cold water, sewage, and electricity are obvious, gas driers are the most cost efficient to use, so an appropriate hook-up is in order. The room should also have good ventilation and air circulation in addition to outdoor vents for exhaust generated by the equipment.

In terms of the equipment itself, programmable microprocessor controls on the laundry equipment are highly recommended. Also recommended are liquid detergent supply systems that can provide pre-set, automatic injections of chemicals, as such devices may serve to remove judgement calls by operators, especially if the operators are part-time helpers (such as students) (Lizarraga, 1991).

Generic Concerns for Building Maintenance

While the foregoing discussion focused on the design parameters of the facilities specifically required for the O&M effort, aspects of sports facility design as a whole should be considered from the maintenance standpoint. These are really non-specific issues that can nonetheless produce significant operating costs.

Figure 10.4 Emergency lighting.

Many of these considerations are quite simple, yet because of their very simplicity, they are easily overlooked as more obvious design considerations hold the attention of the architect and design committee.

We have touched on such matters as building logistics in discussing the custodial complex, yet so much staff time is spent moving equipment around the typical sports facility that further, more specific attention is warranted. Simple accessibility to equipment and fixtures requiring maintenance tends to get short shift in the design process, with potentially disastrous consequences.

Standardizing Building Fixtures and Equipment

By now it should be clear that the variety of building finishes, fixtures, and equipment in a multipurpose sports facility can be staggering. Similarly, the need to inventory and control spare parts and consumable supplies for the maintenance effort can be a very large undertaking. However, by making a conscious effort to standardize building fixtures and equipment during the design phase, the costs of acquiring and carrying building spares can be significantly reduced.

Such reductions are accomplished in two ways. The first is the direct savings realized through a reduction in stocking spare parts. Standardization of finishes and fixtures allows the maintenance manager to reduce the number of items carried in the spare part inventory, which means a smaller financial burden in carrying costs. As a simple example, consider the effect of standardizing light fixtures. If all the fluorescent light fixtures in the building are the same, the number and variety of ballasts and lighting tubes that must be kept on hand can be considerably smaller than if there were a variety of different fixtures scattered throughout the building. Standardization also prevents the cost of wasted labor that results from bringing the wrong replacement tube to the fixture; the chances of this increase with a wide disparity in fixtures.

The second reduction is more indirect, but significant nonetheless. A smaller inventory requires less room for storage. Additionally, a smaller inventory is easier to administer and control, reducing administrative costs and loss through mishandling and pilferage. Concerted efforts can be made in many areas in standardizing building fixtures, including light fixtures and switches, breaker switches and boxes, bathroom fixtures and dispensers, locker room equipment, door hardware, locks and keys, and moveable equipment.

Logistical Concerns

Operating costs can also be realized by taking into account the needs of the maintenance staff in logistical operations. Logistical operations pertains to the handling of furnishings, equipment, and materials within the facility (Heintzelman, 1974).

One area that tends to distinguish sports facilities from other types of buildings is the nature of the equipment contained within. A multi-station weight machine is, by its very nature, a very heavy and bulky piece of equipment to move around, particularly without disassembly. Gymnastics apparatus and mats, wrestling mats, and portable basketball goals are other examples of heavy, unusually configured equipment that is frequently moved around the building. An awareness of these characteristics is important during the design phase of the facility. For example (and as stated on several occasions already), the doors between spaces should line up to reduce cornering, and the doors from the loading dock (or main access from the exterior of the building) and equipment storage rooms should be double doors with flush sills and sufficient height to facilitate equipment movement.

Other design considerations from a purely operational point of view include using ramps between levels in the sports hall, provided the change in level is not too significant. Another approach is to ensure that freight or building service elevators are of sufficient size (including height) to facilitate the movement of equipment between floors. Similarly, making stairwells and landings large enough to handle bulky items, such as boxes of supplies or furniture, will help with logistical concerns.

Lastly, the design phase must recognize all the activities that will take place within the facility. For example, food service or concessions within the building will require the movement of groceries into and garbage out of the building, preferably through service passages.

The author is aware of one sports facility in southwest Asia that was built at a cost in excess of $80 million in which virtually all of these concerns were ignored in the preliminary plan. Fortunately, once construction was underway, a design review was able to rectify the worst of the errors, but only at considerable additional expense. Had not the design errors been caught, the only access to a second-floor food-service facility would have been via the VIP elevator. A worker seeking to get on board with a bag of garbage when the elevator was already occupied by a member of the Royal Family would have been problematic at best. Similarly, the design included three steps between each wing of the building and no way to move equipment between them. It was a situation rectified by the addition of a ramp after the fact.

Access of Building Operating Equipment

As unfortunate as the logistical situation was in this facility, service access to building operating systems was even worse. There was no way to access light and sound fixtures over the pool or the gymnasium floor because of a novel roof design.

The roof in the facility was a translucent, Teflon-coated fiberglass structure designed as an Arabian tent. But the design did not include access by service passages or catwalks to the fixtures suspended from the ceiling. Lights were changed, for example, by erecting scaffolding or using a personal hydraulic lift, both of which were expensive and time consuming. Unfortunately, the hydraulic lift could not be utilized in the pool area, which necessitated the erection of scaffolding in the swimming pool. Thus the only way to change the lights was to drain the pool. This is a classic case of the architect's placing aesthetics before the more pragmatic and mundane concerns of operating the building, with quite costly consequences.

The point of this discussion is that maintenance requirements of building operating systems must be considered during the design of a facility. By taking into account such operational requirements as easy access to equipment, particularly control panels and lubrication ports, which require frequent attention, accompanying labor costs can be substantially reduced.

Utilities

In addition to access to control panels and operating systems for routine maintenance, the astute placement of electrical outlets for cleaning equipment and water spigots for hoses can effectively reduce labor hours in the maintenance effort.

Most floor-care equipment requires electrical outlets, whether they are power scrubbers or vacuum cleaners. Therefore, the placement of electrical outlets needs consideration, particularly in corridors, lobbies, and activity areas. Inappropriately situated outlets can cause considerable additional operating expense, both for labor (the need to continually move power cords) and for supplies (the need to purchase excessive numbers of extension cords). Additionally, the need for exterior outlets on the building should not be overlooked. For example, certain types of window-washing equipment require access to power, as do many other types of maintenance and custodial equipment, such as blowers for grass clippings.

Water spigots on the exterior of the building should be treated similarly to electrical outlets on the interior of the building. Water hoses are commonly used for washing down sidewalks and exterior windows, particularly those located near the ground. Thus careful consideration to the number and placement of spigots similarly warrants close attention in the design phase.

Windows

The whole topic of windows deserves special mention. "The arrangement and proportioning of windows is called fenestration. Consideration of the relationships of lighting, color, use of materials, acoustics, and climate control cannot ignore the importance of fenestration. Thus the size and placement cannot be left to chance, personal whims, or merely traditional use" (Bronzan, 1974, p. 55).

According to Bronzan, the generous use of windows has been in vogue in the past few decades at least in part because of the pleasing visual effects obtained by the architect. But the excessive use of glass in a sports facility may give rise to a host of problems, including high operating costs from heat gain and loss, and inordinate cleaning costs.

Glass is a poor insulator. It causes significant heat gain during summer months through the greenhouse effect and a corresponding increase in air conditioning costs. During the winter, the process is reversed and large glass areas cause significant heat loss with a similar increase in operating costs. Similarly, large amounts of glass tends to increase maintenance costs as dirt is more visible. Any person who has glass patio doors, for example, can attest to how much attention they require when weather conditions make hand prints and streaks more visible. In commercial buildings such as sports facilities, the amount of cleaning required depends on many variables, such as the local environment (rainfall, dust, and pollution) and the extent of the maintenance effort (or, how dirty you are willing to let the glass get?).

Two basic methods are usually used for window cleaning; "over the roof" or "up from the ground." In both cases, special equipment is required for any structure in excess of one story. The cost for these systems can vary from as little as $15 for a garden hose and squeegee with a six-foot handle to as much as $50,000 for a scaffold for "over the roof" work. Regardless of the system used, plans for water and electrical power sources for window washing equipment should be included in the design phase (Heintzelman, 1975, p. 91).

It should be noted that in sports facilities, if windows are to be incorporated in the design, they should be at least 1/16th of the floor area. Additionally, it is recommended that windows be placed nearer the ceiling than the floor (Bronzan, 1974). For a multipurpose gymnasium designed to accommodate both international-level volleyball and team handball, the minimum total area of glass windows would be approximately 66 square meters (over 700 square feet) located some 7 to 12 meters (22 to 40 feet) off the ground. Under these circumstances, accessibility and labor costs related to maintaining an appropriate appearance must be considered during the design phase.

Returning to the sports facility in southwest Asia cited earlier, the architect achieved a stunning visual effect with a bank of blue-tinted windows two meters wide and 50 meters long extending the length of the sports hall wall some 15 meters from the ground and cantilevered at an angle of approximately of 140 degrees to the roof line. However, the design made accessing the windows extremely difficult and in the six years that the author observed the building, the windows were never washed. The result was an originally unique visual effect that was severely degraded because the design did not take maintenance into consideration.

■ Summary

It is not possible to construct a building that is entirely maintenance free. All the elements of a building deteriorate at varying rates, depending on such matters as component quality, location, degree of exposure to the elements, and use. In this regard, the original design, specification, and construction of a sports facility are all of crucial importance to future performance and maintenance liability. For this reason it is highly desirable to obtain some appropriate input into the design process from maintenance specialists. Unhappily, this rarely occurs (Roberts, 1996).

A common misconception of many sports administrators is that planning for maintenance and operations (O&M) takes place once the sports facility has been built and the doors are opened for business. However, this approach overlooks the importance of planning for maintenance during the facility acquisition process. It also overlooks the fact that the expense of properly caring for the building and equipment will represent a major portion of the overall life-cycle cost of the facility. Thus poor planning for O&M will typically result in higher operating expenditures to the facility owner-operator which, in turn, reduces the amount of funding available for conducting programs and activities for which the facility was originally built. Thus it is clear that O&M must be considered during the planning process for the new building.

Learning Objective 1: The student will be able to provide guidelines for planning maintenance-specific facilities into the sports and recreational facility.

The key maintenance-specific area in a sport facility is the central custodial complex. It houses the support area (locker room and break area) for maintenance personnel, administrative offices, workshops, and storage. The size and composition of these maintenance facilities depend on a number of factors including whether the maintenance effort is centralized or decentralized, the size of the facility, and the types of activities conducted.

Learning Objective 2: The student will be able to understand the types of maintenance facilities required in a multipurpose sports facility.

The types of maintenance facilities that should be incorporated into the sports facility were briefly outlined above. Nonetheless, these include a support area for the maintenance staff including a locker room and break area. Management usually finds it desirable to segregate workers from paying clientele in the use of these facilities. Also needed are administrative offices where required documentation can be processed and filed, where the key control box can be monitored, and where maintenance personnel can meet with their supervisors. Obviously maintenance workshops are required where the work can be done as cost efficiently as possible. This means they must be large enough and equipped consistent with the general maintenance strategy (e.g., centralized versus decentralized, etc.). Also required is secure storage for tools, spare parts, and consumable supplies. These facilities are distinguished from sport equipment storage and service areas, which are more program-related than maintenance-related. It should be noted that the facility laundry operation will be most commonly located in or near the sport equipment operation. Lastly, janitorial closets need to be appropriately placed and properly appointed to allow cost-efficient cleaning of the facility to take place.

Learning Objective 3: The student will be able to understand the physical requirements and characteristics for these facilities within the sports facility.

The general specifications and design characteristics for maintenance facilities are typically written to ensure that the maintenance function will be carried out as cost-efficiently as possible. Today most maintenance managerial functions, including the generation, servicing, and archiving of work orders and inventory, are computerized. Thus the administrative offices and, to some extent, inventory storage areas should be wired for a computer network. The building finishes in these areas tend to be simple and reflect they are indeed "work areas." Further, these service and support areas are usually away from client traffic flows where aesthetics are important. Thus concrete floors and painted cinder block walls, which can handle the abuses from moving equipment, water, and chemical spills, etc., are the norm. Similarly the maintenance and support areas must be well ventilated and lit, with access to adequate utility hook-ups such as power and water. Finally, access to the work areas by long wide corridors and lockable double doors without sills or jams is important.

Learning Objective 4: The student will be able to identify strategies for positioning maintenance facilities within the sports facility.

Generally speaking, maintenance service areas should be located in areas of the building where it is easy to restrict client traffic flow. Most maintenance and service facilities are also located on or along the exterior walls of the building. This allows venting of fumes from the work areas (or the dryer in the laundry) without extensive duct work. Also important in this regard is access to the building exterior for the delivery of shipments, removal of supplies and equipment, and other activities such as trash removal. Storage has been distinguished between maintenance-related (tools, spare parts, and consumables) and sports-related (mats, standards, clothing, and balls, etc.). Maintenance storage is generally located in the central custodial complex of the facility, whereas program storage is typically found adjacent to appropriate activity areas. Lastly, janitorial closets should be located in or near restroom and locker room complexes and main building entrances frequented by the general public. Other guidelines include at least one closet on each floor of a facility such that one closet can service about every 10,000 square feet of space.

Learning Objective 5: The student will be able to describe maintenance concerns to be considered within the overall design of the facility.

During the design process, most notably in the development of the facilities program, the maintenance manager should strive toward ensuring standardization of parts and fixtures (e.g., lighting, door hardware, etc.) and finishes so far as it is practicable. The facility design should also address maintenance logistic concerns and access to utilities (e.g., the placement of wall sockets, etc.). Service access to building operating systems and control panels is also needed. The use of glass, both interior and exterior, must be carefully considered against subsequent operating costs associated with operations (e.g., utilities) and maintenance (e.g., cleaning).

■ Self–Assessment Exercise

1. Why is it important to plan for maintenance facilities within recreation and sport facilities?
2. What guidelines would you use in planning for maintenance facilities?
3. What type of maintenance facilities are necessary for multipurpose facilities?
4. What are the physical requirements for a maintenance facility?
5. What are the characteristics of a maintenance facility?
6. What strategies should be used in locating maintenance facilities within recreational and sport facilities?
7. What are the maintenance concerns that should be addressed in the overall design of facilities?
8. What type of storage is needed for maintenance operations?

■ Case Study

You have been hired by Johnny Appleseed Univesity as the maintenance coordinator for physical activity, recreation, and sport facilities (indoor and outdoor). The university has just begun planning a new $20 million student recreation center. You have been asked to provide input regarding the maintenance spaces for the facility and maintenance equipment to be purchased, and respond to general maintenance concerns as the building is being planned. What will be your recommendations regarding maintenance spaces, maintenance equipment, and general maintenance concerns?

■ References

Bronzan, R.T. (1974). **New concepts in planning and funding athletic, physical education and recreation facilities.** Danville: Phoenix Intermedia, Inc.

de Booji, M., & al–Harbi, K. (1993, October). **Managing maintenance operations by computer.** A professional seminar paper on Total Maintenance System Engineering conducted by Future Engineering, Riyadh.

Flynn, R.B. (Ed.). (1993). **Planning facilities for athletics, physical education and recreation.** (2nd ed.). Reston, VA: American Alliance for Health, Physical Education, Recreation and Dance.

Heintzelman, J.E. (1976). **The complete handbook of maintenance management.** Englewood Cliffs: Prentice Hall, Inc.

Roberts, E. (1996). Maintenance. In G. John & K. Campbell. (Eds.), **Handbook of sports and recreational building design: Vol. 2 indoor sports** (2nd ed.) (pp. 22-23). London: The Sports Council.

Walker, J. (1990). Proper equipment maintenance. **American School and University 63**(2).

■ Suggested Readings

Dawes, J.L. (1979). **Design and planning of swimming pools.** London: The Architectual Press.

Lozar, C. (Undated). **Architects design kit for better building maintenance.** Lincolnwood, IL: Architects Equities and International Sanitary Supply Association.

Meier, H. (1989).**Construction specifications handbook.** Englewood Cliffs: Prentice Hall.

Winter, N. (1996). Maintenance management. In G. John & K. Campbell (Eds.), **Handbook of sports and recreational building design: Vol. 3 ice rinks & swimming pools** (2nd ed.) (pp. 152-154). London: The Sports Council.

CHAPTER 11

Electrical and Mechanical

Ed Turner, Appalachian State University ■ Richard J. LaRue, University of New England

Learning Objectives

After reading this chapter, the student will be able to

■ understand lighting and sound in terms of functionality,

■ understand the challenges of implementing electronic technologies,

■ understand climate control concepts in terms of efficiency,

■ recognize the administrative responsibilities related to electronic technology and climate control,

■ understand the challenges of sick building syndrome, and

■ understand both the trends and new technologies in electrical and mechanical engineering.

Introduction

At its best, technology should conform to the way we work, the way we play, and the way we live. Through electrical and mechanical engineering, we have an opportunity to create extraordinary environments through the manipulation of basic components: lighting, sound, and other electronic technologies; heating, ventilation and air-conditioning; and humidity and air quality control. Advancements in engineering these technologies in both indoor and outdoor spaces require planners to understand the basics and expect unlimited potential for new technologies. Planners must avoid setting limits on how far ahead they look. Only a few years ago, the computer was a luxury. Now computers are a necessity of everyday life, operating everything from membership systems to the building automation and HVAC

systems of "intelligent buildings" (Myers, 1997, p. 53). Today's engineering must be about providing for the way we *will* work, the way we *will* play, and the way we *will* live.

Electrical Engineering

A theoretical basis of electrical engineering includes an understanding of circuits, electronics, electromagnetics, energy conversion, and controls. Conceptually, when planners intend to consider lighting and sound, they are also considering the broader areas of illumination and acoustics. Therefore, the planning basics of lighting, sound, and other electronic technologies will also include information relevant to the *design* of electrical systems, which goes beyond electrical engineering in its strictest sense.

Lighting

Lighting is simply a means to illuminate or further brighten an area or space. The two primary lighting options are energy-produced lighting and natural lighting. The product of lighting in combination with other variables, such as the level of darkness, the amount of reflective light (from surfaces), and the color of the lighting, results in illumination. Illumination is measured by the foot-candle. Brightness is the luminous intensity of any surface and is measured by the foot-lambert. Glare, which is an important consideration in physical education and sport facilities, is nothing more than excessive high brightness.

In addition to the amount of light in any given area, the quality of light is of equal importance. Providing efficient illumination is complicated and challenging, and the services of an illumination engineer are recommended in order to obtain maximum lighting efficiency. Gymnasiums, classrooms, corridors, and other specific areas have specific and different lighting requirements. Planning for electric illumination requires that each area be considered relative to specific use.

The foot-candle is a measurement of light intensity at a given point. Light intensity, measured in foot-candles, is one vital factor in eye comfort and seeing efficiency, but intensity must be considered in relation to the brightness balance of all light sources and reflective surfaces within the visual field.

The reflection factor is the percentage of light falling on a surface that is reflected by that surface. In order to maintain a brightness balance with a quantity and quality of light for good visibility all surfaces within a room should be relatively light, with a matte rather than a glossy finish.

The foot-lambert is the product of the illumination in foot-candles and the reflection factor of the surface. For example, 40 foot-candles striking a surface with a reflection factor of 50% would produce a brightness of 20 foot-lamberts (40 x .50=20). These values are necessary when computing brightness differences in order to achieve a balanced visual field. Table 11.1 gives a relative indication as to a comparison of illuminations for specific indoor spaces.

Basic Lighting Considerations

Installation

Lights in arenas, gymnasiums, and other high-ceiling activity spaces need to be a minimum of 24 feet above the playing surface, so they will not interfere with official clearance heights for indoor sports. Indoor lighting systems are generally of two types: direct and indirect lighting. Direct lighting systems face directly down at the floor. Indirect lighting systems face in some direction other than the floor, i.e., side walls or ceiling, reflecting the beaming light in an effort to reduce glare. Indirect lighting is more expensive to operate since with each reflection light is diminished. Therefore more energy is consumed in indirect lighting compared to direct lighting in order to obtain the same final illumination of an area. Both lighting systems should meet the required level of footcandles without causing glare or shadows on the playing surface. The type of lighting—incandescent, fluorescent, mercury-vapor, metal halide, quartz, and sodium-vapor—will likely depend upon the type of space and the way the space will be used (see below). The style of fixture may have more to do with aesthetics than functionality, though the advantages and disadvantages of aesthetics vs. functionality should always be considered.

Designed for Impact

In spaces where the play may involve hitting, kicking, or throwing balls, etc., lighting fixtures should be designed to absorb their impact. Lighting systems are available that include shock-absorbing characteristics. Perhaps more important is the additional protection these lights require in the event that they are struck and the bulb is broken. Falling shards of glass from broken lights should be avoided at all costs. Lights need to be covered with a transparent polycarbonate sheeting (a screen may not be enough) that will catch broken glass bulbs and also protect the bulbs from direct impact. The sheeting or cover should also keep softer, potentially flammable sport implements (i.e., tennis balls, shuttlecocks, and nurf or wiffle-balls) from lodging within the fixture against a high-temperature bulb (Turner, 1993).

Lighting Types

"The incandescent light is instantaneous, burns without sound, and is not affected by the number of times the light is turned on or off. Incandescent lights and fixtures are considerably cheaper in initial cost, are easier to change, and the lamp, within limits, may be varied in size within a given fixture. Incandescent fixtures, however, have excessively high spot brightness and give off considerable heat, a problem when high levels of illumination are necessary.

Fluorescent lamps have the advantage of long life and give at least $2\frac{1}{2}$ times the amount of light that incandescent lamps give for the same amount of electrical current used. They frequently are used in old buildings to raise the illumination level without installing new wiring.

Table 11.1
Levels of Illumination Recommended for Specific Indoor Spaces
Courtesy of Illuminating Engineering Society of North America

Area	Footcandles on Tasks	Area	Footcandles on Tasks
Adapted physical education gymnasium	50	Rifle range	
		Point area	50
Auditorium		Target area	70
Assembly only	15	Rowing practice area	50
Exhibitions	30-50	Squash	70^2
Social activities	5-15	Tennis	70^2
Classrooms		Volleyball	50
Laboratories	100	Weight-exercise room	50
Lecture rooms		Wrestling and	
Audience area	70	personal-defense room	50
Demonstration area	150	Games room	70
Study halls	70	Ice rink	100^3
Corridors and stairways	20	Library	
Dance studio	5-50^3	Study and notes	70
Field houses	80	Ordinary reading	50-70
First-aid rooms		Lounges	
General	50	General	50
Examining table	125	Reading books, magazines,	
Gymnasiums		newspapers	50-70
Exhibitions	50^2	Offices	
General exercise		Accounting, auditing,	
and recreation	35	tabulating, bookkeeping,	
Dances	5-50^3	business-machine operation	150
Locker and shower rooms	30	Regular Office work, active	
Gymnastics	50	filing, index references, mail	
Archery		sorting	100
Shooting tee	50	Reading and transcribing	
Target area	70	handwriting in ink or medium	
Badminton	50^2	pencil on good-quality paper,	
Basketball	80^2	intermittent filing	70
Deck tennis	50	Reading high-contrast or well-	
Fencing	70^2	printed material not involving	
Handball	70^2	critical or prolonged seeing,	
Paddle tennis	70^2	conferring and interviewing	50

These standards have been developed by a panel of experts on facilities for health, physical education, and recreation after careful consideration of the activities involved. In all instances, the standards in this table are equal to, or exceed, the standards which have been recommended by the Illumination Engineering Society, American Institute of Architects, and National Council On Schoolhouse Construction. ^{2}Care must be taken to achieve a brightness balance to eliminate extremes of brightness and glare. ^{3}Should be equipped with rheotstats. ^{4}Must be balanced with overhead lighting and should provide 100 lamp lumens per square foot of pool surface. **Courtesy of Illuminating Engineering Society of North America.**

continued.

Table 11.1 — Cont'd
Levels of Illumination Recommended for Specific Indoor Spaces.
Courtesy of Illuminating Engineering Society of North America.

Area	Footcandles on Tasks	Area	Footcandles on Tasks
Parking areas	1	Swimming pools	
Storerooms		General and overhead	50
Inactive	10	Underwater[4]	
Active		Toilets and washrooms	30
Rough bulky	15		
Medium	30		
Fine	60		

Mercury-vapor lighting is expensive in terms of initial installation. The overall cost of mercury-vapor lighting, however, is cheaper than incandescent lighting. The primary objection to mercury-vapor lighting is its bluish color. However, when incandescent lighting is used in addition to mercury-vapor, a highly satisfactory lighting system results. Mercury-vapor lights are being phased out in favor of metal halide lights.

Metal halide lights do not last as long as mercury-vapor lights but give a better light output and operate more efficiently. Metal halide lights do not have the bluish tint of mercury-vapor lights. Quartz lights and high-pressure sodium lights are outdoor lights. It has been only over the past few years that these lights have been utilized indoors. Quartz lights are not much different than incandescent lights, except they have a slight bronze color and are slightly more efficient. High-pressure sodium lights might well be the indoor activity light of the future. They have long life expectancy; they are highly efficient and give the best light output of all the lights mentioned. The only problem with high-pressure sodium lights is the yellow-bronze hue associated with them.

Lighting Levels

A number of systems exist that allow different levels of lighting so that special events or lighting requirements can be met. The Jack Breslin Student Events Center at Michigan State University (opened in 1989) affords such variety using an intricate Holophane lighting system.

The lighting levels are turned up or down through a computerized control system, which is pre-programmed for different lighting and uniformity levels. On another control panel, the lights can be adjusted by a single button designated for one of eight different pre-programmed scenes. For example, facility personnel can press one button to set the lighting for televised basketball games, another for non-televised games, another for pre-game set-up, and so forth (Rabin, 1993, p. 6).

When the Dan and Kathleen Hogan Sports Center at Colby-Sawyer College went on line in 1991, the NCAA lighting standard was 60 foot-candles at the water's surface. Today 100 foot-candles of illumination are required for U.S. swimming and collegiate championship events. Because the planners decided upon a higher-than-minimum level for lighting the natatorium at the center, the facility continues to meet required lighting standards without any modification.

Using Natural Lighting

Windows and other translucent materials allow natural light into a facility. Natural lighting can reduce operational costs and enhance the aesthetics of an indoor space. The major problem with windows is that it is very difficult to control the glare that they allow to enter. Avoid windows in any activity area where visual acuity is an important commodity for both learning activity skills and safety. However, other translucent building materials are available that do several things windows cannot:

COMPARATIVE AVERAGE LUMENS PER LAMP WATT

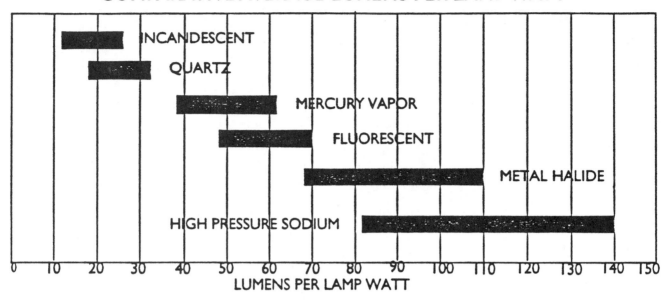

COLOR OF LAMP UNIT

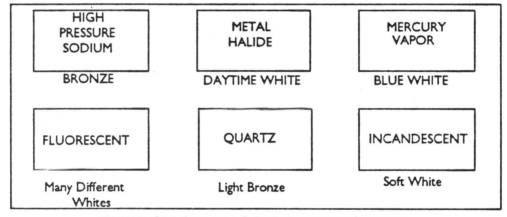

ENERGY SAVINGS COMPARISON*

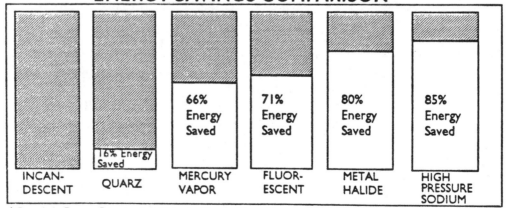

* Based on Energy Required to Maintain Identical Lamp Lumens

Figure 11.1 Comparisons of typical lighting systems.

- provide higher values for insulation reducing both heat loss (during colder seasons) and/or heat gain (during warmer seasons),
- diffuse the light that comes through, reducing glare, and
- provide greater resistance to breaking so they are safer to use in spaces where broken glass is a serious problem, and they are harder to break into from a security standpoint.

Translucent materials are not perfect. Translucent panels or blocks in a high-moisture area, will still allow moisture to condense on the inside surface if it is colder outside and they do not allow clear images to transfer. Windows can also have movable shades, shutters, curtains, or blinds that assist with controlling glare and can improve insulating levels. Skylights are acceptable in "slow movement areas" and vertical skylights are reommended in order to keep both glare and leakage to a minimum. Regardless of the materials used, natural light seems a worthy goal, when the facility is designed and used appropriately.

Maintenance

Planning must also take into account the need to change bulbs or replace fixtures. Unless there is a catwalk or crawl space in the ceiling, the lights will need to be changed from the floor using poles, ladders, scaffolding, or hydraulic hoists. Experience informs us that changing all the lights in a space at the same time, is the most cost-effective approach to maintenance. However, if your lighting fails to meet required levels whenever a single fixture is out, you will be forced to change your bulbs more frequently. Consider adding a couple of fixtures in each space, more than is required; i.e., if the space/activity standard calls for 50 foot-candles on task, you may wish to exceed this standard by four fixtures, so that you can lose up to four lamps and still meet the minimum. And when four bulbs are gone, it is probably time to replace all the bulbs in the space. As you plan for the need to change bulbs and replace fixtures, remember the characteristics of the space. Even telescoping poles need minimum clearance to get inside a space. Racquetball courts with standard-sized doors may allow the use of a small hydraulic hoist rather than a giant stepladder. Finally, direct-lighting bulbs can sometimes be changed using only a pole (standing on the floor), while indirect lighting can only be changed using a catwalk, crawlspace, or more time-consuming approach. Therefore, when planning your lighting system maintenance, you should consider designs that will serve the facility without being labor intensive.

Unique Lighting Settings—Issues

Unique settings in sport and recreational facilities require either special lighting systems, special fixtures, or carefully planned designs. In spaces with a higher level of moisture (pool areas, shower and toilet areas, locker rooms, etc.) vapor-proof lighting units are recommended. Remember that broken glass in any such area is a mini-disaster. If a bulb breaks in spaces where participants are often barefooted, extensive cleanup will be required. Locker rooms and athletic training rooms are two examples of spaces where light placement will directly affect the quality of the environment. Fixtures should be placed to enhance the areas between lockers in locker rooms, to afford clear reflections at mirrors, and to brighten places where visibility is critical to the activity in athletic training rooms.

Aquatic Facilities

Lighting indoor swimming spaces has never been the easiest part of natatorium design—although frequently, and with regrettable results, it has been treated that way. With today's multipurpose aquatic centers frequently accommodating diverse programming activities in a shared environment, it has become an even greater creative challenge to get the light right. Natural light is an increasingly attractive option for indoor aquatic facilities. Large windows or open fenestration can be energy-efficient ways to supplement artificial heat and lighting, and they add interest for users and a much appreciated connection to the outside for employees who work all day in an enclosed environment. With all its advantages, however, natural light can be accompanied by an undesirable partner-glare (Hunsaker, 1998, 51).

If windows are used in aquatic areas, the glare trade-off must be addressed during the planning stages. Glare is not an exclusive problem of natural lighting. Glare can result from improperly located artificial lighting when the lights reflect off either the water surface or side walls. With safety a major consideration in aquatic facilities, every effort must be made to control for glare and/or the blind spots caused by glare. Underwater lighting can reduce some of the glare problem and can further enhance visibility in deeper water (underwater lighting is required in some jurisdictions). And in aquatic facilities, there are maintenance issues related to the location of light fixtures over the pool (the preferred location for competitive facilities). The YMCA's Walter Schroeder Aquatic Center in Milwaukee, Wisconsin, was able to locate light fixtures directly over the 50-meter indoor pool after determining that by using the two movable bulkheads, a hoist could be positioned anywhere a fixture required relamping. This avoided the added construction expense of a catwalk or crawl space and the labor intensiveness of using a scaffolding setup in an empty pool to replace bulbs. Finally, artificial lighting in pool areas must consider the variability of water depth.

Outdoor Lighting

Outdoor lighting for sports fields can have some very specific requirements. "Sport lighting should provide a specified quantity and quality of light on the playing surface. For a football field, the quantity (level) of light is determined by the player's skill level, the number of spectators and any television requirements" (Rogers, 1994, p. 53). Although specific considerations apply when planning illumination of a specific-use field, for the purpose of this chapter, the concepts of outdoor lighting will focus on multipurpose installations.

Multipurpose sports fields are more complicated to light [than single purpose fields], but you'll save money by combining activities on one field. Several issues need to be addressed when lighting a multipurpose field. Light levels and pole placement become big factors, and design decisions become critical. Controlling spill and glare is also very important. Lighting a multipurpose field is extremely cost-effective. By sharing poles and fixtures among several sports, initial costs can be reduced by 40% or more. At some point, making the decision to use the field for both sports increases the land's productivity and so will the decision to give it light" (Rogers, 1996, p. 51).

Planning steps include the following:

■ "Determine the layout of the field and all its potential uses. The most common multipurpose fields combine football with soccer, or football or soccer with softball" (Rogers, 1996, p. 51).
■ Determine the quantity (level) as well as the quality needed (Rogers, 1996). The Illuminating Engineering Society of North America (IESNA) publishes light-level guidelines for outdoor sports (see IESNA web site for further information:, http://www.iesna.org).
■ Determine the type of lamp desired (Rogers, 1996). Figure 11.3 shows comparisons of typical lighting systems.
■ Determine the number of luminaire assemblies (luminaire assemblies consist of lamp reflector, ballast mounting, crossarm and mounting hard-

ware) and poles required to light the playing surfaces while avoiding spill and glare (Rogers, 1996).
■ Decide on the type of poles to be used: wood, concrete, and steel are the standard options. Each has advantages and disadvantages.
■ Consider all aspects of safety. The lighting system must comply with the National Electric Code as well as state and local codes and use luminaire assemblies that have the Underwriters Laboratory approval (Rogers, 1996).
■ Establish switching controls that allow for maximum flexibility and maximum efficiency.
■ Recalling that some activities require more lighting than others, switches should afford higher and lower levels of illumination. "Switching capacity becomes even more important with overlapping fields" (Rogers, 1996, p. 54).

Outdoor sports lighting should be

safe, simple and efficient. Basic requirements include one transformer and a simple service entrance with a basic feeder and branch circuit. Grounding at the service center and at each pole is needed to ensure the safety of anyone who comes in contact with the pole or electrical equipment. Grounding for lighting protection should be designed and installed according to the National Fire Protection Association (NFPA) Code 780. Safety disconnects on each pole provide additional protection for service crews. Individual fusing of each fixture avoids gang failure of the lights, eliminating costly emergency repairs (Rogers, 1994, p. 56).

Finally, the planner should consider and compare the warranties offered by different manufacturers: the length of the warranty, the items included, and those not included. "Manufacturers that offer a multi-year warranty are making a strong statement of confidence in their product" (Rogers, 1994, p. 56).

Supplementary and Special Lighting Requirements

It is advisable to provide supplementary lighting on such areas as those containing goals or targets. Supplementary light sources should be shielded from the eyes of participants and spectators in order to provide the proper brightness balance. Other special lighting requirements include:

■ *Night lighting*—lights that remain on 24 hours per day (can be the same circuit as the emergency lighting), lighting large spaces, lobbies, corridors, stairwells, and classrooms.

■ *Exit lighting*—located at all exits (including exit-only locations), should be mounted according to local and state codes. Because these lights remain on 24 hours per day, cost savings can be realized if fluorescent bulbs are used instead of incandescent bulbs or LED (light-emitting diode) signs are used as both fluorescent bulbs or LED fixtures have much longer lives. All exit lighting should be on special circuits that will remain on, even if the power is lost.

■ *Emergency (white) lighting*—should be provided for exits (including exterior open spaces to which exits lead). This lighting should be on a special emergency circuit (battery powered) that will power-up whenever power is lost.

Lighting Controls

When planning for lighting, the methods of control are also an important to consider. The central light switch box should be located at a major entrance area, and all teaching [or activity] spaces should have individual light switches. A relatively unusaul approach to controlling illumination in spaces where lighting is only on as needed (i.e., individual racquetball or squash courts, rest rooms, etc.) is motion sensor or "occupancy sensors" switching. If the sensor detects no movement over a period of 10 to 15 minutes, the lights automatically switch off. The lights come back on as soon as someone enters the room. Light-level sensors are also available for use indoors as well as outdoors. These sensors adjust the lighting level in response to the amount of natural lighting. Replacing the all-or-nothing on/off switch in parking areas or skylit rooms can give just the right amount of artificial light needed as the natural light fades.

Trends in Lighting

On the horizon, if not already here, is the use of Circadian lighting systems in 24-hour operations. Ciradian lights facilitate true physiological adaptation to working nights and sleeping during the day. These system installations have proven "entirely successful in providing a means in keeping the shiftworkers awake (industrial settings) and alert while on-shift, improving the safety of the commute home, improving the day sleep of the shift worker, and having a positive impact on family life" (Murphy, 1998, p. 1). In other words, Circadian lighting systems have proven to have a positive biological effect on users in a 24-hour, three-shift environment. More research will be needed to determine the possible use and effects of Circadian lighting in more traditional settings.

Sound

Sound is an important part of everyday life, and subsequently it is an important part of sport and recreation. From the public address system to the telemetric microphone, the ability to hear what is going on is almost as critical as seeing what is going on; frequently, one sense will support another in completing the act of communication. From the sound quality we need in aerobic dance studios to the sound system required for a half-time show at the Super Bowl, technology is advancing the availability of high-resolution sound (Fenton, 1997).

For the sport or recreational facility, sound design starts with creating a suitable sound environment. Beginning in the lobby, where users first enter, several approaches can be utilized:

■ Design a small audio/video system that plays videos (either cable or tape), with the audio portion of the videos distributed to other areas as well.

■ Building on the first approach, include a video wall in the workout area that receives the same video as the unit in the front lobby,

■ Have your sound distribution originate in a workout space such as an aerobics studio, and then distribute this sound or allow it to "drift" to the lobby and/or other areas of the facility (Hall, 1993).

In strength-training spaces, the major sound considerations are:

even distribution, the ability to overcome background noise, and low-fatigue factors. Correct selection and placement of appropriate speakers will provide even distribution, reduce the impact of background interference, and satisfy low-fatigue requirements. Wall-mounted speakers usually work best, although clubs that have a lot of tall equipment in rooms with low ceilings should use ceiling speakers. Whenever possible, include in your design a dedicated sound system for free-weight areas to increase your flexibility in sound sources and level control (Hall, 1993, p. 42).

In cardiovascular areas, "the most satisfactory approach for most clubs is to supply each exercise station with a headphone outlet and flexibility in source selection, along with one or more video monitors visible to several stations at once" (Hall, 1993, p. 43).

The aerobics room is the one area where your members [users] most expect to hear sophisticated, high-quality sound. Achieving this in a room full of hard surfaces and highly active people is difficult. A well-designed and properly operated sound system will add precision and impact to your classes, establishing a sense of timing and inspiration without fatigue, stress or hearing damage created by distortion and excessive volume levels (Hall, 1995, p. 42-43).

Four categories of components have a very direct effect on these various factors:

1. speakers;
2. cassette decks/turntables/CD players;
3. amplifier, receiver, and equalizer (soft limiter); and
4. wireless microphone and microphone mixer (Hall, 1991).

Selecting the correct components is easier when you understand the elements of a high-quality sound system. However, it is important to seek the advice of individuals and/or companies who are familiar with the specific needs of an aerobic studio when choosing components for your new studio or when upgrading your current system (Hall, 1991, p. 40).

Acoustics

Because of the amount of noise and sound that emanates from the activities in physical education and sports, acoustics and sound are of paramount importance in building design. Acoustical treatments in building design are the domain of the acoustical engineer. An acoustical engineer should be consulted when dealing with absorption and reflection qualities of all surfaces within a facility.

Acoustical treatments must both enhance sound so that we can hear easily, and absorb sound. Background noise, basically unwanted sound that originates either in the teaching station itself or intrudes from another area, must be controlled. Internal background noise might consist of "squeaking" chairs sliding on a floor, reverberation or "echoing" of sound, and reflective sound. All sound travels spherically. When a space is to be acoustically treated, walls, ceilings, floors, and other surfaces within that space must be considered for appropriate materials.

Internal Treatments

There are four common modes of internal acoustical treatment of spaces. The use of walls and other barriers is one method of controlling sound. Air space itself is an acoustical treatment. The larger the space, and therefore the farther sound travels, the more it is absorbed. The use of soft acoustical materials on various surfaces is a major means of sound control. Acoustical clouds suspended over large open arenas is still another means of controlling sound. Extending walls beyond dropped ceilings can afford better acoustical control than stopping internal walls at the dropped ceiling height.

External Treatments

External background noise or unwanted sound from outside the teaching space also must be planned for acoustically. Unwanted sound or noise may be transmitted into the room by means of ventilating ducts, pipes, and spaces around pipe sleeves. The transmission of sound through ducts can be reduced by the use of baffles, or by lining the ducts with sound-absorbent, fire-resistant materials. The ducts also may be connected with canvas or rubberized material to interrupt the transmission through the metal in the ducts. Pipes can be covered with pipe covering, and spaces in the pipe sleeves can be filled. Sound also can be transmitted through the walls, floors, and ceilings. This can be reduced to a desirable minimum by the proper structural design and materials. In conventional wall construction, alternate studs can support the sides of the wall in such a manner that there is no through connection from one wall surface to another. This sometimes is known as double-wall construction. The space inside the walls can be filled with sound-absorbing material to further decrease sound transmission. Sometimes three or four inches of sand inside the walls at the baseboard will cut down the transmission appreciably. Likewise, sound absorption blankets laid over the partitions in suspended ceiling construction frequently can reduce the sound from one room to another. Machinery vibration or impact sounds can be reduced by use of the proper floor covering and/or by installing the machinery on floating or resilient mountings. "Sound locks," such as double walls or doors, are needed between noisy areas and adjoining quiet areas. Improper location of doors and windows can create noise problems. It is imperative to consider the location of the facility itself and also to consider the placement of internal areas of the facility for sound control. Placing physical education and sport facilities in a semi-isolated area of a school helps control acoustics. This same theory needs to be applied internally within the sports facility. The placement of "noisy" areas such as weight-training areas, aerobic areas, locker rooms, swimming pools, gymnasiums, and spectator areas must be planned for in relation to quiet areas such as classrooms and offices.

It is not good acoustical planning to have a weight room above or next to a classroom. Care must be taken in the maintenance of acoustical materials. Oil-base paint reduces the sound-absorbent qualities of most materials. Surface treatment for different acoustical materials will vary. The most common treatment of acoustical-fiber tile is a light brush coat of waterbase paint. Most acoustical materials lose their efficiency after several applications of paint.

Exterior Treatments

Sometimes the exterior of a space or building must be acoustically treated. If a gym is located on the landing flight path of a local airport, or if it is located next to a fairly steep grade on a major truck thoroughfare, exterior acoustical treatment might be needed. Utilize the same acoustical principles as inside, with an exterior twist. Keep hard surfaces such as paved areas and parking lots to a minimum. Use shrubbery, trees, and grass wherever possible. Walls, solid fences, berms, and water are all good exterior acoustical items. It is important to plan for acoustics and sound control in a variety of ways. Think spherical, think internal, think external, and think exterior in order to best acoustically treat a facility.

Many acoustical problems can be avoided from the start if sound transmission concepts are kept in mind at the initial planning stage of a recreational facility. Keeping noisy spaces separated from quiet areas is easy to achieve in the initial design phase; correcting problems due to improper space adjacencies is more difficult. Even the best sound-isolating construction techniques cannot completely solve the problems created by improper adjacencies. The final results will always be more acceptable if serious acoustical issues are solved in the schematic design" (Whitney & Foulkes, 1994, p. 58).

Other Electronic Technologies

Electronic Communication

The standard communication tools in sport and recreation facilities include an intercom system and two-way audio systems to various activity and office spaces. Additionally, telecommunication has advanced tremendously, allowing for the integration of telecommunications devices for the deaf (TDDs), text typewriters (Tts) or teletypewriters (TTYs), and faxing capabilities to standard telephone installations.

Audio and visual communication needs for the 21st century require many facilities to be integrated for computerization and satellite/cable television reception. Any space that might utilize a computer or video connection should be part of this integration. Fiberoptics are the current standard for such integration. However, a thorough planning process will also consider future technologies. Minimally, appropriate conduits should be installed during facility construction to afford the broadest range of future choices.

Within spaces, especially those used for instruction, the planning process should also consider the electronic technologies required for distance education, such as two-way audio and visual communication tools (I see you-you see me, I hear you-you hear me), computer links for internet and computer presentation, conference-call telephones, digital ds and laser disc players, LCD overhead projectors, keypads for student responses, etc.

Scoreboards and Electronic Timing Systems

The science and technology of scoreboard design has changed the entire sport spectator experience. A scoreboard can not only provides spectators with game data, but it can be configured with a giant video screen and message system, and integrated with the facilitiy sound system (Bradley, 1994). Large indoor sports arenas are using giant four-sided scoreboards that literally pay for themselves with sponsor advertisement. If timing is your need, recent advances in video systems allow sport races to be judged fairly, regardless of the hundreths of seconds between finish times or the failure of conventional timing equipment (Goldman, 1995).

Elevators and Other Hydraulic Lifts

Elevators and other hydraulic lifts are necessary design features of many sport and recreational facilities. Besides offering physically challenged users federally mandated access to facilities, they enhance the ability of staff to move equipment (possibly reducing the potential for worker-related injury), and they facilitate deliveries. To determine if your facility is required to provide elevators and/or hydraulic lifts, refer to Chapter 8: Designing for Inclusion.

Security

Effective facility security begins with building designs that control access to the facility through a main-desk control area and egress-only doors that do not allow re-entry. A number of electronic technologies can further affect the security of a facility, including

■ entrance/exit (access/egress) controls and alarms such as card systems; electronically controlled doors and gates, check points with metal detectors (magnetometers), and annunciators (egress door alarms). Card access "can also be used to gather enlightening and useful data on the facility's clientele" (Patton, 1997, p. 64);

■ closed ciruit television monitor systems; and

■ motion-sensor alarms for controlled areas such as pools (sensor detects water motion).

It is important to remember that as electronic technology is applied to security, any power failure will disrupt such systems unless they are backed up by battery or emergency generator systems.

Emergency Alarms

Facility safety begins with smoke/fire and emergency alarm systems that appropriately warn building users in the event of fire and warn facility staff in the event of a life-threatening emergency. Smoke and fire alarms include those that are user-activated, smoke- or heat-activated, and water-pressure-activated (usually found in wet sprinkler systems). Special alarms for the pool or other exercise area have been designed to notify facility staff in the event of a life-threatening emergency; these are staff activated. Weather or disaster notification will usually utilize an existing intercom system to warn facility users. Emergency alarms, especially those that are designed to warn users, must also be backed up by battery or emergency generator systems.

Emergency Generators

With an increasing reliance upon some of the above electronic technologies and/or the use of air-supported roofs for indoor sport spaces, power outages will require an emergency generator back-up to ensure the safety of facility users and the well-being of the facility. There generators need only provide minimum levels of power (to be determined by the specifications of the facility) to be effective tools. However, where electric energy is at a premium, it is possible that some sport or recreational facilities will plan on a bank of generators to provide unrestricted energy service.

Trends in Electronic Technologies

Illuminated game lines on sport courts and underwater pace lights in swimming pools are two of the more innovative uses of electronic technology. And,

with laser technology, it is only a matter of time before distances in field events, etc. are determined using a laser rather than a tape measure.

Web-to-telephone calling combines the convenience of IP telephony [IP telephony is the use of an IP network to transmit voice, video, and data] with the flexibility of traditional calling. The Web-to-phone interface works via a Web browser plug-in that can be downloaded from a Web site. There is no software to buy. Once call center components are in place, people browsing a company's Web page can use the Web-to-phone plug-in to speak over the Internet directly with someone (Dresner, 1998, p. 42).

Finally, Cable Microcell Integrators (CMIs) are in the news, turning terrestrial television cable systems into communications networks for overcrowded cellular systems. A unique characteristic of CMI technology is the independence of signal coverage from the number of base transceiver stations. In other words, service providers need not build excess capacity to handle occasional, but regular, surges in demand. "Fans and reporters who clog a professional football stadium eight Sundays out of the year might require an additional cell tower/base station to use their telephones, but a CMI system can handle this demand surge without an additional physical plant" (Ackerman, 1997, p. 21). Facility planners may well consider checking with area wireless communication companies to see if a CMI installation is appropriate for their facility. It is fair to say that as technology looks to the 21st century, new ideas will result in wonderful advances.

Mechanical (HVAC)

"Mechanical engineering includes the science and art of the formulation, design, development, and control of systems and components involving thermodynamics, mechanics, fluid mechanics, mechanisms, and the conversion of energy into useful work" An overview of mechanical engineering at Berkley, 1998 [on-line]. Unless facility planners are trained as mechanical engineers, it is likely that the planning process will include one or more of these specialists. Still, there are still a number of important concepts that planners should understand as they address a sport or recreational facility. This section provides an overview of those mechanical engineering concepts.

Environmental Climate Control

Environmental climate controls related to heating, ventilation, and air-conditioning affect the quality of our work and play environments. Sport and recreational facilities, specifically, must provide an environment where fresh air is exchanged and effectively circulated, where air temperature and humidity are controlled in a manner that promotes good health, and where the air quality is safe.

There are four factors that, when combined, give an optimal thermal environment:

1. radiant temperature where surface and air temperatures are balanced,
2. air temperature between 64° and 72° F,
3. humidity between 40 and 60 percent, and
4. a constant air movement of 20 to 40 linear feet/per/min. at a sitting height.

These factors must all be considered to achieve an optimal thermal environment. However, they are only part of the planning that must go into providing indoor environments that are technically sophisticated and also enhance user effectiveness, communication, and overall user satisfaction—the best definition of an "intelligent building" (Tarricone, 1995). Intelligent buildings link such technologies as "HVAC, fire detection and alarm, access, security, elevator, and communication systems to one computer . . . " (Tarricone, 1995). Although this section deals specifically with HVAC, it is important to consider the advantages of creating the intelligent building with a single computer control. This concept has been implemented in both new designs and retrofits. The key is planning ahead.

Additionally, a number of building design characteristics directly impact the optimal thermal environment in buildings. These interior and exterior characteristics include:

. . . building envelopes that reduce heat loss and gain through insulation, barriers and thermal mass; moisture control through vapor barriers and external shading devices; properly glazed windows that have good insulating and glare reduction properties; double- or triple-paned glazed windows that prevent condensation on windows. [a facility that is] adequately sized, ventilated, cooled, and designed for easy access, future growth, and reconfiguration; and passive heating, cooling, and lighting methods" (Myers, 1997, p. 52).

And when considering building automation and HVAC systems, there are additional choices to make, including

. . . centralized or decentralized HVAC systems; centralized heating systems (such as boilers) and cooling systems (such as chillers and cooling towers); ventilation systems; substation sensing; humidification and dehumidification control; facility energy management programs such as Night Cycle, Night Purge . . . (Myers, 1997, p. 53).

What used to be simply stated as HVAC has advanced beyond the basics of heating, ventilation, and air-conditioning to environmental air quality. Dr. James E. Woods, co-chair of the Healthy Buildings/IAQ '97 conference, said, "Building professionals require an understanding of the conditions that contribute to the collection of indoor air pollutants by the design of certain systems or through the operation and maintenance of a building's HVAC equipment and systems" (Giometti, 1997, p. 2).

Facility ventilation is directly tied to the indoor air quality (IAQ). The IAQ is a product of the quality of the fresh air introduced into the ventilation system and the quality of the existing indoor air that is recycled.

Typically, HVAC systems re-circulate as much conditioned air [warm or cooled] as is allowed by health and building codes in order to maximize energy efficiency and reduce the size of mechanical and electrical equipment. In facilities where health and indoor-air-quality issues are paramount [or in facilities where no energy-recovery system exists] as much as 100% of the conditioned air may be exhausted. Such facilities in climates with significant indoor/outdoor temperature differentials in winter and summer can exhaust tens of thousands of dollars in otherwise reclaimable energy (Fabel, 1996, p. 36).

Energy recovery in HVAC systems involves transferring heat from one airstream to another. In summer months, intake air at a higher temperature rejects heat to cooler exhaust air prior to being mechanically cooled by the chilled-water or direct-expansion coil [of the air-conditioning process]. Conversely, during the winter, intake air is warmed by transferring heat from exhaust air. Approximately 60% to 65% of the available sensible heat may be recovered; latent heat is not recovered (Fabel, 1996, p. 36).

"Use of mechanical dehumidification systems is an efficient way to manage room humidity and contribute to better air quality" (Flynn and Schneider, 1997, p. 57).

Sick building syndrome is the result of poor indoor air quality. The basics of IAQ seem to minimally require that potential indoor pollutants are controlled at the source and that the building's HVAC system—including all the equipment used to ventilate, heat and cool; the ductwork to deliver air; and the filters to clear air—are well maintained (Anonymous, 1998). In older or poorly designed HVAC systems that merely recirculate conditioned air without exhausting enough air and/or introducing enough fresh air, the IAQ can become compromised. Indoor air quality can be managed, even in older systems, if a proactive approach is used to address the IAQ issues. This includes controlling pollution at its source, from both indoor and outdoor sources.

One low-cost way to prevent IAQ problems is to stop potential sources of indoor air pollution where they originate. Known as source control, this process manages pollutants by removing them from the building, isolating them from people by using physical barriers, and controlling when they are used (Anonymous, 1998, p. A10).

Another approch is maintaining ventilation systems that which include

all the equipment used to ventilate, heat, and cool; the ductwork to deliver air; and the filters to clean air. HVAC systems significantly affect how pollutants are distributed and removed from a building. These systems can even act as sources of pollutants, through dirty or damp air filters or uncontrolled moisture in air ducts or drip pans. Proper maintenance of HVAC systems not only contributes to better IAQ, but can decrease operating costs since properly maintained equipment runs more efficiently" (Anonymous, 1998, p. A10)

And, John Spengler of Harvard University, at the same conference, reported that

...changes to a building's design during construction often contributes to indoor air pollution. In the process of constructing a building, changes are made at the construction site that affect the design of the HVAC system and produce unrecognized problems which later have implications on the quality of indoor air" (Giometti, 1997, p. 2).

All of this does not negate the need for design planning that includes the choice of heat or energy source: fossil fuels (coal and heating oil), and heat or energy alternatives (propane/natural gas, wood, electricity, below grade heat-pumps, and solar or wind energy). Factors in these choices include geographic location and heat and energy resource availability. Additionally, the start-up or installation costs of some systems are more expensive, but cost less to operate and/or maintain over the long term; and vice-versa for installation of other systems. If the facility is located in a rural area with clean extended air make sure windows are openable. In polluted enviornments such as urban ares, non-openable windows are acceptable.

Propane/natural gas, solar, power wind, heat pump, and nuclear power are all considered "clean" sources of heat or energy and are worth thinking about, considering the depletion of ozone in our atmosphere of fossil fuels. These sources of heat or energy may ultimately reduce operating costs including the "scrubbing" of exhausted air from your building. Finally, the actual selection and type of heating, ventilation, and air-conditioning should consider the economy of operation, flexibility of control, quietness of operation, and capacity to provide desirable thermal conditions.

Planning for the Future

Jim Moravek (1996) has further complicated the decision-making process with the concept that technologies no longer outlast buildings:

Designing for flexibility in buildings rather than for specific technologies is the best way to overcome obsolescence of the structure in the future. Buildings often outlast the most current technologies, and new consideration must be given to making buildings and technologies work together. Flexible design has both structural and system components. Buildings require ample space—both vertically and horizontally—so old systems can be removed and new systems installed quickly, without affecting structure, exits, or life-safety systems. Heating, ventilating, and air-conditioning (HVAC) and power-distribution systems need the capacity to service existing loads and the ability to respond to future requirements" (p. 28).

However, no project can be considered without planning for HVAC. And this planning should be done by an engineering professional and based upon the technical data and procedures of the American Society of Heating, Refrigerating and Air-conditioning Engineers, Inc. (ASHRAE) and appropriate federal regulations.

An example of an ASHRAE standard appears in Appendix L. This standard, and others, are in constant review by the ASHRAE based upon various changes in technologies and government regulations. The ASHRAE also issues position statements, e.g., Indoor Air Quality Position Statement (approved by ASHRAE Board of Directors, February 2, 1989). This ASHRAE document states the importance of indoor air quality and energy conservation and its impacts, with the belief that "indoor air quality should be maintained at levels expected to protect occupants from adverse effects and discomfort" (p. 1).

Challenges and Future Trends in HVAC

The challenge of HVAC is clearly to increase energy savings without compromising indoor air quality. The most recent enhancement is mandated "open architecture" under the Building Automation and Control Networks (BACnet) standard. TheBACnet standard, initiated by ASHRAE in 1987 and passed in 1996, establishes a communications protocol to facilitate information sharing between HVAC equipment and controls from multiple vendors. Additional trends in HVAC involve continued research in evaporation cooling and the compliance with ever-changing standards, i.e., federal and ASHRAE.

■ Summary

The technologies of mechanical and electrical engineering are constantly changing. However, facility planners should become familar with concepts related to the function of HVAC, sound, and lighting, etc.

Learning Objective 1: The student will be able to understand lighting and sound in terms of functionality.

Lighting and sound should serve in the creation of extraordinary places to work and play. They can enhance the quality of experiences, or cause harm. When planning sport and recreational facilities, lighting is expected to effectively and efficiently illuminate indoor and outdoor spaces. Properly designed, lighting should improve visibility and safety, heighten performance, intensify the moment, and aesthetically usher users to and from the facility. Quality sound and acoustics will treat the user to a friendly environment where activity is encouraged, learning supported, and distractions kept at a minimum. For lighting and/ or sound to be safe, simple, and efficient it must function for the user. Therefore, a significant investment in planning is the best way to ensure a successful program.

Learning Objective 2: The student will be able to understand the challenges of implementing electronic technologies.

Electronic technology is advancing faster than we can raise the money to purchase, install, utilize, maintain, and subsequently replace its products. Because some technologies are essential to good communication and management, facility planners must become knowledgeable about these advances and to ask such questions as these: What do we really need? What is required? What can we wait on?

Learning Objective 3: The student will be able to understand climate control concepts in terms of efficiency.

Climate control relates to heating, ventilation, and air-conditioning; the humidity and air quality in our systems; and the overall environmental air quality. Climate control begins with the facility design, is further enhanced with engineering, and is finally affected by the way we control the tools. The goal continues to be an environment where fresh air is exchanged and effectively circulated, where air temperature and humidity are controlled in a manner that promotes good health, and where users are provided environmental air quality that is safe.

Learning Objective 4: The student will be able to recognize the administrative responsibilities related to electronic technology and climate control.

Although everyone benefits or suffers from the planning and implementation of a facility's electronic technologies and climate control, the facility manager responsibile for providing users with a technologically sensible and environmentally sound system. The user of the 21st century will continue to place higher and higher demands upon our limited resources. Administratively, we must own our decisions and responsibly invest in our collective future. We must strive to acquire the knowledge and understanding necessary to manage our facilities successfully.

Learning Objective 5: The student will be able to understand the challenges of sick building syndrome.

The essence of sick building syndrome is poorly managed indoor air quality resulting from poor mechanical design, poor IAQ management, and/or a poor source of air. The basics of good IAQ require that potential indoor pollutants be controlled at the source, and that a clean and well-maintained HVAC system deliver air that is properly conditioned.

Learning Objective 6: The student will be able to understand both the trends and new technologies in electrical and mechanical engineering.

The trend in electrical and mechanical engineering is to develop new technologies that improve or enhance the quality of life in our work and our play. We must manage both the acquisition and implementation of these new technologies to avoid poor choices, thereby making responsible use of our limited resources.

■ Case Study

The architect for a sport facility at a small college is looking for your recommendation concerning the lighting requirements for the facility's swimming pool area. The area (diagramed below) has both a spectator balcony area, program space on the pool deck (under the balcony), and the main pool (25 yards by six competitive lanes). Current U.S. Swimming and collegiate championships require 100 foot-candles at the water's surface; therefore, the architect was planning to meet this level of lighting.

1. What should be the footcandles at the water's surface? Should the facility rely on the U.S. Swimming and collegiate standards?
2. What other sources of light must be taken into consideration when determining the facility's needs?
3. Are there different levels of lighting required for competition pools and leisure pools?
4. Would you choose direct or indirect lighting, and why?
5. If you choose direct lighting, what types are appropriate and what other considerations are important?
6. If you choose indirect lighting, what types are appropriate and what other considerations are important?
7. Detail a maintenance program for your recommended lighting system in this facility.

■ References

Ackerman, R. K. (1997). Television cable provides wireless communications. **Signal, 51**(8), 21-23.

Anonymous (1998). **Making indoor air quality work for you. P.M. Public Management, 80**(8), A10.

An overview of mechanical engineering at Berkeley. (1998). [On-line]. Available: http://www.me.berkeley.edu/overview.html

Dresner, S. (1998). Just pick up your computer and dial. **Communication News, 35**(2), 42-43.

Fabel, B. K. (1996). Airing out the facts on HVAC energy recovery. **Consulting-Specifying Engineer, 20**(3), 36.

Fenton, B. C. (1997). Super sound. **Popular Mechanics, 174** (5), 44-46.

Flynn, B., & Schneider, R. (1997). Energy audit. **Athletic Business, 21**(8), 51-52.

Giometti, A. (Oct. 10, 1997). Healthy buildings/IAQ '97 reports. [On-line]. Available: http://204.7184.20/about/iaqwrap2.htm

Goldman, J. D. (1995). A sense of timing: Electronic timing and scoring takes meet management to new level. **Aquatics International,** May/June, 12-13.

Hall, K. (1993). Sound. **Fitness Management,** May, 42-44.

Hall, K. (1991). Aerobics sound. **Fitness Management,** May, 34-36.

Hunsaker, S. (1998). Getting pool light right. **Athletic Business, 22**(3), 51-54.

Moravek, J. (1996). Preventing future shock in today's buildings. ConsultingSpecifying Engineer, 20(5), 28-32.

Murphy, N. (April 17, 1998) Biological effects of lighting—Shouldn't all you designers know about this? In **IESNA Public Forum** [On-line]. Available: http://www.iesna.org

Myers, C. (1997) Intelligent buildings require a smart pitch. **Facilities Design, 16**(9), 52-55.

Patton, J. D. (1997). Mission: Control—A host of passive and active control measures bring security and comfort within the grasp of recreation facilities. **Athletic Business, 21**(8), 63-68.

Rabin, J. (1993). Locker room bulletin board: Light years ahead. **Athletic Management,** July, 6.

Rogers, J. (1996). Light. **Athletic Business, 20**(5), 51-54.

Rogers, J. (1994). Bright prospects: Proper field lighting can bring a sunny outlook to every night game on the gridiron. **Athletic Business, 18**(12), 53-56.

Tarricone, P. (1995). The brains behind the building. **Facilities Design & Management, 14**(11), 54.

■ Suggested Readings

Beck, P. E. (1991). M/E engineering for Chicago's new baseball gem. **Consulting-Specifying Engineer, 10**(1), 32.

Berg, K. (August 23, 1997). Energy savings from lighting system. In **IESNA Public Forum** [On-line]. Available: http://www.iesna.org

Bradley, M. (1994). Buying time. **Athletic Management,** June/July, 36.

Conroy, M. W., & Zamojcin, R. (1997). BACnet standard can lead to smart building O&M. **Facilities Design & Management,** 16(9), 32.

Dilouie, C. (1996). Lighting & HVAC interactions add up to savings. **Facilities Design & Management,** 15(7), 29.

Eisenhower, C. (1998). Outdoor air introduction & humidity control. **Engineered Systems,** 15(4), 66-70.

Ellis, R. T. (1998). Many variables go into defining commissioning cost. **Engineered Systems,** 15(9), 42.

Galland, L. (1998). Sick buildings, sick people. **Total Health,** 20(2), 38.

Grubb, D. & Diamantes, T. (1998). Is your school sick? Five threats to healthy schools. **The Clearing House,** 71(4), 4.

Hall, K. (1995). A healthy sound. **Fitness Management,** April, 42-43.

Hansen, W. (1998). Going by the book. **Engineered Systems,** 15(7), 72.

Horsey, K. (August 19, 1997). Energy management through lighting retrofit. In **IESNA Public Forum** [On-line]. Available: http://www.iesna.org

Johnson, D. (1998). A cure for sick buildings? **The Futurist,** 32(5), 12-13.

Jonas, C. (1998). Coaching in the digital age: The four classes of technical innovations. **Coach & Athletic Director,** 67(9), 30.

Maloney, J. (1998). Digital TV. **Digital (a supplement of Time),** 3(3), 50-53.

Maloney, L. J. (1990). Sports lighting: The design process. **Athletic Director,** February, 24-25.

Peterson, J. A., & Tharrett, S. J. (1991). Making your facility environmentally sound. **Fitness Management,** October, 44-46.

Rembert, T. C. (1998). Living filters. **E. The Environmental Magazine,** 9(4), 44-45.

Siderius, K. (May 3, 1998). Metal halide is closing the gap. In **IESNA Public Forum** [On-line]. Available: http://www.iesna.org

Spicer, R. C. (1998). Watch out for other sources. **Engineered Systems,** 15(5), 46.

Stone, K. B. (1997). The how-to in facility and upgrade. **Broadcast Engineering,** 39(5), 92-98.

Thieken, H., & Love, G. (1995). Let there be light. **Athletic Management,** April/May, 26-30.

Watkins-Miller, E. (1997). Energy codes under scrutiny. **Buildings,** 91(2), 62-63.

Whitney, T. W., & Foulkes, T. J. (1994). Keep the noise down! **Athletic Business,** 18(12), 57-60.

Woods, P. M. (1998). Is your job making you sick? **Essence,** 29(5), 46-50.

Wright, M. (1997). DVD: Breathtaking sight and sound, significant challenges. **Boston,** 42(17), 47.

Web Sites:

American Society of Heating, Refrigerating, and Air-conditioning Engineers (ASHRAE): http://www.ashrae.org

American National Standards Institute (ANSI): http://www.ansi.org

Electrical Engineering: WWW Virtural Library Index: http://arioch.gsfc.nasa.gov/wwwvl/ee.htm

Electric Technology Resource Center (ETRC) at the University of South Florida, Tampa, FL: http://www.teco.net/etrc.htm

Illuminating Engineering Society of North America (IESNA): http://www.iesna.org

CHAPTER 12

Signage — Environmental Graphics

Ed Turner, Appalachian State University

Learning Objectives

After reading this chapter, the student will be able to

■ understand the importance of signage,

■ know how to design effective signage,

■ know the type of sign needed for a given situation,

■ understand the cost and maintenance factors of signage, and

■ understand the place of graphics in facility architecture.

Introduction

Signs and signage have been a part of facilities for years. Until recently, signage has been relegated to a back seat in facility planning. Today's large and complex facilities, great number of sport facility users, guidelines of ADA and OSHA, and a litigation-oriented society are all moving signage to the forefront. Increasing computer technology, the use of electronic signs, and architectural signage will be the basic areas to develop rapidly in the near future.

Type of Signs

The basic purpose of all signs is to impart information. The information that is imparted varies with the type of sign used. Five categories of signs are presented in this discussion:

■ warning, danger, caution, and emergency,
■ notice and standard operational signs,
■ directional signs,
■ rules and regulations, and
■ sign graphics.

Even though signage is divided into five distinct categories, the groups overlap. A sign could fall into just one category or it might fall into two or three categories depending on its purpose and the type of information it is conveying.

Importance of Signs

Signs are an essential part of a facility and should be an integral part of the planning process in a new facility. Signs have come a long way in the last decade. New materials, colors, and graphics have changed the signage world. Many architectural firms now refer to a signage system as the "environmental graphics" of a facility. All sport facilities include a wide variety of signs. It is important to identify facility entrances and to direct individuals to concourse levels and seating sections. Rest rooms, concession areas, first aid stations, locker areas and exits must be clearly designated. Information concerning parking area locations must be located near exits. Traffic flow direction information must be imparted by external facility signage. The parking area, if large, will need to be sectioned off by effective signs.

Elevator and room designation signs must have raised-letter markings for visually impaired users. The center of these signs should be placed 60 inches above the floor. Other facility signs should also have raised letters, even though at this time this is not an ADA requirement. Where diverse populations exist, signs must be designed in multiple languages. The use of international graphics can also help in designing signage for multiple languages.

Many sports facilities are large, sprawling one- or two-floor facilities. If the facilities have been around for a number of years, there is a good chance additions have enhanced them. Add-ons can create logistic nightmares, and signs become paramount to direct individuals through a facility. It is not uncommon to find sport facilities with interiors of more than 200,000 square feet. Sport facilities are also among the most heavily used facilities on campuses and related sites. Large sport facilities, such as arenas and stadiums, with large numbers of users, call for a well-planned signage system.

Figure 12.1 Handicap signage.

Designing Signs

If at all possible, design your signs during the planning process of your building and its surroundings. If you are renovating or making additions to your building, this is a prime time to plan for all new environmental graphics in your complex. Make your signs an aesthetically pleasing part of your facility.

Signs need to be simple and understandable, and they need to attract the facility users' attention. Placement, size, shape, repetitiveness, color, and graphics are all important in designing simple, understandable signs that attract user attention.

Placement

Again, signs must attract the facility user's attention. A well-placed sign maximizes its effect. Signs need to be placed in the appropriate area and at the appropriate place and height to have the greatest impact on the user. For instance, a sign stating "No Skateboards Allowed in the Building" will not make its point in the interior of the building. This sign needs to be placed at all building entrances, so it can be seen before one enters the building with a skate-

board. On the other hand, the sign "No Food or Drink in the Weight Area" needs to be posted outside the weight area as well as inside the weight area.

It is also important to place signs in normal sight lines. Placing signs too high, too low, or off to the side makes them less viable. It is important to remember that sight lines vary according to the users' height. Signs for young users should be placed lower than signs for adults. Individuals in wheelchairs need signs placed in their sight lines.

Signs may be on a wall, a ceiling, a floor, suspended, free standing, on columns, or on doors. In some instances, a sign may be on two or more surfaces. It may be partially on a wall and continue on to an adjacent wall or floor. The effect of a sign on multiple surfaces is eye-catching thus attracts attention.

At times signs must be repetitive within a facility. An example of repetitive signage is in an indoor racquet court battery. If there are eight courts, some signs will need to be repeated eight times, once at each court. An example of repetitive signage is "Eye Guards Are Mandatory!"

Materials

Signs may be an integral part of the facility as a permanent part of the structure (painted on walls or other surfaces or formed of tiles of different colors, or they can be attached to a surface by a frame or brackets. Architectural or permanent signs are recommended whenever possible. These signs not only impart information, but they are also an aesthetically pleasing part of the structure of your facility. If architectural signage is used, and planned for carefully,

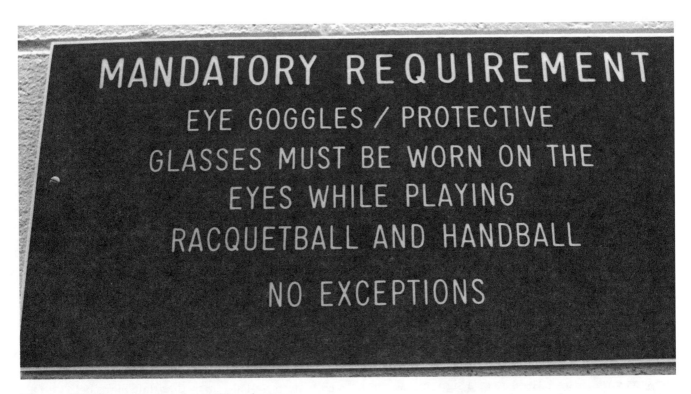

Figure 12.2 An example of repetitive signage.

few signs will need to be added to your facility. It is paramount to plan in advance for successful architectural signage. If mistakes are made in the planning process, they become permanent mistakes, or, at the least, costly mistakes to overcome. Even with the greatest of planning of architectural signage, some will have to be non-permanent and some will have to be later additions. As time and facility use change, signs may need to be changed and updated. Architectural signs are usually made of "like" building material. For instance, a painted wall would have a painted sign, or an asphalt tile floor would have different size, texture, or color inset tiles that form a sign.

Signs may be made of wood, metal, tile, paper, glass, paint, and plastic, or any combination of these. Signs may be electrified, such as lighted signs, billboards, score boards or "running" sign boards. Electrical signs are more expensive than non-electrical signs. An electrified sign, on the other hand, stands out and attracts attention to itself. Electrical signs must be in a secured location since they are easily broken and expensive to repair. If electrical signs are to be used, one must plan carefully for electrical outlets or electrical hookups directly in relation to sign placement. Extension cords running from signs to an electrical power source is unaesthetic, unsafe, and unacceptable.

Shape, Color, Size, and Graphics

Signs do not have to be rectangular in shape. Rectangular signs do afford maximum use of space if the signs contain only words. Other sign shapes have the ability to be eye-catching and/or informational. Take the eight-sided red sign at the end of the street, attached to a metal post, located on the right-hand side of the street. When one sees this sign, it does not need to be read—the octagonal, shape location and color indicate "STOP." Explicitedly shaped signs, can be used in facilities to impart specific information. An example is that all pentagonal signs could indicate classrooms, all circular signs could indicate laboratories, and all diamond-shaped signs could indicate offices.

An X-shaped sign immediately signals a prohibition ("No Diving," "Do Not Run") just by the shape of the sign itself. The idea of effective sign shapes follows a recent international trend toward standard pictorial signs. Facility signs now must convey a universal message to many ethnic populations. A sign featuring graphics will not alienate a facility's foreign users as much will as a sign in English.

Color, as the red in stop signs, can also be an important aspect of signage design. All signs of one color can indicate storage and housekeeping areas. Color in signs can be used to attract the attention of facility users. Bright-colored signs on a bland wall surface, in most instances, attract attention. A colored

Figure 12.3 *An example of signage found in most swimming areas which displays the depth of the water and a reminder not to dive.*

sign will attract a users' attention better than a black and white sign. Think color in your signage theme.

Signs vary in size. The size of a sign, in itself, is a method of drawing the attention of facility users. A very small sign indicating exit is easily seen suspended from the ceiling or wall. Sometimes a large sign is important to house important information and to draw the facility users' attention. "No Lifeguard on Duty -- Swim at Your Own Risk" is effective as a large sign. Vary the size of your signs depending upon the information to be imparted, and make use of sign size to attract attention.

The size of a sign's images and print also are instrumental in how the information is relayed. Words and graphics that are too small make the reader work harder and can result in the sign being ignored.

Just as some signs can be too wordy or hard to comprehend, too many signs posted in a small area also create problems. An overabundance of signs may cause the reader to miss a certain sign that has been placed in a busy array of other signs. Separating and isolating signs is important to their overall effectiveness (Turner, 1994).

The content and message of a sign must be designed for the educational level(s) of the individuals using the facility. Content of a sign for a university will read differently than the content of the same sign for an elementary school. In all cases, it is important to keep signs as *simple* as possible. The simpler a sign, the easier it is to read and understand its content, thus making the sign more effective.

The old adage that a picture or graphic is worth a thousand words is still accurate for sign design. Using a clown figure to enhance a "no clowning" sign in a weight area attracts attention to the sign. A facility

user's attention is drawn to attractive signs, and adding graphics to signs makes them more attractive. A little humor about a serious matter can impart important information.

Signage and the Three Groups It Serves

So far we have directed our attention to signs for facility users. Again, these signs are important to the very large number of individuals who use a facility. They are important to impart information, give direction, indicate warnings and danger, and state rules. The litigious society we live in has placed an increased importance on proper and effective signage in our facilities. Effective signage may prevent an injury from occurring or it may be important in one's defense during a trial. Think of effective signage as both a money- and stress-saver when it comes to litigation.

All of this -information is important not only to facility users, but also to facility staff. Signs help staff acclimate more quickly and safely to their jobs. Good location, direction, and rules signs help new employees adapt to a new environment.

Hazardous materials are found in many facility laboratories and swimming pools. Bio-hazardous waste, toxic chemicals and gases, and nuclear contaminants must be handled routinely by staff. Signage is paramount in these areas. Signs should first indicate the hazard and second inform the employee how to work safely with it. Containers for hazardous material and waste need effective signage in the form of visible labels. Signage should also be placed in break room and work room areas to inform employees of various performance and safety requirements.

Emergency personnel is the third group of individuals for whom signage must be well planned. All of the discussion above is also paramount for emergency personnel. Additionally, signs must be planned so that emergency personnel can find their way easily in a complex facility to save lives or minimize injuries. Emergency personnel should not have to wander around a building before they can complete their job. Clear and effective signage in laboratories and pools indicating specifically what hazardous materials were present when an injury occurred can save a life.

Signage Maintenance

Since signs have been placed throughout the facility, they need to be maintained. If you have electronic signs, you will have to replace bulbs and other elec-

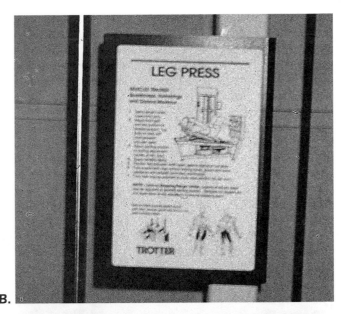

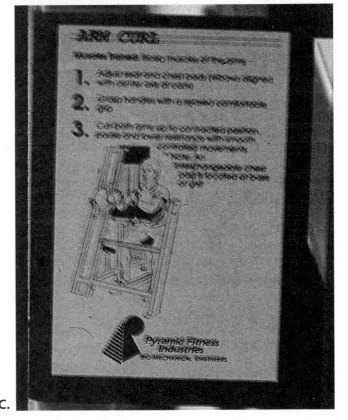

A.

Figure 12.4 A. Too many signs. **B-C.** Specific signs.

Figure 12.5 Using humor to input information. (photo by Lee Bloom).

tronic components. Plan for this in sign placement. Most of these signs can be maintained from the front, however, there are some electronic signs that need to be maintained from the rear or from the top. If electronic signs are small, they are easy to remove and repair. If they are large, heavy, and, cumbersome, one needs to plan for this in their placement. A large rear-entry sign can be placed over a planned opening in a wall to provide easy access for repair work to the rear of the sign, without having to remove it.

Figure 12.6 Emergency signage information.

Signs can break. Breakage may be accidental or intentional. Signs in sport complexes, in particular, take much abuse. Balls rackets, and bats hit them, and they need to be protected. If possible, place signs out range of abuse. Placing signs higher and in areas away from projectiles and hitting devices will help to prolong sign life and reduce maintenance costs. However, signs must be placed in harm's way. Polycarbonate sheeting works best for signs that need to be encased or covered with a clear material. Be careful, though, because the glossy finish of the sign or its covering can create glare problems and take away from its effectiveness as well as provide an unwelcome distraction. Wire mesh (the kind that sometimes covers clocks in school gymnasiums) works as an effective cover on signs whose faces would not be sufficiently protected by plastic sheeting, such as those in the path of balls and other flying objects. If a sign must be covered with a mesh cage, make sure it can still be seen well enough to convey its message (Turner, 1994).

Signs can also be defaced. By placing them out of reach, one can avoid some defacing. Use materials in the construction and covering of signs that deter defacing. The use of polycarbonate sheeting and other slick surfaces will help keep sign defacing at a minimum.

Signs need to be cleaned on a regular basis. Fingerprints, smudges, dust, and other airborne particles need to be removed from signage on a regular routine. Electronic signs need special attention to regular cleaning so they function at an optimal level. Soiled signage of any type can curtail the amount of information imparted by the sign. Set up a regular cleaning schedule.

Miscellaneous Considerations

Signage cost will vary with materials, size, number of signs, and whether the sign is electronic. As mentioned previously, it is suggested that you include your signage cost as a part of your facility construction cost. In some cases, parts of construction costs are bid separately, and signage may be bid after the facility is built. This is not recommended. Repetitive signs will reduce costs since quantity of the same product reduces the cost per unit. It is suggested that you purchase high-quality products, even though these products may be initially more costly than low-quality items. Over the lifetime of facility signage, quality products cost less.

The geographic location of the sports complex will dictate which and how many languages will be used in signs. Inner-city locations and other locations with high ethnic populations will need additioanl languages on signs.

Signs can be affixed to surfaces either permanently or semi-permanently. The method will depend on the philosophy of the design and use of the facility. It will also depend on the longevity of the signage. "Exit" signs, for example, are rather permanent, whereas rules and regulation signs may change over time. Signs may be attached flat onto a surface or they may extend out perpendicularly or horizontally. Protruding signs are sometimes needed for visibility and code adherence. One of the problems with protruding signs is that they are more susceptible to breakage than flush-mounted signs.

Keep in mind that the size and shape of some signs might be dictated by local, state, and federal regulations. Check local fire and building codes to make sure a particular facility includes all the required signs. Additionally, check with state and national offices for signage needed to meet ADA and OSHA requirements.

In some instances, a one-sided flush-mounted sign is not sufficient. Signs suspended from the ceiling may impart information on two, three, or four sides. Protruding signs usually give information on two or three sides. As signage is designed, always think about using signs with multiple sides. Some signs will need to be free-standing in order to be moved from one area to another area of the facility. An example of a free-standing sign would be, "Caution:

Figure 12.7 Art Graphics.

Wet Floor." Free-standing signs can take any shape or form; however, the most common is a two-sided pyramid shape.

Sponsorship in sport complexes is common, and sharing a sign with a sponsor is common in athletics (i.e. rolling sponsorship signs). Scoreboards and other signs are either purchased or rented by sponsors so they can advertise on the sign. This concept of sponsorship can be used for signage in other areas — not just for athletics. Sponsorship or sharing of signage is an important concept and should be studied carefully for all signage in a facility. In any case, sign sponsors and sport complex directors can both obtain mutual benefits by this partnership (Turner, 1994).

A rather new area in signage design is the use of art graphics in a sport complex. Art graphics are permanently painted or inset materials that are designed as integral parts of the facility. Various images can be placed on surfaces in the form of sports art, murals, or basic signage. These images are color-coordinated with the color scheme of the facility. The images can bring life, motion, brightness, and attractiveness to an otherwise plain and dull facility. Currently, there are a number of companies that do art graphic work for sport complexes. Computer imagery is now enhancing the appearance of sports art, graphics, and murals.

■ Summary

Effective signage in a sports complex must be well planned. Signage should be an integral part of facility design. There are various types of signs that will be used in any given sports complex. Well planned, easily maintained, well designed, cost effective signs can help prevent injury and related problems.

Learning Objective 1: The student will be able to understand the importance of signage.

The large size and complexity of today's sport complexes along with a litigious society requires proper signage. Proper signage helps prevent injuries and allows for better traffic flow and rule enforcement.

Learning Objective 2: The student will be able to design effective signage that is simple and understandable.

Signs should be placed so that they can be easily seen and read.

Learning Objective 3: The student will be able to select the type of sign as dictated by need.

Various situations within a sports complex will dictate the type, size, shape, construction material, and placement of signage.

Learning Objective 4: The student will be able to select signs based on cost-effectiveness and ease of maintenance.

Planning for signage in the initial design of a facility will save money over a span of time. Make use of sponsors to help defray signage costs. Use materials in signs that keep maintenance to a minimum.

Learning Objective 5: The student will be able to use art graphics in sport complexes.

Sport art, murals, and computer-generated media should be used in sports complexes. Large and vast walls can be made aesthetically pleasing with the use of graphics.

■ Case Study

A. Divide into groups of three. Each group should visit one portion of your sports complex. (foyer-lobby area, weight area, arena area, etc.). Discuss all aspects of signage in that area. Take notes about the signage. Include signage design, types, placement, construction, shape, use of color and/or graphics, and size. Determine the group of facility personnel for which the signs were designed. Discuss how the signage in this area could be improved upon. Take notes on this discussion. Return to the classroom and share the signage findings from your area to among your the rest of the group. Each group of three then reports to the cass. If time permits, the class can visit each area as the relevant group makes its report.

B. Select a large blank surface in the sports complex. Have the students design an art graphics package for this surface in order to enhance the aesthetic value of the surface and the facility as a whole.

■ Reference

Turner, E. (1994). Vital signs. **Athletic Business**, 18, 65-67.

■ Suggested Readings

Farmer, P.. et al. (1996). **Sport facility planning and management.** Morgantown, WV: Fitness Information Technology.

Horine, L. (1995). **Administration of physical education and sport programs.** Madison, WI: Brown and Benchmark..

Athletic Business, published monthly by **Athletic Business,** Publications, 1842 Hoffman Street, Suite 201, Madison, WI 53704, (608) 249-0186.

CHAPTER 13

Sports Medicine and Rehabilitation

Christopher D. Ingersoll, Indiana State University ■ Thomas H. Sawyer, Indiana State University

Learning Objectives

After reading this chapter, the student will be able to

■ outline the purpose of a sport medicine and rehabilitation facility,

■ describe the various spaces utilized in a sport medicine and rehabilitation facility, and

■ explain the various pieces of equipment needed in a sport medicine and rehabilitation facility.

Introduction

Sport medicine and rehabilitation facilities are common features in indoor and outdoor athletic complexes. Their specific purposes depend on the type of activities and facilities they support. In multipurpose recreational facilities, they often serve as first aid stations for recreational athletes. In athletic facilities, they serve as comprehensive athletic medicine facilities for interscholastic, intercollegiate, Olympic, or professional athletes. If housed in a community they may serve the "weekend warrior." Proper planning and an understanding of the essential components of a sport medicine and rehabilitation facility will make it more effective when completed.

Purpose of a Sport Medicine and Rehabilitation Facility

The activities to be performed in a sport medicine and rehabilitation facility (SMRF) should guide its overall configuration. While the specific activities performed in a SMRF are subject to institutional preference, certain activities are performed in all such facilities. These include team preparation, injury evaluation, injury treatment, injury rehabilitation, and administrative functions. It is important to understand these activities before building or remodeling a structure to house them. The actual square footage for each space will vary depending on the number of athletes using the facility at peak times. Generally, these spaces can never be too large. The more space, the better for servicing the athlete.

The Ideal SMRF at an Institution with an CAAHEP-Accredited Athletic Training Program

The components of this facility will include (1) team preparation area, (2) injury evaluation/treatment space, (3) rehabilitation area, (4) wet space, (5) maintenance area, (6)storage space, (7) office area, (8) examination space (office #2), (9) computer/study/conference area, and (10) classroom (see Chapter 15).

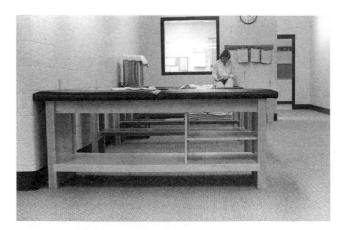

Figure 13.1 Team preparation area, DePaul University.

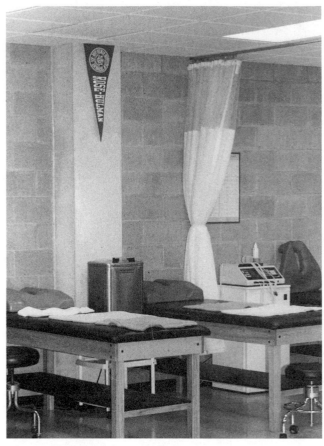

Figure 13.2 Injury evaluation/treatment area at Rose Hulman Institute of Technology.

The needs for each of these areas will be outlined to assist the planner in developing an appropriate floor plan. The environmental requirements will be uniform, including heating, air conditioning, ventilation, and humidity control.

The team preparation area will have tile floor with an appropriate number of floor drains, treatment cabinets with formica tops, a recessed waste receptacle, drawers, and shelves (see figure 13.1). The ceiling height in this area should be 10 feet minimum preferably 11 to 12 feet with fireproof ceiling tiles. The walls should be constructed of blocks and painted with an epoxy paint. There should be a deep, double-basin, stainless-steel, sink in this area. The lighting should be direct, using flourescent tubes. Electrical outlets should be located on all the walls every six feet, and those around the sink should be GFI rated. Finally, this area should have a biohazard waste container and double door entrance and/or exit.

The injury evaluation/treatment area needs different spaces and equipment when performing injury evaluations as well as treatments. The injury treatment portion of this space has three types of activities going on at once, including therapeutic modality applications and manual therapy. Typically, this space includes numerous treatment tables. The tables are used to examine body parts and to do special tests on joints, and to treat various types of injuries. There should be a suspended curtain system that can be utilized for privacy when necessary. Between each table will be a smaller moveable cart to transport therapeutic equipment (e.g., ultrasound machine, muscle stimulator, etc.) and store supplies (see Figure 13.2). The specific needs of this space include a ceiling made of fireproof tiles, with a minimum height of 10 feet,

preferably 11 to 12 feet; cabinets for storage and a deep double-basin, stainless-steel sink; rubberized roll-out sport surface such as Mondo7; block walls with epoxy paint; electrical outlets at each treatment site and above the counter on either side of the sink, all GFI rated; direct flourescent lighting; biohazard waste containers; and double doors entering the area.

The rehabilitation area includes space for therapeutic exercise equipment. This area should be separate from other areas in the complex because of the noise level and the movement of the athletes exercising. The needs of this area include a rubberized roll-out sport floor surface such as Mondo7; free weights; mechanized strength training equipment for exercising shoulders, arms, backs, hips, thighs, knees and ankles; electrical outlets on all walls every six feet; indirect flourescent lighting; a 10 foot ceiling with fireproof tiles; soundproofing in the block walls which are that is painted with epoxy double-door entrance and/or exit; audio system and possibly a video system; and adequate space for running, jumping, and throwing activities.

Figure 13.3 Wet area at Rose Hulman Institute of Technology.

The wet space or hydrotherapy area generally includes whirlpools, ice machines, therapeutic pools, refrigerator, and storage area for large drink containers. This area needs such things as non-slip tiled floor, walls, and ceiling; a ceiling height of 10 feet; an appropriate number of floor drains; recessed plumbing for whirlpools; recessed electrical supply for whirlpools, ice machines, and refrigerator (all GFI rated); storage area for drinking containers; a deep double-basin stainless-steel sink with storage; extra ventilation and humidity control; indirect flourescent lighting; and a close location to the athletic trainer's office so constant visual contact can be maintained.

The maintenance area is where broken equipment is stored and repaired. The needs for this area include shelving; work table; concrete floor with a drain; block walls painted with epoxy; two 8-foot roll-up door entrances (internal and external); ceiling height of at least 8 feet with fireproof tiles; enhanced ventilation; deep double-basin, stainless-steel sink with storage; electrical outlets on all walls a strip above the work bench, and a work bench light; direct flourescent lighting; and storage space for an electric golf cart with an electric charger.

The storage space can never be too large. The needs of the storage space includes humidity control (to protect the tape stored in this area), lockable cabinets, shelves of various heights and lengths, concrete floor, direct flourescent lighting, block walls painted with epoxy paint; double-door entrance or at least a 36-inch door; and allocation adjacent to the trainer's administrative office area.

The office area contains all medical records and serves as the administrative hub for the SMRF. The

Figure 13.4a Water container storage.

Figure 13.4b Ice storage.

needs of this area include a space no smaller than 220 square feet; a location adjacent to the wet and storage areas and a sight line to all other areas in the facility, electrical outlets on all walls, phone outlets, computer outlets, lockable storage cabinets, rug floor, block walls, ceiling height of 8 feet with fireproof tile, and lockable file cabinets.

The examination space is the second office area but also is used as a physician's examination room. The needs of this space include everything suggested for the office area above, examination table, and single sink basin with storage above and below.

The computer/study/conference area will be used by the athletic training students. This space should be no smaller than 220 square feet. The needs of this space include tables for computers and printers, a conference table, shelving for a small library, and appropriate furniture for relaxing and studying. On the outside wall of this area there should be storage lockers for the students' books, coats, etc.

The classroom design should include considerations outlined in Chapter 15.

General Considerations for the SMRF

A number of specific considerations for the SMRF have been discussed. Now some general considerations need to be outlined for the planners of a SMRF. These considerations include the following: The SMFR needs to be located adjacent to team locker rooms. The SMFR needs to be located on an outside wall for easy access to outside sport facilities and emergency medical vehicles. A circular drive should be designed for loading and unloading injured athletes. The entranceway from the circular drive should have a double door that can be operated automatically (similar to a handicapped entranceway) at street level. A janitorial closet and storage area should be located adjacent to or within the SMRF with a large sink and floor drain basin. The SMRF should have a security system that can be utilized when the area is not in use.

Equipment Considerations for the SMRF

The SMRF contains a variety of different and expensive pieces of equipment. This equipment includes (1) free weights C bars, rubberized plates, dumb bells, dumb bell racks, weight trees, weight benches, and squat racks; (2) mechanized strength training apparatus to exercise the following muscles or joints C shoulder, arm, back, abdominal, hip, upper leg, knee, lower leg, ankle, etc.; (3) biohazard waste containers; (4) whirlpools; (5) hydrotherapy pool; (6) portable x-ray unit; (7) ice machines; (8) refrigerators;

(9) portable water containers; (10) electric golf cart; (11) muscle stimulator(s); (12) hydrocollator(s); (13) ultrasound machine(s); (14) dynamometers (e.g., Cybex7, Biodex7, etc.); (15) computer(s), printer(s), monitor(s), and a scanner; and (16) audio equipment.

◼ Summary

The health of athletes is extremely important for a successful athletic program for any organization, amateur or professional. The planners for the SMRF should regularly consult with staff athletic trainers during the planning phase to ensure the construction of a sound facility for treating and rehabilitating athletes.

Learning Objective 1: The student will be able to outline the purpose of a sport medicine and rehabilitation facility.

The sport medicine and rehabilitation facility is designed to maintain and improve the health of varsity athletes, weekend warriors, and student recreators. The SMRF is designed to aid athletic trainers who prepare athletes for practice and games, treat injuries, and rehabilitate injured athletes.

Learning Objective 2: The student will be able to describe the various spaces utilized in a sport medicine and rehabilitation facility.

The various functional spaces within the SMRF include team preparation, injury evaluation/treatment, rehabilitation, wet area, maintenance space, storage, office, examination room, conference/study space, and classroom.

Learning Objective 3: The student will be able to explain the various pieces of equipment needed in a sport medicine and rehabilitation facility.

The SMRF has equipment for the following purposes: (1) therapeutic modality applications (e.g., muscle stimulator, ultrasound machines, and dynamometers), (2) therapeutic exercise (e.g., free weights and mechanized strength training units), and (3) hydrotherapy (e.g., whirlpools and hydrotherapy pools).

◼ Case Study

Colby College has recently received a large donation to construct a multipurpose athletic and recreation facility. You have been the athletic trainer at this institution for the past five years. Your current athletic training room is very small and deep in the center of the old physical education complex. This new facility will be constructed on the fringe of the outdoor athletic facilities. You have been asked to develop a state-of-the-art sport medicine and rehabilitation complex to service the college's athletic and recreational sports program. You have been told that no expense will be spared . You have an open checkbook. Develop a detailed "wish" book for the architects to develop an appropriate floor plan to meet the needs you describe.

■ Suggested Readings

Rankin, J. & Ingersoll, C. (1995). **Athletic training management: Concepts and applications** (p.195-211). St. Louis, MO: Mosby.

Ray, R. (1994). **Management strategies in athletic training** (p. 111-137). Champaign, IL: Human Kinetics.

Secor, M.R. (1984). Designing athletic training facilities or where do you want the outlets? **Journal of Athletic Training, 19**:5, 19-21.

Notes

CHAPTER 14

Ancillary Areas

Hervey LaVoie, Ohlson LaVoie Corporation, Denver, Colorado

Learning Objectives

After reading this chapter, the student will be able to

■ identify ancillary area specialists to be included on the development team,

■ describe design considerations for locker room facilities,

■ explain the concepts of wet and dry areas, and

■ describe the various amenities to be included in ancillary areas.

Introduction

The information in this chapter is intended to assist planners, designers, and administrators in their efforts to create superior locker rooms and training, administrative, laundry, storage, and maintenance facilities. This category of functional uses is referred to as ancillary areas. These are support functions for the primary building attractions such as gymnasiums, pools, and fitness floors. The guidance offered by this chapter will support, not replace, a normal and rigorous planning and design process.

This chapter will aid the planning and design of ancillary facilities by identifying many of the questions that must be asked, along with variables that should be considered as the project team responds to the unique circumstances of each project, each site, and each community of users.

Actual design recommendations for specific solutions will be avoided because the professional planning/design team that follows the analytical guidelines and considerations brought out in this chapter will be well prepared to reach their own conclusions.

Asking the right questions is an essential part of recognizing the best answers.

Design of ancillary areas will require input from the following specialists who are commonly represented on a facility development team:

■ *Owner's project manager:* This individual or company is assigned responsibility to represent the interest of the owner and manage the diverse parties of the development team for the duration of the project.
■ *Facility planner/programmer:* This individual or company is responsible for analyzing the needs of the project owner and producing recommendations as to the mix and magnitude of uses.
■ *Architect:* This is the individual or company responsible for taking the work of the facility planner/programmer and creating a building to accommodate the functional requirements and to express the desired image and aesthetic statement.
■ *Construction cost authority:* This is the individual or company responsible for predicting the cost re-

quired to create the desired building and site improvements.

■ *Operational consultant:* This individual or company is responsible for managing the facility, operating the business, hiring staff, creating programs and providing financial controls. The operational consultant provides input related to staffing, management, maintenance, marketing, specialized FF&E (fixtures, furnishings and equipment), and other operational issues that affect design of ancillary areas.

■ *Component suppliers:* Providers of facility components are the manufacturers of the special products and equipment that will be included in the facility. They are an essential source of information regarding proper application of their products.

For each ancillary area, the following variables will be examined and discussed:

■ issues of size, quantity, and dimension;
■ issues of location and relationship (adjacent/proximate, remote);
■ access and circulation considerations for all users—staff, guests, disabled, users and/or members;
■ matters of style, image, and color;
■ issues of materials, finishes and function;
■ engineering issues regarding lighting, HVAC, and plumbing;
■ gender-specific requirements and other user needs;
■ requirements for expansion and adaptability; and
■ balance of cost vs. benefit.

The most significant variable affecting ancillary areas is that of facility type. As the title of this book suggests, there are many types (and sub-types of facilities), including athletics (sub-types for different sports), physical education (sub-types for different age groups: elementary, junior high, high school, and college), and recreation/fitness (sub-types for university, municipal, and private).

In addition, many facilities try to wear two or three hats; that is, their mission is to serve the programming needs of a variety of users—varsity athletics, intramural athletics, and physical education, for example. Proper design for ancillary areas will be driven by the particular needs of the overall facility type. Therefore, this chapter will discuss locker rooms in general, and then distinguish between the design of locker rooms for specific types of facilities.

Clearly, planning and design of locker rooms should vary according to facility type. Similarly, other kinds of ancillary areas will vary in use and function

for different facility types. The planning and design of training rooms, administrative offices, laundry facilities, storage rooms, and maintenance areas must be viewed in light of their fit to the overall facility mission.

Ancillary, by definition, refers to functions that are necessary to support the primary program activities for which the facility is created.

Locker Rooms

The term "locker room" encompasses a multitude of components and facilities. More than a room of lockers, the modern locker room accommodates a broad range of functions related to dressing, storage, grooming, personal hygiene, therapy, social exchange, information handling, aesthetics, comfort, and safety.

Many aspects of locker room planning and design must be considered in the light of the overall facility type. However, there are some basic principles that apply to all types of locker room regardless of the user. These are the planning and design considerations for such basic components as lockers, toilets, showers, amenities, and grooming stations.

Essential to the accommodation of these functions is the proper location of the locker room within the overall facility and the proper relationship of these components within the locker room itself. Figure 14.1 illustrates the primary relationship that must be considered in properly locating the locker room within the overall facility. Whenever possible, the locker room should be on the same floor as the aquatic facilities.

One wall of the locker room block is often designed to be an outside wall, located so future expansion also can be accommodated by means of internal conversion of "soft" use space, which is located deliberately next to the locker room. Soft space refers to uses that require little or no special provisions (such as plumbing or expensive finishes), and therefore is space that is easily vacated and converted to locker room expansion. Examples include storage rooms, offices, and meeting rooms.

Another approach to expanding existing locker rooms is, for example, to convert the existing women's locker room into an expansion of the men's locker room and at the same time construct an entirely new women's locker room as part of the new building addition.

All but the most primitive locker rooms will have lockers, showers, grooming stations, amenities, and toilet facilities. Figure 14.2 provides a conceptual illustration of the proper relationship of these components. Conventional design wisdom has held that

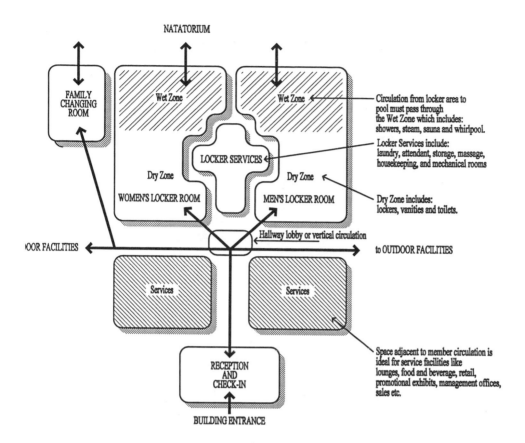

NATATORIUM

FAMILY CHANGING ROOM

Wet Zone

Wet Zone

Circulation from locker area to pool must pass through the Wet Zone which includes: showers, steam, sauna and whirlpool.

LOCKER SERVICES

Locker Services include: laundry, attendant, storage, massage, housekeeping, and mechanical rooms

Dry Zone

Dry Zone

Dry Zone includes: lockers, vanities and toilets.

WOMEN'S LOCKER ROOM

MEN'S LOCKER ROOM

OOR FACILITIES

Hallway lobby or vertical circulation

to OUTDOOR FACILITIES

Services

Services

Space adjacent to member circulation is ideal for service facilities like lounges, food and beverage, retail, promotional exhibits, management offices, sales etc.

RECEPTION AND CHECK-IN

BUILDING ENTRANCE

LOCKER LOCATION

The location of the Locker Rooms within the facility is important. After going through the Reception area users pass through retail areas, promotional exhibits and lounges which help guide them to the locker rooms.

Figure 14.1 The relationship of locker rooms to the facility.

consolidation of plumbing facilities to minimize piping runs is a primary consideration in the layout of locker rooms. In truth, the actual economies of clustered plumbing are not significant, and the resulting consolidation of plumbing can be quite contrary to the principles of user-friendly design. Toilet facilities backed up to showers will save minor quantities of piping, but can result in a mix of wet bare feet from shower traffic with dry street shoes from toilet room users. Lavatory grooming counters near toilets and urinals again will save minor amount of piping, but may result in a loss of privacy for toilet users and a compromised atmosphere for personal grooming functions.

Locker Room Size

The number and size of lockers required will help determine the size of the overall changing room, as will the inclusion of special amenities such as steam rooms, saunas, jacuzzis, baths, lounges, or massage

rooms. A range of 7 to 15 square feet per locker is possible, depending on locker size and other variables. The best way to program accurately the locker room size appropriate for a given facility is to calculate the user capacity of destination attractions (such as gyms, courts, fitness floors, etc.) during peak usage periods. Total occupancy factors are listed below:

■ Aerobics rooms: 1 person per 45 square feet
■ Gymnasium: 12 persons per game court
■ Racquet courts: 2 persons per court
                       (except four for tennis)
■ Lap pools: 4 persons per lane
■ Exercise pools: 1 person per 50 square feet
■ Fitness floors: 1 person per 65 square feet
■ Walk/jog tracks: 1 person per 20 linear feet

When an allowance is made for those who are waiting to participate and those who are finished and showering (25% to 45% of user occupancy), the total demand for lockers can be predicted. Estimates of the

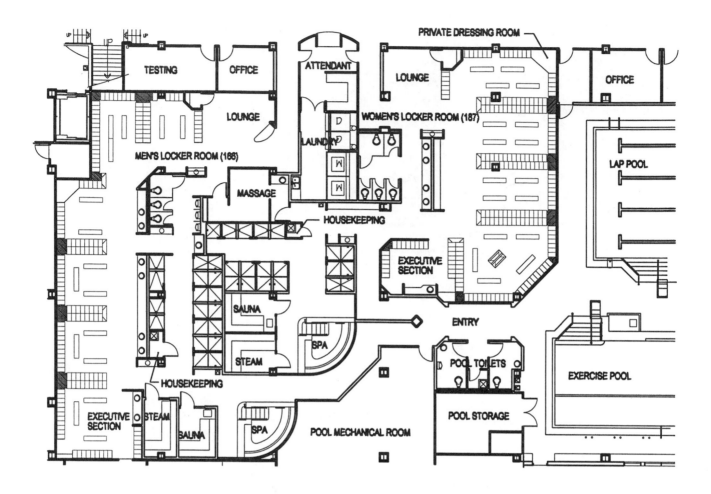

EXAMPLE OF LOCKER ROOM LAYOUT

In this Chicago athletic club the coordination of lockers, wet areas, dry areas and support facilities can be seen. Maintaining separation between men's and women's facilities while entering and exiting through common gatew and promoting user-friendly flow patterns is key to good locker room layout.

Figure 14.2 Conceptual illustration of locker rooms to the facility.

gender ratio of users will allow the total locker count to be distributed between men's and women's locker rooms. Unless special circumstances dictate otherwise, the size of locker rooms for men and women should be the same and each locker count equal to 60 percent of the total predicted demand. This will account for use patterns that may occasionally result in unequal participation according to gender.

The planning objective is to provide a balance between locker room capacity and the total floor capacity of primary facility attractions such as fitness equipment, aerobic rooms, and gymnasiums. An imbalance in this ratio will result in unused capacity in either the locker rooms or the primary attraction areas.

Locker Area

The locker area must provide more than securable storage compartments. A good locker layout will allow for a multitude of functional considerations:

- Provide seated dressing space removed from main circulation paths.
- Provide at least one private dressing cubicle for users with special privacy needs.
- Equip at least one dressing/locker cubicle for use by the disabled.
- Determine size and quantities of lockers by analysis of anticipated user groups. In most cases, it is appropriate and sometimes required to provide

facilities of equal size for men and women, boys and girls.

■ Adhere odor control by means of natural or induced locker ventilation. Management procedures that encourage proper care of locker contents by users also will be beneficial.
■ Provision of swimsuit dryers can help prevent odors and locker damage caused by storing wet suits.
■ Efficiency of locker count can be improved by increasing the height of locker tiers, but caution must be exercised to avoid having lockers so high that they are out of reach of the expected user.

Figure 14.3 illustrates a range of possible locker and bench configurations with recommended dimensions.

When possible, avoid vast and deep maze-like arrays of lockers. Shallow perimeter layouts around two or three sides of a wet core are more user friendly. This will allow shorter distances between locker and shower as well as improved navigation. Supervision of locker areas may be an important consideration for some facility types where vandalism or victimizing behavior can be expected. Avoid hidden alcoves where unobserved activities can take place.

The main locker room access will need to accommodate heavy two-way traffic from users carrying bags or equipment. Therefore, locker room doors should be avoided, and if required by code or security purposes, may be held open with code-approved electro-magnetic devices connected to the fire alarm system. Doorless locker room entries are a commonplace answer to the need for unobstructed two-way circulation in high-volume facilities such as stadiums and airports. The necessary visual screening of locker room interiors can be accomplished easily by blocking sight-lines with corners or wing-walls. These visual baffles should be provided even if doors are installed.

Materials and finishes should be selected with the anticipated maintenance in mind. A variety of impervious floor surfaces is available–ceramic tile, etched terrazzo, vinyl, and synthetics. Considerations should be given to slip coefficients, cleaning techniques, color selection, aesthetics, and cost. If the daily maintenance program will consist of a hosing down or pressure wash, the best choice of flooring for wet areas is ceramic tile or a liquid applied synthetic. Such materials should be fully covered at walls.

Other floor material options for locker room dressing areas include wood and carpet. Wood floors have been used successfully as an accent in upscale club locker rooms. Carpet is a good choice for locker room dry areas, when a proper maintenance program can be assured. The benefits of carpet (quiet, soil-hiding, colorful, durable) will be lost if it is not vacuumed twice daily and steam cleaned at least four times annually. Odor control of carpet can be enhanced by specifying a factory-applied anti-microbial treatment and taking care in planning wet areas to prevent excessive tracking of water to the carpet.

Ceilings should provide for good light diffusion and acoustic absorption. Moisture resistance is also important. If a lay-in grid ceiling is to be specified, an aluminum grid will resist moisture-induced corrosion. Lay-in panels must have sufficient stiffness to resist "pillowing." The aesthetic impact of ceiling treatment should not be overlooked. Consider the possibility of lighting the locker room indirectly by mounting strip light fixtures on top of lockers. Emergency lighting must be provided. Natural day lighting by means of skylights, glass block, or obscure glazing will enhance the locker room environment.

Lockers

Locker systems are available in a variety of materials: painted steel, mesh steel, wood, and plastic laminate-faced particle board or fiber-resin board. The selection of locker material and construction is a function of several factors. Considerations include:

■ cost,
■ appearance requirements,
■ resistance to abuse,
■ resistance to corrosion,
■ availability of desired size and accessories, and
■ installation requirements.

Wood may be most suitable in applications where a traditional or luxury image is desired, and the risk of vandalism is small. A variety of wood stains and door designs are available.

Painted steel may be most suitable in non-corrosive environments where an upscale ambiance is not desired, and abusive behavior is possible. A variety of standard and custom paint colors are available. Choice of door styles is somewhat limited, but painted steel lockers have been the standard choice for applications where economy, utility, security, and durability are the prime concerns.

Plastic laminate-faced board may be the most suitable choice where economy and upscale image are both important. A rich variety of colors, textures, and finishes is readily available for door faces. This type of locker is also a good choice for moisture resistance. Many optional accessories such as shelves, hooks, rods, and mirrors are available. The choice of locking systems must consider the operational challenges and security issues associated

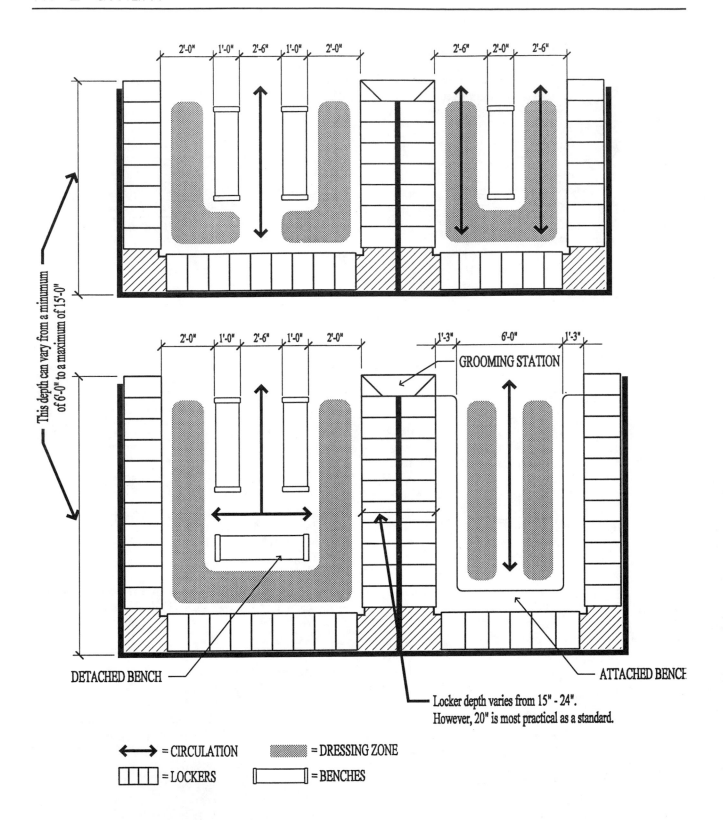

2'-0" 1'-0" 2'-6" 1'-0" 2'-0"   2'-6" 2'-0" 2'-6"

This depth can vary from a minimum of 6'-0" to a maximum of 15'-0"

2'-0" 1'-0" 2'-6" 1'-0" 2'-0"   1'-3" 6'-0" 1'-3"

GROOMING STATION

DETACHED BENCH

ATTACHED BENCH

Locker depth varies from 15" - 24".
However, 20" is most practical as a standard.

◄──► = CIRCULATION   ▒▒▒▒ = DRESSING ZONE

⊞⊞⊞ = LOCKERS   ▭ = BENCHES

LOCKER ALCOVE OPTIONS

Figure 14.3 Possible locker and bench considerations.

Figure 14.4 FLow patterns.

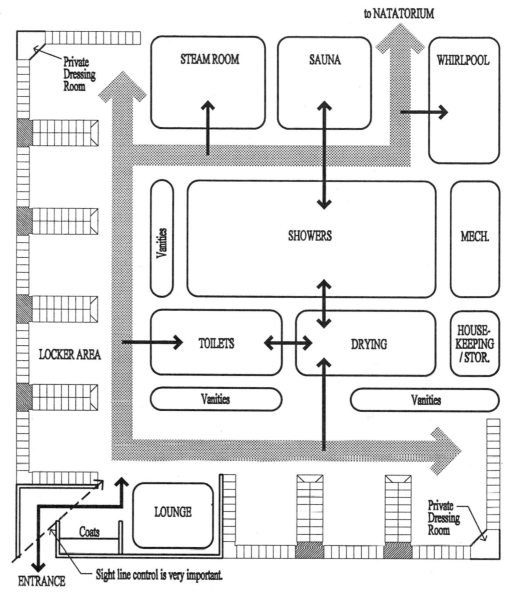

LOCKER ROOM FLOW PATTERNS

with keys, padlocks, cards, and combinations. A new generation of keyless locking systems is becoming available and can offer unique benefits to both users and facility managers.

Toilets

Careful consideration must be given to location of locker room toilets. Will they be used under wet or dry conditions? Are the locker room toilets intended to serve the natatorium? If so, users will be wet, and toilets must be located in the locker room wet area. In this case, other toilet facilities should be provided for

"dry" users in the dry zone of the locker room or in a location outside of the locker room. In any case, mixing dry and wet toilet room traffic should be avoided. Street shoes on wet slippery floors are a hazard, and the presence of bare feet on wet floors that have been soiled by street shoes is unsanitary and unpleasant. Possible solutions are

■ dry locker room toilets near the entry and wet toilets near the shower area,
■ dry locker room toilets near the entry (for convenience of use from outside the locker room) and wet toilets within the natatorium, and

■ dry toilets outside the locker room and wet toilets near the shower area.

Other considerations for planning and designing locker room toilets include the following:

■ Sufficient quantities of fixtures (water closets and urinals) should be provided to meet peak user demand. The unique circumstances of each project must be evaluated in making this determination. Rules of thumb suggest that a ratio of one water closet per 60 lockers is sufficient, but this ratio should be modified to account for special circumstances such as large group use or schedule-driven programs that result in rapid turnover of users.
■ Careful attention should be paid to toilet partition materials and construction. Problems with rusting, delamination, warping, and vandalism are common. This is not the place to cut quality to for the purpose of reducing cost.
■ Lighting of toilet stalls should be placed toward the back of the stall in the form of downlight, wall sconce or valance light. This location will provide the best lighting for cleanliness inspections of the water closet.
■ Maintenance access to piping and valves must be provided. Access panels in plumbing walls are a common solution to this need.

Showers

The quantity of showers and the corresponding capacity of hot-water-generating equipment are the most critical components of an athletic facility's ancillary areas. Shortcomings in any other component can be adapted to or in some way tolerated. Cold showers and/or long lines of people waiting for too few showers will create an extremely negative experience for the facility user.

Unfortunately, rules of thumb for shower count are not always reliable. One shower per 20 lockers is a ratio that sometimes is applicable. However, there will be cases when that ratio will result in too many or too few showers. The best approach is for the project planner to conduct an analysis of anticipated overall user capacity in the facility (similar to the process suggested above for estimating locker quantities) as the basis for predicting the peak shower-taking population at any given time. This projection will, in turn, form the basis of the mechanical engineer's calculation of flow rate and duration of hot water that must be supplied for showers.

The selection of a control valve and shower head should be considered carefully to arrive at the balance of shower quality and water economy most appropriate for a given facility and its users. Control valves can be specified for automatic shut-off, automatic temperature control, variable or fixed volume, and vandal resistance. It is desirable that shower piping and valves be accessible for maintenance and repair without destruction of the enclosing wall and finishes. Access panels can be provided and detailed to coordinate with the overall decor.

Shower rooms must be ventilated and exhausted to prevent odors and moisture accumulation. Air supply points must be arranged to minimize drafts.

A variety of shower types and layouts is possible and are illustrated in Figure 14.5.

Other general guidelines for shower planning and design include the following:

■ Provide drying area adjacent to the showering facility.
■ Provide flush-type recessed hose bibs for cleaning purposes.
■ Walls and floors of the shower enclosure must be completely waterproof.
■ Shower heads should be self-cleaning and water-conserving. Adjustability of spray and angle should be considered on a case-by-case basis.
■ Shower finishes must be impervious to water and easily cleaned. Ceramic tile, stone or etched terrazzo are good choices for floors and walls.
■ Ceilings can be finished with ceramic tile or epoxy paint.
■ Minimum spacing for gang showers is 30 inches. Shower head heights should be set according to anticipated size of users. A variety of heights can be provided if a mix of users is anticipated. Recommended mounting heights for shower heads are as follows (depending on pipe configuration, the actual height of the pipe coming out of the wall can be 4" to 8" higher than the head):

> Men: 6'-8" to 7'-0"
> Women: 6'-2" to 6'-6"
> Children: 5'-6" (or adjustable).

Other design issues affecting wet area finishes are listed below:

■ All outside corners should be rounded and joints of walls and floors covered.
■ Evaluate slippery qualities of a floor material when wet. Most manufacturers can provide a slip coefficient for their products. Avoid the use of curbs, as they can be a safety problem and an access barrier.
■ A finish material will perform only as well as its underlying support. Of the many options for wet-area wall substrate, gypsum board is the least

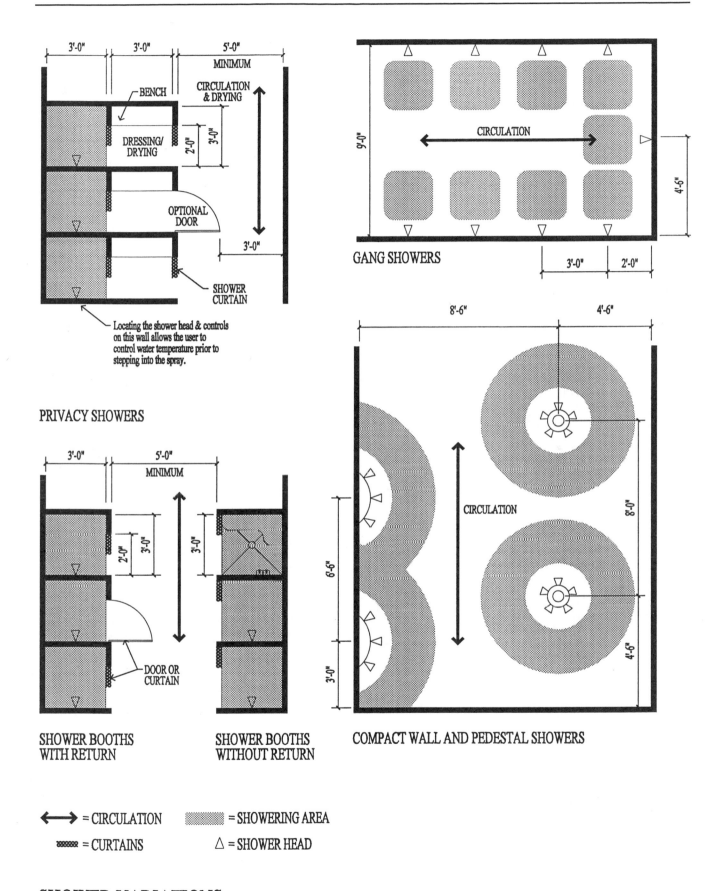

SHOWER VARIATIONS

Figure 14.5 Variety of shower types and layouts.

reliable. Masonry and cement boards are preferred.

■ Floor construction of showers and drying areas must be sloped to perimeter or center drains in order to avoid birdbath-like puddles of water on the floor.

Shower planning also must address the inclusion or exclusion of clean towel distribution, towel hooks, foot rests, amenity shelving, consumable dispensers, used towel collection, and provision, if any, of consumables such as soap and shampoo. A drying zone between shower and locker is important. This area can be equipped with floor mats and drains to prevent tracking of water onto dry-area finishes. The shower area often is positioned to serve users of indoor and outdoor aquatic facilities as well as those using locker room amenities such as the steam room, sauna, and jacuzzi bath. Users of these amenities should be encouraged by the layout and flow to shower prior to use.

Amenities

Steam, sauna, jacuzzi, and cold plunge are the amenities most often considered for an upscale locker room facility. Each of these requires careful attention to a host of planning and design considerations.

Steam Rooms

■ As a guideline, sizing should be based on a capacity factor of one person per 12 square feet or 2.2 linear feet of seat. Steam generators are sized by manufacturers according to the volume of the room.

■ Entrance doors to steam rooms will release large quantities of steam and should be located where this vapor-laden air will not damage nearby fittings and finishes, particularly on the ceiling.

■ Walls, floor, and ceiling of steam rooms must be completely waterproof and finished with non-slip ceramic tile or stone.

■ A glazed door and sidelight will improve supervision and make a more pleasant and open experience for the steam room user.

■ Slope the steam room ceiling at 1:12 to a side wall or uninhabited drip point in order to prevent condensation from dripping on users.

■ All components of steam rooms (lights, hinges, frames, fasteners, etc.) must be corrosion resistant. Plastic and aluminum usually are satisfactory. Stainless steel is not a reliable choice. Avoid painted steel at all costs.

■ Most steam room failures are related to failure of the substrate or wall structures to resist the corrosive effects of the vapor-laden air. Proven steam room construction details are published by the ceramic tile industry and should be followed carefully. Compatibility of components (substrates, bonding agents, adhesives, and finishes) cannot be taken for granted. Any substitutions must be thoroughly researched.

■ Maintenance access to the steam generator room should be available from a mixed-gender corridor so that steam equipment can be serviced without closing off the locker room. Steam room controls, other than a thermostatic sensor, should be located in a staff-only area.

■ The decision to include a steam room must be based on consideration of the operating and maintenance expense, as well as initial construction cost. Periodic staff supervision also is necessary to prevent misuse.

■ Location of steam jets and sensor must be planned precisely to minimize risk of burns from steam and metallic fittings and ensure proper temperature control and heat distribution.

■ Accessories usually include thermometer, hose bib, hose, and clock. An overhead shower head sometimes is included.

Sauna

Saunas are designed to provide dry heat at extremely high temperatures. They are less costly to install than steam rooms but often result in maintenance problems that are difficult to manage. Planning and design considerations follow:

■ Wood-lined walls, floors, and seats are the usual choice; however, tile-lined rooms are easier to maintain and can be used if a means of providing cooled seating and floor surfaces is devised. The high temperatures involved require that users be protected from contact with metal and other highly conductive materials that could cause burns. This protection can be provided by wood battens, plastic mats, or towels.

■ The main problems with wood-surface saunas are staining from accumulated soaked-in sweat and the odors that result. Use of a light colored wood will reduce the unsightliness of the staining problem. The best approach to odor control is to require use of individual towels for seating, and to use daily pressure cleaning. A sauna may not be suitable for many types of public facilities where towels and multiple daily cleaning are not provided.

Figure 14.6 Sauna.

- Glazed doors and sidelights will create a more pleasant and more easily supervised sauna.
- As a guideline, sizing decisions can be based on a capacity factor of one person per 12 square feet.
- Adequate lighting is particularly important for sanitation and maintenance.
- Commonly specified accessories are a clock, thermometer, and water supply.
- A floor drain can be provided for ease of cleaning, but it may need to be a self-priming type to prevent the sauna heat from drying out the trap.

Jacuzzi

Also know as a whirlpool bath, this amenity is a communal body of water (100-104 degrees Fahrenheit) equipped with air and water jets to create a turbulent massage effect for the immersed user. Prepackaged molded fiberglass units generally are unsuitable for the applications addressed in this book. Water quality control is the single most important issue affecting the planning and design of these facilities. Local health regulations will control many aspects of the water purification system, as well as pool and deck materials and configuration. Other considerations:

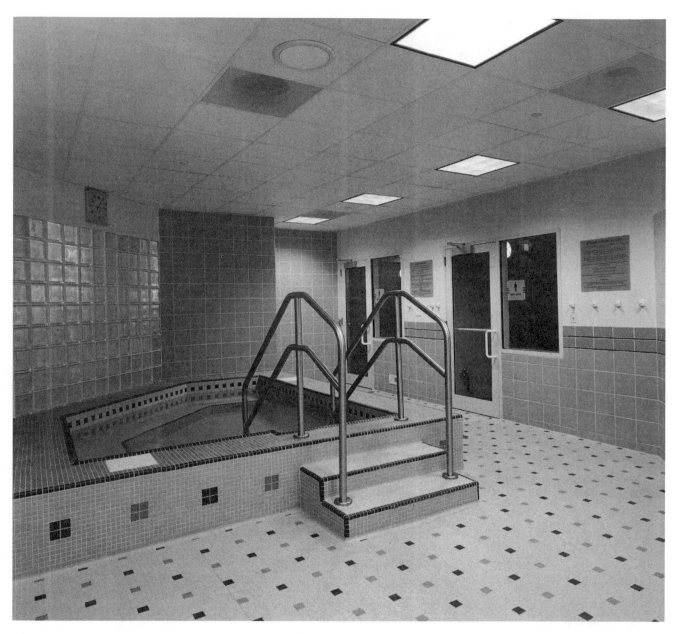

Figure 14.7 Jacuzzi.

- Capacity factors are in the range of 10 to 15 square feet per person.
- Equipment rooms should be located for easy access by maintenance or repair personnel of either gender.
- It is important to encourage users to shower before using the jacuzzi by locating showers convenient to it.
- Pool basins should be completely lined with tile to allow for frequent draining and cleaning, which are necessary to keep a sanitary and attractive body of water. Plaster-lined pools will be more difficult to clean.
- The vapor-laden air of the jacuzzi area will be made more corrosive by the presence of chlorine.

- Even stainless steel eventually will succumb to corrosion in this atmosphere.
- Aluminum, stone, plastic, glass, and ceramic tile will provide more durability.
- It is essential that air-handling systems for the jacuzzi area be designed to produce a negative air pressure relative to surrounding uses. This will prevent the migration of vapor and odor to other parts of the locker room and other parts of the facility.
- Buried piping (which requires jack hammers and shovels to access) is the most economical choice for grade-supported pools. However, access panels must be provided for cleanouts, valves, and stub-outs.

Figure 14.8 Grooming stations.

Grooming Stations

Minimal facilities for a wet grooming station are a sink with hot and cold water, a mirror, and a ground fault-protected power source. Minimal facilities for a dry grooming station are a mirror, a power source, and a small shelf. Optional enhancements of grooming provisions can include such niceties as hand-held hair dryers, wall-mounted dryers, make-up mirrors, stools, soap or lotion dispensers, face towels, paper towels, waste receptacles, and disposable grooming aids such as razors and combs. Each facility must develop its own policy regarding provision of these necessities. Will they be supplied by building management or by each individual user?

General consideration for user-friendly planning and design of grooming stations:

■ The required number of wet and dry grooming stations needed must be analyzed according to the unique circumstances of each project and gender-specific grooming practices. As a rule of thumb, total grooming stations should be approximately the same or slightly less than the shower count. A 50-50 split between wet and dry grooming stations may be varied by some planners to provide more wet stations for men (shaving) and more dry stations for women (make-up).

■ Lighting at mirrors should be arranged to illuminate both sides of a person's face. Provide a color of light that enhances flesh tones, such as incandescent or warm white fluorescent.

- Avoid locating grooming facilities with toilets or placing them too deeply into wet areas. For convenience, they should be located on the seam between the locker dry zone and the shower wet zone.
- Vanity tops must be designed for standing, stool-height seating, or chair seating depending on user preference.
- The design image of grooming stations can be used to convey the intended character of a facility. Upscale club environments should have luxurious grooming facilities. Public recreation facilities may want to convey a more modest but functional character.
- A full-length, wall-mounted mirror should be provided along the locker room exit path.

Locker Room Auxiliary Spaces

Special uses are sometimes incorporated into locker room plans to meet particular project needs. The specific requirements of each must be identified. Examples including social lounges, attendant services, shoe shine, laundry service, workout clothing service, massage, tanning, private telephone cubicles, and personal storage lockers of various sizes. The arguments for and against including each amenity should be examined by the planning team.

Locker Room Accessories

Considerations for a well-equipped locker room include an electric water cooler, clock, scale, automatic swimsuit dryer, telephone, emergency call system, plastic bag dispenser, hair dryers, and vending machines for personal grooming items or beverages.

Special Types of Locker Rooms

Family Locker Room. This is a handy name for an arrangement of changing facilities designed to serve cross-gender couples with special needs:

- Mother and a young son who is too old to join her in the women's locker room and too young to venture into the men's locker room alone,
- Father and a young daughter who is too old to join him in the men's locker room and too young to venture into the women's locker room alone,
- An elderly couple, one of whom needs assistance from the other in preparing for a rehab session or a senior exercise program, and
- An individual man or women with a special privacy need due to a surgical scar, deformity or personal preference. Family locker rooms can be used

for patient changing rooms in facilities that offer clinical services.

The family locker room is an array of individual changing rooms–each one equipped with a shower, toilet, sink and changing space. As many as five or six changing rooms can be provided. An arrangement of storage lockers and benches are provided in a spacious coed common area adjacent to the changing rooms. Grooming, showering, toilet, and dressing functions take place in the privacy of the changing rooms. Storage of clothing and final stages of dressing and grooming take place in the coed locker area. The entire facility should be fully accessible to the disabled and could in itself satisfy the legal requirement for a handicapped-accessible locker facility. Other amenities that can be included in the common area are an electric water cooler, swimsuit dryer, wet vanity, dry vanity, towel station, full-length mirror, scale, diaper-changing platform, coat rack plastic bag dispenser, telephone, waste container, and janitor closet. A selection of full-size and half-size storage lockers works well. Provide at least 10 lockers for each changing room. The family locker room generally works best with direct access to aquatic attractions.

Express Lockers. In any athletic/fitness facility, some members prefer to arrive wearing their workout/sports attire. They have no desire to use the changing/shower/grooming facilities. They prefer to return to their homes for that purpose after working out. These users need only a secure place for their purse/wallet, hat, car keys, gloves, coat, etc. There is no need to force these members into a gender-specific locker room and add to potential congestion.

Express lockers are therefore provided in an area convenient to the ingress/egress flow of members. This is a coed environment that should include a variety of locker sizes (and a coat rack in four-season climates) and comfortable benches for users who need to change shoes. Express lockers have been proven in practice to be a very cost-effective way of diverting unnecessary traffic from overcrowded men's and women's locker rooms. A locker count equal to 1% of the total membership will usually be adequate.

Staff Locker Room. The question of staff changing facilities is important. If staff use the member locker rooms, they may, in effect, displace a member. Yet providing a separate dedicated staff locker room can be space-consuming and costly. Certainly, there is a legitimate need in an athletic facility for staff changing, showering, and grooming functions as well as a secure holding area for their personal effects.

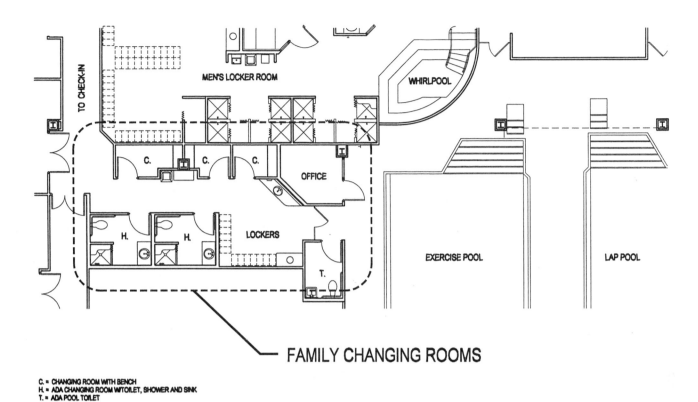

FAMILY CHANGING ROOMS

C. = CHANGING ROOM WITH BENCH
H. = ADA CHANGING ROOM W/TOILET, SHOWER AND SINK
T. = ADA POOL TOILET

FAMILY CHANGING ROOMS
scale - 1"=10'-0"

With the advent of family-oriented facilities, the need is clear for changing rooms which can accommodate cross gender couples (i.e. mothers w/ young sons or fathers w/ young daughters). Parents can help their children change into swimwear as well as get themselves prepared while monitoring their children.

Figure 14.9 Family changing rooms.

Many facilities have found it effective to provide a coed staff lounge with a mini-kitchen, basic furnishings including tables and chairs, and an arrangement of storage lockers for clothing and personal effects. A pair of private unisex changing/shower compartments can be included to allow staff to freshen up after working out without competing with the membership for limited locker/shower availability. A wet vanity/grooming station can also be included. Some management systems will prefer to have staff mingle with the membership and thus perform an ongoing quality check as they use the same locker facilities that the members do. Once again, a case-by-case determination must be made in order to fit the facility design concept to the management concept.

Official's Locker Room. Facilities designed for competitive team sport activities will require locker room accommodations for umpires and referees. These facilities are gender-specific and require a secure location away from contestant and spectator areas.

Administrative Offices

Staff offices must be barrier-free to disabled job candidates and equally accessible to men and women. Staff offices generally fall into two categories of space.

1. Back-office space is required for staff who have little or no regular contact with active facility users. Examples include accounting, administration, and marketing staff.
2. Front-office space is required for staff with supervisory responsibilities and regular contact with active facility users. Examples include management staff, sales personnel, activity directors, and counselors. Other administrative functions that require a mainstream location include

■ reception and check-in for the facility at large,
■ supervision stations for natatorium, fitness floor, gymnasium, racquet sports, and
■ faculty/coaches/instructors' offices.

The size, quantity, and furnishings required by each of these staff offices must be determined by the planner in dialogue with department heads and user representatives. Questions to be considered include:

1. What are the expected number of full- and part-time staff? What are their titles and work descriptions?
2. Which staff members require enclosed private offices? Open but private work stations? Shared work stations (concurrently or alternately)? In-office conference capability?
3. Which staff members require frequent contact with each other? With certain activity areas? With certain users?

With answers to these questions in hand, the designer can begin preparation of a space plan for administrative offices. Design considerations include

■ anticipated traffic patterns;
■ type of partition and extent of glass, if any, in walls and doors;
■ need for acoustic privacy;
■ lighting system for both ambient and task lighting;
■ provision of adequate power, communication, and computer hook ups;
■ provision of year-round heating and cooling and temperature control zones;
■ need for natural daylight or outside view; and
■ computer terminals, computer desks or tables, and wiring for main-frame and Internet access.

Office uses require supplemental spaces for support functions. The design process should bring these questions to the table for discussion by all appropriate parties. Such spaces include

■ utility area for facsimile machines, copiers, printers, office supplies, and storage;
■ employee kitchen area with coffee maker, microwave, refrigerator, dishwasher, and storage, sometimes included as part of a lunch room or staff lounge;
■ conference rooms;
■ coat closets or employee security lockers;
■ designated and specially ventilated smokers' room if operating policies allow staff smoking on premises;
■ staff-only restrooms and shower/locker rooms if desired to maintain separation from customer/users.

In addition, the location and type of central telephone reception and distribution must be determined. Many multi-feature phone systems are available. A mail and message handling system should be planned into the administrative component. Voice-mail phone systems are now an expected and convenient productivity tool for administrative staff.

Laundry

Planning and design of laundry facilities are predicated upon the workload. Just as kitchen design is based on the menu, so laundry design is based on the quantity and type of articles to be processed. Towels and athletic clothing are the most common articles needing to be laundered in a recreation facility. The unit of measure applicable to laundry equipment is the pound. Therefore it is necessary to translate the laundry workload from quantity of articles to their weight in pounds, which must be processed per hour. This is a measure of the actual dry weight of articles to be washed. Without reliable information on weight, quantity, and use rates of laundered articles, the planning of laundry facilities is pure guesswork.

Most equipment cycles allow two loads per hour. Thus it is possible to arrive at a calculation of required laundry capacity by establishing with the facility operator how many hours per day the laundry will be staffed and running. Certainly a double shift operation will get more production from a given quantity of equipment than a single eight-hour work shift, but a double shift may not be practical for other reasons. Once the workload is determined, the size and quantity of washers and dryers can be set. It generally is advisable to select machine sizes that allow at least two washing units and two drying units. In this way, a malfunction in one machine will not completely shut down the laundry operation.

The location of laundry facilities is of great importance. The best locations are close to the storage/distribution place for cleaned articles or the collection point for soiled articles. A ground-level, grade-supported floor slab is preferred for ease of plumbing and control of vibrations from the equipment. Commercial washer extractors work at very high RPMs, which can generate destructive vibrations. Most units must be bolted securely to a 24-inch-thick, grade-supported concrete slab in order to control vibration. If an on-grade location is not possible, it will be necessary to specify an extraction machine with a built-in vibration dampening system. Most manufacturers offer such a unit as an option.

Other factors to consider in selecting a laundry location are listed below.

■ The need for an outside combustion air supply for gas fired dryers may suggest a location along an outside wall.
■ The need for an exhaust flue for both gas and electric dryers may suggest a single-story location with a roof surface immediately overhead. Lint build-up in the exhaust ductwork requires that maintenance access be planned for.
■ The high volume of waste water discharge for most commercial washers requires a high-capacity trench drain recessed into the floor.
■ Consideration should be given to how equipment can be moved into and out of the laundry space. Washer and dryer sizes should be researched carefully prior to sizing and locating access doorways.
■ Accessibility by both male and female staff is needed.

The laundry planner must consider how and by what route both soiled and cleaned articles will arrive at their proper destinations. If carts are used, space must be allocated for storage or holding of extra carts at points of collection, cleaning, and distribution. Folding and sorting of laundered articles is a very labor-intensive process. However, the location of the laundry facility can be planned to allow towel-handling personnel to cover other staff functions such as locker attendant or housekeeping.

Other planning and design considerations for laundry facilities:

■ Confirm that adequate utility capacities exist for electric power, water supply, water temperature, sanitary waste, and gas.
■ Domestic washers/dryers will prove unsuitable for all but the most incidental, low-volume laundry operation.
■ Placement of washers and dryers should be conducive to a logical and efficient work flow.
■ Extractor-type washers use centrifugal force to wring maximum moisture from wet articles prior to drying. This will conserve dryer energy and save time in the drying process.
■ Laundry room floors, walls, and ceilings should be finished with a smooth, easily cleaned impervious coating that will not trap dust and lint.
■ Dryers typically have a greater weight capacity than corresponding washers. A 35-pound washer normally will be paired with a 50-pound dryer.
■ The laundry room must include space for chemical storage, carts, folding counters, a two- or three- compartment sink, and adequate service access space around the equipment.

The final pieces of the laundry puzzle are the washer and dryer themselves. Numerous manufacturers offer commercial units varying in size, power, quality, durability, design, and cost. Selection of the best manufacturers (washers and dryers are not necessarily made by the same company) requires diligent comparisons of actual cylinder sizes, types of motor control capabilities, automatic detergent injection systems, control cycles, and physical construction.

Storage Facilities

Of course, storage rooms should be sized, shaped, and furnished with racks, shelves, binds, etc., as required to accommodate the items to be stored. However, it is not always possible to predict over the life of a facility how much and what kinds of things will need to be stored. Therefore, when it comes to sizing storage rooms, it is best to err on the side of accommodation and provide at least 20% more storage space than can be justified by actual measurement of volume of articles to be stored.

Designers frequently assign the storage function to odd-shaped leftover spaces that are not necessarily conducive to efficient storage. Here are a few simple planning and design guidelines for storage rooms:

■ Within the storage room allow for circulation between actual storage space on each side. The depth of the storage space must be appropriate to the item stored so that it may be retrieved without repositioning intervening stored items.
■ Storage room doors should open out from the room and swing flat against adjacent walls. Double-wide unobstructed door openings should be considered wherever bulky items will be stored.
■ Access to storage rooms should be configured so that large, long articles such as ladders can be maneuvered in and out of the room.
■ Adequate, though utilitarian, lighting is a must.
■ All storage rooms should be ventilated.
■ Provisions must be made for storage of outside field equipment so that access to storage does not result in unnecessary soiling of interior walkways.
■ Code restrictions may impose limits on storage room locations. Many codes, for instance, do not allow use of the dead space under stairway enclosure for storage.

In general, storage rooms should be located close where items will be used. The matter of maintaining storage security and limiting access to authorized persons deserves careful consideration by the design team. Proper door hardware and a well-thought-out keying schedule will enhance storage security. The use of motion detection alarms may be appropriate for storage of high-cost items such as audio-visual equipment.

Maintenance Facilities

In general, two types of assets require maintenance programs:

1. Buildings and landscaping.
2. Fixtures, furniture and equipment (FF&E).

The value represented by these assets is integral to the overall facility mission. No matter how perfectly they are planned and designed, these assets will require a continuing and well-managed maintenance program to sustain their value. This maintenance program will require space allocation and support provisions such as power, lighting, water supply, communications, waste handling, access, FF&E, storage, safety devices, tool storage, and work shops.

An ongoing maintenance program occasionally will require cross-gender access to locker rooms. Planners can anticipate this need and provide subdividable locker rooms that don't need to be completely shut down to allow cross-gender access to a repair site. In addition, planners should not assume that all maintenance staff will be male and must plan accordingly when locating equipment rooms and maintenance access points.

Prerequisite to making a space allocation for a maintenance workshop is the planning exercise of itemizing the assets to be maintained, procedures to be followed, and equipment required. The following checklist will serve as a basic agenda for the dialogue which should take place between the planning/design team and the operations and maintenance director who will have responsibility for the finished assets.

Building Components

Exterior

- landscape improvements
- plant materials (trees, shrubs, flowers, grass)
- pavement (sweeping and snow removal)
- roofing and walls
- window and door openings
- signage and lighting
- irrigation and drainage
- recreational surfaces

- fencing
- pools and fountains
- waste handling equipment
- safety devices

Interior

- floor finishes
- wall and ceiling finishes
- lighting and power
- plumbing
- HVAC
- a variety of fixed/built-in equipment
- built-in accessories
- built-in waste handling equipment
- glass
- elevator
- built-in life and fire safety devices

FF&E Components

- furniture
- exercise equipment
- laundry equipment
- food and beverage equipment
- audiovisual equipment
- communication equipment
- accessories
- waste handling
- signage
- life and fire safety devices

Custodial rooms equipped with floor sinks and space for tools, supplies, and equipment for cleaning should be located conveniently throughout the facility. There should be about 50 square feet of such rooms for every 10,000 square feet of floor space. At least one such room should be provided on each floor. Proper attention to maintenance and housekeeping facilities during the planning and design process will pay dividends for the life of the building.

The remainder of this chapter will examine the ways in which ancillary facilities in general should be customized to meet the unique requirements of each project type: athletic facilities, physical education facilities, and recreation/fitness facilities.

Athletic Facilities

These are the buildings and fields used by educational institutions to conduct competitive, interschool athletic programs. They include facilities for both training and performance. It normally is only at the collegiate level that designated facilities are provided for the exclusive use of the intercollegiate athletic program. High school athletic facilities generally are shared with physical education uses.

When determining requirements for the ancillary areas of intercollegiate athletic facilities, planners must recognize the important role such facilities play in recruiting top-level athletes and coaches and maintaining a successful competitive record.

Locker Rooms

Size, quantity, type, and location of team locker rooms will be determined by the number and size of active sports teams, the timing of practice and competitive seasons, the timing of daily practice sessions, and the location of practice and competition facilities. Other design and planning considerations for team locker rooms:

■ Visiting team locker rooms must be provided for competitive events. Planners must analyze scheduling patterns for all sports with overlapping seasons to determine the number of visiting team locker rooms needed. Security for this area is of utmost importance.

■ Locker sizes for athletics will be determined by the equipment required for a given sport. Of course, football and hockey lockers will be larger than basketball and track lockers. The amount of dressing space allowed also should increase as locker sizes increase to accommodate more equipment. Sports with non-overlapping practice and competition seasons can share the same locker space.

■ Direct outside access to practice and/or game fields may be desirable for sports such as football, soccer, lacrosse, and baseball. The soiling of interior hallways thus can be minimized.

■ Planning efforts must ensure that locker room facilities provide equal opportunities for both men and women.

■ Game day locker facilities should be provided for coaches and officials.

■ Proper locker ventilation for drying stored articles is extremely important in preventing the build-up of unpleasant odors.

■ Competitive sports will require team meetings and "chalk talks," which can be conducted in one or more lecture rooms ideally located close to the locker rooms. Such rooms should be equipped with chalkboards and audiovisual equipment. Video replay and analysis is a key component of most coaching programs and planning for the location and networking of the necessary hardware is essential.

Administrative Offices

The need for staff work stations for athletic team programs can be quite extensive. This is particularly true for the high-profile competitive sports programs found in Division I universities. Each case must be analyzed for its own unique set of requirements, but it is not unusual for multi-sport programs to require defined working quarters for such staff positions as athletic director and assistants, head coaches and assistants, public relations and media coordinators, fundraising and alumni relations director(s), facilities manager, ticket sales staff, recruiting and scholarship coordinator, accounting staff, student advisors, chaplain, transportation coordinator, equipment and supply manager, director of security, secretarial and clerical aides, audiovisual personnel, and part-time or seasonal employees. Allowances should be made for anticipated growth in the scale of the athletic program and the staff to support it.

The planning process must identify all positions requiring a workstation and itemize the needs of each in a document that will be approved by the controlling authority prior to the start of the facility design work. In developing a layout of staff offices, the designer will confront the issue of centralized vs. decentralized administrative offices. This matter is best resolved with input from the users.

Laundry

Requirements for laundry services to athletic team programs goes beyond the provision of clean towels. The laundry service for a team sport facility must deal with the program's need for clean and sanitary towels, practice and game uniforms, protective equipment (shoulder pads, headgear, etc.) personal wear and miscellaneous items such as floor mats, foul weather gear, equipment bags, footwear, and utility items. The laundry is best located at the distribution/collection point for all materials to be supplied by the institution. If the laundry is to be a large central plant shared with other institutional users, a remote location may be required. However, a convenient and secure distribution center then should be created for the team sport facility.

The use of individual mesh laundry bags is an effective way to simplify handling of personal items. Each bag carries an identification tag and can be filled with soiled personal wear, turned in, washed, dried, and held for later retrieval by the user. A numbered storage rack will be helpful in keeping the bags arranged for speedy retrieval.

Storage and Maintenance

Off-season handling of reusable sports equipment must be provided. Planning and design considerations include the following:

■ Adequate space for storage includes shelving and/or racks appropriate for the items being stored. Helmets and shoulder pads, for example, will have a longer useful life if properly racked instead of being dumped into a bulk storage bin. Provide for receiving incoming equipment and issuing outgoing equipment.
■ Adequate space for repair of items before being stored is important. This procedure will allow non-repairable inventory to be identified, discarded, and reordered prior to the next season. Allow cabinet space for tools and spare parts.
■ For team sports, the security of stored items is particularly important. Designers must address the issue of lock keying and access control in coordination with the equipment manager.
■ Storage areas should be kept ventilated and dry to prevent mildew, mold, and odor buildup.

Physical Education Facilities

These are the buildings and fields used by institutions of learning in conducting physical education programs for all ages. Such programs commonly are provided for students of elementary, middle school, junior high, and high schools, as well as at the university undergraduate level. Programming of physical education generally is organized in a class format with one or more instructors. A wide variety of skill development activities must be accommodated. Special considerations for the planning and design of the ancillary facilities that support the physical education program follow.

Locker Rooms

Because of the scheduled class format, physical education locker rooms must be able to accommodate large influxes of user groups occupying and quickly vacating lockers, toilets, shower, and grooming facilities. Planners must analyze these use patterns in terms of class size, class duration, age, gender mix, duration of changeover time between classes, and types of activities being conducted. Not all classes will require use of locker rooms. This analysis will guide determinations such as number and size of lockers; number of toilets, showers, and lavatories; types of locker room accessories provided; and types

of finishes to be used throughout. Designers will reference the same analysis as they create and select provisions for towels, soap handling, energy conservation, grooming aids, handling of refuse, and control of facility abuse. The design strategy for dealing with each of these issues should be developed from the dialogue among planners, designers, manager, faculty, and users.

Other planning and design considerations unique to physical education locker rooms include:

■ Height of locker benches, lockers, and locker security devises should be studied carefully, relative to the average height, reach, and eye level of the typical user. This also applies to heights of water coolers, lavatories, toilets, urinals, and counter tops. In case of a wide mix of users, the design orientation should favor the least able user or provide a mix of accommodations.
■ Many schools have after-hours programs for community use by both adults and children. If the overall facility is going to offer such programs, the toilet facilities portion of the locker room can be positioned to allow access without allowing access to the remainder of the locker room.
■ Locker systems must be customized to meet the special needs of the physical education program being served. The dressing locker and box storage system frequently is used. In this system, a series of small storage lockers is located near a large dressing locker. Security of the storage locker is accomplished with a combination padlock, which is transferred to the dressing locker along with all the contents of the storage locker when the student is in class.
■ Many variations of locker systems have been developed to meet the special needs of physical education facilities. The designer must analyze the unique circumstances of each application before selecting the most appropriate system for a given project.
■ Because these locker rooms may play host to large groups of unsupervised adolescents, the design of all components and finishes should be as abuse-resistant as practical. Plastic laminate, glass and wood veneer, for example, are not considered to be abuse resistant.
■ Avoid creating hidden alcoves where unsupervised behavior could lead to facility damage or personal safety problems.
■ Facility managers may need to inspect locker contents. If this is the case, the use of an expanded mesh locker construction may be the best choice. Otherwise, a means of overriding locker security devices must be planned for.

Staff Offices

The need for physical education staff work stations is limited primarily to faculty office space. The relationship of these offices to those of the athletic teams and administration is the subject of much discussion in schools with both programs. In general, administrative units requiring little or no contact with students may not benefit from close proximity to those with regular involvement with large numbers of students. However, in some cases, interaction and good communication between these groups of staff may produce beneficial results. This is another planning question that defies universal resolution. It must be resolved as a matter of policy, on a case-by-case basis, by each institution.

Laundry

Options for handling the laundry needs of physical education students are the following:

1. Students are responsible for personal laundry needs including towels and/or gym uniforms.
2. The school maintains a laundry facility on the premises for towels and/or gym uniforms.
3. The school contracts to an outside service for towel laundry and/or gym uniforms.

Potential benefits of a school laundry are improved health, reduction of odors, and cleaner uniforms. The feasibility of an on-site laundry must be demonstrated on a case-by-case basis by analysis of all cost factors such as staff, equipment, floor space, maintenance, utility connections, operating costs, and supplies.

Recreation Fitness Facilities

This section addresses buildings and fields created by universities, hospitals, municipalities, and a variety of private clubs to serve the recreational/fitness needs of their respective constituencies. These constituencies include student intramural programs, public recreation programs, and individual fee paying user/members. The basic motivation for these facilities is enjoyment of sporting activities and/or desire for self-improvement and health maintenance through fitness. To be successful, this type of facility must serve the needs of its user/members who are not obligated to participate or who can elect to take their business elsewhere. This service orientation can exist on many levels of quality, image, and cost, but it is clearly an orientation that must be reflected in the substance and style of a facility's ancillary areas. The following summary of special planning and design considerations is directed toward the ancillary areas of recreation/fitness facilities.

Locker Rooms

Comfort, style, and service are matters of concern in recreation/fitness locker rooms. These concerns do not override the basic functional requirements of locker rooms discussed earlier. Depending on the target market of the facility and the operational economics driven by price and volume of user/members, the level of comfort, style, and service must be set by the planning/design team.

The level of comfort is affected by number, size, and spacing of lockers, lavatories, and showers. It also is affected by spaciousness and the kind of seating provided in dressing areas, the lighting, the quality of the heating and cooling systems, and the acoustical ambiance of the space.

The style and image of the locker room is influenced by color, texture, finish materials, and furnishings. These must be selected to ensure compatibility with the overall facility mission and maintain the consistency of the aesthetic statement being made throughout the building. Whether this statement is spartan and utilitarian, luxurious and rich, or high tech and polished, the choices made send a message to the user/member. The designer's challenge is to fit that message to the target market.

The service level of the recreation/fitness locker room is conveyed by the choices made in providing locker security; the system for collecting and distributing towels; the availability of soap, shampoo, lotions and grooming aids; the means of drying hair; and the availability of such amenities as steam, sauna, jacuzzi, telephone, and shoe shine.

Attention to the details of providing comfort, style, and service at a level appropriate to the target market is the key to creating a successful recreation/fitness locker room. Other planning and design considerations unique to locker rooms of this facility type follow:

■ Private shower booths with doors or curtains may be provided.
■ It generally is impractical to offer a permanent full-size private locker to each member.
■ Many facilities of this type have 3,000 to 4,000 members, a number that could require locker rooms of 18,000 to 24,000 square feet. Consider offering a mix of small, private, rental lockers as an extra-cost option and providing a full-size dressing locker to each member for day use.
■ A ratio of 1 full-size day locker per 10 members will be sufficient for facilities with average rates of utilization. Adjustment of this ratio up or down

Figure 14.10 Ambiance
of the locker room.

can be made by planning on a case-by-case basis to respond to higher frequency of use.

Administrative Offices

In general, the administrative departments of a recreation/fitness facility may include the following units: membership sales, management, recreation/ fitness programming, accounting, maintenance/ housekeeping, personnel, food/beverage, and front desk/check-in. There is little benefit to consolidating these offices into a single administrative block. Management and sales offices should be located near the front desk check-in point. Recreation/fitness programming staff should be located close to the activity areas they serve. Accounting, maintenance/housekeeping, and personnel can be placed in a more remote back-office location because they have little need for direct member contact. The food and beverage office should be included within the restaurant/bar area if provided. The front-desk reception station must be equipped to confirm validity of arriving members, control access to the facility, handle telephone reception and routing, confirm activity programming and court reservations, and handle all public inquiries and member service requests. The front desk also may be the best place from which to control lighting throughout the facility and to conduct announcements over the public address system. It is essential that the front desk be positioned to provide clear control of the line separating the public/free-access zone of the facility from member-only zones. This control of access will preserve the value of membership by preventing guests and nonmembers from using the facilities without proper payment and signing of liability release forms.

Multipurpose Facilities

It is not uncommon for a sports facility to be an intercollegiate athletic team center serving student athletics, a physical education center serving all students, and a center for recreation and fitness serving dues-paying alumni and faculty, as well as the student intramural sports system. Facilities that attempt to accommodate a variety of uses must be planned accordingly. With so many diverse groups competing for space and time, conflicts are inevitable. But the economic benefits are obvious. Multipurpose facilities are utilized more fully by avoiding duplication of facilities that may sit idle during large parts of the day. However, scheduling compromises may reduce access by certain user groups to unacceptably low levels. Institutions without the financial resources to fund independent facilities for athletics, physical education, and recreation/fitness may elect to undertake the planning challenges of a multipurpose facility. These challenges involve facility planning, curriculum planning, and schedule planning to accommodate as effectively as possible the needs of each constituency.

Special considerations for the ancillary areas of multi-purpose facilities are primarily applicable to locker rooms. Multiple locker rooms will be needed to allow separate accommodations for disparate user groups as they cycle into and out of shared athletic facilities. Gymnasium space, for example, might be scheduled for early afternoon physical education classes, late afternoon varsity basketball practice and evening student intramural games. It is unlikely that all of these users could be supported by a single pair of locker rooms. Once established, an array of locker rooms could be used with great flexibility to accommodate a broad spectrum of user groups such as men or women's varsity athletic teams (visitor and home teams), physical education classes, intramural sports teams, individual member users, and user groups with access rights by special contract, such as gymnastic classes, martial arts schools, and community youth programs.

■ Summary

In general, the key to creating superior ancillary facilities is a design process that invites input from users, managers, staff, design specialists, and component providers. Such a process will always examine comparable design solutions with a critical eye in a diligent effort to avoid repeating past mistakes and to learn from past successes. It is the mix of solid experience, careful listening, and open-minded inventiveness that allows an architect to produce successful design solutions.

Learning Objective 1: The student will be able to identify ancillary area specialists to be included on the development team.

The design of ancillary areas requires input from the following specialists: owner's project manager, facility planner/programmer, architect, cost authority, operations consultant, and component suppliers.

Learning Objective 2: The student will be able to describe design considerations for locker room facilities.

Many aspects of locker room design must be considered in light of the overall facility type. Nevertheless, some components are basic to all locker rooms, including lockers, toilets, showers, amenities, and grooming stations.

Learning Objective 3: The student will be able to explain the concepts of wet and dry areas.

Careful consideration should be given to the location of toilets, showers, and other wet areas. Toilets should be provided for dry users in the dry zone of the locker area as well. Mixing dry and wet toilet room traffic should be avoided, if possible.

Learning Objective 4: The student will be able to describe the various amenities to be included in ancillary areas.

Amenities often considered for inclusion in a locker room facility include steam rooms, saunas, jacuzzis, and grooming spaces. Each area has specific planning and design considerations.

■ Self-Assessment Exercises

1. Identify and describe the specialists who are commonly represented on a facility development team.
2. Describe the major considerations in designing a locker room facility.
3. Explain the concepts of wet areas and dry areas in planning a locker room.
4. Identify amenities that are often included in a locker room facility.
5. Describe the factors to be considered when designing a training room.
6. What questions should be considered when planning administrative offices?
7. Describe the need for planning appropriate storage facilities.
8. Compare and contrast the planning and design of ancillary areas for athletic facilities, physical education facilities, recreation fitness facilities, and multipurpose facilities.

■ Reference

Flynn, R.B. (Ed.). (1993). **Facility Planning for physical education, recreation, and athletics.** Reston, VA: American Alliance for Health, Physical Education, Recreation, and Dance.

CHAPTER 15

Academic Classrooms
and Research Laboratories

Thomas H. Sawyer, Indiana State University

Learning Objectives

After reading this chapter, the student will be able to

- design a multimedia classroom with distance education capability,

- layout an exercise physiology laboratory,

- design a biomechanics laboratory, and

- plan a motor development/learning laboratory.

Introduction

The nature of institutions of higher education and their objectives and functions will determine in large measure the type, number, size, and relative importance of classrooms and teaching/research laboratories. In institutions offering only services courses in physical education, the need for classrooms and teaching/research laboratories will seldom, if ever, be required. However, classrooms, teaching/research laboratories, and testing equipment become integral components for both physical education-teacher education and adult fitness programs.

A lack of appropriate laboratory space and equipment for teaching/research has hampered many institutions of higher education gaining accreditation from the National Council on Accreditation of Teacher Education (NCATE) and the National Association for Sport and Physical Education (NASPE) in the teacher preparation programs and from expanding their program opportunities in non-teaching areas (i.e., adult fitness, fitness, exercise science). Institutions with graduate programs have a greater need

for the development of teaching/research laboratories. Such facilities are required not only to provide learning experiences for students but also to attract and retain capable research scholars. Therefore, it is not possible to determine the appropriate square footage for a laboratory space. Each institution and its faculty working together should determine what the need shall be for this space. Yet there are some generic considerations for such laboratories that will be outlined in this chapter.

Classrooms

Classrooms need to be designed for multiple uses—from the traditional lecture method aided by multimedia technology to distance education delivery. This requires greater planning and the involvement of multimedia (i.e., sound, video, and graphics) and computer technicians. Classrooms are no longer simple square rooms with adequate lighting, environmental controls, and a blackboard and screen. They have become high-tech instructional spaces.

The ideal classroom is tiered similarly to a theater. The total number of seats will be determined by reviewing typical class sizes over the past five years. Each row should have a counter with the following at each student site—a microphone (for use in televised programming), computer hook-up to mainframe, a 110 V receptacle with appropriate surge-protection, comfortable chairs that can be easily accessed, and space for books and paper. The planner needs to consider providing an appropriate number of handicapped seats.

In the rear or on the side of the room there will be a control room. In the front of the room should be a large counter with a built-in TV monitor, overhead projector, and computer, and controls for the audio-visual equipment . Behind the counter will be a combination screen and grease board that is recessed into the wall and can be pulled out when needed. When not in use, the wall will become a backdrop with an appropriate background for telecasting.

Distance Education Classroom System Features

The following features are needed for a distance education classroom system:

- Three color cameras expandable to four with 12× zoom lens 460 lines of resolution;
- Overhead color Elmo camera graphics stand @ 450 lines of resolution;
- Multiple wall mount monitors for easy student viewing of slides, computer graphics, satellite feeds, and videotape playback;
- One microphone, with expansion capability exceeding 70 microphones, for every two students. This allows student participation in the classroom (16 microphones with 14 for 28 students in classroom, 1 for instructor, and 1 for guest);
- Automatic microphone mixing;
- 35 mm slide-to-video conversion for displaying slides locally and at distant locations;
- PC/MAC multimedia computer (minimum 128 mb RAM and 10 gb hard drive with a CD-ROM, $3^1/_2$" disk, and Zip drive) to video converter for PowerPoint and multimedia presentations;
- Computer interface for multimedia such as CD-ROM and DVD disks;
- Videocassette for playback with freeze frame capability;
- Multiple VCRs for recording class (1 S-VHS VCR playback for presentation, 1 S-VHS VCR for master record, and 5 VHS VCR record for library tapes);
- Character generator and video writer for highlighting 35 mm slides, computer graphics, or video stills;
- Sound system for playback of videocassette, CD-ROM or future DVD, computer audio files, audiocassette, and CD player;
- Switching and mixing control of video and audio for all sources;
- Telephone interface for telephone call in or teleconferencing;
- Wireless microphone for instructor;
- Wired microphone for guest;
- Integrated control system for use by instructor and/or for control of videocassette recorders, camera pan and tilt heads, camera lenses, audio, telephone interface, slide to video converter, video source selection, codec;
- AMX integrated control system for simplified operation and full system control;
- Supplemental lighting;
- A system with the ability to use satellite, fiber, codec, or web video and audio as either a source feed or signal distribution for maximum flexibility and adaptability for future technology; and
- A system with room for expansion to accommodate future requirements and technologies.

The Distance Education system consists of six distance education classrooms connected to a central control center. The system designed for each classroom provides multiple local and remote student participation with complete computer, 35 mm slide, videotape, and other multimedia sources. Each classroom has the capability of using satellite, codec, video via fiber, video via the web, or a combination of any of these. Further, the system is designed for video conferencing with two to four people in a room. It has limited capability to expand to either three cameras or two cameras and a single videocassette machine. Finally, each classroom has an option for an overhead graphics camera stand.

Technology is changing rapidly. No matter how well you plan today it will become outdated in a very short period of time. Therefore, when planning this technical space consider the importance of upgrading the systems in the future and plan for the capability of upgrading the technical components. This planning should include not only the technical equipment itself but the spaces in which the equipment is installed.

Computer Classrooms/Laboratories

This is a space that will be outdated weeks and even months before construction is completed, no matter how much futuristic planning is completed.

Sample Bid Specifications

Two Distance Learning Classroom Systems

Indiana State University
School of Education/School of Business and School of Technology—Distance Education Classrooms

Audio

- Up to 14 student microphones for 28 students, 1 wireless instructor microphone, and 1 guest microphone;
- Room sound reinforcement, audio monitoring at instructor and technical position;
- Audio switching for other sources to include but not limited to computer audio, VCR audio, audio cassette, CD player, codec, and external audio via fiber feed;
- Audio system with automatic level control, gating for student microphones, feedback elimination, and/or echo cancellation;
- Equipment that includes audio cassette player, CD player, telephone interface, all audio mixing, switching, and distribution equipment;
- Record capability for one S-VHS and five VHS videocassette recorders of program audio;
- Outgoing program stereo audio line via fiber;
- Audio monitoring with level control in the podium at the instructor's position;
- Audio monitoring and audio level monitoring at the technical position;
- Amplifier and ceiling mount speakers for listening to incoming telephone calls, instructor sound reinforcement, videotape playback, audio cassette or CD playback, computer audio from either a PC or a Mac, etc.;
- Provision for connection to PicTel or V-Tel codec; and
- Talkback to instructor at podium from equipment racks.

Video

- Three color cameras with horizontal resolution of 460 lines or greater, 12× powered zoom lens with remote control, auto focus, auto tracking/motion detection, and remote controlled quiet operation pan and tilt head. Stable wall mounts are required for all three cameras;
- Video switching for all video sources, including (but not limited) to three color cameras, overhead camera and copy stand, S-VHS playback, slide-to-video, computer video, codec video, and external video via fiber. Video switching should also include picture-in-picture and/or mix and wipe capability;
- Recording capability for one S-VHS and five VHS videocassette recorders of program video;
- Outgoing program video line via fiber;
- Three 27-inch or larger wall-mounted program monitors in technology classroom and four of the same specification in other classroom;
- Provision for a PC and Mac computer video converted to NTSC for use as a single source at a resolution up to 1024 × 768;
- Video source monitoring, multisync SVGA computer monitor, and program monitoring in the podium at the instructor's position;
- All other video monitoring including a waveform/vector provided at the technical operator's position;
- Character generator with internal keyer for downstream use and video writer/pointer device;
- Provision for connection to PicTel or V-Tel codec; and
- Video copy stand with a color camera that has 450 lines or greater horizontal resolution.

Sample Bid Specifications—Cont'd.

Two Distance Learning Classroom Systems

Control System

■ Control system must be AMX with redundancy on power supply and master card.
■ It will control all cameras, switching, audio, CD player, all VCRs, video-to-slide unit, telephone interface, etc.
■ AMX system will be provided with two electroluminescent tilt screen control panels. One panel will be provided for the instructor's position and the other for the technical position.
■ At the instructor's position will also be a touch-screen video source selector.
■ AMX control of codec must be provided.
■ Provision must be made for control of remote router via fiber.
■ Supplier must provide copy of programming for AMX system on 1.44 floppy disk (IBM format) as well as AMX software and software documentation for control system.

Reference

■ Reference system must consist of sync/pulse generator, color bar generator, black burst generator, and identification over color bar signal.
■ All switches will synchronous with no sync disturbance in program signal fed to VCRs or outgoing feed via codec or fiber.
■ All reference video cables will have a red outer jacket to differentiate from other signals.

Fiber

■ Fiber equipment will provide for two-way video, two-way stereo audio, and control of remote router.
■ Fiber equipment will be supplied for both ends of path.

Racks

■ Except for equipment required at the instructor's position, all other equipment should be housed and secured in 19-inch equipment racks.
■ Three of these racks may be of 72-inch rack space. Two other racks should be provided as a technical operator's position in console configuration.
■ All racks should have casters.
■ The racks should be equipped so as to be tip resistant.
■ All cables that run between the racks must be run within the racks or cable chases secured between the racks.

General Technical Provisions

■ All video and audio cable must be digital ready.
■ All cable must be plenum rated.
■ All balanced audio connectors must be Neutrix.
■ All video connectors must be of 75-ohm impedance and the center pin must be of a positive locking type.
■ There must be provided adequate rack space to provide for all equipment mounted in the racks with adequate cooling space as specified by the equipment manufacturers.
■ Supplier must provide a complete set of approval, construction, and as-built prints.

Sample Bid Specifications—Cont'd.

Two Distance Learning Classroom Systems

General Technical Provisions

■ Supplier will also provide as-built prints on floppy disk or ZIP disk (IBM format) from VidCAD version 7.0 or higher within 30 days after completion of each room.
■ Supplier will provide documentation on all system equipment in the form of user manuals, service manuals, and operations manuals.
■ A system operation manual will be prepared and provided by the supplier.
■ Supplier will furnish drawings and specifications for podium and requirements for placement of equipment into podium. Proposed podium layout drawing should be provided with initial proposal.
■ Balanced-to-unbalanced audio and unbalanced-to-balanced audio will be accomplished through active buffer amplifiers.
■ Good engineering standards and practices shall be used throughout the design, construction, and installation of the system.
■ Total power requirements and estimated heat load will be required with initial proposal.
■ The system will be assembled and tested before shipment to the installation site.
■ Engineering personnel from Indiana State University shall confirm supplier assembly and testing prior to shipment.
■ Supplier will provide proof of performance prior to shipment.
■ Supplier will provide instruction for two engineering and two operations personnel at Indiana State University upon completion of assembly at final location of each system.
■ Supplier should provide proof of history and successful completion of similar projects.
■ Two Kinoflo Image 20 lights with lamps and mounts are to be provided for each room.

General Information

■ The control room housing the technical operator and the equipment racks is either adjacent to the classroom or directly across the hall.
■ Cable runs between the equipment racks and the podium will generally be from 100 to 150 feet.
■ Power will be supplied via U-ground outlets.
■ Indiana State University may provide two engineers for assistance in on-site assembly of system.

Computer technology changes dramatically about every three months. The space requirements also change fairly rapidly.

The following are planning considerations for a computer laboratory space:

■ The sub-floor should be recessed and a metal floor installed with removable rectangular floor plates covered with adhesive rug rectangles that can be removed at least 12 times before being replaced. All wiring and cables must be run under the metal floor. The wiring and cables will be accessible through the removable rectangular floor plates.
■ All workstations need to be portable and have appropriate openings for the wiring and cables.
■ The lighting in the space should be reflected off the ceiling (indirect lighting) to reduce glare on the computer monitors.
■ Electrical and cable outlets should be provided in at least two locations in the ceiling to connect an overhead monitor for teaching.
■ The environmental conditions need to be conducive for optimum computer usage.
■ Appropriate security measures need to be planned for to protect the computers from theft and vandalism.
■ A sprinkler system should not be installed in this space. Use an appropriate substitute that will not harm the computers.
■ All electrical supply should be surge protected.

Figure 15.1 Student computer laboratory, Indiana State University.

Science Laboratories

A number of science laboratories should be considered when planning for HPERD teaching facilities. These include exercise physiology, biomechanics, and motor learning and development. Each of these laboratories has special needs.

Exercise Physiology (Human Performance) Laboratory

This space will be used for laboratory classes, research, and human performance testing for a variety of service programs. The size of the actual laboratory ranges from 400 sf to 2,000 sf. This laboratory can never be too large.

The following components maybe necessary for this space:
■ Small office space (200 sf) is needed for the instructor.
■ An environmental chamber is needed, with separate environmental controls that are easily accessible for maintenance.
■ A hydrostatic pool recessed to floor level should have a service crawl space, a winch on an I-beam to suspend and move the chair, and appropriate outlets for cables from the computer to the sensor attached to the chair.
■ The outlets to the computer station should be surge protected.
■ The filter area for the hydrostatic pool must be easily accessible to service personnel.
■ The floor in the hydrostatic area and locker areas should be tile, and the floor in the exercise areas should be multipurpose synthetic flooring.

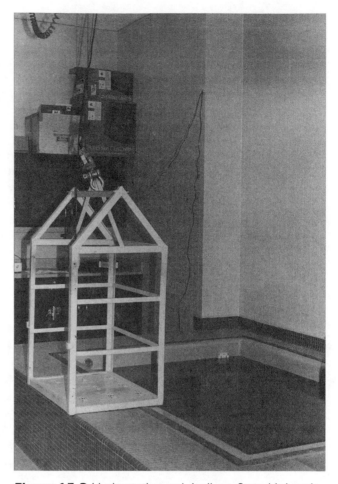

Figure 15.2 Hydrostatic pool, Indiana State University.

■ The hydrostatic area and locker rooms should have an appropriate number of drains in the floor to rapidly remove water.
■ Two small locker rooms are necessary, with toilet facilities for a maximum of ten people.
■ At least one treadmill recessed to floor level is needed (preferably two), with a service crawl space and a ramp to install and remove treadmill.
■ The treadmill(s) should have appropriate 110 or 220 wiring in the recessed area.
■ Electrical outlets should be located at the floor level for data-gathering machines.
■ Both the hydrostatic area and the main laboratory area should have sinks, counter tops, and storage cabinets.
■ Additional electrical outlets should be placed around the perimeter of the laboratory to accommodate other exercise equipment that needs surge protected, electricity;
■ All electrical outlets near the water supplies must be GFI types.
■ All computer stations must be hardwired to the mainframe computer.

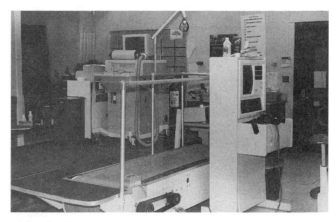

Figure 15.4 Treadmill in Indiana State University's exercise physiology laboratory.

Figure 15.3 Electronics used for motor learning, Indiana State University.

■ All separate spaces within the laboratory area must be capable of closed-circuit TV.

■ Privacy drapes should be suspended from the ceiling for private sections.

■ The height of the room with a recessed treadmill will be 10 feet and 14 feet with a treadmill that is not recessed and has a platform constructed around its perimeter.

■ If the research conducted deals with taking and analyzing biopsies and blood samples, a small chemical laboratory will have to be constructed separate from the main space.

■ Appropriate storage space is necessary.

■ The environment in the laboratory must be conducive to exercise—temperature 68-72 degrees Fahrenheit, 60% or less, and 8 to 12 exchanges per hour.

(Note: Air exchanges should have an appropriate mix of outside and inside air. This mix is usually 10 percent outside air and 90 percent inside air, though a ratio of 40 to 60, outside to inside, is preferred. The specific ratio of outside to inside air (recirculated air) is most often governed by local engineering codes. These codes should be followed when any air-handling system is installed.)

■ Lighting should be indirect to avoid glare on the computer monitors.

■ Appropriate security should be provided to protect all computers and equipment.

■ A sprinkler system should not be installed in this space. Use an appropriate substitute that will not harm the computers.

Biomechanics (Kinesiology) Laboratory

There are many areas in the field of biomechanics in which research may be conducted. The type of research may range from cinematography to human engineering. The size of the space ranges from 600 square feet to 2,000 square feet. This space can never be too large.

The following components may be necessary for this space:

■ An office space (200 sf);

■ A force platform set into the floor in an area where various activities from jumping to running can take place without hindering other activities in the laboratory;

■ Ceiling height of at least 16 feet;

■ Suspended theater lighting;

■ An environment conducive to exercise and cinematography—temperature 68-72 degrees Fahrenheit, 60% or less, and 8 to 12 exchanges per hour;

■ Computer stations for laboratory use and digitizing movement;

■ All computer stations hardwired into the main frame and all electrical outlets surge protected;

- Possibly a dark room to develop film and appropriate storage space;
- Multipurpose synthetic flooring;
- Nets and background drapes suspended from the ceiling that can be lowered and raised electronically;
- Appropriate storage space;
- Indirect lighting (except for theater lights) to avoid glare on the computer monitors;
- Appropriate security to protect all computers and equipment;
- No sprinkler system, but an appropriate substitute that will not harm the computers.

Motor Learning or Development Laboratory

Much of the research equipment found in exercise physiology and biomechanics laboratories can be used in research in motor learning or development and psychology of sport. However, a separate room or facility is necessary, at least 600 sf to 1,000 square feet with at least a 12-foot ceiling. The arrangement of the equipment in the room will depend on the research underway at the moment.

The following components maybe necessary for this space:

- An office space (200 sf);
- An environment conducive to movement activities—temperature 68-72 degrees Fahrenheit, 60% or less, and 8 to 12 exchanges per hour;
- Multipurpose synthetic flooring;
- Curtains and nets suspended from the ceiling that can be lowered and raised electronically;
- Four to six telephone-size cubicles with a counter top, chair, light, and electrical outlets;
- Sound proofing and separate environmental controls;
- Counter top spaces around the perimeter of the laboratory with storage below and above;
- A number of computer stations that are directly wired into the main frame and the outlets surge protected;
- No sprinkler system, but an appropriate substitute that will not harm the computers;
- Appropriate storage space;
- Indirect lighting to avoid glare on the computer monitors; and
- Appropriate security to protect all computers and equipment.

Technician's Office and Workshop Area

The science laboratories in HPERD are very technical, and many researchers and teachers are unable to repair equipment when it malfunctions. This means contacting a repair service. The cost of the repair and other customary charges are expensive and the work not always timely. Therefore, serious consideration should be given to hiring a technician to maintain the expensive equipment in all the laboratories. If this option is taken, a technician's office and workshop must be designed.

The following components maybe necessary for this space:

- An office space (200 sf) with computer, phone, cable TV, and electrical outlets;
- A workshop space (200 sf) with a work bench with multiple outlets, storage cabinets, drawer space, pegboard on wall to hang tools and parts;
- A concrete floor with a painted coarse finish and a floor drain;
- A double-deep sink and cabinets below and above;
- Temperature of 68-72 degrees Fahrenheit, 60% or less, and 8 to 12 exchanges per hour;
- No sprinkler system, but an appropriate substitute that will not harm the computers;
- Appropriate storage space;
- Indirect lighting to avoid glare on the computer monitors; and
- Appropriate security to protect all computers and equipment.

Suggestions for Purchasing Equipment

The manufacture and sale of research equipment has become a very competitive business. As a result, a wide range of the same kind of equipment is frequently available under different brand names. Before purchasing large expensive units, it is worth the time and effort to investigate carefully the various makes. The annual meetings of professional societies generally include exhibits by manufacturers of research equipment appropriate to the particular area of investigation. Consultation with a colleague in the same field who has used the equipment is a good idea before making a purchase.

In considering particular pieces of equipment, determine the following: (a) whether students or trained researchers are to use the equipment; (b) initial and annual servicing cost; (c) whether the equipment is electronically compatible with other equipment now in use or contemplated (often it is more economical to purchase units that match others from the same company so that the responsibility for servicing them rests with one company); (d) what power supply is needed; (e) ease with which the instrument may be calibrated and whether other equipment is needed for the calibration; (g) what service the company is willing to provide and where the service centers are located; and (h) levels of noise, vibration, and heat generated by the equipment. Unbiased answers to these and other questions can sometimes best be found by having discussions with other researchers who have used such installations.

Exercise Physiology Laboratory Equipment Needs

The equipment for the Exercise Physiology Laboratory includes

- crash cart,
- ECG defibrillator,
- spine board,
- treadmill(s),
- stair climber(s),
- bicycle ergometer (s),
- pneumotachmeter,
- gas meter,
- telemetering apparatus,
- electronic gas analyzer(s), either paramagnetic or electrochemical,
- infrared analyzer,
- multichannel recorder,
- Douglas bags,
- barometer,
- thermocouples,
- face mask with two-way non-rebreathing valve,
- disposable pneumotach,
- one-way, T-shaped non-rebreathing valve with mouthpiece and saliva trap,
- metabolic cart,
- cardiopulmonary diagnostic system,
- cardiotachmeter,
- pedometers,
- telepedometer,
- biomotometer,
- accelerometers,
- actometer,
- caltrac,
- electromyography, and
- computers, monitors, and printers (laser).

Biomechanics Laboratory Equipment Needs

The equipment for the biomechanics laboratory includes

- force platform,
- other types of force measuring devices,
- high-speed motion picture camera—motor-driven,

50-500 frames per second,
- stroboscopic equipment,
- videotape recorder with two channels and playback capacity,
- oscilloscope,
- electronic counters,
- amplifiers compatible with measuring and recording devices,
- digitizing equipment,
  - computers, monitors, printers (laser);
  - mirrors; and
  - metal storage cabinets.

Motor Learning and Development Laboratory Equipment Needs

Equipment for the motor learning and development laboratory includes

- multichannel recorders,
- standard electric clocks,
- interval timer,
- steadiness units,
- electronic counters,
- variable power supply,
- electronic kits,
- audio amplifiers,
- microphone,
- audio oscillator,
- oscilloscope,
- telemetry transmitter,
- telemetry receiver,
- voltage stabilizer,
- battery charger,
- seashore test,
- magnetic tape recorder, and
- storage cabinets.

■ Summary

The key academic spaces for HPERD are classrooms and laboratories. These spaces have become very complicated because of technological advances and increased distance education programming. Further, technological advances are changing faster then are the abilities of institutions to keep pace financially. The key words in designing these spaces are flexibility and upgradability.

Learning Objective 1: The student will be able to design a multimedia classroom with distance education capability.

The multimedia age is here to stay. Classrooms must be designed to accommodate not only multimedia needs but also distance education capabilities. The traditional classrooms with just a blackboard and screen are gone. The traditional ways of using a blackboard, a 16 mm movie projector, slide projector, and opaque projector are things of the past. New methodologies require the use of computers, colorful overheads, and audio and film clips. Finally, traditional offerings are quickly being transformed into distance education courses as well. The modern classroom will service synchronous and asynchronous offerings.

Learning Objective 2: The student will be able to lay out an exercise physiology laboratory.

The exercise physiology laboratory has become not only a teaching and research space but also a community fitness testing area. It contains an environmental chamber, hydrostatic weighing pool, cardiovascular testing area, and a small blood testing laboratory. Finally, this laboratory has become vitally dependant on computers.

Learning Objective 3: The student will be able to design a biomechanics laboratory.

The present-day biomechanics laboratory replaces the former kinesiology laboratory. The new laboratory has high-tech lighting and photography equipment as well as computers, digitizers, and force platforms. These are all used to measure forces, angles, and movements of various muscle groups and joints as the human performs physical and sport activities.

Learning Objective 4: The student will be able to plan a motor development/learning laboratory.

Motor development and learning have become very important parts of teaching people how to perform various tasks. The motor development and learning laboratory is used to study how people develop at various ages and how they learn various types of movements.

■ Case Study

You have been selected to be the next chair of the Department of Physical Education at Mark Twain University. The university is in the process of planning a new Health and Human Performance Building to replace an older structure built in 1924. You are part of the planning committee representing physical education. One of the hallmarks of this building will be its laboratory spaces. Physical education has three important laboratory spaces. How will you go about planning for these laboratories and the appropriate equipment needed to make them state-of-the-art? What should be included in these space? What pieces of equipment should be included in each facility?

■ References

American College of Sports Medicine, Tharret, S.J., & Peterson, J.A. (Eds). (1997). Health/fitness facility standards and guidelines. Champaign, IL: Human Kinetics, Inc.

Docherty, D. (Ed). (1996). **Measurement in pediatric exercise science.** Champaign, IL: Human Kinetics, Inc.

Morrow, J.R. Jr., Jackson, A.W., Disch, J.G., & Mood, D.P. (1995). **Measurement and evaluation in human performance.** Champaign, IL: Human Kinetics, Inc.

Montoye, H.J., Kemper, H.C.G., Saris, W.H.M. & Wasshburn, R.A. (1996). **Measuring physical activity and energy expenditure.** Champaign, IL: Human Kinetics, Inc.

Myers, J.N. (1996). **Essentials of cardiopulmonary exercise testing.** Champaign, IL: Human Kinetics, Inc.

CHAPTER 16

Landscape Design and Outdoor Spaces

Richard J. LaRue, University of New England ■ David A. LaRue, Vineyard Gardens, Inc.

Learning Objectives

After reading this chapter, the student will be able to

■ understand landscape design concepts in terms of aesthetics, function, and safety;

■ recognize the planning responsibilities related to groundskeeping management; maintenance, and equipment;

■ understand the design and operation concepts of surface and subsurface irrigation and drainage;

■ understand the concepts related to parking design for aesthetics, function, and safety;

■ understand the difference between standards and guidelines related to chemical handling and storage;

■ understand both the trends and new technologies in landscape design and groundskeeping.

Introduction—The Planning Process and Landscape Design

When planning the outdoor spaces of sport and recreational facilities, adjacent "transitional" space and/or sport fields, the process must include individuals who can lend their understanding and expertise to the process. From a design standpoint, a licensed landscape architect or experienced landscape designer should be employed. If a sports field is the focus of, or is included in the plan, then an experienced sports turf manager is important to the process. Finally, as all outdoor facilities and spaces will require maintenance, a logical planning resource will be the maintenance director and/or an experienced representative of the maintenance staff.

Perhaps the most important individual in the early stages of the planning process is the landscape professional. This person will be invaluable when making decisions related to site selection for the facility and utilization of all adjacent outdoor spaces.

More than any of the other major environmental design professions, landscape architecture is a profession on the move. It is comprehensive by definition—no less than the art and science of analysis, planning design, management, preservation and rehabilitation of the land. In providing well-managed design and development plans, landscape architects offer an essential array of services and expertise that reduces costs and adds long-term value to a project. While having a working knowledge of architecture, civil engineering, and urban planning, landscape architects take elements from each of these fields to design aesthetic and practical relationships with the land. Members of the profession have a special commitment to improving the quality of life through the best design of places for people and other living things (ASLA, 1998, on-line).

Sport fields are truly special facilities. When natural turf is chosen, a sports turf specialist is needed to oversee the development of a total field management program (Lewis, 1994).

A comprehensive program should include the following: 1) selecting an adapted grass for the locality; 2) mowing this selected grass at proper height and frequency; 3) fertilizing at the proper time and rate according to the turfgrass growth; 4) irrigating as needed to encourage establishment and to reduce stress periods; 5) aerifying to relieve compaction or dethaching according to the turf and the amount of play; and 6) using the appropriate preemergence and post emergence herbicides. The goal is to first produce a vigorous turf that will be competitive to the weeds (Lewis, 1994, p. 28).

Such a program will be served by the design of the field, including irrigation and drainage, and the choice of grass, etc. Careful consideration involves knowing the grass and soil makeup, need for aeration, fertilization, top dressing, seeding, and later, weed control (Mazzola, 1998).

Finally, as the ultimate success of the facility planning process is often measured years later, it is important to consider those aspects of groundskeeping that will be predetermined in the design of the fields and other outdoor spaces. Specifically, the labor and equipment required to maintain these spaces can be controlled with a carefully prepared landscape design. Additionally, the life expectancy of the green and hard goods is directly related to the level of quality afforded. Management of money and resources (capital expenditures, debt load, salaries and wages, existing equipment vs. new equipment, etc.) begins with the planning process and the investment decisions made prior to plan implementation (Hughes, Jr., 1996).

To summarize, the planning process must include consideration of both the facility and the adjacent outside or transitional space. Further, the planning process will benefit from the expertise of a certified landscape architect or experienced landscape de-

signer, an experienced sports turf specialist (if planning a formal play space), and a representative of the facilities maintenance staff. The quality of the planning process will be measured against the ability of the facility and all aspects of the plan to meet the goals described in the facility's case statement or building program document.

Landscape Design: Aesthetics, Function, and Safety

Frequently, when money is tight, and/or the facility costs are exceeding expectations, careful development of the adjacent outdoor space is easily ignored. Experience has demonstrated that this is shortsighted, as there are essential components that must be considered exclusive of the site selection of a facility. The design of this transitional space, whether for an indoor or outdoor facility, should consider the following characteristics:

■ the aesthetics of the space relative to all adjacent facilities,
■ the functional characteristics of the space relative to adjacent facilities, and
■ the safety of users (including accessibility) within the space, and relative to adjacent facilities.

Aesthetics

The basics of aesthetics in landscape design are sight lines that bring focus to important features of a facility or space, the use of space (especially spatial relationships), and the ability of the "finished product" to enhance the quality of the experience for all users.

Function

There are critical components to a comprehensive design related to function. The way the implemented design reacts to natural and man-made stresses is indicative of the time and resources invested in the planning process. Further, the long-term demand for maintenance will be affected by the design. And the way the design serves the facility program and user needs is a direct result of the planning process.

In addition to the characteristics described above, site selection is an important part of function for an outdoor facility should also include consideration of:

■ the orientation of play spaces with respect to the sun angle and predominant wind direction,
■ the topography of the developed and undeveloped outdoor space,

- the existing and necessary surface and subsurface irrigation and drainage,
- the appropriate use of natural and man-made barriers,
- environmental concerns, and
- the minimization of normal wear and vandalism (Macomber, 1993).

Safety

It is critical that the planning process for safety results in a landscape design that manages the risk of all adjacent outdoor spaces so that all foreseeable user accidents or injuries can be avoided. This planning for safety and security should include:

- signage in large lettering that clearly identifies pedestrian and vehicular paths, facilities, right-of-way, accessible parking, no parking and fire zones, and any other user-friendly restrictions or expectations;
- perimeter fencing or appropriate use of natural barriers;
- programmable and/or light sensitive night lighting;
- pedestrian and vehicular circulation that is easy to maintain and has reasonable and unobstructed views of cross traffic at every intersection;
- smooth (yet skid resistant) pavements and other path or road surfaces;
- bollards (permanent and removable barriers) restricting vehicular travel on pedestrian paths; and
- surveillance.

Groundskeeping: Management, Maintenance, Equipment Planning Responsibilities

Appropriate to the review of groundskeeping management, maintenance, and equipment are three concepts related to success in these areas: time management, money and resource management, and machinery and equipment management (Hughes, 1996, pp. 2-3). The responsibility for planning related to groundskeeping should be assisted by a seasoned member of the groundskeeping staff. Efficient use of the staff time can be facilitated in a properly planned landscape design. A significant aspect of the plan will be the reduction of labor as it relates to maintenance. If by design, you reduce the employee labor required, you are managing time more efficiently. Secondly, if you demand quality green goods when installing your landscape design, then the money and resources

for your project will be managed more efficiently. Finally, if your planning process includes a design that can be maintained with existing equipment, you are taking responsibility for the future without ignoring the reality of the present! Groundskeeping management must be considered when designing your landscape. And, few people can better assist you with this planning than a knowledgeable representative of your groundskeeping staff.

Surface and Subsurface Irrigation and Drainage

An effective landscape design will consider the operation of surface and subsurface irrigation and drainage. Not having enough moisture can be deadly to your grass and plants. Too much moisture, and no way for the water to drain, can also drown your plants and fields. When rain doesn't come, appropriate irrigation must be available. Irrigation planning is both and art and science. There are extraordinary examples of how, after large amounts of rain and subsequent flooding, the drainage of a sport field has allowed a contest to be held in an amazingly short time (Smith, 1998; Tracinski, 1998).

Parking Design for Aesthetics, Function, and Safety

Parking design will likely be a related part of the planning process, particularly if existing parking does not adequately provide for the needs of the new sport or recreational facility. And, regardless of existing parking, the facility will need its own adjacent accessible parking to meet the Americans with Disabilities Act (ADA). Other vehicular and pedestrian considerations may include a drop-off/pick-up area, emergency access/egress area, and service or delivery area. As in landscape design for a sport or recreational facility, safety (including accessibility) should be considered first and foremost, then function, and finally aesthetics.

Ideally, the parking design should be incorporated into the overall landscape design, especially in terms of aesthetics, function, and safety. However, there are some additional design options to consider:

Aesthetics

The first experience people have at the facility will likely come when they park their vehicle and approach the facility on foot. What are the sight lines, the use of space, and the placement of parking to the facility that make this experience inviting? Can parking be distributed in a way that avoids a large "car lot" look? Are there natural and man-made barriers that can enhance the aesthetics of the parking space(s) without compromising safety?

Function

Will the parking discriminate against users who arrive later in the day? Do plans include large and visible signage, so users understand all allowances and restrictions? Is there adequate parking? Will the facility require a parking garage? Can users exit the parking areas in a timely fashion?

If the parking area must be controlled, there are important decisions to make, including

- parking systems, ticket and ticketless (magnetic stripe, microwave, etc.);
- dispensers, machines, meters, cards or tags;
- attendant booths or valet stands; and
- a van or shuttle system.

It is important to note that parking garages are engineered spaces. The clear advantage of parking structures is that they "...place more of the total parking spaces close to the patron's destination" (*Parking Today,* 1998, p. 28). There is also a science to the vehicular patterns established in parking garages, i.e., the use of a continuous express ramp to reduce back-ups at the entrances and exits (*Parking Today,* 1998). If a parking garage is needed, then the planning process needs to involve an expert consultant in this engineering specialty.

Finally, it might be useful to think about making some of the parking multipurpose, i.e., unused parking space as play space. Provided that vehicular controls are in operation, it is entirely possible to use flat, well-maintained parking surfaces as additional outdoor play space or sport courts. However, the best play spaces are designed as play spaces, and regular use of a parking lot as a play space probably indicates a flaw in the outdoor space planning.

Safety

The safety and security of users are the most important characteristics of parking design. Will facility users circulate between the facility and parking areas secure in the knowledge that they will be safe and their vehicle intact? Will the location of the parking areas mandate use of perimeter fencing? Can pedestrian paths be designed that allow users to avoid walking in vehicular areas in the parking lot? Are permanent or removable bollards required to manage ve-

hicular traffic on pedestrian paths? Is lighting adequate for user safety and security at night? How will surveillance in the parking areas be managed: using closed circuit cameras or parking attendant(s)? Will the parking areas have emergency telephone towers or "call stations"? And, if the lot is gated, will the entrance use pedestrian-safe, one-way traffic controllers with below-grade spikes?

Chemical Handling and Storage Legal Aspects and Recommendations

Besides the Chemical Hazards Act managed under the Occupational Safety and Health Administration (OSHA), both state and federal regulations govern the handling of many of the chemicals used in weed control, insect management, and fertilization. The Chemical Hazards Act requires the employer to properly warn and protect employees using such chemicals. All chemical manufacturers must ship hazardous chemicals with Material Safety Data Sheets (MSDS), which should be kept on file for employees and specifically outline the guidelines for proper use of their products. Other government regulations require groundskeeping staff to be certified in the proper application and handling of chemicals. It is the responsibility of the groundskeeping staff to be knowledgeable in the use and handling of these chemicals and associated equipment. With a knowledgeable resource on the planning committee, the facility can provide for proper storage of chemicals and clean-up of chemical application equipment used in groundskeeping.

Trends and New Technologies in Landscape Design

Finally, the planning process will consider new trends or cutting-edge technologies when designing outdoor spaces. Consider making a significant investment in all aspects of the planning process to reduce short- and long-term mistakes. Once the plan is implemented, the success of the planning process will be easily measured in its ability to meet the needs of the facility program. Include the right people in the planning process. The experts are easy to remember. However, user input is also critical to promote inclusion and a sense of ownership in the process. Users include the people who will manage the facility and outdoor spaces, as well as those who will participate in facility programs, etc. An appropriate number of such people will help build good will and, more important, should serve the planning process effectively because of their unique "user" viewpoint. The long-term reality of maintenance and the cost of labor, materials, and equipment demand that landscape designs provide for low maintenance. A landscape architect or experienced landscape designer as well as a representative member of the groundskeeping staff should provide the expertise to design low maintenance into the outdoor spaces. Finally, the planning process should consider future implementation of the design when it comes to the level of quality selected in green and hard goods. Experience tells us that when purchasing such goods, the better the quality, the better the satisfaction.

■ Summary

When planning a sport or recreational facility, it is imperative that the process include the expertise of a licensed landscape architect or experienced landscape planner. The facility manager should have a significant role in the planning process. Other people who may lend their expertise and/or experience include those responsible for facility maintenance and safety, facility users, and program staff.

Learning Objective 1: The student will be able to understand landscape concepts in terms of aesthetics, function, and safety.

When considering landscape design, the planning process must evolve as a balance among the areas of aesthetics, function, and safety. Each area is important to a successful design or program. However, safety must come first, then function, and finally aesthetics. If the design fails to consider the safety of users, the facility operation may be negligent in its duty to users. If the aesthetics of the design omit features that would provide barrier-free access and egress for the disabled, the facility operation may be out of compliance with the ADA. The landscape architect or planner should be competent in all areas of landscape design (site analysis, planning design, management, and preservation and rehabilitation of the land). However, the spaces of recreation and sport are complex at best, and adjacent spaces need to serve both the facilities and mission of the program. Therefore, every member of the planning committee and every other individual expert involved in the planning process should provide valuable input. Each will have expertise and/or experience relevant to discussion and full consideration of a comprehensive landscape design.

Learning Objective 2: The student will be able to recognize the planning responsibilities related to groundskeeping management, maintenance, and equipment.

Three concepts are basic to success in groundskeeping management, maintenance, and equipment: time management, money and resource management, and machinery and equipment management (Hughes, 1996, pp. 2-3). The responsibility for planning related to groundskeeping should be assisted by a seasoned member of the groundskeeping staff. Efficient use of staff time can be facilitated in a properly planned landscape design. A significant aspect of the plan will be the reduction of labor as it relates to maintenance. If by design, you reduce the employee labor required, you are managing time more efficiently. Second, if you demand quality green goods when installing your landscape design, the money and resources for your project will be managed more efficiently. Finally, if your planning process includes a design that can be maintained with existing equipment, you are taking responsibility for the future without ignoring the reality of the present! Groundskeeping management must be considered when designing your landscape. And few people can better assist you with this planning than a knowledgeable representative of your groundskeeping staff.

Learning Objective 3: The student will be able to understand the design and operation of surface and subsurface irrigation and drainage.

The geography (location) and the landscape design will establish the need for and planning of surface and subsurface irrigation and drainage. When properly designed, surface and subsurface irrigation provides an even distribution of supplemental moisture for plants and turfgrass. Surface and subsurface drainage is necessary to remove excessive moisture (standing water, saturated turf, and/or groundwater).

Learning Objective 4: The student will be able to understand the concepts related to parking design for aesthetics, function, and safety.

The parking design should be an integral component of the total landscape design for the facility. However, there are important considerations relative to aesthetics, function, and safety of the design. Parking should enhance the user experience, not detract from it. If parking is planned properly, the parking area(s) will welcome users, operate in an efficient and uniform manner, and provide users with a safe environment. If a parking garage is needed to fulfill the facility's parking requirements, a specialized engineer should be consulted.

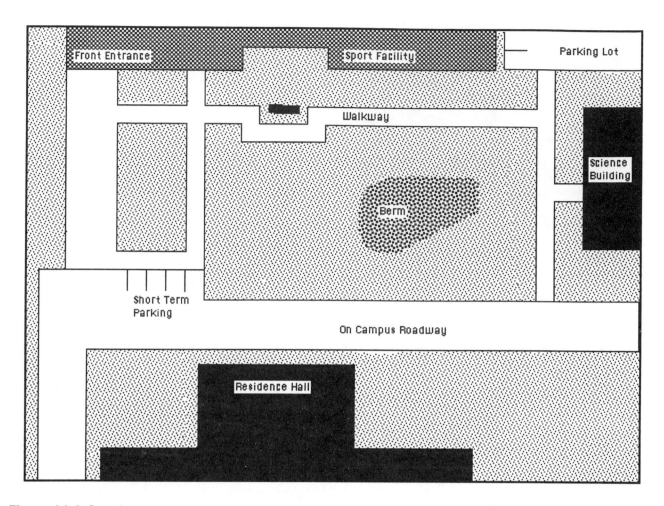

Figure 16.1 Case A.

Learning Objective 5: The student will be able to understand the difference between standards and guidelines related to chemical handling and storage (i.e., legal aspects and recommendations).

A groundskeeper or member of the maintenance staff should be able to provide relative standards (Chemical Hazards Act, etc.) or guidelines (MSDS chemical information) in the handling and storage of chemicals and equipment used to maintain plants and grasses around your facility.

Learning Objective 6: The student will be able to understand both the trends and new technologies in landscape design.

The trends in landscape design include

■ investing in the planning process to reduce mistakes and thereby enhance the success of the facility program;

■ inclusion in the planning process, involving users as well as specialists to develop a sense of ownership among those who will use the facilities;

■ low-maintenance designs to reduce the cost of labor, materials, and equipment required to maintain the outdoor spaces; and

■ quality products (i.e., select the highest level of quality in green and hard goods that the facility can afford, as you truly get what you pay for).

■ Case Study

A. The landscape planner on your facility project has two components that he or she believes will make the front entrance more inviting (see Figure 1 below): an eight-foot berm that will "break-up" the open space in front of the building, and a walkway that extends from the parking lot to the front entrance of the building and "detours" around a bench.

The facility serves a college and community population and is located in New England.

As the facility's first manager, your input is important to the project.

1. Considering the users and geographic location, is there a problem with either or both of the components?
2. How does the walkway design lend itself to snow removal in winter?
3. Should facility maintenance be contacted for input relative to the walkway design?
4. How does the berm component affect the safety of walkway users if campus safety patrols the area by vehicle rather than on foot?
5. Should campus safety have input on the design of the berm?
6. What are your thoughts and recommendations?
7. What steps would you take to justify your opinion?

Figure 1: Case A

B. Your college is planning a sports field for the athletics program. Currently, the athletics department supports women's and men's soccer and women's lacrosse. There are no plans for any other outdoor sports. The college owns one large space that has enough room for one full-size practice field and one competition field or a smaller practice field and a competition field with a track around the field. The athletic director insists that the college will never support a track program. Therefore, the athletic director is pushing for the full practice field and the competition field without a track. A second opinion is that the college should consider the future, placing the competition field so that a track could be added latter, even if it means a smaller practice field.

1. What is your opinion?
2. Should the fields be placed to support the existing program and anticipated plans?
3. Should planning anticipate the possibility of future program changes?
4. Are there other reasonable options?
5. How would you support your opinion?

■ References

ASLA (1998). Landscape Architecture. [On-line]. Available: http://www.asla.org/asla

Hughes, D., Jr., & Higginbotham, J.S. (1996). Systems for success. Cedar Rapids, IA: Dwight Hughes Systems, Inc.

Las Vegas hotel & casino parking. (1998). Parking Today, 3(4), 28-31.

Lewis, W. (1994). Weeding out unwanted growth: Weed problems on athletic fields can be nipped in the bud by implementing a total week management program. Athletic Management, 6(3), 28.

Macomber, B.A. (1993). Outdoor facilities. In Flynn, R.B. (Ed.). Facility planning for physical education, recreation and athletics (2nd ed.). Reston, VA: American Alliance for Health, Physical Education, Recreation and Dance.

Mazzola, G. (1998). Turn your turf into a field of dreams. Scholastic Coach and Athletic Director, 67(10), 36-38.

Merriam-Webster. (Eds.). (1995). Webster's new American dictionary. New York: Smithmark.

Newton, N.T. (1971). Design on the land: The development of landscape architecture. Cambridge, MA: Belknap Press of Harvard University Press.

Smith, D. (1998). Drowned by Bertha, the University at Albany's athletic fields rise to a giant challenge. SportsTURF, 14(3), 32-33.

Tracinski, B. (1998). Milwaukee Brewers' rainy day miracle. SportsTURF, 14(1), 32-36.

■ Suggested Readings

Andersen, M. (1998). Striping and lining. SportsTURF, 14(5), 8-12.

Derr, J.F. (1998). Weed identification and control in sportsTURF. SportsTURF, 14(5), 28-29.

Dossey, B. (1998). From seed to soccer: Bermudagrass you can sink your cleats into. SportsTURF, 14(3), 30-31.

Herbert, F. (1998). Slit drainage: A cutting tool in sports field construction and renovation. SportsTURF, 14(3), 20.

Indyk, H. (1998). Putting tissue tests to work. SportsTURF, 14(2), 20-21.

Kureab, R. (1998). Irrigation management. SportsTURF, 14(4), 14.

Leccese, M. (1998). Let there be light: New advances in both technology and design afford landscape architects greater flexibility for a wide range of lighting requirements. Landscape Architecture, 88(5), 97-101.

Minner, D. (1998). What's in a good sports field? SportsTURF, 14(1), 31.

Minner, D. (1998). Q & A: What are some characteristics of a good sports field? SportsTURF, 12(2), 12.

Trusty, S. & Trusty, S. (1998). ASTM recommendations for skinned area soils are in the works. SportsTURF, 14(2), 10-11.

Trusty, S., & Trusty, S. (1998). Battling compaction. SportsTURF, 14(3), 14-15.

Wallace, V. (1998). Cool-season grasses: Selecting the proper seed variety can improve the overall performance of your turf. SportsTURF, 14(4), 28-30.

Watkins, J.A., & Choate, R.B. (1987). Turf irrigation manual: The complete guide to landscape irrigation design. Dallas, TX: Telsco Industries.

Wilson, W.H.W. (1984). How to design and install outdoor lighting. San Francisco, CA: Ortho Books.

Wrightman, S. (1998). Working up to the Super Bowl. SportsTURF, 14(3), 8-10.

■ Resources

Associations

- Associated Landscape Contractors of America (ALCA): http://www.alca.org
- American Society of Landscape Architects (ASLA): http://www.asla.org
- Interlocking Concrete Pavement Institute: http://www.icpi.org/ICPI
- National Arborist Association: http://natarb.com
- Outdoor Power Equipment Distributors Association: http://www.aip.com
- Professional Lawn Care Association of America (PLCAA): http://www.plcaa.org
- Responsible Industry for a Sound Environment (RISE): http://acapa.org/rise/intro.html
- Sports Turf Managers Association (STMA): http://www.alp.com/STMA
- Snow and Ice Management Association: http://www.sima.org
- The Irrigation Association: http://www.irrigation.org
- Golf Course Superintendents Association of America (GCSAA): http://www.gcsaa.org

Horticulture

- American Horticultural Society: http://www.ahs.org
- PLANTnet a commercial horticulture site sponsored by Florist Insurance: http://plantnet.com
- Farmers Almanac Report: http://www.almanac.com

Industry Related-Government

- Environmental Protection Agency (EPA): http://www.epa.gov
- Federal Department of Transportation: http://www.dot.gov
- Occupational Safety and Health Administration (OSHA): http://www.osha.gov
- Plants National Database: http://plants.usda.gov/plants

Arboretums

- American Association of Botanic Gardens and Arboreta (AABGA): http://www.mobot.org/AABGA/aabga.html

Irrigation

- Irrigation and Green Industry Network: http://www.igin.com

Journals and Periodicals

Landscape Architecture (The magazine of the American Society of Landscape Architects): (800) 787-5267

Parking Today (Circulated free of charge to those who have an interest in the parking industry): (310) 390-5277, http://www.parkingtoday.com

Recreation Resources (Serves the information needs of recreation managers throughout the United States, Canada, and the world): (847) 427-9512 http://www.rec-neet.com

SportsTURF (The official publication of the Sports Turf Managers Association): http://wwwsportsturfonline.com

Other

- The Compost Resource Page: http://www.oldgrowth.org
- Metropolitan Detroit Landscape Association (MDLA): http://www.landscape.org
- The Lawn Institute: http://www.lawninstitute.com
- Crop Science Society of America: http://www.crops.org/cssa.html
- Hot Web-Site Links (Professional Landscape Contractors): http://www.landscape.org/Industry links.html

CHAPTER 17

Playgrounds

Donna Thompson, University of Northern Iowa ■ Susan Hudson, University of Northern Iowa

---

Learning Objectives

After reading this chapter, the student will be able to

■ identify key terms in relation to playground design,

■ recognize the trends in playground design,

■ understand general planning considerations for playground design,

■ identify specific planning steps in a planning a playground,

■ understand the procedures for installing playground equipment and surfacing, and

■ recognize procedures for maintaining, repairing, and inspecting playground equipment and surfacing.

Introduction

Playgrounds[1] are an essential part of children's play. These play sites can be found in a variety of settings including public parks, schools, child care centers, apartment complexes, churches, and commercial establishments. Whatever their settings, all playgrounds should have certain things in common. These include

■ the fostering of a child's physical, emotional, social, and intellectual development,

■ the provision of age-appropriate equipment to meet children's needs,

■ the use of proper surfacing under and around equipment,

■ the placement of equipment that allows for easy supervision by adults, and

■ the regular maintenance of the equipment and the environment.

This chapter will review trends in playground design, general planning considerations, specific planning steps, installation of the equipment and the surfacing, and on-going maintenance, repair, and inspection procedures.

Trends in Playgrounds

In the 1970s, in response to consumer interest and complaints, the United States Consumer Product Safety Commission (CPSC) initiated a process to de-

---

[1]The use of the word "playgrounds" for this chapter refers to designated areas where stationary and manipulative play equipment is located to facilitate a child's physical, emotional, social, and intellectual development.

velop safety guidelines for playgrounds. The first guidelines were produced in 1981. The guidelines came in two handbooks—one designed to give general information to the public, the other to give technical assistance to the manufacturers of playground equipment. These guidelines were revised in 1991 into one handbook for use by the public. In 1988, the American Society for Testing and Materials (ASTM) accepted responsibility for creating a standard based on the refinement of the technical specifications for playground equipment. CPSC has maintained its involvement with the technical standards for public use by assisting ASTM with further development and refinement of these specifications. As a result of these efforts, the first voluntary standard for the playground industry was developed in 1993. This standard, known as F- 1487-93 (Standard Consumer Safety Performance Specification for Playground Equipment for Public Use), provided technical specifications for playground equipment, use zones, prevention of entrapments, and maintenance. The standard was revised in 1995 and in 1997. A surfacing standard was created in 1991(F-1292-91). This standard provides for the testing of the impact attenuation of playground surfacing. Specifically, it provides the methodology to assess the amount of surfacing necessary under and around playground equipment to prevent fatal head injuries of children who may fall to the surface off the equipment. This standard has been revised three times (1993, 1995, 1996).

Both the standards and the guidelines by CPSC (which were revised again in 1994 and 1997) have been instrumental in creating safer play environments for children by providing design criteria for surfacing and equipment. Together, they are essential documents needed for designing playgrounds.

The next major standard that will significantly influence playground design will be the regulation that will interpret the application of the Americans with Disabilities Act (ADA). This regulatory standard is now under public review and is scheduled to be formalized by March of 1999. The standard addresses issues of accessibility to and from play equipment as well as the use of the equipment by children with disabilities.

Other trends in playground design include

■ the growing recognition that equipment for children ages two to five and children ages 5 to 12 needs to be separate,
■ the use of composite play structures rather than stand-alone equipment pieces,
■ the understanding that asphalt, cement, dirt, and grass are not appropriate surfaces to use under and around play equipment, and
■ the movement toward designing safer equipment.

Figure 17.1 *Supervising children on an elementary playground (Lattin Photography).*

General Planning Considerations

In order to design safe playgrounds, four major elements must be considered. They include

■ the placement of equipment and support structures (i.e. benches) which facilitate the **supervision** of children in the play area,
■ the proper positioning of **age-appropriate** equipment to promote positive play behavior,
■ the selection of appropriate surfacing that will absorb the impact of children **falling** from the equipment, and
■ the consideration of **equipment** and surface maintenance issues that contribute to the development of safe playground environments.

Supervision Design Considerations

Supervision requires individuals to be able to see and move through the playground area. Thus, design considerations for supervision include separation of equipment, open sight lines, and zones for play.

Age Separation. It is important to divide the playground area into sections appropriate for different ages of the users. Play equipment for children ages two to five is developmentally different from equipment designed for children ages 5 to 12. Mixing the two types of equipment means that the supervisor will have a difficult time guiding children to use the equipment appropriate for their developmental age level.

Sight Lines. Open sight lines refer to several angles of visual access for the supervisor. Sight lines must occur through equipment and through natural vegetation (see Figure 1). Further, sight lines for play structures should allow visual access to all points of the structure from at least two directions at any one point of observation on the play site (Bowers, 1988, p. 42). Essentially, the ability to respond to emergencies is dependent upon ". . . the ability of the supervisor to approach the structure and get to all the events to provide assistance" using the routes implied by the sight lines (Bruya and Wood, 1997).

Zones for Play. Play sites should also be divided into zones for different activity types. Two types of zones that the designer should pay attention to are activity zones and use zones. *Activity zones* describe the type of play behavior that children might engage in given the space and equipment that is present. Examples of activity zones include areas for social/dramatic play, fine-motor play, gross-motor play, and quiet play.

Use zones refer to the surfaces under and around equipment pieces onto which a child falling from or exiting from equipment would be expected to land. These areas generally extend six feet in all directions with the exception of swings and slides. For descriptions of the exact use zones for equipment consult the CPSC *Handbook for Public Playground Safety* (1997, pp. 6, 24, 28).

Age-Appropriate Design Considerations

Playgrounds should be designed according to the characteristics of the intended user. Therefore, age-appropriate design considerations include selection of the correct size of equipment for children, developmental needs of children, and the physical layout of equipment to support positive play activities.

Correct Size. Size of equipment refers to its height, width and bulk. The *height* of the equipment includes the overall distance from the top of the equipment piece to the surface. It also includes the space between various components such as steps and platforms. Since 70% of reported playground injuries involve falls to surfaces, the height of the equipment becomes a critical factor in designing a safe playground. Experts suggest that equipment for preschool children be no taller than children can reach. Maximum height for most equipment for school-age children should be eight feet (Thompson and Hudson, 1996).

Width of platforms should also allow children to make decisions about how to get on and off equipment safely. A child standing on top of a six-foot slide should have sufficient room to turn around and climb back down the ladder, if that child decides not to slide down.

Bulk is the relationship between the thickness of the material and the grip size of a child's hand. All hand rails, rungs, and other components that children grasp should be between 1 and 1 1/2 inches in diameter.

Developmental Characteristics. Developmental needs of children are also a factor in age-appropriate design. Children grow and develop by stages. The thinking ability of a three-year-old is much different from a seven-year-old. Preschoolers are physically smaller than school-aged children. It is important to consider the developmental needs and abilities of children in planning and designing age-appropriate playgrounds. These needs and abilities include

■ physical (i.e., strength, grip, height, and weight),
■ emotional (i.e. risk-taking and exploration),
■ social (i.e. cooperation, sharing, and accepting),
■ intellectual (i.e., decision-making, inquisitiveness, and creativity), and
■ accessibility (i.e., mobility).

Physical layout. The physical layout of the playground pieces can limit or enhance the play value and safety of children. An interconnected play area is one in which easy movement throughout the play structure is developed through the inclusion of alternate routes of travel (Bowers, 1998). Shaw (1976) investigated interconnection between parts of the structure, which he came to call the "unified play structure." As a result of the Creative Learning Project, he determined that overall use patterns decreased for separate play modules when compared to the "unified" play space. Thus, by unifying or interconnecting play elements in a play space, overall complexity was increased.

As mentioned earlier, it is recommended that equipment for preschool children be separate from equipment for school-age children. In addition, moving equipment such as swings and merry-go-rounds should be placed away from heavy traffic patterns, at the corners or edge of a play area.

Figure 17.2 Age appropriate design—older elementary children using overhead ladder.

Figure 17.3 Falls to surfaces—children replacing appropriate surfacing so the depth is proper for the next class.

Considerations for Proper Surfacing

Surfacing is the third important general design element. Factors that need to be considered include environmental conditions, management requirements, cost factors, characteristics of the user, maintenance requirements, equipment characteristics, and accessibility.

Environmental Conditions. Environmental conditions such as strong winds, rainy weather, high humidity, freezing temperatures, etc., may influence the appropriateness of the type of surfacing selected. For example, strong winds can erode organic loose-fill materials and sand so that they must be replenished often. Wind and dirt tend to form a hard pan or crust in pea gravel that needs to be broken up periodically. When wet, sand tends to stick together and become almost rigid. Some types of unitary materials are susceptible to frost damage. Thus, the climatic conditions of the playground must be considered when selecting a surface material (Mack, Hudson, & Thompson, 1997).

Soil Conditions. Playgrounds located over poor soil will not drain well, causing pooling of water under equipment. In some areas of the country, the shrink/swell characteristics of clay soil can loosen the foundation of play equipment. Shrink/swell conditions can also cause sink holes under playground surfaces. This problem can easily destroy a poured-in-place or other unitary surface. One should check with the local soil conservation district or a county extension agent to check the suitability of the soil for playground development.

Finally, the designer must pay attention to the drainage of the site. Normally, one would want water to run down away from the playground. This might mean that the area around the equipment will need to be slightly raised. Since drainage is also dependent on soil type, as mentioned above, the soil composition should be checked prior to the installation of equipment. One should also be aware of what might drain into the playground area. For instance, if a parking lot is located above the play area, grease, oils, and even gasoline may be washed into the play area during a rainstorm. Make sure that there is good drainage at and around the site to avoid problems.

Management Requirements. Consideration must be given as to how the area will be managed. A site that will have high traffic use will require a surface that will be durable without frequent maintenance. Rubber tiles or poured-in-place surfaces, although initially high in cost, may be more appropriate for these types of areas. Loose-fill materials would be more easily displaced, which would have an impact on the overall safety of the site. However, in areas that have controlled use, loose-fill materials may be appropriate.

Cost Factors. Cost factors of the surfacing material should be pro-rated over the life expectancy of the playground. Materials with low initial cost include sand, pea gravel, wood chips, and bark mulch. However, one should also consider the replenishment costs of these materials along with the initial purchase price. In addition, some method of containment is needed, and the materials cannot be installed over existing hard surfaces such as concrete and asphalt.

Materials with medium initial cost include wood fiber and shredded rubber. Some of these materials are easily installed, while others require professional installation. They may also require a drainage system. Like other loose-fill materials, some type of containment is required, and they cannot be installed over concrete or asphalt.

Unitary materials, such as poured-in-place surfaces, rubber tiles, and rubber mats have a high initial cost when compared to low-cost loose-fill materials. Poured-in-place surfaces are usually the most expensive, with a cost 10 to 15 times higher than common loose-fill surfaces. Rubber mats and tiles typically cost 6 to 12 times that of the cheaper materials. Installation and site preparation costs should also be considered, because these materials must be professionally installed. Unitary materials also require a hard base. If the existing surface is not concrete or asphalt, then a subsurface must be installed prior to the rubber surface. However, if the current surface is concrete or asphalt, installing a rubber surface will avoid the costs of excavating and removing the existing surface.

Characteristics of the User. Certain surfacing materials such as pea gravel are not recommended for young children, who have a tendency to put various objects in their mouths. Ground-rubber products and some wood products may also be inappropriate for the same reasons. On the other hand, the manipulative nature of sand makes it appropriate for younger users and can help enhance the overall play value of the playground.

Maintenance Requirements. A characteristic that is often ignored during the selection process is the amount of time and money needed to properly maintain the surface. Maintenance costs and the needs of surfacing materials vary greatly, with loose-fill materials tending to have much higher maintenance needs. In high-use areas, loose materials may need to be raked daily to replace materials that have been pushed or kicked away. Loose-fill materials need to be regularly inspected for protruding and sharp objects such as glass, pop tops, sharp rocks, and metal objects. These surface materials may also have to be tilled periodically to loosen compaction. Sand should periodically be turned over, loosened, and cleaned. Additionally, loads of loose material may need to be added on an annual or semi-annual basis to keep the surface at an appropriate depth.

While not as time-consuming, unitary materials such as rubber mats, tiles, and poured-in-place surfaces also have maintenance needs. Repairs may need to be made to gouges, burns, and loose areas. Unitary materials may also need to be swept frequently to prevent sand, dirt, rocks, or other loose materials from becoming a slip hazard. Finally, rubber surfaces must be washed occasionally to remove spilled beverages, animal excrement, and other foreign matter.

Equipment Requirements. Equipment requirements also are a factor to consider when choosing the appropriate surface. The CPSC recommendations for the fall heights for various pieces of playground equipment are as follows:

- climbers and horizontal ladders–the maximum height of the structure.
- elevated platforms including slide platforms–the height of the platform.
- merry-go-rounds–the height above the ground of any part at the perimeter on which a child may sit or stand.
- see-saws–the maximum height attainable by any part of the see-saw.
- spring rockers–the maximum height above the ground of the seat or designated play surface.
- swings–since children may fall from a swing seat at its maximum attainable angle (assumed to be 90° from "at rest" position), the fall height of a swing structure is the height of the pivot point where the swing's suspending elements connect to the supporting structure.

It should be noted that equipment that requires a child to be standing or sitting at ground level during play is not expected to follow the recommendations for resilient surfacing. Examples of such equipment

TABLE 1

CPSC Guidelines for Critical Height
Critical Heights (in feet) of Tested Materials

Material	Uncompressed depth			Compressed depth
	6 inch	9 inch	12 inch	9 inch
Wood Mulch	7	10	11	10
Double Shredded Bark Mulch	6	10	11	7
Uniform Wood Chips	6	7	>12	6
Fine Sand	5	5	9	5
Coarse Sand	5	5	6	4
Fine Gravel	6	7	10	6
Medium Gravel	5	5	6	5

are sand boxes, activity walls, playhouses, or any other equipment that has no elevated designated playing surface.

The CPSC uses the term "critical height" to describe the shock-absorbing performance of a surfacing material. The critical height of a surfacing material can be considered as an approximation of the fall height below which a life-threatening head injury would not be expected to occur (CPSC, 1997).

The CPSC has published the following table to help consumers understand the depth of loose-fill material necessary for the height of equipment.

The table should be read as follows: If, for example, uncompressed wood chips are used at a minimum depth of six inches, the height of the equipment can be no greater than seven feet. If nine inches of uncompressed wood chips are used, the maximum height of the equipment is 10 feet. It should be noted that for some materials, the critical height decreases when the material is compressed.

The depth of any loose-fill material could be reduced during use, resulting in different shock-absorbing properties. For this reason, a margin of safety should be considered in selecting a type and depth of material for a specific use. When loose-fill materials are used, it is recommended that there be a means of containment around the perimeter of the use zone (CPSC, 1997).

Accessibility. Accessibility is the final design consideration for surfacing. According to the Americans with Disabilities Act (ADA) of 1990, discrimination on the basis of disability in public accommodations is prohibited in parks, schools, child care centers, or other places of recreation. A revised ASTM standard for playground surface accessibility testing is expected. Until then, the only materials that are generally considered accessible under certain conditions are unitary wood fibers and unitary materials, all of which are commercially available. According to a U.S. Department of the Interior advisory, uniform wood fibers tend to knit together to form an accessible surface while other wood materials (i.e., wood chips, bark mulch, etc.) do not (McCrory, 1994).

Equipment Maintenance Considerations

Considerations about maintenance have to be part of the initial planning process. A poorly built playground is difficult to maintain. Providing good upkeep for a safe play environment begins with planning the playground site. Factors that need to be considered regarding this area include preplanning, materials, inspection, maintenance, and environment.

Preplanning. Prior to any installation of equipment and surfaces, a proper site analysis needs to be conducted. A site analysis addresses natural, manufactured, and aesthetic elements that may affect playgrounds. All of these items will be discussed in greater detail in the next section.

Materials. There is no perfect material for playground equipment. Without good maintenance, wood will splinter, metal will rust, and plastic will crack. Any good maintenance plan should be based on

- Instructions received from the designer/manufacturer,
- Materials used for equipment and surfaces,
- Age of the equipment and surfaces,
- Given frequency of use on the equipment and surfaces, and
- Environmental factors at a specific location.

Make sure that all instructions from the designer/manufacturer are retained in a file and that the schedule of maintenance is followed. Remember, any modification, deviation, or change from these instructions means that liability issues will reside with the agency, not the designer/manufacturer.

Inspection. Inspect all materials prior to installation. Wood products are aesthetically pleasing but will weather faster than metal or plastic. Plastic materials may not be appropriate in areas of great temperature extremes. Metal materials also tend to absorb heat and cold, which can cause problems in hot and cold climates.

Even newly installed playgrounds should be inspected for hazards. Just because a playground is new doesn't mean that problems cannot occur. This is especially true if the equipment was installed improperly or the overall design and placement of equipment is faulty. On the other hand, older playgrounds do need more regular inspections simply because parts may wear out due to age.

Maintenance Schedule. A well-used playground will need more frequent maintenance than one that is used less often. This is especially true with playgrounds that have loose-fill materials as the surface under and around playground equipment. An agency that schedules only one refilling of these materials a year may find that over half its playgrounds are unsafe due to the high usage. Each play area may have its own use cycle and the maintenance schedule should reflect this.

Environmental Factors. Finally, the environmental factors at a specific location are going to determine the required frequency of maintenance. A playground that is located near a shady grove of trees may need to be inspected more frequently because of materials left on the surfacing (e.g., leaves) or other hazards (e.g.,

Figure 17.4 Equipment maintenance a piece of playground equipment that needs maintenance.

overhanging limbs). A playground that is in a wide-open area and exposed to the elements may also experience greater maintenance needs.

It is evident that to maintain a safe playground environment, maintenance practices and procedures need to be thought about at the beginning of the design process. It is also important that these practices and procedures be continually revised and improved.

Specific Planning Steps

The actual planning and design of a playground is accomplished in four distinct phases. They are site analysis, preliminary design, equipment and material selection and final design.

Site Analysis

Site analysis involves the gathering of information and data about the playground site and adjacent properties. "The purpose of site analysis is to find a place for a particular use or find a use for a particular place" (Molnar and Rutledge, 1986). One of the first things that one should do during the site analysis is an on-site visitation. Personal site visits enable one to see how the area is used and how it relates to surrounding land uses (IPRA,1995). It allows the planner to mentally visualize the space available for the project.

During the site analysis, step information about environmental elements, manufactured elements, and hazardous conditions is gathered and analyzed.

Environmental Characteristics. Environment that should be considered during the site analysis include soils, geology, drainage, topography, vegetation, and any other physical characteristics that may have an impact on the development process.

Soils and Geology. Soil type is important because it is directly related to drainage. The playground should be constructed on well-drained soils. A playground constructed on poor soil will be subject to water pooling or standing. It will also tend to erode the foundations of the equipment and cause other problems of equipment stability.

Drainage. In general, water should drain away from the playground. As mentioned earlier, the play area may need to be slightly elevated to accomplish this. One needs to remember that construction of the playground and/or surrounding areas may alter the water movement patterns on the site. If there are questions about preventing or solving water problems, a good source is the local office of the Soil Conservation Service (SACS).

Topography. is concerned the general lay of the land. Playground developments work best within a range of slopes. As a general rule, slopes around and beneath playground should conform to the following guidelines:

■ Slope between 1% to 4% are most suitable for playgrounds (a 1% slope falls 1 foot for every 100 linear feet).
■ Slopes less than 1% may result in drainage problems.
■ Slopes greater than 4% may require site modifications to install and level the equipment (IPRA, 1995).

In addition, slope is an important consideration in providing equal access into the playground for everyone, regardless of physical capabilities. The accessible route into the playground must have a maximum slope of 5% (1 foot of fall for every 20 linear feet) and a maximum cross slope of 2%.

Vegetation is another environmental consideration in playground design. Shade should be an essential ingredient for every playground. If trees are not present, it may be necessary to provide man-made shade such as the placement of shelters . While trees, planted along a western and southern exposure may provide the necessary shade, caution must be taken to ensure that overhanging limbs do not interfere with play activities. "In particular, trees planted inside the playground must be carefully located because they may be used for climbing." (IPSA, p.13). In addition, one should avoid planting tree and shrubs which are messy or likely to attract stinging insects such as bees.

Other environmental considerations include sun orientation, wind patterns, climate, and animal control. Slide surfaces that tend to absorb heat should avoid being placed on a western exposure. The best orientation is north. However, if this is not possible, then natural or manufactured shade needs to be provided.

The direction of the prevailing winds should also be determined. If at all possible, the playground should be located downwind from open fields, farm yards, or areas like unpaved roads where dust from these sites will blow directly into the play area. In addition, if an area is susceptible to strong winds on a routine basis, some type of wind break should be created.

Climatic conditions that affect playground equipment and surfaces include heat and cold, humidity, and precipitation. As mentioned earlier, temperature extremes have a direct influence on different materials used for equipment and surfacing. In addition, humidity may affect certain loose-fill surfaces as well as cause the surfaces of equipment to become slippery and hazardous. An area that has constant precipitation may need to have a cover over the equipment as well as excellent drainage.

Manufactured elements. The second factor to consider in the site analysis is manufactured elements. These include utilities, roads, buildings, adjacent land use, accessibility, and anything else that could affect or be affected by the playground.

Utilities. As a general rule, playgrounds should not be constructed under utility lines. One needs also to pay attention to unused utility easements. There might be a temptation to use these seemingly open areas, but nothing can stop a utility from using the easement at a later date for power lines. Another utility consideration is the support structures that may be found near the playground site. Power poles and towers can constitute an attractive nuisance in the play area. In addition, guidewires or other supporting cables on these utility structures can create a hazard for children in the area.

Roads. The playground should be located far enough away from roads and parking lots that moving vehicles do not pose a hazard for children. A barrier surrounding the playground is recommended, if children may inadvertently run into a street. If fences are used for such barriers, it is recommended that they conform to applicable local building codes (CSPC, 1997).

Use Zones. Proper use zones need to be maintained in relation to any buildings or structures that may be present on the site. For example, a school playground should be located far enough away from the school buildings so that a child on a climbing structure would be in no danger of falling off the play equipment into the building. In addition, close proximity of the playground to windows may encourage vandalism problems.

Land Use. Neighboring land uses need to be considered because they may affect or be affected by the playground (IPRA, 1995). Railroads, freeways, land fills, streams, and rivers may all contribute to a hazardous environment for children. The long-term effects of some of these items (i.e., waste dumps) may not be determined for years. On the other hand, the location of the playground itself may be seen as a less-than-desirable element within the neighborhood environment. Some people may be upset by the perceived increase of noise, vandalism, and traffic they assume a playground will attract.

Access. Accessibility to and from the site is also a consideration. How will project users get to the playground site? Will it involve children arriving on bicycles, walking, or being brought by cars? The answers to these questions will determine the need for bicycle racks, pathways, and parking lots.

Other. Other considerations may include sources of noise such as airports, railroad lines, roadways, heavy machinery, and factories that can detract from the recreational experiences of playground users Odors from factories, sewage treatment facilities, and stagnant ponds can have the same effect. Locating a playground adjacent to such detractors should be avoided (IRPA, 1995, p.15).

Hazardous conditions. A variety of hazardous conditions must be considered before determining the site location of the playground. These include visibility and security, crossings, water, and mixed recreation use zones.

Visibility/Security. Visibility and security are primary considerations. Large shrubs (above four feet in height) should not be planted around a playground since they inhibit the ability to observe children at play. In addition, as already mentioned, low tree branches (below a height of seven feet) should be removed to prevent climbing. Any trees that will be seriously affected by the development of the playground should also be removed before they create a hazardous situation.

Crossings. Children should not be required to use unprotected crossings to reach playgrounds. Railroad tracks are a similar hazard. Fencing or natural barriers may be necessary if alternative solutions are not feasible (IPRA, 1995). Another traffic consideration can occur around schools and child care centers where delivery truck routes may pose a potential hazard for children going to and from the play area. Special care should be given to make sure that these routes do not intersect the play area and are not located nearby.

Water. Water is another site element that may pose a hazardous situation. Children are attracted to ponds, streams, and drainage ditches. Cement culverts or ditches are especially dangerous since their smooth sides may not allow a child easy escape in case of a flash flood. Signage alone will not stop any child from trying to incorporate these areas into their play behavior.

Mixed Use Zones. Mixed recreation use zones can also produce hazardous situations. A soccer field or baseball diamond located too close to a playground is a safety concern because of the chance that errant balls may enter the play area and injure playground users. Locating a playground adjacent to basketball courts, tennis courts, and other similar recreation facilities can also create conflicting access patterns and users.

Preliminary Design

The preliminary design phase is where information about the activity, user, site, and necessary support factors are analyzed and alternative solutions evaluated. At the end of this step, the actual schematic plans will be developed.

Activity Information. What is the purpose of the playground? This fundamental question needs to be answered in terms of performance objectives rather than physical objectives. For instance, if one answers this question by saying the purpose of the playground is to provide slides, swings, and climbing apparatus, then one will limit the possibilities of the play behavior of children. On the other hand, if one answers this question by looking at what children should be able to do, than a different design may result. The philosophical basis for the existence of the play areas must be reflected in the answer to this question. For example, in a school setting, the purpose of the playground should be tied to the educational goals of the total curriculum. Thus, the playground may be designed so that it contributes to a child's understanding of math, language arts, science, and physical education. In a park setting, the playground may reflect the extension of school goals as well as emphasize the physical, emotional, social, and intellectual development of a child. In a child care setting, the play areas should reflect the growth and development of the different ages of young children.

Once the philosophical question about the purpose of the playground is answered, the next step is to decide what experience opportunities should be provided. Experience opportunities are ways that the child will participate in the playground experience. Four different experience opportunities are usually present in the playground environment. They include

■ basic ability level,
■ skill improvement,
■ program participation, and
■ unstructured participation.

Basic Ability

This is especially important in planning play environments for young children. Children do develop in different stages. For instance, in terms of access on play equipment, ramps provide the easiest way for a small child to get onto equipment, followed by stairways, step ladders, rung ladders and climbers. Thus, if one wanted to provide basic skill level opportunities, the design of the play structures would incorporate a variety of ramps and small stairways, as well as be built fairly low to the ground.

Skill Improvement

This allows for children to develop their abilities in incremental steps. For instance, at the age of six, children don't automatically have the upper body strength to control their bodies on overhead ladders. Some intermediate type of equipment is needed between a 6-foot-long and a 20-foot-long overhead ladder, where a child can build up the muscle strength and endurance needed to master the higher and longer apparatus without having the fear of falling.

Program Participation

A playground developed on a school site should be designed to complement the academic offerings of the curriculum. Thus, the design of this playground should have specific equipment pieces and shapes that would supplement the academic program (math, science, art, etc.).

Unstructured Participation

This means an area where children are free to roam, explore, discover, and play. Again, this type of experience opportunity demands some specific design considerations including placement of equipment, open sight lines, and easy access.

Not all playgrounds have to emphasize the same experience opportunities. However, if the designer/planner fails to recognize which opportunities should be present, the playground may become only an area where equipment is randomly placed.

User Information. A brief profile of the intended users is an important aspect of the planning process. Such a profile should include the age distribution of the intended users, developmental and skill levels, known disabilities, and participation time patterns. In addition, information about participation rates per activity period is necessary to determine the design load of the area in terms of needed equipment units, support areas, and services. Seasonal, monthly, and weekly peak participation periods may be additional planning factors in terms of maintenance and operational considerations.

Site Factors. A third consideration in this preliminary design stage is the resource and facility factors that are directly related to the site development. Special requirements, such as the spatial size for the playground area, need to be noted. Preliminary layout of equipment on a grid will allow the planner to visualize traffic flow on and off equipment, relationships of equipment pieces with one another, and space requirements for use zones. Other special requirements may be the location of items such as tree limbs, power lines, and telephone wires that can infringe on air space and cause a hazardous situation.

The solar orientation of the space in relation to the placement of equipment is also an important factor. The primary consideration should be to minimize glare and sun blindness during play and avoid hot surfaces on the equipment.

Support Factors. Items that are auxiliary to the playground but support the area also need to be considered during this preliminary design stage. These items help enhance the overall aesthetic appearance of the are, contribute to the safety of the children, and provide amenities that create an overall positive experience. Trees, bushes, and other vegetation may need to be planted to help provide shade and/or avoid a stark appearance of the playground site. Fencing may be added to keep children safe during play and keep out unwanted animals and others during other times of the day. Benches, water fountains, and shelter areas may provide children and adults with areas to relax and refresh during their visit to the playground. These support factors and others such as bicycle racks, trash and recycling cans, and security lighting will not suddenly appear unless they are planned for in the preliminary design stage. Furthermore, if they are added later, their placement may not be in congruence with the overall design of the area.

Equipment and Material Selection

Equipment for playgrounds should be designed for public use, be durable, and meet requirements for insurance, standards, warranty, age appropriateness, and use. Any equipment purchased should conform to both CPSC guidelines and ASTM Standard F-1487.

Product Compliance. Always require a certificate of compliance with the CPSC guidelines and ASTM Standard from the manufacturer prior to purchase of the equipment. The same type of compliance with ASTM F-1292 should be secured for any surfacing material. If a manufacturer is unable to produce such documentation or will only provide oral assurances as to compliance, purchase equipment elsewhere. In addition, make sure that any equipment purchased for public-use playgrounds is designed for that purpose. Many times, people with good intentions but limited funds will purchase equipment intended for home use and place it in a public setting. This equipment is neither durable nor strong enough to withstand the constant heavy use that is found in public sites. In addition, the standard for home-use equipment is quite different from that for public-use equipment.

Product Materials. Playground equipment is usually made out of one of four types of materials: wood, steel, aluminum, or plastic. Each material has its own advantages and disadvantages.

Wood must be treated to prevent rotting by weather or insects. This is especially true when wood is in direct contact with the ground. Any chemical wood preservative used must be approved for contact with humans. Wood is also subject to splitting and checking, which may eventually weaken the structure. Watch out for evidence of splitting in new wood, especially pieces used as support beams and poles. Sanding and other treatments may be required to avoid injuries from splinters. Although aesthetically pleasing, wooden pieces usually have a lifespan of only 10 years.

Steel equipment pieces should be galvanized and have a protective coating that inhibits rust, such as powder coating and painting. Any paint used should not have lead as a component. It should also be noted that scratches and construction defects are subject to rust. Steel also can heat up to dangerous levels with direct exposure to sun. On the other hand, steel equipment pieces are very durable and have a long life span.

Aluminum components are rust resistant and offer lightweight installation. Aluminum is sometimes more costly at purchase, but the reduced maintenance is often worth the extra cost. Shipping charges will be reduced because of the lighter weight. Like steel, aluminum can heat up with direct exposure to sun.

Plastic can be molded, cut, or formed into a wide variety of shapes for playground use. Because of this, it is a favorite material that is used by many playground manufacturers. However, most plastics do not have the strength of natural lumbers and metals and can sag and bend. It is recommended that UV inhibitors be added to the plastic to extend the life expectancy and color. Plastic components must meet safety standards (IPRA, 1995).

Purchase Factors. One should consider at least five factors prior to purchasing any equipment or surface materials. These include product liability insurance, compliance with standards, product warranty, age appropriateness, and public use equipment.

Product liability insurance protects the buyer against any accident caused by the design of the equipment. However, if the buyer makes any alteration or modification or fails to maintain the equipment properly, the insurance will not cover the agency. The equipment vendor should furnish the agency with certificates of insurance and original endorsements affecting the coverage. As with all documentation, make sure the insurance coverage is in writing and on file.

Compliance with standards should also be documented and on file. Do not buy equipment that does not meet CPSC guidelines and ASTM standards F1292 for surfacing and F1487 for equipment. In addition, a certification of proper installation should be obtained from the manufacturer or his representative following the final inspection. Once the manufacturer agrees that the playground is in conformance with its installation recommendations, ask for a sign-off letter stating the date of inspection. Make sure that you keep this document on file. It is extremely important should an injury occur due to improper design or installation.

Product warranty simply provides the buyer with the length of time for which any products are protected against defects. Many times, the product warranty is a good indication of the product's life expectancy. Again, any modification or repair made without conformance to the manufacturer's guidelines will nullify most warranties.

Age appropriateness of the equipment has already been covered. However, you should notify the manufacturer in writing what the ages of the intended users are to ensure that they have provided you with age appropriate equipment at the time of purchase.

Public-use equipment is the last item to consider. Not all pieces of equipment are recommended for use in a public playground. The following is a list of equipment to avoid primarily because it fails to meet safety guidelines:

- spinning equipment without speed governors,
- tire swings that do not meet requirements for clearance,
- seesaws that do not meet current safety standards,
- heavy swings (metal, wood, animal-type),
- ropes/cables that are not attached at both ends,
- swinging exercise rings and trapeze bars,
- multiple occupancy swings,
- trampolines, and
- homemade equipment.

Final Design

At this stage, one is ready to put all the components together in a scaled schematic drawing that shows layout, use zones, site amenities, access points, and other construction details. Also, one needs to insure that accessible routes to the equipment are present.

The easiest way to begin this process is to use cutouts or round bubbles to represent the actual equipment and place these items on a scale grid plan (see figure 2). In this way, one can visualize how the equipment pieces fit together and where potential conflicts of use may arise. Any moving equipment, including swings, should be located away from other structures, preferably at the edge or corner of anticipated traffic patterns. In addition, make sure to separate preschool (ages two to five) from school-age (5 to 12) equipment.

All equipment has space requirements. By moving the cutouts or squares around, one can make sure that the use zones of the various equipment pieces do not overlap. Remember that these use zones are minimum guidelines. The authors have seen several instances where slide exits were placed directly in front of swing sets. Although the proper use zone was in place, exuberant children who jumped out of the swings landed directly in front or to the side of the slide. Of course, the best way to avoid this situation is not to place these two activities across from one another in the first place.

As mentioned earlier, site amenities should be part of the planning stage. Make sure that the scaled drawings include the placement of benches, bicycle racks, trash cans, etc. If these items are not in the drawings, they will be haphazardly provided later, perhaps at inappropriate spots.

Before finalizing the drawings, make sure that you have considered traffic flow patterns on and off equipment and general access to the area. Every playground should have at least one accessible route to the equipment that will permit children with disabilities the opportunity to be in the playground area and interact with others. Although the final Americans with Disabilities Act regulations have not been finalized, it is important to understand that just getting to the equipment will not be enough to satisfy the law. Once at the equipment, some type of accommodation should be made to allow children on at least some of the equipment as well as to interact with their nondisabled counterparts. Consult the U.S. Access Board for further information on this subject.

Installation

Installation of equipment is an important part of the overall planning process. If equipment and surfacing are installed improperly, the safety of the total play environment will be jeopardized. When dealing with the installation of equipment and surfacing, there are three factors to consider:

1. planning of the installation,
2. actual installation of the equipment and surfacing, and
3. liability issues related to the installation.

Planning of the Installation

Five items need to be considered during the planning of the installation process. These include

1. the manufacturer of the equipment,
2. the manufacturer of the surfacing,
3. the materials needed,
4. who will perform the installation, and
5. budgetary factors.

The Manufacturer of the Equipment. This business must be selected carefully. The decision about which manufacturer to use should be made on the basis of the planning committee's criteria. It is critical that the manufacturer chosen produces equipment that meets the ASTM 1487 current standard and the CPSC Handbook for Public Playground Safety guidelines. After the tentative selection of the manufacturer has been made, the planning committee should talk with others who have purchased equipment from the potential vendor and check the company's competency. The committee should also find out whether the equipment installation process was understandable and reasonable, and most important, how the equipment held up after being installed.

The Manufacturer of the Surface. As with the equipment manufacturer, the surfacing manufacturer should also be chosen with care. Again, any decision should be based on the criteria established by the planning committee. The surfacing manufacturer must be able to provide testing data from an independent laboratory to show the depth of the product needed proportionate to the height of the equipment purchased. The testing procedure used must be based on the ASTM 1292 current standard. In addition, it is a good idea to talk with others who have dealt with the prospective manufacturer to determine the company's competency and service record.

Materials Needed. A third item that needs to be considered in the planning process for installation is the materials needed. It is easier to obtain materials in some areas of the country than in others. This will affect their costs. In a previous section, weather factors have been discussed, but the time of year that installation will occur also needs to be considered. This is especially critical in relation to surfacing and the setting of cement for footings. It also is a consideration for the drying time of preservatives on wood products.

Who Will Install the Equipment and the Surface? The determination of the actual installer(s) is the fourth factor. It is possible to use an installer recommended by the company. If that is the decision, the installer should be trained by the company or be a certified installer recommended by the company. A trained installer adds to the overall cost of the equip-

ment. Thus, many times, in an effort to reduce cost, the purchaser will decide to use in-house agency personnel to install the equipment and surface. If this method of installation is chosen, it is important for liability protection to have a company representative observe the actual installation process or direct the process. Either way, an agency should have the company sign off that the installation process has met the company's specifications.

Budgetary Factor. The budget for installation is the last item that needs attention. The budget will be determined by the cost factors associated with who does the installation, the materials needed, and the time it takes to perform the installation. Cutting costs on installation is many times a short-sighted cost savings. As mentioned before, if the equipment is not properly installed or poor materials are used, the playground will cost the agency more money due to increased maintenance and liability issues.

Installing the Equipment and Surfacing

Four factors should be considered in relation to the actual installation of the equipment and surfacing. They are

■ manufacturer's instructions,
■ coordination of the installation,
■ time needed for the installation, and
■ sign-off by the manufacturer.

The Manufacturer's Instructions. According to ASTM F1487, the manufacturer or designer must provide clear and concise instructions and procedures for the installation of each structure provided and a complete parts list (ASTM-F1487-95, 1995). It is important that these procedures be followed during the installation process. In addition, these instructions should be filed, in case any liability issues arise concerning the proper installation of equipment.

Coordination of the Installation. The next step is to coordinate the installation process. Four potential groups need to interact with one another during installation. These groups include the manufacturer, the owner of the site, the organizer for the personnel who will perform the installation, and the vendors from whom products will be purchased.

Time Needed for Installation. Time is also an important issue that needs to be considered. In particular, the amount of time needed for the installation will influence the number of people involved in the actual installation process. One needs to determine whether or not the community will tolerate weekend installation or if the work must be done during usual work hours or in the evenings. If installation takes a period of time, protecting children from using partially built structures is a priority need.

Manufacturer Sign-off. After the installation is completed, the agency should get the manufacturer of the equipment and surfacing to sign-off that both items were installed according to specifications. This ensures that the structures and the surfacing are safe for children to use.

Liability Issues

Since we live in a litigious society, it is important to protect the agency from being sued. Following appropriate procedures will not prevent lawsuits, but it may reduce the amount of financial responsibility that is imposed, if a suit is upheld. However, the most important thing to remember about following proper installation instructions is not the liability issue, but the safety issue. By following manufacturer's instructions, the agency is being proactive in trying to reduce the potential for children being injured on the playgrounds.

An agency should be concerned with four liability issues regarding the installation of equipment. According to Clement (1988) these are

■ manufacturer's specifications,
■ manufacturer's recommendations,
■ the posting of manufacturer's warnings, and
■ the importance of following manufacturer's instructions.

Manufacturer's Specifications. It is critical that the agency be sure that the installer has followed the manufacturer's specifications for installation. The responsibility for this falls on the manufacturer, if the company performs the installation. If the agency does the actual installation, it assumes the liability and the burden of proof regarding the following of proper procedures.

Manufacturer's Recommendations. Any recommendations by the manufacturer must also be followed. For example, in order to properly deal with the impact attenuation of a surface, it may be recommended that pea gravel be separated from a wood product by use of a fabric. Once installed, it is the agency's responsibility to see that such a separation is continued. Other recommendations may include that bushings on swings be checked annually for wear, or that wood products be covered with a preservative on an annual basis. In each of these cases, it is important that the agency follow the recommendations of the manufacturer.

Posting of Manufacturer's Warnings. The agency must post any manufacturer's warnings that are included with materials. Many manufacturers now place labels on equipment that suggest ages for which the equipment is designed or the proper depth for loose-fill surface materials. In cases where warnings accompany playground equipment, the agency is responsible for replacing the warnings if they become illegible, destroyed, or removed. Diligence on the part of the agency in regard to the posting of the warning label will inform adults about ways to prevent a child from being injured.

Manufacturer's Instructions. Last, following manufacturer's instructions is very important in the installation of equipment. These instructions can include the proper use zone placement of equipment, the installation of the equipment at the proper depths, the correct method of mixing adhesives for surfacing materials, mixing cement in correct proportions with water, and the use of proper tools to lock joints of structures. The agency may need to be able to provide evidence that such procedures were followed.

As adults work with installation, they can conclude that they are dealing literally with the dirt of responsibility, the grit of reality, and the grind of responsibility.

On-Going Maintenance, Repair, and Inspections

The playground area should be perceived as an environment for play that contains many elements including playground equipment (Hendy, 1997). Parking lots, sidewalks, field areas, seating, shelters, and restroom facilities are only a few of the amenities that complement many playground areas. These amenities require maintenance as well. To insure proper long-term maintenance, a comprehensive program must include the total playground environment, not just the equipment.

The basic function of maintenance is to ensure the safety of users by keeping the playground area and equipment in a safe condition. Maintenance also keeps the equipment functioning efficiently and effectively. A track ride is not much fun if the bearings are worn and the mechanism won't glide easily. Maintenance is also performed to keep the area hygienically clean. By keeping an area well maintained, it remains aesthetically pleasing.

A safety audit should be performed when new equipment is purchased and installed to verify that the equipment and installation are consistent with the "Standard of Care" set forth by the agency and the manufacturer. The audit will not need to be repeated unless the Standard of Care changes, the equipment is heavily vandalized, or a natural disaster impacts the equipment.

Inspections

There are basically two types of maintenance inspections that are performed on playground equipment: seasonal (periodic) and daily (high frequency). A seasonal or periodic inspection is one performed two to three times a year. This is an in-depth type of inspection done to evaluate the general wear and tear on the equipment. A daily or high-frequency inspection is done routinely to identify rapidly changing conditions due to weather, vandalism, and sudden breakage. It also identifies surfacing problems typically associated with loose-fill surfacing materials.

There is no magic formula for determining the frequency necessary to perform each type of maintenance inspection. How often the playground is used and by what age group are two of the common considerations that will determine frequency of inspection. The vandalism rate in an area will also dictate the timetable chosen to inspect the playground.

The nature of the area and the environment will influence the need for playground maintenance. The soil type and drainage conditions as well as other geographic and climatic conditions will also influence inspection frequency.

Record Keeping

Documentation of inspections, repairs, and maintenance should be recorded regularly. In addition, the agency must establish a system of work requests that will enable maintenance staff to expedite the ordering of replacement parts and repair services. As part of the overall comprehensive program of playground maintenance, it is important to document all inspections and maintenance procedures. A "fail proof" system of follow-up must be established that enables a supervisor to review the inspection forms, noting

- who performed the inspection;
- items that were corrected on site at the time of inspection;
- hazards that need to be corrected;
- work orders that were issued;
- purchase orders for equipment services, or replacement parts;
- when equipment, parts, or services were supplied or rendered;
- when repair work was completed;
- who performed the repair work; and
- final approval from the supervisor.

■ Summary

Playgrounds should be an important facility consideration for inclusion in schools, child care centers, parks, and other recreation facilities. By following the systematic design process outlined in this chapter, playgrounds can be safe as well as foster children's physical, emotional, social, and intellectual development. By paying attention to age-appropriate equipment, proper surfacing under and around equipment, the placement of equipment for easy supervision, and the regular maintenance of the equipment and the environment, HPERD professionals will be able to design a play environment that allows children to be playful. It will also provide a setting in which children can increase their ability to take appropriate challenges without fear of taking inappropriate risks.

■ Self-Assessment Exercises

1. Which organization publishes safety guidelines about playgrounds for use by the general public?
2. Which organization publishes technical standards about playground equipment and surfacing?
3. What four playground safety areas should influence design considerations? Give an example of how these areas should be incorporated in the planning process.
4. What are the issues surrounding the Americans with Disabilities Act and playground accessibility?
5. Discuss how current trends in playground safety are influencing design.
6. What are the four general planning considerations for playground design?
7. Describe specific planning steps involved in designing playgrounds.
8. What factors should be considered in selecting proper surfacing for playgrounds?
9. What procedures should be followed in order to install playground equipment?
10. What is the function of a maintenance program and how should it be carried out?

■ References

American Society for Testing and Materials. (1993). **Standard consumer safety performance specification for playground equipment for public use. (F 1487).** West Conshohocken, PA.: Author.

American Society for Testing and Materials. (1995). **Standard consumer safety performance specification for playground equipment for public use. (F 1487).** West Conshohocken, PA.: Author.

American Society for Testing and Materials. (1991). **Standard specification for impact attenuation of surface systems under and around playground equipment. (F 1292).** West Conshohocken, PA.: Author.

American Society for Testing and Materials. (1993). **Standard specification for impact attenuation of surface systems under and around playground equipment. (F 1292).** West Conshohocken, PA.: Author.

American Society for Testing and Materials. (1995). **Standard specification for impact attenuation of surface systems under and around playground equipment. (F 1292).** West Conshohocken, PA.: Author.

American Society for Testing and Materials. (1996). **Standard specification for impact attenuation of surface systems under and around playground equipment. (F 1292).** West Conshohocken, PA.: Author.

Bowers, L. (1988). Playground design: A scientific approach. In L.D. Bruya (Ed.), **Play spaces for children: A new beginning** (pp. 22–48). Reston, VA: AAHPERD.

Bruya, L., & G Wood, G. (1997). Why provide supervision on the playgrounds. In S. Hudson & D. Thompson (eds.), **Playground safety handbook** (pp. 38–48). Cedar Falls, IA: National Program for Playground Safety.

Clement, A. (1988). **Law in sport and physical activity.** Indianapolis, IN: Benchmark Press.

Hendy, T. (1997). The nuts and bolts of playground maintenance. In S. Hudson & D. Thompson (Eds.), **Playground safety handbook** (pp. 60–70). Cedar Falls, IA: National Program for Playground Safety.

Illinois Park & Recreation Association. (1995). **A guide to playground planning.** Winfield, IL.: Author.

Mack, M.G., Hudson, S., & Thompson, D. (June, 1997). A descriptive analysis of children's playground injuries in the United States 1990–1994. **Journal of the International Society for Child and Adolescent Injury Prevention, 3,** 100-103.

Molnar, D., & Rutledge, A. (1986). **Anatomy of a park** (2nd ed.). New York: McGraw-Hill.

Shaw, L.G. (1976). **The playground: The child's center learning space** (MH 20743-034A1). Gainsville, FL: The Bureau of Research, College of Architecture, University of Florida.

Thompson, D., & Hudson, S. (1996). **National action plan for the prevention of playground injuries.** Cedar Falls, IA: National Program for Playground Safety.

United States Consumer Product Safety Commission (1991). **Handbook for public playground safety.** Washington, D.C.: Author.

United States Consumer Product Safety Commission (1994). **Handbook for public playground safety.** Washington, D.C.: Author.

United States Consumer Product Safety Commission (1997). **Handbook for public playground safety.** Washington, D.C.: Author.

■ Videos

ABC'S of playground supervision (1997). Cedar Falls, IA: National Program for Playground Safety.

America's playgrounds–Make them safe (1996). Cedar Falls, IA: National Program for Playground Safety.

Inspecting playgrounds for hazards (1992). Fair Oaks, CA.: Information Exchange

Sammy's playground pointers (1997). Cedar Falls, IA: National Program for Playground Safety.

■ Suggested Readings and Other Materials

Frost, J.L. (1992). **Play and playscapes.** Albany, NY: Delmar Publishers.

Frost, J.L., & Sweeney, T. (1996). **Cause and prevention of playground injuries and litigation: Case studies.** Wheaton, MD: ACEI.

Grosse, S.J., & Thompson, D. (Eds.). (1993). **Leisure opportunities for individuals with disabilities: Legal issues.** Reston, VA: American Alliance for Health, Physical Education, Recreation and Dance.

Hudson, S., & Thompson, D. (1997). **Selected annotated bibliography about public playground safety.** Cedar Falls, IA: National Program for Playground Safety.

The following brochures are available from the National Program for Playground Safety, located at the University of Northern Iowa, Cedar Falls, Iowa.

■ Blueprint for Supervision
■ Supervision Means . . .
■ Age Appropriate Design
■ Falls to Surfaces
■ Equipment Maintenance
■ Parent Inspection Checklist
■ Planning a Play Area for Children

CHAPTER 18

Aquatic Facilities

D.J. Hunsaker, Councilman/Hunsaker, Natatorium Planners, Designers, & Engineers

Learning Objectives

After reading this chapter, the student will be able to

- describe aquatic facility trends,

- design and implement a needs analysis for an aquatics facility, and

- describe the technical considerations for designing either a recreational or competitive aquatic facility.

Introduction

The purpose of this chapter is to review current trends in aquatic facilities. The field of aquatics has experienced a broad and comprehensive transition since the early 1980s. From the standpoint of professional programming, activities have been developed for all age groups with attendance increasing mostly among seniors, followed closely by preschoolers. Through the entire age span, North Americans have found aquatic activity in outdoor and indoor swimming facilities to provide entertainment, education, and skill enhancement.

Until the 1970s, swimming/diving activities almost always took place in a rectangular swimming pool that was shallow at one end and deep at the other. The introduction of the wave pool at Point Mallard, Alabama, in the late 1960s demonstrated the opportunity to have more fun and excitement in a manufactured swimming tank that was filled with filtered and hygienically clean water. This new approach led to aquatic entertainment facilities in the commercial sector, called water parks. As private capital underwrote these projects, public agencies at the municipal and county level began to experiment with non-rectangular pools that featured zero-entry water areas, water slides, and children's water play areas. While most of these initiatives with moving water were cautious, the trend in public aquatic recreation definitely is moving toward the design philosophy that is accepted on a broad front in western Europe, Canada, and resort areas in Asia, the South Pacific, and Africa.

Aquatic Center Trends

Leisure Pool Features

Leisure pool features include water falls, fountains, whirlpools, current channels, lazy rivers, and participatory water play apparatus. They must be designed carefully, considering initial costs, operating costs, life-cycle costs, and long-term popularity.

Falling water can be a dramatic focal point in a natatorium or an outdoor aquatic center. An indoor

Figure 18.1 Children enjoying leisure pool activities.

Figure 18.2 Children enjoying leisure pool activities.

facility must be designed with acoustical treatment to reduce the reverberation time of the splash noise. An indoor facility also must be designed to minimize atomization of water. Falling water is different from the misting of sprays. The latter will greatly increase the humidity in the space and increase the water vapor inhaled by people in the natatorium.

Current channels, lazy rivers, and water slides must be designed for safety and economy of operation. Since many states do not have regulations that specifically address these new concepts in aquatic recreation features, designers must work with jurisdictional officials to develop systems, designs, and configurations that reflect the philosophy of the agency. Computer technology is a cost-effective

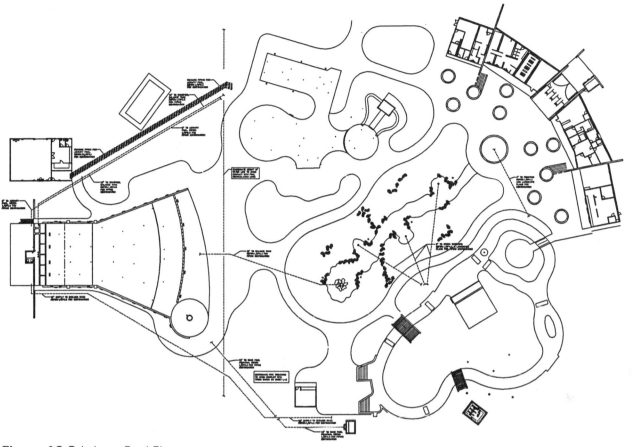

Figure 18.3 Leisure Pool Plan.

component of water features when used to activate and deactivate motors. The motors control the water pumps in an economical sequence that varies at different times of the day, week, and season.

Water slides offer many options for the leisure pool designer. Most installations are engineered by manufacturers based upon the design developed by the architect. The resulting protocol is essentially design/build and allows the configuration to be developed by the organization that is most knowledgeable about this very specialized equipment. In so doing, the manufacturer/designer/constructor accepts the liability for the product.

With few exceptions, the water-slide industry produces only fiberglass flumes. The slides can be open or totally enclosed as tubes. Each year more elaborate designs are produced for large and small venues.

Current channels and lazy rivers can be designed in a variety of ways. The difference between the two concepts is the velocity of the current and the length of the channel. The lazy river is usually a closed loop that allows participants to float continuously at a slow speed, where the current channel is a part of the leisure pool that provides a relatively short flume with a much faster current.

Therapy Pools and Whirlpool Spas

Another new type of pool that is appearing with frequency in North America is the therapy pool. These pools are being included in the construction of new wellness and fitness centers, many of which are being developed by hospitals. The therapy pool usually features an access ramp, recessed stairs, underwater benches, a deep-water area, and hydraulic lifts or movable floors for the non-ambulatory. These pools can be a part of an out-patient facility that specializes in treatment for temporary disabilities (e.g., post-surgical, post-injury or post-trauma, cardiac, etc). Other pools are located in rehabilitation centers for in-patients with permanent disabilities (e.g., paraplegia, quadriplegia, stroke, multiple sclerosis, etc.). Such pools also are in health care facilities that specialize in the treatment and/or care of the physically and mentally disturbed. In many cases the therapy pools are designed for and serve a variety of user groups.

The whirlpool spa has become a standard water feature in many natatoria at municipal, college, and

Figure 18.4 A leisure pool complex.

university sites. However, the spa seldom is seen in high school nataoria. Spas also are popular in health clubs and wellness centers. Their appeal is wide among frequent users of a recreation and fitness center.

Pools and Natatoria

During the mid 1990s a significant increase in the number of municipalities building leisure pools, both indoor and outdoor, occurred to the degree that the water park industry sees its emerging market being the public sector. This new group of developers creates smaller facilities than commercial developers but in much greater numbers. The result is that manufacturers have designed products and systems for the leisure pool complex, which for many companies is now the major market for their products.

A growing number of indoor natatoria are also being built. These facilities are being created frequently in Canada, with its colder climates, as well as throughout the United States. The reasons are several. The year-round benefits are being recognized along with the justification of higher capital costs for the 12-month programs they provide. Other indoor aquatic centers are being constructed at educational institutions to meet expanding demand on the campus and to meet competition from other schools, colleges, and universities, which are targeting the same prospective students.

These indoor facilities, along with others in health clubs, wellness centers, the YMCA, and the JCCA,

etc., are giving their respective populations the opportunity to recreate and develop skills that will enhance the aquatic experience throughout a lifetime. "Moms and Tots" programs introduce infants to the water in the being most secure environment (i.e., in the parent's arms). Preschoolers also have the opportunity to learn to swim and be water safe in a way that provides a foundation for lifelong participation in water sports. Competitive swimming and diving is usually the next plateau that the young person will master, although many youngsters find their enjoyment in unstructured recreational swimming. Other skills are learned in aquatic centers. These include advanced swimming techniques, lifesaving, lifeguarding, and scuba. Many of these skills will carry over into family passtimes and fitness regimens. The latter usually take form as fitness lap swimming on a year-round basis.

Regardless of the reason for creating a new swim center, a definite protocol should be followed to produce the most efficient, cost-effective, and programmable facility. This chapter describes the necessary procedure and discipline for creating a facility that will best meet the owner's needs.

Needs Analysis

While many people believe that the first step is to select an architect, two essential tasks really should be executed before an architect is asked to design a building. The first is to analyze the needs of the orga-

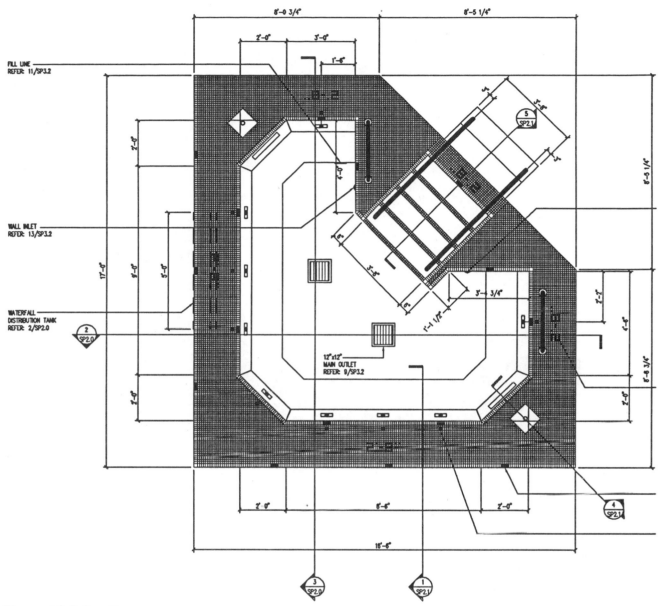

Figure 18.5 Spa Plan.

nization/owner; the second is to develop a design program for the facility. This analysis of needs is executed by identifying current users, potential users, and future users. A description of the activities that these users will want is supplemented by a list of activities and programs that the organization/owner's aquatic staff believes is warranted for the activity program in the new facility.

The analysis of the community's needs is more than a simple list. The data also must show the time and space requirements for proposed activities. This allocation of time and space will reveal potential priorities and demands.

The first step toward the objective is to develop an in-depth understanding of deficiencies in the existing aquatic program and the potential for meeting future demand. This can be carried out best by one or more individuals with experience in this important phase. It is at this time that some organizations/owner groups seek the assistance of a design and planning consultant to help them take the necessary steps toward a commitment to such a complex.

The first phase of the needs analysis is a meeting with staff and administration, followed by meetings with user groups. As a means of developing an understanding of the true core needs of the community, interviews are conducted, public meetings are held, and existing data are reviewed, including previous programs and efforts. Finally, a consensus must be developed among the various parties interested in the project.

Figure 18.6 University of Georgia aquatic facility.

Once the needs have been established and agreed to by all parties, the next step is to develop a design program. The design program is an outline of the features that must be provided in the aquatic center and a designation of the area required for each feature. This process includes not only the natatorium but also the necessary support spaces for the aquatic center.

After the spaces have been identified and have been given surface area values, it is then possible to develop an estimate of the construction cost. This is done by identifying the square footage involved, estimating a cost per square foot by using a conventional formula, and then comparing it to the industry average for recent construction, and adding an escalation factor to reflect the time frame between completed projects and the date of the bidding for the proposed project.

As these numbers are developed, it is essential that a distinction be made between construction costs and project costs. This is an area that is often misunderstood, and construction costs are emphasized when, in reality, the total project cost must be determined. A project cost includes the hard cost of construction, plus all of the soft costs of loose equipment, administration, and design required for the end product.

Once the project cost has been established and confirmed, it is necessary to move on to the source of financing. This may be a capital fund drive, the state legislature (university and college), a bond issue, certificates of participation, a capital expansion budget, donations, a build/lease back, or a combination of the above.

After the source of funding has been identified and a commitment received, the next step is to select an architectural team. There is a protocol that should be followed in this phase of the project. The first step is to develop a request for qualifications, which is a formal communication in letter form that is sent to a number of architectural firms. A formal advertisement is also placed in the newspaper. The firms will determine whether they wish to be considered for such a project. If they do, they will submit by a specified date a package that will reflect information about their selected team, as well as past history and experience with projects of all types including, presumably, those similar to the proposed project.

These submittals will be reviewed, and a selection committee will choose a limited number of firms for an interview. Interviews of the architectural teams will be scheduled for a specific period of time, and the firms will be given a format for their presentation, which usually includes 60% to 75% of the time for a formal presentation and 40% to 25% of the time for answering questions by the interview committee.

The interview process should follow a certain format, and the interview committee should be experienced or at least prepared for a methodical evaluation of the different teams. The important issue is to create a structure whereby all teams are given the same opportunity and benefit relative to presentation time and question-and-answer opportunities. In addition to the interview, it is suggested that the background and experience of each team be researched with former clients.

The final step is to select the architectural team and to sign agreements between the owner and the architectural firm that will lead the team throughout the project. This firm usually is identified as the project architect or architect of record.

What are the tasks and scope of services of the chosen architectural team? At this point an owner's steering committee should be formed, which is made up of individuals representing the users, the administration, the staff, and the owner's project manager. Together, this group must be qualified to make decisions as the process moves forward.

Programming

Much programming is work done when the design program is developed prior to determining funding needs. Once the architectual team is selected, the owner and the architect will confirm the design program surface area needs and requirements developed in the design program stage. The construction cost estimate will be reviewed and confirmed or changed by the project architect. As a result there will be a confirmation of the project cost estimate at this time.

An aquatic center or a community center featuring a natatorium is a very complex building. It is helpful if the organization/owner's steering committee understands the situation and the necessary design process. By comparison, a more simple structure is an office building, which basically repeats floor plans floor to floor and has very few special-use areas in the building. The next level of complexity may be a school, which still has redundancy in the classroom requirements plus several special areas such as a gymnasium, auditorium, lunch room, etc. The next level of complexity is the special-use building, which

describes a community center or an aquatic center. In this type of building there is very little redundancy, and the entire facility is unique unto itself. As a result, the design time is much greater than, for example, the office building. The square foot cost usually is higher because of the special features and characteristics the building must provide.

Once the design program and corresponding budget estimate are confirmed, the architect will develop a series of bubble diagrams and adjacency priorities. This information will be discussed with the steering committee and a consensus reached.

The next step is to develop a schematic floor plan that reflects the data developed in the step above. It is at this point that floor plans, access points, and general operating efficiency are developed.

As these issues are resolved, the schematic plans and elevations (single-line drawings) are developed. The schematics are reviewed by the steering committee, which after discussions and contributions by all members, will arrive at a consensus, resulting in an approved set of schematics. At this point it may be necessary for the architect to create a study model. Some architectural teams prefer to use models as a means of evaluating and studying the total building, both inside and outside. Once the model has been approved, an estimate of construction costs will again be developed.

If the project is on course with budget and program, the design development stage will begin, and more detailed drawings will be created at this time. Outline specifications also will be developed by the architect and various consultants on the design team. These will be reviewed by the steering committee. The outline specifications and design development drawings will be used to provide an update of estimated construction costs. (A constant monitoring of construction cost estimates is necessary to keep the project in line with the budget.)

At this time the steering committee must work closely with the architect until the design development drawings and outline specifications are approved.

Once the design development stage has been completed, the next phase is creation of the construction documents (e.g., drawings, specifications, and general conditions).

When the construction documents are approximately 50% complete, a review should occur again with the various consultants and the steering committee. This is an effective point to estimate again the construction costs and see if there is any necessity for a mid-course correction. When the construction documents reach 90% to 100 % completion, they should be reviewed again by the respective consultants and the

Figure 18.7 Diving center.

owner's steering committee. If all team members are in agreement and there are no omissions or errors, the architect will assist the owner in advertising for bids.

When the bids are opened one of three things will occur:

- The project will be under budget, and the design team will proceed or add any add alternatives that may have been called out in the construction documents.
- The budget will be the same as the accepted bid, and the project will proceed into the next stage.
- The low bid will be over budget, and deduct alternates will be deleted.

In the event of a significant over-budget situation, even after deduct alternates, a common process is to submit the overall design for value engineering and develop a priority of deletions. This usually is done in concert with the low bidder.

When the construction contract has been signed between the owner and the general contractor, the project then moves into the construction phase. At this time it also should be noted that there is an alternative to a general contractor protocol, and that is the owner's use of a construction management firm. In construction management, an experienced management team serves as a contract manager for the owner, in which case the construction management firm is paid a fee for its expertise. As the owner's agent, the construction management company negotiates directly with the respective subcontractors. While

a relatively new concept, the construction management approach does offer some benefits in certain types of projects.

What Happens During the Construction of the Natatorium?

Site Situations. Ideally the site for an aquatic center is level with good-quality soil. Many times, however, the site is not level and there are subsoil problems, e.g., rock, high water table, undesirable types of soil, cuts and fill, compaction, removal and replacement with engineered fill.

Design Options. A swimming pool and/or natatorium may feature several below-grade designs. One is a full basement, another is a tunnel around the pool shell, a third is a pool shell backfilled with no below-grade space, and a fourth is a combination of any or all of the above.

Basements

Benefits. The basement can provide a storage area, equipment area, piping and plenum location, access for maintenance repair, and no hydrostatic pressure on the pool shell. (The problem of hydrostatic pres-

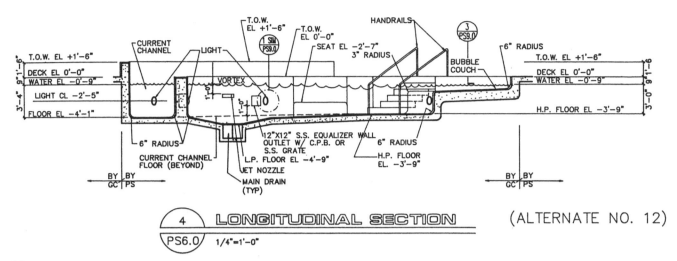

Figure 18.8 Longitudinal section of a pool.

sure under a swimming pool is significant. If there is a high water table, and no means have been created for relieving this pressure, it is possible that the swimming pool can float out of the ground when it is empty for construction or maintenance reasons. For this reason, special considerations must be made and appropriate designs engineered.)

Disadvantages. The below-grade space creates greater costs, delivery problems for mechanical equipment used in the below-grade areas, chemical rooms that are remotely located to filter equipment, and sometimes access problems for maintenance personnel.

Swimming Pool Shell Construction

Cast-in-place concrete

Benefits. The structure can be built above grade or surrounded by a tunnel/basement, and there no backfill is required. It can be included in the conventional concrete work by the concrete contractor. Cast-in-place concrete is advantageous for tile and a paint finish.

Disadvantages. It is costly to create a free-form configuration; water stop and honeycombing leaks are possible, and the wall-to-floor cove is more costly to build compared to pneumatically applied concrete.

Pneumatically applied concrete swimming pool shells

Benefits. This is a relatively economical pool shell construction when the pool walls are constructed

against a soil embankment or cut. Irregular shapes can be constructed efficiently and at a relatively low cost compared to cast-in-place. The wall-to-floor cove is simple and effective. Monolithic pneumatically applied concrete construction has advantages over the cast components in a cast-in-place pool, which depend upon water stop at joints. It is compatible with tile and marble plaster adhesion.

Disadvantages. It is costly and difficult to build a pneumatically applied pool with no earth cavity. The necessary forms needed for this type of construction erode the cost benefit of the process. Sometimes it is difficult to apply tile to the swimming pool interior. When painting is required, multistep preparation is necessary. Often it is difficult to find experienced and qualified contractors in a local bidding market.

Structural Features In the Natatorium

The first choice is structural steel with concrete and masonry walls, plus a concrete roof system. Because of cost, most natatorium roof structures are made of mild steel beams, joists, and trusses. When these steel components are used, they must be coated with highly effective, long-life coating systems. The roof and ceiling systems must be designed carefully to withstand corrosion created by condensation.

Wooden roof structures are effective if humidity is controlled and air circulation in the space is properly engineered.

A concrete roof structure has many advantages over steel and wood. It is noncorrosive and durable. Its cost, however, is greater than the other two lighter-weight options.

Fenestration. Skylights or top lighting are advantageous for location of a natural light source and control of reflective glare on the water. The relation of fenestration to spectator areas, lifeguard locations, and teaching stations is important. Wall and room penetrations for skylights, exhaust ducts, and overhead light fixtures can be the source of problems. As a result, they must be designed, engineered, and constructed with care.

Dehumidification. It is known now that relative humidity inside a natatorium should be maintained between 50% and 60%. This can be done in most areas with the use of outside air or refrigerated dehumidification. Such a design must control the dew point, be operated on a 24-hour basis, control condensation, and control the air velocities in the space along with the fresh air mix for needed ventilation. Physical comfort is most noticeable in this phase of the building system.

Materials and Finishes. Because of the high humidity potential and aggressive chloride conditions that may occur in the natatorium space if mechanical systems are shut down either on purpose or by accident, material choices should be tile, epoxy-coated steel (stainless steel used in some swimming pool components), glass, concrete, and anodized aluminum.

Considerations for maintenance tasks are important in the design process. These consist of daily custodial needs, scheduled repair and maintenance, emergency repair and/or replacement, and future repair and replacement (pool filters/HVAC/dehumidification).

During the construction process a system of inspections and monitoring should be carried out by the owner or his or her representative (e.g., architect/ engineer/consultant). This process is necessary to watch for incorrect installation as well as improper components.

Commissioning

This is the important climax to the entire process that has been executed to date. The general contractor, swimming pool contractor, other contractors, the project architect, engineers, and the swimming pool/natatorium consultants coordinate their efforts and put the facility into operation. In this process, notes are made of any and all problems and/or deficiencies. Responsible contractors will make the proper corrections so that the swimming

pool and all related systems for the complex will operate according to design and in compliance with all jurisdictional codes and regulations. Likewise, the mechanical HVAC/DH systems will be commissioned.

Because most contracts call for a one-year warranty period, it is recommended that a comprehensive inspection be executed just prior to the expiration of the warranty deadline. An independent and qualified inspector should make this audit because a swimming pool system or piece of equipment may be operating, but not as it should. Such a situation should be noted, documented, and reported to the owner's representative, who will notify the responsible contractor for corrective action under the warranty.

Upon the completion of the construction phase and after a final check out (punch list), an orientation of the organization/owner's management and operations staff should take place. This is a step that often is overlooked or minimized. With a multimillion-dollar complex, it is understandable that a thorough and professional set of instructions, including start-up procedures, trouble shooting, and daily operation procedures, as well as periodic maintenance tasks, should be provided in a well-documented, written operations manual. In addition, a resource contact should be provided for working with the operator as the owner takes over and puts the new facility into use.

Technical Considerations

Dimensions. The designer of the swimming pool must select the correct dimensions when creating the bounded water volume of the pool(s). Exact dimensions are required for pools used for swimming and diving competitions. These include

- length,
- width,
- depths (minimum and maximum),
- bottom profiles,
- tolerances and allowances (e.g., touchpad, construction, and bulkhead adjustment), and perimeter overflow tolerance at rim flow.

There is no exception for these types of pools if they are going to be used for organized competition under the sanction of any one of the rule-making entities (e.g., Federation Internationale de Natation Amateur, United States Swimming, United States Diving, United States Synchronized Swimming,

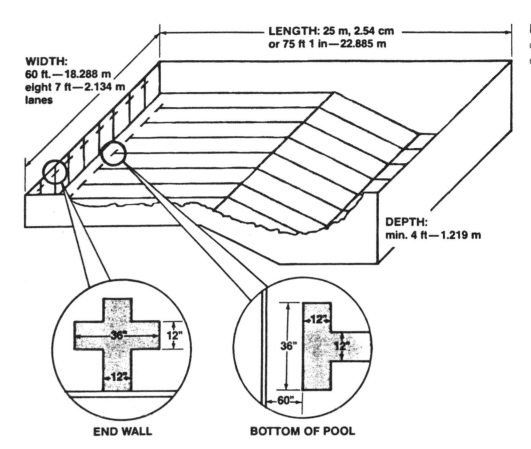

WIDTH:
60 ft.—18.288 m
eight 7 ft—2.134 m
lanes

LENGTH: 25 m, 2.54 cm
or 75 ft 1 in—22.885 m

DEPTH:
min. 4 ft—1.219 m

Figure 18.9 NCAA pool diagram, dimensions and equipment requirements

36" 12"
12"
END WALL

12"
36" 12"
60"
BOTTOM OF POOL

United States Water Polo, National Collegiate Athletic Association, and the National Federation of State High School Associations and Swimming/Natation Canada).The following dimensions are provided as an example, and the reader should contact the appropriate association for accurate and updated information prior to finalizing building plans. Other bodies of water are not as demanding for exact or pre-determined measurements, with the exception of health department safety regulations. These consist of minimum depths in shallow water and in diving areas. Such regulations usually dictate the degree of slope of the pool bottom in the shallow water and in the deep area.

Access for the physically disabled has been a design requirement in swimming pools since the 1970s. Methods of egress for the disabled vary. The most popular is the recessed stair, which is used by all attendees whether or not they are disabled. Other systems include ramps and hydraulic or mechanical lifts. The latter use permanent or temporary anchors in the pool deck. With the creation of new enforcement powers in 1992, more products will become available in subsequent years. Field experience indicates low use of ramps.

Interior Finishes

Ceramic tile is considered the best choice for the interior of a swimming or diving pool. Its durability, appearance, and longevity cannot be matched by the other options. Marble plaster can develop problems on a large pool and/or one that is exposed to construction dust and wind-blown debris. Because plaster should be applied in one continuous process without interruptions, large pools will require large numbers of plaster finishers working simultaneously. Such a large group of skilled craftsmen may not be available in many market areas in North America.

Another problem that must be solved in plastering a large pool is the filling process. For best results, a pool with a green plaster coating should be filled as soon as possible, preferably in 24 to 48 hours after the completion of the plastering phase. This water fill should be uninterrupted to avoid telltale rings around the pool wall.

A painted pool interior is the least expensive process, but such a finish has a short life. As a result, many painted pool interiors must be repainted every three to five years. In some cases, the repainting is more frequent.

POOL DIMENSIONS AND EQUIPMENT

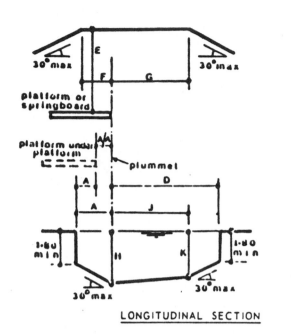

LONGITUDINAL SECTION

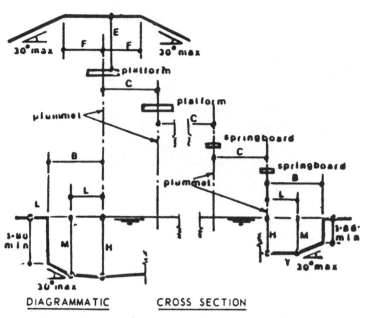

DIAGRAMMATIC   CROSS SECTION

NCAA Dimensions for Diving Facilities	Dimensions are in Feet	SPRINGBOARD		PLATFORM		
		1 Metre	3 Metres	5 Metres	7.5 Metres	10 Metres
	LENGTH	16'	16'	20'	20'	20'
	WIDTH	1'8"	1'8"	5'	5'	6'7"
	HEIGHT	3'4"	10'	16'5"	24'8"	32'10"
Revised to 1st Jan. 1987		Horiz. Vert.	Horiz. Vert.	Horiz. Vert.	Horiz. Vert.	Horiz. Vert.
A From plummet BACK TO POOL WALL	Designation	A-1	A-3	A-5	A-7.5	A-10
	Minimum	6'	6'	4'2"	5'	5'
AA From plummet BACK TO PLATFORM plummet directly below	Designation			AA5/1	AA7.5/3/1	AA10/5/3/1
	Minimum			5'	5'	5'
B From plummet to POOL WALL AT SIDE	Designation	B-1	B-3	B-5	B-7.5	B-10
	Minimum	8'3"	11'6"	14'	14'10"	17'3"
C From plummet to ADJACENT PLUMMET	Designation	C-1/1	C-3/3/1	C-5/3/1	C-7.5/5/3/1	C-10/7.5/5/3/1
	Minimum	8'	8'6"	8'6"	8'6"	9'
D From plummet to POOL WALL AHEAD	Designation	D-1	D-3	D-5	D-7.5	D-10
	Minimum	29'	34'	34'	36'	45'
E On plummet, from BOARD TO CEILING	Designation	E-1	E-3	E-5	E-7.5	E-10
	Minimum	16'5"	16'5"	11'6"	11'6"	16'5"
F CLEAR OVERHEAD behind and each side of plummet	Designation	F-1 E-1	F-3 E-3	F-5 E-5	F-7.5 E-7.5	F-10 E-10
	Minimum	8'3" 16'6"	8'3" 16'6"	9' 11'6"	9' 11'6"	9' 16'6"
G CLEAR OVERHEAD ahead of plummet	Designation	G-1 E-1	G-3 E-3	G-5 E-5	G-7.5 E-7.5	G-10 E-10
	Minimum	16'5" 16'5"	16'5" 16'5"	16'5" 11'6"	16'5" 11'6"	19'8" 16'5"
H DEPTH OF WATER at plummet	Designation	H-1	H-3	H-5	H-7.5	H-10
	Minimum	11'	12'	14'2"	15'	16'
J-K DISTANCE AND DEPTH ahead of plummet	Designation	J-1 K-1	J-3 K-3	J-5 K-5	J-7.5 K-7.5	J-10 K-10
	Minimum	16'5" 11'8"	20' 12'2"	20' 12'10"	26'3" 14'6"	36'2" 15'6"
L-M DISTANCE AND DEPTH each side of plummet	Designation	L-1 M-1	L-3 M-3	L-5 M-5	L-7.5 M-7.5	L-10 M-10
	Minimum	5' 11'2"	6'7" 12'2"	14' 12'10"	14'10" 14'6"	17'2" 15'6"
N MAXIMUM SLOPE TO REDUCE DIMENSIONS beyond full requirements	Pool depth Ceiling Ht	30 degrees 30 degrees	NOTE: Dimensions C (plummet to adjacent plummet) apply for Platforms with widths as detailed. For wider Platform increase C by half the additional width(s).			

Figure 18.10 NCAA Pool Dimensions and Equipment Requirements

Figure 18.11 1996 Olympic Venue

Another problem that sometimes develops is peeling, chipping, or oxidizing, which can be unsightly and cause milky water.

Gutter Systems (Perimeter Overflow Recirculation System)

Numerous gutter configurations are used throughout the world. In most cases, the design has been developed by an architect, an engineer, a builder, or a manufacturer. The purpose of the overflow gutter in modern swimming pools is to receive and capture water that flows over the lip. This water then is transferred to the filter plant, usually through a surge chamber, which helps stabilize the water displacement in the swimming pool.

The gutter cross-section can be created in three basic configurations:

Deep Recessed Gutter

This design often is preferred by competitive swimmers and coaches. The pool deck cantilevers over the gutter trough, with the top of the deck approximately 12 to 15 inches above the water. The overhang provides the competitive swimmer with a visual reference plane for the underwater wall. The recessed gutter captures the wave amplitude very effectively and keeps the pool decks relatively dry. The disadvantage is that the high overhang makes egress from the pool rather difficult, and as a result, most people choose to use one of the pool ladders.

Deck Level Gutter

The deck level overflow system features a gutter lip, a flume, and a grate that is very close to the elevation of the pool deck. This design enables even the weakest swimmer to egress over the water's edge with little effort. The disadvantage of the deck level configuration is that the decks around this type of pool usually are quite wet. Competitive swimmers often dislike this gutter profile because it is difficult to see a reference point above the water that relates to the pool wall under the water. Frequently a swimmer will misjudge the actual location of the turning surface during a race. Backstroke swimmers, in particular, have problems with this situation.

Roll Out

The third concept is the "roll out" gutter profile. This design combines the features of the fully recessed and deck level configurations. It consists of a gutter lip and grate or a very shallow flume at the water level. The pool deck is approximately $7^1/_2$" inches above the water surface, and it forms a curb at the rear of the gutter grate. This curb contains much of the wave action and keeps the pool deck relatively free of water washing up and over the gutter assembly. The low configuration at the water's edge still allows the swimmers to egress easily. A popular concept is to place the roll out gutter design on the long sides of the pool, with a fully recessed gutter parapet at each end of the race course. This arrangement provides competitive swimmers with a good visual reference at the turning walls of the race course and at the same time provides easy access and egress on the sides of the pool for recreational and student swimmers.

In case of a separate diving pool, a roll out gutter profile should be featured on all four sides of the diving pool. The curb will contain waves created by activity in the pool as well as those created by the bubble sprayer for platform diving facilities.

A roll out or deck level gutter often is selected for a shallow water recreation pool because of the ease of ingress and egress by users.

Gutter Construction

Any of these gutter profiles can be constructed in several different ways:

■ cast-in place concrete with tile, paint or plaster finish;
■ pneumatically applied concrete (gunite or Shotcrete) with tile, plaster or paint finish; and
■ stainless steel fabricated with a grate cover made of fiberglass, high impact plastic, or PVC. This system contains a return water pressure conduit as well as the overflow to the surge tank and/or filter system.
■ The cast-in-place concrete is a popular method of construction because
■ it is part of the concrete work on the site and is easily included in that section of work,
■ a tile finish can produce an attractive appearance, and
■ has a long life.

Several other factors should be considered with regard to the cast-in-place system. The gutter flume must feature an outfall system. This can require a periodic gutter drain in the trough or a converter drop at one or more locations in the pool perimeter. The return piping inlet system must be located in the pool walls or in the pool floor.

There are several advantages to a 304 low carbon stainless steel overflow recirculation system:

■ The gutter segments are fabricated at the factory and shipped to the site. A few days' work by a field welder results in the complete installation of the pool perimeter gutter and return piping system. This is beneficial with regard to the scheduling of trades and phases of work.
■ If a floor inlet system is omitted, there is no deep buried piping except that for the main drain. In the event the pressure return conduit, which is part of the gutter assembly, should develop a leak, the water will flow only into the inside of the pool tank. No water will leak into the surrounding soil or into below-grade rooms.
■ When a stainless steel system is installed, the filter system usually is provided by the same manufacturer or distributor. This creates the desirable situation of having one manufacturer responsible for the entire recirculation system.
■ If a movable bulkhead is specified, it usually is provided and installed by the gutter manufacturer. This single-source responsibility can be a desirable situation and will avoid disputes that might occur if different contractors are involved at the gutter/track.

The stainless steel perimeter overflow system must be approved by local regulatory agencies and be manufactured by a company with experience in similar pool installations. The gutter detail should be a stainless steel prefabricated overflow system featuring a handhold with a gutter profile utilizing a PVC, or fiberglass, grate over the gutter trough. The freeboard on the grate side of the handhold should be 3/4".

The trough of the gutter must have sufficient capacity to meet the requirements of jurisdictional agencies.

The hydraulics of the recirculation system, regardless of construction materials, should be such that the gutter trough develops a surge capacity between swimming races when the static surge is nonexistent. Thus the gutter trough subsequently will accommodate the dynamic and static surge during the first length of each race. If a stainless steel perimeter system is selected, at least two converters should be provided for a 50-meter pool, while one is sufficient for a 25-yard or -meter pool.

Parapets and Fully Recessed Gutters

The parapets described above can take many forms. The vertical face toward the race course, however, must provide an orientation that indicates the location of the vertical plane of the race course. Parapets may be temporary or permanent. Parapets result when a fully recessed gutter profile is required to match the above water configuration of the movable bulkhead(s).

Swimming Pool Mechanical Systems

Pool Filters

The selection of a filter system is influenced greatly by the limitations created by the volume of waste water that can be removed from the site. The construction of a holding tank is a common solution if sewer capacity is a problem.

Filter Considerations. There are three basic kinds of swimming pool filtration:

■ sand filtration,
■ diatomaceous earth filtration, and
■ cartridge filtration.

Sand Filters. Sand pressure systems exist in two forms:

■ rapid sand pressure filtration, which operates at flow rate of 3 gallons per minute (GPM) per square foot of filter area, and
■ high-flow (high-rate) pressure filtration, which operates up to a flow rate of 15 GPM per square foot of filter area.

While many manufacturers rate their system at 20 GPM per square foot, field experience suggests that the lower flow rate results in better water quality. The system must be designed to completely turn over the pool volume, as required by the jurisdictional health department. Some manufacturers produce a high flows and pressure system tht features a multiple-cell configuration and operates at approximately $7^1/_2$ GPM per square foot of filter area. These filters are characterized by longer filter runs.

Sand Vacuum Filter Systems

A recent application of sand filter systems to swimming pool water is the vacuum sand system. These units usually require less space than sand systems. While sand systems are very popular because of their simple operation, they have one considerable drawback (besides their high installation cost). That is the large water volume that is discharged during backwash. A multi-cell filter, however, can backwash in stages, and thus produce less volume at one time.

Diatomaceous Earth Filters

Pressure diatomaceous earth (DE) systems have the same requirement for pressurized backwash as does pressure sand. For this reason, they have no significant advantage over pressure sand systems except that DE filters can produce a slightly clearer (polished) water quality.

Vacuum diatomaceous earth filtration with 1-1.5 GPM per square foot of filter area is a viable option. The backwash discharge from the open-top filter tank is by gravity, and the filter elements are cleaned by water jet sprays or by manually hosing off the elements. As a result, only a little more than the volume of the filter tank needs to be discharged via the sanitary sewer system.

Some jurisdictional authorities require a reclamation tank between the DE filter tank and the backwash outfall so that the spent DE is captured and not discharged into the sanitary sewer. This understandably increases labor costs.

One important recommendation with a vacuum diatomaceous earth system is that the top of the tank be slightly above the water level of the pool. The pumps and motors must be below water level for a flooded suction situation.

An open-topped vacuum system should not be installed in a below-grade filter room where the pool water level is above the rim of the filter tank.

A number of quality prefabricated systems are available in the marketplace. Several provide the option of fiberglass or stainless steel tanks, which is essential. Even when coated with special paint systems, mild carbon steel tanks soon can develop corrosion problems, especially if located in the ground with soil backfilled against the walls.

Another common design is for the filter tank to be part of the concrete surge tank with the pump(s) and face piping in the basement level of the natatorium. Such systems usually feature a two-level filter room with open space over both levels.

As a means of avoiding uncontrollable leaks in a fiberglass or metal filter tank below floor level, a concrete well should be built, inside of which the DE tank will sit with space for a person to maneuver around it and be able to look under the tank to locate future leaks. This concrete well must have a floor drain to capture any water that begins to leak from the tank. If the tank walls are backfilled, a subsequent leak can be extremely difficult to repair, especially if multiple leaks develop about the same time.

Chemical Treatment of Pool Water

Swimming pool water must be risk-free for the users. This is accomplished by treating the recirculated pool water with a bactericide. Additional treatment is also required to prevent microscopic plant growth such as algae. Algae, if unchecked, can create an environment that will propagate and harbor organisms that can be harmful to humans in varying degrees.

The most common bactericide and algaecide is chlorine. This chemical has been used for over a century in the treatment of drinking water by municipal water companies. Its application to swimming pools since the early decades of the 20th century is understandable.

Because chlorine creates hypochlorous acid when mixed with water, the product will kill bacteria, and at the same time it will oxidize organic particulant matter in the swimming pool water.

The most popular form of chlorine treatment for public swimming pools historically has been elemental chlorine, which is in gaseous form when it is released from its storage tank and injected into the swimming pool recirculation system. Because chlorine gas can be hazardous if released into the atmosphere and fatal if inhaled in any significant quantity, there is a definite trend away from gas chlorine and toward chlorine compounds. The most popular for public swimming facilities is sodium hypochlorite, which commonly is called liquid chlorine or bleach.

While liquid chlorine does not create some of the risks gas chlorine does, it is not without its disadvantages. The main disadvantages are bulk handling, distribution, and storage, plus the tendency to accumulate total dissolved solids in the pool water. This phenomenon can result in water quality problems.

Dry chlorine products are manufactured and sold in the marketplace and have increased in their share of the public pool demand. The cost of these chemicals is higher than sodium but their handling and storage advantage is viewed by some owners as worth the premium. These chemicals usually are impractical for large-volume pools, especially outdoor pools.

Because of the problems and limitations of the chlorine treatment of swimming pool water, a search for an alternative is underway in the United States market. The one option is the corona discharge ozone generation system. Widely used in western Europe and parts of Canada, as well as isolated locations around the world, the process can reduce many of the disadvantages of chlorine-only treatment, especially indoors. It must be noted that a chlorine or bromine system still is required for pools in order to provide a free bacteriacide residual in the pool at all times. This residual chlorine is surplus bactericide that attacks contaminants and germs that are brought into the water by swimmers. Ozone has many qualities, but it has no sustained residual power after the pool water is treated in the contact chamber. Maintenance in the field has been a challenge for many operators.

Both alternative systems (ozone corona discharge and copper and silver ionization) are in the early phases of market penetration. As a result, the supply and field service after the sale are inconsistent in many locations.

Automation

Automation has been a part of modern swimming pool design for several decades. The application has focused on two systems. The first is water chemistry, and the second is filtration.

The water chemistry of the pool is sampled and analyzed electronically by a microprocessor. The analysis is recorded and compared to two set points previously established by the pool operator. One of the set points is the desired level of free chlorine. The other set point is for pH.

When the analyzer samples the pool water (by means of a sample stream that bypasses part of the recirculation piping), compares the result to the set point for the desired level. If the sample shows that the free chlorine level is above the set point of the analyzer, the unit, which is connected to the chemical feed pump (or a booster pump in the case of chlorine gas), will turn off the chlorine feed pump motor. If the sample reading is below the set point, the analyzer will turn on the feed pump motor if it is off, or it will continue its operation until the pool water in the sample strewn reaches the set point level. In the same way, the analyzer will monitor the sample stream for the pH level and then will energize the chemical feed pump that adds the respective buffer agent (e.g., caustic soda or sodium carbonate [soda ash] to raise the pH, or muriatic acid or carbon dioxide to lower the pH).

There are several benefits to an automated water chemistry feed system. The automated system monitors the pool water constantly, as compared to manual testing by an operator which takes place anywhere from once an hour to once a day. The analyzer begins and ceases the chemical feed system immediately upon demand, as compared to manual adjustments after each manual testing. With manual adjustment, there is no assurance that the change in the rate of feed by the operator will be of sufficient quantity to change the level of chlorine (or pH) to the desired amount. Quite to the contrary, the likelihood is that the chemical level will exceed the desired level before the next manual test is made.

Another benefit of the automatic chemical feed system is the lower chemical cost to the owner. With the constant monitoring of the water and the subsequent activation of the feeders, both on and off, overfeeding is eliminated, and overall chemical costs are lower. This is due to the tendency of a manual set feed system to overfeed the chemical until the next manual test is taken, and a new adjustment is made to the feed pump rate of feed setting.

Modern automatic water chemistry analyzers can be provided with a remote readout, which usually is located in the pool management office. This allows the management staff to monitor the water chemistry levels in the pool water without having to walk to the filter room to visually monitor the system. The system also can be interfaced with the building's environmental monitoring and control systems, in which case a PC computer in the pool office can display pool water chemical levels. In addition, a recorder will tape readings per minute. The paper tape is stored in the analyzer for review by the operator or maintenance service person. Such data are helpful in understanding the impact of bather loads versus quiescent times in the 24-hour cycle of the pool operations.

Movable Bulkhead

Movable bulkheads became popular during the late 1970s and have continued through the 1990s. There are several reasons. The bulkhead, which is usually three or four feet in width and approximately $4^1/_2$ feet in depth, can be moved along a horizontal translation. By moving the bulkhead, different course lengths can be created (i.e., with a movable bulkhead, a 50-meter pool can be converted into a 25-yard or 25-meter race course). When two or more bulkheads are used, duplicate or even triplicate courses can be created. In addition to race courses, other aquatic activity areas can be created at the same time, such as synchronized swimming, water polo, instruction classes, or fitness lap swimming.

While United States bulkheads tend to move horizontally over the length of the pool and are stored at the end of the pool when the 50-meter dimension is in use, European bulkheads usually move only vertically, and they are stored in a floor well when the pool is in the 50-meter mode. The reason for these differences is that the U.S. Swimming competition takes place over several configurations of race course (e.g., 25 yards, 25 meters, or 50 meters).

The bulkheads usually are a fiberglass box girder or a stainless steel truss with a skin of PVC or fiberglass grating. The bulkhead is designed to accommodate live loading both from above and from the side (laterally). These design qualifications are needed to provide a rigid training surface for the athletes, and in the case of starts from a bulkhead, minimal deflection from the simultaneous thrust from swimmers diving from starting blocks mounted on the bulkhead. (It is for this reason that many competitive swimmers prefer starting blocks anchored in the pool deck).

The current generation of bulkhead design features a variable buoyancy chamber. This enables the operator to inflate the chamber, which in turn creates a positive buoyancy in the bulkhead off its resting (bearing points) place on the pool perimeter lip or wall. In this position the bulkhead can be towed to its new position, deflated, and anchored onto the pool perimeter.

Prior to this development, most bulkheads moved on wheels on the pool's perimeter. Difficulty with wheel mechanisms has made some bulkheads difficult to move. It is for this reason that design development has moved toward the variable buoyancy system.

Movable Pool Floors

The hydraulic or mechanically driven pool floor has been popular in western Europe for three decades. Originally developed in Germany, it has the ability to create different water depths, which in turn creates conditions for a greater variety of aquatic activities, making it popular especially in indoor natatoria. The floor creates a variety of pool configurations, all under the same roof with the same operational costs. This has impressive advantages over building several pools with different depths for different activities.

The "floors," which usually are installed at the time that the pool is constructed, have been used in competition pools, both long-course and short-course, as well as rehabilitation centers, wellness centers, and service organizations such as YMCAs and JCCAs.

The majority of movable floors installed in the 1970s and 1980s, used hydraulic rams for the lift translation. During the 1990s, new movable floor systems use a sissor jack mechanism or a cable tension

Figure 18.12 Control Monitor Bypass Line.

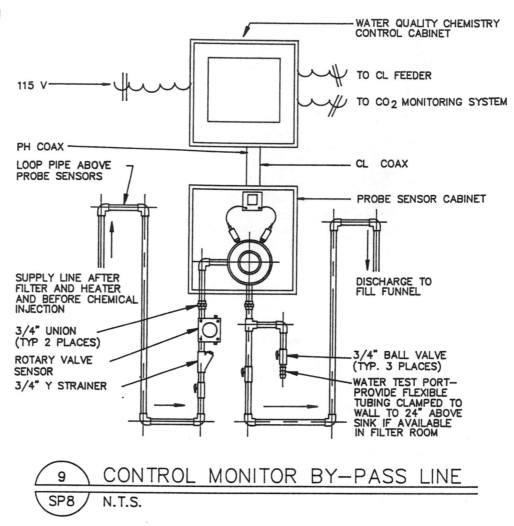

WATER QUALITY CHEMISTRY CONTROL CABINET

115 V

TO CL FEEDER

TO CO$_2$ MONITORING SYSTEM

PH COAX

LOOP PIPE ABOVE PROBE SENSORS

CL COAX

PROBE SENSOR CABINET

SUPPLY LINE AFTER FILTER AND HEATER AND BEFORE CHEMICAL INJECTION

DISCHARGE TO FILL FUNNEL

3/4" UNION (TYP 2 PLACES)

ROTARY VALVE SENSOR

3/4" Y STRAINER

3/4" BALL VALVE (TYP. 3 PLACES)

WATER TEST PORT— PROVIDE FLEXIBLE TUBING CLAMPED TO WALL TO 24" ABOVE SINK IF AVAILABLE IN FILTER ROOM

9 / SP8   CONTROL MONITOR BY-PASS LINE   N.T.S.

system activated by a motor and/or hydraulic ram behind the pool wall in a below-grade room.

The approximate maximum size is usually 75 feet by 42 feet and uses four rams. Such a floor section can be used in a 50 meter-by-25 yard pool and create a functional shallow water area for a number of programs.

A frequent addition to the movable floor is a trailing ramp. This is a plane that is hinged to the floor section with the opposite end of the ramp resting on the pool floor with rollers. The ramp extends from pool wall to pool wall and, as such, creates an inclined slope from the edge of the movable floor to the pool bottom. The ramp prevents anyone from swimming underwater beneath the movable floor when it is in a raised position.

The need for movable floors has become more understandable in the past decade because of the need to locate starting blocks over deep water. A number of young competitive swimmers have been paralyzed when striking the pool bottom with their head after diving headfirst off a starting platform. If the starting blocks are installed at the deep end of the pool along with the diving board supports, the resulting congestion is not desirable. The historic location of starting platforms at the uncongested shallow end of the pool is hazardous when the starting blocks are used over water five feet deep or less. The movable floor solves these problems by creating an ideal situation for the use of starting blocks, while at the same time avoiding the problems of the combined use of the starting blocks and the diving boards at the deep end of the pool.

Diving Facilities

Diving facilities have evolved out of the development and the requirements of competitive springboard and platform diving. The heights of these respective structures have been standardized at one meter and three meters for springboards and 1, 3, 5, 7.5 and 10 meters for rigid platforms. There are sev-

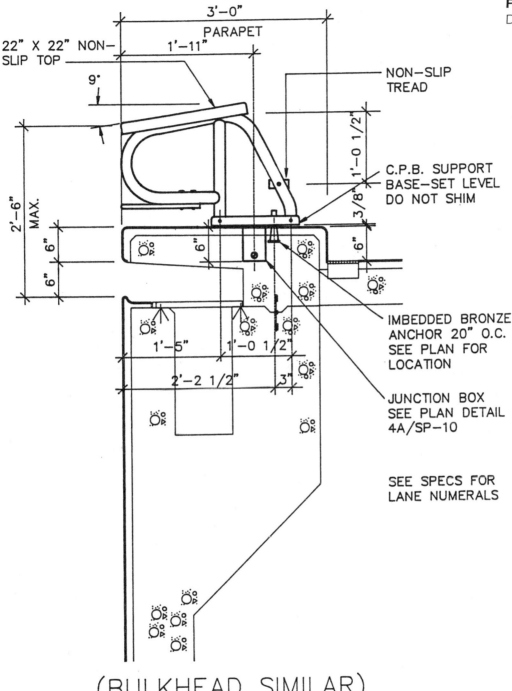

Figure 18.13 Bulkhead Diagram.

(BULKHEAD SIMILAR)

eral dimensional requirements, each promulgated by different organizations (e.g., FINA [Federation Internationale De Natation Amateur] and U.S. Diving and National Collegiate Athletic Association [NCAA]).

Springboard diving competition has been influenced greatly by one manufacturer of diving boards, Duraflex International. Since the 1950s, this company has developed three generations of high-performance springboards. Using a patented aluminum alloy and design, Duraflex International has developed a conventional diving board, a double tapered board, and a double tapered board with holes across a section of the board. As a result, the divers usually are lifted higher in the air, allowing them to execute complicated dives at a higher elevation and with a slightly longer time in the air. Both conditions are advantageous to the competitive diver.

Figure 18.4 IUPUI Natatorium.

The Duraflex board has a reputation for durability and can last for several decades with intermittent resurfacing by the factory. Other diving boards are manufactured by different companies and are sold primarily to the residential pool market, semi-public (motel, hotel, condo, apartment pool market), and the public recreation pool market. These boards usually are fiberglass or vinyl encapsulated wood boards. Other types of diving boards sold to the residential and semi-public market are 100% molded fiberglass.

Diving board supports vary, and the difference is reflected in cost. The least expensive is the cast aluminum stand designed and manufactured by Du-raflex International, called Durafirm. The three-meter unit is relatively rigid, is easy to install, requires no underground footing, and needs only a thickened slab beneath the anchored legs.

A more attractive diving board support, in the opinion of many designers and users, is the cantilevered support pedestal with a stainless steel ship's ladder and handrails. The forward leaning profile creates a dramatic appearance and often is used in public pools, clubs, and schools. Because it has more connected parts, it has a tendency to vibrate and rattle if the bolted connectors are not kept tight by the pool operator. If this type of diving board support structure is specified, it is recommended that the pedestal and flanged ends be 304 stainless steel and painted. It is especially important that the flanges and all bolts not be a mild steel because of the corrosion that will occur. This result is a problem for maintenance personnel who must repaint these components frequently.

The third type of diving board support is a cast-in-place concrete structure for both heights, (i.e., one meter and three meters). This structure has no vibration except from the short stand butt plate and fulcrum base assembly. The overall advantage of the concrete support is the monolithic structure, which will not shake, vibrate, or loosen component connectors. The result is a firm, stable base for the diving board. Understandably, the solid cast-in-place concrete support costs more than the factory-fabricated metal units. This is a result of the labor and materials required and the stair assembly that usually is a part of the design. Because of the greater cost, the concrete supports usually are designed for universities where the budget can accommodate and the diving program justify the expense. Concern over the number of accidents involving children falling down ship's ladders while attempting to climb to a three-meter board has led to the provision of a stair for these high diving boards. Such a stair follows the typical angle of ascent with handrails.

Consideration of diving boards includes the depth and envelope of the water, which are safety issues. Safety for the diver is paramount, which is complicated by the wide ranges of efficiency and skill possessed by different divers. The trained competitive diver consistently will reach a greater depth after entry because of the streamlined body configuration and disciplined movements. Because of his or her experience, injurious impact with the pool bottom is extremely rare. By contrast, the typical recreational diver almost always will enter the water in an inefficient configuration with little or no streamlined characteristics. As a result, this diver will slow body velocity rapidly after entry and will not plunge to the depths that the experienced competitive diver can achieve at will.

While this describes the typical entry of both experienced competitive divers and inexperienced recreational divers, there can be rare exceptions. To anticipate these potentially hazardous experiences by divers, the depth and envelope of the water below the diving boards must be adequate. Standards and/or requirements are promulgated by local health departments and the governing bodies of competitive diving (i.e., U. S. Diving, NCAA, and FINA). While the competitive rule-making agencies dictate water depths that will accommodate experienced divers, municipal and state regulations allow shallower minimum depths and smaller envelopes. Because there is no way of ascertaining the skill level of a diver before he or she executes a dive, or to know the efficiency with which a dive will be executed, shallower water depths may not be appropriate. Another factor that must be considered is the potential for an original low-performance (wood or fiberglass) diving board to be replaced by a high-performance aluminum board. When this occurs, a new set of capabilities is created, and new parameters are required.

The different skill levels and body weights of divers and the different lift characteristics of diving boards suggest that the deeper and larger water envelopes beneath the diving boards (and diving platforms) should be designed for pools that feature regulation aluminum 16-foot diving boards. For this reason, most designers will use the current rules of FINA, U. S. Diving, or the NCAA.

Diving platforms are being built at a noticeably increased rate within new facilities. Most of these are on university campuses and are part of new 50-meter natatoria. This sudden development has been stimulated by the commencement of platform diving at the NCAA Division I Swimming and Diving Championships in 1988. It is anticipated that platform diving will be added to the order of events at conference meets as more platform towers are built at Division I campuses. The rationale for this development is to better prepare U.S. divers for international competition. Diving coaches and platform divers are requesting platforms with three center lines instead of the customary two. In the former, the 10-meter, 7.5-meter, and 5 meter platforms have separate plummet centerlines so that divers can dive from each platform at the same time without conflict. In the latter, the 10-meter platform is directly above the five-meter and one-meter platforms in what is called a stacked configuration. Likewise, the 7.5-meter is stacked above the three-meter platform. The two-centerline design is featured in the great majority of the diving platforms in the world. There are two basic reasons for this. The three-centerline structure is difficult to fit into the desired dimensions of a diving pool, and it is more expensive than the two-centerline design.

Due to budget constraints, tower assemblies sometimes are designed with fewer than the five levels. When this is done, the option most often selected is a single centerline. Other options include a 5-meter, 7.5-meter, and a 10-meter. Sometimes a one-meter is added, thus omitting only the three-meter platform.

If a diving tower is specified, the water depth and envelope beneath the tower should meet or exceed the FINA requirements. Diving platforms usually are located over an independent/separate diving pool.

This is done for several reasons. The first is to avoid conflict with swimming, which would be the case if the water beneath the platforms (landing zone) was part of the bounded water volume of the racecourse. Such a situation is considered undesirable because of conflict during meets as well as during practice. Another important reason is the water temperature desired by divers, which is warmer than that preferred by competitive swimmers.

When there is a separate diving pool, the bottom sometimes is finished with a dark blue color. Platform divers find that the dark color helps them with their orientation as they spin and twist in the execution of their dives.

The deck area that surrounds the swimming and/or diving pool(s) provides the medium of access to the water's edge. This space (and material) is the most important element to the user, other than the pool tanks and their contents. A short observation of a pool in use (especially for recreational free swim) will reveal that the swimmers continually interact with the pool deck and the pool water. As a result, the pool deck takes on a number of important functions:

■ The deck is the surface over which all users must travel to reach the water's edge or reach a diving facility and then into the water. Because of this function, the deck must be smooth enough to be comfortable for bare feet and yet thorough enough to prevent slipping when the deck is wet.

■ Information must be displayed in the deck surface to advise users of potential hazards. This signage will state water depths, warnings, and instructions.

■ Because the swimmers and divers continuously are carrying water out of the pool, which drips and splashes into the deck, a workable deck drainage system must be provided.

There are several basic deck drainage systems that are practical around a swimming pool.

Area Drains. This is the most common. The deck area is divided into sections, and the surface in each section slopes to a low point (usually in the center) where a flush, perforated drain fitting is located. This drain is connected to the other drain fittings in the deck, all of which drain the deck surface water to a sanitary sewer.

Slot Drains. There are a number of varieties of the drain configuration. The feature they all have in common is their concentric location with the pool perimeter. Slot drains usually are located approximately three to five feet from the water's edge. Because the deck slopes away from the pool and toward the slot drain, the great majority of the splashed water and the water carried out by swimmers falls on the upside of the slope from the slot drain and the pool's edge and quickly drains away. The slot in the pool deck can be created in several ways. The primary feature is a conduit that is either level or slopes to an outfall where the deck water that has drained into the slot will flow to the sanitary sewer.

In pools with narrow decks, drainage can occur across the deck to a shallow trough along the natatorium wall, or off the edge of the deck into a French drain if the pool is outdoors.

Building Envelope

A natatorium is a room that contains one or more swimming pools. How the room is constructed is of immense importance. The structural components must be such that they will withstand the normal wear and tear of a public space, as well as the unique demands of an enclosed space above (and below) a large body of water that is treated with chemicals and will evaporate tons of water vapor over the period of a year. This, multiplied by 30 or 50 years, underscores the aggression that the building will be subjected to. Mild steel should be avoided where possible and should be limited to large structural components. These components, if exposed to the natatorium environment, should be coated with an industrial-grade epoxy. If the roof decking is mild steel or even galvanized, it must be coated in the same way to protect the metal from corrosion. Non-metallic building components must withstand the impact of high humidity and aggressive chemically laced air. For this reason, concrete, plastic, glass, and stainless steel are appropriate.

In considering stainless steel, it is important to understand that stainless steel has many grades and alloys. The 300 series usually is used for swimming pool equipment. Even so, certain environmental conditions can adversely affect stainless steel over a period of time. For this reason, it is unwise to use this material for small and yet strategic components that are put under stress as structural components (e.g., fasteners that are part of a roof suspension system). Other than pool gutters, bulkhead, and deck equipment, unpainted stainless steel should not be used in natatoria.

The roof sandwich demands scrutiny in its design so as to avoid problems with the air barrier, the vapor retarder, the insulation, and the moisture membrane. The avoidance of thermal bridging is essential, especially in locales with a cold winter climate. Condensation inside the natatorium can cause many problems if not controlled. The most significant is the creation of hydrochloric acid if vapor with chlorine molecules condenses. The same concerns exist for natatorium walls, and design decisions must take these issues into consideration.

The architectural features in a natatorium may vary depending upon the type of owner, the location, the climate, and the activity program.

Fenestration

The decision to use windows in a natatorium will be influenced by its location. If the facility is located in a park setting or has an attractive view (e.g., mountains, ocean, lake, forest, etc.) wall windows can be a major feature. If, on the other hand, the view is an unattractive cityscape such as a parking lot, blank building walls, or unattractive street scene, there is little reason to introduce light through a wall window because of the glare that will likely develop across the surface of the water. This reflected glare can be a distraction to spectators during a swim meet, a safety problem for lifeguards during recreational swimming, and a heat loss or heat gain. It can also create condensation with possible corrosion damage to window casements and walls. All of these problems can be dealt with if justification for the window and natural light can be established.

One means of avoiding many of the negatives named above is the use of translucent skylights. While this technique will avoid many of the negative aspects of wall fenestration, heat gain still can be a problem, but control can reduce greatly the negative effects. Skylights usually will avoid negative glare on the water surface and at the same time reduce the level of needed artificial light. Artificial light is a very important feature in the design of a poolscape, whether it is indoors or outdoors. Indoor light levels are influenced to some degree by standards or rules set forth by the national governing bodies of competitive swimming, diving, synchronized swimming, and water polo. State and local health department agencies frequently will set requirements for outdoor and indoor pools, both for overhead and underwater light sources. A review of the applicable regulations will enable the designer to meet these requirements.

Acoustics is an issue that must be addressed. Often, acoustics will be overlooked, dismissed, or eliminated because of budget. Reverberating sound is a common problem in natatoria. Sound sources include whistles, gunshots, and diving board impact noises, plus shouts, conversation, and the sounds of splashing. Loudspeakers should be selected and specified by an acoustics and sound consultant. Understand-

ably, the size of the natatorium will influence the acceptable reverberation time in the space.

Outdoor acoustics usually are a factor in the overall design of the poolscape. The pool site can be both a source and a recipient of noise. If the pool is near a residential area or some other land use that should not have excessive sound impact, landscape design can provide buffers. If, on the other hand, off-site noise is produced by an adjacent roadway and/or industrial site, protection must be created for the poolscape.

Support Spaces

While the bodies of water are the focal point of the facility, the design, arrangement, and location of the support spaces are factors of the overall design that will influence the efficiency of the operation and the effectiveness of the programs.

The starting point of the adjacency profile is the user's point of entry. A control point must exist at this location. After passing the control point, the user must arrive at the dressing area. The two dressing rooms should have a dry entrance from the control point area and a wet exit to the pool deck. (The reverse applies for users leaving the pool area.)

The pool office should be located with a visual access of the pool deck area and the exits from the dressing rooms onto the pool deck. Other spaces/rooms can be added to the control area depending upon the size of the pool(s) and programs. The spaces can include an office for lifeguards, a first aid room, and an office for instructors and coaches. Additional spaces may include a swim meet management office, drug testing room(s), and sports technology research offices. If the facility is a university with a physical education major and post graduate studies, other spaces used for research should be considered.

Functional support spaces include filtration and chemical treatment, storage, circulation, and spectator seating. The issue of spectator seating is somewhat complex. It requires the identification of the type of spectator events that will take place, their frequency, the number of spectators, and the type of facilities that will be provided for the spectators. If there are to be spectator events, is it best to provide permanent or temporary seating? The answer to this question will be influenced not only by the issues listed above, but also by budget, available space, and in some cases, the off-site activities of the owner. The difference of the two basic systems (i.e., permanent and temporary) will be reflected in cost. This applies not only to first costs, but also can influence the construction budget in such areas as exits, stairwells, and even parking spaces. Because of the variables, it is important to have a good understanding (and agreement among members of the owner's project committee) of the true purpose of the spectator facilities.

Both indoor and outdoor access to the seating area can be an important design problem, and it can significantly affect the total construction cost.

HVAC-Dehumidification

The environment in an indoor pool can be comfortable to swimmers and spectators if the relative humidity is controlled and maintained at 50% to 55%. An even greater benefit of this range is the lack of aggressive atmospheric conditions relative to the materials in the space. For many years the soaring humidity in a natatorium was controlled by opening the windows and allowing outside air to dilute the moist atmosphere. In this method the laws of physics replaced that warm moist air with cooler, dryer outside air. Understandably the next improvement was the introduction of motorized exhaust fans that mechanically maintained a constant air flow out of the natatorium with a controlled and strategically located introduction of fresh air louvers. This system, which still is in use in the 1990s, is effective if the outside air is at the appropriate temperature and relative humidity level. In some climatic areas, the appropriate level for outside air is available much of the time. Most locations, however, have appropriate levels only a small percentage of the time. During the majority of the time, high levels of temperature and humidity in the outside air result in higher temperatures and humidity levels in the natatorium.

During the 1970s, following the fuel crisis and the escalating cost of energy, modifications were made to the conventional mechanical ventilation systems. These modifications captured the heat that previously was exhausted to the outside and used it to raise the heat of the outside air being brought into the natatorium space. Once again, this worked only if outside weather conditions were correct.

In the late 1970s refrigerated dehumidification was developed. This system is an outgrowth of air conditioning, whereby the warm moist air is mechanically drawn across an evaporator coil. This lowers the temperature of the air and causes it to condense on the cold coil. The dryer air that exits from the other side of the coil has a lower temperature and a lower relative humidity. This air then is reheated and mixes with the natatorium air. In so doing, it stabilizes the temperature in the natatorium at or near the desired level or set point.

Refrigerated systems also use the heat that has been captured and removed from the processed natatorium air to heat the swimming pool water, heat the natatorium space, or even heat the potable shower water. By using the heat that is taken out of the natatorium air as described above, the overall energy costs of the natatorium are much lower. In spite of a higher first cost for the refrigerated dehumidification, the savings in operating costs create an attractive payback to the owner. This is enhanced if energy costs continue to rise.

Designers must consider the human needs for ventilation and fresh air. While dehumidifiers will control humidity without ventilation, fresh outside air is needed for the occupants of the natatorium. If there is a large number of spectators at special events (e.g., swimming meets, tournaments, water-shows, etc.) a separate mode will be required to serve this greater demand for outside fresh air. All modes must meet local building codes and the applicable ASHRAE standards (American Society of Heating, Refrigeration and Air Conditioning Engineers).

There has been a series of complications in natatoria with refrigerated dehumidification beginning in the 1980s and slowly rectified to some degree since. Those complications have occurred because the recycled air in the natatorium, which is necessary for refrigerated dehumidification, does not mix in sufficient fresh outside air to dilute the accumulation of cholramines off-gassing from the pool water. This problem is not as acute with bromine; however, bromine systems seem to have their own complications that frustrate some operators. As this phenomenon became recognized in the industry, several manufacturers of dehumidification systems have modified their equipment to permit greater make-up air capability. Some feature a 25% minimum fresh air introduction into the system as well as a mode of operation for 100% exhaust at times of chloramine build up in the atmosphere, especially at a time of super chlorination.

The difficulty in some systems has led to significant maintenance cost and/or even replacement of components. The problem seems to be a combination of a chlorine system combined with an air handling system that recirculates the interior air without sufficient purging of the natatorium's chloramine-laced atmosphere.

Maintenance and Repair

In planning a swimming pool and/or a nataorium, consideration must be given to the ongoing cost of custodial care, maintenance, and repair. Often this aspect of swimming pool and natatorium design is overlooked. The result is a higher operating cost for each day the facility is in operation, all the way to the end of the facility's life.

Custodial care often is taken for granted by the project committee, and little thought is given to the daily chores that must take place to keep the pool and its support spaces at a high level of cleanliness. The result is greater labor hours expended, which affects the annual budget and at the same time may result in a lower level of cleanliness due to a future mandate to cut labor hours because of budget constraints.

Preventive maintenance is always a task that must be executed if the facility is to be maintained as it should. While budget can have an impact on how well preventive maintenance is carried out, the design of the mechanical systems, support components, working space, and ingress and egress from the mechanical spaces can influence the enthusiasm that physical plant staff will have for practicing preventive maintenance.

The repair of components in the pool and support spaces will be less costly in time and material (and down time of the facility) if parts are available as shelf items. If long lead times are required to obtain some parts, they should be prepurchased and inventoried before the need occurs. This applies to pumps, motors, impellers, chemical feed pumps, air handling units, blowers, and some filter components, etc.

Safety Features

Safety is no accident. It must receive careful consideration by planners, architects, and operators of pools. Many people have been confronted with litigation as a result of an accident in their pools. Lawyers inevitably look for areas of negligence in the operation of the pool or for any defect in the pool's design. Listed below are some essential safety principles, procedures, and policies that should be adhered to in designing the pool and in its operation:

■ Rules governing pool use must be conspicuously posted at all points of entry to the pool.
■ Special rules should be developed and posted for use at such facilities as diving boards, slides, and towers.
■ A lifeguard should be on duty at all times that the pool is open,
■ In areas of the pool with less than five feet of water, signs and warnings should be placed at the edge (coping) of the pool that state, "SHALLOW WATER—NO DIVING." In shallow-water training pools on the edge of the pool, signs should be

posted stating "DANGER SHALLOW WATER—NO DIVING."
■ Where springboards and platform diving is provided, the depth of water and other related measurements must conform to the rules of FINA, USD, NCAA, or the NFHSAA.
■ Starting blocks for competitive swimming should be installed in the deep end of the pools unless the shallow end of the pool is at least five feet deep.
■ Adequate lighting, both underwater and in the pool area, must be provided to enssure the safety of users and meet applicable rules, regulations, and codes.
■ Clarity of pool water is essential and must meet applicable rules, regulations, and codes.
■ Depth markers at least four inches high must be placed in the interior wall of the pool at or above water level. Larger depth markings must be placed on the pool deck as per health department regulations.
■ Never consider the minimum standards for pools promulgated by state governments or the pool industry to be the proper level to achieve in planning a pool. Minimums often become obsolete very quickly.
■ Ladders that hang on the edge of a pool and extend into the water represent hazards to swimmers. All ladders should be recessed into the pool wall.
■ No safety ledge should ever extend into the pool. Instead the ledge should be recessed into the wall at a depth of approximately four feet.

Check List for Use by Planning Committee and Owner

Planning Factors

1. A clear statement identifies the nature and scope of the program and the special requirements for space, equipment, and facilities dictated by the activities to be conducted.
2. The swimming pool has been planned to meet the requirements of the intended program, as well as less frequent special needs.
3. Other recreational facilities are nearby for the convenience and enjoyment of swimmers.
4. An experienced pool consultant, architect, and/or engineer has been called in to advise on design and equipment.
5. The design of the pool reflects the most current knowledge and experience regarding the technical aspects of swimming pools.

6. The pool plans reflect the needs of physically disabled people.
7. All plans and specifications meet the regulations of both state and local boards of health.
8. Provision for accommodating young children has been considered.
9. Consideration has been given to provide a room or area near the pool suitable for video/TV and lectures.
10. Adequate parking space has been provided.

Design Factors

1. The bathhouse is properly located, with entrance to the pool leading to the shallow end.
2. The locker rooms are large enough to accommodate peak loads and meet jurisdictional regulations.
3. The area for spectators has been separated from the pool area.
4. There is adequate deck space around the pool.
5. The swimming pool manager's or director's office faces the pool and contains a window with a view of the entire pool area.
6. There is a toilet-shower dressing area next to the office for instructors.
7. The specifications for competitive swimming set forth by ruling groups have been met.
8. If the pool shell has a tile finish, the length of the pool has been increased by three inches over the "official" size in order to permit eventual tiling of the basin without making the pool too short.
9. The width of any movable bulkhead has been considered in calculating total pool length.
10. Consideration has been given to an easy method of moving the bulkhead.
11. All diving standards can be anchored properly.
12. Separate storage spaces have been allocated for maintenance and instructional equipment.
13. A properly constructed overflow gutter extends around the pool perimeter.
14. Where skimmers are used, they are located so that they are not turning walls where competitive swimming is to be conducted.
15. Drains are at the proper pitch in the pool, on the pool deck, in the overflow gutter, and on the floor of shower and dressing rooms as per local jurisdictional regulation.
16. Inlets and outlets are adequate in number and located to ensure effective circulation of water in the pool.
17. There is easy access to the filter room to permit the transport of chemicals and other supplies.
18. The recirculation pump is located below the water level.

19. The recirculation-filtration system has been designed to meet anticipated future pool loads.
20. Underwater lights in end racing walls have been located $3^1/_2$ feet directly below surface lane line anchors, and they are on a separate circuit.
21. There is adequate acoustical treatment of walls and ceilings of the indoor pool.
22. There is adequate overhead clearance for diving.
23. Reflection of light from the outside has been kept to a minimum by proper location of windows or skylights.
24. All wall electrical receptacles are covered.
25. Proper subsurface drainage has been provided.
26. An area for sunbathing has been provided and oriented for the outdoor pool.
27. Outdoor diving boards or platforms are oriented so that they face north or northeast.
28. The outdoor pool is oriented correctly in relation to the sun.
29. Wind screens have been provided in situations where heavy winds prevail.
30. Lounging for swimmers has been provided for outdoor pools.

Safety and Health

1. The pool layout provides the most efficient control of swimmers from showers and locker rooms to the pool.
2. Toilet facilities are provided for wet swimmers, separate from the dry area.
3. An area is set aside for eating, apart from the pool deck.
4. There is adequate deep water for diving that meets U.S. diving rules.
5. Required space has been provided between diving boards and between the diving boards and sidewalls.
6. Recessed steps or removable ladders are located on the walls so as not to interfere with competitive swimming turns.
7. There is adequate provision for life-saving equipment and pool cleaning equipment.
8. The proper numbers of lifeguard stands have been provided and properly located.
9. All metal fittings are of noncorrosive material. All metal in the pool area is grounded to a ground-fault interrupter.
10. Provision has been made for underwater lights.
11. The chemical feed systems and containers have been placed in a separate room, accessible from and vented to the outside.
12. A pool heater has been included and properly sized.
13. Automatic controls for water chemistry have been specified.

14. Proper ventilation has been provided in the indoor pool.
15. There is adequate underwater and overhead lighting.
16. There is provision for proper temperature control in the pool room for both water and air.
17. The humidity of the natatorium room can be controlled.
18. A fence has been placed around the outdoor pool to prevent its use when the pool is closed.
19. Rules for use of the pool been developed and displayed prominently.
20. Warning signs are placed where needed and on such equipment as diving boards and slides.
21. Starting blocks are placed in the deep end of pool (minimum depth five feet).
22. There is a telephone in the pool area with numbers of rescue and emergency agencies.
23. Emergency equipment, including a spineboard, has been provided.
24. The steps leading into the pool have a black edge to make them visible to underwater swimmers.
25. Bottom drain covers are fastened securely to prevent their removal by interlopers.
26. The diving stands are equipped with guardrails which extend at least to the water.
27. The deck is made of nonslip material.

■ Summary

This chapter was designed to review current trends in aquatic facilities. In past editions, this section was entitled "Swimming Pools and Natatoria." Since the early 1990s the aquatic area has expanded to include not just pools but also a variety of aquatic entertainment centers. Therefore, the chapter was retitled "Aquatic Facilities" to include the increased number of aquatic facilities available to competitors and recreators. The American public loves its opportunities to compete in swimming and to have fun in the water. Water parks have become great family entertainment centers for summer fun.

Learning Objective 1: The student will be able to describe aquatic facility trends.

Over the past 10 years there has been an explosion of entertainment-type aquatic centers, from leisure pools to elaborate water parks with slides, wave pools, current channels, lazy rivers, and much more. The expansion on the competitive side has not been as great, but many changes have occurred in their design to make athletes more efficient and faster.

Learning Objective 2: The student will be able to design and implement a needs analysis for an aquatic facility.

Before beginning to design an aquatics facility a needs analysis should be completed and the results of the analysis used in the planning process. This is true when designing a remodel, upgrade, or new aquatic facility. The focus of any design for an aquatics facility is the program to be implemented in the facility. Therefore, the planners need to throughly understand the programmatic needs of the current program and how that program will change in the future.

Learning Objective 3: The student will be able to describe the technical considerations for designing either a recreational or competitive aquatic facility.

Once the programmatic needs are understood and the size of the pool(s) have been determined, the planners now turn their focus to technical considerations, including, exact dimensions (e.g., length, width, depths, bottom profile, tolerances and allowances, and perimeter overflow tolerance at rim flow), interior finishes, gutter systems, mechanical systems, filter systems, chemical injection and monitoring systems, bulkheads, movable floor, diving facilities, dehumidification system, heating system, speactator seating, storgae, timing systems, building envelope, fenestration, and support spaces.

■ Self-Assessment Exercise

1. What are the trends in aquatic centers?
2. What is a needs analysis?
3. What are the advantages and disadvantages of basements?
4. What are the advantages and disadvantages of cast-in-place concrete versus pneumatically applied concrete?
5. What is fenestration?
6. What is dehumidification?
7. What is important to consider regarding pool interiors?
8. What is important to consider regarding gutter systems?
9. What are the components of a swimming pool mechanical system? Describe each.
10. What is the difference between sand and DE filters? Is one better than the other?
11. Describe the various issues relating to chemical treatment of pools.
12. What has happened over the past 30 years with the development of bulkheads and movable floors?

13. What are the components of a diving facility?
14. Is there a difference between a competitive diving board and a recreational diving board? If there is a difference, explain it.
15. Why is dehumidification important to a swimming pool? What have been the problems with dehumidification systems?
16. What safety factors are important to consider when designing a pool?

■ Case Study

The Butterfield Park Authority (BPA) has approved funds for the development of a plan for a recreational/competitive aquatic complex. The BPA has recently completed a needs assessment, which indicated that the average taxpayer was supportive of an indoor/outdoor aquatic facility that would service the community's competitive, instructional, and recreational swimming needs. The two complexes would be constructed on the same site, and the office, locker rooms, and other service areas would be built between the indoor and outdoor facilities. You are the newly hired aquatic facility director. What steps would you take to develop this new aquatics facility? How will you ensure that this facility is state-of-the-art and energy efficient? How will you program and schedule such a facility? How will you accommodate persons with disabilities, abiding by the ADA and ABA guidelines? What service areas will you include in the aquatic facilities (e.g., lounge, concessions, spectator seating, restrooms, offices, day-care, elder-care, strength training, etc.)?

■ References

Flynn, R.B. (Ed.) 1994. **Planning facilities for athletics, physical education and recreation.** Reston, VA: The Athletic Institute and American Alliance for Health, Physical Education, Recreation and Dance.

NCAA Guides. Overland Park, KS: National Collegiate Athletic Association.

CHAPTER 19

Orienteering Course

Thomas Horne, United States Military Academy

Learning Objectives

After reading this chapter, the student will be able to

- describe orienteering and explain the nature of the sport,

- utilize general orienteering concepts to develop customized orienteering activities,

- identify the equipment required to conduct an orienteering competition,

- organize an orienteering competition,

- apply key concepts and principles involved in laying out a safe orienteering course, and

- develop support materials and procedures needed to conduct an orienteering program.

Introduction

Orienteering originated in Scandinavia as a cross country skiing activity. Later it was modified and done on foot. Orienteering is an outdoor movement activity that requires participants to find the fastest route between a series of terrain features, using a simple compass and a map as navigational aids. Orienteering, an international sport, has standards and procedures that are well established and formalized. Individuals interested in participating in orienteering activities, but not concerned with formal competition, may modify these standards and procedures to meet their individual needs. Orienteers (individuals participating in orienteering activities) decide for themselves whether to focus on wilderness skills, physical training, recreation, winning, or socialization. Even if serious orienteering competition is not the goal, following established basic orienteering procedures will enhance the orienteering activity and make it more enjoyable for participants.

This chapter will focus on how to organize and conduct orienteering activities. Some technical skills will be covered since orienteering activity organizers do need to know some basics to effectively conduct an orienteering event. Adapted and developmental orienteering activities will be covered and additional reference material provided.

Orienteering Basics

The primary facility for orienteering is the great outdoors. Most orienteering events are held in wooded or open terrain, with some obvious features such as fields, water bodies, fences, and trails. Courses will vary depending on the focus of the orienteering activity, the availability of suitable land, and

225

the age, fitness level, and experience of the participants. A map of the event area is normally provided for each participant. A formal topographic orienteering map is required for serious competitions. A series of check points (controls) are located on the course and recorded on the map. The controls are marked with the standard orienteering control marker (a three-dimentional orange and white marker). Orienteers are given control descriptions (clues) on how to locate the controls that must be visited. Normally, the orienteer that completes the course in the shortest time is the winner.

Activities

Types of Activities

Most orientation activities are conducted using one of two general types of orienteering.

Point-to-Point Orienteering. (also called cross country or route orienteering). Point-to-Point orienteering is used for most formal competitions. Point-to-point orienteering consists of a series of controls (check points) in a specific order to be located by the orienteers. These controls are laid out and numbered sequentially and their locations are recorded on an orienteering (topographic) map with a circle. Orienteers use a map and compass to locate all the controls in sequence and get to the finish line as rapidly as possible.

Score Orienteering. Score orienteering is another type of orienteering competition. Similar to point-to-point orienteering, score orienteering participants use a map and compass to locate controls, but the controls are not in a set sequence. Controls blanket the area and each is assigned a point value based on distance to the control and how difficult it is to get to. Competition usually lasts a specific time and participants try to earn as many control points as possible in the designated time. Rogaine is a form of score orienteering that originated in Australia. It takes place on a very large course with controls located much farther apart than in standard score orienteering. Teams of two or more navigate over often rugged terrain during competitions that usually last 12 to 24 hours. The clock runs continuously and the team to earn the most points in the prescribed time is the winner.

Pre-Competitive Activities

String Course. A string course is a relatively short and simple orienteering course where a string or rope designates the course. Control points are located on or very near the string line. Participants simply follow the string that leads them to the control points. A simple string-orienteering map is usually employed to show the course and help participants develop basic map-reading skills and familiarize them with orienteering symbols and map colors.

Landmark Hunt (Kjellstrom, 1976). The purpose of the landmark hunt is to practice locating landmarks that would typically be used in an orienteering competition. Participants gather at a high point where all the landmarks can be seen. They are then given a short list of landmarks with descriptions that must be located on a map. The first person to correctly locate all the landmarks on the map is the winner. A more advanced version of the landmark hunt requires participants to give the correct compass reading to the landmark.

Map Point Walk (Kjellstrom, 1976). Map point walks provide an opportunity for orienteers to practice following a map and locating landmarks on a map. Activity organizers lay out the course on a map leading through a number of easily identified landmarks. Along the route are placed small, brightly colored streamers so that each streamer can be seen from the previous one. Major landmarks will be used for control points and will be distinctly marked, such as with a standard orienteering marker or a different colored streamer. A north-pointing arrow should be placed at each control point to assist participants in orienting their maps. Participants must locate these landmark controls and mark them on the map. Map point walks can be timed if competition is desired. For a Map point walk competition, the individual or group to correctly locate all of the landmark controls in the shortest time is declared the winner.

Map Point Reporting (Kjellstrom, 1976). Map point reporting provides an enjoyable way to practice map-reading skills and heightens the awareness of physical features similar to those used in competitive orienteering. Organizers select 6 to 10 clearly identifiable landmarks on a map. Participants then attempt to locate as many of these as possible in a set amount of time, using the score orienteering format. At each control point, orienteers must answer questions about the terrain or features around the control. Different points will be assigned for each control based on the accessibility of the control and the difficulty of the question to be answered.

Urban Orienteering. If a wooded or country environment is not available, orienteering activities can be conducted in an urban setting. Standard road maps can be utilized and there is an abundance of landmarks and features that can be incorporated into the course. Safety is a special concern when orienteering in an urban setting. A theme can be used for controls. For example, have all controls be emergency agencies (police department, fire station, and hospitals). The course must be carefully laid out to maximize safety in such situations as intersections, congested areas, fast-moving traffic, construction sites, and other dangerous areas.

Levels of competitive orienteering

White Courses. The white courses are the easiest competition courses, and are ideal for younger children, novices, teenagers, and inexperienced adults. They are usually one to three kilometers in length and located on relatively flat terrain. All participants need to know the basic orienteering skills of map reading and using an orienteering compass. Control markers are placed on easily identified features such as trails, junctions, streams, buildings, and large rocks. Younger participants can navigate the course alone or in small groups, or be accompanied by a mature, experienced orienteer.

Yellow Courses. Yellow courses are generally slightly longer than white courses at three to four kilometers. The course should follow easy terrain along distinct features like trails, fences, and open fields. Control points on yellow courses are usually farther from the main trail and more difficult to locate than those on white courses. Adults and teenagers with some experience on white courses should be able to complete yellow courses solo. Novices and younger children can handle yellow course terrain, but will normally need to have an adult or mature experienced orienteer accompany them.

Orange Courses. Orange courses are intermediate courses that are four to five kilometers long. Orange courses begin to go off the trails and into the woods. Controls are still located near large or distinct features, but not necessarily on the trail in obvious locations. Orange courses are for the more experienced orienteers with experience on lower level orienteering courses or other orienteering background. The slightly more challenging terrain and the longer distances require a greater level of fitness to compete successfully at this level. Orange courses are not normally appropriate for younger children, but they may enjoy an occasional outing on an orange course with an experienced adult.

Green, Red, and Blue Courses (expert courses). These expert courses vary in difficulty based on the length of the course (a blue course may be 10 kilometers or longer), difficulty of the terrain, and location of the controls. Successful navigation of a green course (the easiest of the expert courses), red course, or blue course (most difficult expert course) requires considerable experience and a higher level of fitness than are required on the less challenging courses. Expert courses tend to emphasize navigational skills and endurance rather than speed, so adults often excel at orienteering well into middle and advanced age, making orienteering an excellent lifetime fitness activity.

Equipment

Orienteering Maps

A map is a reduced representation of a portion of the earth. A map may be a very simple hand-drawn representation of a specific area or a very detailed scaled representation identifying a variety of features. A map provides five categories of information, the "five D's," which include description, details, directions, distances, and designations (Kjellstrom, 1976).

The type of map chosen for an orienteering activity will depend on the objective of the activity, the experience level of the activity organizer and participants, resources available, and type of orienteering. Most formal orienteering activities and competitions require a *topographical* map—from the Greek *topos,* place, and *graphein,* to write or draw: a drawing or a picture of a place or area. Topographical maps used for orienteering show landforms, water features, linear features, other artificial features, rock features, and vegetation. The International Orienteering Federation (IOF) has established orienteering map symbols (Figure 19.1) that are generally accepted and used for all sanctioned orienteering competition worldwide.

Another standard for topographic orienteering maps is the color coding used to identify the different classes of features. Orienteers often read their five-color orienteering maps while on the move, and the color coding helps them read the map quickly. The IOF standard orienteering map colors are explained below:

■ Black—Artificial features, such as roads, trails, buildings, and fences, plus rock features, such as cliffs and boulders.
■ Brown—Topographic features, such as hills, valleys, ridges, earth banks, and ditches.
■ Blue—Water features, such as lakes, ponds, swamps, and streams.
■ White (the color of the paper)—Normal forest. (This is different from some government maps, which may show fields in white and forest green.)
■ Yellow—Clearings and fields.
■ Green—Vegetation.

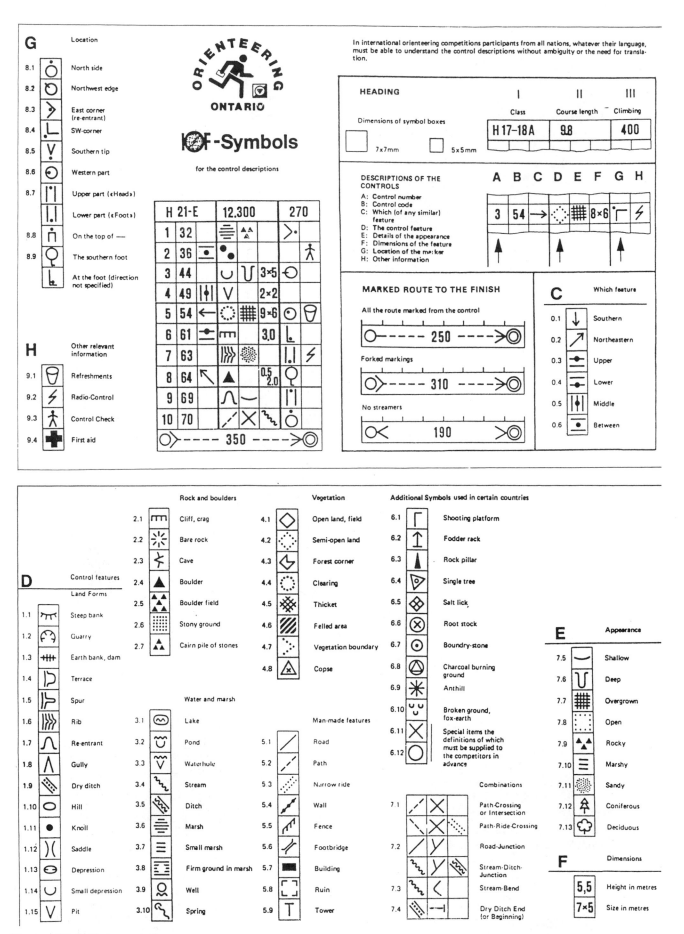

Figure 19.1 Map symbols.

Topographic maps suitable for orienteering may be available from local sports shops, orienteering clubs, or bookstores (Figure 19.2). If an orienteering map is not available at one of these sources, maps of areas in the United States are available through the U.S. Geographic Survey (USGS) by following two steps. The first step is to identify where the orienteering activity will occur and locate a map of the proper area. A *Topographic Map Index Circular* and *Topographic Map* booklet will provide this information and are available from

Branch of Distribution
United States Geographical Survey (USGS)
1200 South Eads Street
Arlington, Virginia 22202

Identify which USGS topographical map includes the orienteering course. The second step is to submit an order for the required map to the USGS (specify "woodland" copies). For maps east of the Mississippi, send a the request to the USGS at the address listed above. For maps west of the Mississippi, send requests to

Branch of Distribution
United States Geographical Survey
Federal Center
Denver, Colorado 80225

Take the map to a blueprint company and ask for a 200% enlargement of the area that includes the orienteering course. Be sure to attach a legend (if desired)

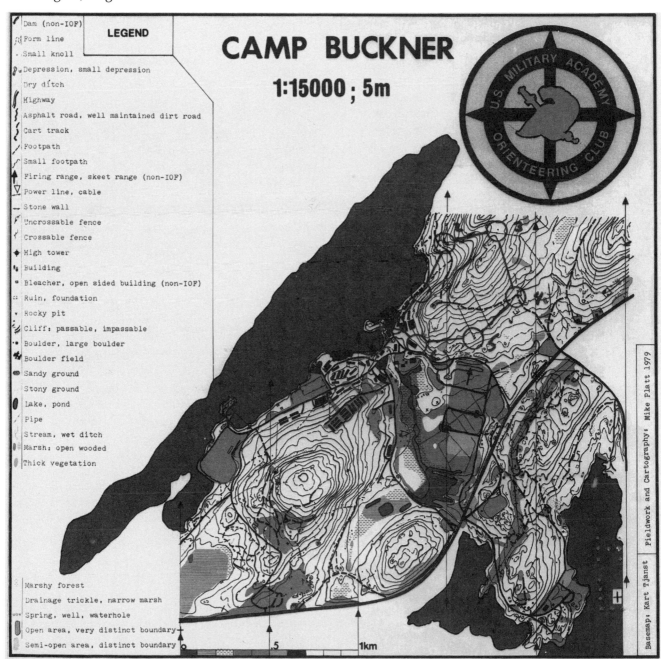

Figure 19.2 Orienteering map.

and the scale indicator from the USGS map to the area being copied.

IOF symbols and color codes are recommended even if a hand-drawn or other less formal map is desired. This will make the orienteering event a developmental exercise and avoid confusing individuals who have participated in more formal orienteering events that used the standardized symbols and colors.

The orienteering course is usually displayed on a large master map near the starting line. Orienteers use the master map to copy the route on their personal orienteering maps if it is not already printed on their maps.

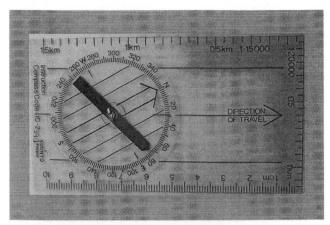

Figure 19.3 Protractor compass.

The Orienteering Compass

A conventional compass can be used for orienteering; however, most competitors use an orienteering compass. Orienteering compasses come in two types, the protractor compass and the NorCompass. The most popular type of orienteering compass is the protractor compass (Figure 19.3). Protractor compasses (also called baseplate compasses) have a clear plastic baseplate with a direction of travel arrow, ruler, and an orienting arrow. The NorCompass (also called a thumb compass) attaches to the orienteer's left thumb (Figure 19.4). Most orienteers find the protractor compass more accurate, but it takes two hands to use it. The NorCompass is not as accurate, but only takes one hand to use. Both compasses are suitable for all levels of orienteering activities. Most orienteers prefer to use their own orienteering compass for orienteering events. If an orienteering event is designed for novices or individuals with limited orienteering experience, event organizers may provide compasses.

Control Markers

Control markers are usually three-dimensional orange-and-white markers that designate the location of the control. For less formal events, control markers may be marked with paint, colored ribbons, or other easily distinguished items.

Control Cards

Orienteers carry control cards with their name, competitive classification, and starting time in a rain- and tear-proof plastic case. (The orienteering map and description sheet are also carried in the protective case.) The control cards are punched with a distinctive mark to verify the orienteer's visit to the control (Figure 19.5).

Figure 19.4 Nor Compass.

Control Descriptions

Attached to each map is a description sheet with details to help locate the controls. Identifying numbers or letters are placed on the control and the description sheet. Beginners' descriptions may be written out in English. Control descriptions for intermediate and advanced competitions normally use International Orienteering Federation symbols (see Figure 19.6, Sample Control Description). A comprehensive copy of all IOF symbols can be obtained from the IOF, local orienteering clubs, Internet sites, and a variety of software programs.

Punch

A punch is a tool used to make a distinctive mark on the control card to verify an orienteer's visit to the control. Most formal competitions use punches with pins arranged in a distinctive pattern. (See Figure 19.6)

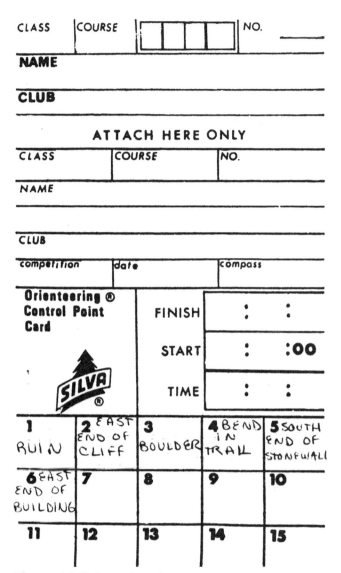

Figure 19.5 Control card.

Organizing Orienteering Events

Organizing and Conducting Orienteering Competitions

Orienteering event organizers must decide which type of orienteering competition they will host and how large the event will be. Then they must select a location for the competition and procure orienteering maps. A simple event for a small number of contestants can be conducted with a few experienced volunteers and limited financial resources. Conducting a large sanctioned competition requires an experienced orienteer and considerable planning time, personnel, and money. Event organizers must decide:

▶ the mode of movement
  ■ standard orienteering (on foot)
  ■ ski orienteering (on cross country skis)
  ■ trail orienteering (varies according to disability)

▶ the nature of the competition
  ■ individual (participants perform independently)
  ■ relay (two or more team members run consecutive individual races)
  ■ team (two or more individuals collaborate)

▶ which age groups and experience levels will be offered
▶ a suitable site location (usually a wooded area with landscape features that will require the use of orienteering skills)

▶ time of competition
  ■ day (during daylight hours)
  ■ night (in the dark)

▶ type of start
  ■ mass start
  ■ staggered start

▶ order in which the controls must be visited
  ■ point-to-point orienteering (controls must be visited in a prescribed order)
  ■ score orienteering (visit as many controls as possible in any order)
  ■ method of determining the competition results
  ■ single-race competition
  ■ multi-race competition (combined results of two or more races, held during one day or over several days, are used to determine results)
  ■ qualification race competition (competitors must qualify for a final race through one or more qualification races; the overall winner is the winner of the final race)

Once the meet organizers have made these decisions, they must develop and distribute invitations and registration forms. Registration forms may include the above information and

■ exact time and date of the orienteering event,
■ registration fee schedule,
■ entry deadlines,
■ sanction number (if sanctioned),
■ host club or organization and event directors (including address and phone number),
■ local accommodations and food,

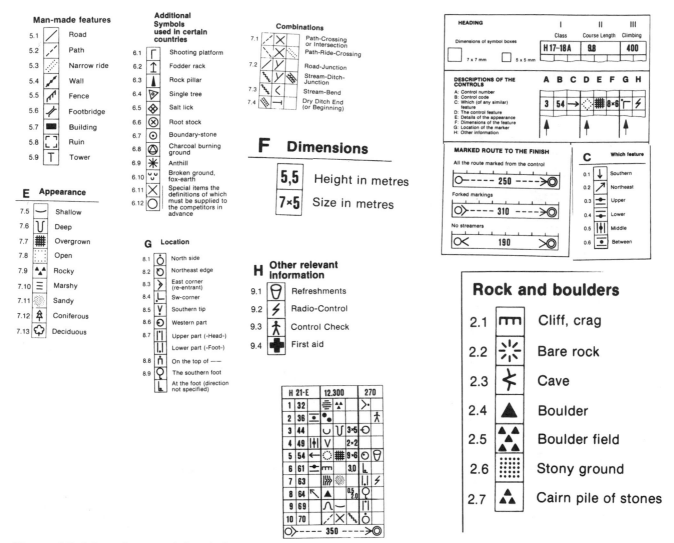

Figure 19.6 Sample control descriptions.

■ general area of the event and map information,
■ details on any practice sessions or clinics, and
■ waiver of liability form.

Checking the course, also called *vetting* the course, is an important part of preparing it for competition. Vetting the course usually takes place the day before the scheduled competition. The event organizer usually marks the location of the controls. Experienced orienteers who are not participating in the competition walk the course to ensure the proposed control points are well located and are designated correctly on the map. Individuals vetting the course should also see if the course is appropriate for the skill level of the participants. Vetting the course minimizes the chance of a control being misplaced or having a course that is too difficult or too easy for the competitors (Schoenstein, 1990).

Staffing and equipping an orienteering event requires proper planning. Recruiting and training meet workers are important tasks. The number of workers needed will vary with the number of participants and the level of competition. Some individuals will contribute primarily with planning tasks, others individuals will simply work on the day of the competition, while others will assist with both aspects of event management. The exact personnel requirement to staff a competition will vary with each event, but most will need workers to accomplish the following tasks:

■ determine the location of the orienteering course,
■ lay out the orienteering course,
■ procure orienteering maps,
■ produce the master maps and maps for participants,
■ prepare meet publicity and registration information,

- collect fees and handle finances,
- acquire compasses if this service is to be provided,
- acquire and place control markers,
- produce the control cards,
- set up required communications (phones, two-way radios, computer support, and fax lines),
- get support materials such as office supplies, signs, tables, chairs, and clocks,
- act as "recorders" (distribute, collect, and check control cards; record the results on a recording sheet and post results on the results board),
- act as "timers" (record start and finish times on the event cards),
- act as "sitters" (individuals that monitor control points),
- act as "course organizer" (verify correctness of names, finish times, and final scores; post scores and account for all orienteers),
- secure numbered bibs so the competitors can be identified,
- purchase trophies or awards, and
- notify media of the event and report the results.

Safety Considerations

Orienteering event organizers are responsible for providing an orienteering course that minimizes danger. Dangerous areas such as cliffs, swamps, and pits or mine shafts must be clearly identified on the orienteering map. The course should not cross busy highways, railroads, or other dangerous features.

Event personnel should develop and be able to implement an emergency action plan. As a minimum, a first aid kit and staff trained to use it should be available. Having medical personnel (doctor, nurse, or emergency medical technician) on site for larger events is recommended. Event workers should know how to contact the local hospital, police, rescue squad, or other local emergency response teams.

Adapted Orienteering Competitions

Ski Orienteering

The main idea of ski orienteering is to locate all the controls marked on the map in the correct order, conventional point-to-point orienteering. The course is organized with cross country ski tracks (printed in green on the map) connecting the control points. Ski orienteers do not simply follow a single track from control to control. Numerous tracks intersect, giving the orienteer the choice of which to take. Skiers must choose the best route based on the length of the route,

the track classification (Figure 19.7) and the altitude. They then ski the chosen route as fast as possible. A typical course will have 30% to 50% continuous lines (wide and narrow), 50% to 70% broken lines and only 1% to 2% dotted lines. Most ski orienteering courses have 10 to 20 controls and up to 200 trail crossings.

Trail Orienteering

Trail orienteering competitions are open to competitors with some type of functional disability that would prevent them from competing on reasonably equal terms with athletes without disabilities. Trail orienteering is also called control choice because trail orienteers must locate the control and then determine which of a number of markers is the one located in the center of the control circle on the map. The winner is the competitor with the most correct answers on his or her control card (Figure 19.8). The total time to complete the course is irrelevant in determining the winner as long as the competitor does not exceed the time limit. The course includes a limited number of timed control points. Personnel staff the timed controls and record on the control card the time required by the competitor to select the correct control marker. Event organizers will use the cumulative time at these time controls to determine the winner in case of a tie. IOF rules for other orienteering disciplines apply except for the following:

- There is be no classification by disability or gender.
- Requested physical assistance is permitted.
- Any recognized mobility aid is permitted except for combustion type vehicles.
- No assistance with navigation or problem solving is allowed.
- The course must be accessible to the least mobile.
- Competitors must stay on the tracks or trails. Other areas are out of bounds.
- Course length is usually from 1000 to 3500 meters.
- Additional personnel will be required to provide permitted assistance and staff the timed controls.

Other Orienteering Variations

The orienteering format can be applied to almost any mode of movement. There are already adapted orienteering competitions done on bicycles and canoes. These forms of orienteering are not as established as standard orienteering and are still developing standard competition rules. Canoe orienteering and cycling orienteering will continue to develop and other forms of orienteering will be tried. Only time will tell which will become established popular forms of orienteering.

Illustration # 7

Classification of tracks

Continuous wide line
- Competition skiing track
- Width at least 2.5 meters
- Very fast to ski

Continuous thin line
- Skating possible
- Width from 1.5 to 2.5 meters
- Fast to ski

Broken line
- Skating impossible
- Width from 1.0 to 1.5 meters
- Good track to ski

Dotted line
- Width less than 1.0 meters
- Slow to ski, possible dangerous slope

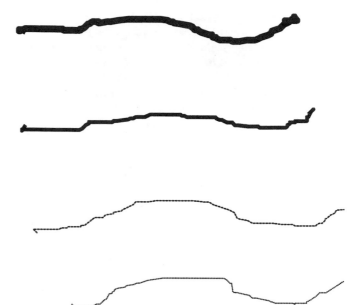

Figure 19.7 Classification of tracks.

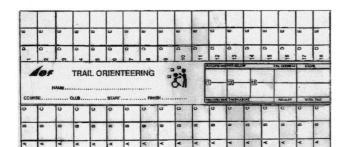

Figure 19.8 Control card.

■ Summary

Orienteering is an outdoor sport movement activity that offers opportunities to (1) develop wilderness skills and improve personal fitness levels, (2) engage in mentally challenging competitions, and (3) enjoy the fellowship and fun of being with others. Participants can select which of these aspects is of most interest and participate in appropriate orienteering activities. Orienteering activities can be highly structured and competitive or very informal and relaxed. Since orienteering requires skill and experience and not just speed, it is suitable for almost any age group. There are adaptations for individuals with disabilities (trail orienteering), lead-up activities for beginners and the very young, and variations done on cross country skis, bicycles, and canoes.

Orienteering requires very little equipment, only a map and compass. All that is needed to conduct an orienteering activity are a few relatively inexpensive pieces of equipment and some open space. Event organizers can follow competition guidelines from the IOF or other orienteering agencies, or they can simply modify the rules to suit their needs.

Learning Objective 1: The student will be able to describe orienteering and explain the nature of the sport.

Orienteering is a sport that combines navigational skills (the use of a map and compass) with physical activity. Orienteers use a map and compass to locate a series of controls (check points) as fast as they can. The person that visits all the controls in the shortest time is the winner (point-to-point orienteering). Another variation is called score orienteering, where the orienteering course is blanketed with controls that may be visited in any order. Controls are assigned a value based on how difficult it will be to get to them. The person with the most points within the designated time limit is the winner.

Learning Objective 2: The student will be able to utilize general orienteering concepts to develop customized orienteering activities.

Orienteering is a very adaptable sport with a wide variety of recreational, competitive, and developmental activities. Developmental outdoor orienteering activities such as landmark hunts, map point walks, string courses, map point reporting, Urban orienteering, and others can be used to develop orienteering skills while having fun. For those interested in competition, there are six levels of orienteering competition beginning with white course competitions (relatively short, easy courses) running through the blue course competitions (designed for experts). Adapted orienteering competitions are available for disabled athletes, cross country skiers, cyclists, and other groups with special needs or interests.

Learning Objective 3: The student will be able to identify the equipment required to conduct an orienteering competition.

All that is needed to conduct a simple orienteering competition is a map, a compass, and some control markers. Larger competitions require more support materials, such as communications links, regulation control markers, control punch, bibs with numbers, large master map, safety whistles, water control points, and a large timing clock. The IOF, the United States Orientation Federation (USOF), commercial suppliers, and local clubs are willing and able to provide assistance in determining equipment requirements.

Learning Objective 4: The student will be able to conduct an orienteering competition.

Like organizing any large athletic event, the organizer of the orienteering event must consider such general organizational issues as parking, finances, equipment, communications, marketing and promotion, media relations, concessions, training and clinics, and food and lodging for contestants. The key to successfully organizing an orienteering competition is to "get good help" and plan completely and early. Orienteering organizations, suppliers, and clubs again provide an excellent source of information.

Learning Objective 5. The student will be able to apply key concepts and principles **involved in laying out a safe** orienteering course.

The first step in laying out the orienteering course is to study the map of the designated area. Identify potentially dangerous areas like cliffs, busy highways, and swamps. Walk the area and determine the long, difficult legs and then connect these long legs with shorter legs. Select a starting point and a finish line in the same general area. Both should be located near drinking water, rest room facilities, and parking. The length and difficulty of the course will depend on the age and experience of the orienteers. An orienteering course should be challenging, interesting, and most important, safe.

Learning Objective 6: The student will be able to develop support materials and procedures needed to conduct an orienteering program.

A compass and map are all that are required to conduct basic orienteering activities. A more sophisticated orientation program, especially one that includes competitions, will need control markers, control cards, orienteering maps, safety whistles, and control punches that are consistent with IOF guidelines. The IOF, USOF, and local orienteering clubs provide detailed rules and guidelines for conducting orienteering programs. If the program includes instruction and developmental activities, the rules used for formal competitions may be adapted, but basic concepts and format of competitive orienteering should be followed.

Self-Assessment Exercises

1. What is orienteering?
2. What is point-to-point orienteering?
3. What is score orienteering?
4. What is a landmark hunt?
5. What is the difference between a map point walk and map point reporting?
6. What is urban orienteering?
7. What are the different levels of competitive orienteering?
8. What are the five categories that an orienteering map provides?
9. What is the difference between a protractor compass and NorCompass?
10. What are control markers?
11. What are control cards?
12. You have been selected to organize the tenth annual orienteering event. How will you go about organizing the event?

13. What are the safety considerations that need to be considered in an orienteering event?
14. What is ski orienteering?

■ References

Kjellstrom, B. (1976). **Map and compass–The orienteering handbook** (4th ed.). New York: Charles Scribner's Sons.

Lowery, R., & Sidney, K. (1989). **Orineteering–Skills and strategies** (3rd ed.). Willowdale, Ontario: Orienteering Ontario.

Schoenstein, R.V. **Organizing informal orienteering meets.** United States Orienteering Federation, Colorado Springs, Colorado.

■ Electronic References

Baker, J. [On-line]. Available: http://ourworld,compuserve.com/homepage/james_baker/htm

Competition rules for international orienteering federation (IOF) events [O-nline]. Available: http://www.orienteering.org/Publications/IntRules.htm

General rules for trail orineteering [On-line]. Available: http://www.orienteering.org/publishing/TrailORules.htm

International orienteering federation address book [On-line]. Available: http://www.orienteering.org/AddressBook/Nations. htm#United States

Introduction to ski orienteering [On-line]. Available: http://www.helsinki.fi/~jkleemol/skio/int/introd.htkl

Orienteering clue symbols [On-line]. Available: http://www.williams.edu:803/Biology/orienteering/clues.html

O–Equipment, services, software [On-line] Available: http://www.us.orienteering.org/cimmercial/index.html

Orienteering [On-line]. Available : http://ourworld.compuserve.homepages/magnus/orient.htm#WhatisO

Orienteering map symbols.[On-line]. Available : http://www.williams.edu:803/Biology/orienteering/legend.html

CHAPTER 20

Combative Areas

Gordon Calkins, Virginia Military Institute ■ Thomas Horne, United States Military Academy

Learning Objectives

After reading this chapter, the student will be able to

- apply general facility planning principles to developing martial arts facilities,

- identify the three general types of martial arts facilities,

- identify the major martial arts styles and determine which of the three facility types is most appropriate for each style,

- list the equipment and key design features for the each type of martial arts facility, design, set up, and properly organize a boxing facility for use as a physical education activity area,

- understand how to utilize the facility as a boxing fitness area, utilizing boxing training activities for the development of physical fitness, and

- understand how to utilize the facility as a training area for the development of basic boxing skills for those interested in learning boxing for self-defense or in competitive boxing.

Introduction

The martial arts are not merely self-defense techniques designed to make invincible weapons of the hands and feet. They are a formulated means by which one can obtain, through diligence and practice, a high level of physical proficiency, a tranquil yet superior mental discipline, and a measurable degree of spiritual enlightenment (Logan and Petras, 1975). Participants from Asia tend to emphasize mental and spiritual aspects, while those from the West tend to emphasize competition and physical development. Most of the modern martial arts have roots that go back to the ancient martial arts of Asia. Differing philosophies, interpretations, and interests of instructors and students have produced the wide range of martial arts practiced today.

Building or renovating a martial arts facility requires extensive planning. This chapter will provide information to assist martial arts facility developers with design and construction decisions. Planners and developers of martial arts facilities must understand at least the general nature of the martial arts if they are to make informed facility decisions. A summary of the major martial arts is included in this chapter to provide this knowledge base.

Facility Planning Concepts

The goal when constructing or renovating a martial arts facility is to produce a facility that is highly functional, cost effective, aesthetically pleasing, safe, and accessible to all. Failure to adequately plan often results in a facility that costs too much and delivers too little. Participatory planning (seeking information from all interested individuals, especially the representative user group) is the recommended planning strategy (Flynn, 1993). The first step is to conduct a needs analysis, which solicits information from the owners and operators, the target facility users, and staff members. The owner and operator may be a person, group of people, or an established organization. The owners and operators often provide all or some of the finances for the project, so they expect and deserve the opportunity to influence construction or renovation decisions. They are often the ones to provide a vision for the facility and leadership in organizing and executing both the planning and construction. Staff members provide an excellent source of information on which features should be included in a new martial arts facility. They have practical expertise and experience and can provide many useful recommendations. Gathering information from the target population is valuable in determining the demand for martial arts activities and identifying which style is most popular. The users, or customers, are often the best source of information on desirable support facilities such as parking areas, locker rooms, concessions, and administrative areas.

Armed with data gathered from the needs analysis, the next step is to persuade higher authority or those providing the funding to support the construction or renovation project. It is important to present the data collected in a professional and convincing manner. Failing to adequately prepare for this phase of planning could result in a poor presentation and abandonment of the project.

Once a project receives support from higher authority, a planning group or a steering committee should be formed. This group will stay actively involved during the entire planning and construction process. It will provide guidance and in some cases make decisions on such issues as:

- renovating an existing facility or building a new facility;
- cost limitations and funding sources;
- promoting the project;
- gathering additional needs assessment data;
- locating the site;
- selecting an architectural firm;
- approving, rejecting, or modifying architectural plans and proposals;
- selecting construction contractor;
- developing construction schedules and phasing;
- specifying material and space requirements;
- ensuring code compliance;

- identifying and solving design and construction problems;
- establishing and implementing maintenance and operation procedures; and
- determining requirements for support and competition areas.

The scope of the project and the complexity of the administrative requirements will determine the magnitude of the planning effort. Whether planning a modest renovation of an existing martial arts room or constructing a new martial arts complex complete with all the support facilities, careful planning will avoid costly mistakes.

Overview of the Martial Arts

Martial arts can be defined as numerous systems of self-defense and offensive techniques that may emphasize sport competition, physical development, mental development, or a combination of these aspects. Initially most martial arts taught in America were taught in wrestling rooms, gymnasiums, multipurpose rooms, or the outdoors. This is still the case in many colleges, recreation centers, YMCAs, and other multipurpose facilities. Martial arts facilities designed specifically for martial arts are now being included in the design and construction of many of these multipurpose facilities. Many commercial martial arts programs are taught in specialized martial art facilities called dojos.

Whether designing a separate commercial facility or a martial arts area in a larger project, planners must decide if the new martial arts facility will be a general combative facility or a facility designed to accommodate a specific style of martial arts. In either case, a general knowledge of the major martial arts will help planners make important design decisions. There are almost as many types of martial arts as there are types of ball games. There are too many types and styles of martial arts to discuss the facility requirements for each one; however, seven of the martial arts represent the major types and styles. A brief summary of these seven major martial arts is provided to assist facility planners in making informed design and construction decisions.

Aikido

Aikido is the art of unarmed self-defense against either an armed or unarmed assailant. The focus of aikido is to develop a healthy mind, body, and spirit, free from bad habits. Aikidoists attempt to use their unlimited spiritual power called *ki*, the

Table 20.1 Overview of Marital Arts

Art	Aikido	Judo	Karate	Kendo	Kungfu Do	Tae Kwan Ch'uan	Tai Chi
Meaning	Way of Divine Harmony	Philosophy of the Gentle Way	The Way of the Empty Hand	Way of Sword	Skill & Effort or Disciplined Technique	The Way of Kicking and Jumping	Grand Ultimate Boxing
Country of Origin School	Japan Aikidajo Dojo	Japan Dojo	Okinawa Dojo	Japan Dojo	China Kwoon	Korea do jang	China Kwoon
Uniforms	Judogi Hakama	Judogi	Karetegi	Ilendogi	Dark Top, Sash Pants & Shoes	dobok	Street Clothes
Competitive	Most Forms No	Yes	Yes	Yes	Traditionally No Some Sport Now	Yes	No
Facility Type	Grappling	Grappling	Striking	Weapons	Striking/ Grappling (weapons)	Striking Wood/	Striking/ Grappling
Flooring	Mat with Submat or Ta Tami	Ta Tami	Wood/ Synthetic Carpet	Wood/ Synthetic Carpet	Wood/Mat Carpet/Mat	Synthetic Carpet	Wood/ Synthetic Carpet

internal energy (Winderbaum, 1977). Most styles of aikido emphasize the art of self-defense and not the sport so there is neither competition nor tournaments. One style of aikido, the Tomiki style, includes organized competitions (*Introduction to Aikido,* Internet).

Judo

Judo was adapted from jujutsu by Jigoro Kano. Kano retained the self-defense, flexibility, mental concentration, and self improvement aspects of jujutsu and discarded the unsatisfactory and dangerous techniques (Winderbaum, 1977). Judo emphasizes throwing and grappling techniques that include pinning, choking, arm locks and striking techniques. Striking techniques are taught but not practiced in the sport.

Karate

Originally, karate was a form of deadly combat, but it is now practiced primarily as a sport. Karate is divided into six major areas: calisthenics, kihon (fundamentals), kata (forms of prearranged movements), kumite (sparring), and weapons (*Karate terms,* Internet). Karate tends to emphasize kicks, punches, and a strong offense as a good defense (Trias, 1973).

Kendo

Kendo, "way of the sword," is a sport version of Japanese fencing. Contestants wear extensive protective armor and try to hit each other on designated parts of the body with simulated weapons (Goodbody, 1969).

Kung Fu

The two distinctive styles of kung fu are the "hard style" (Cho-li-fat) and the "soft style" (Sil-lum). The hard style emphasizes power and strength for debilitating offensive maneuvers. The soft style focuses more on speed and agility to deliver an effective attack on vulnerable areas of the body. Kung fu employs both the arms and legs to deliver kicks, blows, throws, holds, body turns, dodges, leaps, and falls. Weapons are used more in kung fu than karate. Stylized movements are used and some techniques are derived from animal movements.

Tae Kwan Do

Tae kwan do is the art and sport of self defense stressing kicking techniques. Like karate, tae kwan do consists primarily of two components: kata (series of preset movements) and kumite (sparring).

T'ai Chi

T'ai chi emphasizes the harmony of the mind and the body (Perfetti, Internet). The qualities of slowness, lightness, clarity, balance, and calmness characterize t'ai chi activities. T'ai chi is the epitome of organized movement and often is practiced by more mature students for health and exercise (Logan and Petras, 1975). The fundamental moves of this graceful martial art can be practiced almost anywhere with little or no equipment.

Types of Martial Arts Facilities

Martial arts facilities tend to be simple structures with areas free from distractions. These training facilities are often called dojos. Traditional dojos maintain the standards of simplicity and beauty found in the original dojos (Urban, 1967).

There are many different styles of martial arts. No two martial arts programs require the same type of facility and equipment. The major styles of martial arts emphysizes grappling techniques, striking techniques, or a combination of both. Martial arts facilities are divided into three types based on the predominant technique employed.

Types of Martial Arts Facilities

GRAPPLING (G)   STRIKING (S)
GRAPPLING AND STRIKING (GS)
Grappling (G)–throws, chokes, joint locks, wrestling, pushing, pulling, trips, and falling
Striking (S)–kicks, punches, strikes, weapons
Grappling and striking (G/S)–a combination of grappling and striking

Grappling Martial Arts Facilities

Aikido and judo are martial arts styles that involve throwing skills, joint locks, and wrestling type activities. Aikido and judo require protective floor matting. The requirement of floor matting is the distinguishing characteristic of "grappling martial arts facilities." Grappling martial arts often use traditional wrestling rooms with rubberized wrestling mats and padded walls. These wrestling rooms meet the minimum requirements for grappling martial arts, but a two-layer mat system is recommended for any of the grappling martial arts that require throwing. The standard wrestling mat alone does not provide sufficient protection for high-impact activities like throws. A two-layer mat system with a lower layer of foam-type mat-

JUDO COMPETITION AREA

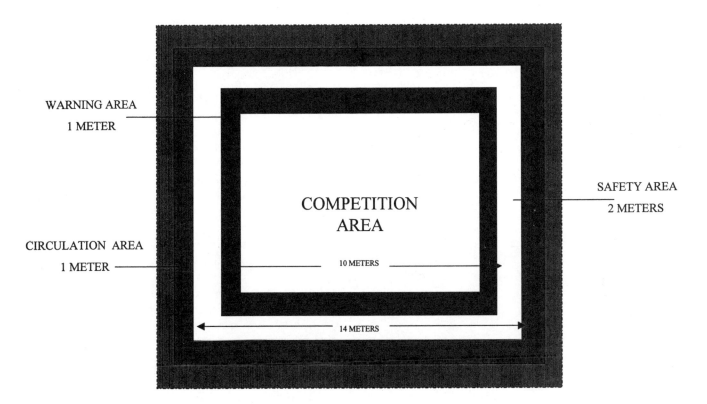

Figure 20.1 Judo competition area.

ting and an upper layer a standard wrestling mat is a versatile option.

When designing a dedicated martial arts facility, include specialized matting specifically selected for the intended activity. Most styles of aikido are noncompetitive and only require a firm mat with shock-absorbing properties. The mat should not be slippery or too rough. The competitive judo mat is a minimum of 14 meters by 14 meters and a maximum of 16 meters by 16 meters. The top layer of matting is usually a green colored "tatami." Tatami mats are normally made of compressed foam and come in sheets one meter by two meters. Judo mats must have a smooth surface without gaps between sections. Competition mats have a competition zone surrounded by a one-meter danger zone marked in red. A three-meter zone on the outside of the danger zone is the safety zone. A resilient wooden platform is the preferred base for judo competitions (*Judo rules*, Internet). Competitive judo venues should also include two scoreboards and three timing clocks.

Striking Martial Arts Facilities

Karate, Kung Fu, Tai Kwon Do, and Kendo are martial arts that employ mostly striking techniques (Roth, 1974). Karate, kung fu, and tai kwon do all utilize a wide variety of kicks with the feet, punches with the hands, and striking skills with other body parts. The majority of these blows are delivered from the feet with full force, but stop just short of the target. Kata, a prearranged series of skills, is also an important aspect of all these styles. Normally, only advanced students participate in contact competitions where they deliver full contact blows against an opponent. Additional protective equipment is recommended when practicing striking techniques with an opponent and is required for full contact competition. The emphasis in each of these martial arts is body control and precise technique. Many of the punching, kicking, and striking techniques are delivered from a spinning or turning motion. The anchor foot must rotate freely when executing these skills.

Kendo is predominately a weapons-oriented style that is normally practiced in a striking type facility.

Both karate and some kung fu also use weapons on a limited basis. Weapons-oriented martial arts require special protective gear and are normally practiced without mats on the floor.

Hardwood, carpeted, or smooth synthetic floors are preferred for striking martial arts. The traditional wrestling mat is often too soft and restricts the required pivoting of the anchorfoot. Small area mats may be used on an as needed basis. Heavy and light bags are usually included in the facility to practice kicking and punching techniques.

Grappling and Striking Martial Arts Facilities

Kung fu and tai chi are martial arts that have a blend of both grappling and striking techniques. If either of these two styles is the predominant form to be practiced in the facility, a firm matted floor is recommended. An area with a hardwood, carpeted, or smooth synthetic, floor should also be available if feasible. If the specific style of martial arts is not known, planners should consider a grappling and striking type facility. This will provide optimal flexibility for use of the facility.

General Features of Martial Arts Facilities

The distinguishing feature of martial arts facilities is the type of flooring and matting required. Yet facility planners have other important decisions to make.

Wall Coverings

The selection of appropriate wall coverings is critical. Most martial arts facilities have at least a portion of the wall covered with mirrors. Mirrors provide a valuable source of feedback for participants. Selecting the best location for the mirrors is often difficult because of conflicting priorities. Placing them too close to the activity area may result in their being broken, posing a safety hazard. Placing them too far from the activity area may make it difficult for participants to see themselves. Walls that do not have mirrors are often covered by protective wall mats to a height of six feet.

Water Fountains

Martial arts activities are very demanding physically, and martial arts participants will need to keep hydrated. A recessed water cooler is recommended for all types of martial arts facilities. A recessed water spigot is often desired to make facility sanitation easier. The spigot may be located near to or as part of the water cooler.

Ceiling

Martial arts facilities tend to be simple functional facilities with few distractions. The simplest and least expensive ceiling is an open ceiling, with the roof or floor above and associated piping, conduit, and duct work left exposed. An open ceiling area is normally a dark color to avoid attracting attention to the ceiling. The open ceiling has advantages for activities that involve weapons and throws. The longer weapons, bos and swords, may damage an acoustic tile ceiling. But the open ceiling is not as aesthetic as an acoustical tile ceiling nor does it have as good acoustic properties. If the facility is to be used primarily as a teaching station, an acoustic tile ceiling may be the ceiling of choice and worth the extra expense. Acoustic tiles in drop ceilings can be equipped with spring loaded clips that will allow the tiles to be contacted without being knocked out of place. The minimum ceiling height is 12 feet high for martial arts facilities, and a higher ceiling is recommended for a martial arts facility used primarily for weapons oriented activities.

Lighting

The recommended lighting level for martial arts facilities is 50 foot-candles. Recessed lights that have some type of protective covering are recommended. If the facility will be used for martial arts demonstrations or shows, equip the lights with dimmer switches.

Storage

Providing adequate storage space for a martial arts facility is an important planning decision. Like storage space in many other facilities, storage space in martial arts facilities is often overlooked or reduced as soon as finances become an issue. Specific storage needs will vary with each martial arts program. The size and type of storage facility required depends upon

- total space available for construction,
- budget constraints,
- type of facility (multipurpose or martial arts specific),
- class sizes,
- whether the mats will need to be taken up and stored,

- whether the uniforms will be stored,
- the style of martial arts to be practiced (Kendo with its weapons will require more storage space than T'ai Chi), and
- desire to include a trophy case to store and display trophies.

If specific storage needs are not available during the planning phase, allow 8% to10% of the total martial arts facility square footage for storage.

Scoreboard

A scoreboard with a clock is a practical feature for many of the martial arts, especially those that involve competition. The specific features of the scoreboard will depend on which style of martial art will use the scoreboard. If a scoreboard is desired, but funds are not available at the time of design, be certain to include the required power source in the plans. Including the power source in the original construction will cost very little and will save both time and money if funds become available to purchase a scoreboard in the future.

Custodial Closet

Martial arts facilities have a lot of skin contact areas, such as rubberized mats, that require regular cleaning and disinfecting. Locating a custodial closet in or close to the martial arts facility will facilitate cleaning and sanitation efforts. A custodial sink is recommended, and a recessed spigot is the minimum source of water for cleaning the facility. The closet needs to have storage space for mops, buckets, cleaning and disinfecting supplies, and a vacuum cleaner (especially for carpeted facilities).

Martial Arts Equipment and Apparel

Armor (kendo)–jacket and pants (hakama) covered by a breastplate (do), heavily padded headguard with steel grill face mask (men), padded fencing glove (kote), and padded waistband (tare), which provide protection while training with weapons

Bag (heavy training)–durable bag used to practice kicking and punching skills (numerous styles)

Balls (double-ended striking)–a padded ball suspended between two bungee cords; used to practice fast punching or kicking

Blockers–padded bat or wand used to block kicks, sweeps, and punches

Bo–staff used as an offensive and defensive weapon

Boots (padded)–padded boot that provides foot protection while sparring

Breaking boards (rebreakable)–boards used for striking practice; can be rejoined and used multiple times

Escrimas stick–staff or wand used to practice stick skills

Focus target–hand-held padded target used to practice striking skills

Hand pads–padded gloves that provide hand protection while striking and sparring

Headgear–heavily padded head protection (numerous styles)

Mats–shock-absorbing floor and wall covering

Mouthpiece–shock-absorbing guard for the teeth

Nunchukus–two sticks connected by a rope or chain used as a weapon

Pads–shock-absorbing coverings for forearms, hands, elbows, shins, ribs and insteps

Shield–relatively large hand-held padded target used in training for striking techniques

Swords–a variety of long-bladed weapons

Uniforms–numerous variations of the judogi (a durable generously cut pant and jacket with a heavy waist belt)

Boxing

This section will provide readers with knowledge and information that will allow them to utilize existing space in their physical education building to design a multipurpose boxing facility that meets existing standards for safety and utilization of proper equipment for boxing.

United States Amateur Boxing Inc. (USA Boxing)

United States Amateur Boxing Inc. (USA Boxing) is the controlling organization for all amateur boxing in the United States. Rules, legislation, and safety regulations are promulgated by USA Boxing and its membership to provide a healthy, safe, and sportsmanlike environment in which young men and women can participate in the sport of boxing throughout the United States.

National Collegiate Boxing Association (NCBA)

The National Collegiate Boxing Association (NCBA) is an umbrella organization under the jurisdiction of USA Boxing that was organized to provide an opportunity for college students to participate in the sport of amateur boxing against other students enrolled in fully accredited institutions of higher learning. Only properly registered students (full-time) from institutions registered with the NCBA may participate in this program, and they may only compete against other full-time college students who meet all the necessary registration requirements. The NCBA is not a member of the NCAA, but is rather an organization of club teams authorized by their respective institutions and registered with both the NCBA and USA Boxing. Numbers of registrations vary from year to year, but there are approximately 30 member clubs (institutions) and over 300 registered participants covering four geographic regions (Northeast, Southeast, Midwest, and Far West). The NCBA conducts educational clinics and annual regional and national championship competitions.

Why a Boxing Facility?

Some may question the use of physical education space for the development of a boxing facility because of boxing's reputation as a violent and potentially dangerous sport. Some of those same people would not think of questioning the use of either outdoor or indoor space for an activity like football, which is statistically far more dangerous than boxing. While one might argue that boxing (amateur as opposed to professional) is one of the safest of the contact sports, that is not the purpose of this discussion. Rather, it is to describe how a facility can be organized for learning and practicing boxing fundamentals and techniques that are ideal for the development of physical fitness and self-confidence.

Boxing is now widely accepted and utilized as a fitness activity. It is universally known that boxers are among the best conditioned athletes and that boxing fitness activities (punching drills, bag punching, plyometrics, associated calisthenics, rope skipping, shadow boxing, distance running, and interval training) are excellent conditioners that reduce stress and are fun at the same time. Add to this the potential for learning the fundamentals of self-defense, and you have an activity that is hard to beat (Bernstein, 1978).

Considerable media attention has been recently given to "white collar" boxing by young professionals, both male and female. Many of these young men and women have traded their jogging and racquet sport shoes for boxing shoes! It is a relatively inexpensive alternative to many other activates and develops not only aerobic capacity but can also increase strength and muscular endurance. It is also a great opportunity for coed fitness training. Conditioning drills and non-contact offensive and defensive fundamentals can be practiced without regard to gender in an environment that can be designed to push participants to reach beyond their previously self-imposed physical limits.

Finally, a properly designed boxing area can be utilized as a multipurpose facility. If it is set up correctly, a boxing space can easily be turned into an aerobics area, a wrestling or gymnastics room, a practice area for cheerleaders, or a conditioning space for just about any team or activity you can name.

How Much Space Is Necessary?

If the space is to be used for boxing only, any space that is 10 feet by 10 feet or larger will suffice. All that is necessary is the proper floor covering, heavy and light striking bags, calisthenic stations, and a small equipment storage area. This area could be categorized as an "all-purpose boxing room" and makes use of almost any available space. The size of a boxing exercise/training area can vary from a large field house, armory, or gymnasium, to a small classroom or similar space suitable for small-group instruction. All that is required for boxing drills/practice is some unobstructed space, adequate ventilation, and sufficient lighting (Deeter, Rubino, and Simmons, 1950).

If a boxing ring is available or you desire a multipurpose room, then some additional space will be necessary. A space 20 feet by 20 feet is required for the ring setup. A good way to organize such a room would be to divide it into the ring area, a striking bag area (heavy and light), and an exercise section. A 30 feet by 50 feet space would be sufficient for this type of room. If you are converting an old swimming pool space (e.g., 20 meters × 10 meters) you should have all the space you need for an excellent boxing/multipurpose exercise room (Deeter, Rubino and Simmons, 1950).

Converting such existing space as a swimming pool into a boxing room is worth considering. Many older instructional pools that no longer meet specifications as competitive venues occupy more than enough space for an excellent boxing facility.

Older pools of this type are usually at least 60 feet by 25 feet (I,500 square feet) with considerable additional space allotted for the pool deck areas. All that is needed is a way to construct a wooden floor over the surface that will support the weight of 25 to 40 participants (100 lbs. per square inch). Your school's buildings and grounds staff along with a local architect can plan and construct this project for less than $10,000.00.

Materials necessary (other than labor) are:

- 2 inch by 4 inch studs,
- 2 inch by 8 foot floor joists,
- Wooden bridging pieces,
- 1/2-inch plywood and 5/8 inch particle board (installed on top of the floor joists), and
- Ensolite® matting to cover the exercise area.

The Virginia Military Institute (VMI) completed such a conversion in the early 1980s. The space provided has been used continuously since that time as both a boxing facility and a multipurpose room. Any questions regarding construction plans, etc., should be directed to the Physical Education Department, Cocke Hall, Virginia Military Institute, Lexington, Virginia 24450.

What Equipment Is Necessary?

If a ring is used, or if contact drills are used, the ring or floor area must be covered with a one-inch layer of Ensolite® AAC or AL closed-cell foam rubber (or a chemical equivalent). The ring padding must be covered with canvas or some similar material, and be tightly stretched and laced securely in place (USA Boxing , 1995). If no contact drills are anticipated, the floor area could be of any type surface, but wood is preferable.

Boxing gloves used for sparring or live contact drills must meet the specifications required by USA Boxing Inc. USA Boxing Official Rules (1995, p. 114) require that the padding inside the gloves be "$^1/_2$ inch Latex, $^3/_4$ inch PVC (Husitonic), $^3/_8$ inch PVC (Rubitex® 313 V) and $^1/_2$ inch Polyfoam or other products which meet the severity (force of blow) index." For instructional purposes, 16-ounce thumbless or attached thumb gloves are recommended. Remember that the purpose of the gloves (in contact work) is to diminish the impact of a blow and to protect the hands.

The purpose of boxing headgear is to reduce the impact of a blow, reduce/prevent facial cuts, protect the ears and substantially reduce impact to the head if a fall occurs. Only headgear approved by USA Boxing Inc. should be used (USA Boxing, 1995). Several manufacturers produce headgear to the proper standard.

During any type of contact drills, use of a mouthpiece is mandatory. The mouthpiece reduces the possibility of jaw injuries, cuts to the inside of the mouth, and injuries to the tongue and teeth. A custom-made or individually fitted mouthpiece must be worn by each participant. Examples of the custom-made and individually fitted are the "dentist-molded" and the clear plastic types, respectively (USA Boxing, 1995).

When contact drills are involved, men and women should wear approved groin or chest protection. For men, his means either a foul-proof protection cup or a jock strap cup. Women should wear a well-fitting breast protector (USA Boxing, 1995).

Handwraps are recommended for all types of striking drills, but need not be required (they are mandatory in competition, however). The purpose of the handwrap is primarily to protect the metacarpal bones of the hand. They are not designed or utilized to add force to a blow. Handwraps can be made of cotton gauze, soft surgical gauze or velpeau material. For ease of wrapping, the velpeau type is recommended. Instruction and practice in proper wrapping technique should be given prior to their.

Heavy bags are vital to the organization of any boxing training facility. They are the single best modality to use for non-contact striking/punching drills and are a must in your training area. They are used to simulate an opponent's body and head and any number of very useful drills can be done with these bags. Several types and sizes are available (canvas, leather, nylon, vinyl) and they can be filled with foam, water, or rags (depending on the type). An inexpensive way to make up a heavy bag is to use a duffle or "sea" bag filled with sawdust, rags, or a combination of the two (Deeter, Rubino, and Simmons, 1950).

Light striking bags are used for advanced drills and are a "nice to have" item in your facility, but the heavy bags are much more practical. Light bags are used for developing speed, timing, and coordination. They are much smaller than a heavy bag, but require that a bag "platform" be anchored to a wall in order to be utilized.

A boxing ring is not necessary for boxing instruction, drills, or conditioning exercises. It is however, an important piece of equipment if any of your participants are interested in competitive boxing. It is also a good way to control the various boxing contact drills or any sparring that is done. Only rings that meet USA Boxing specifications should be utilized. The ring can be either a platform type, elevated about three feet above the floor (not more than four feet), or a floor type built directly upon the floor or on a slightly raised platform that is laid directly on the floor. The platform type is recommended for competition, but for training purposes, many prefer the floor type (Deeter, Rubino, and Simmons, 1950). According to USA Boxing Official Rules (1995, p. 15), "the ring must be not less than 16 nor more than 20 feet square within the ropes, and the apron of the ring floor shall extend beyond the ropes not less than two feet." The ring should be equipped with four ropes that are wrapped in a soft material, and all turnbuckles must be covered with protective padding.

Miscellaneous Exercise Stations

Depending on the specific purpose of your room and the needs of the participants, the number and type of exercise stations you develop is unlimited. At a minimum, however, are recommended exercise stations requiring individuals to use their own body weight as resistance. Among these are pullup bars (six to eight), and sit-up and push-up stations. If the floor is not already padded, some type of matting will be necessary at the sit-up station. An area set up for rope skipping and shadow-boxing (two full length mirrors) can also be provided.

Cost of Various Equipment Items

The cost of equipment items for your facility will vary slightly depending on the vendor you use, but the following rough estimates will enable you to establish a budget to get your facility started. The amount of equipment of course, will depend on the number of participants, but the total cost for this example are based on an expected 25 participants:

Training gloves (16 ounce):	
25 pair @ $175/pair	= $ 4375.00
Bag gloves: 25 pair @ $10-00/pair	= $ 250.00
Training head gear: 25 @ $70 each	= $ 1750.00
Plastic mouthpiece (upper):	
50 @ $1.50 each	= $ 75.00
Groin protection (boxing cups):	
25 @ $15.00 ea,	= $ 375.00
Female chest guards (with support bra):	
25 @ 45.00 each	= $ 1125.00
Handwrap: 25@ $5.00 each	= $ 125.00
Heavy bags (canvas; unfilled):	
8 @ $55.00 each	= $ 440.00
Boxing ring (platform type)	= $ 6,000.00
Boxing ring (floor type)	= $ 2,500.00
Total cost (with platform ring)	= $14,515.00
■ Total cost (with floor ring)	= $11,015.00

It must be emphasized that these prices may vary from vendor to vendor, and you should shop around for the best price. Your facility does not have to be completely equipped for 25 persons. Depending upon how you organize your exercise/practice sessions, equipment and exercise stations can be shared and rotated so that you may only have to be equipped for 10 participants or fewer. You may also be able to purchase used equipment, or construct some of your own.

Organization of the Facility

If you intend to set up a boxing room with a ring, remember that a regulation size ring can be from 16 to 20 feet, inside dimensions of all four sides. Obviously, this means that you will need more space than if you set up the room without a ring. To utilize your available space most efficiently, center the ring on one end of the room, and place heavy bags and light striking bags on the opposite end, thus leaving the space between for drills, calisthenics, plyometrics, or for multipurpose use when the area is not being utilized for boxing. On either end of the room or along the side walls, you can set up permanent pull-up and sit-up stations, using pipe suspended horizontally from the ceiling for the pull-up station and bolted to the floor as an anchor point for feet at the sit-up station. Along one side wall, place full-length mirrors (six by four feet) for shadow boxing and technique drills. This type of arrangement gives you four areas in which to work: a ring area, a bag work area, a alisthenics/conditioning area, and a space in between that can be used as a multipurpose area.

If you decide to set up your facility without a ring, you will save at least 400 square feet of useable space (not to mention the expense of a ring). This will still enable you set up three areas for specific fitness training, including aerobics and circuit training. It also allows you to design your facility in a much smaller space than is possible with a ring. The number of exercise stations in your circuit is then left up to your imagination and the available space. The perimeter of this fitness training facility should be set up for specific circuit exercises, with the center area left open for multipurpose use.

Any boxing facility that does not have a ring (or the space for one), but is going to be used for self-defense contact drills or sparring, should be set up to ensure that participants are protected from the perimeter walls and any objects that may protrude from those walls, and that the floor surface being used is properly matted. Floor surface matting has already been discussed (one-inch Ensolite®) and its main purpose is to protect against traumatic injuries to the head resulting from falls or knock-downs. Perimeter walls should also be padded with one-inch Ensolite® to protect against injuries caused by wall contact. When a ring is not available and the perimeter walls are not matted, you can still conduct contact drills and sparring if you organize the session properly. Participants should form a large circle (16-20 foot diameter) and be instructed to act as a "human ring". This ring should be centered in the exercise area and at least six feet from the perimeter walls. Only two participants should spar at a time and they should begin in the center. Participants on the perimeter of the ring should be instructed to adjust their positions so as to keep the two sparring individuals inside the ring. Any time either of the two boxers makes contact with the ring's perimeter, the instructor should immediately stop the activity and have the participants begin again, in the center. This not only prevents traumatic contact with the perimeter walls, it stops any punching activity when one individual becomes momentarily disadvantaged.

Equipment Storage Concerns

Equipment should be of high quality and meet all published safety standards required by USA Boxing. Properly cared for, boxing equipment will have a long life and replacement costs will be minimal.

Security of the equipment and, in fact, the entire area is of paramount importance. The entire facility should be locked when not in use and access limited to instructors, coaches, and maintenance personnel.

There should be adequate and assigned storage areas for all equipment that is moveable and used on a regular basis. Boxing gloves and head gear, for example, should be stored in an area that is open to circulating air so that the equipment can dry properly. Gloves and head gear should be stowed in open wire racks, on open shelving, or in lockers with steel mesh fronts that allow the circulation of air. Both should be washed with saddle soap and dried thoroughly each week, Both should also be treated weekly with a commercial disinfectant or with a solution of I0% carbolic acid and 90% sweet oil (Deeter, Rubino, and Simmons, 1950). Handwraps should be allowed to dry after each use and should be washed weekly. Obviously, athletic supporters, groin protectors, athletic bras, and chest protectors should be washed thoroughly on a regular basis and stored in a dry, clean area. Usually, this will be the responsibility of individual participants.

Safety Concerns

If contact drills or sparring are part of your exercise program, then it is mandatory that the boxing gloves and headgear utilized meet the safety specifications of USA Boxing. It is also essential that any safety equipment worn be properly fitted to the individual. Protective headgear, especially, should be worn so that it provides the maximum protection possible. All headgear should fit snugly and should not change position on the head if pulled, pushed, or struck. The bottom edge of the padded forehead portion of the headgear should sit just above the top of the eyebrow, approximately $1/2$ inch above the hairline of the brow. The participant's ears should fit snugly inside the ear openings on the headgear and the ears should lie flat against the inside surface. There should be an additional heavily padded area on the rear of the headgear. This should be centered on the back of the head and reach down to the top of the neck. If the headgear has cheek guards, they should fit snugly against the cheeks, tight enough so that they cannot slide up into the eye. Finally, the chinstrap should fit under the chin and be as tight as possible, without causing discomfort.

If plastic mouthpieces (uppers only or doubles) are used, they should be softened and molded to the individual's mouth. This can be done by placing the mouthpiece in a cup of water and then heating it in a microwave oven. When the mouthpiece appears to be softened (flaccid), remove it from the hot water and rinse it with cool water. While it is still soft, have the individual bite down on it until it is "molded" to his or her mouth. This may take a few tries, but it is the most inexpensive way to obtain a fitted mouthpiece.

Handwraps should always be worn when striking drills of any kind are being performed. Cloth (velpeau) handwraps are recommended (Deeter, Rubino, and Simmons, 1950). Further, it is recommended that commercial handwraps can be applied as follows:

1. Place the looped end of the wrap over the thumb,
2. Bring the wrap over the back of the hand to the big knuckle of the wrist,
3. Go underneath the wrist to the base of the thumb in diagonally across the back of the hand to the big knuckle of the little finger,
4. Encircle completely the big knuckles of the hand, wrapping well up toward the middle joints of the fingers,
5. Go diagonally across the back of the hand to the outside wrist bone,
6. Completely encircle the wrist once, angling the wrap slightly upward, stopping at the base of the thumb,
7. Completely encircle the thumb once,
8. Following the normal contour of the hand, bring the wrap over across the back of the hand to the joint of the little finger,

9. Completely encircle the large knuckles of the hand a second time,
10. Carry the wrapping down diagonally across the back of the hand and around to the base of the thumb,
11. Pull it up, completely encircling the thumb for a second time, and
12. Finally, bring the wrap diagonally over the back of the hand to the wrist, and encircle the wrist once using a small piece of tape (one inch by 6 inches) to secure the wrap.

Ensure that participants keep their fingers spread and extended throughout the wrapping process. This will prevent the wrap from being too tight, thus cutting off circulation.

When pairing participants for contact drills, there should be as little weight difference between the participants as possible. A reasonable guideline to follow is to allow no more than an eight pound differential during any sparring or contact drills. It is perhaps even more important to also pair individuals according to their respective skill/experience levels. If a new skill is being learned, it is a good idea to pair an experienced individual with a beginner. The experienced person can control the action and can also act as an assistant instructor for the beginner. If the activity involves sparring or any competitive situations, then it is usually best to pair the individuals according to size (weight) and relative ability.

During any vigorous activity, there is the possibility of injury. There should be a phone located inside the boxing room with clearly posted numbers of the local emergency squad, the school athletic training staff, and the infirmary. In addition, all instructors should be CPR certified and a first aid kit should always be on hand. Identifying injuries should be the responsibility of the professional staff, but guidelines for handling suspected head injuries should also be clearly posted inside the room. USA Boxing Inc. has published the following guidelines for recognizing a possible head injury:

Observe the athlete for:

■ dizziness or headache lasting more than one hour,
■ increasing drowsiness,
■ loss of consciousness,
■ mental disorientation or confusion,
■ unusual or strange behavior,
■ restlessness or irritability,
■ seizure (convulsion),
■ blurred vision or loss of vision,
■ repeated vomiting,
■ blood or watery fluid from ears or nose,

■ inability to control urination or bowel movement, and
■ inability to move an arm or leg.

If any of these symptoms occur (or persist), medical personnel should be contacted immediately.

■ Summary

Planning and designing a martial arts facility is a difficult task because there is no template for such facilities. There are numerous types, styles, and variations of the martial arts, and no two programs will have the same facility requirements. Martial arts programs are often conducted in multipurpose combative facilities, which makes the facility planning even more difficult. Facility planners and designers need to gather information from owners and operators, staff members, and facility users to accurately determine program needs. Having a basic understanding of martial arts will help planners and designers make informed decisions concerning construction of martial arts facilities. Martial arts facilities can be classified as **grappling-oriented facilities with matted floors; striking-oriented facilities** with hardwood, carpeted, or synthetic floors; or **grappling and striking facilities** with partially matted floors.

Designing a boxing room that can also be utilized as a multipurpose facility can be done inexpensively and with a minimum of necessary space. The number of exericse stations and the organization of the facility is limited only by one's imagination and to a much lesser extent, available funding. This type of fitness activity is interesting, a bit different, and most important, pays big dividends in terms of the fitness gains made possible through its proper organization and utilization.

Learning Objective 1: The student will be able to apply general facility planning principles to planning martial arts facilities.

Planning and designing a martial arts facility is a difficult task because there are so many types and styles of martial arts. Utilizing participatory planning will assist facility planners in designing highly functional and cost-effective martial arts facilities (Flynn, 1993).

Learning Objective 2: The student will be able to identify the three types of martial arts facilities.

Every martial arts program is different and requires different facility features. The type of facility flooring required is the most distinguishing feature. Grappling martial arts facilities require a matted floor; a striking martial arts facility is characterized by a wood, carpeted, or synthetic floor; and a grappling/striking martial arts facility should have both.

Learning Objective 3: The student will be able to identify the major martial arts styles and determine which of the facility types is most appropriate for each style.

The wide variety of martial arts is represented by seven major styles. Each of these styles can best be conducted in one of the three types of martial arts facility types.

Aikido	Grappling Facility
Judo	Grappling Facility
Karate	Striking Facility
Kendo	Striking Facility
Kung Fu	Grappling/Striking Facility
Tae Kwan Do	Striking Facility
T'ai Chi	Grappling/Striking Facility

Learning Objective 4: The student will be able to list the equipment and key design features for each of the martial arts facilities.

Grappling-type martial arts facilities have a matted floor, padded walls, and often mirrors. Striking-type martial arts facilities do not have mats on the floor, but do have mirrors, striking bags, and (for some styles) weapons. Grappling/striking facilities can be used for any of the styles, so they may have any combination of equipment and features.

Learning Objective 5: The student will be able to design, set up, and properly organize a boxing facility for use as a physical education activity area.

Boxing activities do not always have to involve contact (striking, punching, etc.) Boxing exercises and training activities are excellent methods of conditioning for both the muscular and cardiorespiratory systems. Proper organization of the facility allows you to have a boxing technique area (ring, bag work), a calisthenics/conditioning area, and a multipurpose area. The facility could then be used as a physical education area for the teaching of boxing fundamentals or as a physical education multipurpose room for use by other sport or classroom activities.

Learning Objective 6: The student will be able to utilize the facility as a boxing fitness area, with boxing training activities for the development of physical fitness.

Boxing exercises can be utilized without any contact drills or sparring. Bag punching, rope skipping, shadow boxing, interval training, plyometrics, non-contact glove drills, and various other exercises (push ups, sit ups), can all be combined into an excellent circuit training program that will provide both aerobic and muscular conditioning.

Learning Objective 7: The student will be able to understand how to utilize the facility as a training area for the development of basic boxing skills, for those interested in learning boxing for self-defense or for competition.

A ring or human circle can be utilized in the facility to teach/practice boxing contact drills and/or sparring. Knowledge of safety fundamentals and use of the proper equipment will enable the individual to participate and learn the necessary skills in a safe and effective manner.

■ Self-Assessment Exercise

1. What is the goal in constructing or renovating a martial arts facility?
2. What is aikido?
3. What is judo?
4. What is karate?
5. What is kendo?
6. What is kung fu?
7. What is tae kwan do?
8. What are the three types of martial arts facilities?
9. Describe a grappling martial arts facility.
10. Describe a striking martial arts facility.
11. What is a combination facility?
12. Discuss the following general features of a martial arts facility—wall coverings, water fountains, ceiling, lighting, storage, scoreboard, and custodial closet.
13. What national organization is responsible for establishing, rules, legislation, and safety regulations for all United States amateur boxing?
14. How much space is necessary for a boxing facility?
15. Describe the three different ways a boxing facility might be utilized for physical education activities?
16. What types of equipment will be needed for the facility?

17. A boxing room (facility) can be organized into four working areas. Name and briefly describe the purpose of each area.
18. Why are mouthpieces and handwraps important pieces of personal equipment?
19. Describe three equipment storage concerns.
20. List five symptoms indicating a possible head injury.
21. Describe two criteria for pairing participants for boxing contact drills or sparring.
22. Describe how you might conduct contact boxing drills without the use of a boxing ring.

■ References

Bernstein, A. (1978). **Boxing for beginners.** Chicago, IL: Conternporary Books, Inc.

Deeter, I.F., Rubino, A.J., & Simmons, R.D. (1950). **Boxing** (Revised by the V-Five Assocation). Annapolis, MD.: U.S. Naval Institute.

Flynn, R. B. (Ed.). (1993). **Facility planning for physical education, recreation, and athletics.** Reston, VA: American Alliance for Health, Physical Education, Recreation, and Dance.

Goodbody, J. (1969). **The Japanese fighting arts.** South Brunswick, NY: A. S. Barnes and Company.

Logan, W., & Petras, H. (1975). **Handbook of the martial arts and self-defense.** New York: Funk and Wagnalls.

Roth, J. (1974). **Black belt karate.** Rutland, VT: Charles E. Tuttle Company, Inc.

Trais, R.A. (1973). **The hand is my sword.** Rutland, VT: Charles E. Tuttle Company, Inc.

United States Amateur Boxing, Inc. (1995). **Coaching Olympic style boxing.** Carmel, IN: Cooper Publishing Group LLC.

United States Amateur Boxing, Inc. (1995). **1995-97 United States Amateur Boxing, Inc. Official Rules.** Colorado Springs, CO: Author.

Urban, P. (1981). **The karate dojo** (12th ed). Rutland, VT: Charles E. Tuttle Company, Inc.

Winderbaum, L. (1977). **The martial arts encyclopedia.** Washington, DC: INSCAPE Publishers.

■ Internet References

AJJF kata contest rules [On-line]. Available: http://www.ajjf.org.rules.html

Frequently asked questions [On-line]. Available: http://www.rain.org/~ssa/judofaq.htm

Index of products [On-line]. Available: http://www.handcrafted.cim/index.html

Introduction to aikido [On-line]. Available: http://www.ii.uib.no/~kjartan/akiidofaq/b_section01.html

Judo rules [On-line]. Available: http://www.rain,org/~ssa/rules.html#2

Karate glossary [On-line]. Available: http:/www.europa.cs.mun.ca/~johnt/glossery.html

Practice guidelines [On-line]. Available: http://www.maui.net/~taichi4u/practice.html

Perfetti, R. **T'ai Chi Ch'uan overview** [On-line]. Available: http://www.maui.net/~taichi4u/overview.html

Recreation:Sports:Martial arts [On-line]. Available: http://www.yaho.com/Recreation/Sports/Martial Arts

■ Suggested Reading

Mullan, H. (1987). **The illustrated history of boxing.** New York: Hamlyn Publishing Group, Limited.

The Diagram Group. (1977). **Enjoying combat sports.** New York and London: Paddington Press, LTD.

CHAPTER 21

Strength and Cardiovascular Training

Thomas H. Sawyer, Indiana State University

Learning Objectives

After reading this chapter, the student will be able to

- assess the needs of an existing or new facility,
- plan and organize an existing or new facility for maximum usage, and
- understand the environmental factors affecting facility development.

Introduction

As a strength and cardiovascular facility coordinator, you are responsible for not only knowing how to organize participants for strength and cardiovascular training, but also for knowing how to arrange equipment safely in order to meet the challenge. In some cases you might be responsible for developing a facility. Planning the facility takes many hours of creating and reviewing floor plans and deciding what equipment will be needed, how space may be best utilized, what surfaces are needed in various areas, and other factors. It is worthwhile to contact professionals in other programs who have built a facility and to compile information on specific needs. A committee of people who represent various areas of expertise may be organized to help in the planning of the facility. Such a committee may consist of an administrator, contractor, lawyer, student-athlete, sport coach, instructors who would use the facility, various experts in the field of sport conditioning, and any other people who could give valuable input on design.

This chapter will focus on a discussion of existing facilities and how you might improve and reorganize

them to best suit the needs of the philosophy (the ideals and values shaping the program), goals (the desired outcome), and objectives (the individual steps toward a goal) of a program, and what would be needed in a new facility.

Assessing the Needs of an Existing Facility

After defining the program goals and objectives, the facility coordinator should assess existing equipment and the needs of the various sport groups that plan to use the facility. As the coordinator, you will need to answer these questions:

- What are the specific training goals of each group?
- What types of training does each require (e.g., circuits, machines. free weights, platform lifts, plyometrics)?
- What are the seasonal priorities of each group?
- What are the training ages (training experience) of the athletes in the groups?

■ When will weight training fit into each group's schedule?

■ What repairs, adaptations, and modifications must be made to meet the athletes' needs?

■ How should the equipment be placed to best utilize the space in a safe and efficient manner?

Planning the Layout of an Existing Facility

An initial step is to determine who will be using the facility and develop a list of existing equipment. Prepare a floor plan to (1) visualize the present and potential locations of equipment; (2) organize for safety and the most efficient use of space, exits, and entrances; (3) identify areas of frequent travel; (4) develop facility flow (pathways in the facility); and (5) select supervisor station locations for maximum supervision of the whole facility, especially areas of increased risk (such as the platform area). Safety should always be a priority.

Station all high-risk activities, including platform lifts, squats, overhead presses, bench and incline presses, and exercises that require spotters, away from windows, mirrors, exits, and entrances to avoid breakage of glass, distraction, or collision with the bar or lifter. Place the equipment for these activities in areas that are readily supervised to ensure safety and the execution of proper technique. Supervision is effective only if all areas of the facility can be observed at any given time. Therefore, locate supervisor stations in places with full visibility of all areas of the facility, to allow quick access to participants in need of spotters or immediate assistance.

Arrange the tallest machines or pieces of equipment along the walls, with the shorter, smaller pieces in the middle to improve visibility (as well as appearance) and maximize use of space. Place weight racks with enough distance away from bar ends and spotter areas for ease of movement without obstruction. Tall pieces of equipment, such as squat racks, may need to be bolted to the walls or floors for increased stability.

The following are guidelines suggested by a panel of safety experts at the National Strength and Conditioning Association (NSCA) and the American College Sports Medicine (ACSM) for the safe and efficient use of equipment (Baechle, 1994; Tharrett and Peterson, 1997):

■ All weight machines and apparatus must be spaced at least two feet (61 cm) from one another, and preferably three feet (91 cm) apart.

■ Platform areas should have sufficient overhead space (at least 12 feet [3.7 m]), which should be free of such low-hanging items as beams, pipes, lighting, and signs.

■ The proper spacing of Olympic bars is three feet (91 cm) between ends (12 feet [3.7 m] $\times$ 8 feet [2.4 m] = 1 platform lifting area).

Maintain a clear pathway three feet (91 cm) wide in the facility at all times, as stipulated by federal, state, and local laws. Machines and equipment must not be allowed to block or obstruct this flow. Place equipment at least six inches (15 cm) from mirrors and mirrors 20 inches (51 cm) above the floor. Place free-weight equipment well away from exits and entrances to avoid obstruction, give participants ample room for passage, and guarantee safety to the pedestrian and lifter. Organize equipment into "priority sections," such as free-weight areas, machine areas, power training areas, and cardiovascular/aerobic areas. This allows the supervisor to identify and focus on the higher risk areas and keep equipment orderly in the facility.

Organizing the Facility for Maximum Usage

When organizing groups of participants, you should consider the size of the facility and assess the needs of each group in terms of the following:

■ specific training needs (e.g., strength, endurance, circuits, and power),

■ seasonal priority (i.e., when sports occur, such as football in the fall and baseball in the spring),

■ group size and equipment availability (i.e., a football team with 150 members may not be able to use a facility efficiently and safely without being split into groups; other sports groups may have to be scheduled at times other than football groups to ensure sufficient use of the equipment),

■ the participant-staff ratio (1:10 to 1:30, depending upon the training group), and

■ a minimum space requirement per lifter of 30 feet (2.8 m) and a maximum of 60 feet (5.6 m) (Baechle, 1994).

Schedule facility usage so that different groups of participants train in the facility at more or less constant "density" throughout the day; avoid large, congested groups, which increase the potential for injury and inefficient use of equipment. If the facility is designed for high school athletes, groups may be organized through physical education classes that offer beginning, intermediate, and advanced strength and conditioning to the students. Teams may organize facility usage time before or after practice according to seasonal priority.

Assessing Existing Facility Surfaces

Two main surfaces need to be assessed—flooring and wall. The following describes exactly what one should look for when assessing these surfaces.

Flooring

Flooring can be composed of such materials as wood, tile, rubber, interlocking mats, and carpet. The assessor will carefully review the surfaces for the following concerns:

Wooden flooring on platforms must be kept free of splinters, holes, protruding nails, uneven boards, and screws. The boards should run in the direction of the bar so that lifters do not catch their feet against the grain of the wood when widening their stance. This is the safest flooring for Olympic-style lifters.

Tile flooring and anti-static, floor should be treated with antifungal, antibacterial agents in the aerobic machine area. The tile should also be resistant to slipping and moisture accumulation, and free from chalk accumulation.

Resilient rubber flooring in the free-weight and machine areas should be similar to aerobic flooring. It must be kept free of large gaps between pieces, cuts, and worn spots.

Interlocking mats must be secure and arranged so as not to pull apart or become deformed (with protruding tabs). The stretching area must be kept free of accumulated dust. Mats or carpets should be nonabsorbent and contain antifungal and antibacterial agents.

Carpet must be free of tears. High-use areas should be protected with throw mats.

All areas must be swept and vacuumed or mopped on a regular basis. Flooring must be kept glued and fastened down properly. Fixed equipment must be attached securely to the floor.

Walls

Wall surfaces include mirrors and windows, exits, storage areas, and shelves. The assessor needs to carefully look for the following regarding wall surfaces:

- Walls in high activity areas must be kept free of protruding apparatus (i.e., extended bars and lighting fixtures).
- Mirrors, shelves, and other fixtures must be fixed securely to the walls.
- Mirrors and windows must be located in an area easily reached for repair and cleaning.
- Mirrors, if present in any area, must be attached to the wall at least 50 inches off the floor, and cracked or distorted mirrors should be replaced.

Environmental Factors

Environmental factors that should be considered in helping make the facility safe and effective include noise control, temperature, ventilation, humidity, lighting, electrical cords and outlets, and posted signs. Music can be a form of motivation for many, but it can also pose a problem if the stereo system is not properly managed. Volume should be low enough to allow for clear communication between spotters or instructors and lifters at all times. The stereo system should be controlled by the facility coordinator and qualified supervisors only.

Air temperature should be kept constant at 68° to 72°F (22° to 26°C) to offer a reasonable training environment. If the room is too cold, athletes may become chilled after they finish warming up; if too hot, participants may become overheated or lose motivation to continue. Proper ventilation is important to maintaining air quality and keeping humidity to a minimum (relative humidity should be less than 60%). The ventilation system should provide at least 8 to 10 air exchanges per hour and optimally 12 to 15 air exchanges. The result should be no detectable strong odors in the room and equipment free of slickness or rust due to high humidity (Tharrett & Peterson, 1997).

Proper lighting of the facility is important for safety and motivation. A facility is well lighted if it is free of dark areas, and all equipment and areas can be observed from one end of the facility to the other. Bulbs, tubes, and other lighting apparatus should be checked and changed on a regular basis; optimum lighting is 75 to 100 foot-candles. Exit signs should also be well lighted and all exits well marked. All extension cords should be large enough for the electrical load and routed, secured, and grounded. Because some aerobic equipment requires 220 V, both 110 V and 220 V outlets are needed.

All safety, regulation, and policy signs should be posted in clear view, in two or three central places within the facility; more postings may be needed in a large facility.

Procedures for Maintaining Equipment

All strength and cardiovascular facilities, whether they are existing or new, should have a well-planned set of procedures for maintaining equipment in specified areas.

Aerobic/anaerobic fitness area. This space contains rowing machines, bikes, sprint machines, stair machines, skiing and climbing machines. In this area, surfaces that come into contact with human skin should be cleaned and disinfected daily. This not only protects participants from unsanitary conditions, but also extends the usefulness and maintains the appearance of equipment surfaces. The moving parts of the equipment should be properly lubricated and cleaned when needed so that they are not stressed unnecessarily. Connective bolts and screws need to be checked for tightness or wear and replaced if needed. Straps and belts should be secure and replaced if necessary. Measurement devices such as rpm meters should be properly maintained (this is usually done by the manufacturer but the life span of the equipment can be extended by wiping off sweat and dirt regularly). Equipment parts such as seats and benches should be easily adjustable.

Machines area. Isokinetic, variable resistance, single-station, multi-station machines are located in this space.

Rehabilitation and special-population machine area. The cleaning and maintenance of both the machines and rehabilitation areas are similar to those processes in the aerobic/anaerobic fitness area. Bench and machine surfaces that come into contact with skin should be cleaned and disinfected daily to provide a clean surface. Padded and upholstered areas should be free of cracks and tears. Moving parts should be cleaned and lubricated (guide rods on selectorized machines cleaned and lubricated two to three times each week). These areas should be free of loose bolts, screws, cables, chains, and protruding or worn parts that need replacing or removal. Pins that were designed for the machines and belts should be kept in stock. Chains and cables should be adjusted for proper alignment and smooth function. Machines should he spaced so that they are easily accessed, with a minimum of two feet (61 cm) on all sides, preferably three feet (91 cm) (Baechle, 1994).

Body weight resistance apparatus area. This area contains sit-up board, pulleys, hyperextension benches, plyometric boxes, medicine balls, climbing ropes, pegboard climb, jump ropes. It should have secured apparatus with well-padded flooring. If mats are used, they should be disinfected daily and free of cracks and tears. The flooring below plyometric boxes and jumping equipment should be padded to protect the jumper from impact with a hard surface. The tops and bottoms of boxes should have nonslip surfaces for safe use.

Stretching area. Equipment in this area includes mats, stretching sticks, medicine balls, elastic cords, wall ladders. Mats in stretching areas should be cleaned and disinfected daily and be free of cracks and tears. Areas between mats should be swept or vacuumed regularly to avoid the accumulation of dust and dirt. The area should be free of benches, dumbbells, and other equipment that may clutter the area and tear mat surfaces. Medicine balls and stretching sticks should be stored after use, and elastic cords should be secured to a base, checked for wear, and replaced when necessary.

Free-weight area. This area includes bench presses, incline presses, squat racks, dumbbells, and weight racks. Equipment should be spaced to allow easy access to separate areas. All equipment, including safety equipment (belts, locks, safety bars) should be returned after use to avoid pathway obstruction. Benches, weight racks, and standards may be bolted to the floor or walls. In the squat area, the flooring should be of a nonslip surface and cleaned regularly. Equipment such as curl bars and dumbbells should be checked frequently for loose hex nuts. Nonfunctional or broken equipment should be posted with "out of order" signs or, if a long delay in repairs is expected, removed from the area or locked out of service. All protective padding and upholstery should be free of cracks and tears, and disinfected daily.

Lifting platform area. Olympic bars, standards, bumper plates, racks, locks, chalk bins. The cleaning and maintenance of the lifting platform includes ensuring that all equipment is returned after use to prevent obstruction of the area and hazardous lifting conditions. Olympic bars should be properly lubricated and tightened to maintain the rotating bar ends. If standards are used in the area, the base of each should be secure and each standard stored out of the way when not in use. Bent Olympic bars should be replaced and the knurling kept free of debris and chalk buildup by cleaning and brushing occasionally. All locks should be functioning, and wrist straps, knee wraps, and belts should be stored properly. The platform should be inspected for gaps, cuts, slits, and splinters (depending on the type of surface) and prop-

Figure 21.1 National Institute for Fitness and Sport, Indianapolis, IN.

erly swept or mopped to remove chalk. The lifting area should be free of benches, boxes, and other clutter to give the lifter sufficient room.

Cleaning supplies should be kept in a locked cabinet located near the office or supervisor station. Supplies should be inventoried and restocked on a regular basis (once or twice each month). These items should be kept in stock (Armitage-Johnson, 1994):

■ Disinfectant (germicide),
■ Window and mirror cleaner,
■ Lubrication sprays,
■ Cleaning sprays,
■ Spray bottles (about four),
■ Paper towels,
■ Cloth towels,
■ Sponges,
■ Broom and dust pan,
■ Small vacuum cleaner,
■ Vacuum cleaner bags,
■ Whisk broom,
■ Mop and bucket,
■ Shower caps (for bicycle meter equipment), and
■ Gum and stain remover (for carpet and upholstery).

Maintenance supplies should be kept in a toolbox located in a locked cabinet. The tool box should contain these items (Armitage-Johnson, 1994):

■ File,
■ Hammer,
■ Pliers (standard and needle-nose),
■ Screwdrivers (Phillips and standard),
■ Allen wrenches,
■ Crescent wrench,
■ Rubber mallet,
■ Carpet knife,
■ Cable splicer parts and appropriate tools,
■ Chain splicer parts and appropriate tools,
■ Heavy-duty glue,
■ Nuts, bolts, washers, nails, and screws in various sizes,
■ Transparent tape,
■ Masking tape,
■ Duct tape,
■ Drill and drill bit set,
■ Lubricant spray,
■ Socket set, and
■ Vise grip.

Planning a New Facility

This area will be one of the most popular spaces in the facility. You should expect a mixture of dedicated bodybuilders, recreational weight lifters, dedicated fitness and body tone people, and novices who are just getting interested in strength training. There will be an equal number of men and women involved in strength training programs. Further, this area needs to include space for free weights, strength training machines, cardiovascular, and stretching equipment. The designer must consider all these variables and create a room that will fit the needs of all groups.

A strength and cardiovascular training area should provide areas for cardiovascular training, resistance training (divided into free weights and machine weights), and stretching. The design and layout of a facility should provide at least 20 to 40 square feet for each piece of exercise equipment (Tharrett & Peterson, 1997). The exact amount of space is determined by the size of each particular piece of equipment and the recommendations of the manufacturer. Further, "a facility should allow for 20 to 25 sf of space for each person expected to be using the facility at any one time" (Foster & Sol, 1997, p. 51). This is not in addition to the space allocation for equipment previously mentioned.

The designer needs to define the use of the space. This is done by responding to the following questions:

■ What programs will be offered, e.g., circuit training, free weights, cardio-vascular?
■ What is the size of the total membership or the membership registered to use the strength training area?
■ What is the approximate peak demand for the area?
■ What is the equipment preference (i.e., a mixture of free weights and machines, free weights only, machines only)?
■ Is there a high demand for separate or coed areas?
■ What type of flooring would be most appropriate?
■ Has the equipment been chosen? If yes, who is the vendor and what are the specific dimensions of the equipment and what is the proposed layout?

Size. The strength training area will include coed free-weight, strength-training, cardiovascular, and stretching areas. A minimum of 9,000 square feet is needed; however, 12,000 square feet is preferred for this space, with at least a 10 foot ceiling. Many new strength and cardiovascular training areas are inadequate when they open, because the designer did not perceive the popularity of the activity during the design stage (Baechle, 1994).

Walls. Three of the walls should be solidly covered with materials that will reduce sound internally as well as externally. The walls should be painted with an epoxy for ease of cleaning. There should be graphics provided to make the walls come alive. Further, numerous mirrors should be placed around the walls.

The fourth wall should be constructed of durable glass and face into the lobby/lounge area (with drapes) to further encourage greater use of the area. Each area should have at least one bulletin board (i.e., cardiovascular, weight machines, free weight, and stretching).

Floor. The facility should provide the following types of floor coverings for the strength and cardiovascular training area (Tharrett & Peterson, 1997):

Cardiovascular area: Anti-static commercial carpet treated with antifungal and antibacterial agents.

Resistance-training area: A rubber-based resilient floor.

Stretching area: Nonabsorbent mats or anti-static commercial carpet with antifungal and antibacterial agents.

Platform. In the free-weight area should be at least one platform, 10 feet by 10 feet by 6 inches, constructed of sturdy materials and covered with a rubberized flooring material to be used for heavy weight activities. This platform should be recessed into the concrete slab. Depending on the number of participants, multiple platforms may be needed.

Ceiling. The ceiling clearance needs to be at least 10 feet. The ceiling should be constructed with acoustical ceiling materials. A drop ceiling can be installed for these spaces; however, ceiling panels are more susceptible to damage by objects or individuals and require considerable maintenance. Therefore, it is recommended that a permanent ceiling be considered rather than a drop ceiling.

Electrical. The electrical needs of equipment (i.e., treadmills, stair climbers, computerized bicycles, etc.) in the facility must be considered as well as the equipment layout. There should be numerous receptacles around the perimeter of the room. The designer will need to provide for audio and video needs in the room as well as for computer access.

The lighting in the area should provide at least 50 foot-candles of illumination at the floor level. The ideal lighting system has both an indirect and a direct component, throwing surface light on the ceiling to give it about the same brightness as the lighting unit itself. It is recommended that fluorescent lamps be installed since they have the advantage of long life and produce at least two and one-half times the amount of light of incandescent lamps for the same amount of current used.

Sound. The strength and cardiovascular training space by its nature and equipment a noisy place.

Therefore, it is necessary to design the room to accommodate the noise generated. Materials in the walls, on the floor, and in the ceiling should have good acoustical qualities. The sound system should provide equal sound distribution to all areas, not exceeding 90 decibels.

Climate control. When people use weights they generate lots of heat, perspiration, and odor. The designer must consider these problems when designing the mechanical aspects of the room. The three most critical concerns are heating and cooling (68-72° F [22-26° C]), humidity control (55%), and ventilation (8 to 12 exchanges per hour with a 40 to 60 mix outside to inside air). Unfortunately, designers and/or owners neglect these concerns and are extremely disappointed after the facility opens. Climate control can make or break a strength training program.

Security. The room should have provisions for emergency and night lighting.

Special Considerations

The following are special considerations planners should include in the planning process for the strength and cardiovascular training area:

■ There should be at least two, 220 volt electrical outlets to service heavy duty cleaning equipment.
■ There should be a provision for a large (40-50 inch) TV with VCR in the cardio-respiratory area.
■ Commercial structures typically have a 60-pound-per-square-foot load-bearing capacity, but exercise areas need at least 100-pound-per-square-foot capacity.
■ The appearance of the room is important. The right ambience entices members to exercise while enjoying their surroundings. Special consideration should be given to the use of mirrors, lighting, carpeting, rubberized flooring, graphics, and skylights.
■ Carpeting that extends on the side to wainscoting height serves as an excellent acoustical buffer as a well as protective surface for the free-weight area.
■ The color schemes of walls, equipment upholstery, flooring, and ceiling must all be coordinated to appeal to users.

Testing Area

A testing area is a must in any strength and cardiovascular training facility. The testing area should include equipment and space to perform fitness appraisals such as body composition, functional capacity, strength, flexibility, and/or exercise stress test analysis. The room should be designed according to the testing that will be conducted. The testing protocol will facilitate the determination of the specific space needs.

Size. The testing area includes a fitness testing space (100 to 180 square feet), counseling room (90 to 120 square feet), and seminar room (20 square feet per participant) all with an 8-foot ceiling (Tharrett and Peterson, 1997). There should be adequate space in this area to house two chairs, a desk, a file cabinet, a storage cabinet, a computer station, a bicycle ergometer, a flexibility tester, a treadmill, control console, crash cart, metabolic cart, 12 lead ECG, ECG defibrillator, cholesterol analyzer, examination table, double sink, spine board, and a storage cabinet for equipment such as skin fold calipers, stopwatches, and stethoscope(s).

Walls. Simple drywall construction, epoxy painted with a pleasing color(s), appropriate graphics for the area, and a bulletin board.

Floor. The floors should be carpeted with a antistatic and antifungal commercial-grade carpet, color coordinated with the walls and equipment in the room.

Ceiling. A suspended acoustical panel ceiling is appropriate.

Electrical. The electrical needs of the equipment in the room should be considered as well as the eventual location of the equipment. There should be numerous electrical outlets around the perimeter of the room. The outlets near the sink should be ground fault interrupters (GFI). The recommended lighting for this area is fluorescent units that will produce at least 50 foot-candles of illumination at the floor surface.

Climate control. These mechanical considerations for this space include heating and cooling (68 to 72° F [22 to 26° C]), humidity control (55%), and ventilation (8 to 12 exchanges per hour with a ratio of 40 to 60 outside to inside air). Due to the activities in this room, careful consideration to cooling, humidity control, and ventilation are necessary.

Plumbing. A facility should ensure that every fitness-testing space either has a sink or access to a sink.

Security. There should be emergency lighting and an audible emergency alarm to alert other personnel to a medical emergency in the testing area.

Equipment for the Strength and Cardiovascular Training Area

The International Health, Racquet, and Sportclub Association (IHRSA), National Strength and Conditioning Association (NSCA), and the American College of Sports Medicine (ACSM) recommend that strength and cardiovascular training area planners should consider providing

■ a variety of types of equipment for the cardiovascular area, including treadmills, mechanical stair-climbing machines, bicycle ergometers, computerized cycles, rowing ergometers, upper-body ergometers, and total-body-conditioning machines;
■ at least one circuit of progressive resistance-training equipment (other than free weights) that includes either a machine or workout station for each of the following muscle groups: gluteus, quadriceps, hamstrings, calves, chest, upper back, lower back, shoulders, triceps, biceps, and abdomen;
■ a circuit for resistance-training in a fashion that allows users to train the largest muscle groups first and then proceed to the smaller muscle groups. All compound movement machines should be placed in the circuit before isolated movement machines involving the same muscle(s); and
■ a variety of types of free-weight equipment, including a supine bench press with safety pins, incline bench with safety pins, Smith type machine, supine bench, adjustable incline bench, cable crossover system, pull-up or pull-down system, abdominal system, dumbbells, and Olympic-style bar and plates.

Equipment for the Fitness-Testing Area

The NSCA and ACSM suggests that a facility should ensure that its fitness-testing area has the following equipment (Baechle, 1994; Tharrett & Peterson, 1997):

In the fitness-testing area. a bicycle ergometer, a treadmill or a fixed step device (e.g., a bench) of a desired height, skinfold calipers or other body composition measurement device, sit-and-reach bench on goniometer, tensiometer or other device for measuring muscular strength and endurance, perceived exertion chart, clock, metronome, sphygmomanometer (blood pressure cuff), stethoscope, tape measure, scale, and first-aid kit.

In the health promotion and wellness area. computer, overhead projector, video system, slide projector, conference table, and chairs.

In the fitness-testing, health promotion, and wellness area. a system that provides for and protects the complete confidentiality of all user records and meetings.

Cardiovascular Equipment Analysis

Kreighbaum and Smith (1995) analyzed commonly used cardiovascular fitness equipment to determine the advantages and disadvantages of each. The following describes the advantages and disadvantages of cross-country ski simulators, stationary cycles, treadmills, rowing machines, stepping machines, and jumping rope.

Cross-Country Ski Simulators

Advantages

■ The potential exists for high-energy expenditure.
■ It is a good off-season conditioning method for competition or recreational skiing.
■ One can listen to music, converse, or watch TV to divert attention and reduce boredom.
■ Simulated skiing is a nonimpact method of exercise that minimizes orthopedic injury.

Disadvantages

■ One has to practice the skill required by a specific machine, which may not be similar to actual snow skiing.
■ Some machines provide only a relatively easy foot sliding motion with friction control for the arms. For optional training and conditioning, the legs should do most of the work.
■ No machine at this time simulates the skating style now used in competition and that of serious recreationalists.
■ The energy expenditure value given by one manufacturer (e.g., 600 calories for a 20-minute workout) is unrealistic for the average user. Unrealized expectations from this type of advertising could lead to discouragement.
■ Many models have instrumentation to tell how many movement cycles have been completed and/or exercise duration. None have the capability to convert exercise effort into repeatable intensity—a major drawback for the serious exerciser.

Figure 21.2 Storage of weights (Photo by Alan Karchmer, courtesy of HOK Sports Facilities Group).

Stationary Cycles

Advantages

■ They are relatively inexpensive (however, some cost several thousand dollars), compact, and portable.
■ One can listen to music, converse, watch TV, or read to divert attention and reduce boredom.
■ Cycling eliminates heel-strike forces (only about 0.6 G vs. 3 G while running).
■ Some models have meters that display the amount of resistance as well as speed and time. Caloric expenditure can be estimated reasonably well from this information.

Disadvantages

■ A "sore behind" can be a problem. Selecting a sex-specific anatomic saddle (broader for females with padding under the "seat bones"), adjusting the seat height properly (almost a straight leg at the lowest pedal position), and using a pressure-reducing seat cover can minimize discomfort. An alternative choice is a model with a chair-like seat (recumbant).
■ Many find indoor cycling boring. (However, reading, listening to music, or watching TV can make time pass more rapidly and even profitably if the distraction is entertaining or educational.)
■ Cycling only works the legs. Supplemental, upper body, and flexibility exercises are necessary for a balanced program. One model does add some push-pull arm exercise but does not incorporate all muscle groups or use a range of motion to replace stretching.

Treadmills

Advantages

■ An exercise session can be precisely controlled by regulating the speed and belt slope— distinct advantage for rehabilitation.
■ Heart rate can be monitored by an inexpensive meter or by pulse count. This feature may be a necessity for the person undergoing cardiac rehabilitation, or a nice extra for the serious trainer.
■ Once adjusted to walking or running on a treadmill, your stride feels very much like normal walking or running.
■ Pace for hills and intervals can be easily set to vary the training session.

Disadvantages

■ Cost. Manufacturers have recently entered the home exercise market with scaled-down versions of institutional models. Although these small treadmills cost much less than the larger models, they are still several times the price of an excellent cycle, rowing machine, or ski simulator.
■ Size. The home treadmill is small and light enough to be used in a room with a standard ceiling. However, the tradeoffs for small size are little or no elevation capability to simulate hills, a belt width that requires attention to maintain a straight gait, and a short belt length that prohibits

safety while running for even an average-sized person. Standard-sized models may be too heavy for house floor supports and require a higher-than-standard ceiling.

■ Noise. Laboratories that use treadmills for testing often are isolated to prevent the sound of the machine from bothering others on the same or adjacent floors. There are newer home models with smaller motors and better sound insulation; however, the durability of a smaller motor and light-duty construction may be questionable under prolonged use, or with a heavy person.

■ Absence of pleasurable distraction while exercising. Treadmill noise may add either excessive background rumble to music, or cause the listener to turn up the volume to a hazardous level.

Rowing Machines

Advantages

■ One uses a larger muscle mass—more than cycling for example.

■ One can use more energy per unit of time is than with cycling.

■ The use of the hip and back extensors, shoulder horizontal adductors, and arm horizontal extensors makes rowing excellent for posture and possibly may help prevent lower back pain.

■ There is no sudden impact stress (as in the foot strike of running).

■ Some machines can be folded into a very compact unit for easy storage.

Disadvantages

■ Untrained rowers with underdeveloped back, shoulder, and arm muscles may fatigue prematurely due to the limitation of these small muscles.

■ The activity may be boring unless attention is distracted (e.g., by listening to music or watching TV).

■ The lack of ground impact on the long leg bones may not provide the bone stress necessary to prevent osteoporosis. However, additional weight-bearing exercise such as normal walking could prevent osteoporotic changes.

Stepping Machines

Advantages

■ Safety is assured, because no jarring contact occurs as in running or tripping while descending stairs.

■ The energy expenditure may be high, comparable to the highest for any aerobic exercise.

■ These machines eliminate body-weight loaded lengthening contraction from descending stairs.

Disadvantages

■ Many people become bored without diversion (such as listening to tapes or watching TV).

■ No upper body or trunk exercise is gained. Climbing should be supplemented with flexibility, trunk, and upper body muscular exercises for a complete program. For example, some devices such as one for wall climbing have been introduced.

■ Stepping machines may aggravate knee pain or injury.

Jumping Rope

Advantages

■ It is inexpensive. Even the fanciest jumpropes are sold for a nominal price.

■ A minimal indoor space requirement or use anywhere outdoors makes rope jumping more convenient than walking, jogging, or running.

■ The energy expenditure rate for most adults will be high enough to meet guidelines established by the American College of Sports Medicine.

■ In addition to other exercise benefits, some exercise is obtained for the upper body, primarily the shoulders.

Disadvantages

■ Rope jumping requires skill. Until sufficiently skilled, you may find exercise intensity too high to maintain; thus rope jumping may be a poor exercise choice for the unconditioned adult.

■ Frequent, long jumping sessions (or even infrequent, short sessions if one is overweight) may lead to injury. (Slow, progressive conditioning, proper shoes, and a resilient floor surface can minimize risk.).

■ The amount of muscle used jumping rope is less than jogging, which somewhat reduces its overall fitness value.

■ Many find rope jumping both difficult and boring, limitations that prevent sufficient frequency and duration to gain significant fitness benefits.

■ Summary

The development of strength and cardiovascular facilities requires a great deal of specific knowledge about the activities to be carried out within the facility. The planners need to be versed in the programs to be offered and the equipment used in the programs. Finally, the planners need to understand any specific requirements for programs or equipment.

Learning Objective 1: The student will be able to assess the needs of existing and new facilities.

The planners need to assess the existing facility to determine what is available for current and future programming as well as equipment. After the initial assessment is completed, the planners need to understand what changes will occur in the programming and what type of new equipment will be purchased. It is also important to gather data from participants describing what their needs are in programming, equipment, and amenities.

Learning Objective 2: The student will be able to plan and organize an existing or a new facility for maximum usage.

The planners need to understand, in detail, the future programming needs and equipment that will be purchased. They will also need to understand the guidelines and standards established by the various national organizations. Finally, the facility must be designed for maximum usage of every square foot.

Learning Objective 3: The student will be able to understand the environmental impact of such a facility.

After all the programmatic and equipment considerations have been thoroughly reviewed, planners will switch their thoughts toward the environmental concerns that might be raised with this facility. The facility and its surrounding environment should be complementary. This is a consideration often neglected or forgotten

■ Case Study

You have been hired by a regional hospital to design a strength and cardiovascular facility. This facility will provide service for local industry, level 2 and 3 cardiovascular rehabilitation, local residents, and in- and outpatient rehabilitation. This will be a new facility constructed adjacent to the main hospital building, connected by a walkway over a main street separating the two buildings.

How will you determine the program needs? How will you determine the equipment needs? How will you determine the size of the facility? Prepare an equipment list for the facility. Prepare a draft floor plan for the facility.

■ References

Armitage-Johnson, S. L. (1994). Equipment maintenance. In T. R. Baechle (Ed.), **Essentials of strength training and conditioning.** Champaign, IL: Human Kinetics.

Baechle, T.R. (Ed.)(1994). **Essentials of strength training and conditioning.** Champaign, IL: Human Kinetics.

Kreighbaum, E. F., & Smith, M. A. (1995). **Sports and fitness equipment design.** Champaign, IL: Human Kinetics, Inc.

Tharrett, S. J., & Peterson, J. A. (Eds.). (1997). **ACSM's health/ fitness facility standards and guidelines** (2nd ed). Champaign, IL: Human Kinetics, Inc

■ Suggested Resources

Aquatics International, 3923 W. 6th Street, Los Angeles, CA 90020, 713/385-3926, FAX 213/383-6658, **www.aquaticsintl.com**

Club Industry, Intertec Publishing, 1300 Virginia Drive, Suite 400, Fort Washington, PA 19034, 215/643-8000, 888/291-5214, FAX 847/291-9002

Athletic Business, 1864 Hoffman Street, Madison, WI 53704, 800/722-8764, FAX 608/249-1153, www.athleticbusiness.com

Notes

CHAPTER 22

Campus Recreational Sport Centers

Thomas H. Sawyer, Indiana State University

Learning Objectives

After reading this chapter, the student will be able to

■ begin planning a new recreational sport center,

■ describe indoor activities and facility needs,

■ outline outdoor activities and facility needs, and

■ describe the security needs for a recreational sport center.

Introduction

Over the past 20 years a number of recreational sport centers have been constructed on campuses to meet the needs of the student body. These centers have been built for recreational purposes, not instructional or athletic. However, recently a number have been built with large aquatic areas (e.g., University of Toledo, Miami University of Ohio, University of Texas, Georgia Tech, University of Michigan, University of Minnesota, and Indiana University) to be used for both recreational and athletic purposes. These centers have been financed primarily with student fees and state and private funds. Most of the facilities include aquatic centers, entrance/lobby area, lounge areas, racquetball/walleyball courts, indoor and outdoor tennis courts, basketball courts, dance exercise areas, indoor running/jogging tracks, strength and cardiovascular training areas, climbing wall, locker rooms, indoor/outdoor rollerblade hockey court, indoor soccer area, administration area, pro shops, concessions, and an area for equipment rental.

This chapter has been designed to provide the planner with an overview of the needs for a campus recreational sport center. The specifics relating to many of the spaces are found in other chapters in this book.

Planning for a New Recreational Sports Center

A common problem is how to secure these new facilities. The following can form the basis from which to justify requests for additional facilities. The initial step in the process of securing any new facility is defining the space requirements. This planning process uses three different types of space used in recreational, intramural, and informal sport programs. The three types are described below:

Type A Space

Type A space includes the following areas:

Indoor teaching stations—space requirements: 8.5-9.5 sq. ft. per student (total under-

Figure 22.1 Model and artist's renderings of proposed Miami University Recreational Sports Facility. (Courtesy of HOK Sports Facilities Group).

graduate enrollment) including a) gym floors, mat areas, swimming pools, court areas, etc.; and b) location adjacent to lockers and showers and within a 10-minute walking distance of academic classrooms (Mull et al., 1997).

Uses: Recreational, intramural, and informal sports participation for student and faculty recreation.

A1 Large gymnasium area with relatively high ceiling (22 ft. minimum) for basketball, badminton, volleyball, etc. (approximately 55% of Type A space).

A2 Activity areas with relatively low ceiling (12 ft. minimum) for combatives, therapeutic exercises, dancing, weight lifting, etc. (approximately 30% of Type A space).

A3 Indoor swimming and diving pools (approximately 15% of Type A space) (Mull et al., 1997).

Type B Space

Type B space includes the following areas:

Outdoor teaching Stations—space require-

Figure 22.2 Multipurpose gym with rounded corners, Central Michigan University (Photo by Balthazar Korab, Ltd. Courtesy of TMP Associates, Inc.)

ments including a) sport fields of all types; b) location adjacent to locker and showers, and within a 10-minute walking distance of academic classrooms.

Uses: Recreational, intramural, and informal sports participation for student and faculty for recreation.

B1 Sodded areas for soccer, touch football, softball, etc. (approximately 60% of Type B space).

B2 Court type areas for tennis, volleyball, etc. (approximately 15% of Type B space).

B3 Specialized athletic areas for track and field, baseball, archery, varsity football, golf, camping demonstrations, etc. (approximately 25% of Type B space).

B4 Swimming pools (included in B3 approximation) (Mull et al., 1997).

Type C Space

Type C spaces include the following:

Sport fields and building, intramural and general outdoor recreation areas—space requirements, 120-140 sq. ft. per student (total undergraduate enrollment) including playing fields and athletic buildings of all types, softball diamonds, tennis courts, field houses, etc. Too far removed from student lockers, showers, living quarters and academic buildings for use as teaching stations.

Uses: Recreation, intramural, and informal sports for students and faculty recreation.

C1 Sodded areas for soccer, touch football, softball, etc. (approximately 40% of Type C space).

C2 Court type areas for tennis, volleyball, etc. (approximately 10% of Type C space).

C3 Specialized athletic area for track and field, baseball, archery, varsity football, golf, camping demonstrations, etc. (approximately 45% of Type C space).

Figure 22.3 Main Street, Student Recreation Center, Central Michigan University (Photo by Balthazar Korab, Ltd. Courtesy of TMP Associates, Inc.)

C4   Swimming pools (included in C3 approximation).

C5   Sports and intramural buildings providing lockers, showers, play space, office space, lounge rooms, etc. (approximately 5% of Type C space) (Mull et al., 1997).

In order to compare a campus with the accepted standards, five steps should be followed: The first step involves the location of existing and potential areas within the boundaries of the campus. This is done by physically canvassing the campus and envisioning the potential of all areas. The initial phase of Step 1 should be the location and identification of all areas that are currently used by recreational, intramural, and informal sport.

The second phase is more difficult and requires more effort and imagination on the part of the observer. Potential areas of expansion are spaces (outdoor and indoor) that can be converted from whatever they are currently being used for to usable recreation areas. Cost of converting each area should be kept at a minimum to further enhance the attractiveness of se-

curing new facilities. For example, the cost of converting a relatively small (50 feet by 100 feet) grassy area to an outdoor volleyball area would only include the installation of two poles and a net. If further funds were available and the sport popular, this area could further be converted to a sand or beach volleyball court at a small additional cost. Providing alternatives or options also enhances the acceptability of the proposal.

Space for conversion should meet the general criteria for Type A, B, or C space before being considered for alteration. For example, an indoor area with an eight-foot ceiling should not be considered for conversion to gymnasium space; however, it could be converted to a dance studio or a karate practice room with the addition of mirrors and mats.

After all available and potential areas have been located, the next step requires computations of the area in square feet. For indoor areas a tape measure is used; however, for large outdoor areas a cross-country measuring wheel is most effective.

When measuring any area, precautions should be taken to allow for a buffer zone of safety around any proposed playing area. An outdoor grassy area measuring 100 yards by 40 yards could theoretically accommodate an intramural football field, but if the boundaries are close to hazards such as chain link fence poles, trees, or buildings, this area should be considered for some other recreational purpose.

The same precautions apply to indoor space. Most areas considered will be fairly easy to measure. Normally, spaces are either rectangular or square in shape. Odd-shaped areas should not be ignored, and their areas should be estimated to the best of the measurer's ability while still allowing for the safety buffer zone. Odd-shaped areas are also sometimes ignored because they do not fit the shape of a standard playing field. These areas may, however, accommodate a combination of two or more sports in that area. Any particular space should not be viewed as usable only for football or basketball, but leftover spaces could easily be used for a frisbee golf course or a single table tennis table.

The square footage for all areas considered should next be classified and totaled under one of the three types of spaces. This total figure of space classified according to type can now be compared with the recommended amount of space. Recommended space is computed by taking current enrollment figures and multiplying them by the median figure in the range of each type of space. For example, a university with an enrollment of 15,000 students should have a recommended space requirement for Type A space of 135,000 square feet (15,000 × 9). The total amount of each type space is then compared with the actual amount to arrive at a figure illustrating the amount above or below recommended standards.

A further breakdown of space within each type into the twelve subclassifications is required to determine the correct "mix" of facilities. This subclassification of space enables the director to specifically locate areas of deficiency.

When standards in terms of square feet per student are used as guides in college or university planning, it is natural to ask where the cut-off begins. Obviously, for a college of 200 students, nine square feet per student of indoor area for sports and athletics would be inadequate. It would not even provide one basketball court. A university or college meeting the space standards for 1,500 students represents the minimum physical recreation space needs of any college institution. As a college or university increases in size, these standards are applicable regardless of enrollment. Also, a ceiling effect applies to some subclassifications of space.

In the beginning phases of planning for recreational facilities, area standards must be developed. A variety of standards relative to size, location, and development of school and recreation areas and facilities has been developed.

The standards provide a useful guide; however, standards can seldom, if ever, be applied completely or without modification. Because a typical or ideal situation is seldom found, standards simply indicate a basis for the intelligent development of local plans.

The third step involves a description of current and potential uses of each area. A description of current uses should be done first. It should include uses by physical education, recreation, intramural sports, and "outside" departments. If a particular area is not being used for any specific purpose, it should be so listed.

Potential uses should be as closely linked to the subclassifications as possible. It is in this phase of the process where the director must make responsible choices as to the development of any given area. A single area must have the potential to be developed into several different types of space. The director must refer to individual program needs and areas of deficiency to make informed decisions as to the development of that particular area. Again, it is important to provide campus planners with options. However, the director should limit the flexibility of the proposal to stay within the most urgent needs of his particular program.

The next step is to determine the cost of converting an area from its current use to its potential use. In some cases the cost of conversion will be zero. This type of space should be accentuated in presenting the proposal before any board involved with campus planning. Often cooperation between two departments regarding scheduling can vastly increase facilities available for recreational use at no cost to either program.

Obtaining other costs of conversion generally involves requesting estimates from the physical plant operations staff on campus or from outside contractors. These estimates should be obtained prior to presenting any proposal. Also, the estimates should enhance the flexibility built into the proposal. That is to say, each options should have its own separate estimate. This allows campus planning boards to examine all suggestions in the proposal in dependenctly of other suggestions in the proposal.

Finally, the last step involves defining the availability for use by the major users. If facilities are shared by two or more users, the priority schedule for usage should also be listed. After all, a program may have access to a facility 40% of the total time available, but if those times are at undesirable hours, the facility is not meeting the needs of the program. If no consideration is given to the prime time needs of students for recreational use, the percentage of availability may be misleading.

Indoor Recreational, Intramural, and Informal Sport Activities

The following is a partial listing of indoor recreational, intramural, and informal sport activities:

Single Function	Specialized or Multipurpose Function	
Archery range	Country club	Gymnasium
Badminton court	Golf	Gymnastics
Basketball court	Swimming	Combatives
Billards	Table sports	Basketball
Bowling alley	Strength training	Volleyball
Combatives room	Tennis	Badminton
Curling rink		Table tennis
Cardiovascular room		
Dance exercise room		
Diving pool		
Electronic games arcade	Fieldhouse	Racquetball club
Fencing salle	Basketball	Strength training
Gymnastics room	Track	Jogging
Handball	Soccer	
Ice rink	Lacrosse	Recreation center
Racquetball court	Jogging	Billards
Rifle-pistol range	Archery	Table sports
Roller skating rink		Table tennis
Rollerblade hockey rink	Fitness center	Swimming
Shuffleboard course	Swimming	Gymnasium
Squash court	Strength training	
Swimming pool	Cardiovascular training	
Table sport room	Jogging	
Table tennis room	Combatives	
Tennis court	Dance exercise	
Strength training room		
Wrestling room		
Volleyball court		

After information has been gathered, supporting documents for the requesting of new facilities must be prepared. The proposal should contain five major parts.

The first part should state clearly the objectives of the study. It should also list all areas and departments of the campus involved in conducting the study. Finally, it should include limitations or qualifications specific to the institution.

The second part should include brief historical developments of the sponsoring program from both a national and campus viewpoint.

The third section is a statement of the problem. In this section, all forces generating the study should be explained. All major problems affected by changing facility structures should be included, as well as the majority of the information gathered in the aforementioned steps. Listing the standards with the organizations using them will lend national support to the proposal. The relationship between the standard and enrollment is explained next. And, finally, the standards are applied to the specific campus in question. The comparison should emphasize those areas in which critical deficiencies exist because the largest deficiencies are not always

Figure 22.4 *Arizona State University aerobics area* (Photo by Larry Smith).

the most critical ones. Section three should conclude with a summary of the work completed on the study and a restatement of those problem areas.

Section four contains recommendations for immediate action and long-term improvements. Flexibility (options) within the overall goals of the organization should be the guiding principle when preparing this section.

Finally, appendices should be prepared to support the proposal. Participation figures may be used in this section; however, the major part of this section should contain a map of the campus with all areas clearly marked. The map should be accompanied by a list of all buildings and rooms investigated. The most precise way of presenting existing and potential areas is according to the following seven-point formula:

1. Location,
2. Area (structure footage),
3. Type of space,
4. Current uses,
5. Potential uses,
6. Cost of conversion, and
7. Percentage of use.

Each area should be listed and explained through this format.

Outdoor Recreational, Intramural, and Informal Sport Activities

The following are common outdoor recreational, intramural, and sport activities:

- Airfield
- Baseball field
- Miniature golf course
- Motocross course
- Basketball court
- Beach volleyball
- Bicycle path
- Boat launching ramp
- Bocce ball course
- Bowling green
- Cross country course
- Curing rink
- Deck tennis
- Diving pool
- Filed hockey field
- Fishing pond/lake
- Fitness trail
- Football field
- Frisbee golf course
- Go-cart track
- Golf course
- Golf driving range
- Handball court
- Horseshoe
- Hydro-slide
- Ice rink
- Lacrosse field
- Marina
- Riding paddock
- Rifle/pistol range
- Rollerblade hockey rink
- Roller skating rink
- Shuffleboard
- Skateboard/rollerblade course and ramp
- Skeet and trap range
- Skiing course
- Soccer field
- Softball field
- Speedball
- Swimming pool
- Speedball field
- Team handball field
- Tennis court
- Toboggan slope
- Volleyball

Indoor Facilities

In planning new facilities, it should be remembered that substand facilities usually result in a substandard program. For this reason, official court and field dimensions should be used whenever possible. The following list identifies the types of areas which should be considered in planning indoor facilities for a campus recreational sports center:

- Main gymnasium—regulation basketball, badminton, tennis, and volleyball courts with mechanical divider nets. The divider nets should be constructed of solid vinyl for the first eight feet and the remainder of a mesh material.
- Auxiliary gymnasiums—regulation basketball, badminton, tennis, and volleyball courts, gymnastics area, rollerblade hockey rink, indoor soccer area, suspended track, fencing, batting cages, and dance exercise. The dance exercise area should have hidden mirrors to protect them when the space is used for other activities (i.e., basketball or volleyball), and a retractable instructor's platform. The planners might consider the possibility of locating two gymnasiums side by side with a storage area between to store equipment, audio system, and retractable instructor's platforms. The storage area should be at least 8 feet wide.

Figure 22.5 A. A good example of a wide open airy entrance lobby with an information center, Recreational Sports Complex, Miami of Ohio University.

B. Consessions area, Recreational Sports Complex, Miami of Ohio University.

C. Artist's rendering of rock-climbing wall designed for University of Miami (Sneary, 1992, Courtesy of HOK Sports Facilities Group).

Figure 22.6 Farley Field House, Bowdoin College (Photo by P. Gobell. Courtesy of Sasaki Associates).

- Swimming pools—50-meter pool, diving pool, and/or instruction pool.
- Combative room—boxing, martial arts, and judo.
- Strength training area—progressive resistance-training equipment, free-weight equipment, and stretching area.
- Cardiovascular area
- Handball/racquetball/walleyball courts
- Golf room—sand trap, putting area, and driving nets.
- Archery/rifle/pistol range
- Games room—billards, table tennis, table games, shuffleboard.
- Administrative area—offices, storage, conference rooms, and audio-visual room.
- Lounge and lobby area—bulletin boards, trophy cases, control center, and art work.
- Concessions, rental, and merchandise area—concession stand, seating area, rental shop, and pro shop. (See figure 22.5b.)
- Training room—treatment area only.
- Locker rooms—student and faculty, gender specific, shower rooms, drying areas, locker space, and common spa area (i.e., hydro-tube, sauna, and steam room)
- Equipment and storerooms
- Climbing wall

Outdoor Facilities

The following list identifies the types of areas that should be considered in planning outdoor facilities for a campus recreational sports center:

- Lighted fields—touch/flag football, soccer, field hockey, softball, baseball, handball, and rugby
- Lighted courts—basketball, badminton, tennis, volleyball, handball/racquetball, and horseshoes

- Lighted rollerblade hockey court
- Lighted jogging/running/walking trails and/or track
- Golf course and lighted driving range and practice green
- Lighted skating rink
- Swimming and diving pools
- Bocci field and horseshoe pits
- Storage building(s)
- Tennis practice boards and soccer kicking wall
- Picnic areas with shelters

Security Issues

The campus recreational sports center will quickly become the focus of campus interest. The center will be used heavily throughout the day and evening. The prime times will be 6 to 8 A.M., 11 A.M. to 1P.M. and 4 to 6 P.M. and 7 P.M. to midnight. The planners need to consider providing adequate security, including appropriate outside lighting at all sites, security cameras, alarmed doors (silent and audible), pool alarms, spa alarms, valuable lockers, fire alarms, sprinkling systems, and appropriate signage.

■ Summary

Recreational sport centers on campuses have become very strong recruiting tools for colleges and universities. Students want to be involved with recreational sports, to relax and play with fellow students. Many colleges and universities are adding new recreational sport centers to their campuses to meet student needs for recreation.

Learning Objective 1: The student will be able to plan a new recreational sports center.

The planner needs to understand clearly how a recreational sports center functions on a college and university campus. The facility must meet the diverse needs of a diverse student body. Programmed activities will require a wide range of facilities.

Learning Objective 2: The student will be able to describe indoor activities and facility needs.

Most recreational sport centers on campuses program a large number of varied activities, from structured intramurals to club sports to informal recreation to instructional non-credit classes. These programs require a variety of activity spaces; they cannot be single purpose areas.

Learning Objective 3: The student will be able to describe outdoor activities and facility needs.

Outdoor programming at recreational sport centers is as detailed as indoor programming. However, outdoor spaces are generally larger and more environmentally sensitive. They range from the various sport fields to running/fitness trails to sport courts to parking to walking and cycling trails. Outdoor facilities, like indoor facilities, cannot be single purpose areas.

Learning Objective 4: The student will be able to describe the security needs for a recreational sports facility.

Security is an extremely important concern for facility managers. The planners need to understand what type of security is necessary for the facility, internally and externally. The planners will use lighting, alarms (e.g., fire, pool, and door), cameras, public address system, card readers, and more.

■ Case Study

You have been hired by XYZ University as the new director of recreational sports. The new president has recently come for another university of similar size, where he learned to appreciate the value of the recreational sports center. It was a great marketing tool for attracting new students. The new president has charged you with the responsibility to develop a plan to finance and construct a new recreational sport center on campus.

What steps will you take to develop the plans for a new facility? What programs will you have, both indoor and outdoor? What program areas will you plan for in the new facility?

■ References

Mueller, P., & Reznik, J.W. (1979). **Intramural-recreational sports: Programming and administration** (5th ed). New York: John Wiley & Sons.

Mull, R.F., Bayless, K.G., Ross, C.M., & Jamieson, L.M. (1997). **Recreational sport management** (3rd ed). Champaign, IL: Human Kinetics.

■ Suggested Readings

Espinosa, C.E. (1990). Planning and constructing a sand volleyball court. **Management strategies in recreational sports** (pp. 51-6). Corvallis, OR: National Intramural-Recreational Sports Association.

Keeny, B.A. (1995). The IHRSA design forum. **Club Business International,** 16(2), 34-47.

Richey, L., & Strong, T. (1987). Energy savings systems for new construction. **National Intramural-Recreational Sports Association Journal,** 11(2), 44-47.

Secor, M.R. (1987). The pitfalls, pratfalls, and problems of facility design and construction. **Cultivation of recreational sports programs** (pp. 102-106). Corvallis, OR: National Intramural-Recreational Sports Association.

Wiles, C. (1995). Join the club. **Athletic Management,** 6(4), 29-34.

CHAPTER 23

Indoor and Outdoor Courts

Bernie Goldfine, Kennesaw State University ■ Ed Turner, Appalachian State University

Learning Objectives

After reading this chapter, the student will be able to

■ identify and describe layout, dimensions, and orientations,

■ identify and describe various materials used in construction, and

■ identify and describe a variety of important specifications and information (e.g., surfacing and lighting) for the courts described in this chapter.

Introduction

Indoor and outdoor courts are popular competition and recreation venues. These venues are continually being modernized and improved. In this chapter a discussion of 14 of the most popular courts will outline important considerations for planners developing new facilities. Two court areas have benefitted from the dramatic growth of competitive and recreational users over the last decade—racquetball and sand volleyball. The planners of these new courts have taken into consideration many important changes in materials regarding lighting, floor surfaces, wall surfaces, ceiling surfaces, ventilation, and safety.

Tennis Courts

Layout, Orientation, Dimensions, Fencing

Tennis was first played in the United States during the mid 1870s. At that time, the game was slow-paced and played on the grass lawns of houses and parks.

The game has now changed to a fast-paced athletic sport. As tennis has changed, so too have the courts on which it is played. Today's outdoor courts are laid out in a manner that minimizes the effects of wind, sun, background vision, and the lay of the land. Tennis courts are constructed of grass, clay, soft and hard composition, asphalt, concrete, and various synthetic materials. Many other features such as accessibility, storage, parking, lighting, and fencing need to be planned for carefully in tennis court construction.

In constructing outdoor tennis courts, prevailing winds must be taken into account in the planning process. If prevailing winds exist, courts should be placed near natural barriers such as woods or hills that act as a windbreak. If no existing barriers are in the area of court construction, a thick stand of staggered trees can be planted to serve as a barrier. Alternately, if existing buildings are near the construction site, they may be used as a wind barrier.

Visual background must be planned for in the layout of tennis courts. The background at both ends of the courts should be natural grass, shrubs, woods, or other natural landscaping. Roads, parking areas, and pedestrian high-traffic areas are not acceptable at the ends of tennis courts. Too many objects moving in front of the tennis player causes lapses in concentration and makes play more difficult. If the busy areas must coexist with tennis courts, they should be at the sides of the courts. Furthermore, tennis complexes should not be placed too far from the remainder of the sports complex or center campus. The more removed the courts are, the more difficulty user access will be. Court layout must also meet ADA requirements for all disabled users.

The contour of the land for proposed tennis court construction also needs careful thought. It is much cheaper to construct tennis courts on flat land than on rolling terrain; it is less expensive in terms of both earth moving and drainage concerns. If courts must be on rolling terrain, they should be laid out with the minimum of cost for earth moving and drainage. Also, hills should serve as natural barriers whenever possible.

Outdoor tennis court planning must also include the sun, which can create visual problems for the tennis player. If tennis courts are to be used mostly between April and October, they should be aligned north to south on the long axis of the court. If courts are to be used year round, the long axis should be northwest to southeast at 22° off true north. These orientations minimize the amount of sun-related visual problems for tennis players (USTA, 1997).

If courts are nonporous, provisions must be made for the drainage of water off the courts. Courts may be sloped from 0.5% to 1.5% depending on the type of surface (USTA, 1997). Any slope greater than 1.5% can be visually detected by the players and is not acceptable. Courts may be sloped side to side, end to end, center to end, or end to center. If only one individual court is constructed, either a side-to-side or an end-to-end slope works well. If a battery of courts is being constructed, the slope should be dictated by the fastest way to drain the most courts as quickly as possible. For example, if five courts are built side by side, an end-to-end slope would be best since all courts would drain and dry simultaneously. If a side-by-side slope were used, the courts on the upper end of the slope would dry quickly, but the last few courts would retain water for a much longer period of time, since the water from the upper end slope courts would have to drain across the courts at the lower end of the slope.

Center-to-end and end-to-center slopes are least desirable. When these types of slopes are used, the water remains on the court and court perimeter playing surface much longer than when side-to-side or end-to-end slopes are used. Additionally, an end-to-center slope requires drains at or near the net. Drains on the court itself are not desirable.

When planning to use slope, natural drainage basins should be used whenever possible. Thus, if a small creek basin or lower land is adjacent to the court area, it is worthwhile to slope courts to these areas to limit artificial drainage and minimize drainage costs.

As outdoor tennis courts are planned, the size of the courts as well as the perimeter space around the court need careful attention. A singles court is 78 feet long and 36 feet wide. Including perimeter space, the minimum size for one doubles court would be 122 feet by 66 feet. These dimensions give minimum safety between the court and the fencing on both the sides and the ends of the court (USTA, 1997).

The minimum distance between side-by-side courts is 12 feet. The minimum distance between the court sideline and the side fence is 15 feet. Finally, the minimum distance between the court baseline and the end fence is 22 feet (USTA, 1997). The shortest distance is between courts since a player has open space (the adjacent court) to run to in order to retrieve a ball. There is more distance between the sideline and the side fence since players can run into he fence. Finally, the baseline distance is greatest since this area is essentially a part of the playing area even though it is not a part of the actual court. Figure 23.1 illustrates these minimum distances, as well as the dimensions of a tennis court.

Tennis courts should be enclosed with chain-link fence. The fence can be either 10 or 12 feet high. The 12-foot high fence is more expensive than the 10-foot high fence; however, those additional two feet of fencing keep in a significantly greater percentage of balls (USTA, 1997).

Chain-link fence comes in a No. 6 or No. 9 gauge. The No. 6 gauge is thicker and thus more costly. Either gauge is acceptable. Fence is also available with a polyvinyl chloride (PVC) plastic coating (most often green). Coated fencing is more expensive; however, in addition to its aesthetic qualities, it does not rust, as will galvanized fencing.

Line posts that hold the fencing must be no farther than 10 feet apart, and all corner and gate posts should be stabilized by cross braces. All line posts should be embedded at least three feet into the ground. If a wind/visual screen is attached to the fence, all line posts should be embedded in a concrete footer.

Adequate gates should be placed throughout the tennis court complex. These gates need to meet the needs of both instructors and players. Each set of courts in a complex must have an external gate and internal gates. Gates are expensive, but compromising on the number of gates will compromise accessibility to the courts, both internally and externally.

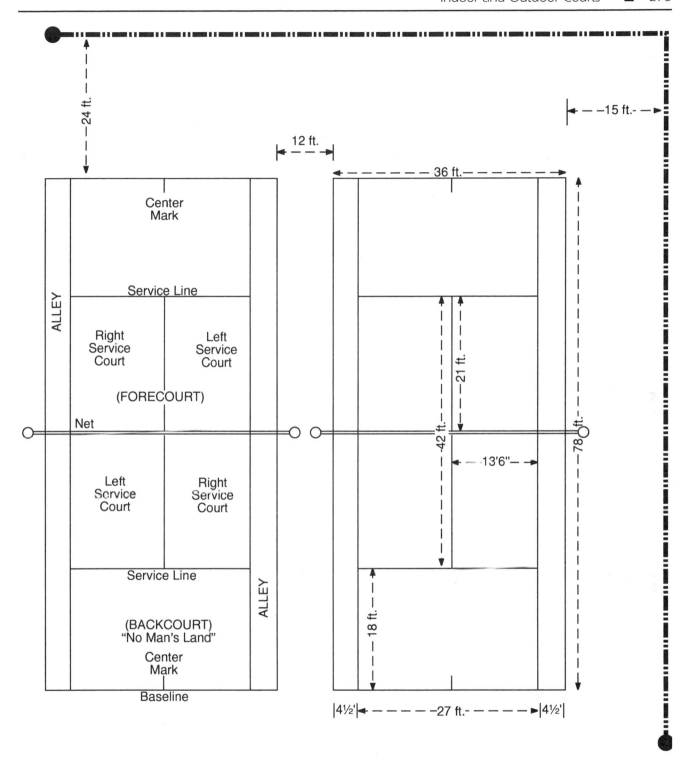

Tennis Court Diagrams and Dimensions

Figure 23.1 Tennis court diagram and dimensions.

Types of Courts

Courts are classified as either porous (those that allow water to filter and drain through the court surface itself) or nonporous (those that do not allow water to penetrate the surface). The sloping as previously mentioned is for nonporous courts, but is sometimes used in porous courts to carry penetrated water into the subsurface drainage system. Clay, grass, soft composition (fast dry), porous concrete, and various synthetics are porous courts. Concrete, asphalt (cushioned and non-cushioned), hard composition (liquid applied synthetic), and various synthetics are nonporous courts. As a group, asphalt courts are composed of (a) asphalt plant mix, (b) emulsified asphalt mix, (c) plant and emulsified mix, (d) asphalt penetration mix, and (e) asphalt bound system (cushioned) (USTA, 1997).

Numerous items must be considered when selecting the appropriate type of court. Initial cost, cost of upkeep, amount of use, area of country, maintenance personnel needed, type of players, level of competition, and age of players must be factored in when determining the type of court to be selected.

Clay, grass, and soft composition courts are much easier on the legs of players and allow for a much slower ball bounce than other courts. These courts are superior for young players, beginning players, and older players. However, they need a high level of maintenance, which is costly in both materials and personnel. Clay courts must be leveled, must have clay added periodically, require watering, and must be kept free of vegetation. Soft composition courts must be rolled, require watering, and need to have screen and base components added often. Grass courts are similar to golf greens and need daily maintenance. Additionally, grass courts that receive heavy use should be alternated daily. That is, a court used on Monday should not be used again until Wednesday. Consequently, more court space is necessary for heavily used grass courts. Grass courts give a skidding ball bounce and sometimes an erratic bounce because of small divots, excessive wear, and taped lines. Overall, clay, grass, and soft composition courts are recommended for commercial clubs where the cost of upkeep can be packaged into member fees. They are not recommended for schools and recreation programs because of upkeep costs.

Asphalt, concrete, and hard composition courts need less maintenance but provide a faster ball bounce and cause more stress on the legs of players. Of the three types, asphalt courts are the most inexpensive to construct, and composition courts are most costly. Hard composition courts take a few months to cure and harden, and they should not be used until they cure out completely. Hard composition courts can be constructed with multiple layers of cushioning material. The more layers in the courts, the greater the resiliency of the surface will be, but each additional layer of cushioning increases the cost. Hard composition courts are smoother than concrete or asphalt; therefore, they cause less wear and tear on balls, shoes, and rackets. Asphalt, concrete, and hard composition courts are recommended for schools and

recreation programs. Hard composition is the optimum choice of the three.

Numerous synthetic court surfaces are available. If synthetic outdoor courts are to be constructed, users should be consulted to determine the advantages and disadvantages of such courts for both players and owners. Also, product descriptions of the material should be studied carefully to help determine which synthetic surface best meets the specific needs of the court under construction.

Regardless of the type of court surface, *it is paramount that a tennis court construction firm be employed* to build the court(s). A local construction firm, with no tennis court building experience, should not be permitted to construct the courts. Typically, a builder inexperienced in tennis court construction does not have the expertise to properly build tennis courts. This lack of expertise results in the use of poor construction techniques; more important, it ultimately results in premature (and costly) repairs and renovations.

Costs for an outdoor court surface and base are diverse, ranging from $10,000 to $15,000 for a clay court to $40,000 to $50,000 for certain synthetic courts. Prices also vary according to the number of courts building (more courts results in a lower cost per court), geographic area of the country, and the amount of grading and drainage required. These costs do not include fencing ($5,000 to $10,000 per court) nor lighting ($5,000 to $10,000 per court). Without a doubt, tennis courts are expensive (USTA, 1997).

Miscellaneous Considerations

All tennis courts should have sufficient secured storage areas, constructed on a concrete base, adjacent to the court complex. The size of the storage area is dictated by the amount and type of equipment to be stored in it. Consider ball hoppers, tennis rackets, fanny packs, ball throwing machines, and other teaching equipment. The storage area must be waterproof and include shelving, bins, racks, and hooks. If maintenance equipment is needed at the courts, a separate storage area must be built for appropriate machines, rakes, hoses, screens, and materials.

Parking areas need to be built in close proximity to the court complex. The size of the parking area is dictated by the maximum number of user vehicles for the complex in addition to sufficient space for spectator parking. If the tennis complex is lighted, the parking area should be illuminated with high-pressure sodium lights.

Night outdoor tennis is popular in many areas of the country. The recommended surface lighting level for recreational tennis is 38 foot-candles—63 foot-candles for tournament tennis. Lighting tennis courts is a necessity in some areas. Information as to the number of light standards and how much light will be needed for the complex can be obtained by consulting the local electric company and a manufacturer (e.g., General Electric). A number of outdoor sports lighting companies install quality tennis court lighting systems. If the cost of ongoing high electric use is of concern, coin-operated light boxes can be installed to defray the electricity cost (USTA, 1997).

Although lighting may be optional, water must be provided at each court complex. One water fountain (refrigerated) and one hose connector are recommended for each set of four courts. Electrical outlets must be provided for each court and for any electrical maintenance equipment. All outlets should be located in the fence area and at the storage areas.

Benches need to be provided outside the fencing for those awaiting an empty court. Unobstructed spectator seating should be provided as close to the courts as possible if tournaments or instruction are to be provided on the courts. Courts used for tournaments and high-level competition also require scoring equipment, officials' seating, tables, benches, concession areas, and a protected area for videotaping.

Finally, court surfaces can be a variety of colors. Synthetics can be found in any color whereas most nonporous tennis courts use a contrasting red and green color scheme. Although many options are available, lighter and contrasting darker greens are easiest on participants' eyes. The actual court is one shade of green; the surrounding surfaced areas are another.

Indoor Tennis Courts

Indoor courts can be practical for tennis. Since the weather can affect the ability to play, tennis is a seasonal sport in many parts of the country. Consequently, indoor courts meet a specific need in certain regions.

The number of courts to be enclosed depends on the number of users and the amount of money available for construction. The type of enclosure varies greatly from complex to complex. Prefabricated steel buildings, air structures, tension membrane structures, and standard brick-and-mortar buildings have all been employed successfully. The use of combination structures has some advantages. A translucent tension membrane that allows light onto the courts combined with a turn-key or one standard structure can save roofing costs as well as electricity costs during the day. The following is a cost comparison of three four-court structures:

■ sports frame metal building—$561,000 ($140,250 per court),

■ tension structure—$422,495 ($105,624 per court), and

■ air structure—$366,000 ($91,500 per court) (USTA, 1997).

Lighting should be indirect so that the tennis ball is not lost in the glare of lights. The background at the end of the courts should be plain. Traffic patterns need careful planning to ensure they do not conflict with play on the courts. Netting must be used between courts since fencing does not exist, and the ceiling height needs to be a minimum of 30 feet. Most indoor court surfaces are synthetic. As with outdoor courts, planning should include storage, parking, water fountains, electrical outlets, seating, concessions, officials' needs, videotaping, and locker/shower facilities.

Summary

Outdoor tennis complexes need special planning in relation to the elements, drainage, surfaces, and playing area dimensions. Fencing and gates are important for both confinement and accessibility to the complex. Storage areas, electrical outlets, and water fountains/outlets need to be provided in each complex.

Paddle Tennis

Dimensions

Paddle tennis courts are 50 feet long by 20 feet wide. The safety space or unobstructed area should be a minimum of 15 feet behind each baseline and 10 feet from each sideline or between each adjacent court. As Figure 23.2 shows, service lines for each side of the court run the entire width of the court, parallel to and three feet inside each baseline. The center service line extends from the service end line, down the middle of the court. The service boxes, therefore, are 22 feet long by 10 feet wide (USPTA, 1996).

An optional restraint line extends the width of the court, 12 feet from the net. These restraint lines are used in doubles play only. All dimensions for paddle tennis court markings are to the outside of the lines with the exception of the center service line, which is divided equally between service courts.

Miscellaneous Considerations

Paddle tennis net posts are located 18 inches outside of each sideline and are 31 inches in height. Unlike tennis courts, the net is strung taut so that the height measures the same (31 inches) at each post and in the middle of the court. Court surfaces are concrete or asphalt, although competition can also take place on hard-packed sand (USPTA, 1996).

Figure 23.2 Paddle tennis court.

Paddle Tennis Court Dimensions With Restraint Line

Paddle Tennis Web

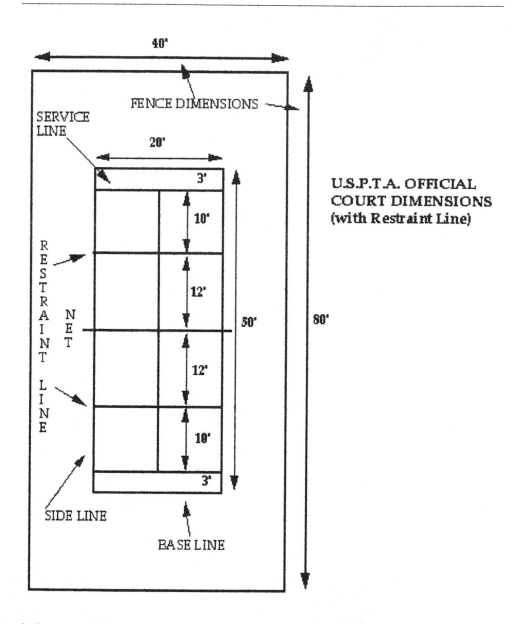

If construction of stand-alone paddle tennis courts is not an option, paddle tennis court markings can be superimposed on a regulation tennis court by using chalk or tape or by painting lighter colored lines, and the net can be lowered to the proper height.

Paddle

Dimensions

The sport of paddle has recently been introduced in the United States and is played in approximately 15 countries. A paddle court is 65 feet, 7 7/16 inches

(20 meters) long by 32 feet, 9 3/4 inches (10 meters) wide, with a plus or minus 1% tolerance level. The net, which divides the court in half, extends to the perimeter fence, where it is anchored to the two center posts of this fencing or to an independent anchoring system. Regardless of the anchoring system, the net must coincide with the perimeter fence. The net measures 37 7/16 inches (0.95 meters) at the posts and is two inches lower at the center of the court (35 7/16 inches or 0.90 meters), where it is held down at the center by a central belt that is two inches wide (APA, 1996).

The service lines for each side of the court run parallel to the net and are placed 22 feet, 9 1/2 inches (6.95 meters) from the net. A central service line, two inches wide, runs perpendicular to the net. This line bisects the court, dividing it into equal service zones on both sides of the net. Each service zone measures 22 feet, 9 1/2 inches long by 16 feet, 4 7/8 inches wide. All measurements for the court markings are made from the net or center of the central, perpendicular service line (APA, 1996).

The paddle court is completely enclosed by backwalls, sidewalls, and fencing on the remaining sideline areas. The backwalls, at the end of each court, measure the width of the court (32 feet, 9 3/4 inches) and are between 9 feet, 10 1/8 inches (3 meters) and 13 feet, 1 1/2 inches (4 meters) in height. The partial side or "wing walls" extend 13 feet, 1 1/2 inches (4 meters) from the backwalls. The wing walls decrease in height from 9 feet, 10 1/8 inches (3 meters) to 5 feet (1.5 meters), beginning at the wing wall's midpoint (6 feet, 6 3/4 inches, that is, two meters from the junction of the back and wing walls) to the end of the wall. This decrease in height on the wing wall should be at approximately a 38-degree angle. The remainder of the court perimeter is enclosed with a wire fence measuring 13 feet, 1 1/2 inches (4 meters) in height from the court surface (APA, 1996). (APA, Paddle Tennis Publication and http://virtual.chattanooga.net/paddle/court.htm)

Miscellaneous Considerations

Paddle court surfaces vary from hard courts to artificial grass. The sport can be played on outdoor as well as indoor courts. If played indoors, however, courts must have a minimum ceiling clearance of 25 feet.

Backwalls and partial sidewalls consist of stucco, concrete, or glass and/or a blindex material that provides for optimum spectator viewing of the court from all surrounding areas.

Portable courts (notinclusive of surfacing) are available for purchase for approximately $25,000. Contact the American Paddle Association at 1-800-861-1539 for further information.

Platform Tennis

Dimensions

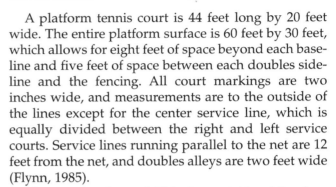

A platform tennis court is 44 feet long by 20 feet wide. The entire platform surface is 60 feet by 30 feet, which allows for eight feet of space beyond each baseline and five feet of space between each doubles sideline and the fencing. All court markings are two inches wide, and measurements are to the outside of the lines except for the center service line, which is equally divided between the right and left service courts. Service lines running parallel to the net are 12 feet from the net, and doubles alleys are two feet wide (Flynn, 1985).

Net posts are located 18 inches outside of the doubles sidelines, and the net height is 37 inches at the posts and 34 inches at the center of the court. Fencing, which measures 12 feet in height, is 16-gauge hexagonal, galvanized, one-inch flat wire mesh fabric.

Miscellaneous Considerations

The total area needed for construction of a platform tennis court is 2584 square feet (68 feet by 38 feet). This allows for the foundation beams at the corners and at the locations of the uprights (Figure 23.4). Specifications for a platform tennis court typically call for four-inch by six-inch foundation beams across the base of the platform. It is recommended that wood beams be waterproofed with creosote. Each beam rests on four evenly spaced concrete blocks; the blocks should be placed such that the beams rest four feet apart (measured from center to center). The foundation beams at the corners and at the locations of the uprights must project far enough to afford a base for the outer support of the uprights. The deck surface should be constructed of Douglas fir planks measuring two feet by six feet. The planks should be laid 1/8 inch to 1/4 inch apart to allow for drainage. The corner uprights and the intermediate uprights must measure 12 feet from their base (i.e., the deck surface) to their top. The corner uprights should be constructed of four-inch-by-four-inch beams; the intermediate uprights should measure two inches by four inches (Flynn, 1985).

The construction of the backstop is a detailed procedure. The tops of the uprights are connected by "top rails"—bars that measure two inches by four inches. These rails are bolted horizontally to the insides of the tops of the uprights and measure two inches by four inches along the sides. Therefore, the rails to which the wire fabric is attached project inside the uprights by four inches at the ends and two inches at the sides. All of the space around the platform is covered by wire except 12-foot openings in the center of each

What a Paddle Court Looks Like ...

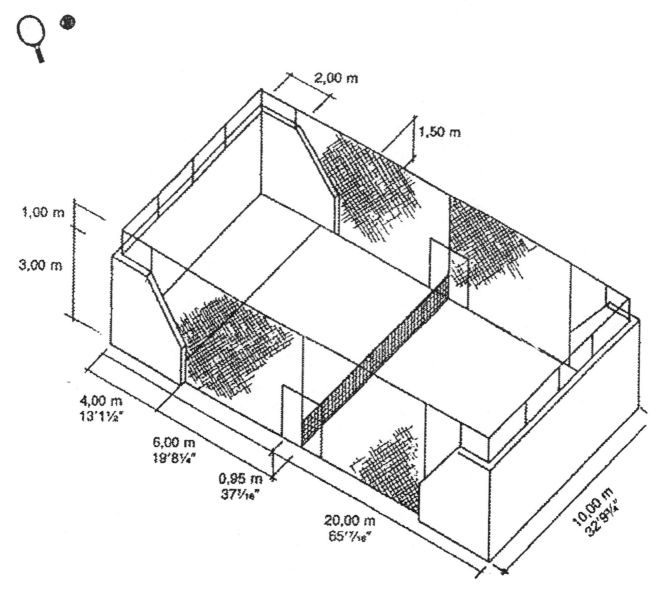

Figure 23.3 Paddle court.

side, at least one of which is closed with either netting. This closure is for containing errant balls. All wiring should be attached vertically on the inside of the uprights and stretched in six-foot widths from the top down to the tension rail below (Flynn, 1985).

Badminton

Dimensions

A badminton doubles court is 44 feet in length by 20 feet wide; a singles court is the same length (44 feet) but three feet narrower (17 feet). All court markings, including the center service line, short service lines, and doubles long service lines, are marked in yellow or white and measure 1.5 inches in width. All dimensions are measured from the outside of the court lines, except for the center service line which is equally divided between service courts.

The court is bisected laterally by a net which is exactly five feet above the ground at the center of the court and five feet, one inch at the net posts. The net posts are placed directly on the doubles sidelines. However, when it is not possible to have the posts

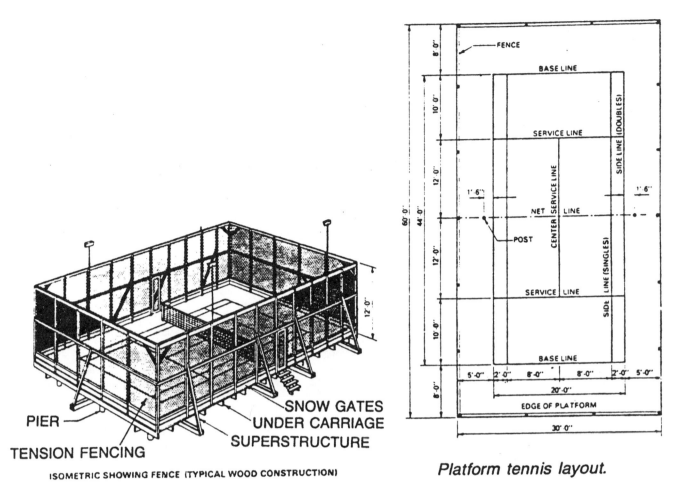

ISOMETRIC SHOWING FENCE (TYPICAL WOOD CONSTRUCTION)

Figure 23.4 Platform tennis court.

Platform tennis layout.

over the sidelines, this boundary should be marked with a thin post or strips of material attached to the sideline and rising to the net cord.

The safety distance or unobstructed space behind the back boundary line should measure eight feet behind and four to five feet outside of each sideline or between courts.

Miscellaneous Considerations

Ideally, ceiling clearance for indoor badminton should be no less than 30 feet over the entire full-court area. This is the standard for international play. However, a 25-foot clearance is the recommended minimum and sufficient for other levels of play.

Basketball

Dimensions

Indoor and outdoor basketball courts vary in size depending upon the level of competitive play. It is recommended that, courts for junior high, high school, and recreational play be 50 feet wide by 84 feet long. Competitive collegiate and professional basketball requires a 50-foot by 94-foot court. Regardless of the level of play, a 10-foot unobstructed or safety space is highly recommended, especially considering today's game and the increased size of the players. However, if a court is constructed with less than 10 feet of safety space (eight feet is a minimum at the end lines and six feet on the sidelines), wall padding should be installed the entire distance of the wall that parallels the side or end line. Another important safety consideration concerns any glass or windows that are part of the surrounding basketball gymnasium. All glass and windows should be shatterproof safety glass. Finally, in a gymnasium setting, especially where other sports can be played, a height clearance of 30 feet is strongly recommended, but a minimum clearance of 23 feet is imperative. Figure 23.6 provides a detailed display of basketball court markings (NCAA, 1997). Concerning the size and colors of the lines, cut several guidelines should be kept in mind:

Figure 23.5 Badminton court.

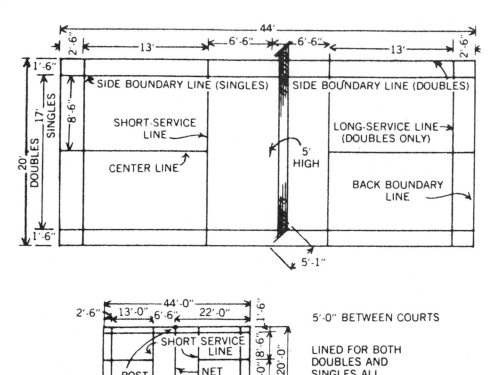

■ All lines must be two inches wide, except for the neutral zones.
■ The color of the boundary lines should match the midcourt markings.
■ The color of the lane space and neutral zone markings should contrast with the color of the boundary lines (NCAA, 1997).

Note: The three-point arch measures 19 feet, 9 inches from the center of the basket for both high school and collegiate competition.

Miscellaneous Considerations

Collegiate competition requires backboards that are transparent and measure six feet horizontally by four feet vertically. The backboard should have a two-inch white-lined target centered behind the goal. This target should measure 24 inches horizontally by 18 inches vertically. The backboard should also have a two-inch thick gray padding on the bottom and up the sides for the players' protection (Head-Summit & Jennings, 1996). Attached to the backboard is an 18-inch (inner diameter) bright orange ring, mounted parallel to and 10 feet above the floor. Although the standard height for a basketball goal (from rim to floor) is 10 feet, adjustable standards that allow the rim to be set at the standard height or lower (i.e., as low as eight feet) provide opportunities for young children to practice shooting at a goal that is more age-appropriate (NCAA, 1997).

The gymnasium flooring is an important consideration. It is imperative that the flooring provide sliding characteristics (the surface friction of a finished floor) and shock absorption that conform to criteria established by the Deutches Institut für Normung (DIN) standards (Table 23.1), to help minimize the possibility of participant injury. Also, the flooring should provide adequate ball bounce or deflection as prescribed under the DIN standards. A final consideration is the placement of padding in appropriate areas, such as the wall directly behind each basketball backboard, especially if the distance between the backboard and wall is less than 10 feet.

Outdoor basketball courts should run lengthwise in approximately a north-south direction. Proper drainage can be insured by slanting courts from one side to the other, allowing "one inch of slant . . . for every 10 feet of court" (Flynn, 1985). If a backboard

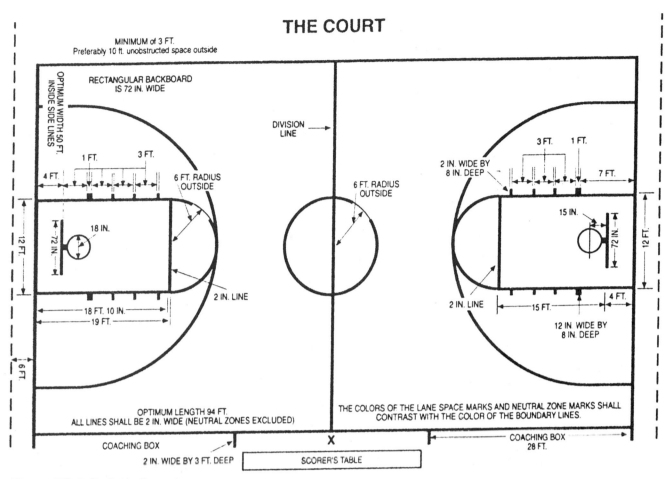

Figure 23.6 Basketball court.

is mounted on an in-ground pole, the pole should be padded. Additionally, the pole should be off the playing court, and the backboard should be extended at least four feet onto the court. Fencing is not a necessity; however, if finances allow, anodized aluminum chain-link should be used. The fence height should be a minimum of 10 feet. The fence posts should be placed six inches to one foot inside the hard surface, and the fence fabric should be affixed on the inside of these supporting posts. Posts should be mounted in concrete such that 35% to 40% of the length of the pole is above the surface (Flynn, 1985). Gates or fences should be constructed large enough to allow maintenance equipment to be brought into the court areas.

Volleyball

Dimensions

Although volleyball courts within the United States traditionally measure 30 feet in width by 60 feet in length, the United States Volleyball Rules (which are those of the International Volleyball Federation) call for the court to measure 59 feet by 29.5 feet (18 meters by 9 meters). Notably, all court dimensions are measured from the outside edge of the lines, and all court lines should be two inches (five centimeters) wide (Sanford, 1997).

A minimum of 6 feet, 6 inches of safety or unobstructed space should surround an indoor court; however, the ideal situation is to provide at least 10 feet from the sidelines and 13 feet from the end lines (NCAA, 1997).

Ceiling clearance is a critical issue. Although United States Volleyball Rules call for a minimum or 23 feet (7 meters) of unobstructed space as measured from the floor, 30 feet of overhead clearance is highly recommended (Neville, 1994, p.6). Figure 23.7 provides a detailed display of volleyball floor markings. Notably, in recent years the service zone has been extended the full width of the court as a result of a rule change permitting players to serve anywhere behind the endline.

Table 23.1 DIN Flooring Standards

The flooring for a multiuse exercise area should adhere to Deutsches Institut für Normung (DIN) standards. These standards require that a floor meet six criteria:

1. Shock absorption—a floor's ability to reduce the impact of contact with the floor surface. The greater the shock absorption, the more protective it is because it reduces impact forces. An aerobics floor, for example, would need more shock absorption than a basketball court.
2. Standard vertical deformation—the actual vertical deflection of the floor upon impact. The greater the deformation, the more the floor deflects downward. Floors with minimal deformation are not good at absorbing impact forces.
3. Deflective indentation—the actual vertical deflection of the floor at a distance 50 cm from the point of impact. The greater the indentation, the more likely impact at one spot will cause deflection at a distant point.
4. Sliding characteristics—the surface friction of the finished floor. A floor with poor sliding characteristics would be inappropriate for aerobics or basketball.
5. Ball reflection (game-action response)—the response of a ball dropped on the floor compared to a ball dropped on concrete.
6. Rolling load—a floor's ability to withstand heavy weight without breaking or sustaining permanent damage.

These DIN criteria are then used to evaluate the effectiveness of a floor. A floor will have one of three functions:

1. Sports function—A floor that serves a sports function enhances athletic performance. Surface friction and ball reflection are important here.
2. Protective function—A floor that serves a protective function reduces the risk of injury (e.g., from a fall) during activity. Shock absorption is important here.
3. Material-technical function—A floor that serves a material-technical function meets the sports and protective functions.

In a health/fitnes facility, the gymnasium and multipurpose floors are classified under sports function or material-technical function. The aerobics floor is classified under protective function, with some sports function characteristics.

A floor surface that has a material-technical function should meet the following DIN criteria:

Shock absorption	53% minimum
Standard vertical deformation	2.3 mm minimum
Deflective indentation	15% maximum
Sliding characteristics	0.5 to 0.7 range
Ball deflection	90% minimum
Rolling load	0337.6 lb

Net Height

The volleyball net height is 7 feet, 11 5/8 inches (2.43 meters) for men's competition and 7 feet, 4 1/8 inches (2.24m) for women's competition, as measured at the center of the playing court. The two ends of the net, directly over the sidelines, must be the same height from the playing surface and may not exceed the official height by 3/4 inch (although a constant height is far more desirable). The net height may be varied for specific age groups in the following ways (Sanford, 1997):

Age Groups	Females/Reverse Mixed 6	Males/Mixed 6
55 years and above		799 5/80 (2.38m)
45 years and above	7'2 1/8" (2.19m)	
15-18 years of age	7'4 1/8" (2.24m)	7'11 5/8" (2.43m)
16 years and under	7'4 1/8" (2.24m)	7'11 5/8" (2.43m)
14 years and under	7'4 1/8" (2.24m)	7'4 1/8" (2.43m)
12 years and under	7'0" (2.13m)	7'0" (2.13m)
10 years and under	6'6" (1.98m)	7'0" (2.13m)

(United States Volleyball Rule Book, 1997-1998, p.14)

The net itself is 39 inches wide and a minimum of 32 feet long. The posts (supporting standards) are fixed to the playing surface at least $19^1/_2$ inches to 39 inches from each sideline. Two white side bands, 2 inches wide and 39 inches long, are fastened around the net vertically and placed perpendicularly over each sideline. Six-foot-long antennas are attached at the outer edge of each side band and extend 32 inches above the height of the net (USVA, 1997).

Miscellaneous Considerations

One of the most important safety factors is to provide poles that are sunk directly below floor level in sleeves or that telescope up from below the floor. Volleyball standards/poles that are on mounted or weighted bases are extremely hazardous. Likewise, volleyball net systems that rely on guy wires are not desirable. If wires are part of an existing volleyball net system, they should be clearly identified and padded. Furthermore, volleyball posts should be padded to a minimum height of six feet, and all official stands should be padded.

Ideally, in a facility built primarily for volleyball, the walls (particularly those behind each endline) should be painted a color that provides some contrast to the color of volleyballs, which are generally white. This contrast in color allows participants to more easily track the flight of the ball during play. Additionally, the ceiling color should be an off-white or other light color that provides a contrasting background for players attempting to follow the flight path of the volleyball.

Light fixtures need to be placed at least as high as the lowest ceiling obstructions to avoid any shadowing effects. Also, lighting needs to be bright (a minimum of 27.9 foot-candles, measured at one meter above the playing surface). The lights, however, should not be closely grouped such that they would create a blinding effect for participants (USVA, 1997).

Outdoor Sand Volleyball Court Guidelines

The dimensions for an outdoor sand court are identical to indoor volleyball court dimensions (i.e., 59 feet (18 meters) long by 29 feet, 6 inches (9 meters) wide, as measured from the outer edge of the boundary lines). Ideally, the court should be constructed with the net running in an east-west direction so that the morning and evening sun does not face directly into the eyes of one team. Outdoor courts should provide a minimum of 9 feet, 10 inches or 3 meters of free space—composed of sand—surrounding the court area. In other words, the complete sand area should measure a minimum of 80 feet long by 50 feet wide. For professional competitions, the court should be centered on an area 93 feet long by 57 feet wide. Standard net heights are the same as for the indoor game: 7 feet 11, 5/8 inches (2.43 meters) for men's and coed play, and 7 feet, 4 1/8 inches for women's and reverse coed play. Children ages 10 to 16 may have the net height adjusted according to the standards listed above regarding indoor volleyball net adjustments (Sandorti, 1995).

Boundary lines are brightly colored 1/4 inch rope or $1^1/_2$-inch webbing tied to the four corners with buried deadman anchors. No centerline is required for outdoor play, but approximately 14 feet of rope will be needed, beyond the 177 feet total necessary for court lines, to anchor the corners (Sandorti, 1995).

Net supports should be made of metal, wood, or other material that will withstand tension. The sup-

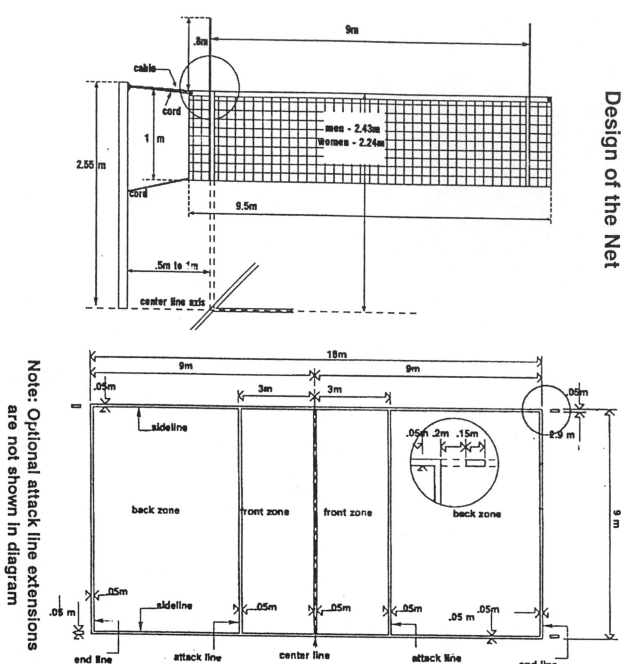

Design of the Net

men - 2.43m
Women - 2.24m

The Playing Court

Note: Optional attack line extensions are not shown in diagram

Design of the Net (Detail)

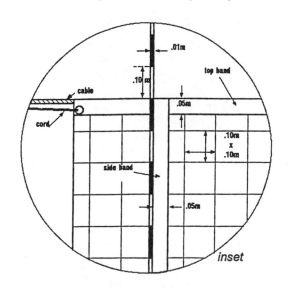

inset

Figure 23.7 Volleyball court dimensions.

ports should be about 14 feet long and should be buried five feet deep using a concrete footing unless the soil is solid, in which case packing in and washing the soil should suffice. These support standards should be set 39 inches (1 meter) from the boundary of the court. Any less space will leave insufficient room for the full net and adjusting cables (Sandorti, 1995).

Suggested specifications for different net supports are as follows. Metal net supports should be four-inch, diameter schedule 40, galvanized steel pipes. Round wood poles should measure eight inches in diameter and should be made of treated, weather-resistant wood. Square wood supports are not recommended because of the potential for participant injury on corner edges. In all instances, padding the support poles is an important safety measure. If the support does not have equal sides, the narrower side should be the net anchor side (facing the court) (Sandorti, 1995).

Hooks, hook-and-eye hardware, and any winch hardware (padded) are necessary to attach the net to the standards. One way to provide for total adjustability of net height is to have four metal collars made that have loops for attaching the net (i.e., the top and the bottom of the net on both sides) that can slide up and down the poles. Holes can be drilled into the collars and set screws inserted, which can be tightened with an allen wrench. Finally, the net should be 10 meters in length with a cable top, although strong rope such as Kevlar also works well. However, the effort of fashioning this system can be avoided by purchasing outdoor standards, now available from a variety of vendors.

Actual sand court construction should start with the excavation of the area with a Bobcat or front-end loader. The court area should be excavated between two and three feet in depth. In low-lying areas, such as shoreline areas of Florida, the court should be excavated only six to eight inches. This will yield an elevated court rather than one that is flush with the ground. Also, the dirt that is excavated should be used to create a slight slope up to the court.

The court perimeter edges can be contained to keep dirt and grass from leaking into the court. Lawn edging material or rubber handrail material from escalator companies seated atop two-inch-by-six-inch wooden boundaries is a good method of providing perimeter boundaries. If railroad ties or similar materials are used, the top edges should be padded to minimize injury potential (Sandorti, 1995).

Drainage of the court under the sand is important. The installation of leaching pipe on the standards with a slant of 14 degrees is highly recommended for a good permanent court. Perforated pipe (approximately two rolls of 250 feet) can be laid perforated side down with the open end at the low point of the court. Each section of the pipe should be wrapped with a flex wrap or "handicap wrap," which can be purchased at plumbing supply houses. This wrap prevents sand from filling up the pipes. Finally, the drainage points should lead away from the court at the lowest point (Sandorti, 1995).

The next step is to set the standards in concrete. Poles should be set at a slight angle outward from the court to allow for any bending caused by eventual net tension. To allow for ease of maintenance or replacement, steel poles should be seated in steel sleeves so that they can be easily removed.

Small pea-sized gravel used for drainage (#56, #57, #2, or #3) should then be placed over the drainage pipe to a depth of about one foot. Approximately 2,600 cubic feet (110 tons) of this gravel is necessary. Plastic landscaping or ground stabilization filter fabric (a woven polyblend that will not deteriorate easily) is placed over the gravel to prevent the sand from washing through (Sandorti, 1995).

The final step in sand court construction is depositing the sand. A good court requires an investment in good sand. Sand comes in a variety of grades; some types are very "dirty" and unsuitable for a court. Washed beach (dune), washed plaster, washed masonry, or washed river sand are the most desirable types of court sand. The most highly recommended sand is silica sand, regionally available by contacting Best Sand at (800) 237-4986. This sand should be deposited and raked level around the court; it should measure one to two feet in depth. The minimum recommended depth of the sand is $19^1/_2$ inches. In essence, a sand court requires approximately 5,200 cubic feet (205 tons of washed sand). The final price tag for the construction of a good sand volleyball court will range anywhere from $6,000 to $10,000 (Sandorti, 1995).

Racquetball, Handball, and Squash Courts

Dimensions and Design Considerations

Four-wall courts for squash and handball have been in sports facilities for over three quarters of a century. Originally, these courts were made from Portland cement with smaller-than-normal doors. Paddleball and racquetball were first played on these courts in the late 1950s and early 1960s. Today's courts are designed for racquetball, handball, and squash, even though other activities may also be played in these enclosed four wall courts (such as walleyball and Bi-Rakits). Today's state-of-the-art courts are constructed of laminated panels and/or tempered glass. In the planning of four-wall courts, teaching, competition, accessibility, and amenities need to be considered (AARA, 1997).

The recommended four-wall racquetball/handball court is 40 feet long and 20 feet wide, with a front wall and ceiling height of 20 feet, and a back wall at least 14 feet high (Figure 23.8). The lower back wall provides a space for a viewing or for an instructional gallery, which may be open with a three-to four-foot-high railing. Clear polycarbonate sheeting should be placed under the railing for seated viewing purposes and safety. The gallery may be totally enclosed with clear polycarbonate sheeting and a small four-foot-square open window. An open gallery is recommended for communication purposes between instructors/officials and the players. But an open gallery poses the risk of spectators being hit by a ball; therefore, appropriate signage should be posted to indicate this hazard.

Squash is becoming very popular in some regions of the United States. The international singles squash court is 21 feet wide and 32 feet long. The old North American standard of an 18-foot-6-inches-wide singles squash court is no longer acceptable and should be avoided. North American doubles squash is played on a larger court measuring 25 feet wide and 45 feet long (Figures 23.9a-23.9c). Squash court wall heights vary compared to the standard 20 foot racquetball/handball wall heights (USSRA, 1997).

When more than a single battery of courts is to be constructed, the batteries should be arranged so the back walls of each are separated by a corridor approximately 10 feet wide and 12 feet high. Courts should be located in the same area of the facility rather than being spread out. Courts should be placed on adjacent walls rather than on opposite walls in order to achieve close proximity, thereby aiding in quality instructional time. Corridors and galleries should be illuminated with indirect light. The minimum number of courts for schools should be dictated by maximum class size and total student enrollment. Normally no fewer than six to eight courts are recommended, which can adequately handle 15 to 20 students at a time. The number of courts for clubs and private usage is determined by the number of users and by the popularity of racquetball, handball, and squash in any given area.

Walls may be constructed of hard plaster, Portland cement, wood, laminated panels, or tempered glass. Laminated panels and tempered glass are recommended. The panels are four-by-eight-foot particle board or resin-impregnated kraft papers covered with a melamine sheet. The panels come in different thicknesses, from 13/16 inches to 1 1/8 inches. The thicker the panel is, the truer the rebound action of the ball

will be; however, the thicker panel is also more expensive. Panels are mounted on aluminum channels or metal studs. Screws that hold them to the wall superstructure are inset and covered with a plug. This creates a monolithic surface for the walls. The panels have a high life expectancy and are easily maintained. Glass walls of 0.5-inch-thick tempered, heat-soaked glass are ideal but expensive. All courts are recommended to have the minimum of glass back walls, and one court should have an additional glass side wall. This will offer good instructional and spectator viewing (Figure 23.12).

If glass walls are utilized, spectator and instructional viewing areas should be planned for carefully. These areas usually are stepped, with carpeted risers along the side wall or back wall of the court. A built-in, two-way audio system should be utilized for this court. Carpet color should not be totally dark and definitely should not be blue or green since player ball visibility through the glass walls is obscured with dark colors as a background. Courts with two glass sidewalls those with glass sidewalls and a glass back wall, and all-glass-wall courts are superior to other courts; however, their cost is prohibitive in most facilities.

Doors are standard size and are placed in the middle of the back wall, not in the corners of the court. The corners are crucial real estate in intermediate and advanced racquet sports, so doors that can cause "untrue" bounces should not be placed there. Door handles should be small and recessed, and all door framing should be flush on the inside of the court. Doors should open into the court, and there should be no thresholds under the doors.

Floors should be hardwood, as in standard gymnasium construction. The more sophisticated the floor system is, the more costly it will be. Resilient wood floors play differently than more rigid system wood floors, but they are more expensive. Any good hard maple floor system is acceptable. Floors should be flush with sidewalls so that no joint is evident. Joints collect dirt, dust, and debris and are a maintenance nightmare. Floors should be resurfaced as needed with a high-grade finish. When floors need refinishing, they become slippery and can be very dangerous. The amount of use, the types of shoes worn during play, and the amount of dirt and grit brought into the courts on shoes will dictate how often refinishing is needed. Floors should be cleaned with a treated mop daily or as needed. Synthetic floors should not be used in racquet courts because they create too much friction and do not allow feet to slide, which is needed for effective and safe racquet sports.

Court line markings should be a lighter color rather than a dark color like blue or black. Again, this helps

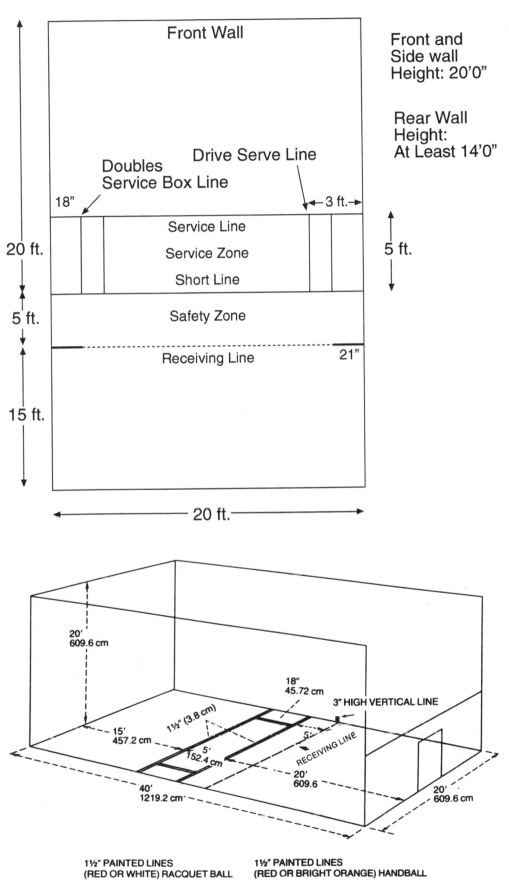

Figure 23.8 Four wall handball and racquetball courts and dimensions.

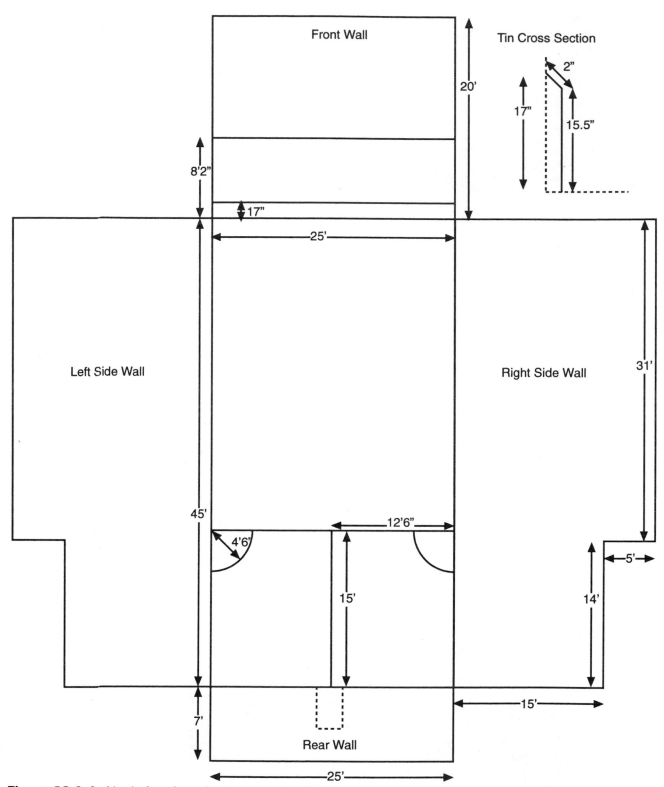

Figure 23.9 A. North American doubles squash court.

the participants' visual acuity in following a dark ball across lighter lines. Off-white, light pastel yellow, or light grey lines are best. Squash lines are red.

For racquetball and handball courts, the first 12 feet of the ceiling from the front wall should be de-

void of any heat or ventilating ducts. This portion of the ceiling must be hard and compatible to the wall surfaces for ball rebounding. Lighting and any other fixtures in the ceiling must be totally flush. The rear eight feet of the ceiling is not as crucial,

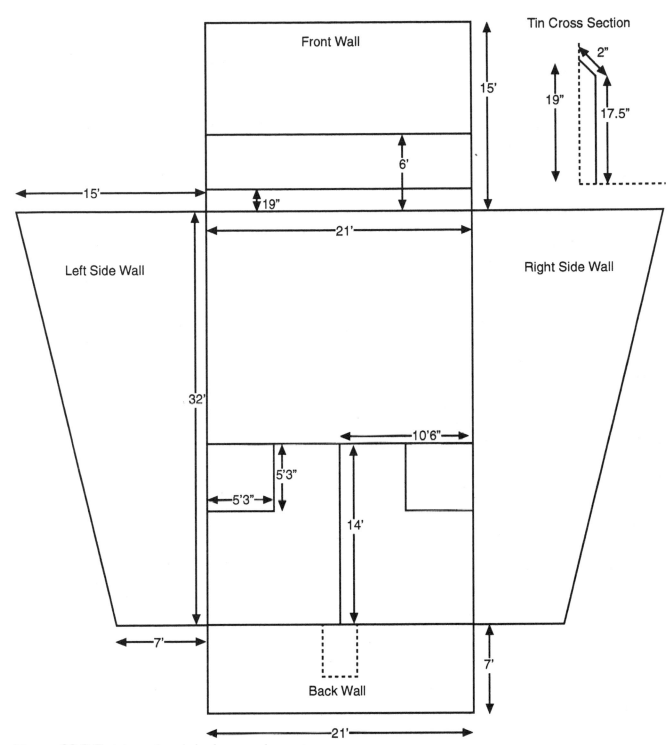

Figure 23.9 B. International singles squash court.

since this part of the ceiling is used very seldom in play.

The ceiling is not used in squash, but it should still be made of an impact-resistant material in case errant balls hit it. Panels or Portland cement would be good for the front 12 feet of the ceiling.

If wallyball is to be played in the court, the ceiling must be strong enough to absorb the impact of the

volleyball. Panels, but not Portland cement, work well in wallyball courts.

Lighting, Acoustics, and Ventilation

All lighting must be flush with the ceiling. Lights should illuminate all portions of the court equally; therefore, they should be spread throughout the ceil-

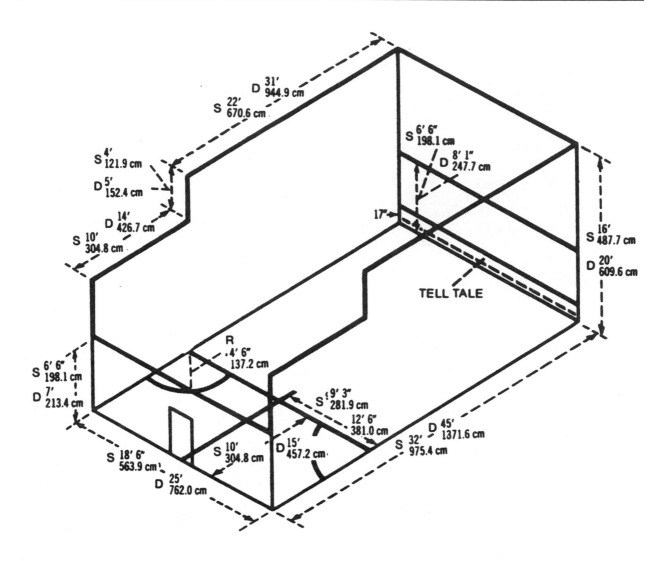

Markings are inside dimensions as lines are out of bounds (except in service areas).

Figure 23.9 C. *Standard squash court.*

**United States Squash Racquets Association
211 Ford Road, Bala-Cynwyd, PA 19004
(215) 667-4006**

ing. Shadows and low-light areas are not acceptable in these courts. Light accessibility for changing bulbs must be planned carefully. Since there is normally a battery of courts, the chore of changing light bulbs is magnified by the number of courts needing a bulb-changing system. The best lightbulb-changing method for courts is to have a crawl space above the ceiling. This enables maintenance personnel to change bulbs from above. This system eliminates the need to use cumbersome hydraulic lifts and/or "A" frame ladders (AARA, 1997).

A metal halide system of lighting is recommended. Metal halide lights give the most light at the least cost. Metal halide bulbs also have a long life expectancy. However, to garner cost savings and longevity, the court lights must be on at *all* times. Turning these lights off and on causes a delay (about six to eight minutes) for the bulbs to obtain full brightness. Turning halide lights off and on also increases the cost of lighting and decreases bulb life expectancy. Metal halide lights should be controlled from a central console, not at each court.

Figure 23.10 Glass back court.

If single courts are not used often, a recommended method of turning the lights on and off is to install switches that are activated by opening or closing the door to the court. This method requires a metal halide lighting system. When the door is closed, lights in the court will turn on. When the door is opened, the lights will turn off automatically, leaving only the night light to burn continuously. Usually, a two- to three-minute delay occurs before the lights go off after the door has been opened, preventing a disruption of lighting during the brief time it takes for players to exit or exchange the court.

A relatively new concept utilizes an annunciator (an electrically controlled signal board) to indicate to the building reservation/control center which courts are occupied at any time. Lights on the signal board are activated by the trip switch on each door as it opens or closes. When lights are to be constantly turned off and on, incandescent bulbs work fairly well. Fluorescent lights should not be used in racquet courts because they tend to flicker and can cause visual acuity problems during play. If wallyball is to be played in the court, stronger light shields and light fixtures will be needed to absorb the impact of a volleyball.

Court walls and floors are hard surfaces, and much sound reverberates in the courts. For non-glass court surfaces, acoustical treatment is important within the surfaces. Insulation in the walls and ceiling will help to buffer sound within a court and also between courts. The rear eight feet of the ceiling should be constructed of acoustical tiles because this area is seldom used in racquetball/handball and never used in squash. Although these tiles provide minimal acoustical treatment, it is very important to attempt to control sound, and they should be considered in each court. If walleyball is played in a court, soft acoustical treatment *cannot* be installed on the ceiling.

Ventilation should be provided by air conditioning. The ventilation of each court is very important so that moisture does not build on wall surfaces, making the courts unplayable. Ample air circulation and dehumidifying the air are major concerns in the ventilation of the courts. Only air conditioning can provide circulation, cooling, and dehumidification. To minimize the potential for moisture, courts should not be built underground with walls exposed to external moisture. Moisture and/or condensation can easily intrude to the interior wall surfaces of the courts. If courts must be built underground, extra waterproofing needs to be completed in this portion of the facility.

All vents for air circulation should be located in the back eight feet of the ceiling for racquetball and handball (Turner 1992), but squash courts may have vents anywhere in the ceiling. The temperature of each court should be controlled by an individual, jar-proof, flush thermostat that is preset and tamper-proof.

Miscellaneous Considerations

Small storage boxes should be built flush with wall surfaces into side walls near the back wall of each court to house valuables and extra balls. The door to this storage box should be constructed of clear polycarbonate sheeting. Storage areas for students' coats, books, and other gear should be provided in an area near the courts. Extra storage must be provided for rain gear and winter gear where applicable. Secured storage for racquetball rackets, handball gloves, squash rackets, eye guards, and balls should be provided near the court area.

All courts should have joints, seams, doors, vents, lights, and corners flush with the surrounding surface. Any unevenness in a court will cause untrue ball rebounds, which are unacceptable in court games. Each court should be equipped with a two-way audio system. Access to this system should be housed in the central console. This audio system can be used to make announcements, to provide music, and for instructional purposes between the court user and the instructor.

Effective external signage is important for all courts. Signs for court rules need to be posted near each court entrance. Rule signs such as "Eye guards are mandatory" and "Only non-marking athletic shoes may be worn in courts" are typical for racquet courts. Other signage includes the designation of a challenge court(s) with rules and a daily sign-up sheet. Courts also must be numbered, and a visible wall clock near the courts is important.

Courts and galleries should be accessible to individuals with disabilities. Doors should be wide enough for wheelchair passage and have no barriers such as thresholds or steps at access points. Additionally, the courts' location within the sport facility and a route from adjacent parking areas must be free of barriers.

University courts should be built at a location with easy access from all points on campus, and ample parking in close proximity of the courts should be carefully planned. Within the sport complex, the courts should be located near the console control area.

In any facility, all courts need to be situated near refrigerated water fountains. In a commercial court complex, an area close to the courts must be designated for a proshop. This area needs to be large enough to accommodate the types of equipment and apparel to be sold. The proshop area must also be able to be secured by either lockable doors or a metal mesh gate since it will not be staffed during all operation hours of the court area.

If there is a hallway access to courts and/or galleries, the hallway must have a ceiling height of 12 feet. A lower ceiling height lends itself to damage from individuals jumping up and hitting it with their rackets. Light shields in these hallways should be flush with the ceiling to deter breakage. Skylights above the court ceiling height, in gallery areas only, add a nice aesthetic touch. The use of a translucent glass or polycarbonate sheeting in skylights will alleviate glare problems.

Movable metal "telltales" can be installed across the front of handball/racquetball courts for use in for squash instruction. However, the courts are racquetball size, not squash size. The floors, walls, ceilings, lighting, heating, and ventilation of squash courts are similar to those of four-wall racquetball/handball courts.

One court at any instructional facility should be a permanent teaching court. There should be a three-foot-by-three-foot front-wall viewing and videotaping square. This "window" should be covered with a single sheet of clear polycarbonate sheeting. The window should be three or four feet high from the floor and closer to one side or the other of the front wall. Access to this window from outside the court must be provided. There should be a small lockable area behind the viewing window, preferably five feet by five feet with a ceiling height of eight feet. An adjustable-height table and chair need to be in this small room, and a small area for storage of a portable video camera, video tapes, and speed gun should be provided there as well.

The teaching court also needs two flush, covered, electrical outlets for power sources. A multimedia projector and a video camera should be mounted *within* the back wall. Both projector and camera need to be protected with a clear polycarbonate sheet. A lockable, flush console should be built into a side wall to house a laptop computer and VCR. This setup allows for slides, videotapes, television, and computer viewing. None of this high-tech equipment ever needs to be moved into or around the courts.

Polycarbonate mirrors, each section measuring six feet long by six feet high, should be placed flush on two adjacent walls. The back wall and a side wall work best for the mirrors. Mirrors are great instructional tools because they allow the students to view themselves.

Foot templates for various movement patterns should be permanently placed on the floor. Different colors may be utilized along with arrows to indicate foot movement direction. Ball flight path patterns should be painted on the floor, and flight paths for a down-the-wall passing shot and/or a cross-court passing shot should actually be templated onto the floor. Again, different colors should be used for different ball paths. An elliptical circle six feet wide and four feet deep should be painted and labeled "center court" in the center court area of the court. An area three feet by three feet by three feet square also needs to be painted and labeled in each back corner. The back corners and center court are the two most important areas in racquet courts.

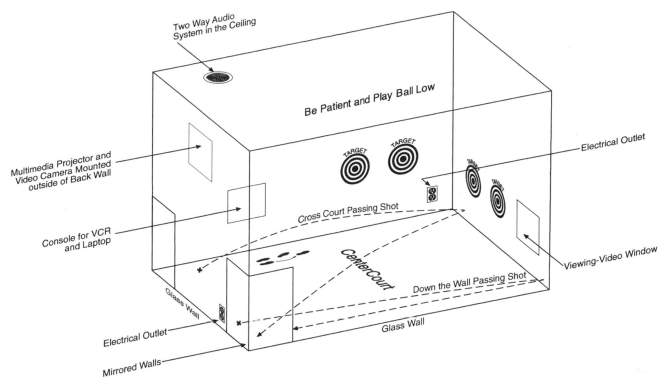

Figure 23.11 Raquetball teaching court.

Targets of varying size and height should be placed on both the front wall and side walls to serve as aiming points for various shots. A few targets also need to be placed on the ceiling near the front wall as ceiling shot templates for racquetball and handball. Skill templates should be placed in a few selected areas of the court, such as "Be patient and play the ball low" and "Culminate all sources of power at ball-racquet impact." These become constant visual educational reminders for students.

Ideally, the teaching court should have one glass side wall and a glass back wall. A glass back wall alone will suffice. A two-way communication system must be in place for the instructor, when in the court, to be able to talk to students out of the court and vice-versa (See Figure 23.11).

Good court construction is paramount for teaching, competition, safety, and maintenance. All court surfaces must be flush. The activity that is played in the court will be a determining factor in both the size of the court and the materials used in court construction.

Shuffle Board

Dimensions

The actual playing area of a shuffleboard court is 39 feet long and 6 feet wide. However, the area outside the court markings includes a six-foot, six-inch standing area at both ends of the court and a two-foot area adjacent to the sideline boundaries. Thus, the entire area for a shuffleboard court should measure 52 feet in length and 10 feet in width (Flynn, 1985).

The shuffleboard court is marked off by lines painted with a black dye, white road paint, or white acrylic stain. The lines measure from 3/4 of an inch to 1 inch in width. The base lines are extended to adjoining courts or two feet beyond the sides of the court (Flynn, 1985).

The separation triangle in the 10/off area measures three inches at the base and extends to form a point in the direction of the scoring area. The outline of the legs of this triangle is 1/4-inch wide, with a clearance of 1/2 inch at both the point and base. Finally, the base of the separation triangle is not marked (Flynn, 1985).

Miscellaneous Considerations

Outdoor shuffleboard courts should be oriented north-south and must be constructed on a level area. A smooth playing surface is essential; therefore, the surface of an outdoor court is typically concrete or asphalt. Furthermore, the courts should be developed over a well-drained area. For proper drainage, a depressed alley should be installed between and at the sides of all courts. The alley must be 24 inches wide and must slope from both base lines toward the

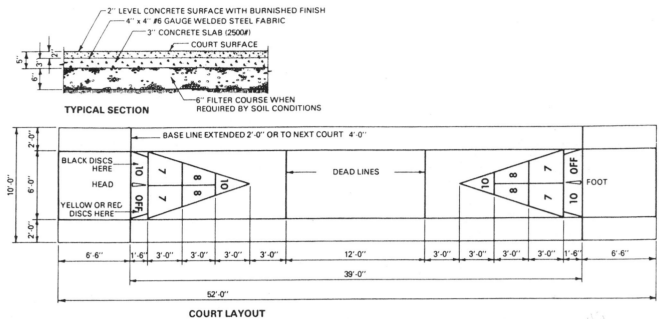

Figure 23.12 Shuffleboard court.

center of the court. To ensure proper flow of rainwater, the alley should descend one inch in depth during the first six inches in length (moving along the alley from each base line toward the center of the court) and gradually increase in depth to at least four inches at mid-court, where a suitable drain should be installed. The court can be lit using a 20-inch hinged pole with a 1500-watt quartzite floodlight. This pole should be erected outside the courts, next to the scoreboard or benches at the base of the courts. Overhead lighting is also an option in recreational areas. Frequently, two-inch-by-two-inch backstops are installed (in a loose fashion) to prevent discs from rebounding back onto the court (Flynn, 1985).

Indoor shuffleboard courts must also be constructed in a level area. Reinforced concrete or any reasonably smooth surface is sufficient. Also, portable courts are available from vendors.

Croquet

Dimensions

The two most common forms of American croquet are six-wicket croquet and nine-wicket croquet. Dimensions, configurations, and layouts are different for each game and are described separately.

The standard croquet court for American six-wicket croquet is a rectangle measuring 105 feet (35 yards) long by 84 feet (28 yards) wide. Boundary lines should be clearly marked, the inside edge of this bor-

der being the actual court boundary. If the area is too small to accommodate a standard court, a modified court may be laid out in accordance with the same proportions as a standard court (i.e., five units long by four units wide; for example, a court could be 50 feet long by 40 feet wide). In fact, in instances where the grass is cut high or beginners are competing, a smaller court such as a 50-foot-by-40-foot court is more desirable (USCA, 1997).

The stake is set in the center of the court (Figure 23.13). On a standard full court, the wickets are set parallel to the north and south boundaries, the centers of the two inner wickets are set 21 feet to the north and south of the stake, and the centers of the four outer wickets are set 21 feet from their adjacent boundaries. On a smaller modified 50-foot-by-40-foot court, the corner wickets are 10 feet from their adjacent boundaries, and the center wickets are 10 feet in each direction from the stake (USCA, 1997).

American nine-wicket croquet is played on a rectangular court that is 100 feet long by 50 feet wide with boundaries, although marked boundaries are optional. However, a court may be reduced to fit the size and shape of the available play space. If the court is reduced, a six-foot separation should be maintained between the starting/turning stake and the adjacent wickets (USCA, 1997).

Miscellaneous Considerations

For further information regarding the construction of courts, rules, or equipment, contact the United

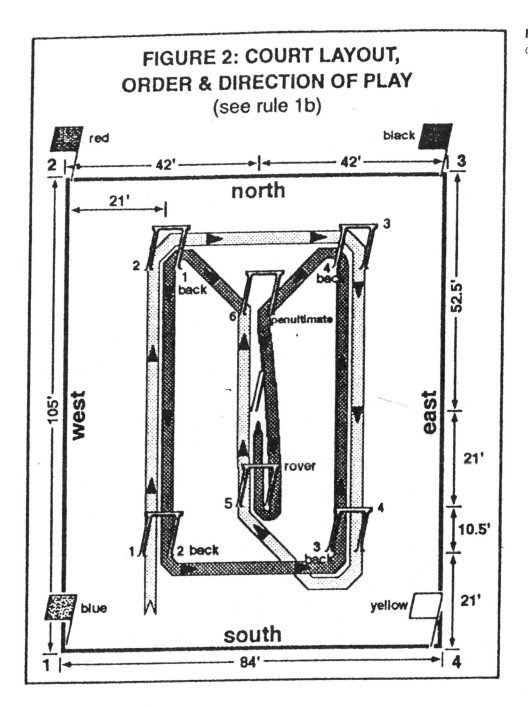

Figure 23.13 Six-wicket croquet layout.

States Croquet Association, 11585-B Polo Club Road, Wellington, FL 33414 (561) 753-9141, E-mail: uscroquet@compuserve.com

Fencing

Dimensions

The fencing court is referred to as the foil strip or piste and is constructed of wood, rubber, cork, linoleum, or synthetic material such as plastic. The strip is from 5 feet, 10 inches (1.8 meters) wide to 6 feet, 7 inches (2 meters) wide and 45 feet, 11 inches (14 meters) long. The strip markings include seven lines which cross the width of the entire strip: one center line; two on-guard lines, one drawn six feet, seven inches (two meters) from each side of the center line; two end lines at the rear limit of the strip; and two warning lines marked three feet, three inches (1 meter) in front of the end lines (Bower, 1980). Portable strips are also an option for those wishing to avoid permanent floor markings. Finally, ceiling clearance should be a minimum of 12 feet.

Figure 23.14 Nine-wicket croquet layout.

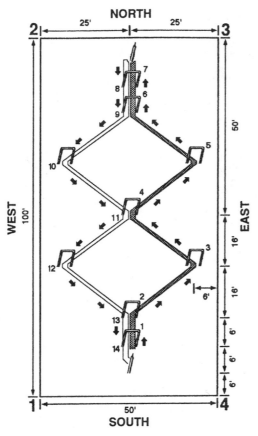

Figure 23.15 Fencing court dimensions.

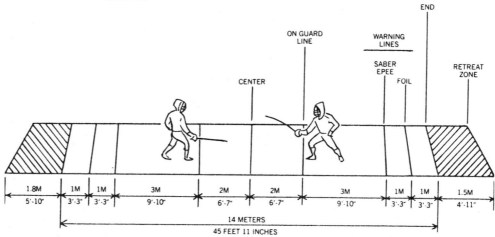

NOTE: The width of the strip shall be a minimum of 1.8 meters (5'10'') and a maximum of 2 meters (6'7''). The length of the retreat zone shall be a minimum of 1.5 meters (4'11'') and a maximum of 2 meters (6'7''). For Foil and Epee, the metallic surface of the strip shall cover the entire retreat zone.

Miscellaneous Considerations

For electric foil and epee, a metallic piste must cover the entire length of the strip, including the extension areas. Electrical outlets and jacks should be located at the ends of the strips to provide power for electrical equipment. For safety, any rackets for mounting fencing targets should be either recessed flush with the wall or fastened to the wall at least as high as seven feet.

■ Summary

Courts, whether they be inside or out, need special planning in relation to playing surfaces, safety issues, playing dimensions, and access. Additionally, planners need to consider storage areas, electrical outlets, lighting, and water fountains.

Learning Objective 1: The student will be able to identify and describe layout, dimensions, and orientation of the commonly used courts.

The layout, dimensions, and orientation of courts are defined by the sport-specific organizations representing each sport. The layout will depend on the space availability and the needs of the client.

Learning Objective 2: The student will be able to identify and describe various materials used in the construction of courts.

Each year new materials are introduced into the building supply market. The planners need to be aware of the new products and modified products that can be used when constructing courts.

Learning Objective 3: The student will be able to identify and describe a variety of important specification information (e.g., surfacing and lighting).

There are a number of court specifications regarding surfacing, lighting, site preparation, fencing, drainage, and access that planners need to be aware of and use in designing the court(s). When multiple court complexes are constructed, including support areas, the number of specifications will increase (i.e., electrical, mechanical, communication, heating, cooling, and ventilation).

■ Self-Assessment Exercises

1. Divide into groups of three and visit either the handball/racquetball courts in your sports complex or those of a nearby complex. Examine the courts for wall, ceiling, and floor construction. Discuss all aspects of construction within your group. Take notes on the discussion. Next, study the flushness of all aspects of the court. Discuss this and again take notes. Examine internal and external storage areas of the court and see if a teaching court is provided. Check the layout of the court battery. Again discuss and take notes. Return to the classroom and discuss your notes as to how improvements could be made to your courts. Each group then shares its comments with the other groups.

2. Divide into groups of three and design a multipurpose gymnasium that includes basketball, volleyball, and badminton courts. Consider all aspects of design presented in the chapter and draw a floorplan that provides gamelines. Also, give an overview of your plan relative to lighting, ceiling clearance, flooring, safety space, and any other factors you deem important.

3. Divide into groups of three and design a racquetball teaching court for clients 10 to 12 years of age. Apply and adapt items discussed in this chapter to this age group. An example might be larger targets and/or the use of cartoon characters in your teaching aids. When this exercise is complete, discuss your design with other class groups.

4. In groups of three, visit three different tennis complexes. Take copious notes regarding design and construction. If possible, take photographs. Present a report of your findings that evaluates these various courts and complexes.

5. In groups of five, attempt to gather information on the costs you would incur if you were to build one of the following courts: paddle tennis, platform tennis, or sand volleyball. Write up your cost analysis and present your findings to the class.

■ References

Bower, M. (1980). **Foil fencing** (4th ed.). Dubuque, IA: William C. Brown.

Flynn, R.B. (Ed.) (1985). **Planning facilities for athletics, physical education, and recreation,** Reston, VA: The Athletic Institute and American Alliance for Health, Physical Education, Recreation, and Dance.

Head-Summit, P. & Jennings, D. (1996). **Basketball fundamentals and team play** (2nd ed.) Dubuque, IA: Brown and Benchmark.

Neville, W. (1994). **Serve it up: Volleyball for life.** Mountain View, CA: Mayfield Publishing.

Sandorti, C.C. (1995). Court cents, **Volleyball Magazine,** 6(8), 114-115, 140.

Sanford, B. (Ed.), (1997). **Official 1997-1998 United States volleyball rules.** Indianapolis, IN: Sport Graphics.

United States Croquet Association (1995). **The official rules of the United States croquet association, 1995-1996.** Wellington, FL: Author.

■ Suggested Readings

Club Industry, published monthly by Sportscape Inc. Framingham Corporate Center, 492 Old Connecticut Path, Third Floor, Framingham, MA 01701, (508) 872-2021.

Fitness Management, published monthly by Leisure Publications Inc., 3923 West 6th Street, Los Angeles, CA 90020, (213) 385-3926.

Turner, E. (1993) Chapter 2, Indoor Facilities (pp. 15-63). In Flynn, R.B. (Ed.), **Facility planning for physical education, athletics and recreation.** Reston, VA: American Alliance for Health, Physical Education, Recreation and Dance.

Tennis Industry, published bi-monthly by Tennis Industry, Inc. 230 West 13th St., Suite 1-B, New York, NY 10011, (212) 242-3687.

■ Organizations

American Amateur Racquetball Association, 1685 West Uintah, Colorado Springs, CO 80904-2921, (719) ■■■-■■■■.

American Paddle Association, P.O. Box 132049, Houston, TX 77219, 1-800-861-1539.

United States Handball Association, 2333 N. Tucson Blvd., Tucson, Arizona 85716, (520) 795-0434.

USA Volleyball, 3595 E. Fountain Blvd., Suite 1-2, Colorado Springs, CO 80910-1740, (719) 637-8300.

United States Squash Rackets Association, 23 Cynwood Road, P.O. Box 1216, Bala-Cynwyd, PA 19004, (610) 667-4006.

United States Tennis Association, 70 W. Red Oak Lane, White Plains, NY 10604, (914) 696-7000.

CHAPTER 24

Dance Facilities

Thomas H. Sawyer, Indiana State University

Learning Objectives

After reading this chapter, the student will be able to

■ recognize the basic needs of a general dance facility,

■ describe the criteria used to determine dance facility needs,

■ outline the construction components for dance areas, including modern dance, ballet, folk dance, social dance, dance production areas, arena stage areas, proscenium stage areas, instructional space, and auxiliary areas, and

■ appreciate the differences between elementary, secondary, and collegiate dance facilities.

Introduction

Elementary School

Dance in education is not a new idea. At all education levels it has existed by virtue of dedicated individuals. In the elementary schools, dance activities under a number of aliases—eurhythmics, rhythms, play party games, singing games, and folk dance—have been offered. Coming into the elementary school curriculum as an offshoot of the playground movement, the dance materials presented were usually happenstance (with a few exceptions in experimental schools). A classroom teacher may have been interested in folk dance or been faced with the necessity to prepare a May Day, a pageant, or a festival.

Within the past few years, many privately administered elementary schools and some public schools have made provisions for dance in the curriculum. By and large, existing physical education facilities are used.

Secondary School

Since the turn of the century, folk dance (usually European in origin) has been offered in physical education classes for girls in secondary schools. When folk dance lessons were first introduced, they were often limited in content and skill and were, as in the elementary school, an outcome of the playground movement. Toward the end of the 19th century, a few secondary schools in large cities had gymnasiums which were primarily equipped for gymnastics and other sports using limited-size courts. The use of these areas for dance was spasmodic and usually occurred in preparation for special events.

In the 1920s dance in education was materially advanced when Margaret H'Doubler initiated the first dance major at the University of Wisconsin. During this period clog and tap dance assumed a leading role in dance education, and Henry Ford promoted a return to the formal square dances of an earlier day, such as the Lancers (NDA, 1985).

By the 1930s, the country was sufficiently removed from its pioneer beginnings to acknowledge the joy and value of square dancing. The teaching of social dance was heavily emphasized as a means of implementing the social values of physical education. Modern dance—stemming from natural dance and from the influences of Martha Graham, Doris Humphrey, Charles Weidman, and others—began a slow but steady growth in curricular offerings. In 1931, great impetus was given to dance in education with the establishment of the National Section on Dance within the American Association for Health, Physical Education, and Recreation (NDA, 1985).

The advancement of physical education programs was not without trauma for teachers and administrators. Until World War I, with its emphasis upon fitness and recognition of the recreational needs of service personnel, it was difficult to finance facilities and staff for physical education. Immediately after the war, mobility and better communications enhanced the athletic program and, as the result of athletic needs, more gymnasiums and stadiums were built. The need for a gymnasium in secondary schools was thereby placed on a firm basis. The depression of the late 1920s and early 1930s, however, curbed these programs and the extensive expansion of facilities. World War II not only emphasized fitness and the recreational needs of service personnel but added a new dimension—recreational needs of war workers in factories, shipyards, and munition plants. The Cold War and the possibility of increased leisure time have reiterated the needs for enriched curricula and additional facilities.

Until recently, studios for dance at the secondary school level had dropped in priority behind athletic and aquatic facilities. At the beginning of the 20th century, dance was often better off than were sports in the low-ceilinged basement rooms and narrow hallways. As gymnasiums were built primarily for basketball programs, dance was relegated to a low priority in the use of these facilities both for class and after-school clubs. Moreover, the finish or seal on gymnasium floors made certain dance activities uncomfortable and precluded others. Within the past 10 to 15 years, there has been a growing consciousness of the needs of girls in secondary schools. As dance has proved its worth as a physiologically demanding and aesthetically rewarding activity, consideration is being given to the employment of specialized teachers and the provision of specialized areas for teaching dance at the secondary level.

Gradually clog and tap dance, natural dance, and later ballroom and square dance as well as modern dance have appeared in the secondary school curriculum. Of significance is the increasing interest of boys in the various forms of dance, especially modern jazz. Frequently, dance programs at the secondary school level are the result of grants from the National Endowment for the Arts (NDA, 1985).

College

As was true in elementary and secondary schools, facilities for dance education at the college level have developed slowly. The gymnasium dominated the scene, with dance scheduled "catch-as-catch-can" during available hours. As emphasis upon dance in teacher preparation increased and as colleges and universities became more involved in all phases of the arts, auxiliary rooms were planned for dance and related activities.

Basic Dance Facility Assumptions

The essential facilities should be supplied in sufficient quantity and quality to provide for all dance activities in the required and elective curriculums and in extracurricular programs. Particular attention should be given to adequate provision for dance performance, observation, and audience spaces.

Related portions of the activity complex should be provided and meet acceptable standards. These will include (NDA, 1985):

- Box office,
- Construction rooms for costumes, props and sets, and music (composing and recording),
- Costume storage areas,
- Custodial space,
- Laundry, cleaning and dying facilities,
- Listening areas,
- Locker-dressing rooms with make-up areas,
- Office space,
- Parking area,
- Public lavatories,
- Rest rooms (remote from toilets and showers),
- Shower area,
- Storage spaces (props and sets),
- Toilets, and
- Training room.

The following should be provided and meet established standards (NDA, 1985):

- Electrical installation,
- Lighting equipment,
- Acoustics,
- Ventilation,
- Heating,
- Floors,
- Walls,
- Sanitation,
- Safety,
- Drinking fountains,
- Sound systems,
- Filming and taping facilities,
- Installation of fixed equipment,
- Movable equipment, and
- Lines of traffic.

Dance facilities should be designed to serve both genders. Further, the dance facility should be readily accessible to outside entrances and be a unit unto itself even if it is attached to, or a part of, another building. Finally, the dance complex should be constructed, decorated, and furnished in an aesthetically pleasing manner and suitable for the pursuit of dance as an art form.

Criteria for Determining Facility Needs

The following criteria can be used to determine the dance facility needs when planning either a stand-alone dance facility or one for inclusion in a larger complex (NDA, 1985):

Total facilities should be determined according to the amount of emphasis placed on various aspects of the dance curriculum such as classes needed and areas for individual work and for extracurricular and concert practice.

Based on the design of the dance curriculum, facilities should be considered in terms of:

- Auxiliary space and equipment,
- Classroom space,
- Dance teaching space,
- Office space,
- Performance space,
- Practice space and choreography,
- Rehearsal space, and
- Research space.

Preferably three distinct areas should be provided: one area for folk and social dance, one area for modern dance, and one area for ballet.

Construction of Modern Dance and Ballet Areas

The following information is provided to assist in the development of state-of-the-art modern dance and ballet areas (NDA, 1985):

Dimensions,

- A minimum of 100 square feet per person is recommended. An area of 3,000 square feet will accommodate 30 students.
- If an area is to serve as an informal theater and instructional area, it should be between 4,800 and 5,000 square feet to accommodate both the class and the needs of the theater section.
- Ceiling height of 16 to 24 feet is recommended for all dance areas. Full height is essential for large dance areas (over 2,400 square feet) and 16 feet is minimum height for small dance areas. There is a feeling of height when the ceiling is high. Some dancers prefer a height of 16 to18 feet but consideration must be given to the total construction in the dance areas. In some instances, any change in the roof line may add prohibitive expense.

Floors

- Dance activities require air space between floor and foundation, and "floating" and/or spring floors for resiliency.
- Floors should be of hardwood (such as maple) of random lengths, and tongue-and -grooved; they should be laid with the grain going in one direction.
- Portable floors (Marly or stage-step) provide flexibility for use when both ballet and modern dance need to be accommodated.
- Floors should be non-slippery and constructed for easy cleaning.
- The finish should provide a smooth surface upon which dancers can glide with bare feet or soft sandals. Tung or linseed oil is considered by most to be a satisfactory finish; an alternative might be several coats of wood sealer. No chemical dust mops should be used to clean such floors, only a slightly damp mop.

Doors

There should be wide double doors to permit traffic flow into and out of the room. The sills of such doors should be level with the floor to allow for moving large equipment such as a piano.

Figure 24.1 Example of a dance exerciser instructor's elevated platform. This one is permanently located in one position; whereas, in some facilities they are portable and can be moved to other locations. Further, some facilities roll them under the wall when not in use so the area can be used for other activities.

Walls

- Walls should be smooth and easily maintained.
- Consideration should be given to having one unobstructed wall of neutral background for filming purposes.
- Stress factors of the walls should be considered to support ballet barres and mirrors.
- Thin walls are inadequate.
- It is desirable to sound-proof walls especially in listening areas.

Lighting

- Incandescent light is preferable to fluorescent light.
- Rheostat lights that also serve as houselights during performances should be controlled from wall switches as well as from the light control board.
- Consideration should be given to natural lighting. Large windows contribute to an aesthetically and phychologically desirable atmosphere. The best location for windows is the north wall to avoid direct sunlight.
- Windows should be curtained so the studio can be darkened for film showing and studio performances.
- When total construction necessitates no windows, the aesthetics may be improved by the use of a pastel color on the walls or draperies serving both aesthetic and acoustical purposes.

Acoustics and Sound Equipment

- When one studio is directly over another or over offices, acoustical treatment is necessary.
- Placement of sound equipment such as record player, turntable, microphones, and speakers should be considered in the initial planning in terms of both performance and security.
- An adequate number of speakers, installed in or near ceiling height, should be located so participants can hear both music and instruction.
- Heavy equipment should be placed on stands of table height equipped with rollers.
- Electrical outlets should be spaced on every wall and located close to where equipment will be used. Four-plex outlets are needed close to the area where most equipment is used (e.g., video-tape recorders, tape deck and amplifiers for performance, and stage manager's desk for cueing lights).

Storage Space

- Locked storage space for sound equipment should be adjacent to the dance area and locked. Storage rooms should have double doors and a flush threshold for easy movement of large equipment such as a piano.
- Built-in storage space for records, sound equipment, tapes, and musical instruments should be provided.
- A sound-proof area for use of students and instructors in listening to recordings and tapes and

Figure 24.2 Ballet bar and mirrors.

viewing videotapes is highly desirable. This area should have adequate acoustics, ventilation, and electrical outlets.

Wiring

- Heavy-duty wiring is essential for all dance facilities. Wiring should be capable of carrying a portable light board as well as phonographs, additional speakers, tape recorders, and projectors. Wall outlets should be plentiful.
- Television conduits should be installed at the time a building is constructed.

Temperature and Ventilation

- Temperature should be maintained at 65° to 72° F (22°-26° C). The thermostat should be located in the studio areas.
- The air should be well circulated and consideration should be given to the use of natural air. Humidity should be no greater than 95%.
- Mechanisms for heating and circulating of air should be as nearly silent as possible to avoid interfering with the quality of sound and its reception.

Accessories

- Leaf-fold mirrors, which can be folded for protection or curtained during performances, may be installed along two adjoining walls so that movement can be analyzed from two directions. Wall mirrors at least six feet high should be installed flush with the wall and raised 1 or $1^1/_2$ feet from the floor.
- Ballet barres should be made of wood, preferably oak or aluminum, and be smooth in texture. The minimum length to accommodate one dancer is five feet. Barres from 40 to 42 inches in height may be installed permanently; they should extend six to eight inches from the wall. If feasible, consider double barres—one at 36 inches, and one at 42 inches. If necessary, barres may be placed in front of mirrors. The barre supports may be screwed into recessed floor sockets just in front of the mirror, thus facilitating the removal of the barre and supports when not needed.
- Custom-made percussion cabinets mounted on rollers are a fine accessory. They may have a carpeted top surface, slide-out drawers lined with

felt for small instruments, and larger partitions to accommodate cymbals and drums.

■ Heavy sound equipment should be built-in or placed on stands of table height equipped with rollers for ease of transportation.

■ Since moving affects the tuning of a piano, this instrument should be placed where it will not have to be moved. A piano should be placed on an inside wall where it will not be subject to extreme heat or cold, and be protected by a suitable cover and lock. It should be placed on a heavy-duty dolly if it is to be moved frequently.

■ Chalkboards and tackboards are useful accessories.

■ Telephone.

■ A glass-enclosed exhibit case for photographs, costumes, costume plates, manuscripts, and other items may be installed near the dance area. A building foyer may be utilized.

■ The atmosphere for dance should be conducive to artistic endeavors. Soft colors, clear lighting, and spaciousness are pleasing to both dancers and spectators.

Construction of Folk and Social Dance Areas

The following information is provided to assist in the development of state-of-the-art folk and social dance areas (NDA, 1985):

Dimensions

■ An area of 5,400 square feet (54 ft. × 100 ft. is suggested) will accommodate a class of approximately 60 students.

■ Dance areas are generally rectangular with a length-width ratio of approximately 3 to 2 (for example, 90 feet × 60 feet).

■ Ceiling height should be in proportion to the size of the room but never lower than 12 feet.

■ An outside entrance into a main corridor of the building will provide for traffic flow of the relatively large groups using the area.

Floors

Floors as described in the section on ballet and modern dance (see p. ●●●) are necessary. However, an epoxy finish, rather than tung oil, will enable the use of street shoes without damage to the floor.

Lighting and Ventilation

■ Acoustics and sound Equipment (see above),

■ Storage space (see above),

■ Wiring (see first point under wiring, above), and

■ Temperature and ventilation (see above).

Accessories

■ Racks for coats and books should be installed either within the dance area or along the outside corridor wall.

■ Tackboards, chalkboards, and display cases are highly desirable.

Dance Production Areas

While a well-equipped theater is the ideal dance performance area, it is not always possible to have such a facility. The alternative is to provide a large area for both instructional and performance activities. The area may be equipped with a balcony for observation of classes and for audience seating during performances. Other seating arrangements such as portable bleachers may also be desirable. A large area may be equipped to provide for arena or proscenium staging, or both.

Arena Stage Area

The planning for an arena stage area should include performance space, seating, lighting, sound equipment, control booths, and wiring. The following describes the specifics needed in each area:

Performance Space

The performance area should contain between 875 and 1,200 square feet (NDA, 1985).

Seating Space

The most desirable seating capacity for performances should accommodate 300 to 500 people. The entire performing area should be visible from all seats. The seating arrangement should be flexible. Seats may be on movable risers so space may be used in a variety of ways. Raked seating is essential. Adequate entrances, exits, and exit lights should be provided for performers and audience in accordance with local fire codes.

Lighting

Lighting should be available from all directions. It should be possible to use gels on all lighting instruments except house lights. All lights should be on separate dimmers. A sufficient number of electrical out-

Figure 24.3 The proscenium arch surrounds the stage like a picture frame.

lets should be available. When possible, all lights should be operated from a single console within the control booth.

Sound Equipment

Equipment should be operated from a control booth. Speakers for amplification should be placed so both performers and audience can hear. Backstage monitors should be used.

Control Booths

Provision should be made for control booths or areas with full view of the stage area to operate lights and sound.

Wiring

Wiring should be adequate to carry a portable light board, a phonograph, tape recorder, speaker system, projector, and follow spots (see local electric codes).

Proscenium Stage Area

The planning for a proscenium stage area should include performance space, seating, curtains, teasers, battens, lighting, sound equipment, control booths, and live musicians. The following describes the specifics needed in each area:

Performance Space

The minimum performance area should be 1,200 square feet (30 feet by 40 feet). The two wing areas combined should be equal to the amount of visible stage space. Space should be provided for musicians, chairs, and lighted music stands. Placement of musicians should not interfere with the visibility of the stage or the sound of the music (NDA, 1985).

Seating Space

A balcony with permanently installed raked seating is desirable, with the possibility of portable risers below. The entire performing area should be visible from all seats. The number of seats should be planned for estimated size of audience.

Curtains, Teasers, Battens

Hand control is preferable to a mechanically controlled front curtain. Side curtains (legs) or flats should be provided on both sides of the stage for entrances and exits. Flexible tracks to move the curtain horizontally should be considered. Asbestos teasers and tormentors are needed for safety and masking. Battens to be used for hanging scenery, sky drop, or film screen should be suspended above the visible stage area. Provision should be made for lowering and raising battens for the attachment of scenery. Lines should be attached to a pin rail located at one side of the stage. Metal grids are also usable. The back wall should be free of visible obstructions and painted white for projections. Curtains and flats should be light, absorbent, and of neutral or dark color.

Lighting Equipment

Provision should be made for side lighting, front lighting, and overhead border lighting. Three separate circuits should be provided to be used singly or in combination. There should be front ceiling beam lighting, balcony lighting, or both. Crawl space should be provided in the ceiling above the beams to permit focusing and repair work. It should be possible to use gels on all lights except house lights. All instruments should be on separate dimmers. A sufficient number of electrical outlets should be located in floor pockets or wall spaces in the wings. A low wattage light should be installed for cueing performers and crew members at the side of the front stage. When possible, all lights should be operated from a single console within the control booth.

Sound Equipment

Equipment should be operated from the control booth. Speakers for amplification should be placed so both performers and audience can hear. An intercom should be used to link the backstage, dressing rooms, and control booth. Telephones to handle outside calls should be located in the box office and backstage. The backstage phone should be equipped with a signal light.

Live Musicians

If feasible, space should be allocated for performance appearances.

Control Booths

Control booths for lights, sound, and projections should be centered at the audience end of the facility and should include soundproofing, a large window for viewing the stage, built-in counters and shelves for storing equipment, and an intercom for communication with the backstage area.

Auxiliary Areas

The following auxiliary areas need to be included in the planning process for a dance facility:

Costume Room

A costume room for constructing, fitting, cleaning, and storing should be a minimum of 400 square feet and be equipped with or accessible to

- Built-in cabinets with shelves and drawers, and racks for hanging and storing costumes,
- Cleaning machine,
- Control room with toilet facilities,
- Cutting table,
- Double door with a flush threshold to facilitate moving costume racks,
- Dress forms,
- Ironing boards and steam irons,
- Laundry tubs and dying facilities,
- Sewing machines,
- Tackboard and chalkboard affixed to one wall,
- Three-way mirror, and
- Washing machine and dryer.

Dressing Rooms

Dressing rooms should be provided for men and women. They should be equipped with costume racks, chairs, wash basins, lighted mirrors, toilets and showers, and a first aid kit.

Make-up Room

The make-up room should be located between the men's and women's dressing rooms and be furnished with lighted mirrors, built-in shelves, make-up tables, chairs, wash basins, and storage space.

Scene and Prop Room

The scene and prop room should be located as close to the stage area as feasible. It should be a minimum of 400 to 500 square feet and have a ceiling height of at least 16 feet, although 24 feet is preferable.

The floor should have a paint-resistant surface. Proper ventilation is necessary to avoid fumes from paint and glue. The room should be furnished with built-in bins and shelves for storage of nails, brushes, screws, paints, and glues; a pegboard mounted flush with the wall for hanging tools; a built-in workbench; a wash sink; outlets for electrical tools; and a chalkboard and tackboard. Storage space for props should be a minimum of 500 square feet with a 16- to 24-foot ceiling; it should be easily accessible to the backstage area (NDA, 1985).

Box Office (Ticket Booth)

The box office should have locked racks for tickets, a locked drawer for currency, a telephone with an outside line, and an intercom to the backstage area.

Foyer

It is desirable to provide a social area where the audience and performers may meet following a production. It should be situated adjacent to the performing area and include attractive decorations, a comfortable seating arrangement, display cases, and an adjoining small kitchen for preparing refreshments.

Additional Instructional and Laboratory Facility Needs Based on the Size of the Dance Program and Curriculum

Three areas need to be planned for in the dance facility, including teaching space, office space, and auxiliary space.

Teaching Space

The following are planning considerations for dance teaching areas:

■ There should be a minimum of one large teaching and performance area. This area should have a 24-foot ceiling and resilient floors, and be equipped with special lighting for performance, sound equipment, a communications media, an observation balcony, and good ventilation and lighting.
■ Two additional areas should be provided: an area for ballet and modern dance, and an area for jazz, social, and folk dance.
■ Provision should be made for well-designed and -equipped classrooms and seminar and lecture rooms for instructional use.

■ In addition to the performance area, there should be rehearsal space that is somewhat larger than the area designed for performance.
■ There should be an area for practice and choreography that is equipped with phonographs, tape machines, and video-tape equipment.
■ A library and reference room with an adjoining study area for books, music, records, tapes, and copying machine should be available.
■ Provision should be made for a soundproof recording studio large enough to accommodate a piano and small orchestra, turntables and tape recorder. It should have built-in shelves for storage and be not less than 300 square feet.
■ Storage space for musical instruments should be provided.

Office Space

The dance facility office space should include the following:

■ There should be a centralized office for unified administration.
■ A private office and conference space for the director of the dance program should be available.
■ There should be office space for faculty members and for technical personnel.
■ Supporting space for office equipment and storage should be provided.
■ Laboratory space for faculty should be available.

Auxiliary Space

Additional auxiliary space might include the following:

■ It is desirable to have a reception-social room (with adjoining kitchen) for use by students, faculty, and community groups on special occasions.
■ Locker-shower areas should be available for students and faculty of both genders.
■ A faculty conference room should be provided.
■ A rehabilitation or therapy room is desirable.

Adaptation of Dance Facilities and Equipment

Since local conditions may demand modification of ideal dance facilities while a dance program is being developed, this section describes some of the adaptations that may be feasible.

Elementary School

Current Practices

Small gymnasiums are used most frequently, with cafeteria-gymnasiums, multipurpose rooms, and auditorium-gymnasiums following in close order. The size of classes ranges from 25 to 70 pupils, with 30 being the average size.

With regard to floor surfaces used for the instruction of dance, hardwood predominates, with linoleum tile running second. The floors in winter should be heated.

As far as equipment was concerned, all schools but one have a record player with convenient electrical outlets, but just over half the schools report having sufficient recordings. The same is true of movable tables with rollers for record players, and of controlled speeds and amplification of recordings. Tape recorders are available in approximately half the schools. There is some evidence of percussion equipment, principally rhythm band instruments, with a few schools having either a Chinese tom-tom or a Gretsch dance drum. Three-fourths of the schools report chalkboards and nearly half of them report bulletin boards in use as teaching aids. Approximately half of the schools cite that storage space is available for recordings and percussion instruments.

Use of Limited Facilities and Equipment

Practically speaking, it is impossible to secure ideal dance facilities in all situations at the elementary school level. Community socio-economic conditions virtually negate such a dream. Lack of ideal facilities and equipment is no reason to omit dance experiences for children. An outstanding authority on children's movement experiences has stated that a multipurpose room is quite adequate for the dance program. Another expert found that children can be taught to move lightweight classroom furniture efficiently so that dance space is available. By constant attention to opportunities for renovations in a school (or a school system), one may ask for use of renovated space, for installation of bulletin boards and electrical outlets, and even for changes in floor surfaces. Teacher initiative is a priority if space for dance is to be acquired.

Recommendations

Dance areas for elementary school children should be large enough to accommodate approximately 30 students. Rooms below ground level are inadvisable because of possible dampness and lack of adequate ventilation. As increasing numbers of elementary schools are built on a one-floor plan with outdoor exits for individual classrooms, basement facilities will gradually vanish.

Hardwood is advised for dance floors. Tile floors, which frequently are laid directly on cement or concrete, are cold to the touch, often slippery, and conducive to injury. Because tile flooring allows no resiliency for foot action, it can lead to painful shin splints.

There is no answer to the exact type of dance facility that should be provided. Except under unusual circumstances, economics rule out the provision for a dance studio. The combination gymnasium-lunch room is not recommended because of loss of time for classes before, after, and during lunch hours, and the health hazards of dust on food and lunch debris in the activity area. The stage-auditorium, stage-gymnasium, small gymnasium, multipurpose room, or large playroom may be used if adequate electrical outlets and wiring for record players, tape recorders, and minimal stage lighting can be provided.

The rather informal dance programs presented at the elementary school level can often be accommodated by seating the children on the floor and visitors on chairs around three sides of one end of the dance area. Usually storage space for recordings and simple percussion equipment is available in, or adjacent to, such areas. Many physical education items can be used in the dance program. Jumping ropes, balls, boxes, benches, mats, and other play apparatus lend themselves to creative uses.

Dance for children has become an established activity in elementary school programs. It can only take place, however, when space and equipment are provided, time is allocated, and leadership is available.

Secondary School

Current Practices

It is extremely difficult to secure detailed information on dance programs at the secondary school level. The size of areas used for dance varies from extremely small to extremely large, with a rectangular shape being most common. In height, the areas vary from 8 feet to 40 feet. Record players and tape recorders are usually available. Percussion instruments, drums predominating, are also in use. Some schools have closet space set aside for costumes and even a full costume room. Ballet barres and mirrors are in use. Wooden floors predominate. One school reports that excellent additional practice space is available, and several schools note that smaller additional space is available, and several schools note that smaller additional space is available only when not in use by other groups.

Use of Limited Facilities and Equipment

Few secondary schools have specialized facilities for dance. One reason is that there has not been adequate emphasis on dance in the secondary school curriculum. There is some indication, however, that specialized concentrations (dance, sports, aquatics, gymnastics) in teacher preparation, and a cultural emphasis upon the arts are beginning to alter this pattern, particularly in suburban areas and in certain consolidated school districts. As these programs begin to establish their value, obtaining facilities will become easier.

Meanwhile, the standard gymnasium can be used. Teachers who are interested in providing dance experiences for their students can plan curricular units, secure a few portable barres, borrow a record player and/or tape recorder from the audiovisual supply room, find storage area for a few percussion instruments, and secure space for a costume closet. The floor with the usual gymnasium seal on it is not ideal but can be used. The battle for time allotments and space assignment is perennial. Interest and effort can perform wonders.

Recommendations

A minimum dance facility should provide 100 square feet per student, one dimension to exceed 60 feet; full-length mirrors at a corner for analysis of skill from two directions; a speaker system designed to distribute sound evenly throughout the room; a control system for record players and microphones; and practice barres on one wall at heights of 34 inches and 42 inches. For modern dance, the floor should be of hard northern maple that has been sealed and then buffed with fine abrasive. Additional suggestions follow (NDA, 1985):

Equipment. As in the case of the elementary school, physical education equipment such as balls, ropes, and gymnastic apparatus may be used. Stall bars, if available, are an excellent substitute for ballet barres and a fine medium for creative activity.

By wise planning, basic equipment (recordings, percussion instruments, and portable lighting boards) can be floated from school to school for production use.

Portable percussion racks made in an industrial arts department solve the problems of easy storage and efficient class and program use. Portable mirrors, six feet tall and eight feet wide, can be constructed 1^1/$_2$ feet from the floor on rollers and moved into the dance area if wall-mounted mirrors are not feasible. Portable ballet barres of lightweight aluminum are desirable when unobstructed wall space is at a premium.

Floors. Poor floors should be covered by Marly dance flooring rather than a ground cloth.

Areas. Investigation of the following areas may reveal available spaces for dance: adaptive rooms, gymnastic rooms, weight control rooms, recreational game rooms. Careful pre-planning of new facilities suggests the possibility of combining two or more of these. Two community resources are feasible—churches and local theater groups. Churches are now interested in dance. Either temporary or permanent use of a large classroom or a church auditorium may be possible. Community theatre groups are adding dance experiences for all age levels to their gamut of activities. It may be possible to arrange for use of their areas during the school day.

The possibility of pooled resources in the performing arts—dance, drama, music—opens wide potential in the development of excellent facilities, economy in their use by several departments, and rich experiences in multimedia.

Performing Arts for Modern Dance or Ballet

The following specific recommendations are made for modern dance and ballet areas (NDA, 1985):

■ The stage should be situated at the end of the room that can best provide entrances for the dancers. The dancers' entrances should be out of the audience's view.
■ The stage can be formed by curtains or flats.
■ A back curtain should have a center opening and be hung at least three feet forward of the back wall to provide crossover space for the performers.
■ In the case of a raised stage, the front curtain should be set back about four feet from the raised edge to provide an apron (forestage).
■ Side curtains or flats should be provided.
■ If curtains cannot be used, an open stage is advisable. The folding mats used in physical education can be set on edge to form entrances and exits. Flats and portable screens are alternative possibilities.

Performing Area for Folk and Social Dance

The following specific recommendations are made for folk and social dance areas (NDA, 1985):

■ Roll-away bleachers can be installed at one end of the room.
■ Provision should be made for storage of folding chairs, which can be placed along the side walls.
■ An auxiliary performing space can be a patio or other outdoor area, such as a dance green or a

broad, level surface at the entrance to a school building, which can be adapted for occasional use for dance performances. Marly dance floorings may be placed on the cement surface to protect the dancer's feet and legs.

As in the case of elementary schools, specific dance facilities are not feasible in all secondary schools. Dance is possible, however, depending on the teacher's interest, effort, and ability to adapt to the situation.

College/University

As new facilities have been constructed and older facilities remodeled in the larger colleges and universities, there seems to be little excuse for omission of areas specifically planned for dance. The increasing emphasis upon dance as a major field and the increasing interrelationships among the performing arts have placed dance in a position of importance in college planning.

■ Summary

Dance facilities are often ignored and provided facilities that are not even close to adequate. This chapter has provided information to assist the planners of HPERD facilities at the elementary, secondary, and collegiate level in properly planning appropriate and adequate dance facilities.

Learning Objective 1: The student will be able to recognize the basic needs of a general dance facility.

The planner needs to be aware what the facility requirements are for elementary, secondary, and college dance programs, as well as private dance programs taught outside the school. It is important to understand the programs and recognize the needs of the teachers and participants.

Learning Objective 2: The student will be able to describe the criteria used to determine dance facility needs.

The planner needs to be aware of the criteria established by the dance profession for the various dance facilities (i.e., elementary, secondary, and postsecondary, as well as modern, ballet, folk, and social dance). The criteria for an instructional setting are different than for a performance area. The planner needs to understand the differences clearly.

Learning Objective 3: The student will be able to outline the specific construction components for the various dance facility areas.

The dance facility planner must first understand the dance program before the facility can be constructed. Once the program is established, the components can be planned. Generally the components of a dance program include instructional space, performance space, storage and office areas, dressing space, and dance production areas. The planners need to consider the best types of walls, ceiling, floor, environmental controls, lighting, acoustics, and sound systems.

Learning Objective 4: The student will be able to appreciate the differences between the three levels of educational dance programs.

There are distinct differences between instructional programs at the elementary, secondary, and postsecondary levels. Planners must understand these differences before planning a dance facility.

■ Case Study

You have been selected by a state university to assist in the planning of a dance facility that will service students from preschool to the university level. Currently, a small dance facility is located in the aging laboratory school, which is adjacent to a small park connecting the laboratory school with the university theater and fine arts building. The university has decided to develop a BS in dance in conjunction with the theater department. There will also be a traveling dance troupe to promote dance, theater, arts, and the university.

The university has received a $10,000,000 gift from a wealthy alumnas who loves the theater and arts and is especially taken with dance. She wants the money to be used to renovate the older facility and construct a new connecting facility for the new dance major. Your task will be to develop plans for a dance facility that will be used for instruction from pre-schoolers to college students and older adults in the community. The facility will include instructional spaces, a performance area, dressing area, storage spaces, offices, ticket booth, lobby, etc. There will also be an outdoor performance space developed in the park area.

■ Reference

National Dance Association. (1985). **Dance facilities.** Reston, VA: American Alliance for Health, Physical Education, Recreation, and Dance.

CHAPTER 25

Field Spaces

Arthur H. Mittelstaedt, Jr., Recreation Safety Institute ■ Thomas H. Sawyer, Indiana State University

Learning Objective

After reading this chapter, the student will be able to

■ design a safe outdoor sport field complex.

Introduction

Sport fields generally require the largest amount of space in an outdoor complex. The activities that can be conducted are varied and require a variety of sizes. Additional acreage is required for spectators, officials, service personnel, and service areas (i.e., concessions, restrooms, equipment storage, score boards, and press box).

The usability of the areas, particularly at night and after inclement weather, often requires substantial support utilities such as communication, drainage, irrigation, lighting, security, and sewer systems. Further, the surface material, synthetic or natural, and its substructure systems are also critical.

The various sport field venues that will be highlighted in this chapter include baseball/softball, boccie, cricket, crochet, field hockey, football, lacrosse, lawn badminton, lawn bowling, lawn volleyball, rugby, soccer, and team handball. The beginning of the chapter will highlight common planning challenges for all fields, and the latter portion will cover specific needs for the various fields.

Safety and Fields

The owner of a potential ballfield property must apply the sound and proven guidelines for planning a facility that are outlined in this text to reduce the athletes' exposure to risks (Chapters 2 and 3.) The planning process should include an analysis of the causation of injuries. The following are common causes for injuries on field spaces:

1. Location
   a. The size of the field area is critical. A field should have *10-yard* safety buffers around the perimeter to protect athletes and spectators.
   b. Neither athletes nor spectators should be exposed to any of the following hazards, and planners need to consider each concern when selecting a location for a field:
      1) *Streets* should not be located any closer than 100 yards to a facility.
      2) *Railroad tracks*, like streets, should not be any closer than 100 yards to a facility.
      3) *Water courses*, man-made culverts, or natural streamways can contain deep, fast-moving water that can trap or entangle

people who slip, walk, or slide into them. They should not be any closer than 100 yards to a facility.

4) *Trenches or gulleys* can be a hazard holding deep muck, hidden snakes, reptiles, or rodents, or containing wires, quicksand, or reinforcing rods that can pierce or entrap a person. They should not be any closer than 100 yards to a facility.

5) *Settlement ponds or basins* can contain toxic liquids, silt, or flammable materials and should not be any closer than 100 yards to a facility.

6) *Storage yards,* with old concrete or other culvert pipes that can roll and crush, junk cars and machinery that can cut or pierce, old wood and metal junk piles, and hazardous drums of liquids (i.e., lead paint, paints, sealants) or acids that can explode or burn, should not be any closer than 100 yards to a facility.

7) *Climatic noise, odors, smoke, and dust* should be avoided.

c. The protective perimeter of the area should consist of fencing, landscaping, or walls to keep spectators away from the playing field and to keep players within the playing field.

d. The area must not consist of soils that are toxic, poor-draining, decaying, or of poor structure. They should be free of debris and glass.

e. In order to protect the athletes and spectators, the field space should be located in an area that has no other activity spaces in close proximity.

f. The visibility of the entire area should accommodate foot and vehicle security.

g. The area should be illuminated at critical times to facilitate supervision and security.

h. Multipurpose fields that are used for baseball or softball as well as soccer, field hockey, or football can, have ruts that create dangerous high-speed bounces on the baseball or softball playing surface.

i. The games of baseball and softball have three major concerns for spectators and parking areas—foul balls, home runs, and overthrows.

2. Users

a. The participants' age, gender, skill levels and/or experience must be considered in creating facilities for all participants.

b. The area must be accesible to physically and mentally challenged participants and spectators.

3. Site Conditions

a. Concealment areas caused by shrubbery or tree canopy or adjacent structures should be eliminated to deter improper activity.

b. The public comfort for players and spectators must include rest room facilities close to supervised areas, properly designed and positioned litter containers, benches, and drinking fountains.

4. Space

a. The safety or buffer zone around the field and its appurtenance and equipment must be large enough to keep players from hitting stationary objects along its perimeter.

b. The padding or other accepted proven standards, such as releaseable or yieldable devices for outfield fences, stanchions, fences or walls and all other perimeter stationary obstructions, must be used and/or have sufficient buffered perimeter areas.

c. The safety glazing of nearby windows, observation panels, and doors is a necessity.

d. The relationship of fields and appurtenance among facilities should be harmonious and complimentary in encouraging and facilitating play.

5. Circulation

a. The traffic flow of users from one field or appurtenance to another should be designed to be safe.

6. Materials

a. The durability and maintainability of the types of appurtenances within and adjacent to the field must be considered.

7. Access

a. The pedestrian, player, and spectator traffic around the activity field is important. The field must be located so that there is no interference with the traffic of people, buses, automobiles, service vehicles, vendors, and bicycles. Pedestrian traffic should be routed to have easy access to comfort stations, security, refreshments, lockers, and other related facilities.

b. The automotive and service (i.e., lawn mowers, maintenance vehicles) driveways should not bisect or parallel open play or human access areas.

c. Immovable barriers should be installed to separate any automotive traffic routes from all activity areas.

d. Maintenance vehicle access to fields should have the correct sub-base and surface materials installed so as to limit wear and irregular surfaces.

8. Utility Lines

a. The utility lines, above, on, or below ground should be positioned so as not interfere with players, the game, or spectators, nor to be accessible to contact with any person.

b. Storm drains are frequent hazards, often within the field limits or directly adjacent to them. Players can have their feet entrapped by such street-sized drains.

c. Irrigation heads for pop-up or quick-couple sprinklers can cause tripping if not designed properly.

d. Relocatable aluminum irrigation pipes and sports equipment left on the field are also hazardous.

e. Power lines, poles, transformers and control panels must not be in proximity to playing and/or spectator areas. They should be in remote and inaccessible, secure locations.

f. Fire hydrants and even drinking fountains must not be placed in the vincity of the area of play.

Field Turf

Two types of turf are used on sport fields—synthetic and natural. (See Chapter 16 for a complete discussion of natural turf.) Between the late 1960s through the late '80s many natural turf fields were converted to synthetic fields. These conversions were intended to reduce the cost of maintenance and to provide flexibility to sport schedulers without concern about the wear and tear on the natural turf being used by numerous sport teams and "mother nature." Since the late 1980s the conversion back to natural turf has increased to reduce injuries.

Synthetic Surface

Synthetic materials can be soft or firm. They can be piled, turfed, graveled, or smoothed. They can be rolled or poured, paneled or sprayed. The ingredients of the turf can be rubber, polymer, pigment, PVC, thermset, theromsplastic, and a host of other new high-tech materials. Synthetic products have substrates that are also of varied ingredients.

Synthetic turf is attractive to players for a number of reasons, including that the surface and footwear interact well for better footing, the surface stays in place, it is resilient, balls bounce well, the surface dries rapidly, and it has a cooling effect. It also has distractions for players, including that the surface has little resiliency, balls respond inconsistently, the surface affects the speed of the ball (making it faster), and the surface is very hot on hot days.

Attractions for operators include that the surface is repairable, picturesque, portable, durable, stable, and paintable, and drains rapidly. However, the greatest detractor of synthetic surfaces for the operator is life of the surface, approximately 15 years.

Seating

All fields must have adequate seating for spectators. Numerous types of seating are available, from concrete stands to steel or wood bleachers of various heights, to portable aluminum bleachers. The seating has changed from 18 inches wide to 20 inches to accommodate the spectators' larger backsides. Many of the seats are fiberglass rather than wood and some are aluminum. The seats are contoured for greater comfort and some areas have soft theater seating. The choice comes down to the size of the purchaser's pocketbook.

The planners need to consider the following safety suggestions when developing seating for spectators for outdoor events: (1) conforming to ADA guidelines (see Chapter 8), (2) providing railings for each side and the top row to prevent falls, (3) closing areas under each row of seats to prevent children from falling through or climbing, (4) enclosing the structure to gain space for storage, concessions, or rest rooms and at the same time preventing children from playing under the bleachers, and (5) providing aisles with railings for ease of accessing seating.

Lighting

Lighting (illumination) is critical to safety and revenue generation. The illumination level for baseball and softball is 20 foot-candles for the outfield and 30 for the infield. The lighting for other team sport fields (i.e., field hockey, football, lacrosse, rugby, and soccer) requires a minimum of 30 foot-candles. If sporting events are to be televised, the lighting requirement will be much different. However, if this happens only occasionally, portable-lighting companies can be

Figure 25.1 Examples of bleacher seating, Rose Hulman Institute of Technology.

Figure 25.2 Example of outdoor lighting, Indiana State University.

Figure 25.3 Example of safety considerations for outdoor fencing, DePauw University.

hired to provide additional lighting requirements. The air should be monitored for contaminantes that can cause the reflector surface to change by increasing diffusion and decreasing total reflection. This results in less total light energy leaving the face of the light, with less lumens. There should be no shadows on the field that create unsafe catching, nor should there be any glare or irregular bright patches. All stanchions or poles must be outside the field of play.

Orientation

There are various thoughts as to the orientation of baseball and softball fields. It depends on where the field is and the time games are to be held. One school of thought is that the back of home plate should be set to point south to southwest or have the baseline from home plate to first base run in an easterly direction. The theory is for the batter to look into the sun, which implies the catcher as well. Another thought is for the batter to look away from the sun. Presently, the orientation is probably the least of the safety problems. However, since batter/catcher and pitcher are in the most hazardous positions, they still require consideration. A line through these positions would be the axis for orienta-tion for either position. After locating the axis, locate the sun's position at sunrise, early morning, late afternoon, and sunset. Establish an orientation for the field that avoids the batter/catcher and pitcher from facing directly into the early morning or late afternoon sun.

All other fields should run north to south to avoid the direct movement of the sun from east to west. However, if all contests are played in the evening after sundown, the sun does not become a factor.

Fencing

The entire field must be fenced. The height of the fence ranges from four feet for youth fields to eight feet for interscholastic and up. A number of fields have six-foot fences, which is acceptable but not ideal. The fence should be sturdy enough to withstand an athlete's weight as well as serve as a wind screen. The fence should start at eight feet as it leaves the backstop around the circumference of the field, including in front of the dugouts. The top of the fence should be covered with a colorful vinyl tube to protect the players from injury and as a reference point. The fencing should be attached on the field side of the poles, with all attachments and prongs on the outside of the fence. The fence should be stretched down from the top to the tension rail on the bottom. The fence is meant to protect players as well as spectators. It should be no closer than 25 feet to the sidelines or foul line but preferably 50 to 75 feet.

Drainage and Irrigation

A properly constructed sport field has a good drainage system so that play can resume after a short

Figure 25.4 French drains.

waiting period and the turf is not destroyed when played upon in a wet condition. Turf that is too wet or too dry will be compromised. The subsoil of the field should be composed of sand (80–90% sand base) to improve the speed of drainage. The playing field should be crowned to allow the heavy rainwater that cannot be absorbed to drain to the sidelines. The slope on either side of the crown should not exceed $1/_4$ inch per foot toward the sideline drainage area. The sideline drainage area should be at least five yards from the playing field, contoured and sloped to catch the runoff to direct it to large drains (see Figures 25.4a, b) that are approximately 20 yards apart along the sidelines. These drains should be approximately 15 to 20 feet deep with a three- to five-foot diameter filled with gravel and covered with a metal grate. Marketers always say the key to sales is "location, location, location." The key to a great field is drainage, drainage, drainage.

The irrigation of a field is very important in dry climates. There are basically three types of irrigation systems available for fields, including underground with sprinkler heads throughout the field space, underground with sprinkler heads on the perimeter of the field, and above ground with portable piping and sprinkler heads or hoses. The latter option is very la-

bor intensive and requires a lot of equipment storage. The other options are the most convenient and least labor intensive.

The planners of the irrigation system need to consider the following: (1) the safety of the participants (i.e., perimeter or within-field sprinkler layout), (2) type of sprinkler heads, (3) the watering pattern layout (i.e., the number of overlapping zones needed, based on the available water pressure, to reach all areas of the field evenly), (4) the source of water (i.e., wells with a pumping system or government or private water company), (5) a timing system, (6) a plan for winterizing in climates that have temperatures below freezing, (7) tie-ins for drinking fountains and hose bibs, and (8) the possibility of a liquid fertilization option.

Planning Tip for Sport Fields

1. Have good construction specifications.
2. Have good communications between all parties throughout the project.
3. Be able to compromise and solve problems as they develop.
4. Use sound agronomics including planning surface and subsurface drainage, doing a good job of soil preparation, and planting turfgrass adapted to the conditions and intended use.
5. Follow a good fertilization, irrigation, and mowing program during establishment of the turf.

Sport Field Service Areas

Sport field service areas include concessions areas, press box, restrooms, score boards, and storage. These areas are very important to spectators and support staff. If the service areas are well designed and maintained, they will increase fan loyalty.

Concessions Area

The concessions area should be centralized behind home plate or on both sides of the field. The area can be constructed from wood or concrete block. It should have plenty of counter space for preparation of products and to service the patrons. The floor should be concrete with numerous drains. There should be at least one double sink and ample cabinet space for storage. The area should have numerous electrical outlets and GFI outlets near water sources. The lighting should be flourescent. The equipment in the area should include refrigerator, freezer, stove top with at least four cooking elements, microwave, pop-

Figure 25.5 A. Irrigation system control box. **B.** Draining irrigation system. **C.** Footbball press box **D.** Baseball press box, DePauw University.

corn popper, hot dog cooker/warmer, coffee maker, soda fountain dispenser, ceiling fans, shelving for merchandise, sign board for advertising, and cash register.

Press Box

The press box is important for the press, scouts, scoreboard operator, and those filming games. The press box should be located higher than the highest part of the bleachers. The size will be dependent upon the number of users. It should have an unobstructed view of the playing field. The following should be available for the press: (1) table to write on or broadcast from; (2) comfortable chairs; (3) phone hook-ups; (4) computer hook-ups; (5) electrical outlets; (6) refrigerator; (7) coffee maker; (8) separate areas for press, radio announcers, scorekeeper, PA announcer, coaches, and scouts; and (9) an area above the press area exclusively for filming games. These facilities are generally constructed of wood with flourescent lighting.

Rest Rooms

There need to be numerous restrooms provided, preferably not portable. The number of facilities for women should be twice as many as that provided for men. Each restroom should provide changing areas for babies, with adjacent waste disposal units. Each restroom area should be handicapped-accessible, or at least an appropriate number of restrooms needs to be handicapped-accessible and so labeled. These facilities are generally constructed of concrete block with concrete floors with drains for cleaning. The lighting should be flourescent. The rooms should be adequately ventilated.

Scoreboards

There are a number of reliable scoreboard companies. The planners need to consider first what the function of the scoreboard will be—to depict score and time remaining only or to provide entertainment and information as well. Scoreboards can be simple or very complex in nature. The planners need to consider what they want the scoreboard to depict before determining the type of scoreboard to be purchased. The choices include (1) score; (2) periods or innings; (3) injury time or penalty time remaining; (4) times and places by lanes; (5) diving score by judge, degree of difficulty, total points scored, ranking after "x" number of dives; (6) balls, strikes, outs; (7) roster; (8) players vital statistics; (9) advertising; (10) PA system; (11) multiple functions for various sports using the field complex; (12) close-ups of players and specta-

tors; (13) time of day; (14) scores from other games; and much more depending on the planner's imagination.

Storage

As is true with indoor facilities, there is never enough storage. The planners need to consider what items need to be stored. These include but are not limited to (1) various types of riding lawn mowers; (2) push mowers; (3) tillers; (4) weed eaters; (5) shovels, rakes; and hoes; (6) utility vehicles; (7) irrigation pipes; (8) hoses and sprinkler heads; (9) field liners; (10) goals; (11) field flags; (12) benches; (13) waste containers; (14) protection screens; (15) pitching machines; (16) tarps; (17) fertilizers, insecticides, and talc; (18) paint; (19) chains, yard markers, and padding for goal post for football; and much more.

Storage areas generally are constructed out of concrete blocks with concrete floors and an appropriate number of drains for cleaning. The space should have flourescent lighting with an adequate number of electrical outlets. There should be a separate work area with a workbench and an adequate amount storage with shelving. The entrance should be an automatic roll-up door at least eight-feet high. The ceiling height should be at least 10 feet. The voids under bleachers should be enclosed (these spaces make inexpensive storage areas). The space for chemical storage must meet OSHA guidelines.

Baseball/Softball Fields

Baseball and softball facilities are important aspects of sport in public schools (grades 5-12), colleges and universities (varsity competition as well as recreation), community recreation programs, Babe Ruth Leagues, Little Leagues, Miss Softball Leagues, corporate recreation programs, and military recreation programs. Due the alarming number of injuries reported to the Consumer Product Safety Commission (CPSC), safety is a principal concern. This concern places pressure on field operators, turf managers, maintenance managers, and others to have a safe playing field. A "field of dreams" is created from a consistent set of proven guidelines and safety standards to ensure consistency around the country. It is important for the planners to be aware of the field specifications described in the various rules books that govern these two sports (i.e., National Federation of High School Activities Association, National Collegiate Athletic Association, National Intercollegiate Athletic Association, National Junior College Athletic Association, Softball USA, International Softball Federation, National Associa-

Figure 25.6 Scoreboard at Sycamore Field, Indiana State University.

Figure 25.7 Example of a structure that contains consessions, press box, restrooms and storage.

tion for Girls and Women's Sports, Little League Association, on so on). These rule books are the "gospel" in regard to the specific dimensions for the fields, and most rule books are revised annually.

Bases

The base areas must be level, with all irregularities eliminated. The type of base used in either baseball or softball varies and the rule books stipulate what types are permissible. The planner should contact the American Society of Testing and Materials (ASTM) for detailed information regarding the appropriate standards for bases. Presently the ASTM F-8 Committee on Sports Equipment and Facilities is establishing standards and classifications for bases.

Bases are intended to be a reference point on a baseball or softball field. They are an integral part of the game. There are four types of base designs used, including permanent or stationary bases, modified stationary bases, release-type bases, and throw-down bases. The type of base usually refers to how the base is secured to the playing field, or its function.

Stationary Base. This base uses a ground anchor permanently installed in the playing field. The anchor measures either 1 inch or $1^1/_2$ inches, installed a minimum of 1 inch below the playing surface. The base is designed with a stem that fits into or over the ground anchor and holds the base securely in place.

The base should be constructed of permanently white material, which can be rubber, polyvinyl,

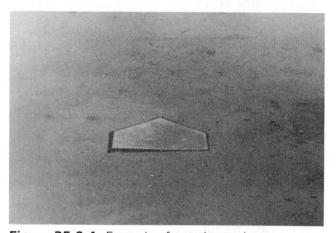

Figure 25.8 A. Example of a stationary base.

polyurethane, or other synthetic material to increase service life. The base top should have a molded tread pattern to increase player traction and reduce slippage. Base size and color should conform to individual governing organizations. Permanent or stationary bases can be used on fields by players with more advanced or higher skill levels only after (1) the players have been throughly warned that they can be seriously injured for life if they make a mistake in judgement or miscalculation, and (2) they have been made thoroughly aware of other options (i.e., the tapered side base or low silhouette which tapers to the ground eliminating impact of a sliding player against a vertical surface and uses that momentum to slide over the base). Bases are the number one cause of injuries to

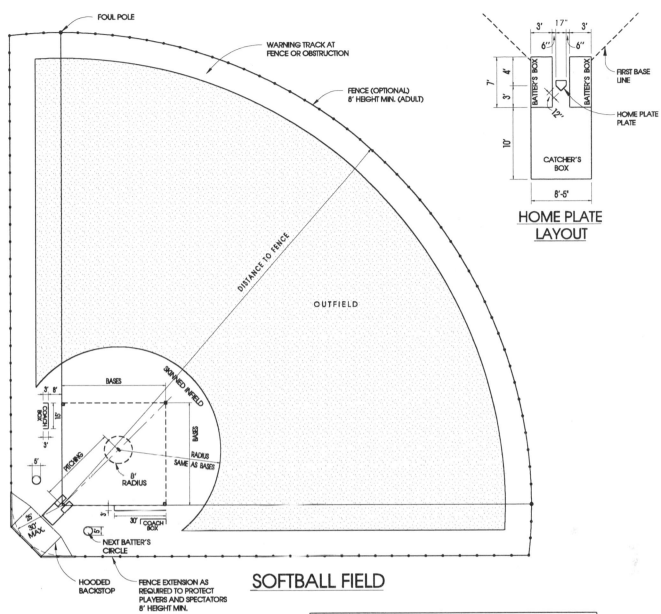

FOUL POLE

WARNING TRACK AT FENCE OR OBSTRUCTION

FENCE (OPTIONAL) 8' HEIGHT MIN. (ADULT)

DISTANCE TO FENCE

OUTFIELD

BASES

SKINNED INFIELD

COACH BOX

BASES

RADIUS SAME AS BASES

PITCHING

8' RADIUS

5'

3'

30' COACH BOX

NEXT BATTER'S CIRCLE

25'

30' MAX.

15'

HOODED BACKSTOP

FENCE EXTENSION AS REQUIRED TO PROTECT PLAYERS AND SPECTATORS 8' HEIGHT MIN.

SOFTBALL FIELD

3' 17" 3'

6" 6"

7' 4'

3'

10'

12"

BATTER'S BOX

BATTER'S BOX

FIRST BASE LINE

HOME PLATE PLATE

CATCHER'S BOX

8'-5'

HOME PLATE LAYOUT

FIELD DIMENSIONS

ADULT				FENCES	
GAME	DIVISION	BASES	PITCHING	Min.	Max.
FAST PITCH	WOMEN	60'	40'	200'	250'
	MEN	60'	46'	225'	250'
	JR. MEN	60'	46'	225'	250'
MODIFIED	WOMEN	60'	40'	200'	
	MEN	60'	46'	265'	
SLOW PITCH	WOMEN	65'	50'	265'	275'
	MEN	65'	50'	275'	315'
	COED	65'	50'	275'	300'
	SUPER	65'	50'	325'	NO MAX.
16 INCH SLOW PITCH	WOMEN	55'	38'	200'	
	MEN	55'	38'	250'	
14 INCH SLOW PITCH	WOMEN	60'	46'		
	MEN	60'	46'		

SOURCE: AMATEUR SOFTBALL ASSOCIATION OF AMERICA

YOUTH				FENCES	
GAME	DIVISION	BASES	PITCHING	Min.	Max.
SLOW PITCH	GIRLS - 10 UNDER	55'	35'	150'	175'
	BOYS - 10 UNDER	55'	35'	150'	175'
	GIRLS - 12 UNDER	60'	40'	175'	200'
	BOYS - 12 UNDER	60'	40'	175'	200'
	GIRLS - 14 UNDER	65'	46'	225'	250'
	BOYS - 14 UNDER	65'	46'	250'	275'
	GIRLS - 16 UNDER	65'	50'	225'	250'
	BOYS - 16 UNDER	65'	50'	275'	300'
	GIRLS - 18 UNDER	65'	50'	225'	250'
	BOYS - 18 UNDER	65'	50'	275'	300'
SLOW PITCH	GIRLS - 10 UNDER	55'	35'	150'	175'
	BOYS - 10 UNDER	55'	35'	150'	175'
	GIRLS - 12 UNDER	60'	35'	175'	200'
	BOYS - 12 UNDER	60'	40'	175'	200'
	GIRLS - 14 UNDER	60'	40'	175'	200'
	BOYS - 14 UNDER	60'	46'	175'	200'
	GIRLS - 16 UNDER	60'	40'	200'	225'
	BOYS - 16 UNDER	60'	46'	200'	225'
	GIRLS - 18 UNDER	60'	40'	200'	225'
	BOYS - 18 UNDER	60'	46'	200'	225'

Figure 25.8—Cont'd B. Softball field.

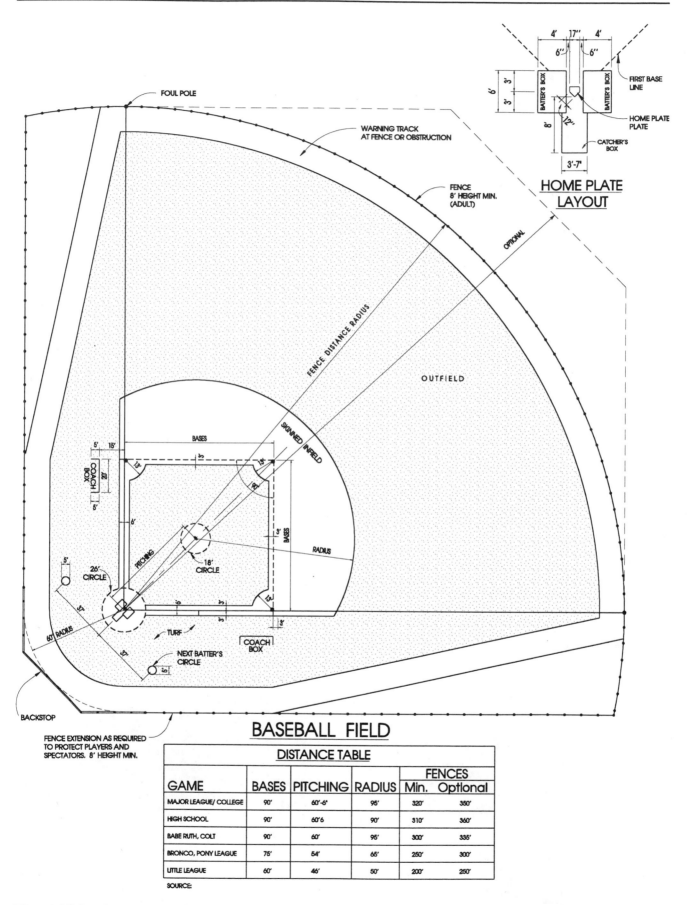

HOME PLATE LAYOUT

BASEBALL FIELD

DISTANCE TABLE

GAME	BASES	PITCHING	RADIUS	FENCES Min.	Optional
MAJOR LEAGUE/ COLLEGE	90'	60'-6'	95'	320'	350'
HIGH SCHOOL	90'	60'6	90'	310'	360'
BABE RUTH, COLT	90'	60'	95'	300'	335'
BRONCO, PONY LEAGUE	75'	54'	65'	250'	300'
LITTLE LEAGUE	60'	46'	50'	200'	250'

SOURCE:

Figure 25.8—Cont'd C. Baseball field.

ankles and other body parts, especially stationary, modified-stationary, and poorly designed release-type bases.

Modified Stationary Bases. The flexible base is a one-piece base that uses a fixed anchor system for secure placement. It is constructed with interdependent ribs that allow the base to compress and absorb energy generated by a sliding player. The cover allegedly flexes inward and downward but does not release.

The *strap-down base* or tie-down base must be held in place by four spikes inserted into the ground. Straps attached to the base are inserted through loops in the spike head and tightened down. The base is constructed of vinyl-coated nylon or canvas filled with a foam or other resilient material. If installed properly, a portion of the base will remain somewhat stable. However, it has a tendency during play to loosen and move. This style is low cost relative to other base styles which accounts for its popularity.

Release-Type Base. The release-type base is designed to reduce the chance of injury to a sliding player by releasing from its anchor system on the impact of a hard lateral slide. The release base must use a permanent ground anchor securely positioned below ground for installation. There are two-piece and three-piece designs. The release-type must not expose hidden secondary hazards after the primary above-ground base portion releases.

Throw-Down Base. This base is a thin square, sometimes using a waffle design on the bottom, usually constructed of canvas or synthetic material with little or no padding. It is not physically attached to the playing surface, and therefore, is dangerously subject to moving when a player steps on or rounds a base. Throw-down bases are not recommended for basic skills teaching in a gym, such as physical education class.

Specialized Bases. The *flush or recessed base* (except home plate, which is mounted flush with the playing field) is usually not considered for the following reasons: (1) difficulty in keeping the base visible and clean; (2) difficulty for umpire in making a call at the base when the base is not visible; (3) the change in the nature of the game; and (4) the fact that it is not widely used.

Double First Base. The double first base uses a securely positioned ground anchor system. The base is designed to reduce or eliminate the contact between the first baseman and base runner. It is a unit equal in size to two bases side by side, one-half white mounted in the normal first base position, and one-half colored, mounted in foul territory.

Home Plate. The home plate, batter's box, and catcher box and their correct dimensional size and positioning must conform to the game and the rules of the appropriate governing body. The area should be well compacted, properly tapered, and level with no irregularities. The plate must be firmly anchored and any undermining or ruts corrected before play begins.

The home plate is a reference point on the playing field. It establishes the horizontal limits of the strike zone used by the umpire in calling balls and strikes. It is imperative that all home plates have a white surface that measures 17 by $8^1/_2$ by $8^1/_2$ by 12 by 12 inches flush with the surrounding playing surface. Further, all home plates must have a periphery black bevel that does not exceed 35 degrees. The outermost edge of the bevel must be sufficiently below the playing surface. It does not matter how the plates are field mounted as long as they remain flat and flush with surrounding playing surfaces with no sharp corners or sharp nails exposed.

There are four styles of home plate, including buried, staked, anchored, and throw down.

Buried. A rubber or synthetic plate 2 inches or more thick is buried and the uppermost white surface is installed flush with the playing surface. It can be mounted in a concrete sub-base to provide greater leveling stability.

Staked. A rubber or synthetic plate $^3/_4$ inch to 1 inch thick has an installed white surface flush to the playing surface. It can be mounted in a concrete sub-base for better anchoring.

Anchored. A rubber or synthetic plate has a stem built into the bottom that fits into a permanent ground anchor. The uppermost white surface must be installed flush with the playing surface.

Throw Down. A rubber or synthetic thin mat sometimes using a waffle design on the bottom is laid down on the playing surface and is not mechanically held in place. Throw down home plates are not recommended for basic skills teaching in a gym, such as physical education class.

Skinned Infield

With an eye to player safety, begin the outfield slope 20 feet back into the outfield, lessening the transition from the infield to outfield (this is for both synthetic and natural fields). The infield slope should be established at 0.5%, the outfield slope at 1.3% all the way around to further speed drainage. The infield should a 80/20 premixed sand to clay material at a depth of three inches. The demarcation between skinned area and turf must be smooth and firm. The skinned areas must maintain the proper pitch to eliminate puddling and erosion. Irregular clumps of turf, uneven edges, and undermining of skinned materials are among some of the causes of ankle and leg injuries in the game.

Skinned areas could be just cut-outs around the bases, home plate, and pitchers mound or include base lines or the entire infield area. In all cases, the skinned areas must be continuously inspected and groomed. All irregularities must be eliminated, particularly around bases where sliding groves the area.

Clay is most often used as such a skinned area; however, other materials and mix of materials have been used depending upon local sources and preference. Most fields should be designed to be playable within 15 to 20 minutes after rain. A higher percentage of sand may be needed to achieve that without underground drainage.

Turf Infield and Outfield

In Chapter 16 is a discussion regarding natural turf as well as irrigation concerns. However, it needs to be noted here that natural turf in the infield and outfield should be Tifway II® Bermudagrass. It should be overseeded (see base paths) with Topflite® perennial ryegrass.

Pitchers Mound

The pitchers mound and its plate must meet the requirements of the games governing body. The height of the plate, the pitch of the slope within the circle toward home plate, the radius of the circle, the level plate length and width size are all critical to safety in any type of designated and designed fields and must be checked and maintained before any game.

Base Paths

A regular maintenance concern is the rutting of the base path. Like the infield, the base path should be free of ruts and irregularities in the surface. Periodically hand rake the base paths between first and second and second and third to identify any low spots. The base paths between home and first and first and third can be composed of clay and sand like the infield, or natural turf or synthetic material. If the base path is composed of natural turf, it should be overseeded with Topflight® perennial ryegrass prior to

the season, periodically during the season, and at the conclusion of the season, as well as early fall. Prior to overseeding in the early spring and early fall the area should be aerated, then de-thatched to provide good seed-to-soil contact. The seeded area should be fertilized first with 10-10-10 fertilizer, and one month later with a slow-release 30-16-10.

Warning Track

The warning track should encircle the entire playing field and provide noticeable surface variations in feel and sound to provide ample warning to players chasing a fly ball who are unaware of the perimeter and any obstacles. The track can be made of clay or crushed (M-10) granite or brick. The crushed brick will add color for enhanced TV coverage. The warning track and/or buffer zone should be equal in width to 5% of the distance from home plate to the deepest part of the playing field (e.g., 200' × .05 = 10' or 400' × .05 = 20'), and completely encircle the field. Care should be taken than any edge between the track and the turf be smooth and even.

Backstop

The backstop is a key element of a field for safeguarding the players and spectators. The basic purposes of backstop include (1) keeping the ball within the playing area, (2) protecting the spectator, (3) safeguarding others involved in the game (i.e., batters in the on-deck circle, bat persons), and (4) protecting nearby activities from conflict with pop-ups (i.e., adjacent ball fields, concessions areas, rest rooms, parking areas).

When designing the backstop, the planners should consider the following: (1) using small mesh to discourage people from climbing the structure; (2) ensuring the parking and traffic areas are not close; (3) installing a double mesh to prevent fingers, faces, and other body parts of spectators from being crushed by errant balls or thrown bats; (4) keeping the mesh free from any barbs or penetrating parts to ensure safety for players and spectators; (5) ensuring the distance between home plate and the backstop is not less than 25 feet but preferably 60 feet to ensure player safety; (6) using ground materials of either turf with an appropriate warning track composed of clay or crushed granite (M-10) or crushed brick, or no turf with either clay or crushed granite (M-10) or crushed brick; and (7) ensuring the height of the backstop is at least 18 feet, preferably 20 feet, with a four- to six-foot overhang at the top with a 45° angle.

The most frequently used backstop consists of three 12-feet wide panels that are 18 to 20 feet high covered with a $1^1/_2$-inch galvanized wire mesh mate-

Figure 25.9 Warning track, DePauw University.

Figure 25.10 Backstop, Indiana State University.

rial. These panels can be made of steel, aluminum, or wood. One panel is placed directly behind home plate and the other two on each side flaring at 30° with the center panel. The fencing on either side of the side panels should gradually taper down to eight feet behind the players' bench area to provide greater pro-

tection for the spectators in bleachers on the other side of the fence. The top of the backstop will have three panels, 4 to 6 feet by 12 feet, attached to the upright panels and positioned at a 45° angle to contain errant balls. This overhang will be covered with the same material as the uprights.

Figure 25.11 Bullpen area, Indiana State University.

Player's Bench Area

There are two types of player bench areas commonly constructed for baseball and softball. These areas dugouts and field level shelters. The safer of the two is the dugout, but it is also the most expensive to construct. The dugout is usually 4 feet deep, constructed of poured concrete and concrete blocks with drains to remove water quickly. It has an elevated players' bench area, entrance to locker rooms (if in a stadium complex), drinking fountain, communication, bat rack, other storage space, lights, and electrical outlets. Recently, to better safeguard the players, either shatter-proof plastic or wire mesh has been installed to repel errant balls and bats. The roof is constructed so as to discourage people from sitting or climbing on it.

The field level shelter is at field level with a poured concrete floor and concrete block walls. It has a wire mesh fence at least 6 feet high to repel errant balls or bats. The space should have a bat rack, communications, a drinking fountain, additional storage, lights, and electrical outlets. The roof should be constructed to discourage sitting and climbing.

Batting Cage

The batting cage should be located outside the fenced playing field. It should be constructed of either steel, aluminum, or wood. The minimum size for one batter should be 10 feet wide, 100 feet long, and 10 feet high. If more than one batter is going to be hitting, then the cage needs to be wider (i.e., 10 feet wider for each batter) with a separating mesh curtain.

The space must be completely covered by mesh netting to protect other players and spectators. There needs to be a source of electricity and numerous GFI electrical outlets. The floor surface should be similar to home plate for the batters and natural mounds for the pitchers.

Bull Pen

The bull pens should be located either down first and third into the outfield area or in right and left center fields. These areas should be protected from errant balls and the spectators. The area behind the catcher should have a protective fence to protect the spectators. The pitching mounds should be exact replicas of the actual playing field mound. There should also be a home plate area. Finally, there should be benches available for the players.

Size

The area required for a baseball or softball field will vary from 260 to 460 feet depending on the level of play anticipated. Since baseball and softball are now often scheduled on the same fields, the age group and type of activity govern the field size. It is recommended that if multiple age groups are to play on a field, it should be sized for the optimum use. Many fields have been planned for a size for high school play, only to have young adults scheduled for the same field. This creates numerous incidents with players colliding with obstacles or other players. Ideally, if funding is available, there should be separate facilities for the various age groups.

Multi-field Complex

It is common to see multi-field complexes for baseball, softball, and combination baseball and softball. The most common multi-field complex contains four fields. If one were to view the complex from an airplane it would resemble a wheel with four spokes coming from a central hub.

The central hub would contain a two-story building with each side facing a different backstop and field. The first floor would contain a concession area, rest rooms, storage for game and maintenance equipment, and a first aid space. The second floor would have four large screened windows, four scorer tables, four scoreboard controls, communication center, and field light controls. The pathways leading to the various fields would contain either crushed granite (M-10) or crushed brick. The parking area would be located at least 100 yards from the nearest outfield fence. All fields would be lighted.

Field Hockey, Football, Lacrosse, Rugby, Soccer

Fields for field hockey, football, lacrosse, rugby, and soccer have a number of common requirements. For example, a drinking fountain should be available for each team to use near the team benches. A utility structure should be placed at mid-field, set back from the field 25 feet, to store equipment and house the scorer and controls for the field lights and score board. Shade must be available for the teams at halftime, preferably from a deciduous tree grove at either end or side of the field and about 25 yards away from the playing field.

Specific considerations by sport include the following:

Field hockey: This sport needs sleeves in the ground for corner flags and goal posts. The actual field dimensions are similar to those diagrammed below. Official rule books can be purchased from the NCAA or NAGWS; rules are revised annually.

Football: There should be sleeves in the ground for the end zone flags. The goal posts (usually a single pole with uprights) need to be centered and secured at the end line. Actual field dimensions are similar to the ones diagramed below. Official rule books can be purchased from the NCAA; rules are revised annually. Planners should review carefully the ASTM publication "Safety in Football."

Lacrosse: There should be sleeves in the ground to hold the goals. Actual field dimensions are similar to the ones diagramed below. Official rule books can be purchased from the NCAA or NAGWS; rules are revised annually.

Rugby: There should be sleeves in the ground for the end flags and the goal posts. Actual field dimensions are similar to the ones diagramed below. Official rule books can be purchased from the United States Rugby Association; rules are revised annually.

Soccer: Sleeves in the ground are needed for the flags for the corner kick area, substitute area, and the goal posts on the end line. Tie-down hooks should be inserted at least 1 foot into the ground for securing the nets to the ground. There should be a drinking fountain available for each team to use near the team benches. Actual field dimensions are similar to the ones diagramed below. Official rule books can be purchased from the NCAA; rules are revised annually.

Planning Checklist for Fields

The following is a checklist to be used by field planners when designing field spaces:

- Define the use of the field complex (i.e., single or multiple sport users; youth, adolescent, or adult; amateur or professional).
- Pay careful attention to slope on fields to encourage proper and adequate drainage.
- Ensure drainage requirements are met and the type as well as placement of drainage outlets are well out of the playing area and swales are beyond safety or buffer zones.
- Make sure fences on the perimeter are offset beyond safety or buffer zones. The height of the fence should be at least eight feet. Fences should be flexible, resilient, and padded. Further, ensure that fences are placed in front of players (i.e., dugouts and field level shelters) and spectators.

Table 25.1 General Activity Space Requirements

Activity			Dimensions Play Area	Dimensions Total	Area Sqft
Archery	Min		50' × 300"	110' × 40"	44,000
Badminton	Singles		17' × 44"	27' × 54"	1,458
	Doubles		20' × 44"	30' × 54"	1,620
Baseball	Official		350' × 350"	400' × 400"	160,000
	Pony		250' × 250"	300' × 300"	90,000
	Little League		200' × 200"	250' × 250"	62,500
Basketball	Official		50' × 94"	62' × 114"	7,068
	High School		50' × 84"	62' × 104"	6,448
	Recreation		40' × 70"	52' × 90"	4,680
Croquet			35' × 70"	45' × 80"	3,600
Deck Tennis	Singles		12' × 40"	20' × 50"	1,000
	Doubles		18' × 40"	26' × 50"	1,300
Field Hockey			180' × 300"	200' × 320"	64,000
Football			160' × 360"	180' × 380"	68,400
Lacrosse	Men	-Min	160' × 330"	180' × 350"	63,000
		-Max	180' × 330"	200' × 350"	70,000
Lacrosse	Women	-Min	150' × 360"	17' × 380"	64,600
		-Max	150' × 420"	17' × 440"	74,800
Soccer	Men	-Min	195' × 330"	115' × 350"	40,250
		-Max	225' × 360"	245' × 380"	93,100
Soccer	Women	-Min	120' × 240"	14' × 260"	36,400
		-Max	180' × 300"	200' × 320"	64,000
Softball	Fast Pitch		225' × 225"	250' × 250"	62,500
	Slow Pitch	-M	275' × 275"	295' × 295"	87,025
		-W	250' × 250"	270' × 270"	72,900
Tennis	Singles		27' × 78"	51' × 120"	6,120
	Doubles		36' × 78"	60' × 120"	7,200
Volleyball			30' × 60"	50' × 80"	4,000

*Refer to recent regulations for changes.
**The area above does not include space for support facilities.

The fence should be sturdy enough to attach a wind-screen or sun-screen. Finally, the mesh on the fences should be of a size to discourage climbing.

■ Provide gates for security and for separation of different practice areas.
■ Design warning tracks to provide advanced warning of perimeter barriers and ensure they are wide enough and of appropriate material.
■ Ensure that light poles, fence poles, and foul poles are not in the field of play.

■ Plan that mowing or maintenance strips along fences are inserted so they are not hazardous.
■ Place all shrubs and tree plantings well outside the playing area.
■ Ensure that the turf (artificial or natural) is suitable for different weather conditions (i.e., hot, cold, dry, or wet).
■ Install the scoreboard well outside the playing area.
■ Design the irrigation system so that it will not interfere with play and that all valves, distribution boxes, and other utilities are well outside the field of play.

- Make sure that vehicular and pedestrian traffic flow patterns prevent conflict and interference, and that bike and vehicle parking is marked and controlled.
- Ensure that emergency call stations are placed at strategic locations and emergency vehicle access is available for immediate response.
- Plan the field area so that hazards are not nearby (e.g., major highways, railroad tracks, waterways, culverts, ravines, industries, woods, uncut roughs, and utility lines).
- Create the field area so that security vehicles have easy access and surveillance.
- Understand the importance of field orientation relative to the movement of the sun and prevailing wind patterns.
- Configure spectator seating to ensure the best viewing of the game as well as easy access and exit.
- Ensure each space has the appropriate safety or buffer zones.
- Review the plan to ensure that the field dimensions are accurate and meet the specified association rules.
- Configure all field spaces to include metal sleeves for goal post, goals, and flags.
- Encourage the owners to ensure that regular maintenance and inspections are done to eliminate ruts, ridges, and depressions in the fields after use; remove debris and rocks from the playing area as well as safety zones; ensure all hooks on goal posts, foul line posts, and fencing are recessed; eliminate all sharp edges on posts, rails, and welds; and make sure benches, seats, and bleachers are protected by screening or barriers.
- Create backstops that protect players, spectators, and other game personnel from injury from errant balls or bats.

■ Summary

Designing safe sport fields is important to athletes of all ages, genders, and skill and experience levels, as well as to spectators and parents. The number of sport fields being built each year has increased dramatically. Sport field complexes with multiple fields will become the norm rather than the oddity.

Learning Objective 1: The student will be able to design a safe outdoor sport field complex.

When designing a safe outdoor sport field complex, designers consider the following generalized aspects: (1) field turf (i.e., synthetic or natural turf), (2) seating (i.e., spectators and players), (3) lighting (i.e., fields and adjacent areas), (4) orientation (i.e., sun and prevailing wind), (5) fencing and barriers, (6) drainage, (7) irrigation, (8) sport field services (e.g., concessions area, press box, rest rooms, scoreboards, and storage), (9) location, (10) users, (11) materials to be used in construction, (12) access to field areas, (13) warning tracks, (14) backstops, (15) safety or buffer zones, (16) utility lines, (17) security, and (18) equipment.

■ Self-Assessment Exercise

1. What are the common causes of injuries on outdoor field spaces?
2. Describe the two common types of surfaces.
3. What is important to know and understand about the orientation of sport fields?
4. What should the designer know about fencing for sport fields?
5. Describe how you would ensure a sport field will drain quickly and adequately.
6. What is important to understand about irrigation of sport fields?
7. List the common services areas found at outdoor sport field complexes and describe each.
8. What should the designer know about spectator seating?

■ Case Study

You are a member of a newly formed community youth baseball association. The organization is nonprofit. You have indicated some knowledge about field design and construction. The group elects you as chairman of the building committee. As chairman you are responsible for designing the new four-field youth baseball facility. Prepare a checklist for the design, a diagram of the new facility, and an outline of the details for the facility.

Notes

CHAPTER 26

Winter Sports

Larry Horine, Professor Emeritus, Appalachian State University, Retired

Learning Objectives

After reading this chapter, the student will be able to

- develop planning strategies encompassing appropriate location, scope, and resource allocation for winter sports facilities,

- select the essential directional orientation, topography, hydrology, and market factors for winter sports facilities,

- recognize the historical trends in user statistics and ski operations equipment as these factors affect design,

- develop the important aspects of design and layout of ski areas,

- identify essential aspects of ice rink design, and

- understand various options of axillary winter sports facilities.

Introduction

Winter sport areas and facilities have been promoted in the United States since the 1930s. Some of the early breakthroughs were refrigeration systems that allowed for year-round indoor ice skating, and rudimentary rope tows to carry skiers uphill. In recent years, scientific and engineering advances in ice and snow making have been the major factors in increasing the number of participants in order to support increasing facility development. Other advances in user equipment, maintenance equipment, computer-assisted design (CAD), marketing, and new construction techniques and materials have promoted growth in winter sports facilities. Rapid growth of winter sports participants continued until the 1970s in the U.S., but since then, the growth has been limited. Recent trends have shown a consistent and substantial growth in snowboarding, and the disappearance of family-owned areas, as conglomerates have moved in with large interrelated and integrated multi-recreational and leisure complexes.

Ski and Snow Boarding Areas

Strategic planning

The primary initial need is to determine the clientele for the area. This need should be determined by answering the following questions:

- Will the users be day trippers or will this be a destination resort with participants staying for several days or longer?

Participant Numbers

	National Sporting Goods Association	American Sports Data
Alpine skiing	9.8 million	13 million
Cross country	3.4 million	4.6 million
Snowboarding	9.6 million	4 million
Snowshoeing	6 million—	

(Rowan, 1996).

Participant Numbers by Ability Levels

	Alpine skier	Snowboarder
Novice	05.8%	39.%
Beginner	06.%	04.2%
Intermediate, low.	18.1%	14.8%
Intermediate, adv.	36.6%	16.2%
Advanced	22.3%	11.7%
Expert	12.9%	07.%

(Spring, 1996).

■ What ability level will be targeted, and what age and gender distribution will there be?
■ What will be the economic mix of the clients?
■ What will be the transportation mix of cars to buses?
■ What will be the estimated maximums and minimums of attendance weekdays and nights, as well as weekends?

Next, the planners must match these factors to resources and capitalization. Undercapitalization—failure to obtain sufficient resources to provide the facilities and operational costs expected by the target clients—is a major reason for ski area failures. Once appropriate capitalization is assured, the three most important considerations are LOCATION, LOCATION, and LOCATION. In addition to all other reasons location is vital, the location will also allow the match of the balance of the slopes (beginner, intermediate, expert) to the target clients. Failure to provide

this balance is another major reason for ski area failure (Farwell, 1996).

Planning a ski and snowboarding area is similar to planning for the development of a small city. It is immensely complicated. For this reason, to plan for an area larger than a small one-slope beginners area, the employment of a consulting firm is a must. Refer to any issue of *Ski Area Management Journal* for listings. In addition, if the consulting firm is from outside the region, also employ a local consultant.

Ski and snowboarding area site selection

In the best of worlds, the planner will have matched the needs of the target clientele with capitalization, and then be able to purchase free and clear the land to make the perfect fit. More likely, the land available will only partially match the needs. The planner may be forced to work with land that doesn't have much of a match at all. For example, a university may have been given some land that is minimally suitable for a ski area for its students, and the planner must make do. If the fit is so poor that even with the most creative design the user results will be poor, the planner must call a halt to the project before it's started.

In selecting the location, the planner must consider the transportation systems already in place, such as highways and airports, again matching the needs of the target clients. For example, for a destination resort, a commercial airport is a distinct asset, while the highway infrastructure would be vital to an area that expects mostly clients who will stay for only a day or so. What housing, restaurants, and other support providers are already in the area, or can be expected to be attracted? Is it necessary to provide housing, and is the capitalization sufficient to accommodate this? A major reason for mid-sized ski areas failure is associated with incorporating real estate sales in the development plans.

Latitude, snowfall, winter humidity, and elevation are critical factors. Naturally, the higher the latitude, the greater the snowfall, and the lower the humidity, the better. Generally, higher elevations are desirable so long as the elevation isn't so great as to cause high altitude sickness or equipment failures. If one or two of these factors are negative, then the others must be strong.

Prime consideration must be how the physiographic and topographic variables match with what the target clientele will need. Seventy percent of skiers are attracted to grades (slope incline) of 20-40% (Farwell, 1996). If half the clients will be attracted to intermediate slopes, does the location allow for this type of development? Is there sufficient water available for both domestic use and for snow making? Many major ski and snowboarding areas have found that they did not plan for sufficient water for snow making and have had to adopt costly alternative plans. Are other utilities available at reasonable costs?

Topography and Orientation

Topography refers to the surface features of the site, which will include variations in elevation. Hydrology refers to the study of the patterns of water flow above and below surface. The decisions on where the land allows natural development of beginner, intermediate, and advance slopes will be made using both of these factors. The control and capture of natural water flow and melting snow is essential. This planning will also determine the best location for creating ponds to capture the water, or to improve or enlarge existing ponds. Snow making requires enormous quantities of water. The planner will be fortunate if a flowing river is on the property, which reduces the problems of finding sufficient water for snow making.

Orientation of the slopes is vital. The greater the protection from the sun between mid-morning and mid-afternoon, the better. The orientation should thus be north or northeast except in the very coldest climates. A southwest orientation should be avoided. If a west orientation is included, it should be protected by outcropping or vegetation. The effects of wind must also be studied. High winds will adversely effect snow making; cause chair lifts, trams, or gondolas to be shut down from swinging; and affect attendance numbers because of the cold.

Layout

Referring back to the needs of the expected clientele will determine many layout decisions. A local day trip-type area will need careful planning for parking and drop-off arrangements, while a destination resort may have most patrons arriving on shuttles or walking from nearby accommodations. Plan carefully for bus drop-off and bus parking. Busloads of clients are great for business and take less space than patrons in individual cars.

Be generous in the space provided for beginners. These clients will have difficulty maneuvering and thus need more room. The beginner slopes may be quite consistent in gradient, and can be more straight line than others. Future business will depend to a great degree on how pleasing the experience is to the beginner.

Plan slopes parallel to the fall line or perpendicular to the contour, since side hill runs create routed trails on the lower side. Increase wind and sun control through the use of trees on the south side of slopes. Vary the design of the runs as to gradient and to the type of sides. A feathered side incorporates an uneven cut resulting in an aesthetically pleasing look. Adopting curves adds to interest and excitement. If possible, plan for some gladed areas by thinning the forest to allow for tree skiing and boarding. Allow for wider areas on the steeper aspects of the intermediate slopes.

For a variety of reasons, limit slopes running under lifts. If any are created, check state codes and insurance standards for minimum clearance between the snow surface and the bottom of the lift. Separate types of runs so that an expert run doesn't cross or end in a beginner area. Create a dedicated area for racing training and a park for snowboarders. Slope terminals should be flat, and chair lift egress ramps need special planning to be gentle with generous run-out distance. This has become more important with snowboarders

Figure 26.1 Examples of a variety of types of slopes: straight, undulating curve, wide, narrow, gladed and feathered. River Run Ski area, ME.

who have more difficulty exiting steep off-loading ramps than do skiers.

Plan to groom and plant hardy grass on all slopes that will receive the most use. The grass will decrease erosion during the off season. Install diagonal water-intercepting run-off bars utilizing drain pipe and gravel. Clients can ski or snowboard on four to six inches of packed snow on a groomed slope, while an ungroomed slope may require three times this depth of snow. Mowing these slopes in the off-season must be done with care to avoid damage. One solution to this is to equip a standard grooming machine with a custom frame and modified flail mover on the front that can follow contours of the terrain just like it does on snow (Faster, 1996). Consult with local authorities as to whether the water and air lines should be buried underground. This depends on climate and soil conditions.

A variety of landscape features incorporated into the area will make it unique and create additional marketing avenues. Bowls, broad ridge, flat bottom, side hills, or undulating terrain may all be turned into positive attributes. Generally, gullies, rock outcroppings, and chutes create poor qualities.

Achieving the greatest aesthetic blend with the surrounding environment is usually very difficult to visualize. Utilizing new techniques through computer-assisted design (CAD), planners can see what the whole scheme will look like. It only takes about 40 hours of work to create such a picture. This realistic picture can help elicit approval from both local approving boards and regulatory agencies. This tech-

nique was used to create new trails on Pioneer Ridge at Steamboat Ski area to show what the new additions would look like viewed from the town of Steamboat Springs, Colorado (Jackson & Kaden, 1997).

Lodges and Support Facilities

A careful traffic flow system must be planned that uses the lodge as the center. All client traffic should flow into and out of the lodge. If the area will be huge, several lodges at the bottom of primary mountains should be planned. These should be connected both by roads at the bottom and by interconnecting trails on the mountains. Killington Ski Area in Vermont is a good example of this, where each base lodge area has a primary focus, such as one directed toward families, and another to accommodate parking buses and handling group processing.

In the planning process, it is suggested that the general layout be determined by visualizing that you are driving up to the area. What is your order of needs, and how do you find them? At some well-known major areas, parking is a guessing game because of inadequate signage. Repeat clients will not be encouraged if they must walk across a long distance of gravel or mud in expensive ski boots to get from parking to the ticket sales area. If a long distance cannot be avoided, incorporate drop-off circles near the ticket windows with a safe system of leaving equipment for a short time. In some areas it has proven to be less expensive to install roundabouts, rather than traffic lights and rerouting ramps (Best, 1996). Consideration should be

Figure 26.2 Aesthetically pleasing base area and lodge. Wildcat Ski Area, NH.

given to automatic people movers (APM) similar to those used for many years in airports.

The success of a winter sports facility depends greatly on the strategic planning and placement of the support facilities. It is beyond the scope of this text to delve into the details of planning each of the support facilities. Only a summary of some of the important assets will be presented. After parking, the second requirement for clients will be to purchase their lift tickets. Great care should be given to make this experience as painless and efficient as possible. Locate ticket windows in adequate numbers to handle the largest crowds and so that ticketing brings patrons to the lodge, but not into it. Ticketing will be the first detailed impression patrons get from the facility, so make it a good one.

In close proximity to the ticket purchasing windows should be the rental shop and the ski school contact area. Organizing the rental shop is both an art and a science. Avoid creating a noisy, confusing area that leaves a negative impression. The storing, maintenance, and drying of equipment requires careful planning. In general, ski schools have not generated as much revenue as they could. Some small ski areas have aggressively marketed their product and have generated far greater revenues than some of the major ski areas.

Inside the Lodge

Good design for changing space, lockers, picnic areas, retail sales stores, administrative suites, and food service, and perhaps game rooms should be planned. Like airports, major ski areas will learn that their lodges should be more like shopping malls to generate the most revenue. Ski areas have generally scored very poorly for their food service. Consider employing a designer of fast food businesses to plan the food service aspects of the lodge.

The remaining service components that require planning are the compressor and pump house, maintenance center, ski school instructors' locker and staging area, and the ski patrol area. If a large number of groups will be booking lessons, plan an inside lecture room in the ski school facility. Careful placement of both the ski school staging area and the ski patrol facility are important. The ski school needs visibility so that business will be stimulated. The ski patrol facility needs easy double access—one directly from the slopes on skis—and one at the other side for emergency vehicles to load victims. In both of these areas plan sufficient lockers, storage, and eating space. Note that eating and first aid treatment areas must be separated.

Participant Equipment

In most sport facility design, neither the equipment that the participants use, nor operational equipment directly affects the design of the facility. Not so in ski and snow boarding areas! An example of this is the recent explosion of snowboarding, which has created the need for snowboard parks built into slopes. Just a few years ago snowboard parks didn't even exist.

While it is not possible to present details of these facets, a brief overview of each is in order. In many ways, the changes in skiing and snowboarding equipment, lift design, lighting, snow making, and grooming machines have all directly affected ski area design and operation. For example, in alpine skiing, there has been a consistent evolution of equipment, from long and heavy wooden skis with ankle-high lace-up leather boots and "bear trap" bindings to today's high-technology equipment. Skis have evolved through plastics, metal, and fiberglass to space-age composites. The length of skis has run from long and heavy, to very short (made popular through the Graduated Length Method [GLM] of instruction in the 1970s), back to longer skis in the 1980s, and then a return to the somewhat shorter narrow-waisted parabolic skis of the 1990s.

The bindings have improved, with fixed-toe plates and movable cables at the rear, step-in bindings with unidirectional rear release, step-in bindings with rear and front unidirectional release, whole plate release systems, and finally multidirectional front and rear releases with sensing devices.

Hard-shell ankle-high plastic boots with snap-lever fasteners came on the market in the 1960s. Higher boots evolved, with fiberglass replacing plastic in a variety of fastening devices. In the 1980s, rear-entry and heated boots came into use, along with a variety of adjustment options for forward lean, pressure, and canting.

The evolution of snow boarding and Nordic skiing (cross country) equipment has also affected the design of winter sports facilities. For Nordic skiing, the change in the equipment has been slow and steady since the sport was active for many years in Europe. Cross country skiing was stimulated greatly in the early 1940s with the training of large numbers of military troops for operations in the Nordic countries. The evolution of Nordic equipment paralleled that of alpine. The skis went from all wood, to wood with steel edges, to fiberglass construction. Telemark skis became a popular diversion, allowing more aggressive downhill turns. Bindings and boots followed the cycle of alpine skiing improvements.

Snowboarding equipment will likely change most in the future since it is a relatively new sport. Almost all large ski areas now embrace snowboarders. This in an excellent example of how new equipment and a new form of an existing sport change the design of the areas. As snowboard participants grew in number, ski areas scrambled to develop parks with lifts dedicated to this new venue.

Operations Equipment

Lift design changes have also greatly affected the design of winter sport areas. The first single chair lift in the world used for skiing was installed in Sun Valley, Idaho in 1936. Between 1934 and 1964, 240 new non-rope tows were installed in North America. The first double chair lift was installed at Berthoud Pass, Colorado, in 1947. Triple chair lifts were common in the 1970s, and quad (four-person) lifts were in common use in the 1980s. The first detachable chair lift in the U.S. was in Breckenridge, Colorado, in 1981. The first six-person chair was installed in Quebec, Canada, in 1991.

Snow-making technology has also affected the design of ski areas. How is snow made? Machines break the water into small particles, cooling the water by causing the particles to move through cold air, nucleating the water particles, and distributing the resulting snow on a surface. Why is it necessary to make snow? To get open, to stay open, to provide a base, to give the best skiing conditions possible, and for cosmetic purposes. In the beginning, more ice than snow was made. Some of the air compressors used for the early snow-making operations in the early 1960s came from, or were similar to those used in ice plants.

The guns for early snow making were light and small so they could easily be moved up and down hills. As the power of the air compressors and water pumps increased, and snow cats became more powerful, the size of the guns increased. The guns changed from standing on tripods to being mounted on skids so they could be towed about. In the late 1960s and early 1970s, the somewhat misnomered large fan airless guns (almost all require piped compressed air or manufactured their own air) came into use. These behemoths frequently had a full-sized automobile engine mounted on the unit for power. They were costly, operated more quietly, but required lower temperatures for efficient operation. Recently, more fixed guns, movable fan machines, and tree- or tower-mounted machines have been utilized for snow making. In colder climates, new, efficient, small, lightweight guns on tripods have reappeared.

The development of grooming machines has paralleled farm machinery in becoming larger, more powerful, and having more accessories for moving (farming) snow and pulling a variety of grooming devices. The compressors and water pumps for snow making have become more powerful and efficient. Cooling systems have been incorporated so that the compressed air is cooled before being sent uphill. Additives are being introduced into the water supply to allow snow to be made at higher temperatures and in increasing amounts.

Even the improvements in lighting have affected the design of ski areas. There were few ski slopes

Figure 26.3 A.-C. Examples of excellent gentle off-loading ramps.

Figure 26.3—Cont'd D. Example of excellent gentle off-loading ramps.

Figure 26.4 A. Pole-mounted swivel fan-type snow gun, Appalachian Ski Mountain, NC.

Figure 26.4—Cont'd B.
Pole-mounted fan type snow gun.

Figure 26.4—Cont'd C.
Fan-type snow making machine mounted on top of a lift house.

with night skiing in the 1950s. Some areas experimented with night skiing in the 1960s, but as more efficient lighting became available, many ski areas situated near urban areas initiated night skiing in the 1970s. By the 1980s, even large destination areas had at least the lower slopes open for night skiing, and now many have installed lighting to the top of the slopes.

Ice Rinks

Strategic Planning

If the rink will be commercial, the two most important factors will be location and population base. Within the clientele cohort, one must consider the sociological/cultural background. Has this public a his-

Figure 26.5 Outdoor skating rink. Appalachian Ski Mountain, NC.

tory of ice skating and ice hockey? If not, this can be overcome with astute marketing, but it will be an up-hill battle. To gather an accurate estimate of costs, the following information should be gathered.

■ In what geographic area do you plan to build your rink?
■ Is your rink for public skating or theatrical use?
■ Is your rink to be a permanent structure?
■ If it will be portable, what will be the range of temperatures in which it will be used?
■ Will the rink be indoor, outdoor, or a combination of both?
■ If the rink will be in an existing building, how well is that building insulated, and is it air conditioned?
■ What type of construction will be planned (metal, masonry, air structure)?
■ What are your average winter and summer temperatures?
■ What is your elevation?
■ What is your power source (e.g., 220 volt, 3 phase 60 cycle)?
■ If you will install the rink in an existing building, what type floor exists in this building?
■ What size ice skating surface do you wish to build? (Standard hockey rink is 200 by 85 feet—cost of operation is relative to the size.)
■ If you plan to play hockey, will it be for teaching and recreational play, or will it need to meet professional standards (Ice Rink Engineering, 1997)?

■ What will be the maximum spectator seating required (theater type seating or bleachers)?

Ice Rink Size and Geographical Considerations

The amount of the power costs will be directly related to rink size and other factors. Rinks can be built indoors or out, operated year-around or seasonally, and in cold or hot climates. Obviously, the warmer the climate, the greater the operating costs. The buildings housing the rink can be insulated or not. If the rink will be installed in an existing building, it can be applied over a concrete floor.

Allow sufficient ceiling height to safely operate gasoline powered equipment. For spectators, a round building is recommended; if little spectator seating will be needed, a rectangular building will be more economical.

Ice Making

Ice about $\frac{1}{2}$ inch thick is required for beginning figure skating, while ice hockey can be played on a little less. Water to a depth of about one-fourth inch is sprayed on a concrete floor. A brine solution is circulated through the pipes at a temperature below 18 degrees Fahrenheit. When the water is frozen, a paint is sprayed on the surface before another layer of water is applied. This is to give the proper color for aesthetics and for the puck in hockey to show clearly. Compressors are needed to remove the heat from the brine that will be circulated through the miles of pipes. Water

Figure 26.6 Well organized skate rental area. Appalachian Ski Mountain, NC.

pumps will be required to provide the power of moving the brine. It is recommended that an extra compressor and pump be installed for emergencies and alternate use. A common floor system utilizes refrigeration-grade fiber tubing, which remains flexible at all temperatures. Usually the floor will be delivered on steel reels and can be laid in place and removed easily. The same floor is used in permanent or portable installations.

The quality of the refrigeration system is vital. This should be a solid-state totally automatically controlled system, which should require little maintenance. Ensure that all components carry standard warranties, and that the selling firm will install and service all equipment (Ice Rink Engineering, 1997).

Sides of Ice Rinks

For safety and maintenance, care must be used in selecting the sides of the rink. At ice level, kick boards should be installed of oak or similarly strong material about eight inches to a foot high to act as a buffer for the skate blades. If the rink will be used for hockey, dashers are installed to a height of four to five feet to protect spectators. The dasher material is usually polycarbonate sheeting or shatter-proof glass.

Some of the essential maintenance equipment will include an ice resurfacer, such as a Zamboni or Jimbini machine, with an extra blade. It should have the capability of cutting a 48 inch or greater width, and to cut and water at the same time. Other key equipment or areas to be considered are an appropriate level of lighting for activities offered (such as TV), an inventory of skates, skate sharpener, ice tools, hand rails, changing and rest rooms, storage and maintenance space, sound system, food service, and rubber walkway mats. If the rink will be used for hockey competition, shower and locker rooms, coaches' box, penalty box, and a timer's box will be required, with all having appropriate protection.

Artificial Ice

For many years, artificial ice panels have been used. These are made of sandwich board with plywood covered with thin layers of synthetic skating material. These panels allow heat build-up from the skate blades and have a short life span and are thus not recommended for a facility with daily skating. New products are constructed with solid skating material throughout, which allows skating on either side. They last several times as long with little heat build-up. The panels are constructed so that they interlock and are much lighter than the old type, making for simple installation. In addition, new spray-on, friction-reduction products are now available (Ice Rink Engineering, 1997).

Auxiliary Winter Sport Activity Areas

Nordic skiing (cross country) has had a long history in Europe and the United States. Most Nordic areas have been established separate from ski areas, but this is not a requirement. In general, cross country operations have been successful on a commercial basis only where snowfall has been substantial and temperatures low. Numbers of Nordic skiers increased in the 1970s, paralleling jogging's popularity because of the well-documented cardiovascular benefits of the sport. Generally the most popular Nordic areas include trails that are protected from the wind and sun, and include a variety of terrain with aesthetically appealing views.

While commercial Nordic areas require expensive grooming machines, and possibly snow making capability, many non-commercial trails can be identified and successfully utilized by recreation programs on open fields, golf courses, hiking trails, remote roads, and bike/jogging greenways. Ancillary facilities range from simple parking and warming huts to full-scale overnight lodges, equipment rental and repair services, and complete food service provisions.

Recently, many smaller ski resorts (and a few large) have installed commercial sledding or tubing slopes. While a slope ticket must be purchased, and many provide a dedicated lift, the charges are usually less than for a full mountain lift ticket. Many charge by the hour or by the run, and most rent sleds or tubes. A word of caution is that the commercial adaptation of sledding and tubing may present additional liability vulnerability (Heck, 1997; Best, 1997).

From time to time, new types of devices are introduced for participants to use to slide down a mountain. These range from bike-like contraptions with two short runners to snow skates, short "feet"-like skis, fat miniskis, and ski boards. Ski boards are about one-third the length of regular skis, wider, and lighter. Generally none of these devices requires changes in the slope design; however, some (skibikes) require adaptations of lift loading and unloading.

Provisions for ice climbing or ice fishing may be considered as part of the ski area design. While the numbers of participants may be small, there may be marketing and publicity advantages to including them. Because of recent advances in the equipment, snow shoeing has gained more popularity. Many gentle hiking trails can be utilized for this activity with little adaptation. If the area is appropriate, snowmobiling may be accommodated.

While mountain biking is not generally a winter sport, this growing activity should be considered in the design of any new ski area. Ski areas throughout the world are experiencing great interest in their sum-

mer use for both recreational mountain bike use and competition. Some ski areas have developed a full summer season, including lift operations, around mountain biking.

■ Summary

Winter sport areas and facilities have been promoted in the United States since the 1930s. Some of the early breakthroughs were refrigeration systems that allowed for year-round indoor ice skating, and rudimentary rope tows to carry skiers uphill. In recent years, scientific and engineering advances in ice and snow making have been the major factors in increasing the number of participants in order to support increasing facility development. Other advances in improved user equipment, maintenance equipment, computer-assisted design (CAD), marketing, and new construction techniques and materials have promoted growth in winter sports facilities. Rapid growth in winter sports participation continued until the 1970s in the U.S., but since then, growth has been limited. Recent trends have shown a consistent and substantial growth in snowboarding and the disappearance of family-owned areas as conglomerates have moved in with large interrelated and integrated multi-recreational and leisure complexes.

Learning Objective 1: The student will be able to develop strategies encompassing appropriate location, scope, and resource allocation for winter sport facilities.

The three most important aspects of any facility project include location (i.e., site and site development), scope (i.e., size and programming considerations), and resource allocation (i.e., costs for land, site development, professional fees, construction costs). Additional considerations would be orientation, topography, hydrology, and equipment.

Learning Objective 2: The student will be able to select the essential directional orientation, topography, hydrology, and market factors for winter sports facilities.

It is important to consider directional orientation, topography, and hydrology when planning a winter sports facility. If the facility is oriented inappropriately and the slopes are too steep, the project will face certain financial disaster in a short period of time. Further, it is necessary to complete a through marketing study to assure the financiers that the project is financially feasible.

Learning Objective 3: The student will be able to recognize the historical trends in user statistics, and participant and ski operations as these factors affect design.

Part of the marketing analysis should include a review of the historical trends including user statistics, economic conditions in the area, and population demographics within a 100-mile radius. It is always to important understand historical trends when developing a feasibility anaysis.

Learning Objective 4: The student will be able to develop the important aspects of design and layout of ski areas.

The key points in designing a ski and snowboarding area include directional orientation, slope, water flow above and below surface, sun and wind control, orientation of slopes, slope grooming, traffic control, parking, transportation, snow making machines, ski lifts, support facilities (e.g., lodge, locker rooms, restaurant, shopping area, administrative offices, storage, rental area, and equipment needs).

Learning Objective 5: The student will be able to identify essential aspects of ice rink design.

The essential aspects of ice rink design include year-round or seasonal operation, operations in cold or hot climates, structure housing the ice rink, spectator or non-spectator, ice making or artificial ice, ice rink floor design, support areas (e.g., storage, administrative offices, concessions, luxury suites, press area), ADA issues, etc.

Learning Objective 6: The student will be able to understand various options of axillary winter sports facilities.

The area of axillary sports increases every year. Planners for winter sports facilities must be flexible in the design of facilities.

■ Self-Assessment Exercise

1. What questions need to be answered prior to developing a ski and/or snowboarding area?
2. Why is location so important when developing a ski and/or snowboarding area?
3. What are the prime considerations relative to topographic and orientation variables when developing a ski and snowboarding area?
4. How should the slopes be designed?
5. What type of support facilities should be planned for the ski and/or snowboarding area?
6. Which equipment will most likely change the most—skis, bindings, and boots or snow boards? Why?
7. What type of operations equipment is necessary for a ski and/or snowboarding area?
8. What needs to be considered when constructing an ice rink?
9. What is important to understand about ice making?
10. How should the ice be maintained?
11. What is artificial ice?

■ Case Study

A. A good friend's father and a number of other investors have requested that you develop a strategic plan for the development of a ski and snowboarding area in the Rocky Mountains of Northern Montana approximately 60 miles from the Canadian boarder. Prepare the strategic plan for the development of the Havre Ski and Snowboarding Resort. This plan should include need statement, topography variables, physiographic variables, orientation analysis, plan for slopes, outline of support facilities, and equipment needs.

B. Mark Twain University is considering adding women's ice hockey to its athletic program. As the athletic director, you are to prepare a report for the president and board of trustees describing the costs of an ice rink.

■ References

Best, A. (1997). That's entertainment! Ski Area Management Journal, 36, 66-67, 89.

Best, A. (1996). Roundabouts solve traffic problems. Ski Area Management Journal, 35, 46-47, 88.

Farwell, T. (1996). The secret to modest success. Ski Area Management Journal, 35, 54-56.

Faster, M. (1996). Mountain mowing. Ski Area Management Journal, 35, 42-44.

Heck, T. (1997). On the road to new profits. Ski Area Management Journal, 36, 54-55.

Ice Rink Engineering and Manufacturing Co. (1997). Personal correspondence, 1727 E. Salufa Lake Road, Greenville, SC 29611.

Jackson, M.S. & Kaden, S.A. (1997). Beyond visualization. Ski Area Management Journal, 36, 56-57, 72.

Rowan, D. (1996). Skiing down, boarding up. Ski Area Management Journal, 35, 34-35, 73.

Spring, J. (1996). More days/more fun, but shrinking numbers. Ski Area Management Journal, 35, 44-45.

■ Suggested Reading

Ezersky, E.M., & Theibert, P.R. (1976). Facilities in sports and physical education. St. Louis, MO: C. V. Mosby.

Jubenville, A. (1976). Outdoor recreation planning. Philadelphia, PA: W. B. Saunders.

Ski Area Management Journal. All current issues. Circulation Office: 1093, A1A Beach Blvd. # 396, St. Augustine, FL 32084. Tel. (904) 461-4403.

CHAPTER 27

Ice Facilities

Jack Vivian, JRV, Inc.

Learning Objectives

After reading this chapter, the student will be able to

■ appreciate the historical development and recent popularity of skating, hockey, and the ice arena industry,

■ understand the variety of ice and dry-floor events and activities that can be programmed in an ice facility,

■ understand the basic design and layout requirements of ice arenas,

■ recognize the organizational structure, management requirements, and responsibilities of those who operate ice arenas, and

■ learn sources of management training, product information, and reference materials for this unique industry.

Introduction

Skating dates back to ancient times and is depicted in nearly every civilization and continent of the world through modern times. According to historical records, it became popular in the Scandinavian countries over 3000 years ago. Skates at that time were very primitive, with blades made of smoothed animal bones, wood, and later, steel. Initially, the skaters needed pushing poles to aid them in moving over the ice. In the nineteenth century, skates were made of metal fastened to wooden sole plates. According to Proctor (1969), the next evolution of skates was a clamp-on metal version held on by leather straps laced through slots and tied around the ankle. Next came ornately designed blades with curved pieces at the toes and, later, special shoes for skating with the blades attached by screws. Modern-day hockey and figure skates are made comfortable by high-quality leather with solid ankle support and are built with sophisticated blades made of stainless steel and, in the case of hockey, encased in plastic holders attached to lightweight boots.

In Belgium and Holland, skating was first employed by those who traveled across the frozen rivers and dykes delivering products and mail to surrounding communities. Naturally, as this became a way of life, there began contests for speed and thus the development of speed skating. Later, skating clubs were formed for both speed and leisure skating. The first organized club dates back to 1642 in Scotland.

The early settlers of Canada and the United States brought the sport of hockey to North America, although many historians claim the Indians played a game like hockey in the winter as a substitute for their favorite sport, lacrosse. Moreover, Great Britain is credited with introducing field hockey, and Ireland the sport of hurley (the hurley being the hockey stick) to Canada, making it difficult to determine the exact origin of hockey. What can be proven is that the sport of ice hockey evolved in the Dominion of Canada and retains its cultural importance to that country today.

By the late 1800s hockey was played in Canada and, shortly thereafter, several colleges in the United States began to play. The first recorded and organized indoor ice hockey game took place in Montreal on March 3, 1875, in the Victoria Skating Rink (Fischler, 1991). In 1892 the first intercollegiate hockey game between Harvard and Brown was played in Boston. By the early 1900s, hockey and figure skating became popular and were featured in the 1924 Olympic Games in Chamonix, France.

Sonja Henie of Norway is credited with helping popularize the ice resurfacer called the Zamboni, named after its inventor Frank Zamboni. Furthermore, her appearances in ice shows all over the world helped introduce the sport of figure skating to the masses. Skating recreationally has been popular ever since.

The production of films and the invention of television further helped in selling the sports of hockey and figure skating in the United States and around the world. This encouraged the building of indoor ice facilities. Today, there are over 1500 community-sized ice arenas in the United States, with rapid expansion due to the recent popularity of hockey and skating fueled by the expansion of the National Hockey League and minor league hockey and the popularity of figure skating on television. In 1996, Vivian (1996) conducted a national survey of community ice arenas and learned that 59% are owned by the public sector (cities, counties, colleges and universities and the states), while 41% are owned by private and nonprofit entities. Up to now, about 80% are single-surface facilities, however, recent trends indicate the building of dual-surface, family-oriented complexes.

Ice skating and hockey are no longer relegated to the cold northern regions of the country. The advent of steel and long-span arena structures and advances in ice-making technology and refrigeration allow ice activities to take place year round in practically every geographic location of the world. Because of this technology, skating has turned into a year-round activity, and public or open skating has become popular summertime recreation in the warmer climates of the South.

Summer hockey and skating camps attract a host of students and high-quality instructors and turn into profitable and popular summertime recreation for area youth. With the growth and promotion of college hockey and major and minor league professional hockey, the star players in these leagues make excellent instructors and role models for young players just learning the game. Besides, the quest for more recreation and free-time activities and the international television coverage of figure skating and hockey, especially during Olympic years, have similarly contributed significantly to the demand for more ice sport facilities. Furthermore, skating and hockey are seen as growth sports of the future, especially as facilities are built in the sun-belt areas of the country.

The demand for more ice facilities and professionally trained and competent managers for a new breed of dual-surface and multipurpose facilities has never been higher. This chapter will introduce the sport management student to the activities and events held in ice arenas, provide insights into the unique designs of these facilities, and identify the important management responsibilities and competencies needed by successful managers in the ice arena industry.

1. *What are the activities and ice sports that are traditionally held in an ice facility during the ice season? How has the demand for these activities changed over time?*

National interest in ice sports is growing rapidly. Ice is used for the activities suggested in Table 27.1. The biggest demand for ice is from individuals or organizations that rent it for the activities described in the following pages.

Hockey

Ice hockey can be played either formally in schools or leagues or informally in "pick-up" groups. According to the National Sporting Goods Association, 2.5 million Americans played ice hockey on some level in 1997, a 29.2% growth in only one year. Each segment creates different ice-time demands and will be discussed separately.

High School Hockey

To date, high school hockey has been limited to the northern region of the United States, with Massachusetts, Minnesota, and Michigan having the highest participation rates. Teams are generally funded by the school systems, but some teams that are not funded rely on booster club membership and fund raisers to cover costs of uniforms, equipment, and ice rental. Unlike other major sports played in high school, most of the coaches are volunteers.

Table 27.1 Potential Ice Uses for a Multipurpose Facility

Ice Activities

Hockey
Youth hockey leagues
    Youth
    "Minor leagues"
Adult hockey leagues
    Over 35 year old
    Under 35 year old
Drop-In hockey
Tournaments
    Youth
    Adults (men and women)
Sledge hockey (handicapped)
School Activities
P.E. Classes
School hockey-team practice
    Boys and girls
Collegiate teams and games
    Men's and women's
Collegiate P.E. Classes
Broomball
    Youth—boys, girls, co-rec.
    University—men, women, co-rec.
    Adult—men, women, co-rec.

Speed Skating (men and women)
Public Skating
General (5-7 2-hr. sessions/wk.)
Adult (daytime/late evening)
Figure Skating
Parent/tot skating
Learn-to-skate lessons (youth & adult)
Patch, freestyle and dance sessions
(for competitive skaters)
Figure skating clubs
    Figure
    Freestyle
    Dance/ballet
    Precision team
    Ice Shows and exhibitions
    Competitions
Icercise

Amateur Hockey Leagues

Throughout the 1990s, hockey as a whole has shown steady increases in popularity throughout the United States, as Figure 27.1 demonstrates. The National Hockey League's expansion from 21 to 30 teams in the 1990s has helped to spur this interest.

Teams are generally classified by age and ability, with AAA representing the most advanced players. Players try out for the various teams at the beginning of each season. The levels of play are shown in Table 27.2.

Hockey leagues give participants an opportunity to play competitive hockey with their peers. Leagues range from 4 to 30 teams. Each team consists of approximately 15 to 17 people, although no more than six people per team are allowed on the ice during a competitive game. During practice sessions, however, skating and shooting drills involve all team members.

Players range in age from 5 to 50 years, depending on the league. The majority are between 6 and 17 years old.

Demand for ice time from league hockey peaks during hockey season, which normally begins in October and lasts through mid-March. Recent interest in hockey is steadily increasing the length of this peak demand period. During a season, each team practices about 17 to 20 hours and plays approximately 20 to 24 two-hour games.

Hockey is a relatively expensive sport because of the cost of renting ice and buying and maintaining equipment. Players typically come from middle to upper-middle class families. Those who cannot afford the costs may need to be funded by a local association or some other local group.

Hockey players frequently travel up to 65 miles to participate on a team, although they prefer to play

USA Hockey Team Registration, 1971-1997*

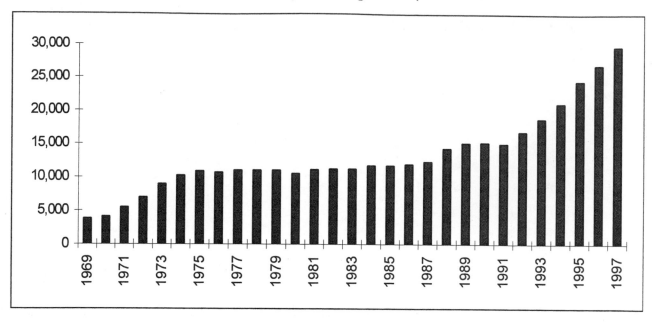

Figure 27.1 USA Hockey Team Registration, 1971-1997.

Table 27.2 USA Hockey Levels

Classification	Boys/Men	Girls/Women
Initiation Program	5 or under	
Mite	8 or under	
Squirt	10 or under	12 or under
Pee Wee	12 or under	15 or under
Bantam	14 or under	
Midget	17 or under	19 or under
High School	19 or under	
Senior Novice	18 & over	
Senior U.S.	20 & over	20 & over
Senior Open	20 & over	
Senior Non-Checking	20 & over	
Over 30	30 & over	

close to their homes. Hockey players prefer to rent ice after 5:00 p.m. and until 12:00 a.m. during the week, after work or school, and from 8:00 a.m. to 2:00 a.m. on the weekends. Typically, most arenas rent ice to the youth leagues in the early evening and to the adult leagues after 9:00 or 10:00 p.m.

Pick-Up Hockey

Pick-up hockey is an informal game for players who drop in at a time scheduled just for this activity. These players are not necessarily affiliated with a league. Pick-up groups typically consist of 12 peo-

Table 27.3 Growth of USA Women's Hockey

Year	Number of Female Teams	Estimated Number of Players
1996*	710	20,214
1995	498	17,537
1994	352	12,577
1993	269	8,991
1992	232	6,805
1991	154	5,573
1990	149	4,800
1988	169	5,100
1986	142	4,500
1984	114	3,000

Source: USA Hockey   *As of 5/20/96

ple (six on each team) who range in age from 15 to 35. Due to the informal status of pick-up games, the players are more price-sensitive than players in organized hockey leagues. Pick-up groups typically play during off-peak times, such as early morning or after midnight, when ice rental rates are reduced. These groups are seldom willing to travel as far as league players, preferring to skate at rinks close to their homes. Pick-up hockey groups rent ice an average of one or two times a week throughout the year.

Women's Hockey

For many years, women's hockey lagged far behind the men in terms of participation and interest. Now, this segment of the hockey market is growing even faster than men's hockey. As seen in Table 27.3, women's membership in USA Hockey has increased threefold in the 1990s. Of the women playing hockey, the majority is under the age of 20. The largest individual age segment, according to USA Hockey, is girls under the age of nine. With the United States Women winning the gold medal at the 1998 Winter Olympics in Nagano, Japan, women's hockey at all ages is expected to grow dramatically in the years ahead.

For the 1994-95 season, the NCAA had nine Division I, and six Division III teams. At the end of the 1995-96, season the NCAA expanded to 12 Division I, and 11 Division III teams, with the number of Division III teams expected to rise to 14 by 1998. This has prompted the NCAA to label women's hockey as an "emerging sport" that they hope to develop into a national championship level. But to do so, the NCAA requires that 40 teams achieve varsity status before sponsoring a national championship.

The dominant college hockey league for women is the Eastern Collegiate Athletic Conference (ECAC), which splits their women's hockey program into two leagues: the ECAC Women's League and the ECAC Women's Alliance. The Women's League has 12 teams and play 22 games, while the Women's Alliance is directed at schools with emerging varsity teams that don't want such a demanding season. Currently, the Women's Alliance is made up of 11 teams and is expected to grow to 14 in 1998-99. In addition, the Midwestern Collegiate Women's Hockey Alliance (MCWHA) consists of 12 club teams. The newly formed Central Collegiate Women's Hockey Association (CCWHA) fields eight club teams from Michigan, Ohio, and Illinois. In addition to these three leagues, there are 20 club teams currently playing throughout the country.

Just as women's hockey is growing at the collegiate level, the sport is also growing at the high school level. On March 21, 1994, the Minnesota State High School Association sanctioned girls' ice hockey as a varsity sport, making Minnesota the first state to do so. In its inaugural season, 1994-95, 24 schools formed girls' varsity teams.

Sledge Hockey

Sledge hockey is a team sport developed in Norway during the early 1960s to give persons with disabilities an opportunity to participate in ice sports. Participants sit on low sleds, or "sledges," mounted on 10-inch metal skates. Participants propel themselves with short ice picks, which are also used to pass and shoot the puck. Sledges can be adjusted to fit the needs of individual participants. Players are secured onto the sledges with Velcro straps and seat belts; sledges may also have backs for support. Numbering the sledges helps players find the right size quickly.

Sledge hockey is a full-contact sport played on a regulation-size ice surface, with regulation-size nets. A game consists of two 20-minute periods of effective play between two teams of six players each. Able-bodied participants can also use the sledges, and mixed competitions are possible. Rules for the game have been established by the Canadian Wheelchair Sports Association and are very similar to regular hockey.

Figure Skating

Figure skating has experienced similar increases in popularity, particularly among young people and females because of the publicity created by the Olympics and the many ice skating shows now on television. In a report released in February of 1997 by ESPN and Chilton sports, a survey of females responded that their favorite sport is ice skating. Another report published by USA Today stated that figure skating was the fourth most popular spectator sport, behind football, basketball, and baseball.

The United States Figure Skating Association (USFSA) is the governing body for the sport of amateur ice skating in the United States, and it is the national body that sanctions skaters for national, world, and Olympic competitions. Since 1921, the USFSA has directed and encouraged the development of figure skating skills instruction, and it has supervised the competitive aspects of the sport.

The USFSA uses an established test structure to measure individual achievement and abilities of skaters in four main areas:

Figures. The act of following a trace on the ice in the form of the Arabic number eight or a more complicated figure. The area on the ice surface where these figures are practiced is referred to as a "patch."

Freestyle. Individual skating that includes a required number and type of jumps, spins, and other moves.

Dance. A man and a woman performing a choreographed dance on ice; the man must not lift the woman above his waist or throw her.

Pairs. A man and a woman performing jumps, lifts, and throws (the man pushing the woman from him).

Figure skating is normally administered by a skating club that collects dues from individual skaters. The club then rents ice and coordinates all classes, tests, and competitions. The skating club, in turn, is a member of either the Ice Skating Institute (ISI) or the USFSA. Both of these national organizations provide members with uniform national standards. This lets skaters who practice at different ice rinks with different teachers gain the same skills as any other ISI or USFSA member. Typically, the ISI provides a set of standards for less experienced skaters; more advanced skills are covered under USFSA programs.

Skating sessions, typically two hours in length, are divided into 45-minute patchwork sessions and 45-minute freestyle sessions with a dance or stroking session. Each hour is subdivided into a 15- or 20-minute lesson with 35 to 40 minutes of practice time. On the average, lessons range from $12 to $18 per 15 minutes. Skaters attend two to three two-hour sessions per week under normal circumstances. When they are training for a specific event, attendance is increased to two sessions a day four to five times each week. The high costs of lessons and fees associated with club membership make recreational skating an expensive sport. As such, the majority of the participants come from middle- to upper-middle-class families who can afford the expenses.

Figure skaters generally rent ice on weekdays in the early morning between 5:30 a.m. and 7:30 a.m. and in the late afternoon between 4:00 p.m. and 6:00 p.m. The number of recreational skaters on the ice during a two-hour session is limited by the number of patches or figures that fit on a standard rink at one time (approximately 680 square feet per patch). Therefore, a maximum of 24 people can be on the ice during a skating session. Figure skaters normally live near the ice rink where they skate. Nationally, they represent 20% of the ice rental segment.

The demand for ice to practice pair and dance skating is considerably less than for freestyle and figure skating. Because there are few male figure skaters in the 5-to-18-year age bracket, most pair and dance skating is limited to women who work on these skating maneuvers on their own. A few have partners. Some clubs let pair and dance skaters practice during the freestyle sessions, while others try to schedule ice for them early in the morning, after school, or late in the evening.

Table 27.4 ISI Speed Skating Levels

Level	Age
Senior	18 years & up
Intermediate	16 and 17 years
Junior	14 and 15 years
Juvenile	12 and 13 years
Midget	10 and 11 years
Pony	8 and 9 years
Bantam	7 years & under

Many skating clubs have separate adult skating sessions where dance skating is the central part of the program. Those introduced to skating at a later age and those who cannot risk the jumps and spins of freestyle skating enjoy one or two hours once a week of dance skating. Knowledgeable arena managers accommodate this important group into the ice schedule, as they are often the prime organizers of the club, and they provide the leadership and direction to the entire figure-skating program.

Like USA Hockey, USFSA has experienced astronomical growth within its membership in the 1990s. Their members include clubs that foster amateur figure skating, individual figure skaters who are not members of the club, associate members, and honorary members. Since 1987 the basic skills category has experienced the most growth of USFSA memberships. This is significant because basic skills is a program designed for persons of all ages who wish to learn the skills and techniques for recreation or competition. These classes are not held at specific skating clubs, but at any arena throughout the country that offers learn-to skate-classes. It is an inexpensive and enjoyable program of group lessons for all members of the family.

Speed Skating

Speed skating is a form of racing that emphasizes balance, rhythm, and drive on the straightaway and around turns. Speed skaters can reach up to 30 miles an hour around a specialized or specifically modified track. Participants perfect their time and distance through training, practice, and competition. Skaters of all ages and abilities can participate in speed skating since they can compete either in races against each other or against their own times. While specialized skates have been developed for speed skating, many skaters begin with equipment they already have for other forms of ice skating.

The Ice Skating Institute (ISI) offers guidelines for learning and competing in speed skating. Their guidelines introduce skaters to the basic strokes and to procedures for conducting races. Participants begin by learning and perfecting the straight-away stroke. They develop the balance, rhythm, and drive that give speed skating its speed and grace. When these straightaway skills are perfected, skaters then learn to navigate turns without losing speed.

Formal races consist of a series of heats over long and short distances. Champions are chosen by their performance in both types of events, not just one or the other. Points are awarded by place, with five points for first place, three for second, two for third, and one for fourth. Competitors are matched by sex and age in several different levels:

Speed skating has traditionally been performed on a special surface designed and built for that purpose. With the development of "short track" speed skating, which is based on a 100-meter course laid out on a regular indoor rink, and with the building of more Olympic-size ice arenas, speed skaters will demand more ice time.

Broomball

Broomball is a fast-paced, exciting ice game and a great answer for summer athletic teams looking for a dynamic sport to keep themselves in shape over the winter. Broomball is played on ice without skates. It is similar to hockey, except that players wear sneakers and use brooms instead of skates and hockey sticks. It is great exercise and popular for all ages.

There are six players on the ice at one time: three forwards, two defensive players, and a goal-tender. Corecreational leagues usually require that at least two females be on the ice at all times. Games are 50 minutes long, divided into two 25-minute halves. The game is played like hockey, with the objective being to score the most goals. On-ice referees wearing skates assess penalties for such infractions as tripping, high-sticking, cross-checking, and boarding. The penalized team plays shorthanded until the player(s) can return. Some arenas organize two games at the same time with goals set up across the width of the rink, inside the blue lines.

Serious players purchase knee pads (like those used in volleyball), elbow pads, and even special shoes. Most leagues like to play on rough ice (already cut up) rather than freshly made ice. Many arenas require or provide helmets with or without face masks, and many provide brooms. Some even build special goals larger than hockey goals to enhance scoring. Teams usually like to socialize after the game and can be good clients for concession areas and party rooms.

Learn-to-Skate Programs

Learn-to-skate programs are typically administered by arenas that hire local skating professionals to teach the lessons on an hourly basis. One instructor can typically teach 10 to 20 students, and it is possible to have four or five groups and instructors on the ice at any one time. The ice surface is divided up by the ability level of the participants.

The length of the group lessons may vary from a suggested minimum of 6 weeks to a maximum of 20 weeks. Lessons are normally taught on Saturday or Sunday so parents can transport their children to the arena and even take lessons themselves. Some programs, especially in new facilities, give specialized youth lessons after school and adult lessons during weekday evenings to accommodate adults who want to learn the basics of skating on their own, without children. Weekday adult lesson programs typically evolve into adult skating clubs, often specializing in dance skating.

The United States Figure Skating Association and the Ice Skating Institute both have beginning lesson programs with various levels of tests to reward the progress of each skater. Tests need to be carefully spaced so that pupils can take them frequently and experience the satisfaction of accomplishment and earning a badge.

A well-run, well-publicized learn-to-skate program is an excellent way to introduce the pleasure of skating to a community when a new facility is opened. Participants generally take several series of lessons. Once they master the activity, they become excited by skating and advance into a skating club or hockey organization.

The management of a new facility should keep in mind the importance of having a complete line of well-maintained rental skates available for this program. Most new participants rent skates until they begin to like the sport and decide to invest in skates of their own. Some arenas provide the skates as a part of the lesson fees and work hard at seeing that this initial experience is positive. A good learn-to-skate program can be a big money maker for the arena as well as an excellent way to introduce new participants to the facility and recruit them into the sports of hockey, figure skating, and speed skating.

Public Skating

Public skaters can be those who do not skate regularly, skating enthusiasts, and individuals associated with organized groups. This segment includes families, school and religious groups, and other groups from the surrounding area. They skate one or two times a month.

Public skaters normally live in the immediate area of the ice rink, but some will travel up to 25 miles to skate. These skaters represent different socioeconomic levels and typically do not own ice-skating equipment and therefore must rent ice skates. They usually prefer to skate in the late afternoon and early evening hours (4:00 p.m. to 8:00 p.m.) on weekdays, and in the afternoon and early evening hours on weekends (12:00 p.m. to 6:00 p.m.). Public skaters pay up to $5.00 per session for adults and expect to receive senior citizens' and children's discounts of 10% to 20%. They will pay $2.00 to rent skates.

Traditional public-skating sessions last for about two hours and are offered 6 to 10 times a week. Attendance at these sessions ranges from 25 to 400 people, depending on the season and time of day. The annual average is 150 persons. At many arenas, the public skating segment represents a sizable portion of the total hours of prime-time ice use; it also represents substantial income for the facility.

Private Ice Rental

Renting ice to youth and adult groups, organizations, and local companies not directly affiliated with skating and hockey can be an excellent source of additional income and a good way to introduce various ice sports to potential new users. Service organizations like to sponsor programs for their members and families, especially around holiday periods. Local businesses are searching for wholesome activities for employee parties. Moreover, many youth organizations look for activities to stimulate involvement and excitement in their organization. Skating, pick-up hockey, and broomball, where the essential equipment is provided by the facility, fit their needs well. These rentals, especially those at the holiday periods, fit into an arena schedule since most of the hockey and figure-skating organizations like to reduce their hours at this time of the year.

2. *What can ice arenas be used for in the off-season when ice skating and hockey are not in demand?*

The large, open space of a community-sized ice arena makes it an ideal location for activities other than ice skating and hockey. Many outdoor sports, such as soccer and lacrosse, have been adapted to indoor areas the size of typical arenas. These activities, as well as special events such as shows, exhibits, and meetings, represent potentially profitable uses of arena facilities at times of the year when the demand for ice is low. A sampling of dry-floor uses is presented in Table 27.5, and characteristics of the activities are described more fully in the following materials.

Table 27.5 Potential Dry-Floor Uses for a MultiPurpose Facility

Dry-Floor Activities

Sports/Recreation
Indoor soccer
  Youth
  High school
  College
  Community leagues
  Adult
Indoor lacrosse
  Youth
  College
In-line skate hockey
Basketball
Tennis
Volleyball
Pre-season baseball
Roller-skating
In-line skating
Batting cages
Golf driving range
Archery
Fencing
Exercise classes
Gymnastics
Walking/running track
Dance classes

Shows
Animal (cat, dog, horse)
Antiques
Arts and crafts
Boats
Collectibles
Fishing and hunting goods
Flea markets
Home and garden
Sporting goods
Vehicles

Social Gatherings
Banquets
Commencements
Community organizations
Dances
Food fairs
Picnics and parties
Table games (cards, bingo)

Recreational Sports

In areas of the country where the weather interferes with or shortens the season for outdoor sports, many recreational sports have been adapted indoors. Soccer and lacrosse, both popular sports, can be played indoors. Other activities that require large, open spaces, such as in-line skating, volleyball, or golf driving cages, can also be adapted if demand warrants.

In-Line Hockey

In-line hockey is one of the fastest growing sports in North America. These players are not draining the ranks of ice hockey players, however. According to the NIHA, 20% of in-line hockey players were ice hockey players, but 80% had never played hockey before.

Although the sport began almost 10 years ago, the NIHA was formed in 1993 to standardize and promote the sport in affiliation with the International In-Line Skating Association (IISA). In 1994, USA Hockey In-Line was created by the governing body of ice hockey, USA Hockey, and was also a member of the IISA. These two organizations governed the sport of in-line hockey separately until December of 1996, when USA Hockey In-Line acquired NIHA and merged the two organizations into one. This firmly established USA Hockey In-Line as the largest in-line program in the world, with the potential for more than 80,000 registered members and 600 teams.

Along with offering a variety of memberships, USA Hockey In-Line is also partners with the National Hockey League (NHL) in presenting the NHL Breakout Tour. The tour features tournaments, skills clinics, and special appearances by NHL stars intended to boost the interest of people in both in-line skating and the NHL. In the summer of 1996, the tour visited 16 cities and attracted more than 225,000 participants.

With rules similar to those for ice hockey, in-line hockey can be played on any smooth, clean, dry surface that is at least 145 feet by 65 feet and no more than 200 feet by 100 feet. The preferred size is 180 feet by 80 feet, which is close to the size of a regulation ice rink (200 feet by 85 feet). Dasherboards at least eight inches and no more than four feet high must surround the surface. Major differences between in-line hockey and ice hockey include five players per team instead of six, no offsides, two 22-minute halves instead of three 20-minute periods, a zero-tolerance rule against violence that is strictly enforced, and a playing piece that can be either a ball or a puck.

In-Line Skating

In-line skating is a rapidly growing sport that combines roller skating and ice skating by placing the wheels of roller skates in a single line that looks and functions like an ice skate. Since these skates can be used on any smooth, hard surface, they are popular with hockey players and speed skaters, who use them for cross-training. The activity has developed rapidly over its brief life, creating opportunities for multipurpose recreational facilities, such as hosting in-line races, stunt competitions, and public in-line skating. Competitive events are now being developed that take advantage of the unique performance characteristics of in-line skates.

Indoor Soccer

Indoor soccer is an exciting game, with high scoring, four quarters, and a fast-action format. Unlike other sports that require expensive protective gear or playing equipment, soccer, indoor or outdoor, is also low-cost, a factor that explains its worldwide popularity. It is a year-round sport, but in colder climates, outdoor play is sometimes impossible; indoor soccer allows players to consistently train and compete.

The demand for indoor soccer playing facilities has been rising steadily since professional indoor soccer was introduced by the Major Indoor Soccer League. Ice arenas, because of their dimensions and design, are easily transformed into indoor soccer facilities.

Indoor soccer in the United States has two professional leagues: the National Professional Soccer League (NPSL), started in 1984, and the Continental Indoor Soccer League (CISL), founded more recently in 1993. Their version of soccer allows for fewer players due to the smaller field size. An indoor soccer field is usually no larger than 200 feet by 85 feet (size of an NHL ice rink), while an outdoor soccer field is at least 110 yards by 60 yards. This results in a high-speed sport sometimes referred to as "pinball soccer." Although indoor soccer is not as popular as outdoor, both the NPSL and the CISL have drawn crowds exceeding 10,000 spectators for their games.

Soccer is governed internationally by the Federation Internationale de Football Association (FIFA). FIFA holds authority over the World Cup and the Women's World Championship, as well as soccer involvement in the Olympics. The United States belongs to a continental subgroup of FIFA, the Confederation Norte-Centroamericana y del Caribe de Futbol (CONCACAF). The United States Soccer Federation (U.S. Soccer), which is linked with FIFA, directly governs American soccer. U.S. Soccer is grouped into smaller divisions, including the Unites States Youth Soccer Association (USYSA) and the United States Amateur Soccer Association (USASA). In addition, the American Youth Soccer Organization (AYSO) and the Soccer Association for Youth (SAY) are both national affiliates of U.S. Soccer. Currently,

Indoor Soccer has no governing body and is not sanctioned by any of the above national organizations. Some indoor soccer leagues, however, are sanctioned by local and state organizations. And a national indoor soccer tournament has been taking place for several years and is sponsored by Mitre (a soccer apparel company).

Cities with facilities for indoor soccer have found that these venues can be booked easily for a large majority of the day. Peak indoor soccer seasons vary, some lasting from October through April, others from December through May. During an average week of the indoor soccer season, more than 72 games can be played. The facilities can also be used year-round to host a large number of tournaments, special events, and championships.

Although ice-related activity seasons and indoor soccer seasons overlap, the two sports can be combined through careful scheduling. Ice facilities may be transformed into indoor soccer facilities in a very short time, without removing the ice. Portable sections of indoor soccer flooring or special carpeting can cover an ice surface and convert it to an indoor soccer surface in approximately 90 minutes. This allows a facility to book soccer and ice activities on alternating days without difficulty.

Indoor ("Box") Lacrosse

Lacrosse is the oldest sport in North America, dating back 1000 years. It is often referred to as the fastest game on two feet. In the 1400s Jean de Brebrief witnessed a Huron contest and likened the stick with which the Indians played to the "crosier" carried by bishops at religious ceremonies. By the 1800s the French standardized field dimensions. In the 1900s lacrosse became an Olympic sport, and the United States Intercollegiate Lacrosse League (USILL) was formed.

Lacrosse, which is usually played outdoors in the spring, is a fast-paced sport with long sprints, abrupt stops and starts, and body checks. Advances in protective equipment have made lacrosse one of the safest contact sports. The object of the game is to put a 5 1/4-ounce solid rubber ball into the 6 foot by 6 foot goal of the opposing team. The ball can be carried, thrown, batted or rolled with the crosse (lacrosse stick), or kicked in any direction. Lacrosse complements football, soccer, basketball, and hockey and gives young athletes a genuine choice of team sports to play in the spring.

Lacrosse is popular with both men and women. Men like lacrosse because of the running and contact, while women value the grace and beauty of the sport. Six players are allowed on the field at once, but because of the sport's free substitution rules, many more players can participate in each game.

Many consider lacrosse to be one of the fastest growing of all sports. The United States Intercollegiate Lacrosse Association (USILA) reports a strong growth in men's college varsity programs since 1983, as does the Intercollegiate Women's Lacrosse Coaches Association's (IWLCA) for women's varsity collegiate programs. According to the National Interscholastic Lacrosse Association (NILA), high school lacrosse is now the fastest-growing segment of the sport. In addition, USWLA membership, representing girls' high school varsity lacrosse, has experienced comparable growth since 1988.

As in indoor soccer, many of the statistics available are only for outdoor lacrosse, or outdoor and indoor combined. However, in cold weather, outdoor lacrosse players may become interested in indoor play, and could become a possible market.

The Major Indoor Lacrosse League (MILL) was formed in 1986 as a viable professional indoor lacrosse league. Indoor lacrosse is played in an enclosed area much like a hockey arena. It is played under different rules than field lacrosse, allowing more physical contact. MILL has six teams. In 1994, MILL contracted a six-year national broadcast agreement with both ESPN and ESPN2. The MILL reached new attendance records in 1995, averaging close to 11,000 fans per game for an overall attendance of just 300,000.

The fast-paced style of lacrosse and its increasing popularity seem to fit well with the off-season uses for an arena. Like indoor soccer, "box" lacrosse can be played on a hockey arena, either on the dry floor or on a rug placed over the ice. This is a sport of the future and an excellent use of an arena's off-season.

Other Indoor Sports

The smooth, dry floor of an ice arena is a good surface for many other physical activities. Basketball, volleyball, and tennis are some of the team sports that fit well in dry arenas. Other individual activities, such as roller-skating, archery, fencing, skateboarding, batting cages, and golf driving ranges or exercise areas, can also be accommodated easily.

Meetings and Trade Shows

Meetings and trade shows create special design requirements for a facility. Multipurpose sport and recreational facilities, because of their large open space, can be used to host these events if their design requirements are taken into consideration during planning; amenities and decoration that might be suitable for serious athletes might not be attractive to meeting participants.

Trade shows are expositions that generate sales for a particular industry. Sponsors are usually trade associations, industry groups, or private entrepreneurs. For these gatherings the sponsors are generally concerned about exhibit space only. Because attendance is often limited to members of a single industry, however, the attendees are usually drawn from a wide geographic area, so they often need overnight accommodations near the show.

Public shows, such as boat shows, antique shows, and craft shows, draw attendance from the general population. Like trade shows, public shows primarily require exhibit space. Demand for overnight accommodations is limited to exhibitors, as the attendees normally come from nearby.

Sporting events and cultural events also create demands for space. The requirements for these events are often very specific and must be considered when the facility is designed.

The needs of trade shows and public shows tend to be less complex, with flat, open space being the prime requirement. This market segment is more interested in maximum space availability than flexibility. Athletic events have space needs specific to the given sport. The most adaptable space for this type of event is an arena, but no single space configuration can appeal to all segments of the market.

3. *What special equipment is required to sharpen skates?*

Provisions for handling the public's figure and hockey skates and the facility's rental skates must be provided and properly located within the facility. A dual- or triple-headed sharpening machine is usually located in the main lobby area adjacent to the skate rental room and connected to the pro shop, allowing one attendant, trained in the art of skate sharpening, to maintain both customer and facility skate sharpening needs. A triple-headed machine with one grinding wheel each for hockey and figure skating and one for cross grinding is the best solution although there are a number of skating sharpening models available with only one wheel. That means that the sharpener must dress the wheel before switching to sharpening hockey or figure skates.

For control and record-keeping purposes, most arenas use a ticket system similar to the local shoe repair shop. Customers either drop off their skates and leave them to be sharpened or the attendant is able to service them immediately. A secure area with shelves is provided for storing customer skates. However, during high usage periods, the arena normally has a skate sharpener in attendance to immediately take care of the customer skates. During slow periods, the attendant can do the necessary preventative maintenance and sharpening for rental skates and work in the pro shop selling or stocking merchandise. Skate sharpening and care of rental skates are important duties that require specific training and an interest in learning about the intricacies of skating and boot care.

From a business standpoint, skate sharpening is a very important function and a good source of revenue with little or no operational costs. Once the skate sharpener has been purchased and paid for, personnel cost and a small amount of electricity are the only expense items. Furthermore the revenue from skate sharpening justifies having a person available and greatly reduces the cost of operating the pro shop since one person can normally perform both functions in a well-laid-out venue.

4. *How is artificial ice made?*

The freezing of an ice sheet is usually accomplished by the circulation of a heat transfer fluid through a network of pipes located in a concrete or sand-based floor below the ice surface. Community-sized ice arenas are designed primarily for recreational use, in which the ice is normally left in for lengthy periods of time, ranging from a couple of months to years. Large-seating-capacity public arenas, auditoriums, and field houses, on the other hand, are used for a variety of spectator events, which generally requires that the ice be produced in 12 to 16 hours and removed easily or covered with an insulated floor to accommodate non-ice events. For these settings, a specially designed floor and removal system is required to properly remove the ice in 20 to 24 hours.

The heat transfer fluid is predominantly a secondary coolant, such as ethylene or propylene glycol, methanol, or calcium chloride. Freon-22 and ammonia are used most frequently for chilling secondary coolants although new products (i.e., R134a) are being looked at as CFC refrigerants are projected to be phased out due to environmental concerns.

There are both direct and indirect refrigeration systems, although direct systems, in which the refrigerant circulates in the floor, are being phased out as most rink designers prefer to use an indirect system. In the past, ammonia or freon had been used as a direct coolant for freezing the floor.

Properly designed indoor arenas can be operated year-round without a shut down period. Some arenas operate 8 to 10 months and close because of maintenance, the inability to control indoor conditions, or unprofitable operation during part of the year. Today's technology allows the rink designer to provide sufficient refrigeration capacity for year-round operations in almost any type of climate, provided that the facility is designed to address humidity and other operating conditions.

Once it is determined that ice is to be made, the refrigeration plant is started, taking several days to pull the temperature of the refrigerant down to 18 to 20 degrees (most arena operators try to reduce the temperature 2 to 4 degrees per hour). This freezes the concrete floor or sand-based floor. Once at 20 degrees, water can be applied to the surface (sand-based floors are thoroughly saturated during the temperature reduction process) and freezing of the ice slab begins. Once one quarter inch of thickness is developed, the ice is painted white with a water-based paint. The hockey lines are then painted on top of this layer and the ice built up to one inch of thickness before it is ready to be skated on. After the operator reaches three quarters of an inch in thickness, flooding of the ice can be accomplished with the ice resurfacer instead of hoses.

The wise arena manager tries to maintain the ice at one-inch thickness to reduce the cost of producing good-quality ice. It stands to reason that the thicker the ice, the more costly it is to maintain. In fact, it is estimated that each one-tenth of an inch of ice represents about 1000 gallons of water; therefore one inch of ice contains approximately 10,000 gallons of water which has to be frozen. Since the ice is being resurfaced hourly in most cases, with a thin layer being taken off and replaced, it is important to maintain the one-inch thickness and for weekly depth readings and ice maintenance to occur.

5. *How are ice facilities managed? What skills and competencies are required to run these unique facilities?*

The key to the successful operation of an ice arena is the people within the organization. The better the staff is organized into a smooth running unit and the better staff members know their jobs and how they relates to other aspects of the facility's operation, the better they will perform and the better service they will provide those who use the facility. Competent and knowledgeable facility employees go a long way toward providing safe and satisfying surroundings and experiences for users of ice arena facilities.

Below is a typical two-surface ice arena organizational structure showing the various positions and job titles required to operate a facility with modern-day amenities.

Regardless of the size of the arena or number of ice surfaces, the day-to-day management of the facility should be under the direction of a full-time manager supported by a number of assistants. Normally, the manager is responsible for the business aspects, personnel, booking, and contracts, while the assistant managers oversee the various profit centers (concessions, pro shop, skate rental, sharpening) and operations, programming, and supervision of events and activities. The development of programs in start-up situations is an important task for the entire management team over the first several years of operation. The financial success of any new ice arena setting will depend in large part on the manager's ability to introduce and attract new participants to skating and hockey.

There are two important considerations in putting together a management team and opening, operating, and developing dynamic programs for a new facility. The first is to hire a mature management team capable of overseeing a seven-day-per-week, 16-to-20-hour-per-day operation. These facilities are used around the clock in some settings and even if they are not, the equipment operates 24 hours a day to hold ice and must be monitored and maintained daily.

The second is to establish a compete set of policies and procedures governing financial, operational and programming aspects of and ice and dry-floor facility. In today's litigious society, risk management and safety issues are of utmost importance, as are the training and daily operation of the refrigeration, ice resurfacing, and various profit and service centers in the facility. Few new managers have the knowledge to design these policies and procedures, and it is normally necessary for a new arena to hire consultants or experienced managers from other settings to assist with structuring the management systems.

The major responsibilities of an ice arena management team are as follows.

A. Human Resources Management
  1. Recruit, orient, train and schedule a diverse team of employees to supervise and provide services.
  2. Supervise and evaluate these employees on a regular basis.
  3. Work with volunteers and support service personnel.

B. Policy Administration
  1. Develop and consistently administer policies and procedures.
  2. Recommend changes in policies and communicate these to staff, user groups, personnel, and support services.

C. Marketing, Public Relations and Contacts
  1. Direct, counsel, and interact with user groups.

Ice Arena Organization Structure

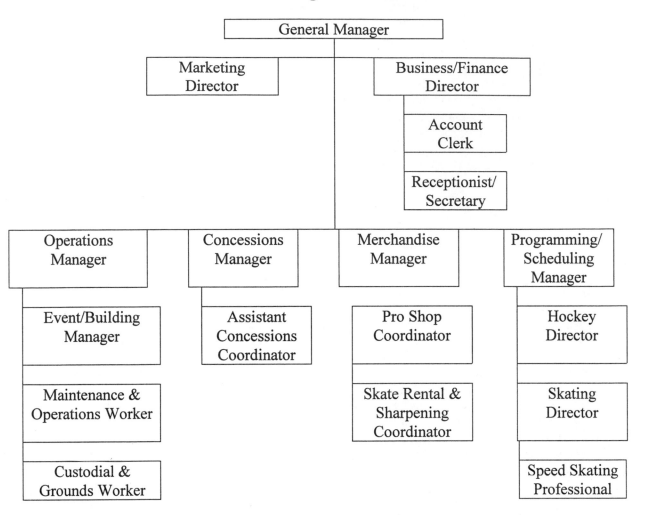

2. Develop and publish literature, brochures and promotional material on the programs and activities of the facility.

D. Scheduling and Contract Administration

1. Provide leadership to insure maximum efficient multi-purpose use of facilities.

2. Oversee the signing of contracts and collect of insurance certificates.

E. Fiscal Accountability

1. Be responsible for fiscal operations and controls.

2. Project and monitor budgets.

3. Generate income from sales, rentals and programs.

4. Assume responsible for inventory and supplies management.

F. Event Management

1. Coordinate and provide personnel, equip-

ment, and supervision for a wide variety of regularly scheduled and special ice and dry-floor events.

2. Serve as a liaison to local security and safety support agencies.

G. Safety and Security

1. Provide a safe and appropriate environment for activity to take place.

2. Address all risk management concerns and take corrective action whenever possible.

3. Report and follow up on injuries and incident reports.

H. Program Supervision

1. Provide leadership for user group programs and activities.

2. Initiate and develop new skating and hockey programs.

3. Host facility sponsored programs such as learn-to-skate, hockey clinics, freestyle and dance sessions.

I. Maintenance

1. Oversee and coordinate all custodial, services, preventative maintenance, and repairs.

2. Supervise outside service contractors.

J. Capital Improvements

1. Project and develop requirements and program statements for capital improvement projects.

2. Act as a liaison between the facility and contractor when capital projects are undertaken.

K. Organizational Liaison

1. Act as liaison to agencies such as building services, health center, public safety, contract groups, etc., on matters of common interest.

2. Serve as a spokesperson for the organization.

6. *Where do ice arena managers get their training and what associations/organizations do they join.*

The ice arena industry is a very small and fragmented business with limited sources for formalized training beyond the normal college or university business, sport management, or leisure and recreation degree. Currently, there are only two settings offering opportunities for specialized training in ice facility or general public assembly facility management.

In Canada, the Ontario Recreational Facilities Association (ORFA) annually conducts a one-week school for arena managers and operators at the University of Guelph in Guelph, Ontario. This school is designed to provide management training and certification to operators of arenas and pools in the province of Ontario. In Canada, arena owners are required by law to have a certified operator with refrigeration training present when the ice plant is operating.

Ontario Recreation Facilities Association Inc.
1185 Eglinton Avenue East
North York, Ontario M3C 3C6
Canada
(416) 426-7062

There is also an opportunity in the United States for formalized facility management training for ice arena management professionals. The International Association of Assembly Mangers (IAAM) conducts an annual school for managers of arenas, stadiums, auditoriums, and convention centers each year at Oglebay in Wheeling, West Virginia. This school is taught by practicing assembly managers and specializes in advancing the careers of public assembly managers with many topics that would enrich ice arena managers.

Public Assembly Facility Management School
Oglebay Division of Continuing Education
Rt 88, Hubbard House
Wheeling, WV 26003
(800) 624-6988

Professional and Trade Associations

Numerous trade and professional associations conduct annual meetings and conferences, which identify and discuss problems beneficial to ice arena managers. Below is a list of those that arena managers might wish to attend.

National Recreation
and Parks Associations (NRPA)
22377 Belmont Ridge Road
Ashburn, VA 20148
(703) 858-0784

International Association of Assembly
Managers Inc. (IAAM)
Annual Conference and Trade Show
4425 West Freeway, Suite 590
Irving, TX 75067-5835
(972) 255-8020

Ice Skating Institute (ISI)
Annual Conference and Trade Show
355 West Dundee Rd
Buffalo Grove, IL 60089-3500
(708) 808-7528

USA Hockey
4965 North 30th Street
Colorado Springs, CO 80919
(719) 599-5500

United States Figure Skating Association
(USFSA)
20 First Street
Colorado Springs, CO 80906
(719) 635-5200

ISI was originally formed to represent ice arena managers, although this organization is more noted now for its beginning figure skating and hockey programs. USA Hockey and the USFSA are the official governing bodies of hockey and figure skating and are in charge of national, international, and Olympic competitions and sanctioning. NRPA has state and regional organizations, which attract community recreational professionals.

Regional Ice Arena Manager Associations

Due to the absence of a dynamic national ice arena managers organization, regional ice arena management associations have evolved to share information, solve mutual problem and promote skating and hockey. These associations charge dues, produce newsletters, and hold annual meetings and trades shows and generally look out for the welfare of the industry in their region of the country. The leadership of these associations comes from current operating ice arena managers and is shared from year to year with those who will serve.

Minnesota Ice Arena Managers Association (MIAMA)
8020 80th Street South
Cottage Grove, MN 55016
(612) 861-9351

Wisconsin Ice Arena Managers Association (WIAMA)
4001 S 20th Street
Milwaukee, WI 53221
(414) 281-6289

Michigan Arena Managers Association (MAMA)
7330 Highland Rd
Waterford, MI 48327
(248) 666-1911

Mid-Atlantic Ice Arena Managers Association (MAIAMA)
505 Larimer, #7
Turtle Creek, PA 15145
(412) 823-6642

North East Ice Skating Manager's Association (NEISMA)
c/o N. Yarmouth Academy
Box 1137
Yarmouth, ME 04096
(207) 846-9441

Amenities and Common Development Characteristics of Ice Facilities

In order to understand the amenities included in ice arenas, the reader would do well to study the steps and procedures in the planning of a facility. After conducting a feasibility study, a program statement is usually prepared by the planning committee to indicate the desired programs and events and how the various spaces relate to each other. This statement is used by the architects and engineers in the initial planning and layout of the facility. Below is a typical two-surface ice arena program statement.

Program Statement for a Typical Two-Surface Ice Arena

1.0 GOALS

The primary intent of this program statement is to provide the planning criteria for the typical two-surface ice arena project based on current and forecast market demand for these facilities. The organizers are contemplating a 800-seat multipurpose arena capable of hosting a wide variety of sport activities and events.

1.1 General Considerations

A feasibility and market study concluded that the planning committee should develop a multi-purpose arena with the following principal functional areas:

■ Olympic ice arena
  with dry-floor capabilities   23,000 sf
■ Seating area (assume 1,200 seats)   4,000 sf
■ Meeting/general purpose room   1,500 sf
■ Regulation ice arena (85' × 200")   20,000 sf

The facility must also contain all necessary ancillary spaces to support these principal functional areas. These spaces, as outlined in this program, include lobbies, ticket areas, offices, skate rental/sharpening area, concourses, food service, a special figure-skating workout room, locker rooms, and storage, mechanical, service, and freight handling areas.

All public spaces are to be attractive and highly functional. The decor and furnishings shall be of a quality consistent with standards in moderately appointed facilities.

All public spaces are to be well lighted, air-conditioned and heated. They must meet all ADA requirements for handicapped persons. Restrooms, drinking fountains, telephones, and other conveniences shall be located throughout the facility.

All office areas and meeting rooms are to be sound isolated. Special attention must be given to reducing the noise levels of heating and ventilating systems.

The following basic design issues, summarized here and expanded in the text, will contribute to the success of the ice arena.

1.1.1 Program and Function

Programmatic Relationships—The facility will only be as successful as the organization and relationship of its parts.

Marketing Flexibility–Layout flexibility is essential to accommodate the diverse skating, hockey, recreational sports, and events needed to fill the facility's calendar.

Identity of Spaces–Major spatial components (lobby, pro-shop, snack shop, and meeting spaces) must retain their primary identity while providing overall flexibility and free-flowing circulation.

Operational Efficiency–Sequential and simultaneous activities must be accommodated with minimal compromise to management, concessions, pro-shop tenants, users, and spectators.

Service Efficiency–The speed and independence with which simultaneous but separate activities are supervised, served, and cleaned up have direct impact on the activity calendar and ultimately the financial success of the center. This includes adequate restrooms, food service, meeting, and public assembly provisions.

Contiguous Space–All spaces, from the smallest locker room to the largest lobby area, must fit within a hierarchy of contiguous space to promote maximum flexibility and efficient utilization.

Adequate Systems–It is imperative that electrical systems, lighting, HVAC, audiovisual telecommunications, and life safety systems all reflect the most cost-effective solution from a total life-cycle cost to ensure a competitive, operational center.

1.1.2 Architecture

Image/Marketability–The complex must reflect design ingenuity and excitement that can motivate skating, hockey, interested spectators, fans, recreational sport, and event attendees to return for future activities and events. Further, the design must capture the spirit and personality of the region.

Lobby Identity/User Orientation–The most successful facilities create a high level of user comfort through design techniques that promote identity and orientation, both inside and out. This includes using stimulating site environments, views, and access.

Integrity–All aspects of the solution must enhance and complement the constraints provided by the site, functions, design, costs, and program.

1.1.3 Site Design

Development Impact–The complex must be compatible with its setting, both initially and in the future.

Climate–The design of the complex must take into consideration the climate, through landscape design, internal development, and external envelope design.

Vehicular Traffic–Users, services, and background densities must be acknowledged and accommodated to create easy access.

Service Access–Approaches, coupled with internal service access, should be separate from public circulation to reduce conflict and allow simultaneous event service and attendance with no noise or visual interference.

Pedestrian Flow–Arrival by foot, private automobile, taxi, bus, or other public conveyance must flow to an integrally planned pedestrian system.

Active Image–The highly active areas of the complex should be easy to see from the exterior without compromising control of activity space, thus maximizing self-advertising through visible and active use.

1.1.4 Operational Insight

Activity Knowledge–Of paramount importance in creating a successful complex is the ability to meet skating and hockey participants' needs as well as the needs of those producing and attending trade and consumer shows and other activities. These needs includes easy access to the arenas, locker room and restroom facilities, food service, skate rental, skate sharpening, and pro shop. For exhibitors, easy access to unloading, storage, and display space is especially important.

Understanding the Visitor–To compete successfully, the complex must accommodate a diverse mix of patrons and visitors. Easy flow, quick access, visible and readable graphics, environmental comfort, and exciting architectural and site design are several of the prime ingredients associated with making visitors welcome.

Service Factors–The complex must easily accommodate a variety of delivery vehicles for trade and collectible shows, food service, waste disposal, and building maintenance. Adequate storage for these components must also be available.

1.2 Facility Functions and Uses

The primary functions and uses of the facility include:

1.2.1 Hockey Programs and Events

Amateur Youth Hockey: (October–March) weekly practice sessions and games, drop-in hockey, invitational tournaments, play-offs (league, regional, state, national).

Adult Hockey: (October–March) weekly practice sessions and games, drop-in hockey, invitational tournaments, play-offs (league, regional, state, national).

High School Hockey: (October–March) weekly practice sessions and games, play-offs (league, regional, state).

College Hockey: (October–March) weekly practice sessions and games, play-offs (league, NCAA).

1.2.2 Figure Skating: (October–March) patch, free style, dance sessions, competitions (invitational, regional, national), skating shows and exhibitions.

1.2.3 Speed Skating: (October–March) practices, short track competitions.

1.2.4 Indoor Soccer: (Year-round) practice sessions and games.

1.2.5 Recreational Sports: (Year-round) volleyball, tennis, lacrosse, batting cages.

1.2.6 Conventions: large meetings with the number of delegates reaching into the thousands.

1.2.7 Trade Shows: exhibitions involving booths and other displays presenting a wide variety of high technology, educational, medical, materials handling, and other equipment, processes, and trades.

1.2.8 Consumer Shows: exhibitions of goods, such as antiques, apparel, home products, travel information, and vehicles, at which public admission is charged.

1.2.9 Seminars, Technical Sessions, and Religious Conferences: meetings where attendees range from a few dozen to thousands.

1.2.10 Banquets and Receptions: food and beverage service ranging from small groups to 2,000 persons or more.

1.2.11 Major Community Events: a wide variety of civic celebrations, arena activities, festivals, dances, school activities, etc.

1.2.12 Miscellaneous Entertainment Events: concerts and other events for which public admission is normally charged.

It is inevitable that certain events will fall into more than one of the above categories, requiring some combination of exhibits, meetings, ice sports, and food service. For example, there may be conventions that have exhibit requirements and consumer shows that need some meeting space for lectures, film presentations, and other related activities. There will also be times when ice sports will be conducted in one arena while dry-floor events are going on in the other. The goal is that the facilities be flexible and capable of housing virtually every conceivable type of activity in a broad range of event sizes without compromising full use of the facility.

2.0 General Design Considerations

The main challenge of designing an ice arena is to create an ideal facility for ice sports that can be converted to accommodate the mix of events hosted in the off-season. This program will detail the ice sports, and exhibition and meeting room requirements for this type of multi-purpose space.

2.1 Main Entrance

The main entrance must be on grade, allowing unobstructed and free access from the exterior and permitting easy, well-lighted conditions for crowd dispersal.

2.2 Ticket Sales

The ideal entrance and foyer should provide a direct and obvious path to two or more ticket sales windows to allow visitors free access to the main arena after purchase, without having to cross another line of people. Many arenas have two separate ticket outlets and several have a ticket outlet for game or event nights, in the central part of the foyer; this allows access from two sides, along with access from the regular windows along the sides of the foyer.

The public skating ticket and sales office is usually adjacent to the arena manager's office. This is more efficient for the staff who can handle advance ticket sales or provide information easily from a central location. Money-counting areas and cash-handling safes should be out of public view and may double as the safe for concessions, pro shops, and building operation income.

2.3 Lobby and Viewing Area

The lobby should have direct visual access to the arena floor, concessions, rest rooms, and have some view of the ice sheet(s). Public telephones should be provided in a prominent position, either near an exit or in the lobby of the arena.

Skate Preparation. This area often serves as a pre-function space for events or concerts as well as an area for putting on skates, storing coats on portable coat racks, and for rental lockers to store valuable items while skating.

The lobby should contain one or two television monitors programmed for providing electronic daily, weekly, and special events schedules, and for playing videotapes. Such monitors can provide good advertising and relieve arena staff from answering many simple questions about schedules and upcoming events. It is also a potential income source as advertising space for local merchants can be alternated with arena information.

2.4 Public Rest Rooms and Drinking Fountains

Rest rooms and drinking fountains should be conveniently located throughout the lobbies, concourses, and corridors.

The distribution of rest rooms and public pay phones and house phones should correspond to the occupancy load centers they serve, and should be arranged to achieve a balance when the facility is subdivided for multiple uses. These facilities should not be concentrated close to the entrance or skate rental areas, as this will increase congestion at times of heavy traffic. All restrooms shall provide accessible facilities according to ADA.

Restroom facilities should have high-quality, low-maintenance finishes. Adequate floor drains and nearby custodial closets are desirable.

The lobby should lead directly to the arenas to ease crowd flow at peak periods. The overall design and location of major areas should minimize the distances from one arena to another.

2.5 Meeting Room/General Purpose Room

This room can be used for meetings, birthday parties, registrations for conferences and trade shows, and for youth hockey, figure skating and adult hockey board meetings. The room may have state-of-the art computerized conferencing capabilities and will have an adjacent control and storage room. This room should be capable of being subdivided into smaller areas, each having separately controlled lighting.

2.6 Finish Considerations

Floor–The lobbies, public rest rooms, concourses, locker rooms, and corridors should be covered with a rubberized surface to accommodate skate blades. Entry areas should have special flooring to reduce slipping hazards from snow, ice, water, and mud. Where carpet is used, the color, pattern, and texture should be able to withstand the high traffic volume as well as food and beverage spills. Light-colored, monochromatic carpets should be avoided.

Walls–Vertical surfaces should be of materials and finishes that can be easily maintained and resist heavy wear and tear.

2.7 Public Address/Score Boards/Safety/Security

A public address system, controlled from the main arena office, should be available throughout for paging, announcements, and background music. The system should be zoned for control during simultaneous events.

Due to the large number of exterior doors required, the variety and broad distribution of valuable items that are housed in the facility, from time to time and the variety of people having access to the facility during activity times as well as attendees during shows, adequate security systems must be incorporated into the facility. Securing the building perimeter, lobbies, and concourses through the use of a door alarm system, access control systems, and the like must be coordinated with the building administration's operations and staffing. Coordination with local police and fire departments may also be required.

A large scoreboard with advertising panels and a message board should be located so the spectators, the players and official in their respective bench area can see the clock and perform their duties. A control panel, goal judge system for hockey and soccer, and remote tape deck, plug-in and volume control for figure skaters must also be provided.

2.8 Vehicle Access and Maintenance

All corridors and concourses should be wide enough and high enough to permit passage, including turning of light maintenance vehicles, floor scrubber, telescoping ladders, food service equipment, etc.

Electrical outlets should be available throughout the concourse and lobbies for use with janitorial equipment. Custodial closets and other maintenance facilities should be uniformly and conveniently distributed throughout the facility.

2.9 Acoustics

Wall and ceiling finishes should provide sound absorption to reduce excessive noise when the lobbies and concourses are crowded.

2.10 Main Arena

The architectural design should recognize the intended activities and programmed use of the arena.

The surface for Olympic size is 100 feet by 200 feet and NHL surface regulation size is 85 feet by 200 feet.

Arenas of this nature have no windows, skylights, or other openings for outside light. Some new facilities have broken with this tradition, and it is our understanding that natural light has been well received, especially by dry-floor users. If windows or other openings are considered, they must include appropriate devices for blackout to accommodate ice sports and traditional shows with "black box" requirements. If natural light is desired in public assembly and lobby spaces, acoustics must be considered and outside noise should be prevented from entering the space.

The minimum clear height of 27 to 30 feet to any trusses, catwalks, overhead lights, or other equipment is recommended in the main arena.

Access:

The main arena should have at least one oversized drive-in freight door to allow direct access by semi-tractor-trailers to the floor. The door should be approximately 16 feet wide and 12 feet high. If a freight access door to the loading dock is incorporated, it should be 16 feet wide and 12 feet high and should be placed along the dockside of the arena to reduce fork-lift congestion at the loading dock. Ramps or other changes in elevation needed for drive-in doors should be accommodated outside the facility or in service areas, not within the arena space.

2.11 Capacity for Ice

Criteria related to the ice surface, compressors, subsoil heating systems, dasherboard construction, penalty boxes, scorer's table, and team boxes should meet the following minimum conditions:

- A complete and automatic flooded indirect refrigeration system should be capable of producing and maintaining ice conditions year round. This system should have an evaporative condenser for outdoor service and be sized for year-round use.
- A subsoil and snowmelt pit heat system is required to recover heat from the compressors.
- All refrigeration and distribution piping for the floor should be located within the rink area; supply and return headers should be curved to comply with the radius of the rink corners.
- The entire rink floor will be one continuous pour with no cold joints; it should be capable of supporting a wide variety of activity loads and equipment, such as tractors and trucks, and should be machine or hand-finished so as not to be slippery. *It must be within 1/8 inch of a true level plane.*
- The dasherboard system should be constructed of lightweight aluminum and should be easy to dismantle and store on stackable dasherboard-panel and protective-glass carts. The system should use protective acrylic glass with end glass heights of eight feet and side glass heights of six feet. The dasher boards should be tightly fastened to the perimeter concrete with a system employing brass screw-in plugs with flush tops for when the boards are removed. The system should be capable of removing the dasherboards and keeping the ice in by way of an ice dam.
- Player, penalty, scorer and goal judge boxes should also be portable and easily stored.
- The following accessories should be included in the ice rink installation:
  —Goal post anchors to be placed at 11 feet (professional) and 15 feet (college) from the end of the rink for optional goal placement.
  —Tennis and volleyball net post floor-anchor inserts with four bolt-down, inside-threaded anchors welded to the base plate and supplied with flush brass screw plugs.

■ Indoor soccer and lacrosse can be accommodated using the inserts for hockey and by removing sections of the dasher boards.

Energy Conservation:

Maximum energy conservation can be achieved by installing a low-emissivity ceiling over the main arena ice surface. Furthermore, a central heating, dehumidification, and air conditioning system to treat air for a year-round ice operation will be required. The radiant and conductive energy loads must be calculated and addressed during the design phase.

2.12 Seating Area

The seating capacity for the typical community-sized arena should be between 350 and 500 seats, depending on design and financial considerations. If possible, these seats should be located along one side of the ice surface, easily accessible for those entering the facility, and close to the dasherboards, as these seats will be primarily scheduled for hockey and figure skating events and small concerts.

2.13 Dressing Rooms, Showers, Toilets

There should be a minimum of four dressing rooms per ice surface with two dressing rooms sharing common toilets and showers. Youth and adult hockey associations, along with a successful figure-skating program, all impose a heavy demand for dressing room facilities so when possible, additional large dressing rooms should be provided.

Including coaches and other team personnel, a dressing room can easily attract 24 people or more at one time and therefore should be designed for 24 players plus coaches. All benches should be made of wood or plastic and supported from the walls to facilitate cleaning of the floors. Lockers are usually only provided in very large arenas or for college or professional teams. Clothing and equipment hooks should be made of steel strapping or rods and secured to the wall or directly to a steel plate that is permanently bolted to the wall. A wooden or metal shelf above clothing equipment hooks is very useful.

The flooring in dressing rooms should be able to withstand skate blades and should be rubberized to protect blade edges. Bare concrete is unsuitable since it is subject to damage as well as being extremely damaging to skates. Unpainted concrete becomes dirty and unsightly and creates dust.

Doors need to be able to withstand rough use and be wide enough to accommodate players carrying large hockey bags. Steel doorjambs and heavy-gauge steel doors are the most useful and practical.

With a high volume of traffic in and out of the dressing rooms, security is a concern. Some operators provide security by installing heavy-duty hardware (without doorknobs) or hasps with padlocks for team/locker rooms.

Ceilings in the locker area should be plywood, concrete, or other equally durable material. Acoustic tile or other soft material is not suitable. All ceiling lights should be flush with the ceiling and covered with durable glass or impact-resistant plastic, such as Lexan. There should be no exposed pipes, unless the ceiling is at least 10 feet.

2.14 Showers and Toilets

It is common to design one shower-toilet area common to two dressing rooms with a doorway leading to the shower-toilet from each room. Most shower rooms have at least six shower heads with 30-second or longer control taps and a mixing valve set to 110°F. Materials resistant to moisture and condensation on the walls and ceiling include ceramic tiling and concrete walls painted with sprayed or epoxy paint. Adequate ventilation to the outside reduces air moisture. By separating or dividing the shower room from the dressing room, a drying area can be provided. The number of toilets and washbasins must be closely calculated to fit the number of users in each area.

2.15 Referees' Room

The referees and linemen should have a small dressing room accessible to both ice surfaces, preferably with a single shower, washbasin, toilet, several chairs or a bench with wall hooks, and a mirror. The referees' room should be located away from the locker rooms, the lobby, and, if possible, away from the main entrance. Access for officials to the ice through an ice entrance opposite the players and coaches is desirable.

3.0 General Offices/Operation Areas

Properly programmed and effectively designed office suites and workrooms create efficient working relationships among the various user groups and enhance the success of the facility. When office spaces and service areas provide a pleasant environment and a functional setting in which to work, staff members' morale and motivation build, which fosters increased productivity.

Administrative offices should be centrally located with easy access from main entrances. A reception area, controlled by clerical assistants, should be available for guests and for scheduled appointments. It may be advisable, since all of the ice time may not be rented prior to the season, to plan a combined reception office/supervision station close to the ice arena(s) to facilitate working with the users during the weekend and evening hours. This station should have direct sight lines and should contain the lighting and sound controls for the arena's surface.

Administrative office space, including spaces for the general office, the general manager's office, two assistant manager's offices, an account clerk's office, and one or two program/marketing offices, should be provided. A general storage area could contain space for a copier, a floor safe, and cash-counting area with shelves for office and building promotional supplies.

3.1 Food Service/Vending

Concessions or food services are a normal part of every ice arena/events operation, large or small. The only difference between various arenas is in the scale of operation. A large arena may have several outlets as opposed to just one in small arenas. At least one stand should be located in the main lobby, adjacent to the office and skate rental area. This area will be designed like a "village of shops" to give the customer the impression of a sequenced order of the concession, office, and skate rental, but so one person can serve all areas during non-peak periods. Cash registers or computerized point-of-sale systems should be located at strategic service points to facilitate good cash and inventory control.

A well-laid-out food service area can increase food and drink profits since the time between periods of a hockey game, hockey practice sessions, concerts, trade shows, and conventions is always at a minimum. The concessions should be designed so the soft drink and food sections are convenient to each attendant, eliminating cross traffic and increasing efficiency.

Vending machines supplement crowded concession counters as well as eliminate the need for concession staff during off-peak or low-attendance hours. This area should be recessed so it can be closed off when the concession stands are open, and it should be in view of the office, skate rental counter, etc.

3.2 Pro Shop

The facility should include a full-service pro shop that would stock a complete line of hockey sticks, tape and protective equipment, athletic supports, mouthpieces, skate guards, laces, tape, etc. The shop would also carry a complete line of figure skates and apparel as well as area university, college, and high school products. This area may be leased to an outside vendor or operated by another party and should have a separate, controlled entrance, ample storage, and a security system.

3.3 Skate Sharpening

Management will have a trained skate sharpener and machine available for the immediate skate sharpening needs of customers. For this to be cost effective, this attendant must be able to work at some other function, such as skate rental or even concessions, during non-peak periods. The skate sharpening attendants must develop a reputation of doing the best job in town.

There should be a separate room designated for sharpening, repair, and maintenance of hockey, figure, and speed skates. The skate sharpening equipment should be equipped with a powerful filtering and vacuum system. Storage space should be provided for extra grinding wheels, skate holders, and blades as well as work space for blade straightening, eyelet replacement, and repair equipment.

3.4 Skate Rental

Most two-surface arenas should have approximately 600 to 800 pairs of hockey and figure skates for rent. This will require a room with proper shelving and a service window. This space must be well ventilated and should be designed to be near the office area, concession stand, and pro shop. One person in off-peak times should be able to serve all of the areas.

The shelves in the skate rental room should be adjustable in height to fit different sizes of skates. Shelves (box-style storage cabinets are not acceptable) must be numbered to coincide with skate numbers and should be able to hold the shoes of the patrons while they have rental skates out. The design should allow the attendant to reach a variety of skate sizes with a minimum of travel.

3.5 Mechanical and Electrical

This section of the building must be designed to enclose the electrical control panels and main switch gear in a separate room. The mechanical room must be large enough to contain and provide for maintenance of the hot water tanks and the total building HVAC equipment.

3.6 Storage

Storage should be provided in several areas for such general items as chairs, tables, dasherboards (one or two sets), dasherboard glass, and hockey, soccer, soccer rug, broomball goals, and tennis nets and posts during the off-season. Some storage must be provided for other equipment, supplies, and the many items that must be stowed from the public in this type of multipurpose facility.

3.7 Ice Resurfacer Room

The building design should provide a secure, well-lit ice resurfacer storage room away from spectators and dressing rooms (preferably so that patrons never cross the path of the resurfacers to reach the ice) and able to serve both surfaces. This room must have a snow disposal area and floor drainage close to the ice resurfacer parking. To save energy, the snow-melting pit should be connected to the heat recovery from the compressors. Sufficient head room and width should be provided for front-end as well as side-dump machines. Head room should be at least 14 feet for a front-end dump machine. A side-dump machine requires about 12 feet of horizontal width space with a ceiling height of 10 feet. Electricity should be provided for electric ice resurfacers.

The resurfacer room should have a work area for changing the resurfacer's blades and general maintenance. In addition, the room could provide storage space for the ice spuds, scrapers, and hoses used for leveling, cleaning, and flooding the ice.

The temperature of the water used for flooding is important to the final ice surface quality. The water should be between 150° and 180°F for best resurfacing. As much as 180 gallons of hot water will be needed for normal flooding every hour. For ice machines that serve two arenas from different directions, hot water connections are needed on both sides of the resurfacer room, as are floor drains immediately off each ice surface outside the exit doors.

3.8 Refrigeration Room

A separate, enclosed, and well-ventilated room should be provided for the ice refrigeration equipment and related items sufficient to serve both ice surfaces. The room must have a gas detector, alarm, and automatic ventilation system to meet code requirements for refrigerant gases. This room is best located at an outside wall with a lift-out wall panel to ease installation and maintenance of the total refrigeration skid. A workbench and a parts storage area should be included. This room should be located as close to the ice resurfacer room as possible to coordinate and reduce piping. It is best located between and at the ends of the two ice sheets.

3.9 Figure Skaters' Warm-Up, Exercise, and Dressing Room

A room should be provided adjacent to the ice sheets as a dressing and warm-up/exercise area for figure skaters. This room should have mirrors, a ballet bar, and a videotape recorder/player to allow study of performances and practices. This room can function as a regular locker room for other activities, but it should provide washroom facilities, lockable lockers, and a small lounge for the professional skating staff.

3.10 Signboard/Building Signage

Outside the main entrance, there should be large flagpoles and a signboard displaying the upcoming events of the facility. The ideal signboard system would be a computerized board with a control located in the arena office. This would make it easier to change the message and would attract greater attention of people passing the facility. This system also provides opportunities to sell advertising, thus increasing income.

Internal building signage should be uniform, located in strategic areas so patrons can easily find specific locations and seats and easily exit the facility after events. The trend toward computerized internal building signage suggests that this option be investigated during design.

3.11 Special Lighting

Provisions for reduced mood lighting for public skating should be included in the original design and wiring of the Olympic arena. Lighting of both ice surfaces should be of a dual-ballast, zoned design to reduce energy consumption.

Electrical service should be planned for television cameras, stage lighting for concerts, spotlights for ice

Load Source	Approx. Max. Percentage of Total Load (%)	Max. Reduction Through Design & Operation (%)
Radiant loads		
Ceiling radiation	28	80
Lighting radiation	7	40
Convective loads		
Arena air temperature	13	50
Arena humidity	15	40
Conductive loads		
Ice resurfacing	12	60
System pump	15	60
Ground heat	4	80
Headers heat gain	2	40
Skaters	4	0
Total	**100**	

Source: American Society of Heating, Refrigeration, and Air Conditioning Engineers (ASHRAE), 1992

shows, and a control sound and lighting area for some concerts. At least one platform for ice show spotlights should be built into the structure of the facility.

3.12 Parking

Visitors' impressions of a facility begin when they first arrive. Clear directions to the building's entry points should be achieved through the use of graphics and marquees. Changeable graphics are desirable to give a clear understanding of the location of each particular event and to give each event its own identity.

The drop-off zone should be designed to accommodate large volumes of pedestrian traffic transferring to buses and automobiles. Weather-protected arrival and departure areas should be provided for each entry point. Marshaling areas for buses should be provided. The area should ideally be designed to accommodate peak-load conditions and allow the collection of parking fees without causing traffic backups (especially if Phase II is completed). Ease of access and departure forms the first and last impressions of a facility in the public's mind and, as such, deserves careful attention in its design. An irrigated, well-landscaped exterior always creates a favorable impression and is relatively in-expensive when one considers the positive image created.

The Importance of Energy Conservation

To meet today's energy-saving expectations, ice arena owners and operators need to understand how to curb energy use without affecting the quality of their ice. Knowledge about and technology for ice arena refrigeration systems, lighting, and water quality for ice-making has improved dramatically in the last few years.

To understand how an ice arena uses energy, it is important to understand the various heat loads and energy needs for making and maintaining ice; for heating, air conditioning, and dehumidifying arena air; for lighting the facility; and for providing water for ice-making.

The refrigeration system in an ice arena consumes the majority of energy used in the building. Since refrigeration is a process of removing heat, the various heat loads in an arena should be closely examined. Most arenas are large metal, block, or brick structures that protect the ice sheet from the effects of weather. All of these conditions have a direct affect on the cost of maintaining the ice surface, as well as the climate inside the arena. The following table shows the sources of the heat loads that affect an arena and the type of energy savings that could be achieved by addressing these sources.

Radiant Loads

Ceiling Radiation

Heat radiating through the ceiling is the largest single heat load in an indoor ice arena. Controlling this source would therefore result in the greatest energy savings. The heat load from the ceiling comes from the sun's infrared energy lighting on the large roof of an arena, as well as from the outdoor air temperature whenever it is above the temperature of the arena.

The amount of heat radiated into the building can be controlled by installing an aluminum and fiberglass fire-resistant barrier called a low-emissivity ("low-e") ceiling. A low-emissivity ceiling is normally installed over the cables in the interior roof structure, reducing the radiant heat load by as much as 80%. In addition, it can reduce ceiling condensation and increase illumination in the building by approximately 20%. These savings alone can pay for the cost of the ceiling and its installation in two to three years.

Lighting Radiation

Lighting systems in ice arenas are complex and expensive. To achieve maximum efficiency, both arena designers and operational personnel must anticipate the needs of the programs and activities in the arena. Energy efficient lighting can only be successfully implemented if the objectives of the lighting system are clear when they are installed.

Radiation to the ice from light fixtures, although only 7% of the total heat load, can be controlled by reducing the number of fixtures over the ice. Many older arenas have 40 or more inefficient, 1000-watt mercury-vapor lights. These can be replaced with as few as 28 high-efficiency, dual-ballast fixtures using 400-watt metal-halide bulbs. Lighting levels will be dramatically improved, energy consumption reduced, and the amount of radiant heat on the ice reduced by as much as 40%. The new lighting system can be designed to let the facility's management select the proper lighting level for each activity.

Convective Loads

The convective loads placed on an arena's refrigeration system come primarily from the arena's humidity (15%) and temperature (13%). To conserve energy, both the temperature and humidity levels must be properly monitored. When humidity is high, the ice surface becomes a condensation point. This increases the load on the compressors. This condensation can be likened to the moisture that collects on the outside of a glass of ice water on a warm, humid day. In an arena, the ice-making system must work harder to freeze this condensation.

Heating, Air Conditioning, and Dehumidification Systems

There are basically three types of heating, air conditioning, and dehumidification systems presently on the market. First, there is the self-contained, air-cooled compressor-type packaged dehumidifier. The second type is the desiccant drier with gas or electric regeneration. The final type is the central heating and air conditioning system commonly used in most buildings.

The optimum temperature for skating and spectator comfort in an arena is 58° to 60° Fahrenheit. To achieve this temperature without causing excessive loads on the refrigeration system, infrared space heaters or forced-air systems must be directed away from the ice surface. Even when these systems are properly adjusted, the ice will still be affected by a heat load because skaters' movement circulates arena air toward the ice. According to calculations by ASHRAE, skaters represent 4% of the total heat load. These loads cannot be avoided since skaters' comfort is an important part of doing business.

The central heating and air conditioning systems and space dehumidifiers commonly found in ice arenas operate by collecting and passing humid air over cold coils. This causes the moisture to collect on the cold coils, where it is then removed. Most dehumidification systems have separate compressors to cool the solution used in the coils; some central systems use the ice-floor freezing system for this purpose.

The cooled, dehumidified air is then reheated by passing it over a set of hot coils before it is returned to the arena. These reheating coils often contain brine or water heated by electricity or gas. Occasionally this air is reheated by heat recovered from the ice-floor compressors.

Desiccant systems dehumidify air without cooling it by passing humid air over a desiccant—a substance that absorbs humidity. Once dehumidified, the air is then returned to the arena. The moisture is removed from the desiccant by using waste heat from the compressors, solar collectors, natural gas, water heaters, or forced-air heaters.

Controlling the humidity in an ice arena is a delicate process. With too much humidity in the air, moisture may collect on the steel building structure. This moisture can drip on the ice as well as damage the structural integrity of the facility. Taking too much moisture out of the air, however, can make the ice brittle and crisp, as natural evaporation from the ice will be speeded up. When this happens, the top layer of ice deteriorates in quality. Since humidity represents approximately 15% of the total heat load of a typical arena, arena managers must experiment and determine optimum conditions for their facility.

Sources of Moisture

There are several sources of moistures in an indoor ice rink. Moisture is introduced into the rink environment by ventilation, infiltration, people, combustion (ice resurfacer, gas heaters), and flood water evaporation. The visible effect of high humidity is fog near the ice surface and condensation on the ceiling. The moisture travels from warm areas to cold areas, since the vapor pressure is lower on a cold surface.

Therefore, the first step in dealing with high humidity in an ice rink is to address each moisture source. For example, the infiltration moisture load can be minimized by keeping the doors to the outside closed as much as possible and installing proper weather-stripping and caulking throughout the building. The moisture created from the combustion processes can be minimized by keeping equipment properly tuned and by operating this equipment only when needed. Flood water evaporation can be minimized by installing a demineralization system, which uses less flood water and freezes at higher water temperatures, thus resulting in higher overall ice surface temperatures.

Ventilation of outside air represents the greatest source of moisture in a rink. Therefore, ventilation should be the minimum required for the building occupancy load and ice surface area, which still, however, maintains an acceptable indoor air quality. Reducing the moisture produced from these sources will often help eliminate the problem or reduce the capacity and operation of any dehumidification equipment.

Fog on the Ice Surface

Fog is formed when the moisture laden air at the ice surface is cooled at or below its "dewpoint" temperature. Dewpoint is the temperature at which moisture will condense out of the air. Therefore, moisture will condense on anything (boards, glass, speakers, ceiling, flags, etc.) in the rink that has a surface temperature below the dewpoint. Even the ice surface itself actually acts as a large dehumidifier, condensing moisture from the air. However, this process increases the refrigeration load on the ice-making equipment, which in turn wastes energy.

A far better approach is to use dehumidification equipment. When sized and installed properly, dehumidifiers will virtually eliminate fog near the ice surface, eliminate moisture from forming on the boards and glass, prolong building life, and provide improved comfort conditions.

Ceiling Condensation and Drip

The cold ice surface literally draws the heat out of the ceiling by a process known as radiation. Not only does this process dramatically increase the refrigeration load on the ice-making equipment, but the ceiling surface temperature often falls below dewpoint, and thus condensation and dripping occurs.

Low-emissivity ceilings are designed to reduce this radiation effect and raise the ceiling temperature above dewpoint. Heat that would normally be radiated to the ice now stays up at the ceiling, which raises ceiling temperatures. Furthermore, low-emissivity ceilings will drastically reduce refrigeration loads and energy usage by about 25% (ASHRAE 1994 Refrigeration Handbook, Chapter 33).

Ice-Making Water Temperature

Ice resurfacing represents one of the highest conductive heat loads in ice arena operations. Flooding the ice with water temperatures between 140° and 180°F accounts for about 12% of the total refrigeration requirements. While using hot water improves the quality of ice by removing air from the resurfacing water, it causes an additional load on the compressor system. Managers can experiment with lowering the flood-water temperature. Lower floodwater temperatures may not make much of a difference in most properly dehumidified facilities, but it does mean that the water will freeze faster, thus eliminating wet spots on the ice at the start of the next scheduled use. Furthermore, savings can be realized because the water doesn't have to be heated to as high a temperature.

Ice Temperature Controls

Typically, the refrigeration plant represents about 70% to 80% of the total electrical energy usage in an ice rink. In the past, inaccurate, cheap, cumbersome, and inefficient controls were used to maintain ice temperatures and control the operation of the refrigeration plant. In addition, the control sensor was usually installed in the return brine line (indirect systems) or in the concrete or sand for direct systems. These control strategies made it difficult for the operator to maintain good ice quality for all activities (hockey, skating) and created high energy and operating costs. However, advanced refrigeration control technology has been developed that drastically improves the quality of the ice and helps to reduce operation costs. These products include variable-speed pump drive and infrared ice temperature control refrigeration systems.

In the past, control systems for ice rinks tried to control the ice surface by monitoring and controlling return brine or slab temperatures. As a result, the brine and slab temperatures could be maintained within 2° F to 3° F, but the actual ice surface temperature would vary considerably (4° F to 8° F). In addition, the operator never really knew what the actual ice surface temperature was.

These poor control systems for ice rinks cause the surface temperatures to vary considerably. This variation in ice temperature would also help to explain why many operators are reluctant to turn up their ice temperatures during unoccupied periods, skating events, or warm weather. They have experienced soft ice and are concerned about ice quality and losing the ice.

In comparison, the ice surface can be maintained within 1° F of the setpoint, using advanced control and infrared technology, as thermal lag is minimized and brine or refrigerant temperatures can vary to satisfy the magnitude of the actual heat load.

Infrared Ice Temperature Control

Ice temperature control has come a long way from the old brinestat or slab sensor control strategy. Now, it is possible for the operator to monitor and control from the actual ice surface. Operators can now tell exactly what the ice surface temperature is at all times and can easily adjust the setpoint to match the activity on the ice.

This advanced technology is commercially known as an infrared ice temperature control. Using a state-of-the-art electronic temperature controller and infrared sensor installed above the ice surface, the technology can be used to improve ice quality and reduce operating costs of any direct (ammonia, freon) or indirect (brine, glycol) refrigeration system. Additional savings and benefits are possible when this technology is integrated with a variable-speed brine pump control or a computerized building energy management system.

The infrared ice temperature controller can maintain precise ice temperatures based on the setpoint chosen by the operator. With this type of control system, ice arena operators can take advantage of the tremendous energy savings without the danger of affecting ice quality or losing their ice. The benefits of being able to easily adjust the actual ice surface temperature in response to the various activities on the ice cannot be overstated. Not only does this technology provide improved ice temperature control and quality, but the energy savings can also be substantial.

Conductive Loads

Additional savings and benefits can be achieved by incorporating a variable-speed pump drive into the refrigeration system. Variable-speed pump drives will help to reduce the cost associated with the operation of the brine pump on indirect systems.

Arenas with indirect refrigeration systems and brine pumps produce pipe-and-pump friction heat loads representing approximately 15% of the total refrigeration load. Most brine systems have one or more pumps driven by 25-horsepower motors. These pumps and motors run continuously, circulating the brine through the ice slab's piping. There are two methods to investigate for reducing these conductive loads:

1. Install variable or two-speed brine pumps with high-efficiency motors controlled by the ice temperature. This will reduce the friction loads in the pipes and pumps, especially in the winter when the system doesn't need to run that much. It will also allow the system to respond to the actual heat loads of the ice surface.

2. Develop an automatic or manually controlled system to set the brine temperature higher when the building isn't occupied late at night or in the middle of the day, when the arena is used less (most infrared systems have a computer to help with this process). With the temperature set two to three degrees higher, the compressors, brine pumps, and motors will run less. Care should be taken not to develop a plan that runs the ice compressor system more heavily when peak-demand rates are being charged; this could easily offset the potential savings earned from raising the temperature.

Demineralized Water Systems

Using demineralization technology allows operators to maintain a thinner ice sheet and higher ice and refrigerant temperatures, use less energy to heat the flood water, and create a smaller heat load on the refrigeration system. This translates into substantial energy and operating savings for ice rinks.

It is often said that ice is as good as the water it is made from. Anything dissolved in the water resists a phase change. This means that contaminants (organic or inorganic) steadily increase in concentration in the liquid portion of the ice sheet, which is the last to freeze. The ice stratum nearest the surface will always have a higher mineral content than that close to the floor, and the effect is cumulative in nature, with successive floods guaranteeing an increasing salt concentration in the skating surface as the season progresses. The result is slower ice, expensive freezing, reduced hardness, and higher salt content and pH.

Demineralized systems (either reverse osmosis or deionization) are designed to remove impurities from the municipal water source. Both systems also have the effect of forcing air out of the water (the reason for heating the water is to remove air) thus allowing for lower temperature and improving the opacity of the ice. The results are realized in energy savings and better looking ice with clearer lines and in-ice logos.

Learning about the energy-saving technology and techniques available today is important for ice arena managers. Each facility is unique, so managers need to study their energy consumption patterns, experiment with various energy reduction methods and techniques, and train their staff on the importance of energy conservation. The savings and benefits will be critical in the years ahead.

■ Summary

Ice arenas are unique and complex facilities to operate and program. To successfully manage this type of facility, it is important to understand general business practice, the technical aspects of making and maintaining ice, and the wide variety of ice and dry-floor programming that must occur for year-round use of the facility. Furthermore, these facilities must have teams of professionals with competencies in a variety of areas: marketing, programming, operations, concessions, equipment sales, maintenance, and rental. The facility operates many hours during the ice season; therefore, the management team must be capable of sharing supervision and leadership roles in order to have a smooth-running operation.

Up to now, most ice arena managers have been self-taught. However, today's sport management programs are preparing young people with basic skills and competencies to managing sport and recreational facilities. All that is needed to manage an ice facility is to acquire the specific refrigeration and programming knowledge. With the projected expansion and the trend to building bigger and more complex facilities, it will be important for all sport and recreational professionals to understand the basics of ice facility operation.

■ Self-Assessment Exercises

1. How has the ice arena industry developed over time?
2. What impact have skating and hockey had on the development of ice arenas?
3. What are the primary ice activities that can be hosted at indoor ice facilities?
4. How are ice facilities used in the off-season?
5. What are some of the unique design features of ice facilities?
6. What is done to offset the high cost of making and maintaining ice?
7. How are ice facilities organized and managed and what are their primary responsibilities of the management teams that operate these facilities?
8. Where do ice arena managers get their formal training?
9. Compare and contrast the responsibilities and duties of managing ice sport facilities with other recreational and sport facilities.

■ References

Blades, R. W. (1992). **Modernizing and retrofitting ice skating rinks.** Atlanta, GA: American Society of Heating, Refrigerating & Air-Conditioning Engineers, Inc.

Cimco Lewis. (1994). Things you should know about ice rink construction and operation. [Brochure]. Toronto, Ontario: Cimco Refrigeration.

Fischler, S. (1991). **Great book of hockey: More than 100 years of fire on ice.** Lincolnwood, IL: Publications International, Ltd.

Proctor, M. (1969). **Figure skating.** Dubuque, IA: Brown Company Publishers.

Ontario Recreation Facilities Association Inc. (1992). **Refrigeration and ice making.** Aylmer, Ontario: The Aylmer Express Ltd.

■ Suggested Readings

Center for Study of Responsive Law. (1993). Athletic facilities. **Energy Ideas, 1** (9), 1-15.

Cimco L. (1994). **Things you should know about ice rink construction and operation.** [Brochure]. Toronto, Ontario: Cimco Refrigeration.

Moore, D. L. (1995, March/April). Advancements in Ice Paints. **On Ice, 3** 3.

Maloy, P. & Vivian, J. (1992). Risky business. **Athletic Business, 6** (5) .

Ontario Recreation Facilities Association Inc. (1993). **Refrigeration and ice making** (2nd ed.). Aylmer, Ontario: The Aylmer Express Ltd.

Vivian, J. (1992). Maintenance: A year-round process, an everyday thing. **Skating, 69** (5).

Vivian, J., Daugherty, D., & Dunn, R. (1994). Bloodborne pathogens. **Facility Manager, 10** (2) 17-19.

Vivian, J. R. (1994, December/January). Energy conservation in ice arenas. **On Ice, 2** (3, Pt. 1).

Vivian, J. R. (1994, February/March). Energy conservation in ice arenas. **On Ice, 2** (4, Pt. 2).

Vivian, J. R. (1990). **The perceived importance of managerial and professional job functions of selected ice arena managers.** Unpublished doctoral dissertation, Bowling Green State University, Bowling Green, OH.

Vivian, J., & Dunn, R. (1996) Hot ice. **Athletic Business, 20** (11) 31-40.

Vivian, J., & Watkins, B. (1993). What it takes to run a successful arena. **Recreation Canada, 51** (1) 36-38.

Vivian, J., Stevens, S., & Wootton, G. (1994). Energy freeze. **Leisure Management, 14** (11), 46-48.

CHAPTER 28

Track and Field/Cross Country Facilities

John McNichols, Coordinator Track and Field/Cross Country & Head Men's Coach,
Indiana State University ■ John Gartland, Head Women's Track and Field/Cross Country
Coach, Indiana State University ■ Thomas H. Sawyer, Indiana State University

---

Learning Objectives

After reading this chapter, the student will be able to

■ select an appropriate site for a track and field complex as well as a cross country course, and

■ properly design a track and field complex and cross country facility.

Introduction

A track and field competition complex (See Appendix J) is complicated at best when compared to other outdoor or indoor sport spaces, such as an indoor basketball/volleyball court or a baseball, football, or soccer field. The track and field complex includes areas such as throwing, jumping, running, relaxation and warm-up, spectator, timing and recording, storage, and officials' dressing room. The areas are basically the same for an indoor facility.

A cross country course (See Appendix J) requires appropriate planning to service both girls and women, and boys and men. The distances differ for genders and level of competition (i.e., interscholastic and intercollegiate).

This chapter will describe the facilities needed for indoor and outdoor track and field, and cross country. Further, it will describe various pieces of equipment needed to assist and protect the athletes. The text in this chapter is based on the NCAA Track and Field/Cross Country Men and Women rules.

Site Selection and Planning the Track

Building a running track can be a formidable task, since few athletic facilities are as complex and yet have so many acceptable building options. With so many choices, no two track projects are the same. Each is a product of site constraints, owner preferences, location, budget, and availability of materials and expertise.

Faced with the task of building a track, an owner or facility manager can become overwhelmed by the choices and concerned about the possibility of costly mistakes. The first step, then, is identifying all decisions that must be made in planning a track facility and learning what to expect from the construction project. The success of the project will depend on proper site analysis, quality design and engineering, expert construction—including construction of proper drainage, a stable, well-built base and a quality synthetic surface—and accurate marking.

The first stage in the construction of a running track is choosing a site and designing a track to fit the site. In calculating the accuracy of a finished 400-meter track, no minus tolerance is acceptable and a plus tolerance must be no more than $1/2$ inch in any lane. These very small tolerances and the numerous design and site factors to be considered make track design extremely complex and demanding. Owners should begin by deciding what size and shape of track is needed. A 400-meter, six- or eight-lane track is the standard for high school and college competition, although a few high school and many large college tracks are 10 lanes wide.

There are two basic shapes. An *equal quadrant track* has two 100-meter straightaways and two 100-meter curves, while a *non-equal quadrant* track has two straightaways of one length and two curves of another length, totaling 400 meters. In the latter case, the result is a track with either a slightly stretched or compressed oval shape.

Recently, a third design—the so-called *broken-back track*—has come into use. This design features a more square track with shorter straightaways and rounded ends made of double curves. This design creates a larger infield that is large enough for an NCAA soccer field (which neither of the two more common designs can accommodate) and is useful for sites where one of the more common track designs will not work. Generally, an equal quadrant track is desirable, but site factors will determine which design is most feasible.

Will the track have a curb? Most high school tracks are built without curbs, but curbs are required on tracks where NCAA record events will be conducted. The curb will require additional area on the inside perimeter of the track.

How large a site is available? A track will require a site of no less than five acres, a minimum of 600 feet long by 300 feet wide. Additional area must be allowed for grading, curbs and drainage, and for amenities such as grandstands, bleachers, lighting, walkways, and fencing.

Will the track be built around playing fields? Many tracks are built around football or soccer fields. In addition to allowing space for the field itself, space must be allowed for player seating, walkways and other associated facilities. Artificial turf fields require additional space for anchoring detail at the perimeter.

Will the construction project include field events? Most track projects built today include construction of a high jump pad; long jump runway and pit; pole vault runway and landing area; shot put, discus, and hammer throwing pads and landing areas; and sometimes a javelin runway and a triple-jump runway and landing pit. It is more economical to construct field event areas at the same time as the track.

It is during the design phase that the design team must consider where the field events will be located. Placing the field events in the infield of the track may facilitate spectator viewing, but may mean more traffic over the runways. *Wind* must also be considered. Straightaways should be parallel to prevailing winds—which is especially important for dashes and hurdle races. For athlete safety, jumping events should also take place with the wind, since crosswinds are particularly dangerous. Multiple-jump runways should be considered because of the addition of the women's pole vault and time constraints during competition, when there is only one runway for men and women for the long jump and triple jump.

Throwing events should be located so that participants are throwing into the wind. Likewise, for safety reasons, it is essential that high jump and pole vault runways be located so that the athlete does not have to look into the sun or artificial lighting.

There are a number of other important considerations in site selection:

■ Does a potential site allow for proper drainage and storm water management? Water should drain away from the track. It is best to locate a track on a relatively level plain, higher than surrounding areas. Additional filling or drainage work required by a low site may add substantially to construction costs. Even under the best site conditions, tracks should be constructed with a perimeter drain on the inside of the track to remove storm water that has drained from the track and playing field.
Note: No expense should be spared in developing a good, solid base.

■ Is the site reasonably level? While the track will be sloped slightly for drainage, for all practical purposes, the track must be level in the running direction.

■ What type of soil exists at the site? Poor soil conditions often lead to excessive settling, heaving caused by freeze/thaw action and drainage problems. The best soil is hard, well-drained and non-heaving. Locations with peat, clay, topsoil, shear sand, or other organic materials at a depth of 8 to 12 inches should be avoided.

■ Where are underground utilities located? While the finished facility will require utility service, it is better to avoid constructing the track over underground utilities.

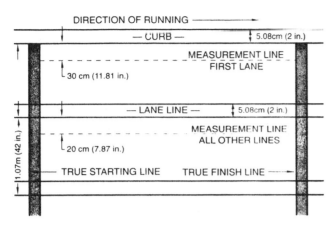

Figure 28.1 Track measurements.

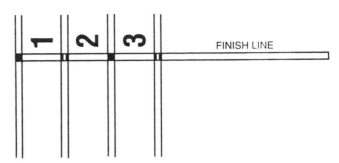

Figure 28.2 Finish-line intersections.

Many track projects are reconstruction or renovation projects. These projects can be even more complex to design than a new facility because of existing constraints.

Track and Field Facilities

Measuring Distances

The distance to be run in any race is measured from start to finish between two theoretical hairlines. All distances not run in lanes are measured 30 centimeters (11.81 inches) outward from the inner edge of the track if a regulation curb is in place. If no curb is used, lane one is measured 20 centimeters (7.87 inches) from the left-lane as in other lanes. For all races in lanes around one or more curves, the distance to be run in each lane is measured 20 centimeters (7.87 inches) from the outer edge of the lane that is on the runner's left, except that the distance for the lane next to the curb is measured 30 centimeters (11.81 inches) from the curb. If no curb is used, lane one is measured 20 centimeters (7.87 inches) from the left-hand line as in other lanes (NCAA, 1997).

Visible Starting Line

The visible starting line, 5.08 centimeters (2 inches) wide, is marked on the track just within the measured distance, so that its near edge is identical with the exactly measured and true starting line. The starting line for all races not run in lanes (except the 800 meters) is curved so that all competitors run the same distance going into the curve. (Figure 28.1)

Visible Finish Line

The visible finish line, 5.08 centimeters (2 inches) wide, is marked on the track just outside the measured distance so that its edge nearer that start is identical with the exactly measured and true finish line. Lane numbers of reasonable size should be placed at least 15.24 centimeters (6 inches) beyond the common finish line, positioned facing the timing device. The intersection of each lane line and the finish line is painted black in accordance with Figure 28.2. Finally, a common finish line is recommended for all races. Lines in the finish area should be kept to a minimum. If additional lines are necessary, they should be of a less conspicuous color than the finish line, so as not to cause confusion.

Except where their use may interfere with fully automatic timing devices, two white posts may denote the finish line and be placed at least 30 centimeters (11.81 inches) from the edge of the track. The finish posts should be of rigid construction, approximately 1.4 meters (4.59 inches) high, 80 millimeters (3.15 inches) wide and 20 millimeters (0.79 inches) thick (NCAA, 1997).

Note: The white posts have been deleted from new facilities and should be removed from older facilities because virtually every track has installed automatic timing devices.

The General Track Area (See Figure 28.1-28.3)

Outdoor. In constructing track and field facilities metric measurements must be used. The construction of track and field areas will follow the International Amateur Athletic Federation rules with respect to grade or slope: "The maximum inclination permitted for tracks, runways, circles, and landing areas for throwing events shall not exceed 1:100 in a lateral direction and 1:1000 in the running and throwing direction." In the high jump, the maximum inclination of the approach and takeoff area not exceed 1:250 in the direction of the center of the crossbar. Prevailing wind conditions should be considered when constructing field-event areas (NCAA, 1997).

Indoor. Tracks, runways, and takeoff areas should be covered with synthetic material or have a wooden surface. These surfaces should be able to accept 6 millimeter (0.25 inch) spikes for synthetic surfaces and 3 millimeter spikes (0.13 inch) for wood (NCAA, 1997).

Running Track

Outdoor. The running track should not be less than 400 meters in length nor less than 6.40 meters (21 feet) in width, which allows six hurdle lanes of 1.07 meters (42 inches) each. It may be bordered on the inside by a curb of concrete, wood, or other suitable material a minimum of 5.08 centimeters (2 inches) in height and a maximum of 10.16 centimeters (4 inches)in width (figure 3). The edges of the curb should be rounded (NCAA, 1997).

Indoor. ■ *Straightaways*—Maximum lateral inclination in the running direction should not exceed 1:250 at any point and 1:100 overall. Lanes should all have the same width, with a recommended minimum of 1.07 meters (42 inches) and a maximum of 1.25 meters (48 inches) including the white line to the right. There should be a minimum of 3 meters (9 feet, 10 inches) behind the start line and 10 meters (32 feet, 9.75 inches) beyond the finish line free of any obstruction. It is recommended that clearance beyond the finish line be at least 20 meters (65 feet, 7.5 inches) (NCAA, 1997).
■ *Oval Track and Lanes*—Indoor tracks may vary in size, with 200 meters as the preferable distance. The track consists of two horizontal straights and two curves with consistent radii, which should be banked. The curves should be bordered with a curb of suitable material approximately 5.08 centimeters (2 inches) in height (NCAA, 1997).

Where the inside edge of the track is bordered with a white line, it should be marked additionally with cones at least 20 centimeters (7.87 inches) high. The cones should be placed on the track so that the outward face of the cone coincides with the edge of the white line closest to the track. The cones should be placed at distances not exceeding 2 meters (6.56 feet) on the curves and 10 meters (32.81 feet) on the straightaways (NCAA, 1997).

The track should have a minimum of six lanes. Lanes should have a recommended minimum of 91.44 centimeters (36 inches), including the lane line to the right. Lanes should be marked by lines 5.08 centimeters (2 inches) wide (NCAA, 1997).

It is recommended that a maximum angle of banking should be not more than 18 degrees for a 200-meter track. This angle may vary based upon the size of a track. The angle of banking in all lanes should be the same at any cross section. Further, it is recommended that the inside radius of the curves on a 200-meter track should not be less than 18 meters (59 feet, 0.75 inches) and not more than 21 meters (68 feet, 10.75 inches) (NCAA, 1997).

Track Markings

Outdoors. It is recommended that the following color code be used when marking the track: (NCAA, 1997)

■ Starting line (white): 55 meters, 55-meter hurdles, 100 meters, 100-meter hurdles, 110-meter hurdles, 200 meters, 300 meters, 400 meters, 1,500 meters, mile, 3,000 meters, steeplechase, 5,000 meters, 10,000 meters
■ Starting line (green): 800 meters
■ Starting line (red): 800-meter relay
■ Starting line (blue): 1,600-meter relay
■ Finish line (white): all (A common finish line is recommended for all races.) Except where their use may interfere with fully automatic timing devices, two white posts may denote the finish line and be placed at least 30 centimeters (11.81 inches) from the edge of the track. The finish posts should be of rigid construction, approximately 1.4 meters (4.59 feet) high, 80 millimeters (3.15 inches) wide and 20 millimeters (0.79 inch) thick
■ Relay exchange zones: 400-meter relay (yellow), 800-meter relay (red), 1,600-meter relay (blue), 3,200-meter relay (green)
■ Hurdle locations: 100 (yellow), 110 (blue), 300 (red), 400 (green), steeplechase (white), break line (green)
■ Lanes shall be marked on both sides by lines 5.08 centimeters (2") wide
■ The lanes shall be numbered with lane one on the left when facing the finish line
■ Relay zones: in all relays around the track, the baton exchange must be made within a 20-meter (65.62 feet) zone, formed by lines drawn 10 meters (32.81 feet) on each side of the measured centerline. All lines and/or boxes or triangles should be inclusive within the zone (NCAA, 1997).

Hurdles

Hurdle lanes should be at least 1.07 meters (42 inches) in width. If no hurdle lanes are marked on the track, they should be judged as equivalent to 2.54 centimeters (1 inch) wider than the total width of the hurdles (NCAA, 1997).

Placement of Hurdles

Distance	# Hurdles	Distance to 1st hurdle	Distance between Hurdles	Distance last hurdle to finish
55-meter/60-yard Indoor (m)	5	13.72 m	9.14 m	4.72 m
55-meter/60 yard Indoor (w)	5	13	8.5	8
100-meter	10	13	8.5	10.5
110-meter	10	13.72	9.14	14.02
120-yard	10	15y	10y	15y
400-meter	10	45 m	35 m	40 m

Steeplechase (see Figure 28.3)

The standard distance for the steeplechase is 3,000 meters, with 28 hurdle jumps and seven water jumps. The water jump should be the fourth jump in each lap. If necessary, the finish line should be moved to accommodate this rule. The following measurements are given as a guide, and any adjustments necessary shall be made by lengthening or shortening the distance at the starting point of the race. The chart below assumes that a lap of 400 meters or 440 yards has been shortened 10 meters (32.81 feet) by constructing the water jump inside the track. If possible, the approach to and exit from the water-jump hurdle should be straight for approximately seven meters (NCAA, 1997).

Placement of Hurdles on Track—The hurdles, including the water jump, should be placed on the track so that 30 centimeters (11.81 inches) of the top bar, measured from the inside edge of the track, will be inside the track (see Figure 4). It is recommended that the first hurdle be at least 5 meters (16 feet, 4.75 inches) in width, and that all hurdles weigh at least 80 kilograms (176.4 pounds) (NCAA, 1997).

Water-Jump Construction—The water jump should be 3.66 meters (12 feet) in length and width. The water should be a minimum of 70 meters (2.29 feet) in depth immediately after the hurdle, and the pit should have a constant upward slope from a point 30 centimeters (11.81 inches) past the water-jump hurdle

Possible Steeplechase Measurements

Lap of 390 meters

Distance from starting point to commencement of 1st lap, to be run without jumps	270 m
of 1st lap to 1st hurdle	10 m
From 1st to 2nd hurdle	78 m
From 2nd to 3rd hurdle	78 m
From 3rd to water jump	78 m
From water jump to 4th hurdle	78 m
From 4th hurdle to finish line	68 m
390 m × 7 laps =	2,730 m
	3,000 m

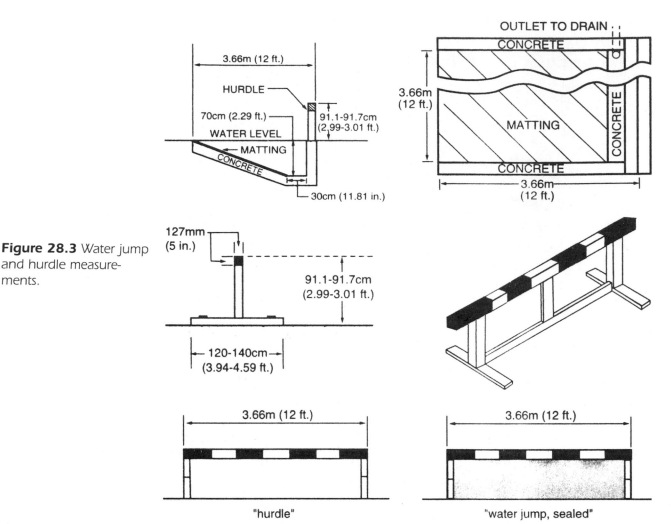

Figure 28.3 Water jump and hurdle measurements.

to the level of the track at the far end (see Figure 28.4). The hurdle at the water jump should be firmly fixed in front of the water and be of the same height as the other hurdles in the competition. It is recommended that the water jump be placed on the inside of the track. The landing surface inside the water jump should be composed of a nonskid, shock-absorbent material. The area between the vertical uprights of the water-jump hurdle should be sealed with a solid, rigid material to provide safety and to aid the athlete with depth perception. A water source needs to be installed to fill the water-jump and a drain installed to drain the water-jump after use (NCAA, 1997).

Jumping Areas (Indoor and Outdoor)

High Jump

It is recommended that the approach be an octagon or square with a surface of at least 21 meters (68.90'). The minimum length provided should be 15 meters (49.21'). The length of the approach run is limited.

The takeoff area is the semicircle enclosed by a 3-meter (9.84 foot) radius whose centerpoint is directly under the center of the crossbar. For a record to be approved officially, no point within this area may be higher than the tolerances (NCAA, 1997).

Pole Vault (see Figure 28. 5)

The vaulting box in which the vaulting pole is planted should be constructed of wood, metal or other suitable materials. Its dimensions and shape should be those shown in the accompanying diagram (see Figure 28.5). The box should be painted white and immovably fixed in the ground so that all of its upper edges are flush with the takeoff area. The angle between the bottom of the box and the stopboard (see Figure 28.6) should be 105 degrees. The vaulting runway needs a minimum length of 38.1 meters (125 feet). It is recommended that the width of the runway be 1.22 meters (4 feet) (NCAA, 1997).

Figure 28.4 Water jump, Indiana State University.

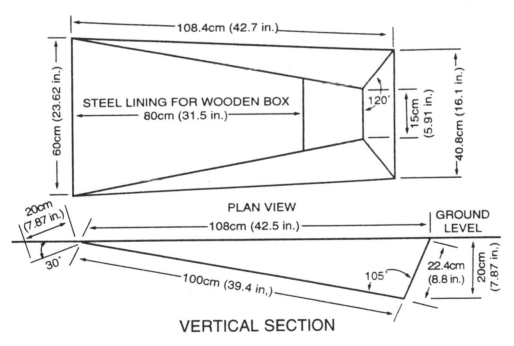

Figure 28.5 Pole vault box.

Long Jump and Triple Jump

The minimum length of the runway for the long jump and triple jump should be 39.62 meters (130 feet) from the edge nearest the pit of each event's takeoff board. It is recommended that the width of the runway be 1.22 meters (4 feet). The construction and material of the runway should be extended beyond the takeoff board to the nearer edge of the landing pit. When the runway is not distinguishable from the ad-jacent surface, it is recommended that it be bordered by lines 5.08 centimeters (2 inches) in width from the start of the nearer edge of the landing pit (NCAA, 1997).

The landing area should be not less than 2.74 meters (9 feet) in width and identical in elevation with the takeoff board. The area should be filled with sand. Figure 28.6 shows an approved device for ensuring proper sand level (NCAA, 1997).

Figure 28.6 Control of sand level in long jump and triple jump.

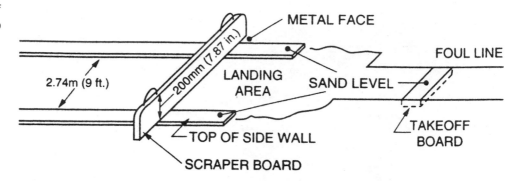

Figure 28.7 Long jump and triple jump takeoff board and foul marker.

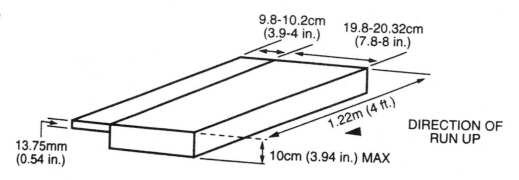

In the long jump, the distance between the takeoff board and the nearer edge of the landing area should not be less than 1 meter (3.28 feet) or greater than 3.66 meters (12 feet). The distance between the foul line and the farther edge of the landing area should be at least 10 meters (32.81 feet).

In the men's triple jump, the nearer edge of the landing area should be at least 10.97 meters (36 feet) (12.5 meters or 41 feet is recommended) from the foul line.

In the women's triple jump, the nearer edge of the landing area should be at least 8.53 meters (28 feet) (10.36 meters or 34 feet is recommended) from the foul line.

The takeoff should be a board made of wood or other suitable rigid material 19.8 to 20.32 centimeters (7.8 to 8 inches) wide, at least 1.22 meters (4 feet) long, and not more than 10 centimeters (3.94 inches) thick. The upper surface of the board must be level with the runway surface. This board should be painted white and be firmly fixed in the runway. The edge of the takeoff board nearest the landing pit should be the foul line. For the purpose of aiding the calling of fouls, the area immediately beyond the foul line may be prepared as shown in Figure 28.7. A tray 10.2 centimeters (4 inches) wide filled with plasticene or other suitable material may be used. The plasticene or other material should be of a contrasting color to, and level with, the takeoff board (NCAA, 1997).

Surfaces for Track and Runways

Once the basic design work is completed, a track surface must be selected. Natural-material track systems, such as cinder and clay, used to be common. These tracks were relatively inexpensive to construct, but they required constant maintenance and were rendered soggy by rains, often causing postponement or cancellation of meets. In recent years, the growing cost of transporting the materials used in these tracks has increased their price to a point where they are nearly as expensive as more modern systems.

All-weather surfaces, the first modern track surfacing systems, became popular in the late 1960s. Their development meant that systems were now available that were relatively durable and unaffected by ordinary weather. Called asphalt-bound, these systems consisted of a combination of rubber with asphalt emulsion, sand and asphalt, or roofing asphalt.

Although many asphalt-bound tracks are still in use, these tracks (like cinder tracks) are no longer being constructed in large numbers because their disadvantages are no longer balanced by a significant cost savings. Asphalt-bound tracks are affected by temperature—they become quite soft in the summer and hard in the winter. More important, asphalt becomes harder as it ages, so that despite its rubber content, an older asphalt-bound track is no more resilient for runners than an ordinary street.

At the same time, the cost of an asphalt-bound track has increased because it has become increasingly difficult to find an asphalt plant willing to manufacture the special mix required at an affordable price. Existing asphalt-bound tracks in good condition are often sealed to prolong their life. An asphalt-bound track in good condition can be used as a base for a more modern all-weather surface.

Today, most tracks are constructed of rubber particles bound with latex or polyurethane. The latex or polyurethane surface is installed to a depth of $3/8$ to $1/2$ inch on top of an asphalt or concrete base. The rubber used may be black or colored. Black rubber particles may be granular or stranded and they may be made from natural rubber, styrene-butadiene rubber (SBR), or ethylene-propylene-diene rubber (EPDM), virgin or recycled. Colored rubber particles are almost always made of virgin EPDM rubber and come in granular form only. The relative costs and performance characteristics of the rubber types used are beyond the scope of this article. In general, though, virgin rubber is more expensive than recycled rubber and colored rubber is more expensive than black rubber (Bardeen, et al., 1992).

Latex-bound tracks provide good performance and durability at an affordable cost. Depending on the specific type of system, color, and location, latex tracks cost from $8 to $25 per square yard (Bardeen, et al., 1992). They can be installed in multiple layers or in a single layer, creating a permeable, resilient surface. In some systems, the rubber is spread over the track surface, which is then sprayed with the latex binder. In other systems, the rubber particles and binder are premixed and then spread. Virtually all latex systems are permeable to some degree.

The basic, and least expensive, system is black, but three types of colored systems are available, including colored binder with black rubber; color sandwich, which has colored rubber and colored binder in the top layers over black rubber/black binder or black rubber/colored binder; or full-depth color, where both the rubber and latex binder are colored throughout the surface.

Polyurethane systems are more expensive than latex systems, costing from $14 to $55 per square yard, but they are considered to be more durable. In addition, their resilient but slightly firmer surface is often preferred by track athletes, so they are often used for world-class competitive tracks. Polyurethane surfaces can be either permeable or impermeable. They are most often mixed and installed on site, though pre-manufactured systems are available for locations where on-site mixing and spraying is not feasible (Bardeen, et al., 1992).

Polyurethane surfaces may be colored or black. There are four types. The basic polyurethane-bound system consists of rubber particles bound with polyurethane to form a base mat. The base mat may be used alone, or it may be enhanced by the addition of a structural spray consisting of a mixture of polyurethane and rubber sprayed on top of the mat, which creates a textured surface. Alternatively, the base mat may be coated with a flood coat of polyurethane and rubber, creating an impermeable, textured surface. Or, a full-pour system may be used, where each layer is mixed and poured in place. Full pour systems are impermeable and textured.

With so many systems available, it is important to consider initial cost, maintenance cost over the expected life of the surface, life expectancy, surface wear, repairability, and performance characteristics of the surface.

In the first step of the construction phase, the track is staked out on the site and all measurements are carefully checked. Elevations and grades are set. Next, excavation begins. The sod and topsoil are removed, and the track area is excavated to a depth of 8 to 12 inches. The area of excavation is wider than the finished track will be. The asphalt courses and synthetic surfacing also will extend beyond the actual dimensions of the track lanes. This pavement extension serves several purposes—it allows for drainage of the track and infield, and serves as a control point for leveling, grading, and establishing the correct length and width of the track (Bardeen, et al., 1992).

In some locations, subsoil must be sterilized after excavation and prior to base construction. If weed growth under or through asphalt surfaces is a problem, herbicides should be considered.

Once excavation is completed, a grader is used to establish the appropriate slope and pitch. Normally tracks are pitched to the inside, with a slope of not more than 1% or $1/8$ inch in 1 foot. (A slope of 2%—$1/4$ inch in 1 foot—is acceptable for a high school track.) Finally, a heavy vibratory roller is used to tightly compact the sub-base, which prevents settling that may cause cracking in the finished surface (Bardeen, et al., 1992).

After completion of the preliminary site work, the measurements must be rechecked. The allowable tolerances of the finished track are so small that measurements should be checked at each stage of construction to prevent problems at a later stage.

A base course is then laid. The base course is usually aggregate, but asphalt or penetration macadam also are used. The base course should be no less than four inches thick; more in colder climates. Once spread to uniform thickness, aggregate should be compacted with a tandem roller. After compaction, the grade of the base course must again be verified.

Next are the leveling and finish courses. Asphalt is commonly used for these layers, although concrete can be used. A recent development in track design is the dynamic base track, which uses a rubber, stone, and polyurethane binder mix in place of the solid asphalt or concrete track structure.

A leveling course of hot plant-mix asphalt is applied to the aggregate base to build an asphalt track. This leveling—or binding—layer contains fairly coarse aggregate to provide stability to the finished track. It is rolled and compacted to a thickness of not less than one inch. On top of the leveling course, a surface or finish course of finer asphalt is applied. Like the leveling course, the finish course is compacted to a thickness of not less than one inch. The proper type of asphalt will vary from location to location. State highway department standards can provide some guidance in choosing an asphalt mix.

The finish course is rolled and compacted to complete base construction. Once completed, the asphalt or concrete base must be cured prior to application of the surfacing system. Asphalt is usually allowed to cure for 14 days, while concrete normally cures for 28 to 30 days.

The cured surface is then inspected one last time. The finished surface must not deviate more than $1/8$ inch in 10 feet from the specified grade. Its surface may be flooded to check for low areas, called bird baths, to complete the inspection of the base. The base is then cleaned to remove loose particles, dirt, or oil and, for most surfacing systems, primed.

Next, the synthetic surface is installed. The track surface must be installed in strict compliance with the specifications for that particular type of surface and, for layered systems, each layer must be properly cured prior to the installation of the next one.

The last step in constructing a track is calibration and marking. Various options—such as color code, and design or markings—must be considered in light of the type of competition that will be held on the track. The governing bodies of high school, college, national, and international amateur track have all agreed that the 200-meter race should be marked in such a way that all racers start on a turn–but for some events, the governing bodies differ, so the markings will differ. Once such decisions are made, a track-marking specialist should perform all necessary computations and measurements, marking the required distances on the track. Today, track calibration and marking is frequently computer-assisted to ensure its accuracy.

Permanent markings are then painted on the track, indicating the various distances, start and finish areas, exchange zones, lane numbers, photo timing marks and similar symbols. The track striper then certifies that the marking and striping meet the specifications agreed to by the owner and designer and the requirements of the appropriate governing body. For most high school tracks, certification by the striper is considered sufficient. If the track is to be used for high-level competition, it must be measured and certified as accurate by a professional engineer or licensed land surveyor.

From start to finish, a track project involves many steps. The planning phase of the project can take several months, while actual construction will take at least eight to 12 weeks, without delays caused by weather or other factors. Do your homework—the investment of time and energy now will yield a quality facility in the future.

Throwing Areas (Indoor and Outdoor)

Throwing Circles

The circles in throwing events should be made of a band of metal or suitable rigid material (as described in Figures 7, 9, and 11), the top of which should be flush with the concrete outside the circle. The interior surface should be of concrete or similar material and should 20 millimeters (0.79 inches), plus or minus 6 millimeters (0.24 inch), lower than the surface outside the circle (NCAA, 1997).

The following is the procedure used for determining a 40-degree sector: The level of the surface within the landing area should be the same as the level of the surface of the throwing circle.

The inside diameters of the shot-put and hammer-throw circles should be 2.135 meters (7 feet), plus or minus 5 millimeters (0.20 inch), and the diameter of the discus circle should be 2.5 meters (8.20 feet), plus or minus 5 millimeters (NCAA, 1997).

The circle should be made of metal or suitable rigid material 6 millimeters (0.24 inch) in thickness and 19.05 millimeters (0.75 inch) in height, plus or minus 6 millimeters, and be firmly secured flush with the throwing surface.

The insert should be made of metal or suitable rigid material (rubber is not suitable). The top of the insert must be flush with the concrete outside the circle.

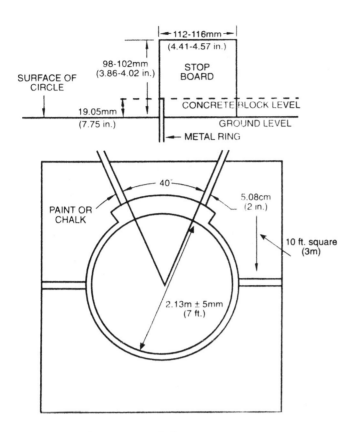

Figure 28.8 Shot put circle.

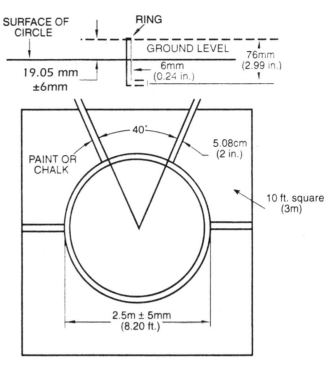

Figure 28.9 Discus circle.

All circles should be divided in half by a 5.08 centimeter (2 inch) line extending from the outer edge of the circle to the end of the throwing pad and measured at right angles to the imaginary center of the throwing sector. There should be no lines painted within any throwing circle.

Shot-Put Area

The circle should be constructed in accordance with Figure 28.8. The stepboard is an arc of wood, or other suitable material painted white and firmly fixed so that its inner edge coincides with the inner edge of the shot-put circle. It should measure 1.22 meters (4 feet) in length along its inside edge, 112 to 116 millimeters (4.41 to 4.57 inches) in width and 98 to 102 (3.86 to 4.02 inches) in height (see Figure 28.8) (NCAA, 1997).

Radial lines 5.08 centimeters (2 inches) wide should form a 40-degree angle extended from the center of the circle. The inside edges of these lines should mark the sector. The surface within the landing area should be on the same level as the throwing surface. Sector flags should mark the ends of the lines (NCAA, 1997).

Discus Area

All discus throws should be made from an enclosure or cage centered on the circle to ensure safety of

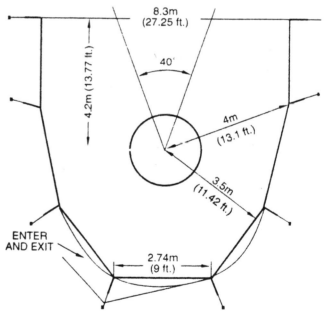

Figure 28.10 Contruction for discus cage.

spectators, officials, and competitors (see Figure 28.9). The height of the discus cage should be at least 4 meters (13 feet 1.5 inches). A discus cage is designed to provide limited protection for spectators, officials, and competitors. It does not ensure their safety due to the nature of the event(NCAA, 1997).

The circle should be constructed in accordance with Figure 28.10. The throwing sector for the discus should be marked by two radial lines 5.08 centimeters (2 inches) wide that form a 40-degree angle, extended from the

Figure 28.11 Contruction
of hammer cage.

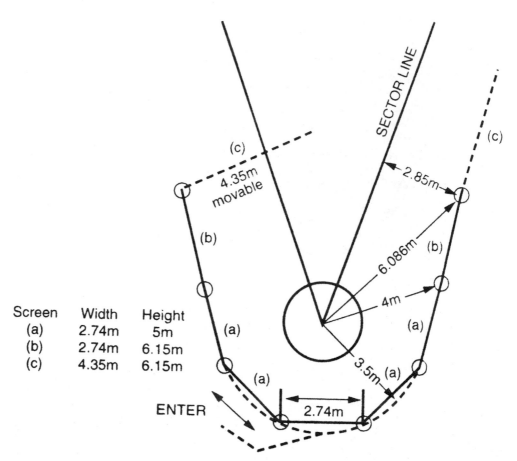

Screen	Width	Height
(a)	2.74m	5m
(b)	2.74m	6.15m
(c)	4.35m	6.15m

center of the circle, and the inside edges of these lines should mark the sector. The surface within the landing area should be on the same level as the throwing surface. Sector flags should mark the ends of the lines. The sector should be centered within the enclosure.

Hammer Area

All hammer throws should be made from an enclosure or cage centered according to the dimensions in Figure 28.11 to ensure the safety of spectators, officials, and competitors. The cage shall be constructed as follows (NCAA, 1997):

■ There should be two movable panels at the front of the screen at least 4.20 meters (13.78 feet) but not more than 4.35 meters (14.27 feet) in width.
■ These panels should be attached to a fixed vertical support that is 2.85 meters (9.35 feet) away from the sector line and 6.086 meters (20.08 feet) out from the center of the circle. The height of the movable panels should be 6.15 meters (20.18 feet).

The circle should be constructed in accordance with Figure 28.12. The throwing sector for the ham-

mer should be marked by two radial lines 5.08 centimeters (2 inches) wide that form a 40-degree angle, extended from the center of the circle. The inside edges of these lines should mark the sector. The surface within the landing area should be on the same level as the throwing surface. Sector flags should mark the ends of the lines. The sector should be centered within the enclosure.

Javelin Area

It is recommended that the runway be constructed of an artificial surface for a width of 4 meters (13.12 feet) for the entire length of the runway. The minimum length of the runway for the javelin should be 36.58 meters (120 feet). If an artificial surface is used, it is recommended that the runway be extended 1 meter (3.28 feet) beyond the foul line for safety reasons. The runway should be marked by two parallel lines 5.08 centimeters (2 inches) in width and a minimum of 1.22 meters (4 feet) apart for 21.34 meters (70.01 feet), widening to 4 meters (13.12 feet) apart for the 15.24 meters (50 feet) before the foul line (NCAA, 1997).

The foul line should be 7 centimeters (2.76 inches) wide and painted white, in the shape of an arc with a

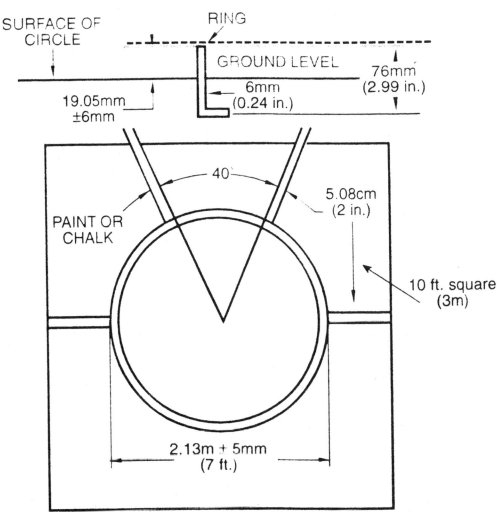

Figure 28.12 Hammer/weight throw cirlcle.

radius of 8 meters (26.25 feet). The distance between its extremities should be 4 meters (13.12 feet) measured straight across from end to end (NCAA, 1997).

Radius lines 5.08 centimeters (2 inches) wide should be extended from the center of the circle of which the arc of the foul board is a part through the extremities of the arc. The inside edges of these lines should mark the sector. The surface within the landing area should be the on the same level as the throwing surface. Sector flags should mark the ends of the lines (see Figure 28.13) (NCAA, 1997).

Other Structures/Facilities
Finish Line Towers

Tower A

The finish line is the control center for running events. The finish line tower should be directly across from the finish line. It should be a two-story enclosed structure, 20 feet by 40 feet square with eight-foot ceilings and a roof designed as a deck with railings. The first-floor area will contain space for restrooms, a small storage area with a small roll-up door, and concessions. The second-floor will have picture windows facing the finish line. The second floor area will have space for the press, announcer, and the automatic timer, computers, and cameras (Flynn, 1993).

Tower B

This will be a duplicate of Tower A, except the first floor will be dedicated to the storage of hurdles, implements, and pads. The first-floor storage area will have a large roll-up door to accommodate the large landing pads.

Both towers should have hot and cold water, sewer connection, communications lines (i.e., telephone, computer, and television), electricity, and appropriate ventilation.

Figure 28.13 *Javelin throwing area.*

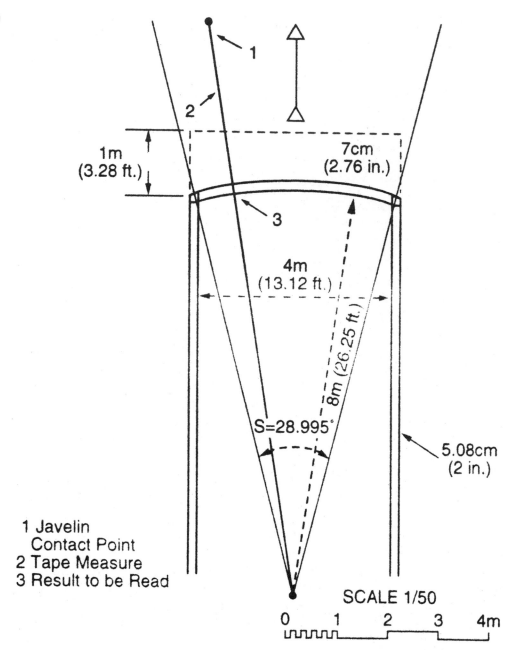

1m
(3.28 ft.)

7cm
(2.76 in.)

4m
(13.12 ft.)

8m (26.25 ft.)

S=28.995°

5.08cm
(2 in.)

1 Javelin
   Contact Point
2 Tape Measure
3 Result to be Read

SCALE 1/50

0   1   2   3   4m

Lighting

The track and field area should be lighted for security at a minimum, but serious consideration should be given to lighting the area for evening competition.

Fencing

The entire facility should be fenced so it can be secured when not in use. The fence should be at least 10 feet high, plastic/vinyl coated, painted to match the surrounding paint patterns. The fence should have gates in appropriate locations for athletes, spectators, and maintenance vehicles (Flynn, 1993).

Fences need to be installed to protect athletes and officials from throwing areas (e.g., discus, hammer, and javelin). These fences need to be at least six feet high. They should also be constructed with plastic/vinyl-coated material.

Spectator Seating

Spectator seating is a necessity. The planners should design seating for both sides of the track. The running track will have two finish lines going in opposite directions. Depending on the prevailing wind, a decision will be made as to which direction the races will be run. Therefore, it is necessary to provide seating on both sides of the track for spectators.

The total number of seats should be based on historical data regarding spectator involvement over the past five years. The seating can either be permanent, constructed of metal, wood, or other appropriate materials, or be portable aluminum bleachers. The higher the bleachers, the greater the liability concerns. If money is not a problem, construct concrete seating large enough to incorporate storage areas underneath the seats and a press box on the upper level (Flynn, 1993).

Starting System

Modern timing systems are connected to the starter's gun. Therefore, the hard wiring that is required should be placed underground and junction boxes made available at the various starting lines for the races. These junction boxes should be at least four feet off the ground.

Landscaping

There should be an irrigation system designed to provide water to all grass areas, shrubbery, and flowers. When planning the irrigation system, careful consideration needs to be given to providing additional water to drinking fountains throughout the complex and water for the water jump. The track and field area should be large enough to provide at least a half-acre shaded area for athletes between events. The areas at the end of the straightaways should have trees to provide a wind break for the athletes (Flynn, 1993).

Track and Field Equipment

Starting Blocks

Starting blocks must be made without devices that could provide artificial aid in starting. They may be adjustable but must be constructed entirely of rigid materials.

Hurdles

Hurdles should be constructed of metal, wood, or other suitable material. The hurdles should consist of two bases and two uprights supporting a rectangular frame, reinforced by one or more crossbars. The top crossbar should be wood or other suitable material, with beveled edges, and a height of 70 millimeters (2.76 inches). The center of the crossbar should be directly over the end of the base. The surface facing the starting line should be white in color with two vertical or diagonal stripes. A center chevron should be added to help contestants determine the center of the lane (NCAA, 1997).

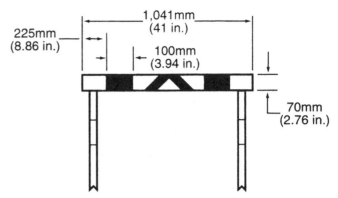

Figure 28.14 Hurdle measurements.

Pull-over force refers to the 3.6 kilograms (8 pounds) of steady pulling force required to overturn a hurdle when applied to the center of the uppermost edge of the top crossbar and in the direction of the finish line. If the weights cannot be adjusted to the required overturning force, it is recommended that the next greater setting be used, since records will not be allowed when the overturning force or the weight of the hurdle is less than the required minimum (NCAA, 1997).

When no definite counterweight setting for intermediate hurdles has been made by the manufacturer, it is sometimes possible to attain the correct adjustment by setting one weight as for the 106.7-centimeter (42 inch) height and the other weight as for 76.2-centimeter (30 inch) height. A difference of 3 millimeters (0.12 inch) above or below the required height will be tolerated (see Figure 28.14) (NCAA, 1997).

Steeplechase Hurdles

Hurdles should be constructed of metal, wood, or other suitable material. Steeplechase and water-jump hurdles should not be less than 91.1 centimeters (2.99 feet) nor more than 91.7 centimeters (3.01 feet) high and should be at least 3.66 meters (12 feet) in width. It is recommended that the first hurdle be at least 5 meters (16 feet, 4.75 inches) in width. The section of the top bar of the hurdles and the hurdle at the water jump should be 127 millimeters (5 inches) square without sharp edges or with a 6.35-millimeter (0.25 inch) bevel. The weight of each hurdle should be at least 80 kilograms (176.4 pounds). Each hurdle should have on either side a base between 12 meters (3.94 feet) and 1.4 meters (4.59 feet) long (NCAA, 1997).

High Jump

The high jump pad should be a minimum of 4.88 meters wide by 2.44 meters deep (16 feet by 8 feet). It should be high enough and of a composition that will provide a safe and comfortable landing. A minimum height of 66.04 centimeters (26 inches), including the top pad unit, is preferred (NCAA, 1997).

The horizontal supports of the crossbar should be flat and rectangular, 4 centimeters (1.6 inches) wide and 6 centimeters (2.4 inches) long, and friction-free. Each support should point toward the opposite upright so that the crossbar will rest between the uprights along the narrow dimension (3.81 centimeters [1.5 inches]) of the support (NCAA, 1997).

The uprights should extend at least 100 millimeters (3.94 inches) above the support of the crossbar. The crossbar should be circular and made of suitable material. The ends of the crossbar should be smooth and not be covered with rubber or any other material that has the effect of increasing the friction between the surface of the crossbar and the supports. The diameter of the bar must be at least 25 millimeters but not more than 30 millimeters (0.98 to 1.18 inches). The crossbar should be constructed in such a way that a flat surface of 25 to 30 millimeters (0.98 to 1.18 inches) by 150 to 200 millimeters (5.91 to 7.87 inches) is designed for the purpose of placing the bar on the supports of the uprights (NCAA, 1997).

Pole Vault

The pole vault pad measurement beyond the vertical plane of the stopboard should be a minimum of 4.88 meters wide by 3.66 meters deep (16 feet by 12 feet). It is recommended that the front portion of the pad be the same width as the back units, 4.88 meters (16 feet), extending 91.44 centimeters (36 inches) from the back edge of the stopboard to the front edge of the vaulting box. Measured across the bottom of the cutout. The back of the cutout should be placed no farther than 36 millimeters (14.17 inches) from the vertical plane of the stopboard. A height of 81.28 centimeters (32 inches), including the top pad unit, is required. Suitable padding should be placed around the base of the standards (NCAA, 1997).

Any style upright or posts may be used for the pole vault, provided the style is rigid and supported by a base not to exceed 10.16 centimeters (4 inches) in height above the ground. Cantilevered uprights are recommended. The distance between the vertical uprights or between the extension arms where such are used should be 4.32 meters (14.7 feet) (NCAA, 1997).

The crossbar should rest on round metal pins that project not more than 75 millimeters (2.95 inches) at right angles from the uprights and have diameters of not more than 13 millimeters (0.512 inches). The upper surfaces of these pins should be smooth, without indentations or aids of any kind that might help to hold the crossbar in place. The crossbar should be circular and made of suitable material. The ends of the crossbar shall be smooth and not be covered with rubber or any other material that has the effect of in-

creasing the friction between the surface of the crossbar and the supports. The diameter of the crossbar must be at least 29 millimeters but not more than 31 millimeters (1.14 to 1.22 inches). The crossbar should be between 4.48 and 4.52 meters (14.7 to 14.83 feet) in length. The maximum weight shall be 2.25 kilograms (4.96 pounds). For the purpose of placing the bar on the supports of the uprights, the ends of the crossbar should be constructed in such a way that a flat surface of 29 to 35 millimeters (1.14 to 1.38 inches) by 200 millimeters(7.87 inches) is provided (NCAA, 1997).

Other Accessory Equipment

The following pieces of equipment will be very useful for both indoor and outdoor track and field facilities (NCAA, 1997):

■ Pole vault standards base protection pads,
■ Countdown timer,
■ Wind gauge—now required for all collegiate 100. 200. 110 & 110 hurdles, long jump, and high jump,
■ Implement certification unit,
■ Aluminum water jump,
■ Foundation tray,
■ Blanking lid,
■ Take-off board with plasticine insert,
■ Long jump/triple ump aluminum pit covers,
■ Throwing rings,
■ Toe boards,
■ Concentric circles,
■ Stainless steel or aluminum pole vault box,
■ Pole vault covers,
■ Finish post,
■ Aluminum track curbing,
■ Rotating track gate,
■ Hammer cage,
■ Discus cage,
■ Indoor throwing event cage,
■ Lane markers,
■ Distance marker boxes,
■ Long jump/triple jump distance indicator,
■ Performance boards,
■ Lap counter,
■ Wind display,
■ Awards stand,
■ Judges' stand,
■ Starter's rostrum,
■ Hurdle carts,
■ Platform cart,
■ Starting block caddy, and
■ Implement carts—shotput cart, hammer cart, javelin cart, discus cart, combo cart.

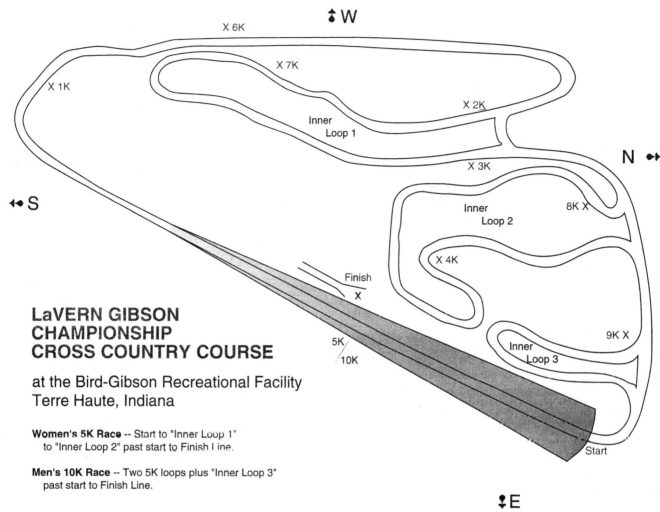

Figure 28.15 LaVern Gibson Championship Cross Country Course.

Cross Country Facility

The Course (see Figure 28.15)

The length of the cross country course varies as follows:

■ Men—The length of a cross country race should be from 8,000 to 10,000 meters, unless otherwise mutually agreed upon by coaches or determined by the games committee
■ High school—5,000 meter standard, some variations are found between state associations.
■ Women—5,000 meters; high school—3,000 to 5,000 meters.

Course Layout

The course should be confined to fields, woods, and grasslands. Parks, golf courses, or specially designed courses (see Figure 28.15) are recommended. The turf should be a quality to promote safety and freedom from injury to the runners, keeping the following in mind:

■ Dangerous ascents or descents, undergrowth, deep ditches, and in general any hindrance detrimental to the contestants must be avoided.
■ Narrow gaps must be no less than two and preferably five meters in width for non-championships courses. Obstacles and other hindrances should be avoided for the first 600 to 800 meters as well as the last 200 to 300 meters of the race.
  Note: Championship course must be at least 10 meters wide at all points.
■ Continuous traversing of roadways should be avoided.
■ The direction and path of the course shall be defined clearly for the runners.
■ All turns must be gradual.

Course Markings

The course should be properly measured along the shortest possible route that a runner may take, and it must be marked clearly by at least two of the following methods, presented in order of preference:

▶ Sign posts not less than seven feet high, with large directional arrows on boards fastened to the tops of the posts so that the arrows will be visible plainly at a distance to competitors approaching the posts. The posts must be placed at every point where the course turns, on the side of the direction of the turn, and wherever there is any doubt as to the direction of travel.

▶ A single white or colored line for directional purposes only—not to be assumed as the measured line—or two lines that mark the outside borders of the course, one on the measured course marking its shortest perimeter and the second such that runners cannot vary from the proper course. In addition, these two lines serve as restraining lines for spectators. Lines on the turns must vary in color from the color of lines approaching the turn.

▶ Flags, sign posts, or stakes that meet the following conditions:

■ markers at least seven feet above the ground level,

■ a turn to the left marked by a red flag or arrow of direction on a sign post or stake,

■ a turn to the right marked by a yellow flag or arrow of direction on a sign post or stake,

■ a course continuing straight marked by a blue flag or arrow of direction on a sign post or stake, and

■ all flags, sign posts or stakes marking the shortest perimeter of the course.

Finally, all of the above course-marking devices must be placed on the edge of the measured line when lines and flags, sign posts, or stakes are used to mark the course.

■ Summary

A track and field competition complex is complicated at best when compared to other outdoor or indoor sport spaces, such as an indoor basketball/volleyball court or a baseball, football, or soccer field.

Learning Objective 1: The student will be able to select an appropriate site.

The most important decision in building a track and field complex is site selection. The substrata for the track most be solid so that a good base can be developed before constructing the running surface. If the running surface is not optimal the complex will be considered substandard.

Learning Objective 2: The student will be able to design proper track and field and cross country facilities.

After the site is selected, the planners need to shift their thoughts to designing a solid plan for the track and field and cross country facilities. The planners need to consider each event carefully. The track and runways need to be fast. The throwing areas must be safe. The finish line and time area must be efficient and clear of congestion.

■ Case Study

You have been hired as the new track and field and cross country coach for Advanta University, a medium-sized private liberal arts college in the Midwest. The university uses a local high school facility to practice and compete. The director of athletics has informed you that in the five-year capital campaign the university just completed included funds for a new track and field facility as well as a cross country course. You have been appointed the chair of the university's design committee for these two new facilities. Describe the steps that you will take in planning these facilities, and outline what you will request to be part of the facilities.

■ References

Bardeen, J., Renner, M.P., Ediger, R., Lemons, B., Parks, S., Petrucelli, J., & Rauch, T. W. (1992, November). Precision tracks. **Athletic Business**, 16(11), 49-56.

Flynn, R.B. (Ed.) (1992). **Planning facilities for athletics, physical education, and recreation** (2nd ed.). Reston, VA: The American Alliance for Health, Physical Education, Recreation, and Dance.

NCAA. (1997). NCAA men's and women's track and field and cross country rules. Overland Park, KS: Author.

■ Suggested Readings and Resources

The United States Tennis Court and Track Builders Association has available a number of informative publications dealing with track construction. Contact USTC&TBA, 720 Light St., Baltimore, MD 21230, or call (410) 752-3500.

Berg, R. (1990, November). Getting on the right track. **Athletic Business, 14** (11), 63-67.

Blueprints of an NCAA-commissioned 400-meter track and meter layout may be purchased for $4 each from NCAA Publishing, P.O. Box 7347, Overland Park, Kansas 66207-0347.

Notes

CHAPTER 29

Trends in Stadium and Arena Design

Todd L. Seidler, University of New Mexico

Learning Objectives

After reading this chapter, the student will be able to

■ be familiar with the concept of the retractable roof stadium and understand its advantages,

■ identify the three main types of fabric structures and list the advantages and disadvantages of each,

■ describe the importance of designing luxury suites and club seats in new spectator facilities,

■ identify the advantages of wooden domes, and

■ identify the new arena design features intended to speed the change-over from one event to another.

Introduction

This chapter will present an overview and analysis of certain recent trends and innovations in stadium and arena design. It is by no means a complete look at these unique sports facilities; many others are covered in other parts of this book. This chapter will merely try to highlight certain significant trends and concepts that should not be overlooked.

A New Breed of Facilities

The fundamental purpose and design of stadiums and arenas has changed radically in the last decade. These changes are so dramatic that many facilities have become obsolete, and even young ones 10 to 20 years old are facing the wrecking ball. The basic idea behind this change is that modern arenas and stadiums are no longer just places to watch an event, but are now designed to provide a total entertainment experience.

Historically, most large arenas and stadiums have been funded by city or state governments, or by colleges and universities. Recently these entities have had tighter budgets and, more than ever, must rely less on public funding. The current trend is more toward private funding (Jewell, 1992). In order to maximize return on such a large investment, every effort must be made to ensure that the facility be able to accommodate as many events and different kinds of activities as possible. Recent design improvements have focused on optimally supporting each event and being able to change over from one event to another as quickly as possible. Whereas some older facilities would rely on 8 to 10 football games or 40 basketball games per year as their main source of revenue, some facilities now schedule from 250 to 600 events per year, including sporting events, concerts, conventions, trade shows, rodeos, monster truck shows, and professional wrestling. Efficient design can allow a crew to change the set-up for one kind of event to another in a matter of hours. This means that more than one event can take place in the same day. Several aspects of design that allow a facility to accommodate a wide variety of events and also to quickly alter the set-up for different events include

■ versatile lighting and sound systems that can adequately handle the wide variety of events,
■ ramps that allow semi-trucks to back all the way to the floor. Even better, some facilities provide floor access for two or more trucks at a time so that one can be loaded while another is unloaded,
■ heavy-duty lighting grids that can be lowered to the floor in order to enhance the placement of sound and lighting equipment for concerts, and
■ fixed, pre-wired camera positions that for allow for quick and easy set-up for television broadcasts. Many new arenas have a full television production studio, which permits a television network to broadcast a game without bringing in their semi-trucks full of production equipment.

Another trend in arena and stadium design that is designed to maximize revenue is the move toward more upscale facilities and greater service and convenience for spectators. Some aspects of this trend include the following:

■ Providing more rest rooms. In the past, many spectator facilities provided only enough rest rooms to satisfy the local code requirements. This often resulted in long lines and frustration on the part of the spectators. Many facilities are now being designed with up to twice as many rest rooms as the minimum required. Since some events may draw a disproportionate number of men or women, consideration should be given to designing some rest rooms that can serve either gender simply by changing the sign on the door.
■ Taking into consideration the requirements of customers with disabilities. With the advent of the Americans With Disabilities Act, full accommodation of the needs of the disabled is now federal law. Recent lawsuits have established new standards for the placement of handicapped seating. All wheelchair-accessible seats must now be located so that users can see over the heads of the spectators in front of them even when they stand.

■ Building larger concourse areas and adding separate concourses to serve different levels. Improved access and less crowding make these areas more attractive. Some concourse areas are being designed to resemble a mini-mall by offering many different choices of food and novelty items.
■ One of the most significant trends in stadium and arena design is adding luxury suites and club seating. Luxury suites are small, private rooms opening toward the court or field that are usually leased to individuals or companies who desire a semi-private lounge area, typically large enough to accommodate 12 to 20 guests. Suites are normally leased on multi-year contracts and are often furnished and decorated by the tenant. The prevalence of these luxury suites is growing rapidly primarily because they are such good revenue producers. The Palace of Auburn Hills is a good example of how important suites have become to the economics of this type of facility. The original plans called for 100 luxury suites to be built as part of the arena. About one-third of the way through construction, all of the suites had been leased. Some quick design changes by the architect produced an additional 80 suites, which were also leased by the time the Palace opened. Total construction cost was about $63 million and the income from the lease of the suites alone was almost $12 million per year (Gordon, 1990).

This incredible increase in revenue can make a big difference in the profitability of a team and can be a huge advantage over other organizations that do not have it. It also has become an essential part of the equation for financing a new facility. The Palace generated enough revenue just from leasing the suites to pay for the facility in less than six years. That is not including revenue from ticket sales, concessions, parking, etc. Luxury suites have become a significant design feature and not only make the construction of future arenas and stadiums more economically feasible, but are becoming a necessity for many sports organizations to remain financially competitive.

Club seats are usually exclusive seating areas where the right to buy tickets may be purchased through a permanent seat license (PSL). Club seats are typically larger and have more leg room than regular seating and include special considerations such as waiters who take orders and deliver food right to the seat. Income from PSLs and club seats can be significant and an important source of revenue.

Innovations in Materials and Methods of Construction

Recent innovations in the techniques of enclosing large areas without support pillars and posts that interfere with spectator comfort are providing many more options for the construction of stadiums and arenas. Stadiums with retractable roofs, tension fabric structures, air-supported fabric structures, wooden domes, and cable domes are examples of building designs that have been successfully used to enclose large sports facilities.

Retractable Roof Stadiums

One of the biggest innovations in stadium design is the concept of having a stadium that is open to the elements when the weather is nice but can be quickly covered when needed. The first attempt at a retractable roof stadium was Olympic Stadium in Montreal, built for the 1976 Olympic Games. The original plan was to build a huge concrete mast next to the stadium that would support a fabric roof on steel cables. The roof was supposed to be lifted off the stadium and suspended from the mast, thereby becoming an open-air stadium (Holleman, 1996). The roof could then be lowered back on top of the stadium to enclose it again when desired.

The design never did work correctly, but this ambitious idea eventually led to the successful designs we are seeing today. It is estimated that adding a retractable roof to the design of a new stadium will increase the cost between $30 and $70 million.

Examples:

■ SkyDome—Located in Toronto, Ontario, Sky-Dome was the first stadium to have a fully retractable roof. Opened in 1989, SkyDome can completely open or close the entire steel-trussed roof in 20 minutes. This is accomplished by three movable roof sections, two of which slide and another that rotates. The stadium seats 50,600 for baseball, 53,000 for football, and has different seating arrangements for concerts ranging from 10,000 to 70,000. It also contains 161 luxury Sky-Boxes, a 348-room hotel and health club, full broadcast facilities, underground parking, and a 110 by 33 foot state-of-the-art video screen. Original estimates of the cost for SkyDome were $184 million (Canadian) but it ended up costing about $585 million. So far, the roof has only been closed about four or five times a season due to inclement weather (Gordon, 1990).

■ Bank One Ballpark—Opened for the 1998 season, BOB is the home of the Arizona Diamondbacks, located in downtown Phoenix, and is the first retractable-roof stadium to be built since SkyDome. This air-conditioned, retractable-roof stadium is designed primarily for baseball and seats 48,500. It is a natural grass stadium and was built for a cost of $349 million with 68% coming from public financing. With a total of 69 private suites, six party suites and 5,592 club seats, there is something for everybody, including 350 bleacher seats that are sold for $1 per game. As with many of the new stadiums, it is more than just a place to watch a ballgame. BOB contains two micro-breweries and two 10,000-square-foot beer gardens, a mini hall-of-fame fashioned after Cooperstown, a 4,000-square-foot team store, 110 picnic tables, and 212 concession stands. The new stadiums are meant to provide a quality entertainment experience, not just a place to watch a game.

As of the time of this writing, construction has already begun on retractable-roof stadiums for the Houston Astros, Milwaukee Brewers, and Seattle Mariners. The new stadium for the Detroit Tigers is being built so that a retractable roof can be added at a later date. Discussions are also underway by at least four other teams—the Minnesota Twins, the Florida Marlins, the New York Mets and the Montreal Expos—who are considering construction of retractable-roof stadiums. It appears that the retractable-roof stadium is now coming into its own and we will probably see many new examples in the coming years.

Fabric Structures

A fairly recent development in the area of physical education, recreation, and athletic facilities is the concept of fabric structures. The fabric used most commonly is a Teflon® coated fiberglass material. The fiberglass yarn used to make the material is pound for pound stronger than steel and is also less expensive. It can be designed to allow either a large amount or very little natural light to penetrate. The fabric can withstand temperatures of 1300 to 1500 degrees Fahrenheit and is not adversely affected by cold or the ultraviolet rays of the sun. Fabric structures offer a number of possible advantages and disadvantages when compared with standard construction.

Advantages

■ Lower initial cost—initial costs are usually lower than with conventional construction. Several factors contribute to this, the primary one being weight. A fabric roof is 1/30 the weight of a conventional steel-truss roof. This reduced weight means that the walls, footings, and foundations

Figure 29.1 Toronto Skydome.

are not required to be nearly as strong as in a conventional building.

■ Less construction time—the amount of construction time is directly related to the initial cost of the structure. The total time necessary to build a fabric structure is usually less than for a conventional roof.

■ Natural lighting—Since the fiberglass fabric material that is used is translucent, it results in a large amount of interior natural lighting. Without using artificial lights during the day, the light intensity inside can vary anywhere from 100 to 1000 footcandles, depending on weather conditions, design, and choice of fabric. The interior light is considered to be of high quality because it is non-glare and shadow-free.

■ Possibly lower energy costs—in some climates or regions, energy costs may be substantially reduced by the fabric's translucency. The large amount of natural light may reduce or eliminate the need for artificial light during the daytime. This may also reduce the need for air-conditioning required to overcome the heat generated by the artificial lights.

■ Less maintenance—The non-stick characteristics of Teflon® allow the fabric to be washed clean each time it rains.

■ Full utilization of space—depending on the fabric structure's configuration and support, the area that can be enclosed is almost limitless.

Disadvantages

■ Life span—the fabric envelope in use today has a life expectancy of up to 25 years, with longer-life materials being tested. All other items such as the foundation, flooring, and mechanical equipment have the life span of a conventional building.

■ Poor thermal insulation—in cold climates there may be an increase in energy cost when compared with conventional construction due to lower insulating properties of the fabric roof. The insulating value of a typical fabric roof is about R-2 but can be increased substantially (see Lindsay Park Sports Centre). The cost of heating is a significant factor and should be evaluated against that for a conventional building over time. During winter months when the heat is required to melt the

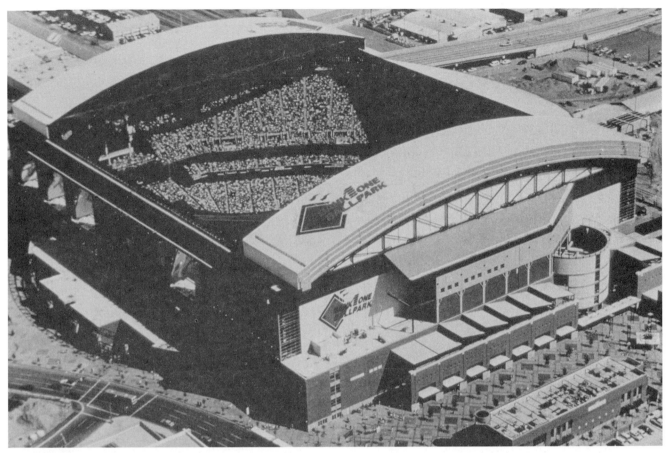

Figure 29.2 BankOne Ballpark.

Figure 29.3 MetroDome.

snow or to cause it to slide off, a safe level of temperature will have to be maintained at all times, which has an impact on heating costs. If the bubble is not to be heated during inactive hours, it will have to be supervised constantly for the dangers of unexpected snowfall. In the summertime the heat gain of the air-supported structure may pose a cooling problem.

■ Acoustic problem—the curved shape of the air-supported structure produces a peculiar acoustic environment. This may pose limitations on its use for large gatherings and open-plan arrangements for different groups.

■ Restriction due to wind—in winds of hurricane velocity, most codes require that the structure be evacuated.

There are three basic types of fabric structures in use: tension structures, air-supported structures, and cable domes. Tension structures are made by stretching fabric between several rigid supports. Air structures are sealed buildings that, through the use of fans, maintain a positive internal air pressure that supports the roof. These structures are actually inflated like a balloon and must maintain the positive air pressure to remain inflated. Cable domes are the newest type of fabric structure. The cable dome is actually a modified tension structure that uses a complex network of cables and girders to support a fabric roof.

Tension Structures

Some projects lend themselves more naturally to tension structures than to air-supported structures or cable domes. Some of the conditions in which tension structures may be more favorable are as follows:

■ Free and open access from the sides is desirable or required.
■ A unique design or aesthetics are of importance.
■ The facility will be largely unattended or not monitored.
■ Possible deflation of an air structure would constitute a severe operational or safety problem.
■ A retrofit to an existing building or structure such as a swimming pool or an outdoor stadium is desired.
Examples
■ Knott Athletic Recreation Convocation Center—Located at Mount Saint Mary's College in Emmitsburg, MD, the Knott Center is a unique combination of standard construction and a fabric tension structure. Completed in 1987, most of the facility is built with standard brick construction, with the tension-structure field house connected onto one side of the building. The fabric roof covers 30,000 square feet of activity space including a multiple court set-up and a 10-lap-per-mile running track. Rising to a height of 40 feet, the double-layered roof allows for almost exclusive use of natural light during the day. Also included within the facility are four racquetball courts, locker rooms, and a 25-yard pool.

■ La Verne College—La Verne College in La Verne, CA, contains the first permanent enclosed fiberglass structure in the United States. The tent-like structure covers 1.4 acres, with the fabric roof having been erected in just three days. Called the Campus Center, it contains a gymnasium that seats 900 people, men's and women's locker rooms, offices, the campus bookstore, and lecture areas. A smaller separate tension structure houses the drama department. This facility was completed in 1973.

■ Lindsay Park—The Lindsay Park Sports Centre in Calgary, Alberta, Canada, houses a 50-meter pool, a diving pool, a fully equipped 30,000-square-foot gymnasium, and a 200-meter running track. The roof is unique in that it was designed with insulation that is rated at R-16. This compares with a typical fabric roof that has about an R-2 rating. Despite the great improvement in insulating qualities, the fabric roof is still translucent enough to allow for an interior illumination of about 200 footcandles. This facility was completed in 1983.

■ McClain Athletic Training Facility—Completed in 1988, this field house is located at the University of Wisconsin at Madison, WI. Due to site restrictions, this $9.5 million facility contains a 90-yard football field instead of a full-size field. Most of the 76,380-square-foot field is covered by a 42,000-square-foot fabric-tension roof that admits up to 750 foot-candles of natural light into the structure. When comparing the fabric roof to standard construction, it is estimated that the increased cost for heating and the reduced cost for artificial lighting result in an overall saving of about $21,000 per year. Below the synthetic turf field lies a full 64,320-square-foot basement that contains locker rooms for football, track, and coaches; weight room; training facilities; and therapy pool. The therapy pool is 15 by 40 feet and goes from four to seven feet in depth. Also included in the facility are an auditorium, six meeting rooms, and a film room.

Figure 29.4 Knott Center-Exterior.

Figure 29.5 Knott Center-Interior.

Figure 29.6 McClain Athletic Training Center, Univeristy of Wisconsin, Madison.

Air-Supported Structures

There are two basic types of air-supported structures, large permanent structures and smaller, more portable structures.

Air-supported fabric structures are supported by a positive air pressure within a totally enclosed building. This positive air pressure is produced by a group of large fans. In conventional buildings the foundation, walls, and internal columns must support a roof weight of between 10 and 40 pounds per square foot. On the other hand, in air-supported structures, a roof weight of about one pound per square foot is transmitted directly to the ground by the increased pressure. This increased air pressure of about four or five pounds per square foot greater than ambient pressure is usually unnoticed by the building's occupants. Some of the instances when an air structure may be preferable to a tension structure or standard construction are:

■ when column-free spans of greater than 150 feet are desired,

■ when large, column-free spans are desired at a cost that is greatly reduced compared to conventional structures. In fact, cost per unit area usually decreases as the size of the span increases, and

■ when a low silhouette is desired.

Examples

■ Dedmon Center—Located at Radford University in Radford, VA, the Dedmon Center was constructed for a cost of $6,750,000 and opened in 1982. Encompassing 110,000 square feet, it has 5,000 temporary seats for basketball. Used for physical education, athletics, and recreation, the center provides five full basketball courts, weight room, pool, locker rooms and offices.

■ Thomas E. Leavey Activities Center—This physical education and athletic complex is located at the University of Santa Clara in Santa Clara, CA. It contains a 5,000-seat arena for basketball and volleyball along with racquetball courts, wrestling, gymnastics, weight training and conditioning areas, conference rooms, staff offices, and

Figure 29.7 Pontiac Silverdome.

a 25-meter swimming pool. The pool is covered by a separate air-supported fabric roof that can be removed in the summertime, converting it into an outdoor pool. This facility was completed in 1978.

■ DakotaDome—Located at the University of South Dakota in Vermillion, SD, the DakotaDome contains five basketball/volleyball courts, two tennis courts, an eight-lane 200 meter track, four racquetball courts, a six-lane 25-meter pool, locker rooms, classrooms, and the offices for the athletic department. The main floor is a synthetic surface that is used for most court activities and has an artificial turf football field that can be rolled out for football, soccer, and other field events. When the facility is set up for football, there is seating for 12,000 spectators. The entire facility was built for the bargain price of about $51 per square foot in 1978.

■ Carrier Dome—The Carrier Dome, located in Syracuse, NY, is the home of Syracuse University athletics. The stadium seats 50,000 for football and over 30,000 for basketball. Also a great bargain, total construction cost was $27,715,000, which figures out to $554 per seat. This is very inexpensive

when compared to conventional covered stadiums. This facility was completed in 1980.

■ Silverdome—The Silverdome, located in Pontiac, MI, has the largest capacity of any indoor stadium in the world. Opened in 1975, the Silverdome has permanent seating for over 80,000 spectators for football and has accommodated over 90,000 for special events. The inflated fabric roof covers an area of 10 acres and is maintained at a height of 202 feet above the playing surface. The Silverdome is owned by the city of Pontiac and is currently the home of the Detroit Lions. The Lions are designing a new stadium in Downtown Detroit and should move soon after 2000.

Other examples:

■ Steve Lacy Field house—Milligan College, Milligan, TN–1974,

■ Uni-Dome—University of Northern Iowa, Cedar Falls, IA–1975,

■ Sun Dome—University of South Florida, Tampa, FL–1981,

Figure 29.8 Dedmon Center, Radford University.

■ Metrodome—Minneapolis, MN–1982,
■ B.C. Place Amphitheater—Vancouver, B.C., Canada–1983, and
■ RCA Dome—Indianapolis, IN–1984.

Since the concept of fabric structures is still quite new, not all the problems have been resolved. However, each new fabric structure appears to have fewer problems and to be an improvement over those built previously. In spite of the many advantages of the large air-supported structures, their days may be numbered. The primary disadvantage of air-supported structures is the need for the constant positive air pressure. Since this positive pressure is what supports the roof, if there is even a temporary loss of pressure, the fabric will hang down on the supporting cables. Although this alone should cause no damage to the facility, this is when the structural system is the most vulnerable. Even light winds, snow, or rain may cause extensive damage to a fabric roof in the deflated position.

These facilities must be constantly monitored and all precautions must be taken to ensure that all systems are functioning properly. Cable domes appear to have the same advantages as the large air-pressure structures but with fewer problems. It is entirely possible that we have seen the last large air-supported structure that will ever be built (see Cable Domes).

Combining Air-Supported and Tension

A recent development in the construction of fabric structures is the idea of combining both an air-supported roof and a tension roof in the same building. An example of this concept is the Stephen C. O'Connell Center. This physical education, recreation, and athletic complex is located at the University of Florida at Gainesville. This was the first structure to combine both air-supported and tension roofs in one building. The center or main arena is covered by a large air-inflated roof, while the outer areas of the building are the tension-covered spaces. The main arena has an indoor track and can seat 10,400 spectators for basketball. Located under the tension supported areas are a gymnastics area, dance studio, weight room, locker rooms, offices, and a 3,000-seat, 50-meter natatorium. Like most fabric structures, this facility was a bargain. The total construction cost was $11,954,418, which comes out to about $49 per square foot. This facility was completed in 1980.

Temporary Air Structures

This section will outline the merits of the smaller and more portable air structures. Air structures work well as environmental covers placed over existing recreational areas and, for many organizations, the 'bubble' is the answer to an increasing need for large covered activity areas at a nominal cost. Cost savings are in proportion to the size of the space to be covered. Spaces over 300 square feet usually bring a cost savings when compared to conventional roofing. Because of heat gain, which seems to present a more severe problem than heat loss, the northern areas of the United States seem better suited for environmental covers. There are numerous playing fields within communities and around schools and colleges that lend themselves easily to enclosure by a fabric air structure. Some of the additional advantages and disadvantages of using small air-supported structures are as follows:

Advantages:

- Speed of erection—the actual erection of the structure usually takes only one or two days. However, additional time is required for the ground work, site services, foundation, anchorage, flooring, and installation of mechanical and electrical equipment. Only minimal field labor is needed.
- Ease of deflation, inflation, and repair—deflation and inflation of the fabric envelope usually do not require skilled labor.
- Portability—when deflated and packed, the fabric envelope can be stored in a small space or easily transported elsewhere for storage or use. Depending on the size of the dome, deflation and packing usually require one or two days.
- Adaptability for temporary functions—for temporary use, the air-supported structure has definite physical and financial advantages over a conventional building.
- Long-span and high-ceiling features—clear and unobstructed spaces is an inherent feature of the structure. Conventional long-span and high-ceiling structures are much more expensive.
- Integrated heating, ventilation, and air-pressure system—the integrated heating, ventilation, and

air-pressure system is simple and less expensive than conventional systems. Lengthy duct and pipe works are not required.

Examples

- Memorial Stadium—A portable inflatable fabric bubble is used to cover the entire football field at the University of Illinois in the winter. First erected in 1986, it was purchased for $1.5 million. With an average inside winter temperature of 55 degrees, the field is used heavily by several departments across the campus. The concept of a portable dome over the game field adds extra use to a facility that would otherwise sit empty much of the year.
- University of Santa Clara—The swimming pool at the Thomas E. Leavey Center is covered by a portable air structure. It is removed for use as an outdoor pool in the summer months and then re-inflated for the winter to transform the pool for indoor use.

Cable Domes

Cable domes are the most recent innovation in fabric structure technology. Through a complex system of cables and girders, very large spans can be inexpensively covered by a fabric roof without the need for columns or fans to maintain integrity. Engineers predict that the cable dome concept is feasible for spans of at least 1,000 feet. Cable domes incorporate most of the advantages of fabric structures when compared to standard construction, and fewer of the disadvantages. Many experts in fabric roof technology believe that cable domes will replace the air-supported structure as the design of choice for the future. There will probably not be any more large air structures built because of the inherent advantages of the cable dome. Some of these advantages are as follows:

- Huge column-free spans can be covered.
- There is no need for expensive energy consuming fans.
- A passive system means no need for someone to constantly monitor the facility.
- The structure has an extremely low silhouette.

Examples

- Redbird Arena—Opened in 1991, Redbird Arena is on the campus of Illinois State University in Bloomington-Normal, IL. This multipurpose arena can seat 10,500 spectators for basketball, with the ability to provide an additional 1,500

Figure 29.9 Redbird Arena.

seats on the floor for concerts or commencement. The lower sections of seats are portable bleachers that can be removed to provide 36,000 square feet of space on the main floor. Built for a cost of $20,000,000, Redbird is the first cable dome to be constructed on a college campus, but probably won't be the last.

■ Tropicana Field—Tropicana Field is located in St. Petersburg, FL and was opened in 1990. This multipurpose stadium was designed primarily for baseball, yet with the flexibility to accommodate football, basketball, soccer, and tennis, as well as concerts and trade shows. In addition to 50 private suites, a variety of seating arrangements allow the facility to function as an 18,000-seat arena or a 43,000-seat stadium for baseball. The unique movable grandstands contain built-in concession stands and public toilets. The fabric roof is 688 feet in diameter and was constructed on a tilt of 60. This tilt is designed to allow more clearance for the trajectory of fly balls and allows the roof to reach a height of 225 feet in front of home plate.

The cable truss roof system is capable of supporting 60 tons of lighting and sound equipment for concerts, yet weighs a mere six pounds per square foot. Tropicana Field was built for a cost of $132 million and is the new home of the expansion Tampa Bay Devil Rays.

■ Georgia Dome—Located in downtown Atlanta, GA, the Georgia Dome was completed in August 1992. This $210 million structure was the site of the Super Bowl and the Olympics in 1996. The Teflon-coated fabric roof covers 8.6 acres, weighs 68 tons, and incorporates 11.1 miles of steel support cables. This multipurpose facility seats 70,500 for football and is the new home of the Atlanta Falcons. A total of 202 luxury suites are located on different levels around the stadium that range in price from $20,000 to $120,000 per year for a 10-year lease. During the planning process it was estimated that changing the design from an open air stadium to a fabric-covered dome would increase the cost of the project by only 20% or less.

Figure 29.10 Tropicana Field.

Wooden Domes

Another recent development in encapsulated spaces is the wooden dome. These spherical wooden structures have several advantages over conventional structures. Column-free spans of up to 800 feet are possible, and they are generally easier to build. There are several wooden dome structures around the country ranging from high school gymnasiums to very large stadiums. Some of the advantages of wooden domes when compared with standard construction may include:

■ efficient construction of huge column-free spans,
■ lower initial cost when compared with conventional construction,
■ less construction time,
■ full utilization of space, and good insulation and acoustical properties.

Examples

■ Round Valley Ensphere—Located in Eager, AZ, this wooden dome is the only high school

domed football stadium in the world. Opened in 1991, it was built for a total project cost of only $11.5 million and is unique in many respects. The 113,000 square feet of unobstructed floor space provide a full-size synthetic turf football field with seating for 5,000; a six-lane, 200-meter, synthetic-surface running track with 100-meter straight away; seven combination basketball, volleyball, or tennis courts; and a softball field; as well as offices, training room, and four full locker rooms. The wooden roof is insulated to a value of R-28 and is very energy and acoustically efficient. One of the most interesting features of the dome is that it contains a large skylight in the center of the roof. This skylight is made of clear Lexan and provides good illumination of the activity areas even on overcast days. At an elevation of over 7,000 feet, the Round Valley area experiences extremes in weather, including snow-packed winters. During these colder months, the skylight also acts as a solar collector, helping to make the Ensphere very energy efficient.

Figure 29.11 Georgia Dome–Exterior.

Figure 29.12 Georgia Dome–Interior.

Figure 29.13 Round Valley Ensphere–Exterior.

Figure 29.14 Round Valley Ensphere–Interior.

Figure 29.15 Superior Dome–Exterior.

■ Walkup Skydome—This laminated wood dome is located in Northern Arizona University in Flagstaff, AZ. Opened in 1977, the Skydome is 502 feet across and covers 6.2 acres. It contains a full-size, roll-up, synthetic football/soccer field, a professional-sized ice hockey rink, a 1/5-mile running track and a portable wood basketball court, and has seating for more than 15,000 people. The total construction cost was $8.3 million, or about $620 per seat.

■ Tacoma Dome—The Tacoma Dome in Tacoma, WA, was opened in 1983. This $44-million multi-purpose complex is 530 feet across and for eight years was the largest wooden dome in the world. It can seat 20,722 for football and 25,138 for basketball and contains a full-size permanent ice rink.

■ Superior Dome—Constructed on the campus of Northern Michigan University in Marquette, MI, this state-owned wooden dome was opened in the fall of 1991. With a diameter of 533 feet, the 14-story, $21.8-million structure was envisioned in 1985 as an Olympic training center. It has a 200-meter track and a full-size football field and is home to the NMU football team, with seating for 8,000 spectators. Designed to be constructed in phases as funding becomes available, the facility will eventually include an additional 5,000 seats; an ice rink for hockey, speed skating, and figure skating; locker rooms; sports medicine facilities; and public use areas.

■ Summary

The fundamental purpose and design of stadiums and arenas has changed dramatically in the last decade. These changes are so radical that many facili-

Figure 29.15 Superior Dome Interior.

ties built in the last 20 years have become obsolete. The basic idea behind these changes is that modern arenas and stadiums are no longer just places to watch an event but are now designed to provide a total entertainment experience.

Learning Objective 1: The student will be familiar with the concept of the retractable-roof stadium and understand its advantages.

The retractable structures where born in the 1970s. The main advantage is being able to play during inclement weather.

Learning Objective 2: The student will be able to identify the three main types of fabric structures and list the advantages and disadvantages of each.

The three main types of fabric structure include tension, air-supported, and cable domes. The advantages include lower initial cost, less construction time, natural lighting, lower energy costs, less maintenance, and full utilization of space. The disadvantages are shorter life span, poor thermal insulation, acoustical problems, and restrictions due to high winds.

Learning Objective 3: The student will be able to describe the importance of designing luxury suites and club seats in new spectator facilities.

The cost of operating professional sport teams has grown dramatically over the past two decades and shows no signs of slowing. Therefore, it is imperative that professional sport venues include a variety of income-generating aspects. Luxury suites and club seating are among the many new streams of revenue for the cash-hungry professional franchises. These areas cater to big-dollar clients and guarantee bonds used in funding the new facilities.

Learning Objective 4: The student will be able to identify the advantages of wooden domes.

The advantages of wooden domes include huge column-free spans, lower initial costs, less construction time, full utilization of space, and good insulation and acoustical properties.

Learning Objective 5: The student will be able to identify the new arena design features intended to speed the change-over from one event to another.

The new modern facilities are designed to accommodate a wide variety of events and also to quickly alter the set-up for different events. The planners included such things as versatile lighting and sound systems, ramps, heavy-duty lighting grids, and fixed, pre-wired camera positions to improve the change-over efficiency of these facilities.

■ Self-Assessment Exercises

1. Identify the three main types of fabric structures.
2. About how much does it cost to add a retractable roof to the design of a new stadium?
3. List three design features of new arenas that are meant to enhance the change-over for events.
4. List three advantages of fabric structures over standard construction.
5. List three disadvantages of fabric structures compared with standard construction.
6. Why is it that we may not see any more large air-supported structures built?
7. Why has the addition of luxury suites become so important in arena and stadium design?
8. What is the primary purpose of modern stadiums and arenas today?

■ Suggested Readings

Cohen, A. (1991). Back to the future. **Athletic Business, 15** (7), 31-37.

Dethlefs, D. (1991). Multiple cheers. **College Athletic Management, 3** (3), 28-33.

Gordon, J. (1990). The suite smell of success. **Skybox, 1** (2), 6-9.

Holleman, M.A. (1996). Scoring with stadiums. **Athletic Business, 20** (9), 45-49.

Johnson, R. (1991). All in one. **College Athletic Management, 3** (3), 28-33.

Krenson, F. (1988). Crowd-pleasing arena design. **Athletic Business, 12** (9), 66-69.

Meagher, J. (1985). Eliminating the negative in sports facility design. **Athletic Business, 9** (1), 32-35.

Staff. (1998). Stadiums: Today' bargaining chips. **Sports Business Journal, 1** (1), 19-36.

Jewell, D. (1992). **Public assembly facilities** (2nd ed.) Malabar, FL: Krieger Publishing Co.

Whitney, T. (1992). A house divided. **Athletic Business, 16** (3), 44-51.

Wolfe, R. (1987). Designing facilities to meet future needs. **Athletic Business, 11** (9), 48-55.

Appendix A

Field and Court Dimensions

FACILITY SPECIFICATION GUIDE

(The information contained in this guide, based on information provided by various associations and governing organizations, is intended merely as a guide and is not applicable to all situations. Contact the appropriate organization for further information.)

FACILITY SPECIFICATION GUIDE
BASEBALL

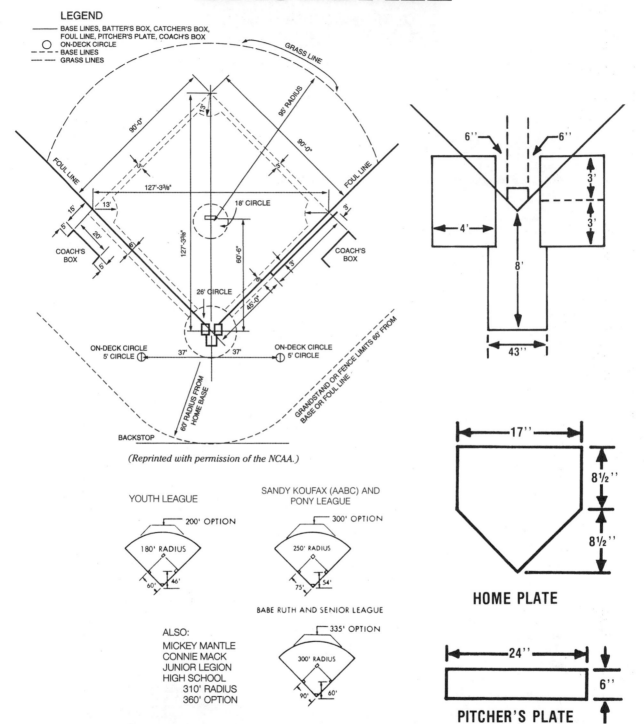

(Reprinted with permission of the NCAA.)

LEGEND
— BASE LINES, BATTER'S BOX, CATCHER'S BOX, FOUL LINE, PITCHER'S PLATE, COACH'S BOX
○ ON-DECK CIRCLE
--- BASE LINE
--- GRASS LINES

YOUTH LEAGUE
200' OPTION
180' RADIUS
60' 46'

SANDY KOUFAX (AABC) AND PONY LEAGUE
300' OPTION
250' RADIUS
75' 54'

BABE RUTH AND SENIOR LEAGUE
335' OPTION
300' RADIUS
90' 60'

ALSO:
MICKEY MANTLE
CONNIE MACK
JUNIOR LEGION
HIGH SCHOOL
310' RADIUS
360' OPTION

HOME PLATE
17''
8½''
8½''

PITCHER'S PLATE
24''
6''

(Diagrams courtesy of USA Baseball.)

For more information contact:

USA Baseball
Hi Corbett Field
3400 E. Camino Campestre
Tucson, AZ 85716
(520) 327-9700
Fax: (520) 327-9221
www.usabaseball.com

American Amateur Baseball Congress
118 Redfield Plaza
P.O. Box 467
Marshall, MI 49068
(616) 781-2002
Fax: (616) 781-2060
www.voyager.net/aabc

National Collegiate Athletic Association
6201 College Blvd.
Overland Park, KS 66211-2422
(913) 339-1906
www.ncaa.org

FACILITY SPECIFICATION GUIDE

BASKETBALL

PROFESSIONAL COURT

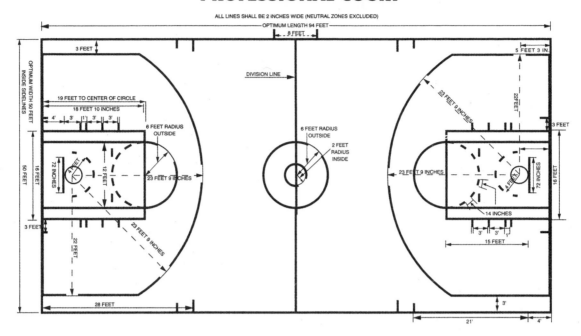

ALL LINES SHALL BE 2 INCHES WIDE (NEUTRAL ZONES EXCLUDED)

HIGH SCHOOL & COLLEGE COURT

Note: The optimum length of the high school court is 84 feet. If court is less than 74 feet long, it should be divided by two lines, each parallel to and 40 feet from the farther end line.

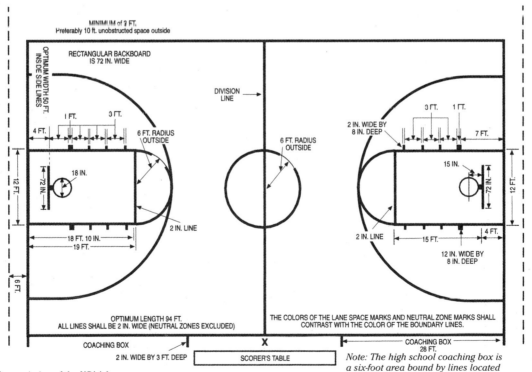

(Reprinted with permission of the NCAA.)

National Basketball Association
Olympic Tower
645 Fifth Ave.
New York, NY 10022
(212) 826-7000
www.nba.com

National Federation of State High School Associations
P.O. Box 20626
Kansas City, MO 64195-0626
(816) 464-5400
Fax: (816) 464-5571
www.nfhs.org

National Collegiate Athletic Association
6201 College Blvd.
Overland Park, KS 66211-2422
(913) 339-1906
www.ncaa.org

PROFESSIONAL

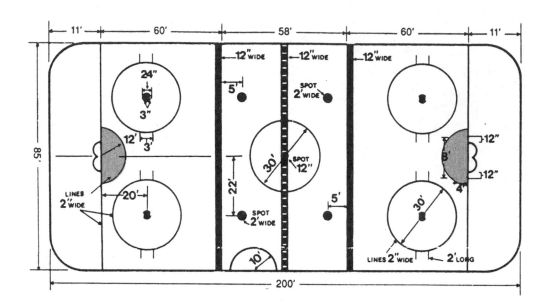

COLLEGE AND HIGH SCHOOL

Commercial, institution or conference logos and/or names are allowed in the ice only in the nuetral zone.

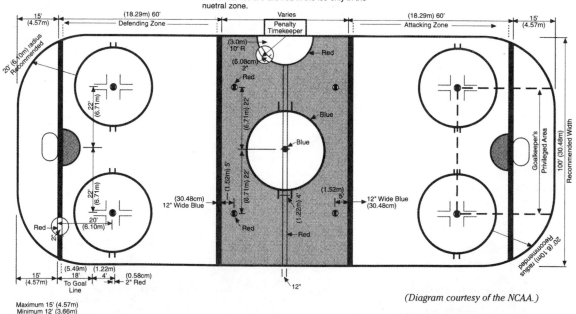

(Diagram courtesy of the NCAA.)

For more information contact:

National Hockey League
75 International Blvd., Room 300
Rexdale, Ontario M9W 6L9
(416) 798-0809
Fax: (416) 798-0819
www.nhl.com

**National Federation of State High
School Associations**
P.O. Box 20626
Kansas City, MO 64195-0626
(816) 464-5400
Fax: (816) 464-5571
www.nfhs.org

**National Collegiate Athletic
Association**
6201 College Blvd.
Overland Park, KS 66211-2422
(913) 339-1906
www.ncaa.org

RACQUETBALL/ HANDBALL

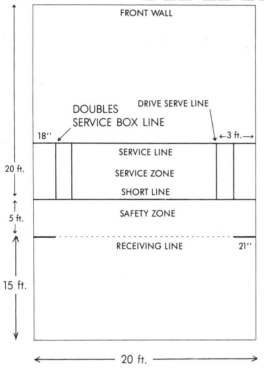

FRONT WALL

FRONT AND SIDE WALL HEIGHT: 20'0''

REAR WALL HEIGHT: AT LEAST 14'0''

DRIVE SERVE LINE

DOUBLES SERVICE BOX LINE

18''

←3 ft.→

SERVICE LINE

SERVICE ZONE

5 ft.

SHORT LINE

20 ft.

SAFETY ZONE

5 ft.

RECEIVING LINE

21''

15 ft.

←——— 20 ft. ———→

For more information contact:

United States Racquetball Association
1685 W. Uintah
Colorado Springs, CO 80904-2921
(719) 635-5396
Fax: (719) 635-0685
www.racquetball.org

SQUASH

NORTH AMERICAN COURT

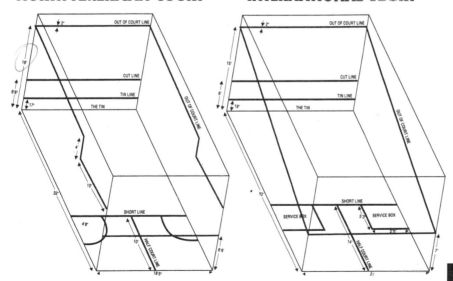

INTERNATIONAL COURT

DOUBLES COURT

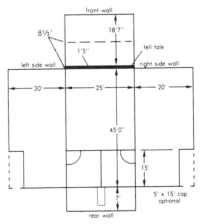

For more information contact:

United States Squash Racquets Association
23 Cynwyd Road, P.O. Box 1216
Bala-Cynwyd, PA 19004
(610) 667-4006
Fax: (610) 667-6539
www.us-squash.org/squash

WOMEN'S LACROSSE

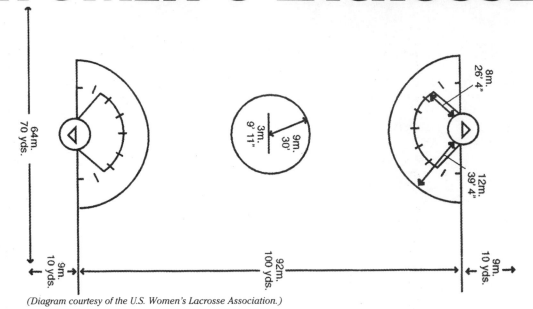

(Diagram courtesy of the U.S. Women's Lacrosse Association.)

For more information contact:

U.S. Women's Lacrosse Association
35 Wisconsin Circle, Suite 525
Chevy Chase, MD 20815
(301) 951-8795
Fax: (301) 951-7082
www.USWLA.org

US Lacrosse Inc.
113 W. University Pkwy.
Baltimore, MD 21210
(410) 235-6882
Fax: (410) 366-6735
www.lacrosse.org

MEN'S LACROSSE

1997
The Lacrosse Field of Play

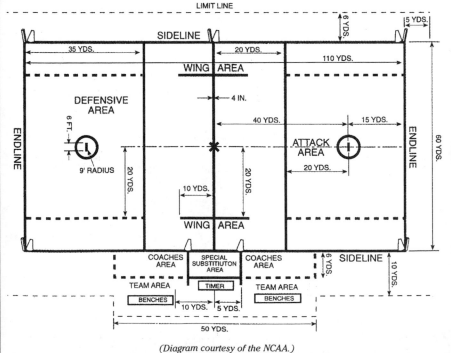

(Diagram courtesy of the NCAA.)

For more information contact:

US Lacrosse Inc.
113 W. University Pkwy.
Baltimore, MD 21210
(410) 235-6882
Fax: (410) 366-6735
www.lacrosse.org

National Collegiate Athletic Association
6201 College Blvd.
Overland Park, KS 66211-2422
(913) 339-1906
www.ncaa.org

POLE VAULT LANDING AREA DETAIL

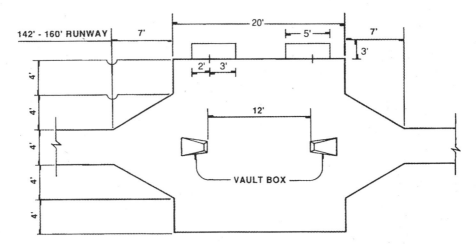

LONG JUMP/TRIPLE JUMP PIT PLAN

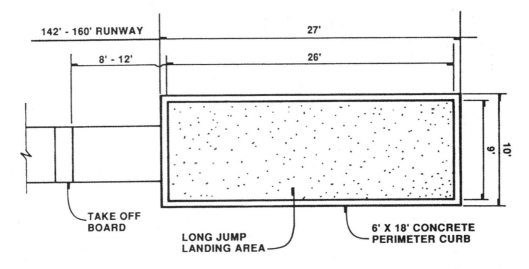

TAKE OFF BOARD

LONG JUMP LANDING AREA

6' X 18' CONCRETE PERIMETER CURB

HIGH JUMP DETAIL

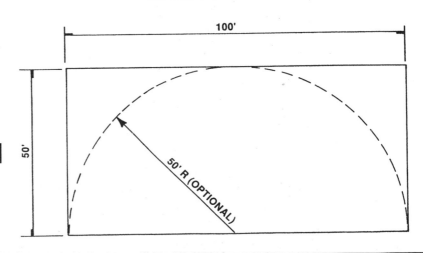

All diagrams reprinted with permission of the USTC&TBA.

For more information contact:

**U.S. Tennis Court and
Track Builders Association**
3525 Ellicott Mills Drive, Suite N
Ellicott City, MD 21043-4547
(410) 418-4875
www.ustctba.com

TRACK & FIELD

Dimensions for track and field events appearing in the following diagrams are based on requirements set forth by the National Federation of State High School Associations (NFHS). There are variations of requirements for facilities governed by the National Collegiate Athletic Association (NCAA), USA Track and Field (USAT&F) or the International Amateur Athletic Federation (IAAF). Please consult the appropriate governing body or the U.S. Tennis Court and Track Builders Association (USTC&TBA) for specific information.

TRACK USE ONLY

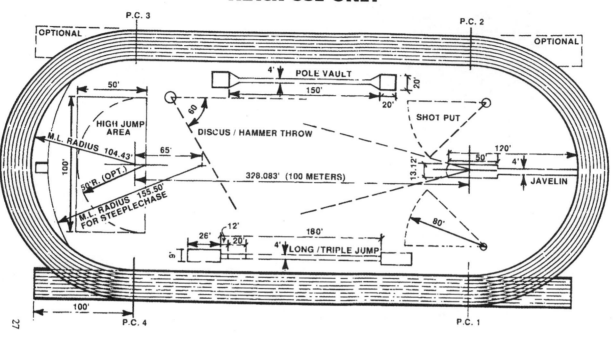

400 METER EVENTS

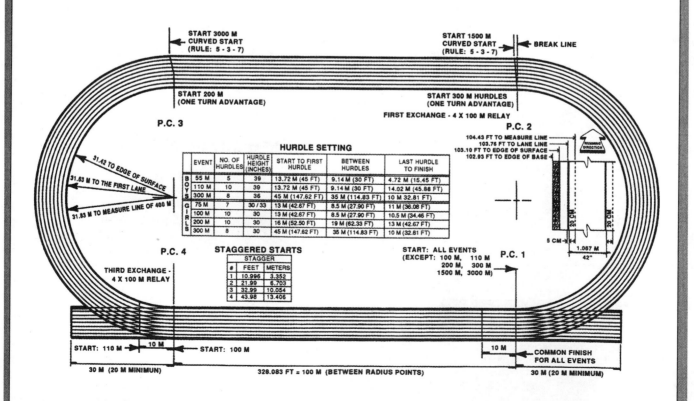

HURDLE SETTING

	EVENT	NO. OF HURDLES	HURDLE HEIGHT (INCHES)	START TO FIRST HURDLE	BETWEEN HURDLES	LAST HURDLE TO FINISH
B O Y S	55 M	5	39	13.72 M (45 FT)	9.14 M (30 FT)	4.72 M (15.45 FT)
	110 M	10	39	13.72 M (45 FT)	9.14 M (30 FT)	14.02 M (45.88 FT)
	300 M	8	36	45 M (147.62 FT)	35 M (114.83 FT)	10 M 32.81 FT)
G I R L S	75 M	7	30 / 33	13 M (42.67 FT)	8.5 M (27.90 FT)	11 M (36.08 FT)
	100 M	10	30	13 M (42.67 FT)	8.5 M (27.90 FT)	10.5 M (34.46 FT)
	200 M	10	30	16 M (52.50 FT)	19 M (62.33 FT)	13 M (42.67 FT)
	300 M	8	30	45 M (147.62 FT)	35 M (114.83 FT)	10 M (32.81 FT)

STAGGERED STARTS

STAGGER		
#	FEET	METERS
1	10.996	3.352
2	21.99	6.703
3	32.99	10.054
4	43.98	13.406

328.083 FT = 100 M (BETWEEN RADIUS POINTS)

TRACK & FIELD

STEEPLECHASE HURDLES

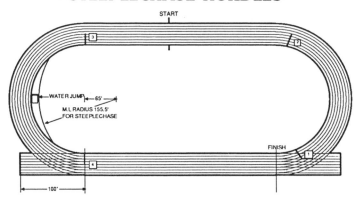

Distance for Junior
Events—2,000m

SHOT PUT PAD (HIGH SCHOOL)

THROWING SECTOR

90° RADIUS

1/4" STONE CHIPS
12" DEPTH

TOE BOARD

2" WIDE PAINTED STRIPE OR
3/4" RECESSED CIRCLE

1/8" SAWCUTS

4" REINFORCED CONCRETE
SLAB WITH
LIGHT BROOM FINISH

10'

1/8" SAWCUTS

10'

NOTE: INSTALL 1/8" SAWCUTS ON
RECESSED CIRCLE ONLY

DISCUS CAGE
(HIGH SCHOOL)

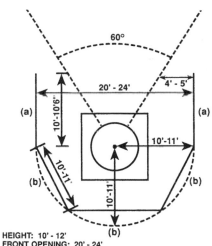

HEIGHT: 10' - 12'
FRONT OPENING: 20' - 24'
4' - 5' : DISTANCE CORNER
POST TO SECTOR LINE
10' - 11' : DISTANCE CENTER
OF CIRCLE TO FENCING

JAVELIN THROW

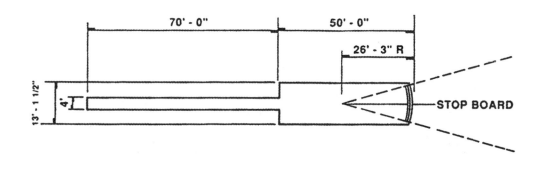

SWIMMING & DIVING

INTERNATIONAL AND NATIONAL COMPETITION

There are a number of sanctioning organizations for national and international amateur competition. Included here are the facility standards of FINA (the Federation Internationale de Natation Amateur) and one of its U.S. affiliates, United States Swimming Inc.

FINA STANDARDS

• Length—50m. When touch panels or electronic timing devices are used, the pool must be of such length that ensures the required distance between the panels.
• Width—25m preferred.
• Depth—1m minimum.
• Number of lanes—8. For Olympic Games and World Championships, 10 lanes are required.
• Width of lanes—2m minimum with spaces of 0.2m outside first and last lanes. A lane rope must separate these spaces from the first and last lanes.

U.S. SWIMMING STANDARDS

• Length—Long course, 164'½" (50m); short course, 82'¼" (25m) or 25 yds.
• Width—Eight lanes, 8'2½" (2.5m) minimum (centerline to centerline), with approximately 1'6" (0.45m) outside first and last lanes.

• Water depth—For national championships and international competition, 6'7" (2m) throughout the course. Minimum water depth for racing starts during competition and practice shall be measured for a distance 3'3½" (1m) to 16'5" (5m) from the end wall. Starting requirements and height of starting blocks shall be as follows: (1) In pools with water depth less than 3'6" (1.07m) at the starting end, the swimmer must start from the deck or from within the water; (2) In pools with water depth 3'6" (1.07m) to less than 4' (1.22m) at the starting end, starting platforms shall be no more than 18" (0.46m) above the water surface; (3) In pools with water depth 4' (1.22m) or more at the starting end, starting platforms shall meet the following height requirements: A. Long course: The front edge of the starting platforms shall be no less than 1'8" (0.50m) nor more than

2'5½" (0.75m) above the surface of the water. B. Short Course: The front edge of the starting platforms shall be not higher than 2'6" (0.762m) above the surface of the water.

NOTE: Local, state and municipal statutes, ordinances, rules and regulations may have depth limitations in conflict with the above. The LSC and all member clubs should check for this at all times.

For more information contact:

United States Swimming Inc.
One Olympic Plaza
Colorado Springs, CO 80909
(719) 578-4578
Fax: (719) 575-4050

STANDARD DIMENSIONS FOR PUBLIC SWIMMING POOLS

The following are the currently recommended standard dimensions for Class B and Class C public swimming pools, not designed for sanctioned competition.

MINIMUM DIMENSIONS FOR DIVING PORTION OF CLASS B AND C POOLS
(This drawing does not show the shallow portion of the pool)

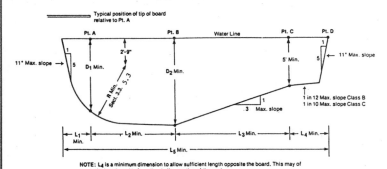

NOTE: L4 is a minimum dimension to allow sufficient length opposite the board. This may of course be lengthened to form the shallow portion of the pool

POOL TYPE	RELATED DIVING EQUIPMENT		MINIMUM DIMENSIONS								MINIMUM WIDTH OF POOL AT:		
	MAX. DIVING BOARD LENGTH	MAX. BOARD HGT. OVER WATER	D₁	D₂	R	L₁	L₂	L₃	L₄	L₅	PT. A	PT. B	PT. C
VI	10'	26" (⅔ meter)	7'-0"	8'-6"	5'-6"	2'-6"	8'-0"	10'-6"	7'-0"	28'-0"	16'-0"	18'-0"	18'-0"
VII	12'	30" (¾ meter)	7'-6"	9'-0"	6'-0"	3'-0"	9'-0"	12'-0"	4'-0"	28'-0"	18'-0"	20'-0"	20'-0"
VIII	16'	1 Meter	8'-6"	10'-0"	7'-0"	4'-0"	10'-0"	15'-0"	2'-0"	31'-0"	20'-0"	22'-0"	22'-0"
IX	16'	3 Meter	11'-0"	12'-0"	8'-6"	6'-0"	10'-6"	21'-0"	0	37'-6"	22'-0"	24'-0"	24'-0"

L2, L3 and L4 combined represent the minimum distance from the tip of the board to pool wall opposite diving equipment.

For board heights exceeding 3 meters, see Article 3.5.4.

* NOTE: Placement of boards shall observe the following minimum dimensions. With multiple board installations minimum pool widths must be increased accordingly.

Deck level board to pool side . . . . .8'
1 meter board to pool side . . . . .10'
3 meter board to pool side . . . . .11'
1 meter or deck level board to 3 meter board . . . . .10'
1 meter or deck level to another 1 meter or deck level board . . . . .8'
3 meter to another 3 meter board . . . . .10'

DEPTH

• Swimming—In Class B and C pools, water depths at the shallow end of the swimming area shall be 3' minimum with 3'6" minimum for racing pools. Exceptions may be made in a recessed area of the main swimming pool, outside of the competitive and/or swimming course, when the pool is of an irregular shape with the permission of the state or local authority.
• Diving—Class B and C pools intended for diving shall conform to the minimum water depths, areas, slopes and other dimensions shown in Article 4.7 and shall be located in the diving area of the pool so as to provide the minimum dimensions as shown in Article 3.6.1. Competitive diving equipment shall not be installed in Class B and C pools.

There shall be a completely unobstructed clear vertical distance of 13' above any diving board, measured from the center of the front end of the board. This area shall extend horizontally at least 8' behind, 8' to each side and 16' ahead of point A. (See diagram.)

According to a spokesperson for the National Spa and Pool Institute (NSPI), this standard has been approved by the American National Standards Institute. American National Standards, once approved, may be revised at any time. Make sure that you have the latest edition of this standard by ordering the NSPI-1 Standard for Public Swimming Pools from the NSPI.

For more information contact:

National Spa and Pool Institute
2111 Eisenhower Ave.
Alexandria, VA 22314-4678
(703) 838-0083
Fax: (703) 549-0493
www.poolspaworld.com

SWIMMING & DIVING

The following are NCAA standard pool dimensions. These are recommended dimensions for collegiate competition only, and specifications are subject to annual review and change.

POOL CROSS-SECTION

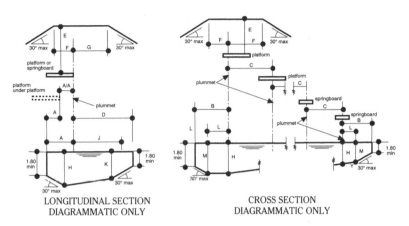

LONGITUDINAL SECTION
DIAGRAMMATIC ONLY

CROSS SECTION
DIAGRAMMATIC ONLY

DIVING CHART

NCAA Recommended Dimensions for Diving Facilities		Dimensions are in Feet	SPRINGBOARD				PLATFORM					
			1 Meter		3 meters		5 meters		7.5 Meters		10 Meters	
Revised to March 3, 1991		LENGTH	16'		16'		20'		20'		20'	
		WIDTH	1'8"		1'8"		5'		5'		6'7"	
		HEIGHT	3'4"		10'		16'5"		24'8"		32'10"	
			Horiz.	Vert.	Horiz.	Vert.	Honz.	Vert.	Horiz.	Verth.	Horiz.	Vert.
A	From plummet BACK TO POOL WALL	Designation	A-1		A-3		A-5		A-7.5		A-10	
		Minimum	5'		5'		4'2"		5'		5'	
		Preferred	6'1"		6'1"		4'2"		5'		5'	
A/A	From plummet BACK TO PLATFORM plummet directly below	Designation					A/A5		A/A7.5		A/A10	
		Minimum					2'6"		2'6"		2'6"	
		Preferred					4'2"		4'2"		4'2"	
B	From plummet to POOL WALL AT SIDE	Designation	B-1		B-3		B-5		B-75		B-10	
		Minimum	8'3"		11'6"		10'8"		14'		17'3"	
		Preferred	8'3"		11'6"		12'4"		14'10"		17'3"	
C	From plummet to ADJACENT PLUMMET	Designation	C-11		C-331		C-531		C-7.5531		C-107.55531	
		Minimum	6'7"		7'3"		7'5"		8'3"		9'1"	
		Preferred	7'1"		8'3"		8'3"		8'3"		9'1"	
D	From plummet to POOL WALL AHEAD	Designation	D-1		D-3		D-5		D-7.5		D-10	
		Minimum	29'7"		33'8"		33'8"		36'2"		44'4	
		Preferred	29'7"		33'8"		33'8"		36'2"		44'4"	
E	On plummet from BOARD TO CEILING	Designation		E-1		E-3		E-5		E-75		E-10
		Minimum		16'5"		16'5"		10'8"		10'8"		13'2"
		Preferred		16'5"		16'5"		11'6"		11'6"		16'5"
F	CLEAR OVERHEAD behind and each side of plummet	Designation	F-1	E-1	F-3	E-3	F-5	E-5	F-7.5	E-7.5	F-10	E-10
		Minimum	8'3"	16'5"	8'3"	16'5"	9'1"	10'8"	9'1"	10'9"	9'1"	13'2"
		Preferred	8'3"	16'5"	8'3"	16'5"	9'1"	11'6"	9'1"	11'6"	9'1"	16'5"
G	CLEAR OVERHEAD ahead of plummet	Designation	G-1	E-1	G-3	E-3	G-5	E-5	G-7.5	E-7.5	G-10	E-10
		Minimum	16'5"	16'5"	16'5"	16'5"	16'5"	10'8"	16'5"	10'8"	19'9"	13'2"
		Preferred	16'5"	16'5"	16'5"	16'5"	16'5"	11'6"	16'5"	11'6"	19'9"	16'5"
H	DEPTH OF WATER at plummet (minimum requried)	Designation		H-1		H-3		H-5		H-7.5		H-10
		Minimum		11'		12'		12'2"		13'6"		14'10"
		Preferred		11'6"		12'6"		12'6"		14'10"		16'5"
J-K	DISTANCE AND DEPTH ahead of plummet	Designation	J-1	K-1	J-3	K-3	J-5	K-5	J-7.5	K-7.5	J-10	K-10
		Minimum	16'5"	10'10"	16'5"	11'10"	19'9"	11'10"	26'3"	13'2"	36'2"	14'
		Preferred	16'5"	11'2"	19'9"	12'2"	19'9"	12'2"	26'3"	14'6"	36'2"	15'7"
L-M	DISTANCE AND DEPTH each side of plummet	Designation	L-1	M-1	L-3	M-3	L-5	M-5	L-7.5	M-7.5	L-10	M-10
		Minimum	5'	10'10"	6'7"	11'10"	19'11"	11'10"	12'4"	13'2"	14'10"	14'
		Preferred	9'11"	11'2"	8'3"	12'2"	11'6"	12'2"	14'10"	14'6"	17'3"	15'7"
N	MAXIMUM SLOPE OF REDUCE DIMENSIONS beyond full requirements	Pool depth Ceiling Ht.	30 degrees 30 degrees		Note 1: Dimensions C (plummet to adjacent plumet) apply for Platforms with widths as detailed. For wider Platforms increase C by half the additional width(s). Note 2: All dimensions rounded up, even if ony fractionally greater than the enxt lowest inch.							

Reprinted with permission of the NCAA.

LONG COURSE SWIMMING POOL
• Preferred—The racing course should be 164'1½" (50m, 2.54cm) in length by 75'1" (22.89m) in width, providing for eight 9' (2.74m) lanes with additional width outside lanes 1 and 8. A minimum water depth of 7' (2.13m) is desirable for competition. Optional markings: nine 8' (2.44m) lanes or ten 7' (2.13m) lanes.
• Acceptable—The racing course may be 164'1½" (50m, 2.54cm) in length by 60' (18.29m) in width, providing for eight 7' (2.13m) lanes with additional width outside lanes 1 and 8. The water depth may be no less than 4' (1.22m) at the starting end of the racing course and no less than 3'6" (1.07m) at the opposite end. However, a water depth of no less than 4' (1.22m) is recommended throughout the entire length of the racing course.

SHORT COURSE SWIMMING POOL
• Preferred—The racing course should be 75'1" (22.89m) in length by at least 60' (18.29m) in width, providing for not less than eight 7' (2.13m) lanes with additional width outside lanes 1 and 8. A minimum water depth of 7' (2.13m) is desirable for competition.
• Acceptable—The racing course may be 82'1¼" (25m, 2.54cm) in length by at least 45' (13.72m) in width, providing for six 7' (2.13m) lanes with additional width outside lanes 1 and 6. The water depth may be no less than 4' (1.22m) at the starting end of the racing course and no less than 3'6" (1.07m) at the opposite end. However, a water depth of no less than 4' (1.22m) is recommended throughout the entire length of the racing course.

DIVING POOL
• Preferred—The diving facility should be 60' (18.29m) in length by 75'1" (22.89m) in width. It should be equipped with two 1-meter and two 3-meter springboards and a diving tower, providing takeoff platforms at 5, 7.5 and 10 meters. Recommended dimensions for diving facilities are specified in the table on the left.
• Acceptable—The diving facility may be separated from or incorporated with the swimming pool. Recommended dimensions for diving facilities are specified in the table on the left.
Note: The above dimensions may be incorporated in "L," "T," "Z," and "U" shaped pools.

For more information contact:

National Collegiate Athletic Association
6201 College Blvd.
Overland Park, KS 66211-2422
(913) 339-1906
www.ncaa.org

TEAM HANDBALL

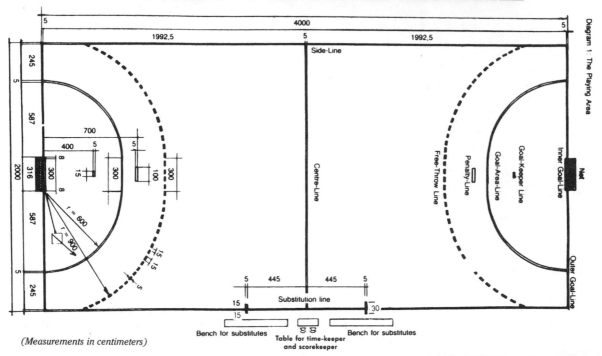

(Measurements in centimeters)

For more information contact:

United States Team Handball Federation
1903 Powers Ferry, Suite 230
Atlanta, GA 30339

FIELD HOCKEY

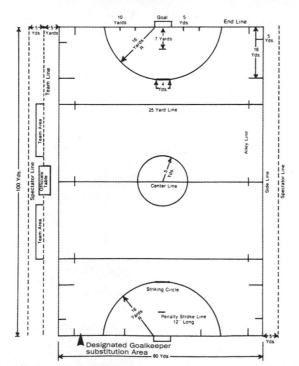

For more information contact:

National Federation of State High School Associations
P.O. Box 20626
Kansas City, MO 64195-0626
(816) 464-5400
Fax: (816) 464-5571
www.nfhs.org

TENNIS

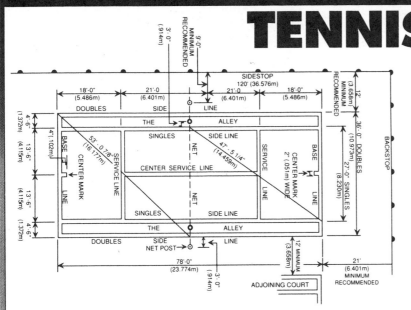

TRUE PLANE
SLOPE
REQUIREMENTS:
SIDE TO SIDE → *(preferred)*

END TO END

DIAGONAL

The recommended court slope should be:

Fast Dry:
Minimum 1" in 30' (0.28%) (preferred)
Maximum 1" in 24' (0.35%)

Hard Courts:
Minimum 1" in 10' (0.833%) (preferred)
Maximum 1" in 8.33' (1%)

○ MARKER FOR SINGLES STICKS
OR SINGLES NET POSTS

LINE WIDTH: 2" 5CM
4" 10 CM
NOTE: BASE LINES CAN BE 4" WIDE

(Reprinted with permission of the USTC&TBA.)

Lines should not vary more the 1/4" (.64cm) from exact measurement.

For more information contact:

U.S. Tennis Court and
Track Builders Association
3525 Ellicott Mills Drive, Suite N
Ellicott City, MD 21043-4547
(410) 418-4875
www.ustctba.com

United States Tennis Association
70 W. Red Oak Lane
White Plains, NY 10604
914/696-7000
www.usta.com

BADMINTON

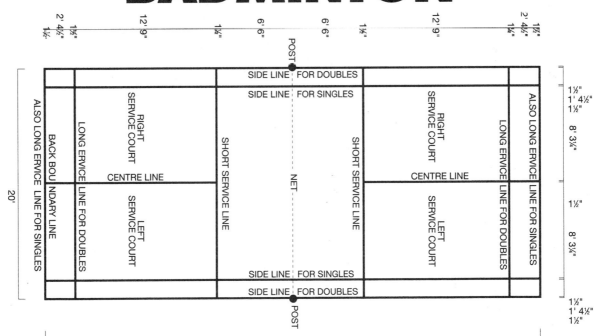

For more information contact:

USA Badminton
One Olympic Plaza
Colorado Springs, CO 80909
(719) 578-4808
Fax: (719) 578-4507
www.usabadminton.org

Note: Court can be used for both singles and doubles play.
Dimensions determined by the International Badminton Federation.

FACILITY SPECIFICATION GUIDE
SOCCER

LAW I. — THE FIELD OF PLAY
The Field of Play and appurtenances shall be as shown in the following plan:

Note: For players under 16 years of age, the size of the field of play, as well as the width between the goal posts and the height of the cross-bar may be modified.

OUTDOOR FIELD

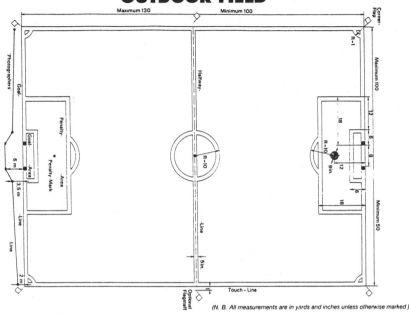

(N. B. All measurements are in yards and inches unless otherwise marked)

Note: The length of the touch line must be greater than the length of the goal line.

INDOOR FIELD

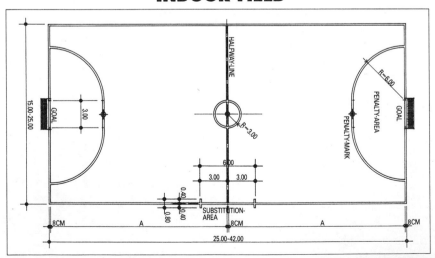

For more information contact:

United States Soccer Federation
1801-1811 S. Prairie Ave.
Chicago, IL 60616
(312) 808-1300
www.us-soccer.com

American Youth Soccer Organization
5403 W. 138th St.
Hawthorne, CA 90250
(800) USA-AYSO
Fax: (310) 643-5310
www.ayso.org

US Youth Soccer
899 Presidential Drive, Suite 117
Richardson, TX 75081
(800) 4-SOCCER

FACILITY SPECIFICATION GUIDE
SOFTBALL

OFFICIAL DIMENSIONS FOR SOFTBALL DIAMONDS

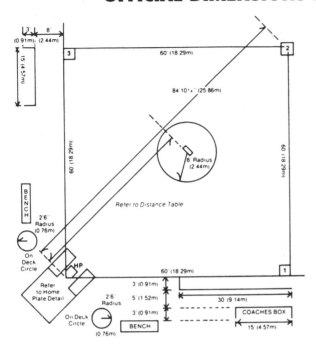

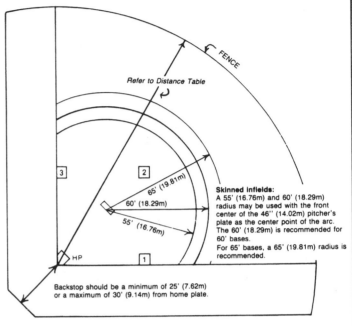

Backstop should be a minimum of 25' (7.62m) or a maximum of 30' (9.14m) from home plate.

Skinned infields:
A 55' (16.76m) and 60' (18.29m) radius may be used with the front center of the 46'' (14.02m) pitcher's plate as the center point of the arc. The 60' (18.29m) is recommended for 60' bases.
For 65' bases, a 65' (19.81m) radius is recommended.

(Diagrams courtesy of the Amateur Softball Association of America.)

DISTANCE TABLE

ADULT

GAME	DIVISION	BASES	PITCHING	FENCES Minimum	FENCES Maximum
Fast Pitch	Women	60' (18.29 m)	40' (12.19 m)	200' (60.96 m)	250' (76.20 m)
	Men	60' (18.29 m)	46' (14.02 m)	225' (68.58 m)	250' (76.20 m)
	Jr. Men	60' (18.29 m)	46' (14.02 m)	225' (68.58 m)	250' (76.20 m)
Modified	Women	60' (18.29 m)	40' (12.19 m)	200' (60.96 m)	
	Men	60' (18.29 m)	46' (14.02 m)	265' (80.80 m)	
Slow Pitch	Women	65' (19.81 m)	50' (15.24 m)	265' (80.80 m)	275' (83.82 m)
	Men	65' (19.81 m)	50' (15.24 m)	275' (83.82 m)	315' (96.01 m)*
	Co-Ed	65' (19.81 m)	50' (15.24 m)	275' (83.82 m)	300' (91.44 m)
	Super	65' (19.81 m)	50' (15.24 m)	325' (99.06 m)	No Max
16 Inch Slow Pitch	Women	55' (16.76 m)	38' (11.58 m)	200' (60.96 m)	
	Men	55' (16.76 m)	38' (11.58 m)	250' (76.20 m)	
14 Inch Slow Pitch	Women	60' (18.29 m)	46' (14.02 m)		
	Men	60' (18.29 m)	46' (14.02 m)		

YOUTH

GAME	DIVISION	BASES	PITCHING	FENCES Minimum	FENCES Maximum
Slow Pitch	Girls 10-under	55' (16.76 m)	35' (10.67 m)	150' (45.72 m)	175' (53.34 m)
	Boys 10-under	55' (16.76 m)	35' (10.67 m)	150' (45.72 m)	175' (53.34 m)
	Girls 12-under	60' (18.29 m)	40' (12.19 m)	175' (53.34 m)	200' (60.96 m)
	Boys 12-under	60' (18.29 m)	40' (12.19 m)	175' (53.34 m)	200' (60.96 m)
	Girls 14-under	65' (19.81 m)	46' (14.02 m)	225' (68.58 m)	250' (76.20 m)
	Boys 14-under	65' (19.81 m)	46' (14.02 m)	250' (76.20 m)	275' (83.82 m)
	Girls 16-under	65' (19.81 m)	50' (15.24 m)	225' (68.58 m)	250' (76.02 m)
	Boys 16-under	65' (19.81 m)	50' (15.24 m)	275' (83.82 m)	300' (91.44 m)
	Girls 18-under	65' (19.81 m)	50' (15.24 m)	225' (68.58 m)	250' (76.02 m)
	Boys 18-under	65' (19.81 m)	50' (15.24 m)	275' (83.82 m)	300' (91.44 m)
Fast Pitch	Girls 10-under	55' (16.76 m)	35' (10.67 m)	150' (45.72 m)	175' (53.34 m)
	Boys 10-under	55' (16.76 m)	35' (10.67 m)	150' (45.72 m)	175' (53.34 m)
	Girls 12-under	60' (18.29 m)	35' (10.67 m)	175' (53.34 m)	200' (60.96 m)
	Boys 12-under	60' (18.29 m)	40' (12.19 m)	175' (53.34 m)	200' (60.96 m)
	Girls 14-under	60' (18.29 m)	40' (12.19 m)	175' (53.34 m)	200' (60.96 m)
	Boys 14-under	60' (18.29 m)	46' (14.02 m)	175' (53.34 m)	200' (60.96 m)
	Girls 16-under	60' (18.29 m)	40' (12.19 m)	200' (60.96 m)	225' (68.58 m)
	Boys 16-under	60' (18.29 m)	46' (14.02 m)	200' (60.96 m)	225' (68.58 m)
	Girls 18-under	60' (18.29 m)	40' (12.19 m)	200' (60.96 m)	225' (68.58 m)
	Boys 18-under	60' (18.29 m)	46' (14.02 m)	200' (60.96 m)	225' (68.58 m)

Note: The only difference between college and high school is the pitching distance.

high school	fast pitch male	..........46'
	slow pitch male	...........46'
	slow pitch female	..........46'
	fast pitch female	..........40'
college	...............................43'	

For more information contact:

Amateur Softball Association of America
2801 N.E. 50th St.
Oklahoma City, OK 73111
(405) 424-5266
www.softball.org

FOOTBALL

PROFESSIONAL

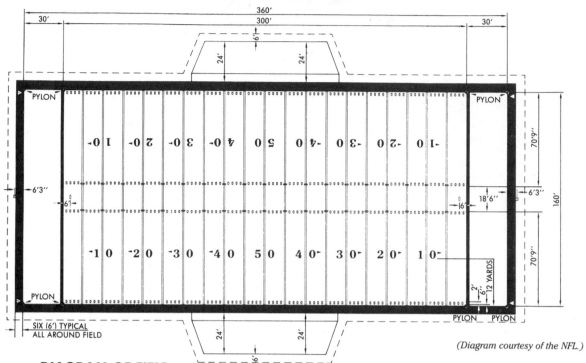

(Diagram courtesy of the NFL.)

DIAGRAM OF FIELD

COLLEGE

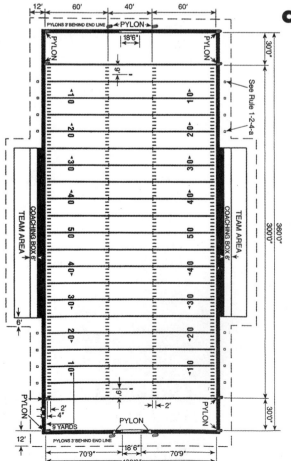

(Diagrams courtesy of the NFHS.)

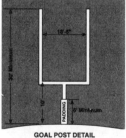

GOAL POST DETAIL

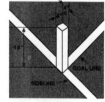

PYLON DETAIL

RECOMMENDED YARD-LINE NUMBERING

END ZONE DETAIL

For more information contact:

National Football League
410 Park Ave.
New York, NY 10022
(212) 758-1500
www.nfl.com

National Collegiate Athletic Association
6201 College Blvd.
Overland Park, KS 66211-2422
(913) 339-1906
www.ncaa.org

FOOTBALL

HIGH SCHOOL

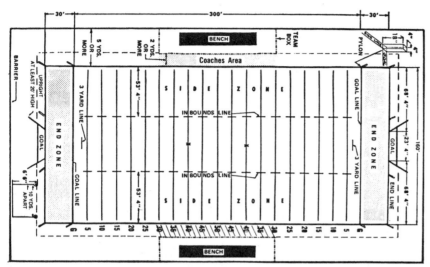

(Diagram courtesy of the NFHS.)

Note: Both team boxes may be on one side between the two 45- and 20-yard lines. End lines and sidelines should be at least 4 inches wide. Other field dimensions should be 4 inches wide.

Note: Recommend the area between team boxes and sidelines be solid white or marked with diagonal lines.

Note: Inbounds lines should be 24'' long and 4'' wide.

Note: Recommend the field slope from center to each sideline at 1/4-inch per foot.

Note: A 4-inch wide broken restraining line may be put around the entire field, 2 or more yards from boundaries.

For more information contact:

National Federation of State High School Associations
P.O. Box 20626
Kansas City, MO 64195-0626
(816) 464-5400
Fax: (816) 464-5571
www.nfhs.org

VOLLEYBALL

Note: NFHS rules require standards to be 3' (1m) outside the court.

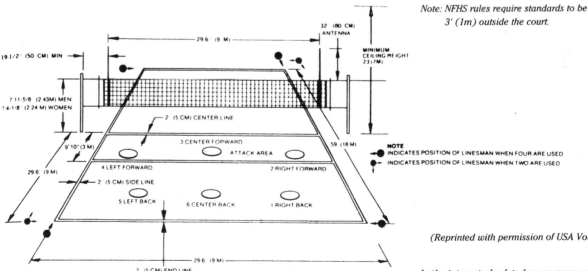

(Reprinted with permission of USA Volleyball.)

In the interest of safety for age group and scholastic competition, the height of the net shall be that specified for male competition. This height requirement shall not be modified.

For more information contact:

USA Volleyball
3595 E. Fountain Blvd.
Colorado Springs, CO 80910-1740
(719) 637-8300
www.volleyball.org

The following net heights are currently in practice for the below indicated age groups and scholastic levels of competition:

AGE GROUPS	GIRLS	BOYS/COED
18 years and under	2.24m (7'4⅛")	2.43m (7'11⅝")
16 years and under	2.24m (7'4⅛")	2.43m (7'11⅝")
14 years and under	2.24m (7'4⅛") or 7'0"	2.24m (7'4⅛")
12 years and under	2.10m (7'0") or 6'6"	2.10m (7'0") or 6'6"

SCHOLASTIC LEVELS	GIRLS	BOYS/COED
Grades 1 thru 6 (Elementary School):	1.85m (6'1")	1.85m (6'1")
Grades 7 and 8 (Middle School):	2.24m (7'4⅛")	2.24m (7'4⅛")
Grades 9 thru 12 (Sr. High School):	2.24m (7'4⅛")	2.43m (7'11⅝")

Appendix B

Planning Checklist for Outdoor Spaces

The following is an abbreviated list of items to be considered during the planning process:

Circulation

- ■ **Types:** Vehicle (cars, trucks, buses, maintenance, etc.); pedestrians (handicapped, different teams); participants (different teams, players, coaches, officials, etc.); main entry; secondary entries; control and security points, etc.
- ■ **Roadway:** Type of vehicles (trucks, cars, buses, etc); quantity of traffic (conduct survey); type of roadway system (single or two directional); roadway width (vehicle size and number of lanes); surface systems (materials); protection devices (bollards, guard rails, etc); etc.
- ■ **Parking:** Type of vehicles (trucks, cars, buses, etc.); quantity of vehicles; sizes (length and width) of vehicles; drainage (surface or subsurface, water collection/detention areas); snow removal (storage areas); protection devices (bollards, guard rails, tire bumpers, etc.)
- ■ **Walkways:** Type of use (pedestrian and/or vehicle); walkway widths; surface system (materials); elevation changes (walks, ramps, stairs and lifts); railings.

Activity Areas

- ■ **Landscaping:** Type of surfaces (grass, etc.); type of plantings (ground cover, shrubs, plantings, etc.); etc.
- ■ **Game Standards:** Applicable Association regulations for each sport; etc.
- ■ **Activity Configuration:** Areas (separate or combined activity); orientation; flexibility; etc.
- ■ **Surfaces:** Type (natural, synthetic, or combination); grading and drainage (surface and subsurface); etc.

Sports Areas

- ■ **Diamonds:** Type of sport(s); type (game and/or practice); size; quantity; etc.
- ■ **Courts:** Type of sport(s); type (game and/or practice); size; quantity; etc.
- ■ **Fields:** Type of sport(s); type (game and/or practice); size; quantity; etc.
- ■ **Ranges:** Type of sport(s); type (game and/or practice); size; quantity; etc.

Structures

- ■ **Tickets:** Type (fixed or portable); surfaces for portable types (pads); utilities; quantity of units (location on site); etc.
- ■ **Security:** Type (fixed or portable); surfaces for portable types (pads); utilities; quantity of units (location on site).
- ■ **Medical Treatment:** Type (fixed portable); surfaces for portable types (pads); utilities; quantity of units (location on the site); etc.
- ■ **Storage:** Type (fixed or portable); Surfaces for portable types (pads); utilities, quantity of units (location on site); type of storage (equipment and tools); etc.
- ■ **Communications:** Type (fixed or portable); utilities (supplemental); quantity of units (location on site); type of systems; etc.
- ■ **Concessions:** Type (fixed or portable-owner or vendor-supplied); surfaces for portable types (tent pads, trailer pads, etc.); utilities; quantity of units (location on the site); etc.
- ■ **Seating:** Type (standing and/or seats); persons (spectators, teams, officials, etc); natural (beams, sloped areas, etc.); artificial (prefabricated bleachers, type of seat, guard rails, etc.); etc.

Signage

- **Vehicle:** Type (direction, information, safety, etc.); etc.
- **Pedestrian:** Type (direction, information, safety, etc.); etc.
- **Activity:** (by sport, area, etc.); etc.
- **Scoreboard:** activity (single or combined use); type (manual or electronic); size; etc.

Barriers

- **Vehicle:** Type (sound, visual, safety, etc.); natural (plantings, berms, depressed areas, etc.); artificial (walls, fending, railings, etc.);
- **Person:** Type (sound, visual, safety, etc.); natural (plantings, berms, depressed areas, etc.) artificial (walls, fencing, railings, etc.) etc.
- **Security:** Type (gates, juxtaposition, or open); etc.

Utilities

- **Power:** Site lighting (pedestrian and vehicle); activity lighting; structures (tickets, security, storage, communications, concessions, etc.); etc.
- **Water:** Irrigation; sanitary; drinking fountains (hot and cold), etc.
- **Sanitary:** Type of units (fixed or portable); etc.
- **Storm Drainage:** Type (surface and subsurface); etc.
- **Communications:** Scoreboards; team sidelines to observation booth; public address for game; telephones for public and private use; broadcasting for television and radio; portable communications for security personnel; emergency; etc.

Appendix C

Surface Selection Process

A systematic approach must be followed to conduct a search to determine the appropriate surface. The following guidelines will assist in the decision-making process:

1. **Definition:** Define the characteristics required to meet specified needs. These characteristics should be material, system, and activity-specific, such as, the effects of sunlight on synthetic materials, the internal filtration of water through the system, or the bounce of a ball on the surface, respectively. This task may seem research-intensive, but it usually isn't since many of these questions already have been addressed by the manufacturers in their literature.

2. **Solicitation:** Don't allow a cost limitation to prevent review of all available systems. Request information from as many manufacturers as possible to obtain literature. The information contained in the literature will provide you with a broad knowledge of different systems, a basis to compare systems, and instill a curiosity to question system design. Project costs as well as material estimates should be obtained. References, list of installers, and locations of systems should be furnished with the literature.

3. **Comparison:** Review and compare each system after receiving the manufacturers' literature. Categorize the information by type and desirable qualities, such as natural versus synthetic or resiliency, etc. A table of desirable attributes is most helpful in comparing the systems.

4. **Visitation:** After the type of products has been narrowed to a few systems, the sports professional should plan to visit various sites to inspect the products, as well as discuss the performance and maintenance factors with the users.

5. **Selection:** Select a system based on research to this point. Although this may be the system eventually purchased, other factors still have to be considered and may influence the final selection.

6. **Quality:** Defining the quality of a system may become difficult since several systems may be very close in design. Quality refers to the materials as well as the installation of the system.

7. **Manufacturers:** What type of reputation does the manufacturer have? Ask for references, but don't be surprised if they give the manufacturer and the installer high marks. Some manufacturers have provided products to clients at reduced rates in exchange for their marketing assistance. How many years has the manufacturer been in business? What type of technical support is available through the manufacturer and the local representative? Ask for information regarding the manufacturer's method of monitoring quality control in the plant as well as in the field.

8. **Installer:** The installer should be recommended by the manufacturer to be assured that the installer is familiar with the products and installation. The installer should be asked questions similar to those asked of the manufacturer.

9. **Maintenance:** Since maintenance can be a considerable portion of the operating budget, it is important to define the extent of the system. Questions, such as these will help with planning: What type of maintenance is required? What is the frequency of each type of maintenance?

10. **Initial Cost:** What is the "total" initial cost of the system? Ask if two systems are considered the same, then why is one system more costly than the other? It may be that the quality of the materials or the system or both are the reason for the cost reduction. In some instances, the product name will increase the cost of the system, or hidden costs will be identified by the low bidder after the work has been awarded.

11. **Life Cycle Cost (LCC):** This is a comparative analysis of each type of surface which considers the initial cost, the operation and maintenance cost, the operation and maintenance cost, and the replacement cost, if necessary, during an established time period. The figures generated from the analysis provide the anticipated total costs. Generally, the more expensive systems (initial cost) will be comparable to the less expensive systems when all factors are considered.

12. **Bidding:** When the owner is required to conduct competitive bidding for products or services, attention should be directed to the writ-

ten specifications, to insure that the products and methods of installations are clearly and accurately described. Too often the specifications make assumptions which permit systems of lesser quality to be considered as equals and therefore acceptable.

13. **Installation/Installer:** Up until this point, the owner has had control over the selection process. However, this phase is where additional expertise will be required. It is in the owner's interest to require the manufacturer to perform periodic on-site supervision of the installer to insure compliance with the manufacturers' specifications.

Appendix D

Indoor Activity Dimensions

Activity	Play Area in Feet	Safety Space in Feet*	Total Area in Feet	Minimum Ceiling Height
Archery	5 × 60	15e	5 × 75	12
Badminton	20 × 44	6s, 8e	32 × 60	24
Basketball				
Jr. High instructional	42 × 74	6s, 8e		24
Jr. High interscholastic	50 × 84	6s, 8e		
Sr. High interscholastic	50 × 84	6s, 8e	62 × 100	
Sr. High instructional	45 × 74	6s, 8e	57 × 90	
Neighborhood E. Sch.	42 × 74	6s, 8e	54 × 90	
Community Junior H.S.	50 × 84	6s, 8e	62 × 100	
Community Senior H.S.	50 × 84	6s, 8e	62 × 100	
Competitive—College & University	50 × 94	6s, 8e	62 × 110	
Boccie	18 × 62	3s, 9e	24 × 80	
Fencing, competitive	6 × 46	9s, 6e	18 × 52	
instructional	4 × 30	4s, 6e	12 × 42	12
Handball	20 × 40			
Racquetball	20 × 40			20
Rifle (one pt.)	5 × 50	6 to 20 e	5 × 70 min.	20
Shuffleboard	6 × 52	6s, 2e	18 × 56	12
Squash	18.5 × 32			12
Tennis				
Deck (doubles)	18 × 40	4s, 5e	26 × 50	
Hand	16 × 40	4½s, 10e	25 × 60	
Lawn (singles)	27 × 78	12s, 21e	51 × 120	
(doubles)	36 × 78	12s, 21e	60 × 120	
Paddle (singles)	16 × 44	6s, 8e	28 × 60	
(doubles)	20 × 44	6s, 8e	32 × 60	
Table (playing area)			9 × 31	
Volleyball				24
Competitive and adult	30 × 60	6s, 6e	42 × 72	
Junior High	30 × 50	6s, 6e	42 × 62	
Wrestling (competitive)	24 × 24	5s, 5e	36 × 36	

*Safety space at the side of an area is indicated by a number followed by "e" for end and "s" for side.

Appendix E

Indoor Activity Area Planning Checklist

Checklist for Planning and Designing Indoor Activity Areas

A checklist has been prepared to aid those responsible for planning facilities for athletics, physical education, health and recreation. The application of this checklist may prevent unfortunate and costly errors.

General

_____ 1. A clear-cut statement has been prepared on the nature and scope of the program, and the special requirements for space, equipment, fixtures, and facilities have been dictated by the activities to be conducted.

_____ 2. The facility has been planned to meet the total requirements of the program, as well as the special needs of those who are to be served.

_____ 3. The plans and specifications have been checked by all governmental agencies (city, county, and state) whose approval is required by law.

_____ 4. Plans for areas and facilities conform to state and local regulations and to accepted standards and practices.

_____ 5. The areas and facilities planned make possible the programs that serve the interests and needs of all the people.

_____ 6. Every available source of property or funds has been explored, evaluated, and utilized whenever appropriate.

_____ 7. All interested persons and organizations concerned with the facility have had an opportunity to share in its planning (professional educators, users, consultants, administrators, engineers, architects, program specialists, building managers, and builder)—a team approach.

_____ 8. The facility will fulfill the maximum demands of the program. The program has not been curtailed to fit the facility.

_____ 9. The facility has been functionally planned to meet the present and anticipated needs of specific programs, situations, and publics.

_____ 10. Future additions are included in present plans to permit economy of construction.

_____ 11. All classrooms and offices are isolated from background noise.

_____ 12. Ample numbers and sized storage areas are built-in flush with walls at all teaching stations.

_____ 13. No center mullions or thresholds are on storage room doorways.

_____ 14. All passageways are free of obstructions; fixtures are recessed.

_____ 15. Storage areas are well ventilated, dry, and cool.

_____ 16. Buildings, specific areas, and facilities are clearly identified.

_____ 17. Locker rooms are arranged for ease of supervision.

_____ 18. Offices, teaching stations, and service facilities are properly interrelated.

_____ 19. Special needs of the physically handicapped are met, including a ramp into the building at a major entrance.

_____ 20. All "dead space" is used.

_____ 21. The building is compatible in design and comparable in quality and accommodation to other campus structures.

_____ 22. Storage rooms are accessible to the play area.

_____ 23. Workrooms, conference rooms, and staff and administrative offices are interrelated.

_____ 24. Shower and dressing facilities are provided for professional staff members and are conveniently located.

_____ 25. Thought and attention has been given to making facilities and equipment as durable and vandal-proof as possible.

_____ 26. Low-cost maintenance features have been considered.

_____ 27. This facility is a part of a well-integrated Master Plan.

_____ 28. All areas, courts, facilities, equipment, climate control, security, etc., conform rigidly to detailed standards and specifications.

_____ 29. Shelves are recessed and mirrors and supplies are in appropriate places in restrooms and dressing rooms.

_____ 30. Dressing space between locker rows is adjusted to the size and age of students.

_____ 31. Drinking fountains are placed conveniently in locker room areas or immediately adjacent areas.

_____ 32. Special attention is given to provision for locking service windows and counter, supply bins, carts, shelves, and racks.

_____ 33. Provision is made for repair, maintenance, replacement, and off-season storage of equipment and uniforms.

_____ 34. A well-defined program for laundering and cleaning towels, uniforms, and equipment is included in the plan.

_____ 35. Noncorrosive metal is used in dressing, drying, and shower areas, except for enameled lockers.

_____ 36. Antipanic hardware is used where required by fire regulations.

_____ 37. Properly placed house bibbs and drains are sufficient in size and quantity to permit flushing the entire area with a water hose.

_____ 38. A water-resistant, covered base is used under the locker base and floor mat and where floor and wall join.

_____ 39. Chalkboards and/or tackboards with map tracks are located in appropriate places in dressing rooms, hallways, and classrooms.

_____ 40. Book shelves are provided in toilet area.

_____ 41. Space and equipment are planned in accordance with the types and number of enrollees.

_____ 42. Basement rooms undesirable for dressing, drying, and showering, are not planned for those purposes.

_____ 43. Spectator seating (permanent) in areas that are basically instructional is kept at a minimum. Rollaway bleachers are used primarily. Balcony seating is considered as a possibility.

_____ 44. Well-lighted and effectively displayed trophy cases enhance the interest and beauty of the lobby.

_____ 45. The space under the stairs is used for storage.

_____ 46. Department heads' offices are located near the central administrative office which includes a well-planned conference room.

_____ 47. Workrooms are located near the central office and serve as a repository for departmental materials and records.

_____ 48. Conference area includes a cloak room, lavatory, and toilet.

_____ 49. In addition to regular secretarial offices established in the central and department chairmen's offices, a special room to house a secretarial pool for staff members if provided.

_____ 50. Staff dressing facilities are provided. These facilities also may serve game officials.

_____ 51. The community and/or neighborhood has a "round table" for planning.

_____ 52. All those (persons and agencies) who should be a party to planning and development are invited and actively engaged in the planning process.

_____ 53. Space and area relationships are important. They have been considered carefully.

_____ 54. Both long-range and immediate plans have been made.

_____ 55. The body comfort of the child, a major factor in securing maximum learning, has been considered in the plans.

_____ 56. Plans for quiet areas have been made.

_____ 57. In the planning, consideration has been given to the need for adequate recreational areas and facilities, both near and distant from the homes of people.

_____ 58. Consoles for security, information, and checkout have been ideally located.

_____ 59. Every effort has been exercised to eliminate hazards.

_____ 60. The installation of low-handing door closers, light fixtures, signs, and other objects in traffic areas has been avoided.

_____ 61. Warning signals—both visible and audible—are included in the plans.

_____ 62. Ramps have a slope equal to or greater than a one-foot rise in 12-feet.

_____ 63. Minimum landings for ramps are five-by-five feet, extend at least one foot beyond the swinging arc of a door, have at least a six-foot clearance at the bottom, and have level platforms at 30-foot intervals on every turn.

_____ 64. Adequate locker and dressing spaces are provided.

_____ 65. The design of dressing, drying, and shower areas reduces foot traffic to a minimum and establishes clean, dry aisles for bare feet.

_____ 66. Teaching stations are related properly to service facilities.

_____ 67. Toilet facilities are adequate in number. They are located to serve all groups for which provisions are made.

_____ 68. Mail services, outgoing and incoming, are included in the plans.

_____ 69. Hallways, ramps, doorways, and elevators are designed to permit equipment to be moved easily and quickly.

_____ 70. A keying design suited to administrative and instructional needs is planned.

_____ 71. Toilets used by large groups have circulating (in and out) entrances and exits.

_____ 72. All surfaces in racquetball, handball, and squash courts are flush.

_____ 73. At least one racquetball, handball, or squash court has a tempered glass back and side wall.

_____ 74. All vents in racquetball, handball, and squash courts are located in the back one-third of the ceiling.

_____ 75. Standard size doors are utilized on racquetball, handball, and squash courts.

_____ 76. All aspects of safety are planned carefully for the weight areas.

_____ 77. Racks are provided for all lose plates, dumbbells, and barbells in weight areas.

_____ 78. Special attention is paid to acoustical treatment in weight areas.

_____ 79. Ample walk areas for traffic flow are planned around lifting areas in weight rooms.

_____ 80. Concession areas are planned for and built flush with existing walls.

_____ 81. Adequate numbers of concession areas are planned.

_____ 82. Concession stand cash handling methods have been planned carefully.

_____ 83. Storage and maintenance has been planned for concession areas.

_____ 84. Classrooms are planned by instructors, students, and maintenance staff.

_____ 85. Classrooms are planned for the numbers of users and the styles of teaching to be utilized in the room.

_____ 86. Careful attention has been paid to storage areas in classrooms.

_____ 87. Faculty offices should be private and secured.

_____ 88. Storage areas and windows are planned in faculty offices.

_____ 89. Laboratories need to be planned for both teaching and research utilization.

_____ 90. Ample space and subdivisions within laboratories are planned carefully.

Climate Control

_____1. Provision I made throughout the building for climate control—heating, ventilating, and refrigerated cooling.

_____ 2. Special ventilation is provided for locker, dressing, shower, drying, and toilet rooms.

_____ 3. Heating plans permit both area and individual room control.

_____ 4. Research areas where small animals are kept and where chemicals are used have been provided with special ventilating equipment.

_____ 5. The heating and ventilating of the wrestling gymnasium has been given special attention.

_____ 6. All air diffusers adequately diffuse the air.

_____ 7. Storage area ventilation is planned carefully.

_____ 8. Humidity and ventilation are balanced properly in racquetball, handball, and squash courts.

_____ 9. Thermostats are located out of the general users' reach and/or are secured.

_____ 10. The total energy concept has been investigated.

Electrical

_____ 1. Shielded, vapor-proof lights are used in moisture-prevalent areas.

_____ 2. Lights in strategic areas are key-controlled.

_____ 3. Lighting intensity conforms to approved standards.

_____ 4. Adequate numbers of electrical outlets are placed strategically.

_____ 5. Gymnasium and auditorium lights are controlled by dimmer units.

_____ 6. Locker room lights are mounted above the space between lockers.

_____ 7. Natural light is controlled properly for purposes of visual aids and to avoid glare.

_____ 8. Electrical outlet plates are installed three feet above the floor unless special use dictates other locations.

_____ 9. Controls for light switches and projection equipment are located suitably and are interrelated.

_____ 10. All lights are shielded. Special protection is provided in gymnasium, court areas, and shower rooms.

_____ 11. All lights must be easily accessible for maintenance.

_____ 12. The use of metal halide and high pressure sodium lighting has been investigated.

_____ 13. All areas have been wired for television cable and computer hookups.

_____ 14. Indirect lighting has been utilized wherever possible.

_____ 15. All teaching areas are equipped with a mounted camera, 25-foot color monitor, and tape deck securely built-in flush with the existing walls.

Walls

_____ 1. Movable and folding partitions are power-operated and controlled by keyed switches.

_____ 2. Wall plates are located where needed and are attached firmly.

_____ 3. Hooks and rings for nets are placed (and recessed in walls) according to court locations and net heights.

_____ 4. Materials that clean easily and are impervious to moisture are used where moisture is prevalent.

_____ 5. Shower heads are placed at different heights; four feet (elementary) to seven feet (university) for each school level.

_____ 6. Protective matting is placed permanently on the walls in the wrestling room, at the ends of basketball courts, and in other areas where such protection is needed.

_____ 7. Adequate numbers of drinking fountains are provided. They are properly placed (recessed in wall).

_____ 8. The lower eight feet of wall surface in activity areas is glazed and planned for ease of maintenance.

_____ 9. All corners in locker rooms are rounded.

_____ 10. At least two adjacent walls in dance and weight areas should have full length mirrors.

_____ 11. Walls should be treated acoustically 15 feet and above.

_____ 12. Walls are reinforced structurally where equipment is to be mounted.

_____ 13. Flat wall space is planned for rebounding areas.

_____ 14. Walls should be flat with no juts or extruding columns.

_____ 15. Pastel colors are utilized on the walls.

_____ 16. Windows should be kept to a minimum in activity areas.

Ceilings

_____ 1. Overhead support apparatus is secured to beams that are engineered to withstand stress.

_____ 2. The ceiling height is adequate for the activities to be housed.

_____ 3. Acoustical materials impervious to moisture are used in moisture-prevalent areas.

_____ 4. Skylights are gymnasiums, being impractical, are seldom used because of problems in waterproofing roofs and of controlling sun rays.

_____ 5. All ceilings except those in storage areas are acoustically treated with sound-absorbent materials.

_____ 6. Ceilings should be painted an off-white.

Floors

_____ 1. Floor plates are placed where needed and are flush-mounted.

_____ 2. Floor design and materials conform to recommended standards and specifications.

_____ 3. Lines and markings are painted in floors before sealing is completed (when synthetic tape is not used).

_____ 4. A cove base (around lockers and where all and floor meet) of the same water-resistant material that is used on floor is found in all dressing and shower rooms.

_____ 5. Abrasive, nonskid, slip-resistant flooring that is impervious to moisture is provided on all areas where water is used (laundry, swimming pools, shower, dressing, and drying rooms).

_____ 6. Floor drains are located properly, and the slope of the floor is adequate for rapid drainage.

_____ 7. Hardwood floors are utilized in racquetball, handball, and squash courts.

_____ 8. Maintenance storage is located in areas with synthetic floors.

_____ 9. Floors should be treated accoustically when possible.

_____ 10. Hardwood floors should be utilized in dance areas.

Appendix F

Metric Conversion Formulas

Converting from Metric to English:

To Obtain	Multiply	By
Inches	Centimeters	0.3937007874
Feet	Meters	3.280839895
Yards	Meters	1.093613298
Miles	Kilometers	0.6213711922

Converting from English to Metric:

To Obtain	Multiply	By
Centimeters	Inches	2.54
Meters	Feet	0.3048
Meters	Yards	0.9144
Kilometers	Miles	1.609344

Appendix G

General Resources for Planning Facilities

Books and Guides

Council of Educational Facility Planners (CEFP), International. 1985. *Guide for Planning Educational Facilities,* Columbus, OH: Council of Educational Facility Planners.

DeChiara, J. and Callendar, J. H. 1990. *Time-Saver Standards for Building Types* (3rd ed.), New York: McGraw-Hill.

Gillis, John (Editor). 1992. *National Federation Court and Field Diagram Guide,* Kansas City, MO: National Federation of State High School Associations.

Gonsoulin, Sid (Editor). 1988. *Outstanding Sports Facilities,* Corvallis, OR: National Intramural-Recreational Sports Association.

National Collegiate Athletic Association Rules and Interpretations Guides, Overland Park KS:
   —Baseball
   —Basketball
   —Illustrated Basketball
   —Football
   —Ice Hockey
   —LaCrosse
   —Rifle
   —Skiing
   —Soccer
   —Swimming & Diving
   —Track & Field/Cross Country
   —Water Polo
   —Wrestling

Sol, Neil and Foster, Carl (Editors). 1992. The American College of Sport Medicine's *Health/Fitness Facility Standards and Guidelines,* Champaign, IL: Human Kinetics Books.

Periodicals

Athletic Business. Published monthly by Athletic Business Publications, 1842 Hoffman Street, Suite 201, Madison, WI 53704, (608) 249-0186.

Athletic Management, Published bimonthly by College Athletic Administrator, Inc., 438 West State Street, Ithaca, NY 14850, (607) 272-0265.

Club Industry. Published monthly by Sportscape Inc., Framingham Corporate Center, 492 Old Connecticut Path, Third Floor, Framingham, MA 01701, (508) 872-2021.

Fitness Management. Published monthly by Leisure Publications, Inc., 3923 West 6th Street, Los Angeles, CA 90020, (213) 385-3926.

Journal of Physical Education, Recreation and Dance. Published monthly except in July by American Alliance for Health, Physical Education, Recreation and Dance, 1900 Association Drive, Reston, VA 22091, (703) 476-3400.

Parks and Recreation. Published monthly by National Recreation and Parks Association, 3101 Park Center Drive, Alexandria, VA 22302, (703) 820-4940.

The Physician and Sports Medicine. Published monthly by McGraw-Hill Co., 4530 W. 77th Street, Minneapolis, MN 55435, (612) 835-3222.

Recreation Resources. Published monthly by Lakewood Publications, 50 South Ninth Street, Minneapolis, MN 55402, (612) 333-0471.

Sports Medicine Digest. Published monthly by PM, Inc., P.O. Box 10172, Van Nuys, CA 91410, (818) 997-8011.

Tennis Industry. Published monthly by Sterling Southeast Inc., 3230 West Commercial Blvd., Fort Lauderdale, FL 33309, (305) 731-0000.

Appendix H

Associations Pertinent to Planning Recreation, Sport, and Physical Education Facilities

Aerobics & Fitness Association of America.
15250 Ventura, Suite 310
Sherman Oaks, CA 91403, (818) 905-0040

American Alliance for Health, Physical Education, Recreation and Dance (AAHPERD)
1900 Association Drive
Reston, VA 22091, (703) 476-3400

American Amateur Racquetball Association
815 North Weber, Suite 101
Colorado Springs, CO 80903, (719) 635-5396

American Association of Cardiovascular and Pulmonary Rehabilitation
7611 Elmwood Avenue, Suite 201
Middleton, WI 53562, (608) 831-6989

American Athletic Trainers Association and Certification Board, Inc.
660 W. Duarte Road
Arcada, CA 91006, (818) 445-1978

American College of Sports Medicine
P.O. Box 1440
Indianapolis, IN 46206-1440, (317) 637-9200

American Council on Exercise
6190 Cornerstone Court East, Suite 202
San Diego, CA 92121

American Heart Association
7320 Greenville Avenue
Dallas, TX 75231, (214) 373-6300

American Massage Therapy Association
1130 West North Shore Drive
Chicago, IL 60626

Association for Fitness in Business
310 N. Alabama, Suite A100
Indianapolis, IN 46204, (317) 636-6621

Athletic Institute
200 Castlewood Drive
North Palm Beach, FL 33408, (408) 842-3600

Illuminating Engineering Society of North America
345 E. 47th Street
New York, NY 10017, (212) 705-7926

International Council for Health, Physical Education and Recreation (ICHPER)
1900 Association Drive
Reston, VA 22091, (703) 476-3400

International Dance Exercise Association (IDEA)
6190 Cornerstone Court East, Suite 204
San Diego, CA 92121, (800) 999-IDEA

International Racquet Sports Association
253 Summer Street
Boston, MA 02210, (800) 228-4772

Maple Flooring Manufacturers Association
60 Revere Drive, Suite 500
Northbrook, IL 60062, (708) 480-9138

National Archery Association
1750 East Boulder Street
Colorado Springs, CO 80909, (719) 578-4576

National Association of Concessionaires
35 East Wacker Drive, #1545
Chicago, IL, 60601, (312) 236-3858

National Collegiate Athletic Association
6501 College Blvd
Overland Park, KS 66211-2422, (913) 339-1906

National Employee Services and Recreation Association
2400 S. Downing Avenue
Westchester, IL 60154, (708) 562-8130

National Institute for Occupational Safety and Health
944 Chestnut Ridge Road
Morgantown, WV 26505

National Intramural-Recreation Sports Association
850 Southwest 15th Street
Corvallis, OR 97333-4145 (503) 737-2088

National Recreation & Park Association
3101 Park Center Drive
Alexandria, VA 22302 (703) 820-4940

National Rifle Association
1600 Rhode Island Avenue, N.W.
Washington, DC 20036 (202) 828-6000

National Strength & Conditioning Association
P.O. Box 81410
Lincoln, NE 68501 (402) 472-3000

National Swimming Pool Foundation
10803 Golfdale, Suite 300
San Antonio, TX 78216 (512) 525-1227

National Wellness Association
University of Wisconsin
Stevens Point, WI 54481

President's Council on Physical Fitness and Sports
450 5th Street, N.W., Suite 7103
Washington, D.C. 20001 (202) 272-3421.

Sporting Goods Manufacturers Association
200 Castlewood Drive
North Palm Beach, FL 33408 (407) 842-4100

United States Badminton Association
920 "O" Street, Fourth Floor
Lincoln, NE 68508 (402) 438-2473

United States Fencing Association
1750 East Boulder Street
Colorado Springs, CO 80909 (719) 632-5737

U.S. Golf Association
P.O. Box 708
Far Hills, NJ 07931 (201) 234-2300

U.S. Gymnastics Federation
Pan American Plaza, Suite 300
201 South Capitol Avenue
Indianapolis, IN 46225 (317) 237-5050

U.S. Handball Association
930 North Benton Avenue
Tucson, AZ 85711 (602) 795-0434

U.S. Squash Racquets Association
P.O. Box 1216
Bala-Cynwyd, PA 19004 (215) 667-4006

U.S. Tennis Court and Track Builders Association
720 Light Street
Baltimore, MD 21230 (301) 752-3500

U.S. Volleyball Association
3595 East Fountain, Suite 1-2
Colorado Springs, CO 80910-1740 (719) 637-8300

Wellness Council of America
7101 Newport Avenue
Omaha, NE 68152 (402) 572-3590

YMCA of the USA
726 Broadway, 5th Floor
New York, NY 10003 (212) 614-2827

YWCA of the USA
101 North Wacker Drive
Chicago, IL 60606 (312) 977-0031

Appendix I

Associations Pertinent to Planning for Accessibility

American Coalition of Citizens with Disabilities
1346 Connecticut Avenue, NW, Room 814
Washington, DC 20036
(chapters in states)

American Council of the Blind
1211 Connecticut Avenue, NW, Suite 506
Washington, DC 20036
(chapters in states)

Arthritis Foundation
1212 Avenue of the Americas
New York, NY 10036

Association for the Aid of Crippled Children
345 East 46th Street
New York, NY 10017

Disabled American Veterans
3725 Alexandria Pike
Cold Spring, KY 41076
(state and local units)

International Society for the Rehabilitation of the Disabled
219 East 44th Street
New York, NY 10017

Muscular Dystrophy Association of America
1790 Broadway
New York, NY 10019

National Association of the Deaf
814 Thayer Avenue
Silver Spring, MD 20910
(local chapters)

National Association of the Physically Handicapped
76 Elm Street
London, OH 43140
(local chapters)

National Congress of Organizations of the Physically Handicapped
6106 North 30th Street
Arlington, VA 22207

National Easter Seal Society for Crippled Children and Adults
2023 West Ogden Avenue
Chicago, IL 60612

National Foundation for Neuromuscular Diseases
250 West 57th Street
New York, NY 10019

National Multiple Sclerosis Society
257 Park Avenue South
New York, NY 10010

National Paraplegia Foundation
333 North Michigan Avenue
Chicago, IL 60601
(state and local chapters)

Paralyzed Veterans of America
4330 East West Highway, Suite 300
Washington, DC 20014
(state and local chapters)

United Cerebral Palsy Association, Inc.
66 East 34th Street
New York, NY 10016

Appendix J

Track and Field and Cross Country Layouts

TRACK & FIELD

OVERALL DIAGRAM OF FIELD EVENTS

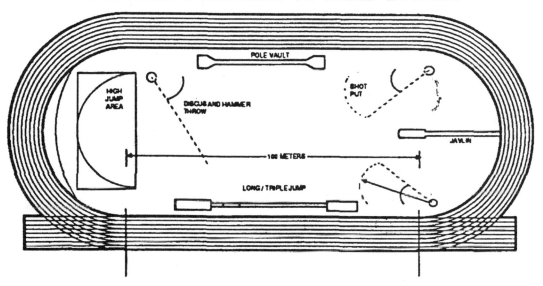

STANDARD 400M TRACK

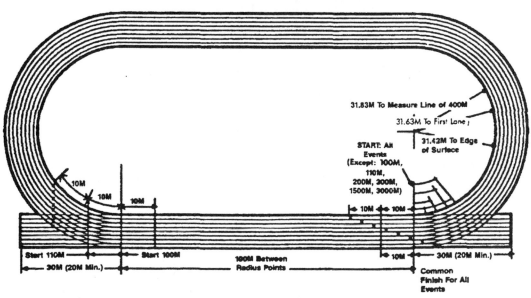

Appendix K

Renovation, Retrofitting or Replacing Facilities

Renovation, Retrofitting, or Replacing

The practice of buying-using-discarding has become an unacceptable practice today. This not only applies to paper, aluminum cans, and glass, but to facilities as well (CEFP, 1985). Due to the high cost of new construction, upper level administration, whether it be in the private sector, at a university, municipal agency, or in a public school system, has the responsibility of making the wisest use of existing buildings. In meeting this obligation, it is necessary for administrators, with input from knowledgeable resource persons, to consider the feasibility of either renovating or retrofitting an existing building, or of constructing a new facility.

By definition, the renovation of an existing facility is the rehabilitation of the physical features of that building, including the rearrangement of spaces within the structure. Retrofitting, on the other hand, is the addition of new systems, items, features, materials, and/or equipment to a facility which were not installed at the time the building was constructed. These changes may be minor, or they could be significant to the point of changing the primary function of the facility. (Figure 1.6.)

To accurately ascertain whether renovation, retrofitting, or new construction is the most prudent alternative, administrators have a myriad of factors to consider. One of the more important is the effect that the construction process has relative to ongoing programs. Consideration must be given to program modifications and adaptions that may occur during the construction process. A close scrutiny of the advantages and disadvantages of both the present and the possibility of a new building should be undertaken. The following is an adequate representation of the factors to consider:

Cost Considerations

A. What is the cost of new construction to provide comparable space?

B. What is the cost of construction needed to bring the existing facility up to compliance with safety codes/accessibility?

C. Does the cost of renovation or retrofitting exceed 50 percent of the cost of new construction?

D. Will the increased cost of maintaining an older building justify renovation instead of constructing a new facility?

E. Could the existing facility be sold or leased to a private entity to help defray the cost of new construction?

F. If the amount of construction time becomes critical, which method, renovation or new construction, could be completed in the least amount of time?

Site Considerations

A. Is a site available, and how effectively does the site meet the agency's immediate and long-range goals?

B. Is the location of the present structure easily accessible?

C. Is the parking adequate at the present site?

D. How efficient is the sewer and storm water control?

E. How is the soil-bearing performance of the present site?

F. What is the general condition of the grounds?

G. Is there sufficient area for all program activities?

H. Are vehicular drives well located for safe ingress and egress?

I. Are the existing utilities on or near the site adequate to provide the needed services?

Architectural and Structural Considerations

A certified architect and engineer should be sought to determine the following structural factors:

A. Is the present facility aesthetically appealing and structurally sound?

B. Does the existing facility meet current and long-range program goals and, if not, would renovation or retrofitting realistically elevate the facility to acceptable standards?

C. What is the availability of utilities?

D. How energy efficient is the present facility? Does it meet all updated energy codes?

E. Are there signs of deterioration of footings, foundations, or piers?

F. Are structural members adequate and in serviceable conditions?

G. Is the exterior masonry sound? Are there structural cracks, water damage, or defective mortar?

H. What is the condition of the roof and roofing surfaces, roof drains, and skylights?

I. What is the condition of flashing, gutters, and downspouts?

J. What are the conditions of doors and windows?

K. What are the conditions of door hardware and panic devices?

L. What are the locations, numbers, types, and condition of plumbing fixtures?

M. What is the condition and capacity of the present water supply, sewage lines, and drainage systems?

N. Is the present HVAC System adequate and energy efficient? Does it meet updated codes?

O. What is the condition and adequacy of lighting and power distribution systems?

P. Do the existing light fixtures provide adequate illumination in all areas?

Q. Are stairways, circulation patterns, and exits safe and adequate in number?

R. What is the present condition of fire alarms and inter-communication systems?

Educational Considerations

A. Is the building now meeting the agency's program?

B. What is the current inventory of rooms and their sizes?

C. Are laboratories adequately served by all required utilities?

D. Is the library adequate to house the required book collection and to provide media and related services?

E. Are food service facilities adequate to meet present and projected needs?

F. Are physical education, recreation, and athletic areas usable or capable of being retrofitted if required?

Community Considerations

A. Will the renovation of the building be consistent with present zoning requirements and policies?

B. What are the plans for the area served by the program as projected by city or area planning agencies?

C. Is the building on or eligible for placement on the National Register of Historic Places?

D. Will a new facility constitute a political problem with businesses in the private sector?

Before deciding on the wisdom of renovation, retrofitting, remodeling, or replacing, factors concerning the existing and proposed facilities should be evaluated in detail, both individually and collectively. It also would be beneficial for administrators to project a reasonable life expectancy of the facility, taking into account factors such as:

—increased or decreased populations served by the programs within the facility,

—growth and development of areas surrounding the facility, and

—the potential reorganization, community re-zoning, or consolidation of schools in the district.

A decision on whether renovation or retrofitting is advantageous over new construction then should be rendered, based on a composite of all the factors. (Figure 1)

Facility Evaluation

Figure 1. Facility Evaluation (Permission to print by the Council of Educational Facility Planners, International)

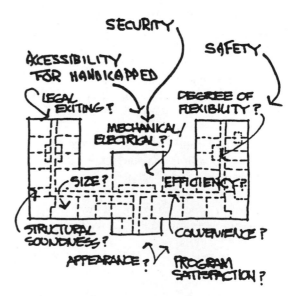

FACILITY EVALUATION

Appendix L

Sample ASHRAE Standard

ANSI/ASHRAE/IESNA 90.1-1989—Published standard

Addenda 90.1b-1992, 90.1c-1993, 90.1d-1992, 90.1e-1992, 90.1f-1995, 90.1g-1993, 90.1I-1993, 90.1m-1995 to ASHRAE/IESNA 90.1-1989 (Addendum 90.1n-1997 approved for publication by ASHRAE BOD 97/07/03 [Publication pending])

Energy Efficient Design of New Buildings Except Low-Rise Residential Buildings

1 PURPOSE

1.1 The purposes of this standard are to: new buildings so that they may be constructed, operated, and maintained in a manner that minimizes the use of energy without constraining the building function nor the comfort or productivity of the occupants;

   (a) provide criteria for energy efficient design and methods for determining compliance with these criteria; and

   (b) provide sound guidance for energy-efficient design.

1.2 This standard shall not be used to circumvent any safety, health, or environmental requirements.

2 SCOPE

2.1 This standard sets forth design requirements for the efficient use of energy in new buildings intended for human occupancy. The requirements apply to the building envelope, distribution of energy, systems and equipment for auxiliaries, heating, ventilating, air conditioning, service water heating, lighting, and energy managing.

ASHRAE Standard

2.2 This standard applies to all new buildings or portions of buildings that provide facilities or shelter for human occupancy and use energy primarily to provide human comfort, except single- and multi-family residential buildings of three or fewer stories above grade.

2.3 This standard does not apply to:

   (a) areas of buildings intended primarily for manufacturing or commercial or industrial processing:

   (b) buildings or separately enclosed identifiable areas having an combination of dedicated space heating, service water heating, ventilating, air-conditioning, or lighting systems whose combined peak design rate of energy usage for these purposes is less than 3.5 Btu/(h · ft²) of gross floor area; or

   (c) buildings of fewer than 100 ft2 of gross floor area.

2.4 Where specifically noted in this standard, certain other buildings or elements of buildings may be exempt.

Standing Standard Project Committee 90.1 (Project Committee originally authorized 83/01/23 and changed to standing committee 83/09/16) (TPS revised 97/07/02)

Maintenance and revision of ASHRAE/IESNA 90.1 with revised TPS.

Energy Standard for Buildings Except Low-Rise Residential Buildings

   1 PURPOSE. The purpose of this standard is to provide minimum requirements for the energy-efficient design of buildings except low-rise residential buildings.

2 SCOPE.

2.1 This standard provides:

ASHRAE Standard

   (a) minimum energy-efficient requirements for the design and construction of:

      1. new buildings and their systems,

      2. new portions of buildings and their systems, and

      3. new systems and equipment in existing buildings.

   (b) criteria for determining compliance with these requirements.

2.2 The provisions of this standard apply to:

   (a) the envelope of buildings provided that the enclosed spaces are:

      1. heated by a heating system whose output capacity is greater than or equal to 3.4 Btu/h · ft² (10 W/m²), or

2. cooled by a cooling system whose sensible output capacity is greater than or equal to 5 Btu/h · ft² (15 W/m²);

(b) the following systems and equipment used in conjunction with buildings

1. heating, ventilating, and air-conditioning,
2. service water heating,
3. electric power distribution and metering provisions,
4. electric motors and belt drives, and
5. lighting.

2.3 The provisions of this standard do not apply to:

(a) single-family houses, multi-family structures of three stories or fewer above grade, manufactured houses (mobile and modular homes),

(b) buildings that do not use either electricity or fossil fuel, or

ASHRAE Standard

(c) equipment and portions of building systems that use energy primarily to provide for industrial, manufacturing or commercial processes.

2.4 Where specifically noted in this standard, certain other buildings or elements of buildings shall be exempt.

2.5 This standard shall not be used to circumvent any safety, health or environmental requirements.

Glossary of Terms

Access. A way or means of approaching, entering, getting, using, etc.

Acoustical Engineer. Individual responsible for the design of large and small spaces that are appropriate for good sound (i.e., being able to hear in any seat in a large arena or aquatic complex, or not damaging to one's ears while playing racquetball).

Acoustical Treatments. Applications designed to control/absorb sound.

Addendum. A written or graphic instrument issued by the architect prior to the execution of the contract which modifies or interprets the bidding documents by additions, deletions, clarifications, or corrections. An addendum becomes part of the contract documents when the contract is executed.

Advertising Rights. Rights sold to various entities who wish to advertise to the spectators within the sport facility.

Aesthetics. A branch of philosophy dealing with the nature, creation, and appreciation of beauty.

Alternate Bid. The amount stated in the bid to be added to or deducted from the amount of the base bid if the corresponding change in the work, as described in the bidding documents, is accepted.

Ancillary Areas. Areas that provide support functions for the primary building attractions.

Annunciator. An electronically controlled signal board that indicates to the building control center, which courts/areas are occupied at any time.

Application for Payment. A contractor's certified request for payment of amount due for completed portions of the work and, if the contract so provides, for materials or equipment delivered and suitably stored pending their incorporation into the work.

Architectural Barriers. Obstacles which prevent parties from entering a facility or any architectural restraint that hampers moving throughout a building.

Area—Elastic Surfaces. Allow for dispersion of impact, where a bouncing object, or an individual jumping, is felt approximately 20 inches around the point of impact.

Area of Deflection. The amount of impact that is felt in the vicinity of the points of contact.

Asset-Backed Securities. Investments secured by expected revenue.

Attractive Nuisance. It is a doctrine that holds if a person creates a condition on his/her premises which may reasonably be construed to be the source of danger to children, he or she must take precautions as a reasonably prudent person would take to prevent injury to children of tender ages whom he or she knows to be accustomed to frequent the area.

Baffles. A mounting or partition used to check the transmission of sound waves.

Base Bid Specifications. The specifications listing or description of those materials, equipment, and methods of construction upon which the bid must be predicated, exclusive of any alternate bids.

Base Bid Sum. The amount of money stated in the bid as the sum for which the bidder offers to perform the work described in the bidding documents, prior to adjustments for alternate bids which are also submitted.

Bearing (azimuth). A direction stated on compass degrees.

Bequests and Trusts. Agreements made with specific individuals that upon their deaths a certain amount of their estates will be given to the organization.

Bid. A complete and properly signed proposal to do work or designated portion thereof for the amount or amounts stipulated in the proposal and submitted in accordance with the bidding documents.

Bid Bond. A form of bid security executed by the bidder and by a surety to guarantee that the bidder will enter into a contract within specified time and furnish any required performance bond, and labor and material payment bond.

Bid Form. A form furnished to be a bidder to be completed, signed and submitted as the bidder's bid.

Bid Opening. The opening and tabulation of bids submitted within the prescribed bid time and in conformity with the prescribed procedures.

Bid Price. The amount stated in the bid for which the bidder offers to perform the work.

Bidder. A person or entity who submits a bid, generally one who submits a bid for a prime contract with the owner, as distinct from a sub-bidder, who submits a bid to a prime bidder. Technically, a bidder is not a contractor on a specified project until a contract exists between the bidder and the owner.

Bidding Documents. The bidding documents include an invitation to bid, instructions to bidders, the bid form, other bidding and contracting forms, and contract documents including any addenda issued prior to receipt of bids.

Bond. An interest bearing certificate issued by a government or corporation, promising to pay interest and to repay a sum of money (the principle) at a specified date in the future.

Bond Period. Most government projects and some larger projects require the contractor to post not only a performance bond, but a one-year (or some other specified time) warranty on the quality of the work.

Brightness. The luminous intensity of any surface.

Broken-Back Track. Track configuration that features a more square track with short straightaways and rounded ends made of double curves.

Builder's Risk Insurance. A specialized form of property insurance which provides for loss or damage to the work during the course of construction.

Building Permit. A permit issued by appropriate governmental authority allowing construction of a project in accordance with approved drawings and specifications.

Bulletin. A document issued by the architect after the contract is awarded. It may include drawings and other information used to solicit a proposal for change in the work. A bulletin becomes part of the contract documents only after being incorporated in a change order. A bulletin may also be referred to as a request for a change.

Cash Allowance. An amount established in the contract documents for inclusion in the contract sum to cover cost of prescribed items not specified in detail, with provision that variations between the established amount and the final amount of the prescribed items will be reflected in change orders.

Cash Discount. The amount which can be deducted from a seller's invoice for payment within a stipulated period of time.

Cash Donation. Donation of cash to an organization for a general or specific use in return for a personal tax deduction.

Certificate of Insurance. A document issued by an authorized representative of an insurance company stating the types, amounts and effective dates of insurance in force for a designated insured.

Certification of Occupancy. A document issued by a governmental authority certifying that all or a designated portion of a building complies with the provisions of applicable statutes and regulations, and permitting occupancy for its designated use.

Certificates of Participation. Involves a governmental entity buying a facility. The government entity then leases portions of the facility to the general public.

Certificate of Substantial Completion. A certificate prepared by the architect on the basis of an inspection stating that the work or a designated portion of the work is substantially complete as of a particular date. This establishes the date of substantial completion with respect to the responsibilities of the owner and the contractor for security, maintenance, heat, utilities, damage to the work, and insurance.

Change Order. A written order to the contractor signed by the owner and the architect, issued after the execution of the contract, authorizing a change in the work or an adjustment in the contract sum or the contract time. The contract sum and contract time may only be changed by a change order. A change order signed by the contractor indicates the contractor's agreement therewith, including the adjustment in the contract sum or the contract time.

Changes in the Work. The changes ordered by the owner within the general scope of the contract, consisting of additions, deletions or other revisions, which result in the contract sum and the contract time being adjusted accordingly. All such changes in the work shall be authorized by a change order, and shall be performed under the applicable conditions of the contract documents.

Checkpoint. An obvious feature shown on the map that helps orienteers determine their progress along the course.

Civil Engineer. Individual who is responsible for the following tasks: grading and land movement plans, geometric layout of new improvements, plans for new roads and street pavements, utility plans, and plans for water collection system and sanitary sewers.

Comprehensive General Liability Insurance. A broad form of liability insurance covering claims for bodily injury and property damage, which combines under one policy coverage for all liability exposures (except those specifically excluded) on a blanket basis and automatically covers new and unknown hazards that may develop. Comprehensive general liability insurance automatically includes contractual liability coverage for certain types of contract.

Concessionaire Exclusivity. The sale of the exclusive rights for all concessions within a spectator facility for a specified number of dollars over a specified period of time.

Construction Document Phase. This phase is based on the design development phase. The architect prepares final drawings and construction specifications.

Construction Phase. The final phase is the construction phase. The architect shall (1) visit the site at least twice monthly at appropriate intervals at various stages of construction, (2) certify payments for work completed, (3) authority to reject work which does not conform to the contract documents, (4) review and approve all submittals such as shop drawings, product data, and samples, (5) prepare all change orders and construction change directives with supporting documentation and data deemed necessary, (6) conduct periodic observations to determine the date or dates for substantial completion, and receive, review, and forward all records, and written warranties to the owner, and (7) interpret and decide matters concerning performance of the contractor.

Contingency Allowance. A sum included in the project budget which is designated to cover unpredictable or unforeseen items of work, or changes in the work subsequently required by the owner.

Contract. A legally enforceable promise or agreement between two or among several persons.

Contract Award. A communication from an owner accepting a bid or negotiated proposal. An award creates legal obligation between the parties.

Contract Sum. The sum stated in the owner-contractor agreement, which is the total amount payable by the owner to the contractor for the performance of the work under the contract documents. The contract sum may be adjusted only by a change order.

Contractor's Liability Insurance. Insurance purchased and maintained by the contractor to protect the contractor from specified claims which may arise out of or result from the contractor's operations under the contract, whether such operations are by the contractor or by any subcontractor or by anyone directly or indirectly employed by any of them, or by anyone for whose acts any of them may be liable.

Control. One of several events to be visited by the orienteer.

Control Card. A card carried by orienteers used to verify that the competitor visited the control.

Control Description (Clue Card). A sheet or card with a brief description of the control location, control number and other clues for locating controls. The International Orienteering Federation control symbols are the internationally recognized symbols for orienteering.

Control Marker. A distinct marker that identifies the control, usually a three dimensional orange and white nylon marker.

Control Punch. A small clipper used to make a distinctive mark on the control card to verify visiting the control.

Cost Plus Fee Agreement. An agreement under which the contractor (in an owner-contractor agreement) is reimbursed for the direct and indirect costs or performance of the agreement and, in addition, is paid a fee for services. The fee is usually stated as a stipulated sum or as a percentage of cost.

Critical Path Method (CPM). A charting of all events and operations to be encountered in completing a given process, rendered in a form permitting determination of the relative significance of each event, and establishing the optimum sequence and duration of operations.

Date of Agreement. The date stated in the agreement. If no date is stated, it could be the date on which the agreement is actually signed, if this is recorded, or it may be the date established by the award.

Date of Substantial Completion. The date certified by the architect when the work or a designated portion thereof is sufficiently complete, in accordance with the contract documents, so the owner can occupy the work or designated portion thereof for the use for which it is intended.

Deduction. The amount deducted from the contract sum by a change order.

Deductive Alternate. An alternate bid resulting in a deduction from the base bid of the same bidder.

Desiccant. A substance that absorbs humidity.

Design-Build Process. A process in which a person or entity assumes responsibility under a single contract for both the design and construction of the project.

Design Development Phase. This phase is based on the results of the schematic design phase. The architect prepares, during this phase, drawings including floor plans, mechanical and electrical systems, and structural design; outline of materials to be used; landscape designs; parking lot designs; and other such documents as may be appropriate.

Dewpoint. The temperature at which moisture will condense out of the air.

Drainage. Surface and subsurface removal of water and groundwater. When properly designed, surface and subsurface irrigation eliminates standing water and relieves saturated turf. Further, it will maintain the proper amount of subsurface moisture.

Drawings. Graphic and pictorial documents showing the design, location, and dimensions of the elements of a project. Drawings generally include plans, elevations, sections, details, schedules, and diagrams. When capitalized, the term refers to the graphic and pictorial portions of the contract documents.

Egress. A way out to grade level around a building.

Electrical Contractor. The individual who will provide all electrical wiring, boxes, switches, receptacles, equipment hook-ups, conduit for all telephone wires, computer cable, television cable, security wiring, and public address system.

Eligible Individuals. Those individuals who have a physical or mental impairment which substantially limits a major life activity.

Equal quadrant Track. This type of track configuration features two 100-meter straightaways and two 100-meter curves.

Estimate. It is a forecast of construction cost, as opposed to a firm bid, prepared by a contractor for a project or a portion thereof. A term sometimes used to denote a contractor's application or request for a progress payment.

Estimate of Construction Cost, Detailed. A forecast of construction cost prepared on the basis of a detailed analysis of material and labor for all items of work, as contrasted with an estimate based on current area, volume, or similar unit costs.

Extra. A term sometimes used to denote an item of work involving additional cost.

Fee. A term used to denote compensation for professional ability, capability and availability or organization, excluding compensation for direct, indirect and/or reimbursable expenses, as an agreement based on a professional fee plus expenses. Sometimes denotes compensation of any kind for services rendered.

Fenestration. The arrangement and proportioning of windows.

Fixed Limit of Construction Cost. The maximum construction cost established in the agreement between the owner and the architect.

Fluid Mechanics. The study of the flow properties of liquids and gases.

Footcandle. A measurement of light intensity at a given point.

Footlambert. The product of the illumination in footcandle and the reflection factor of the surface.

Force Account. A term used when work is ordered, often under urgent circumstances, to be performed without prior agreement as to lump sum or unit price cost thereof and is to be billed at the cost of labor, materials and equipment, insurance, taxes, etc., plus and agreed percentage for overhead and profit; sometimes used to describe work performed by owner's own forces in a similar manner.

Foreseeability. The reasonable anticipation that harm or injury is a likely result from certain acts or omissions.

Function. Measuring satisfaction of purpose; where function is the particular purpose for which a person or thing is specifically fitted or used or for which a thing exists.

General Conditions. That part of the contract documents which sets forth many of the rights, responsibilities, and relationships of the parties involved, particularly those provisions which are common to many construction projects.

General Contractor. Individual responsible for constructing and finishing floors, walls, ceilings, steel structure, built-in cabinets, sidewalks, driveways, doorways, windows, and other things not completed by the electrical and mechanical contractors.

General Obligation Bonds. A full-faith and credit obligation bond. Refers to bonds that are repaid with a portion of the general property tax.

Glare. Excessive high brightness.

Groundskeeping. The management and maintenance of the outdoor spaces including landscaped grounds and play spaces.

Guaranteed Maximum Cost. The sum established in an agreement between owner and contractor as the maximum cost of performing specified work on the basis of cost of labor and materials plus overhead expenses and profit.

Guidelines. An indication or outline of policy or conduct.

Hydrology. Refers to the study of the patterns of water flow above and below the surface.

Inclusion (Designing for). A concept that supports full facility-full program access to all people.

Indirect Expense. These are overhead expenses (i.e., general office expense) indirectly incurred and not directly related to a specific project.

Indirect Lighting. The act of reflecting light off the ceiling to create a clean and pleasant form of light arrangement in an indoor space.

Indoor Air Quality. A product of the quality of the fresh air introduced into the ventilation system and the quality of the existing indoor air that is recycled.

In-Kind Contribution. An organization, business, or craftsman donates equipment or time to the project in return for a tax deduction.

Instructions to Bidders. Instructions contained in the bidding documents for preparing and submitting bids for a construction project or designated portion thereof.

Interior Designer. This individual will assist in selecting paint colors, wallpaper, rugs (color, texture/thickness), furniture, accessories, artwork, and other items to make spaces comfortable, functional and aesthetically pleasing.

IP Telephony. The use of an IP network to transmit voice, video, and data.

Irrigation. Surface and subsurface supplemental watering. When properly designed, surface and subsurface irrigation provides an even distribution of water for plants and turfgrass.

Invitation to Bid. A portion of the bidding documents soliciting bids for a construction project.

Invited Bidders. The bidders selected by the owner, after consultation with the architect, as the only ones from whom bids will be received.

Labor and Material Payment Bond. A bond of the contractor in which a surety guarantees to the owner that the contractor will pay for labor and material used in the performance of the contract. The claimants under the bond are defined as those having direct contracts with the contractor or any sub-contractor.

Landmark. An easily recognized obvious feature in the landscape.

Landscape Architect. Individual who provides information such as: specifications and designs for landscaping a building or green area, types of trees to be planted, types of flowers to be planted, number of walkways, specifications and designs for the irrigation system, and types of grass to be planted or sod to be installed.

Landscape Architecture. The art or science of arranging land, together with spaces and objects upon it, for safe, efficient, healthful, pleasant human use.

Latent Heat. The heat liberated or absorbed by a substance as it changes phase at a constant temperature and pressure.

Lease Agreements. A program to lease facilities to other organizations during the off-season or additional spaces within the facility not used for the sporting activity, such as office space or retail space.

Legend. A section of a map that provides an interpretation of map symbols.

Letter of Agreement. A letter stating the terms of an agreement between addressor and addressee, usually prepared to be signed by the addressee to indicate acceptance of those terms as legally binding.

Letter of Intent. A letter signifying an intention to enter into a formal agreement, usually setting forth the general terms of such agreement.

Liability. An obligation recognized and enforceable by the courts.

Liability Insurance. Insurance which protects the insured against liability on account of injury to the person or property of another.

Life Insurance Packages. A program to solicit the proceeds from a life insurance policy purchased by a supporter to specifically benefit the organization upon the death of the supporter.

Low Bid. A bid stating the lowest bid price for performance of the work, including selected alternates, conforming with bidding documents.

Lowest Responsible Bidder. A bidder who submits the lowest bona fide bid and is considered by the owner and the architect to be fully responsible and qualified to perform the work for which the bid is submitted.

Lumen. A unit of measure for the flow of light.

Luminaries. Floodlight fixtures with a lamp, reflector, etc.

Luxury Suites. These areas have been designed for VIP use and leased by large corporations to wine and dine their clients as well as to provide them entertainment.

Magnetic Lines. Lines on an orienteering map pointing toward magnetic north.

Master Map. Large orienteering map near the start line that shows the course and controls.

Mechanical Contractor. Individual who is responsible for all plumbing (hot and cold water, sewage), humidity control, heating and cooling systems, ventilation systems, and pumps.

Mechanical/Electrical Engineer. The individual who provides such information as: specifications for heating and air conditioning equipment, drawings and specification for power and lighting, determinations of plumbing requirements, and the design of any communication system (e.g., security, public address, music, closed circuit television, etc.).

Mechanic's Lien. A lien on real property created by statute in all states in favor of persons supplying labor or material for a building or structure for the value of labor or material supplied by them. In some jurisdictions a mechanic's lien also exists for the value of professional services. Clear title to the property cannot be obtained until the claim for the labor, materials or professional services is settled.

Modification. This is a written amendment to the contract signed by both parties. It is a change order. It is a written interpretation issued by the architect. Finally, it could be a written order for a minor change in the work issued by the architect.

Municipal Bonds. Bonds issued by a government or a subdivision of a state.

Named Insured. Any person, firm or corporation, or any of its members specifically designated by name as insured(s) in a policy, as distinguished from others who, although unnamed, are protected under some circumstances.

Naming Rights. Corporations vie for the right to place their name on the facility for a specific sum of money for a specific number of years.

Negligence. The omission of that care which a person of common prudence usually takes of his own concerns.

Negotiating Phase. Phase in which the architect assists the owner in obtaining bids or negotiating proposals and assists in awarding and preparing contracts for construction.

Non-Equal Quadrant Track. This track configuration resembles a stretched or compressed oval shape with two straightaways of one length and two curves of another length.

Non-Guaranteed Bonds. These bonds are sold on the basis of repayment from other designated revenue sources.

NorCompass (Thumb Compass). An orienteering compass that attaches to the left thumb of the orienteer.

Nonconforming Work. Work that does not fulfill the requirements of the contract documents.

Optimal Thermal Environment. Provides conditions which make it possible to dissipate body heat in the most effortless manner. Combines radiant temperature where surface and air temperature are balanced; air temperature between 64 and 72 degrees F; humidity between 40 and 60 percent; and, a constant air movement of 20 to 40 lineal feet/minute at a sitting height.

Orienteer. A person who participates in the sport of orienteering.

Owner-Architect Agreement. Contract between owner and architect for professional services.

Owner-Contractor Agreement. Contract between owner and contractor for performance of the work for construction of the project or portion thereof.

Owner's Representative. The person designated as the official representative of the owner in connection with a project.

Parking Fees. Fees generated from parking lots that surround the spectator facility.

Performance Bond. A bond of the contractor in which a surety guarantees to the owner that the work will be performed in accordance with the contract documents. Except where prohibited by statute, the performance bond is frequently combined with the labor and material payment bond.

Pert Schedule. An acronym for project evaluation review technique. The pert schedules the activities and events anticipated in a work process.

Plan. A two-dimensional graphic representation of the design, location and dimensions of the project, or parts thereof, seen in a horizontal plan viewed from above.

Point Elastic Surfaces. Maintain impact effects at the immediate point of contact on the floor, with the ball, object, or individual.

Point to Point Orienteering. A type of orienteering where controls must be visited in a specific order and speed in completing the course determines the winner.

Preconstruction Conference. A meeting between the contracting agency and the contractor(s) prior to the commencement of construction to review the contract items and make sure there is an understanding of how the job is to be undertaken.

Preferred/Premium Seating. VIP seating located within the luxury suites or in the club areas of the stadium which are the most expensive seats in the facility.

Prequalification of Bidders. The process of investigating the qualification of prospective bidders on the basis of their experience, availability and capability for the contemplated project and approving qualified bidders.

Prime Contract. Contract between owner and contractor for construction of the project or portion thereof.

Progress Payment. Partial payment made during progress of the work on account of work completed and/or material suitably stored.

Project. The total construction of which the work performed under the contract documents may be the whole or a part; or it could also include the total furniture, furnishings, and equipment.

Project Cost. Total cost of the project including construction, professional compensation, real estate, furnishings, equipment, and financing.

Property Damage Insurance. Insurance coverage for the insured's legal liability for claims for injury to or destruction of tangible property including loss of use resulting therefrom, but usually not including coverage for injury to or destruction of property which is in the care, custody, and control of the insured.

Public Accommodations. A facility, operated by a private entity, whose operations affect commerce. The private entity that owns, leases or leases to, or operates a place of public accommodation.

Public Liability Insurance. Insurance covering liability of the insured for negligent acts resulting in bodily injury, disease, or death of persons other than employees of the insured, and/or property damage.

Readily Achievable. Easily accomplishable and able to be carried out without much difficulty or expense. It constitutes a lower standard than undue burden.

Reasonable Accommodations. Requires that employers and facilities make an accommodation if doing so will not impose an undue hardship on the operation of the business or facility.

Record Drawings. Construction drawings revised to show significant changes made during the construction process, usually based on marked-up prints, drawings, and other data furnished by the contractor to the architect.

Reflection Factor. The percentage of light falling on a surface which is reflected by the surface.

Regulations. An order issued by an executive authority of a government and having the force of law.

Reimbursable Expenses. The amounts expended for or on account of the project which, in accordance with the terms of the appropriate agreement, are to be reimbursed by the owner.

Release of Lien. An instrument executed by a person or entity supplying labor, material, or professional services on a project which releases that person's or entity's mechanic's lien against the project property.

Resident Engineer. An engineer employed by the owner to represent the owner's interests at the project site during the construction phase.

Resilience. The ability to bounce or spring back into shape, position, etc.

Restaurant Rights. The sale of the exclusive rights for all the restaurants within a spectator facility.

Retainage. A sum withheld from progress payments to the contractor in accordance with the terms of the owner-contractor agreement.

Revenue Bonds. A bond that can be backed exclusively by the revenue occurring from the project or from a designated revenue source, such as a hotel/motel tax, restaurant tax, auto rental tax, or a combination of these taxes and others.

Reverberation. Reflection of light or sound waves.

Rolling Load. The capacity of a floor to withstand damage from external forces such as bleacher movement, equipment transport, or similar activities.

Safety Direction (Panic Azimuth; Safety Bearing). A compass bearing or direction to guide the orienteer directly to a road, major trail, or settlement if lost or injured.

Schematic Design Phase. This phase is based on the program developed by the project committee and submitted to the architect. The architect will prepare, for approval by the owner, schematic design documents including drawings (floor plans and mechanicals), scale model, project development schedule, and estimated costs.

Schedule of Values. A statement furnished by the contractor to the architect reflecting the portions of the contract sum allocated to the various portions of the work and used as the basis for reviewing the contractor's applications for payment.

Score Orienteering. A type of orienteering where controls blanket the course and each is assigned a point value based on the distance to the controls and how difficult they will be to find. The individual or team with the most points in the prescribed time is the winner.

Shop Drawings. Drawings, diagrams, schedules, and other specific data specially prepared for the work by the contractor or any subcontractor, manufacturer, supplier or distributor to illustrate some portion of the work.

Site Analysis. The gathering of information and data about a site and adjacent properties. Its purpose is to find a place for a particular use or find a use for a particular place.

Ski Orienteering. Orienteering conducted on cross country skis.

Soft Space. Space in a facility that requires little or no special provisions (such as plumbing or expensive finishes), and therefore is space that is easily vacated and converted.

Special Authority Bonds. These bonds have been used to finance stadiums or arenas by special public authorities, which are entities with public powers that are able to operate outside normal constraints placed on governments.

Specifications. A part of the contract documents contained in the project manual consisting of written requirements for material, equipment, construction systems, standards, and workmanship.

Sponsorship Packages. Corporate support programs pursued whereby large local and international firms are solicited to supply goods and services to a sporting organization at no cost or at a substantial reduction in the wholesale prices in return for visibility for the corporation.

Stipulated Sum Agreement. A contract in which a specific amount is set forth as the total payment for performance of the contract.

Structural Engineer. Individual concerned with determining possible structural systems and materials, providing cost of preferred systems and materials, and designing final structure to meet architectural requirements.

Sub-bidder. A person or entity who submits a bid to a bidder for material or labor for a portion of the work at the site.

Subcontract. An agreement between a prime contractor and a subcontractor for a portion of the work at the site.

Subcontractor. A person or entity who has a direct contract with the contractor to perform any of the work at the site.

Successful Bidder. The bidder chosen by the owner for the award of a construction contract.

Superintendent. The contractor's representative at the site who is responsible for continuous field supervision, coordination, completion of the work and, unless another person is designated in writing by the contractor to the owner and the architect, for prevention of accidents.

Supplementary Conditions. A part of the contract documents which supplements and may also modify, change, add to or delete from provisions of the general conditions.

Supplementary Lighting. Providing additional lighting on such areas as those containing goals and targets.

Supplier. A person or entity who supplies material or equipment for the work, including that fabricated to a special design, but who does not perform labor at the site.

Thermodynamics. The branch of physics dealing with the transformation of heat to and from other forms of energy, and with the laws governing such conversions of energy.

Topography. Refers to the surface features of a site including variations in elevation.

Topographical Map. A precise map that designates altitude of the land with contour lines.

Trade (Craft). An occupation requiring manual skill or members of a trade organized into a collective body.

Trade Shows. Expositions that generate sales for a particular industry.

Trail Orienteering (Control Choice). A modified type of orienteering designed for orienteers with disabilities.

Undue Hardship. Requiring significant difficulty or expense, considering the employer's size, financial resources and the nature and structure of the operation.

Unit Price. The amount stated in the bid as a price per unit of measurement for materials or services as described in the bidding documents or in the proposed contract documents.

Vendor/Contractor Equity. Vendor or contractor returns to the owner a specific percentage of the profit generated by the firms during the construction process.

Vetting. Checking the orienteering course before competition.

Waiver of Lien. An instrument by which a person or organization who has or may have a right of mechanic's lien against the property of another relinquishes such right.

Walk-off Area. The first 12 feet on the inside of an entry doorway that functions exactly as the name implies; it is within this radius that dust, dirt, oil from the parking area and water from rain and melting snow are deposited.

Workers' Compensation Insurance. Insurance covering the liability of an employer for compensation and other benefits required by workers' compensation laws with respect to injury, sickness, diseases or death arising from their employment.

Index